Spooks

To the memory of
Harry George Thomas
1947-1993

omnia vincit amor

Spooks

The Unofficial History of MI5
From Agent Zig Zag to the
D-Day Deception 1939-45

Thomas Hennessey
& Claire Thomas

AMBERLEY

Acknowledgements

The authors which to thank a number of people without whose assistance this book would have taken considerably longer to complete: in particular the staff of The National Archives of the United Kingdom; the Imperial War Museum; the Northern Ireland Political Collection, the Linen Hall Library, Belfast; and to the Security Service for permission to use material from their website. We would also like to thank Linda Herviel, Elizabeth Cantello, Janet Allen and Su Bradley; particular thanks go to Kate Marsh and Simon Mills; Lesley Clay; Marion and Derek Hall; and Ross Gower of Nineteen80 Design and Illustration. Finally thanks to Emma, Susannah, Sam and John for putting it all in persprective.

This edition first published 2010

Amberley Publishing Plc
Cirencester Road, Chalford,
Stroud, Gloucestershire, GL6 8PE
www.amberley-books.com

© Thomas Hennessey & Claire Thomas 2009, 2010

The right of Thomas Hennessey & Claire Thomas to be identified as the Author of this work has been asserted in accordance with the Copyrights, Designs and Patents Act 1988.

British Library Cataloguing in Publication Data.
A catalogue record for this book is available from the British Library.

ISBN 978 1 4456 0184 7

Typesetting and Origination by Amberley Publishing.
Printed in Great Britain.

Contents

1. SNOW: The First XX Agent 1939–1942   6

2. 'The Truth in the Shortest Possible Time': Camp 020   44

3. The End of an Era: Kell's Fall & Petrie's New Order 1940–1941   64

4. DOUBLE-CROSS   112

5. SUMMER, RAINBOW & TATE   138

6. The Fall of SNOW   163

7. MUTT & JEFF; HAMLET, PUPPET & MULLET   206

8. Enter BRUTUS   241

9. CARELESS Whispers   278

10. ZIGZAG Drops In   322

11. Turf War: MI5's Battle with SIS Over ISOS   358

12. DREADNOUGHT & ARTIST   377

13. Turn of the Tide: Preparing to Liberate Europe 1942–1944   399

14. Finest Hour: The Liberation of Europe 1944–1945   423

15. The ROCK   455

Select Bibliography   484

Notes   486

1

SNOW
The First XX Agent 1939–1942

On 18 August 1939, Mrs Arthur Owens, accompanied by her son, walked in to Metropolitan Police headquarters, New Scotland Yard, in order to make her statement concerning her husband, Arthur. She alleged that her husband was a German spy; although she had had it in mind to inform the police of his activities for some considerable time she had 'refrained from doing so on account of their children'. But now Mr and Mrs Owens had quarrelled and he had left her; although this, she claimed, was not the cause of her sudden decision to give information. Arthur, she said, had tried to persuade his son, her brother's stepdaughter and another friend to join him in his 'despicable business' of spying and had threatened to shoot Mrs Owen and ruin her family should she reveal any information about him.

Mrs Owens described her husband's background to the Police: he was born in Wales, later migrating to Canada where, after five years of residence, he automatically became a Canadian citizen. He often used the name 'Wilson' as an alias. In 1933, he returned from Canada and now described himself as an inventor. Around 1935, revealed Mrs Owens, he became a British Intelligence agent and while so engaged got to know several German Secret Service agents. Arthur had, around this time, met a millionaire named Hamilton who formed a company called the Owens Equipment Co., to make car batteries and it was in this business that he was now supposed to be engaged; however, it was merely a cloak for his other activities. Through Hamilton, and his own activities for British Intelligence, Owens had met a man called Peiper around 1936. Peiper was believed to be an American Jew in the employ of the German Secret Service. The two men exchanged notes and Owens was persuaded to join the German Secret Service while still apparently working for the British. Owens's company formed a subsidiary company in Germany, which, Mrs Owens claimed, had never actually done any business but was used as an excuse for his frequent visits to Germany. The correspondence Owens received, presumably from the company because its letter paper was used, Mrs Owens alleged to be in code. Owens was paid for his services in English money, which was supposed to accrue to him from the profits of this company.

Owens had taken his wife and the family to Ostend a little over a year before, for a holiday and, while there, he had received a letter calling him to Hamburg. He and his wife went, leaving the children in the hotel manager's care. In Hamburg they met a German whom they addressed as 'Doctor' to whom Owens had to report. He was alleged to be 'one of the Chiefs on the German Secret Service' and efforts – which appeared to have been somewhat feeble and amateurish – were made to inveigle Mrs Owens into becoming a German agent. While the Owens were in Germany, Peiper visited their hotel in Ostend and endeavoured to 'blackmail' the children. The manager, however, intervened and, on the Owens return shortly afterwards, Mrs Owens threatened to have Peiper arrested. He disappeared and she had not seen him again.

Mrs Owens complained to the police that her husband was now trying to inveigle her brother's stepdaughter, to go to Germany with him and join the German Secret Service. He had made her extravagant promises of rewards. Mrs Owens had spoken to the girl and she was prepared to give police a statement of all she knew. It was about three days before coming to the police that Mrs Owens learned her husband had given an address to which a letter containing money could be sent to him from Germany. The said letter, addressed to 'Mr Wilson', had not arrived, but a messenger had called the previous day, on 17 August. Mrs Owen complained that her husband was also making a similar attempt to entice another female friend to join the German Secret Service by making extravagant promises to her as well. He said he would take her to Germany and, as far as Mrs Owens knew, they might now be there as Arthur was supposed to be on holiday at Golden Sands Holiday Camp, Great Yarmouth. The girl's mother, Mrs Owens believed, was German by birth. Mrs Owens was also angered by the fact that, about two years previously, her husband had asked her brother (now deceased), who was then employed by Short Brothers, the aircraft manufacturers, in Rochester, to obtain certain secret information for him. The request was refused. Most damaging of all, Mrs Owens claimed that a wireless transmitting set had been sent to her husband from the German Secret Service in February 1939, which he had disposed of on or about 29 July. The code used in connection with this set which was based on the word 'CONGRATULATIONS' each letter bearing a number.

From their new informant, the police learnt that Arthur Owens, it seemed, had a very good knowledge of many British aerodromes and had passed information concerning them to Germany. Mrs Owens revealed that he recently had in his possession some 1937 RAF codebooks, which she had destroyed so that they should not fall into German hands. She alleged that her husband had, and might still have, in his possession some new RAF codebooks, which were quite recently reported to have been stolen. She feared that he intended to take them to Germany. Mrs Owens claimed that her husband was 'very clever and carries coded messages covered in tin foil either in his mouth or in the petrol cavity at the end of a cigarette lighter. He is the chief of a number of agents who operate under his orders.' Quite recently (apparently during the Munich crisis of 1938), when he arrived at Harwich from a German trip, a railway employee warned Owens that he was likely to be searched and followed; he 'chewed up the evidence and spat it out of the carriage window'. The incident, it seemed, had scared Owens who said thereafter he intended to reveal all he knew to the British Secret Service.

Mrs Owens concluded her statement by revealing that she had not seen her husband for about ten days; but before leaving her he had thoroughly searched their house including her handbag and destroyed every possible scrap of evidence that might be used against him. She revealed that her husband had been drinking heavily for some time past and 'he had not been sober for weeks'. Mrs Owens feared her husband might use violence towards her and requested police protection. Special Branch, who by this stage was involved, promised support, asking the local police to pay special attention to the Owens address. As the Branch began their enquires they found, according to the last police report they could lay their hands upon, that Arthur Owens had left Dover for Ostend on 11 August and had not yet returned to the country.[1]

In actual fact British Intelligence were already well aware of Arthur Owens and his work for the British – and the Germans – as an agent; but they were unaware of his latest alleged shenanigans. They had even given him a codename: SNOW. His firm had been the holder of a number of Admiralty contracts and SNOW travelled frequently to Germany on business; he was in the habit of bringing back a certain amount of technical information which he passed on to the Admiralty. At the beginning of 1936, SNOW told his contact there that he would like to work regularly for His Majesty's Government and was therefore passed on, through Naval Intelligence, to an SIS officer who employed him for a short while as an agent, apparently with good results. Towards the end of the year, however, a letter from SNOW to Postbox 629 Hamburg, a known German cover address, was intercepted in transit. This letter made it clear that SNOW had been, previously, in contact with German Intelligence and was about to have a meeting with them at Cologne. This appointment he kept, and further letters were observed to pass between him and the Germans. No action was taken against SNOW himself as it was anticipated that he might presently confess. In December 1936 he did in fact do so. But it was behaviour such as this – and the suspicion of dubious loyalty to Britain compounded by his overt Welsh nationalism – that hung over SNOW throughout the forthcoming war. British Intelligence could never be quite sure which side SNOW was batting for.

SNOW admitted his contacts with Peiper – whom he described as a German engineer – from whom he had attempted to obtain information. The information, which Peiper had supplied, had not been wholly satisfactory and, after a while, SNOW had found himself unable to continue to pay Peiper's expenses. At this point Peiper had proposed to him that he, SNOW, should work as an agent for the Germans rather than the British. SNOW had fallen in with this suggestion in order, so he said later, to penetrate the German Secret Service in the British interest. Peiper had accordingly arranged meetings for him with the Germans at Cologne and elsewhere, and they had accepted SNOW as an agent. This had occurred before he became an agent of SIS. But there seemed to be little doubt that the Germans were aware of his subsequent connection with SIS, though according to SNOW they believed him to have broken off this connection before he took service with them. At all events they did not subsequently make any attempt to employ him in the capacity of a double agent, but rather to use him as a straight forward reporting agent. As there were some difficulties in the way of legal proceeding against SNOW, on account of his previous connection with SIS, no action was taken against him by the British authorities and SNOW continued his association with the Germans. A great part, however, though not all, of his correspondence continued to be intercepted and from time to time SNOW volunteered information either to SIS or latterly to Special Branch, about the contacts which he had made with the Germans and the information which he was asked to supply. Substantially, from the end of 1936 until the outbreak of war SNOW worked as a straightforward German agent, whose activities, although known to the authorities were not interfered with in any important respect.

SNOW's principal contact in Germany was known only as the DOCTOR. During the time that SNOW knew him he appeared to occupy the position of the Lieter of I. Luft, Hamburg, and SNOW's work therefore consisted largely of collecting airforce information. From time to time however, he supplied information both for the naval and the military sections in Hamburg. At one moment also he seems to have made an approach on the Germans' behalf to the BUF, putting forward a scheme for the establishment of four secret transmitters in

England for the purpose of disseminating propaganda in time of war. Although MI5 could not be certain on this point, it seemed from his own account that SNOW successfully represented to the Germans that he possessed a number of sub-agents in England, amounting perhaps to a dozen or fifteen men. The Security Service noted: 'It is probable, though not certain, that all these persons existed only in SNOW's imagination.'

In January, 1939 SNOW informed Special Branch that he expected to receive a wireless transmitter from Germany. Later in the same month he did receive a letter which contained instructions for the working of such a set and a ticket from the cloakroom at Victoria Station where the wireless set had been deposited for him in a suitcase. This set was handed over by SNOW to Special Branch, and examined by SIS, and then returned to him.[2] Observation on SNOW was taken up on Friday, 10 February 1939, but he was not seen until Monday 15th, on which day he left his home address at 9.50 a.m. and went to Morden Station. He was followed, and proceeded by underground to Queen's Park, and thence on foot to 75 Chevening Road, NW6, where he knocked on the door and was admitted at 11.05 a.m. Watch was continued on the address until 5.50 p.m. but he was not seen to leave. Meantime, another Watcher had taken up observation at Morden, and SNOW was seen to leave the station there at 5.10 p.m., carrying a brown paper parcel measuring approximately 8in.x 4in.x 4in. He then walked to his address, being joined on the way by a young girl in school dress; both entered the house at 5.15 p.m., and nothing further of interest was seen up to 7 p.m. when the watch was withdrawn.[3]

In his contacts with Special Branch, at this time, SNOW expressed his regret that the authorities did not wish to utilise his service.[4] The intelligence agencies were not impressed by the fact that SNOW was indiscreet. He informed the authorities that he was going to take photographs of certain British coast defence batteries, which he announced that he was going 'to take over to the other side'. As one observer commented to the Air Ministry: 'I hope you do not think I am making an unnecessary fuss, but I have never yet heard of a genuine agent talking so much about his job and knowing the man to be a very considerable perverter of the truth has aroused very grave suspicions in my mind.'[5] This merely confirmed to the Air Ministry what they were already aware of as they had 'a considerable adverse record' of SNOW while British Intelligence was aware that SNOW was 'a bad lot, requiring very discreet handling'.[6]

By March 1939, MI5 were taking a closer interest in SNOW. From their sources they were aware that he travelled, frequently, between

England and Hamburg and that he boasted that he was not now worried by the British authorities. He appeared to have plenty of money and journeyed from place to place in taxicabs. SNOW also made no secret of the fact that he was paid by the Germans 'with whom he is working and speaks very highly of them in every way'. In explanation of this attitude, he had told a source that he was 'very bitter against England' because his father, his brother and himself were responsible for the invention of a special steel which was used against Zeppelins during the war but which the British authorities cheated them, both out of any credit for this and, also out of hundreds of thousands of pounds.

It was noted that SNOW, at this stage, appeared very anxious to get information concerning any political scandals in which leading politicians were involved, such as Eden and Churchill. This, he explained to another source, was required for use in the German press and for wireless propaganda. SNOW also wanted information concerning Communist activities against Germany; and any information of people in Germany who were in touch with refugees in Britain, particularly with regard to smuggling German currency. On the military side, he wanted details of a new explosive that was being tried out, which it was said was more powerful than any other as yet known. He was also anxious to obtain a copy of any instruction book dealing with any branch of the army; he would only require the book to loan for twenty-four hours and would guarantee its safe return. Items of general information which SNOW said he also required, included details of works and ammunition dumps in south and central Wales; details of the new Sunderland bomber; and information of any secret experiments in 'the new wireless idea for bringing down hostile aircraft'. With regard to the latter he said he was aware that experiments had now reached a definite stage and were referred to as 'the wireless cloud'. SNOW was quite open with regard to communicating with Hamburg by wireless and promised that liberal payments would be made for any information received.[7]

SNOW had, by now, installed the German wireless transmitter (W/T) in his own house and attempted to establish wireless communication with Hamburg. It appeared from his intercepted correspondence, however, that he did not succeed – the result, apparently, of some defect in the set itself. It was at this point, August 1939 that SNOW and his new female friend, Lily, left for Germany.[8]

For some time – acting on instructions – Special Branch maintained contact with SNOW, and submitted the information he gave to MI5. On Friday 1 September 1939 – the day Germany invaded Poland – a

Detention Order under Regulation 18B of the Defence Regulations 1939 was made against SNOW. Inspector Holmes, of Special Branch, made enquiries with a view to effecting SNOW's arrest, but this was not possible because he had left his regular address, and he could not be traced. But, about noon on Monday 4 September – the day after Britain had declared war against Germany – SNOW telephoned his Special Branch contact – a Superintendent – to make an appointment. With Inspector Holmes, the Superintendent met SNOW at Waterloo Station at 4 p.m. SNOW explained that he wished to offer his services to the British Government, but declined to reveal his address. The policemen arrested SNOW on the spot and he was taken to Wandsworth Prison, where the Detention Order was served on him. Just before he entered the prison SNOW gave his address and added that a transmitting set would be found in his bathroom.

The Special Branch men, accompanied by TAR Robertson from MI5, called the same evening at the address and there saw Mr and Mrs 'X' the occupants of the flat where SNOW was staying with Lily. At first the Xs denied all knowledge of SNOW, but later admitted he was living there as the husband of Lily. A search of the flat was made, but the transmitting set could not be found. In a cupboard in the bathroom, however, a two-valve receiving set that had been made by SNOW was discovered. After sharp questioning, Mr X admitted that Lily had arrived home about 5 p.m. the same day, and asked him to 'get rid' of a parcel belonging to SNOW. He was aware that SNOW was living apart from his wife, and claimed that he was under the impression that the parcel was something to do with SNOW's domestic quarrel with his wife. He had buried the parcel in a corner of the garden, without investigating its contents. Mr X pointed out the spot to Robertson where the transmitting set was found, in a paper carrier. By this time Lily had returned to the house, and she and Mr X were taken to Kingston police Station, where statements were taken from them.

From these statements it appeared that SNOW had suggested that he could put various commercial agencies in Mr X's way, and for that purpose invited him to Hamburg. Mr X accompanied SNOW and Lily to Hamburg where they arrived about 10 p.m. on 11 August 1939. He was introduced to various men by the names of Kurtz, Schneider, 'Herr Doctor' and Leitz. Nothing materialised in the way of business from these meetings, but Leitz asked X to meet him at the Great Eastern Hotel, Liverpool Street on Thursday 17 August. X kept the appointment, but was informed that Leitz had returned to Germany by air. SNOW and Lily had stayed on in Germany, returning to Britain on 24 August, and had lodged at the X's Parklands address since. On 4 September, the couple left the house at about 3.15 p.m. and the girl arrived back at about 5 p.m. She informed X that SNOW 'had been taken away'. X admitted that he was 'highly indiscreet in burying the parcel, and being evasive when first seen', but thought he was assisting SNOW as he knew he was having a lot of trouble with his wife.

During questioning, Lily explained how she had been introduced to SNOW about Easter last, and became friendly with him. She had been 'intimate' with him since, and they had lived together. SNOW invited her to go for a holiday with him to Germany and, as stated by X, the party arrived at Hamburg on 11 August. After X had returned to England, SNOW and Lily went on to Berlin, and left Germany for home on 23 August. Lily stated that she saw nothing suspicious while in Germany, but had met several people there who were known as 'doctors'. Meanwhile the transmitting set – which was the 'parcel' buried in the garden – was reunited with the receiving set, and both were taken possession of by TAR Robertson and MI5.

On 5 September, Robertson visited SNOW at Wandsworth Prison with Lieutenant Colonel J.F. Yule of MI1 – specialists in radio technology. SNOW was examined as to his proficiency in Morse Code. He said during the interview that the 'doctor' he saw in Hamburg was a Dr Rantzau, and that another man he met there was named Theiler. The latter individual, according to SNOW, was in charge of the radio section of the German Secret Service, and had promised to send him another transmitting set and a receiving set which would be addressed to him c/o Mr X, Parklands. These would only be sent providing SNOW agreed to have them. He added that 4 a.m. would be the time that the Germans would transmit to him on a wavelength of 60 meters, but he could get in touch with them any of hour of the day or night. SNOW admitted that Rantzau gave him £40 for his expenses. The reference to expenses seemed connected with something that X had mentioned earlier that day: namely that, before he left Hamburg, SNOW asked him to collect a letter from a Southampton address in the name of Wilson. X was to open the letter, extract £11 and give the money to Lily's mother. X went twice to collect the letter, but was told it had not been delivered.[9]

After hearing this TAR Robertson made a proposal to SNOW: that his wireless set should be used from the prison to re-establish contact with Germany under MI5's direction. SNOW jumped at the chance and the wireless set was installed in his cell.[10] Having put the set in order, Robertson arranged to come to SNOW's cell at 6 p.m. on Friday 8 September and MI1G were advised to listen, not only to report upon the prisoner's transmission but also for a reply from Germany. Unfortunately, SNOW, in looking over his set to satisfy himself – at Robertson's request – that it was set up exactly in the manner, which he had been instructed, pushed a switch at the base of the set which caused a fuse to blow. This 'ended our activities for the day' as he was unable to repair the set before the following morning.

On Saturday, 9 September, Robertson again went to Wandsworth and succeeded in transmitting at 6 p.m. and 7.45 p.m. with SNOW keying. The message keyed was sent out in code and was: 'ALL READY HAVE REPAIRED RADIO SEND INSTRUCTIONS NOW AWAITING REPLY.' It was reported by those monitoring at MI1G that the transmission was poor and no reply was picked up. According to SNOW's information, the reception station in Germany would be more likely to be listening for him at 4 a.m. in the morning than at any other time in the day. Robertson therefore came back again at exactly 4 a.m., but unfortunately the transmission was reported by MI1G as unidentifiable. No reply was picked up by MI1G.

During Saturday, and in the early hours of Sunday morning, Robertson had various conversations with SNOW. He made it abundantly clear to SNOW that it was in his interests to use his best endeavours to get in touch with Germany. Previous to this conversation 'it had been my impression that he was not telling us by any means all he knew, and furthermore, there were inconsistencies in his interpretations of various points in the code of transmission. It is now my impression that, since that conversation, he is doing all he can to get in touch with Germany, although I would not be prepared to say whether he is now still withholding a certain amount of knowledge from us.' What seems to have shifted SNOW's position was an incident during his conversation with Robertson between 6 p.m. and 7.45 p.m. on the evening of the 9th: SNOW was sitting in the cell in which the transmitter was rigged up, the door was left ajar and a warder was standing outside. The warder pushed the door further open and asked Robertson whether he minded someone, unspecified, coming down the passage outside – 'as I discovered afterwards, apparently for hanging up curtains or some other purpose'. Both SNOW and Robertson interpreted his remark at that moment to mean that the prisoners along that passage were going to be returned to their cells, and would therefore be passing the open door of the cell in which SNOW was sitting. SNOW 'became very white and was obviously terrified, and said to me, "don't let them see me – whatever happens don't let them see me". I therefore shut the door and told him that there was nothing whatever to be frightened of as he would be absolutely safe where he was.

I then asked him what had upset him so much.' SNOW replied that he had met a certain prisoner, whose name he did not give, in the prison that morning and that he had taken SNOW into a corner and told him that he knew he had been 'quizzed by the Intelligence cops' the day before, and had tried to get out of him what he had said. SNOW denied this. Robertson 'did not ask him the man's name as I did not wish to appear to be curious. The result being that he continued to talk of the man and said that he knew him well and also that he had only just returned from Germany.'[11]

SNOW was now very eager to co-operate. As a reward, on the evening of 11 September, SNOW was removed from Wandsworth Gaol and taken to Kingston police station, where it was arranged that he should be treated as a special prisoner. The aim was to set SNOW and Lily up in a flat somewhere in the Kingston district so he could transmit to the Germans while controlled by Robertson. On 12 September, SNOW and two Special Branch detectives went flat hunting, and obtained a flat. With the help of MI1G they managed to put up SNOW's set, with the aerial concealed in the roof. 'Having fixed up the set SNOW transmitted a message to Germany at 11.30: "Must meet you Holland at once. Bring weather code radio town and hotels. Wales ready".' This message was allowed to go after SNOW had explained that, in accordance with the instructions he had received from Rantzau, he was to meet him in Holland as soon as possible in order to pick up the weather code which would enable SNOW to give the Germans information regarding the state of the weather over certain places in England, which they intended to bomb. The reference to Wales was explained by the fact that Rantzau was anxious to get hold of a Welshman who was a member of the Welsh Nationalist Party. Apparently, Rantzau wished to use this organisation to create disturbances in Wales. Once Rantzau had established this link, he proposed to supply them with arms, which would be brought up the Bristol Channel in a submarine. Unfortunately, no reply to this message was received; so Robertson decided to send it again at 4 a.m.; this time they immediately received a reply, which was prefaced by the call sign OEA, which was the call sign used by Hamburg Station when they wished to get in touch with SNOW. The message sent by the German Station was undecipherable, 'so we asked for a repeat, whereupon the German Station replied that they wanted a repeat. After this last message we decided that it was high time we gave it up.'

On the 13th, Robertson discussed the case with his colleagues at MI5, Colonel Hinchley-Cooke and Jasper Harker, who both agreed that it would be as well to allow SNOW to go to Holland, in order to contact Rantzau. Harker also obtained permission from the Home Secretary for the suspension of the Detention Order against SNOW. Robertson then went down to see SNOW at Kingston and took with him a passport and permit form. Hinchley-Cooke arranged with Superintendent Foster, of Special Branch, that MI5 should borrow the services of two Watchers from the Police, whose duty it would be to keep an eye on Lily and SNOW. On 14 September, Robertson went to the passport office in order to have SNOW's passport regularised and then again went down to see SNOW at Kingston and arranged for furniture, for the flat, to be brought from Mr Chapman, a furniture dealer. Special Branch had in the meantime collected Lily and she was given instructions to furnish the house with everything she required.

Robertson handed SNOW his passport and told him that the next boat was leaving for Flushing from Tilbury on Saturday, and that he must leave from Fenchurch Street Station the next day, the 15th, not later than 5 p.m. He also explained to SNOW that on no account when he returned to Britain was he to give the impression that he was on a special mission, but was to conform in every way to the requests of the immigration authorities. SNOW, in turn, asked that Robertson produce someone by the next day, before he left England, who was a member of the Welsh Nationalist Party. He would have to give his name and address to Rantzau, who would then get in touch with him.[12] The last point was short notice but MI5's Aliens Branch believed it had found a suitable candidate, from Swansea, whom they thought 'would be an admirable person to go over to Holland as a representative of the Welsh Nationalist Party'. MI5's latest recruit, on his return to Swansea, decided to 'make it his business to attend their meetings and become au fait with their customs and so on'. The agent could speak Welsh and struck his MI5 contact 'as being an extremely determined type of individual, and I should imagine he would serve our purpose admirably'.[13] His codename was WW.

SNOW made his way to Rotterdam; when he returned to Britain he was interviewed by MI5, on 21 September. SNOW recalled how, on arrival, he made contact with Rantzau who, according to SNOW's account, asked whether he had received the money they had sent over to him. SNOW replied all except the first £17. Rantzau said he had £80 for him, 'and as much as I require in London, where it would be delivered to my new address'. He asked SNOW what work he had done, 'and I told him that my time had been occupied with getting a new address, and having [the] radio installed and put into working order'. SNOW then told Rantzau that he had made three trips to Wales to organise the 'Welsh Nationalist Bombing Scheme'. He had contacted a gentleman there (in South Wales) – 'just an ordinary sort of man, not very flush with money' – who was in touch with the head of the Welsh Nationalist Party, and was working from North Wales. SNOW gave him the gentleman's name and address. Rantzau asked SNOW if he was 100 per cent reliable. SNOW replied: 'Definitely, they need not worry on that account.' Rantzau then asked for SNOW to arrange a meeting between the Germans and the gentleman, in Brussels in approximately two to three weeks time. 'He said right away if I could. I said that there were certain other things to be arranged first and that I could not just pick up a man and send him without knowing anything about him, though so far as I know, he is perfectly reliable. I will spend a week checking up, and they will do the same.' The meeting between the 'Welsh Nationalist Party' and German Intelligence was to take place at the Savoy Hotel in Brussels. The gentleman from Wales would arrive before SNOW did, carrying with an identification coin. The Germans would then identify the coin and check his passport. SNOW was to go in later.

In the meantime SNOW had to investigate, in South Wales, the best method of shipping in explosives and rifles and ammunition, by U-boat, and of storing them. All contacts would be through SNOW's radio. SNOW had to arrange where the U-boat could land the material. SNOW was also told that, from 21 September, his weather reports from London '<u>must</u> go through every night. That is the basis of my broadcast at the moment.' The Germans were very interested in getting the numbers of RAF squadrons located in England, especially between London and South Wales, in the districts around Bristol and Gloucester. They also required information regarding reports of troop movements for, according to Rantzau, there were reports of very large concentrations of British and French troops on the Belgian-French frontier. SNOW reported to MI5 that the Germans were 'afraid of British and French troops making a dash through Belgium and Holland' and they were 'trying to make arrangements to go into Belgium and Holland first'. With regard to air raids on London, SNOW described how Rantzau had told him: 'I would advise you, as soon as raids start, to get out of the way. You are to go away for two or three days. We shall try to destroy the new works of Hawkers at Kingston. Have you a gas mask? Get a service gas mask, you can buy one in London.' SNOW was unclear as to German intentions, but the reference to a gas mask might have implied something which led to him concluding that 'if everything else fails the Germans will resort to bacteriological warfare against this country'. He believed that they were 'fully prepared in this direction'. When he returned to England, SNOW also gave MI5 a description of the mysterious Rantzau or 'DOCTOR': 'He was 6ft, well built, clean shaven, broad shoulders, fair haired and 'looks like an American, gold tooth on top right side.' By now SNOW was eager to go down to Swansea to establish contact with WW before going over to Belgium; he was particularly anxious to have WW 'under his tuition so as to be able to coach him and prepare him for all eventualities'.[14] Unfortunately, for reasons unknown, WW was no longer able or willing to take the journey to Belgium with SNOW; so, MI5 had cast their net for someone else. Soon, they thought they had their man:[15] G.W., a retired police inspector from Swansea.[16] In the meantime, MI5 had to clear the sending over of weather reports with the Air Ministry. SNOW was allowed to continue with the proviso that should he get a request from the Germans to furnish them with a weather report on any particular town other than London, MI5 was to get in touch with the Ministry immediately.[17]

At 9.15 p.m., on 26 September, two MI5 officers arrived at SNOW's flat for his nightly transmission to the Germans. They had come to brief SNOW about his next trip to the Continent to meet Rantzau. The Security Service men parked their car outside Norbiton Station and, upon walking through the subway, 'noticed several people hanging about, but no one particularly suspicious'. On arriving at SNOW's flat they found that he was not in and left some batteries for his transmitter, covered up outside his door; they then left. On returning at 9.35 p.m. the officers saw a car draw up and three men and a girl get out; two of them were SNOW and Lily. Not knowing whom the other occupants might be, one of the officers returned through the subway and rang up TAR Robertson who was told: 'I noticed a girl hanging about and also I was aware that I was being followed by a man.' Robertson said that the car, being a Vauxhall, was probably that of a Special Branch Inspector he knew. The MI5 officer again returned through the subway towards SNOW's flat. The girl was still hanging about at the mouth of the subway. She was 'fairly thick set, short, aged about 25–30, wearing a dark blue felt hat and a dark coat in some tweed material with, I think, a leather belt. In the darkness of the subway I could not be certain of the colour of her hair although I passed very close to her, but my impression was that it was dark.'

On arriving at SNOW's flat the MI5 officer found the said Special Branch Inspector accompanied by a sergeant and discovered that the man who had been following him was in fact the sergeant whom the Inspector had asked to tail him after becoming 'suspicious of my walking past the flat'. By this time it was about 9.50 p.m. 'and the whole performance caused an immense rush to get out code message on the air at 10 o'clock. More so as I had the key of the wireless room and had also intercepted the [MI5 appointed wireless] operator and prevented him from going into the building. Both [transmitting and receiving] sets, therefore, also had to be prepared.' At 10 p.m. a message, using the full 'CONGRATULATIONS' code was sent to the Germans on behalf of SNOW: 'Leaving for Wales. Will radio on Friday night at 12.' After two requests for a repeat the Germans signalled the reception of the message and, after a lapse of time, 'while presumably they were decoding our message', they sent the following reply: 'Need military and general news urgently daily.' This message was sent in the full 'CONGRATULATIONS' code. SNOW then sent a weather report and after two repeats the Germans signalled their reception. The exchange then ceased with the German Station sending 'Goodnight, old boy'.

As preparations were discussed to send SNOW back to the Continent – the rendezvous with the Germans was to be in Belgium – the agent told the MI5 officer that he thought it necessary that whoever was sent over with him should be able to speak fluent German, as he was unable to understand the various asides during his conversations with Rantzau made to the other members of Rantzau's entourage, since his German was not up to scratch. SNOW was also clear that it was absolutely necessary that the MI5 agent 'should look, speak and act like a Welshman', and should at least have a slight smattering of the Welsh language. While the Germans did not understand Welsh – SNOW had tried it out on them – 'they knew what it sounded like and would not easily be taken in by an impostor'. One of the Special Branch men then suggested 'perhaps rather unfortunately' that one of their sergeants might go over with SNOW as he spoke fluent German. MI5, in the end, did not subscribe to this suggestion, as although the sergeant 'certainly has the appearance of a Welshman', it was not thought that it would probably be possible to 'coach him sufficiently in the Welsh speech and habits in the time at our disposal (perhaps a fortnight)'.

SNOW, when asked during the conversation, what type of military and general information he thought the Germans would require, replied that he had been asked to obtain as much knowledge as possible about all troop movements, particularly those pertaining to avenues obviously leading to the coast and indicating the movement of troop abroad in large quantities. When asked why the German were so keen to have the information, SNOW's reply was, 'to say the least of it, surprising'. He said that Rantzau, although realising that the scheme could only have a moral – i.e. psychological – effect, had decided, when the majority of troops had left England, to send over large flights of aeroplanes to drop German troops in England, armed with machine guns and any other light weapons. SNOW impressed on MI5 that Rantzau had lived a lot in America and 'has acquired the American outlook of showmanship. He said that Rantzau fully realised that the German troops dropped in this country would have no hope of surviving and would probably do little actual damage, but that Rantzau realises the immense effect on the general populous of England of seeing German troops in German uniform actually on English soil.'

Apart from this extraordinary statement, SNOW also revealed that one of the things he had been asked, for months, to find out was the exact position of all reservoirs in the country and especially those around London. He said that, although he himself had not given them this information, he knew that they had acquired it through various minor agents in the country. Questioned as to why the Germans should consider this information of paramount importance, SNOW repeated that Rantzau had told him that, although it would be the last weapon they would use, 'if all else failed they were going to start a concentrated bacteriological warfare upon this country and that as far as he could gather, their main objective would be the reservoirs, into which they would endeavour to drop bombs charged with bacteria'.

As the conservation drew to a close, SNOW particularly asked that any letters arriving addressed to him c/o Expanded Metal Company, Burwood House, Tothill Street, Westminster, SW1 should be intercepted and held by MI5 until his return from Wales. He explained that these letters would contain the names and addresses of the various agencies abroad that would in effect be 'spy bases' and it was essential that these should not get into the hands of the Expanded Metal Company. The MI5 officer asked him if he wished them to be opened or not and SNOW immediately said, 'Oh yes, certainly open them if you like. Then you will have the information immediately.'

The officer made a note of how SNOW had numbered that night's message as no.13 report and the message from the Germans as no.1. It was, therefore, 'most important that the next message sent out should be no.14, as if the numbers of messages sent out are not consecutive it will mean that the sender is suspicious and that everything is not right. Similarly if the Germans are not satisfied, they will number their message 3 instead of 2.' As arranged with Robertson on the telephone, the officer intimated to SNOW 'that we were suspicious that someone had been watching us, possibly a girl, and told him to keep his eyes open and to let us know if he was suspicious that anyone was following him at any time. He said he would be specially careful, but I am afraid the news appears to make him somewhat nervous.'

An alarming fact that the MI5 officer discovered, in the course of the conversation with SNOW, was that the latter had the greatest respect for Rantzau's 'brains and ability and he says that his power is quite extraordinary, not only in Germany but outside. He says that Brussels is infested with German S [ecret] S[ervice] men and that Rantzau can do exactly what he likes there. When he was out there he asked Rantzau how he had got in. Rantzau laughed and said that he could go anywhere, and that in this case he had been made a director of a big hemp manufacturing company in Germany the week before and was in Brussels for the purpose of selling hemp.'

Reflecting on the fact that MI5 were unaware that Special Branch was intending to appear as SNOW's flat the Security Service officer present pointed out that the presence of the two parties 'very nearly resulted in a major calamity, as had I been unable to get in touch with Mr Robertson', who was able to identify the Special Branch car 'we should not have entered the flat in time to come up at 10 o'clock as arranged. SNOW has frequently impressed upon me that the Germans will accept no excuses for delays or mistakes and that were he to be late in coming up one evening it might destroy the whole of our programme. He was certainly in a fever last night, so much so that I had to code most of his messages myself.' The officer thought it of 'paramount importance that such a misunderstanding should not occur again. I also think it essential that the minimum possible number of people' should be allowed to enter and leave SNOW's flat, 'and it is taking a quite unnecessary risk' to allow the Special Branch Inspector 'in a large and shiny car, which he parked outside the door, accompanied by another SB officer to go in and out this flat as he chooses. His attendance on this occasion was quite unnecessary and only aroused suspicions among the neighbouring tenants. The good lady in the flat opposite did in fact put her head out of the door to see who all the people were going up and down her back stairs.'[18]

SNOW, in the meantime, had what he described as 'a very successful visit to Swansea', where he had met WW for the first time and a 'friend' of his – who was, in fact, GW. He 'strongly approved of both these individuals and said that he thought WW was eminently suitable for the job'. Later they took a car and went for a long drive on the south coast of Wales, as far as Haverfordwest. They discussed places to land arms or submarines. Both WW and his friend knew this coast exceedingly well, as did SNOW and they came to the conclusion, after duly inspecting the site, that Oxwich Bay was eminently suitable for the project.[19] Upon returning to England, SNOW rang up Robertson to confirm that he had been in contact with the Germans and they had agreed to meet in Brussels. Robertson took his passport to SNOW and, with no expense spared by His Majesty's Government, bought him a 3rd class return ticket to Brussels (£4.2s.9d) with his own money. After getting his visa, Robertson and SNOW had a talk about various things connected with his trip. At this point it was envisaged that SNOW would be travelling to the Continent alone and he seemed quite certain that he would be able to get over the difficulty of not taking anyone with him from Wales at this stage. Robertson suggested that in view of the difficulty in getting people out of the country at the present moment, he might say that he would be willing to run the Welsh Nationalist Movement from London and would the Germans give him the necessary instructions? Robertson added that he thought it would be a good thing if he appeared to be a little worried about not receiving, from the Germans, any money yet. He gave SNOW some information which had been cleared referring to the fact that new British Divisions had been sent to France and taken up their position in French defences.[20]

Within a few days it had been decided that there should be a change in the plan: GW would now accompany SNOW to the Continent. As far as the Germans were to be told, GW was, as well as an ardent Welsh Nationalist, an enquiry agent investigating road accidents throughout Wales. What SNOW did not know was that part of GW's remit was to keep an eye on him for MI5. The night before the planned departure GW, WW, SNOW and Lily went out on the town. It gave GW a chance to make an assessment of his travelling companion. SNOW had hired a Daimler car in which he and his two companions were driven to Kingston. On the way with the glass division being closed, and with WW sitting in the front talking to the chauffeur, GW was able to draw SNOW out into conversation.

SNOW told GW that, when on the Continent, he would be introduced to a 'doctor' who was in charge of the 'Secret Service organisation of the Western area, i.e. England and as far as America'. GW must play up to the fact that, in his capacity as an enquiry agent investigating road accidents, he got about Wales a good deal and saw the working conditions of the people and how they were pressed and exploited by measures decided upon in a Parliament largely composed of Englishmen: he must dwell upon his intensely pro-Welsh convictions and also indicated that he had pro-German sympathies. 'Don't be surprised,' said SNOW at this juncture, 'if I am addressed as Colonel. I hold the rank of Colonel in the German Army.' Apparently, GW 'good humouredly' suggested, this must be rather difficult, because, so he understood, SNOW did not speak German – or at least very little. 'Oh,' said SNOW quickly. 'They call me Colonel.' SNOW then went on to warn GW that he would probably be questioned about sites of ammunition factories, oil refineries and steel works in Wales, and also about activity in the various ports. GW, in his Security Service briefing for the trip, asked MI5 for instructions on this point and was told that he could certainly tell about any factory, oil refinery or steel works of which the existence was a matter of local knowledge and comment – for example, the ICI works at Landore, (which GW quoted as an example) and a new munitions factory going up at Bridgend, near Neath, (which GW also quoted).

During their night out SNOW had returned to the U-boat project which was familiar to MI5; but it was new to GW. SNOW said that perhaps anything up to two or three submarines would come over to land explosives for the blowing up of factories, etc. No rifles, in this instance, were mentioned. SNOW explained that GW would be expected to point out on an ordnance map the most suitable place for landing this material. MI5 later told GW that, after due consideration, he should appear, warmly, to approve of this project and express gratitude for anything that could be sent to him confrères in the way of arms, explosives and money to support a rebellion. GW was later shown, by MI5, a sketch map of Oxwich Bay, depicting the character of the coast and adjacent terrain, and indicating two coves towards the eastward end of the Bay as being most suitable for the landing of munitions. The map was not left with GW because he had a good memory, and he was warned by MI5 that what he said would undoubtedly be checked on a German Admiralty chart. GW came up with the idea of attributing his information to what he had heard all his life from fishermen about that part of the coast.

During their evening out with SNOW he had boasted to GW that he knew the approximate position of every German submarine operating outside Germany. 'Oh yeah!' was the MI5 comment when this was reported by GW. SNOW had also stated, confidently, that, if the Germans sent over three or four submarines, they would not be greatly concerned if one or two did not return, as they would take it for granted that the missing ones had been 'bumped off' by depth charges at some stage in their journey. On arrival at Kingston, SNOW took GW and WW into the room in which his transmitting set was installed. He showed them that it could work off the mains or off a battery. He tuned in, and some very rapid Morse was heard, which he said emanated from Berlin. A curious GW asked SNOW whether he could read Morse, and he said: 'Yes, but they send it very slowly for my benefit.' At about 6 p.m. SNOW, GW, WW and Lily went to the Castle Hotel at Richmond for drinks. About 7 p.m. or so, they proceed to Norbiton, where GW and WW were introduced to a youngish man and woman. The woman said her name was Maude. No surname was clearly mentioned, but GW thought he caught the surname. The young man, with whom GW had quite a conversation, was a lighter man by trade. Then they went to a public house some way off; GW and WW did not know where it was. There they stayed drinking and dancing till 9.30 p.m. Apparently, GW got on very well with Lily 'and must have played his part well' for when GW was dancing with Maude, Lily said to WW: 'Mr GW is a grand man.' – or words to that effect. Then they drove back to Kingston, where SNOW at once got busy with his wireless set. Later, Lily went down to the car with them and paid the driver. GW and WW then left and were back in their hotel by 11.15 p.m. Both GW and WW concurred in thinking that SNOW possessed an 'extremely quick mentality and tremendous willpower' particularly as he drank heavily throughout the evening, even mixing his drinks in respect of whisky and beer, and yet remained very clear headed. SNOW later gave GW some Welsh Nationalist literature to read.

GW and WW arranged to meet SNOW by Nelson's Column at 10.30 the next morning. This was supposed to be the day the agents began their trip to Belgium. MI5 were eager to have a quick chat with GW before he met up with SNOW and hear what had transpired the night before. GW, in order not arouse suspicion, had told SNOW he was going to buy a lighter type of suitcase (he had in fact done so already); and was confident that he could easily explain being late by saying that he had missed the way, London being somewhat strange to him. When he met up with his MI5 contact GW was given a telephone number which he memorised. If he did not leave England with SNOW that night, he was to telephone to let MI5 know. An MI5 officer dropped GW and WW at a safe distance from Trafalgar Square and said goodbye to them. The officer then proceed to Trafalgar Square to have a look at what SNOW – who did not know him by sight – was up to. Unseen by any of them, he watched the agents meet, converse for a while, and then walk away up The Strand.[21]

As it turned out, the agents did not begin their trip that day – 17 October. So, the MI5 officer contacted GW outside the Bonnington Hotel at 10 a.m. the next morning and took him for a drive. GW reported that he had met SNOW the day before, at 11 a.m. at Trafalgar

Square and had gone up The Strand with him and WW for a drink. WW then departed to catch the 1.15 p.m. train back to Wales. GW and SNOW proceeded to Thomas Cook travel agents and arranged to leave Charing Cross at 5.08 p.m. and to sail at dawn on Thursday 19 for Holland. But this plan had to be cancelled, because of the difficulty of obtaining a Dutch visa in under three weeks or a month. GW and SNOW then retired to Burwood House, Caxton Street, to get a letter for SNOW. Reading this letter, SNOW kept shaking his head and eventually remarked cryptically; 'sewing machines'. They eventually managed to get visas from the Belgium consulate.[22]

SNOW and GW left Folkestone on Thursday, 19th, and went straight to Brussels, where they arrived late at night, checking in to the Savoy. At about 5 p.m. on 20th, a German describing himself as a 'Doctor' called at the hotel to say that he had been sent by Dr Rantzau. This doctor explained that he was Dr Rantzau's secretary. The secretary explained that Rantzau would contact SNOW before 2 p.m. on the 21st. However, there was some muddle about the message, and the contact was eventually made at 5 p.m., when Rantzau himself met them at the hotel. SNOW was given 2,000 francs to pay his bill, and they left immediately by the 6 p.m. train for Antwerp where they arrived at about 6.20 p.m. Dr Rantzau travelled with them. On arrival at Antwerp, Rantzau left SNOW and GW with instructions that they should go to the first class dining room in the station were they would be contacted. After about ten minutes, Rantzau's secretary met them and they went to the main part of the station where they met a tall, thin, fair-haired German woman wearing a dark green dress and coat. She was aged thirty-eight to forty and spoke good English. The woman explained that she had recently come from London, apparently just before the outbreak of war. After getting a taxi the woman left them, and the secretary, SNOW and GW drove to the docks. After a while they entered the offices of a shipping firm. SNOW noticed that the offices were exactly opposite the S.S. *Pennland*. This boat was at one time owned by the Red Star Line, but was sold to a German company. SNOW recognised it as he had travelled to England from American on it on many occasions. The office itself was situated on the third floor and they went up by lift. There was nothing particularly striking about the office, apart from the fact that it was a typical shipping office with pictures of ships on the wall. They arrived there at about 7 p.m.

They were met by Dr Rantzau, his secretary, a man known as the 'COMMANDER' from Berlin 'and A.N. Other' who was with SNOW for most of the time. First of all a general meeting was held in the board room. Wales, sabotage, and the Welsh Nationalist

Movement were discussed in general terms. After a while, SNOW, Dr Rantzau, the secretary and A.N. Other went into another room, leaving the Commander with GW. During this time the Commander was constantly going into the room in which SNOW was and asking his advice on certain matters. GW stated that he had about thirty men in South Wales upon whom he could rely to do sabotage work, and further the aims of the German Reich. They discussed arrangements for the moving of some of these Welshmen into factories in England for sabotage purposes. The German also wanted some advice on the landing of explosives in Wales, and it was decided that Oxwich Bay was the best spot on the South Wales coast, where the submarine could be brought fairly close into the shore. The Germans had previously suggested to SNOW, 'who had jibbed', that they should drop explosives by parachute from an aeroplane. They also suggested that they should drop pamphlets in Welsh for propaganda purposes. The Germans seemed to be very keen that the explosives should be brought by submarine. At this stage they mentioned that it was quite possible to get explosives into the United Kingdom by ships, especially though Liverpool. The explosives were to be brought in large quantities but packed in small cases and small bottles, so as to make the storing of them very much easier.

The Commander inadvertently remarked at this juncture that this was one of the mistakes they had made with the IRA, but that they had learnt their lesson and were now sending in the stuff in small quantities. MI5 found this 'extremely interesting as it is a fairly concrete example that the IRA are being run by the Germans'. Mention was also made by the Germans that they had made a mistake in paying members of the IRA in American dollar bills. In discussing the landing of the explosives by submarine the Germans said that it would be dangerous for its ship to come too close in to the shore, and they suggested that possibly it would be as well to stay at about a quarter of a mile out, and that a motorboat should go out to fetch the material. SNOW was asked his opinion as to whether it would be better to send a submarine by the north route or through the Channel to South Wales – he said that he thought it would be better by the north route (an MI5 officer's comment, during the debriefing assessment of the mission, was: 'I think this is probably megalomania' on the part of SNOW).

The Commander apparently knew the South Wales coast extremely well and as far as SNOW and GW could gather he was in charge of the sabotage activities in the United Kingdom, and was therefore 'an important man'.[23] No name was given although this did not seem to matter as SNOW, MI5 had already realised, 'sets no store by names'.[24]

In the first place, the explosives were to take the form of a mixture of potassium chlorate, three parts, to one part of sugar, to be exploded by a concentrated sulphuric acid. Other forms of explosives were to come at a later date. Both GW and SNOW were instructed to return to Holland in about three or four weeks where they would be given American passports to enable them to get into Germany. They would spend a fortnight there partly for the purpose of giving GW further instructions with regard to the mixing of explosives, and also for the purpose of giving him instructions in radio telegraphy. They were both to receive new radio sets after they had made their trip to Germany. Apparently the idea of giving GW a radio set was so that he could contact the submarine and act as a substation to SNOW. He was not to be given facilities for contacting Germany direct – at any rate for the present. Between now and the time that GW went to Germany he was to try and brush up his knowledge of Morse. In his debrief, SNOW was emphatic that he was the only radio link between the United Kingdom and Germany, excluding Ireland; he had been given the impression by the Germans that he was to be the general organiser of agents in the United Kingdom. With regards to his payments of money, he was to receive these through a woman whose name he was not given. She was either going to send it to him by post, deliver it personally at the door, or contact him. The meeting ended at around 9.15 p.m.

On Sunday 22nd, SNOW had to go to the Metropole Hotel, Antwerp and waited for Rantzau's secretary to contact him. This he did, arranging to meet later. SNOW then returned alone to the Metropole where he met Rantzau in a room on the fourth floor. The meeting lasted for about fifteen minutes and Rantzau congratulated SNOW on the information that he had sent through about aeroplanes at Northolt. He also said that he liked GW very much and that he would suit their purpose admirably. SNOW's impression was that he and GW were separated for a purpose, so that German agents in Antwerp could watch GW. At 6.30 p.m. SNOW and GW again went to the shipping office with the Commander who had brought with him various instruments for measuring out and weighing ingredients for explosive mixtures. Arrangements were made for a demonstration to take place on Monday evening. On Monday night the Commander again came for them and took them to a flat of a Flemish Nationalist, where the Commander gave a demonstration on mixing the ingredients of the explosive. SNOW's impression from this meeting was that the Flemish Nationalists were well-organised and as soon as an advance was made into Belgium by the Germans, the Nationalists 'will start sabotage and a revolution'. After the demonstration, SNOW and GW left Antwerp for Brussels and returned home. As an MI5 officer assessed SNOW's debrief 'it was clear that his dates are not very accurate. This, I am pretty certain is not intentional on the part of SNOW as he is notoriously bad at getting things into a chronological order in his own mind.' Apart from the fact that he had got his dates slightly wrong, his report coincided with the one submitted by GW.

SNOW was offered some £30,000 in American dollars to take with him to England for the purpose of paying members of the Welsh Nationalist Party for committing acts of sabotage. This he flatly refused to take for it would be too dangerous for him to handle American dollars in England, owing to the exchange-rate difficulties, and he said that it would be far better to pay these men in English currency. It also emerged that a German agent was shortly coming over to England to contact GW. He would make himself known by first of all talking about pictures, and then producing a photograph of GW (while they were on the Continent they were instructed to get their photographs taken). This agent would be moving round the country for a fortnight before actually going to Swansea. The information gathered by SNOW seemed to confirm MI5's fears that the Germans had an agent in the Air Ministry and one in the Admiralty.

As far as GW was concerned, he gathered that he was to be responsible for collecting information about activities in Liverpool and Lancashire, especially with regard to Liverpool, in relation to the number of ships leaving, and the supplies coming in from America.[25] GW was 'now a stamp collector'. He was to get the names and addresses of agencies for stamps all over the world. The Germans were going to use a stamp code. GW and SNOW were to be back in Brussels in about three weeks time. They were both to go from Belgium or Holland across the frontier into Germany, and they would spend two or three weeks where they were to be given American passports. The object of this visit was to school GW in the mixing of chemicals for explosive purposes. The Germans gave SNOW wooden slabs 4in. by 3in. and half an inch thick, which contained detonators. These SNOW brought back with him to Britain in his case. He also had with him three tiny bits of photograph, on each of which there was something typewritten. It was micro-photography. On one of these was a letter of introduction to a man in Liverpool who was a Fellow of the Royal Photographic Society. SNOW was to go up in the near future and contact this man, who was apparently in the pay of the Germans. The other two contained detailed instructions for SNOW; apparently he was to get them developed in Liverpool. The idea of the microphotography was that they were to get instructions out of the country by sticking these under postage stamps on a letter. The letter would be an ordinary business one.[26]

The German agent in Liverpool was codenamed by MI5 as CHARLIE. CHARLIE was of German origin and one of a family of three brothers. He himself acquired British nationality at birth. Of his two brothers, one was still resident in Germany and the other, who was staying with CHARLIE at the outbreak of war, was later interned and died in the *Arandora Star* after it was torpedoed by a U-Boat. CHARLIE and his brother had already come to notice in August 1939 when their address had been found in the possession of a certain Gunther Raydt, who had himself come under suspicion. Subsequently he was arrested for a breach of the Aliens Regulations, and as a result of statements made by him it had become clear that the two brothers had been recruited by another 'doctor' this time – Dr. Hansen – in Cologne in the summer of 1938. Since then they had both worked to some extent for the Germans, though CHARLIE had only done so reluctantly under the threat of reprisals to his brother in Germany. It later appeared that Dr. Hansen was in fact identical with Rantzau and 'there is little doubt that his object in putting SNOW into touch with CHARLIE was that the latter, who was an expert photographer, should be used by SNOW to develop the microphotographs which he was to receive and to reduce SNOW's own reports to the same form for easy transmission to Germany'.[27]

Lieutenant Stopford, of MI5, was despatched to Manchester and CHARLIE was hauled in to a local police station. CHARLIE's house was raided by the police who removed a parcel of documents. When Stopford saw CHARLIE in the evening of 4 November 1939, in a private room at the local police station, he arranged for Superintendent Page to give CHARLIE a parcel of some of the documents taken from the house so that the agent's family should have no suspicion of the real reason for his visit to the police station. Stopford 'thoroughly frightened' CHARLIE at the very beginning of the conversation, 'by telling him that we know all about him and his family, and all their activities, and that if he breathed a word of the conversation to anyone at any time in the future and did not do exactly what I told him, we would see that he and his brothers were "put inside" and further that we would see that a copy of his confession fell into the hands of German S[ecret]S[ervice]'. CHARLIE hastened to assure Stopford that he was entirely British in his sympathies and had lived in England nearly all his life, and would, without question, do anything MI5 asked.

From this interview Stopford was quite confident, both from examination of his correspondence and from his conversation with

CHARLIE, that he was an unwilling agent for Germany, had not done anything much, but had been thoroughly frightened by Dr Hansen when he saw him on his last visit to Germany. Dr Hansen had told him 'several cock and bull stories of people being mysteriously killed in England if they gave the game away'. Stopford felt equally sure that the reason for the Germans approaching CHARLIE at the present juncture was that Hansen was trading on the effect of the fright he gave CHARLIE in Germany and the threat to his brother, Hans, in Germany if CHARLIE did not act for them. CHARLIE revealed to Stopford that Hansen had asked him if he could reduce photographs to a size small enough to go under a postage stamp, and also told him that he would arrange to send an illustration of the proper printing paper enclosed in a sample of ordinary sized paper. CHARLIE claimed that this never turned up. Hansen also told him that he would be contacted by a man from Edinburgh on one of his journeys 'in quite a haphazard way', and that the other man would refer to his family in Germany when introducing himself. This contact, according to CHARLIE, was also not made.

Stopford explained to CHARLIE that MI5 had rather a vague clue of the probability of his being contacted by a German emissary quite unknown to them, and that, in fact, 'we had no idea of the nationality, position, or even sex, of the possible agent'. But if and when this contact was made CHARLIE was to act exactly as he would do if he was on the German side and willing to engage in espionage on their behalf; CHARLIE at this point claimed that if Stopford had not got in touch with him, he would have arrested the emissary himself, if possible, and handed him over to the Police. Stopford did not comment on this and merely made the point that, directly the contact had been made, CHARLIE was to write to him at once. CHARLIE was told to write quite a simple letter mentioning that 'Mr Roberts' had been to see him, was coming to London, and hoped that Stopford would be able to do something towards helping him to find work. Stopford would then get in touch with CHARLIE, arrange to meet him, and he would let him know full details of what the Germans emissary had said and asked him to do. In the event of CHARLIE wanting Stopford to get in touch with him urgently, in his letter he would give Mr Roberts a Christian name. CHARLIE was not to get in touch with Stopford by telephone. Stopford reported back to London Centre that CHARLIE 'absolutely understands that on no account must he disclose to the unknown emissary, or to his brother, or anyone else, that he has been contacted by us; and I think he is much too frightened to do so even if he wanted to, which I do not believe is the case'.[28] As the result of Stopford's successful visit to CHARLIE, it was decided that SNOW should go to Manchester and contact CHARLIE at the Manchester Photographic Society. SNOW was to approach him, using the name of 'Graham' and go to register in a hotel under the name of Wilson. He was also give CHARLIE a cover address, namely, British Columbia House, London, to write to.[29]

It will be recalled that, during his visit to Brussels SNOW was informed by the Germans that he would for the future be paid by a German agent in Britain – a mysterious woman resident near Bournemouth. In fact, during his absence in Brussels two letters had arrived for SNOW, each containing £20.[30] Lieutenant Stopford set himself the task of tracking down this German agent. He noted that three of the four £5 notes paid to SNOW had a rubber stamp on the back marked 'S. & Co Ltd'. This suggested that they had been through the tills at Selfridges department store in Oxford Street. Stopford went to see Mr King, the Chief Cashier at Selfridges to see if he could trace their history. After discussing the matter with him and Miss Oxford, who was in charge of the cashiers there, and examining their banking system, Stopford concluded that as the three notes had not got the stamp of Selfridges's bankers, the Midland Bank, on them and as the date of the post mark on the envelope to SNOW, in which the cash was delivered, was similar to that on the notes, i.e. the 14 November 1939, the notes must have been received into Selfridges and paid out again on the same date. There were only three ways in which the £5 notes could have been paid out, namely: (a) Against a cheque or draft, (b) In exchange for notes of a higher denomination, and (c) In exchange for notes or coin of a lower denomination.

Stopford examined the list of cheques paid into Selfridges, on the 14, 15 and 16 November, and asked for further information in this connection from the Midland Bank; from this he was able to conclude that the notes in question had probably not been paid out against a cheque. There were only four cashiers in the head cash office who would have changed a note of a higher denomination and none of them remembered doing so. Stopford, therefore, questioned the three cashiers, at Selfridges, whose code numbers were marked by rubber stamp on the back of the notes. One of the cashiers remembered taking in a £5 note, from a shop assistant, about the date in question in part payment for a purchase; and she subsequently remembered the same assistant asking her if she had already banked a £5 note as she wished to exchange it for five £1 notes.

The cashier was able to find the assistant in question; and, on Stopford's interrogation, she told him that a tall elderly lady with grey hair, probably wearing glasses, dressed in black or a dark costume with black furs and carrying a dark rather large attaché case, had taken five £1 notes out of an envelope in her handbag and asked if the assistant could get her a £5 note in exchange, as she wished to send it away. The assistant said that the lady was particularly charming and well spoken. The assistant obtained the £5 note from the cashier and gave it to her. The assistant's code number was 2175 in department 21, Ladies' Wear and the cashiers code number was 157. Stopford then found that cashier number 47, whose number was stamped on the back of one of the other £5 notes, also remembered giving a £5 note to one of the assistants about that date in exchange for five £1 notes. Stopford traced the assistant in question and her number was 1571 in the Ladies' Underwear department. She told him that on the day in question, an elderly lady about six feet tall, about sixty years old, with grey hair, rather stoutish build, very charming in manner and well-spoken, dressed in a dark costume, took seven £1 notes out of a purse, concealed either in her stocking or her underclothes, and asked if she could have a £5 note in exchange for five £1 notes, as she was anxious to send it away by post. The assistant said that the lady was carrying a small dark weekend case into which she put the things she was buying. The third cashier was unable to remember giving out a note.

It seemed quite clear to Stopford that the lady in question who got the £5 notes was the person who made the remittances to SNOW, and this tallied with what SNOW had been told in Germany. Her technique appeared to be to draw £1 notes from her bank or somewhere else, and turn them into £5 notes at any suitable place such as a store, thinking that in this way she could not be traced back to a bank. Stopford concluded that: 'She is probably a person of means and probably lives in the country, having come up to London to shop. She may live in the district not far from Bournemouth and Southampton, as two previous remittances were posted at those towns.'[31]

More information was gleaned from an intercepted letter from Wm. H. Muller & Co, Electra House, 78 Moorgate, EC2, to a Mrs Krafft dated 4 December that indicated she might be the German agent dropping money off to SNOW. Stopford took Mrs Longstaff and Miss Beedell, the shop assistants from Selfridges, to Waterloo Station on 7 December. Stopford wanted to see if they could identify Mrs Krafft, who was travelling on the train from Bournemouth to London, as the woman who asked for the £5 notes at Selfridges. They met the train from Bournemouth due at Waterloo at 12.09 p.m. on No.11 platform, which arrived at 12.50 p.m. All the passengers came out of one gate but Mrs Krafft was not identified. They then met the train from

Bournemouth due at 1.07 p.m. on platform 13, which arrived on time. There was a large number of passengers and Mrs Krafft was again not identified, though Stopford personally, from the description he had had of her, thought that he saw her come off the train.

As Mrs Krafft had an appointment with Wm. Muller & Co, Stopford took the two girls to Moorgate and kept observation on Muller's office from about 2.10 p.m. till 3.05 p.m. There was an elderly lady standing in the office talking to two men, and Mrs Longstaff and Miss Beedell walked by the window and identified her as the woman to whom they had given £5 notes in Selfridges. A minute or two later Mrs Krafft walked out of the office of Muller, passed close to Mrs Longstaff and Miss Beedell, who without hesitation recognised her as the lady they had served at Selfridges. She waited on the pavement for a taxi. 'Neither Mrs Longstaff nor Miss Beedell had any doubts as to Mrs Krafft being identical with the woman they had described to me,' recorded Stopford.[32] Mrs Mathilde Krafft's immediate fate is unclear, however an MI5 report later described her as 'now in Holloway Prison'.[33]

SNOW travelled once more to Belgium, arriving back from Antwerp on 19 December. He was debriefed by MI5 on 20 December. Rantzau told him that he had been called to Berlin to explain why SNOW's weather reports had been so bad. Rantzau made excuses apparently and said that his agent could not possibly be expected to 'furnish accurate weather reports at night especially in the blackout!' They pointed out in Berlin that these reports did not tally with those received from Ireland and Holland. SNOW was given instructions to take the weather between 12 noon and 2 p.m. and broadcast it as usual in the evening. His call sign and German station were changed to CTA, i.e. SNOW had to make CTA and the German station had to make OIK. His transmissions had not been coming through at all well: 'at any rate, they cannot compare with the transmissions from Ireland'. Transmissions were to start again at 7.15 p.m. on 26 December.

The weather code was now to be in five letter groups. The first group and the last group were to start with 'X', but the intervening groups were to be as usual, only they had to be made up to five letters by adding two other letters as padding. For example, XVO, which was the original group giving the visibility would now be XVOPQ. The second group giving the height of the clouds would start 'H' with four other letters to follow. The velocity of the wind would be given separately as before but a new code word was to be used to indicate the speed. This was: CHRISTMAS CAROL. C=1, H=2, R=3, I=4, S=5, T=6, M=7, A=8, S+C+A+R=Nulls, O=9, L=0. The direction of the wind was now to be given as: A = North, B = South, C = East, D = West.

As arranged SNOW mentioned that his money had not been paid to him for some considerable time and it was explained to him that the Germans had had trouble with their agent in Britain (Mrs Krafft) and they were making new arrangements. He was given £215 as an advance. During his time in Antwerp Dr Rantzau, the Commander, a Dr Kiess, and an unnamed woman interviewed him. This woman, until just before the war, had lived in Farnborough and London. She also had many contacts in high Fascist circles in Britain. She expressed disappointment that she had not heard from her friends in the BUF for some time and it was considered likely that, if she did not hear within the next few weeks, SNOW would be given the names of a certain number of them and would be asked to contact them. SNOW described her 'as looking like a Canadian'. After consultation with Dick White, Max Knight and others, it was thought almost certain that this woman was identical with a woman MI5 knew to be Mrs Lisa Kruger. White provided a photograph of Lisa Kruger, which was shown to SNOW. He felt that the photograph was very like the woman except that the face in the photograph was a bit too full.

The Germans had asked many questions about GW and said that 'they were not very inspired by him' indicating that he appeared to them to be far too nervous during his visit. SNOW suggested that if they wanted to make use of them they could, but that the best thing would be to do it direct and to cut him out. He said that he was quite satisfied with their *bona fides*. Incendiary materials were to be sent by submarine to South Wales as arranged previously but not until SNOW had given the word go. SNOW had to make arrangements to have explosives loaded in ships leaving the UK for foreign countries. For this purpose the Germans had invented a new type of explosive, which they claimed to be extremely effective. These bombs were to be sent over to SNOW concealed in accumulators. These accumulators would be charged but would not have any distilled water in them. In each of the cells there would be a bomb. These would be operated by a small watch that could be timed to go off any time from one hour to seventeen days. They were also making arrangements for the shipment in false accumulators of wireless parts. As far as this type of business was concerned SNOW was considered to be admirably situated to carry out any correspondence with foreign countries in connection with importing batteries and accumulators. When he was ready for a consignment of these accumulators, he was to write quite an open letter to the Societe Consignation et Affertement, 25–27 Rue Jesus, Antwerp. This firm would then despatch the accumulators to him. The Germans also told him that they had invented a new type of incendiary bomb, which was to be packed in a package of Swedish bread. ('This I think looks something like Ryvita' reported SNOW) When the package was opened a small ring would be found which, when pulled, released the incendiary bombs twenty seconds afterwards. They were trying to perfect this bomb in order to arrange for it to go off three hours afterwards.[34]

German interest in a Welsh Nationalist rebellion continued for some time afterwards, though it gradually became clear that the Germans were losing interest in their Welsh sabotage scheme. The reason for this, considered MI5, was not that the Germans did not trust GW; rather 'it appears more probable that the insurrection in South Wales was designed to coincide with the Germans' invasion of this country and that for this reason action was postponed until that moment, and in the end abandoned entirely'. SNOW continued to transmit wireless messages almost daily and from time to time paid further visits to the Continent for the purpose of consultation with the DOCTOR. Nothing of very great interest happened at most of these meetings. In the meantime, SNOW had been established himself in business in London. His partner in this enterprise was W.N. Rolph, a nominee of MI5. In this capacity SNOW was in correspondence with the Societe de Consignation et Affertement of Antwerp, the firm employed by the Germans as a cover.

All in all it had to be admitted by MI5 that they were more than satisfied with the results shown by the case: 'SNOW's activities had been from our point of view uniformly successful, since they had already resulted in the discovery of not less than three German agents. From the German point of view they had been equally satisfactory, since they supposed that SNOW was now established with a satisfactory sub-agent, CHARLIE, living near Manchester, a link through GW with a promising scheme for sabotage in South Wales, a wireless set and a safe means of payment' through Mrs. Krafft. But, in 1940, events were to shake the Security Service's confidence in their pioneering Double-Cross agent.

SNOW continued his periodic trips over to the Continent. During a meeting, which SNOW had with the DOCTOR in Antwerp in April 1940, it had been suggested by Rantzau that a further meeting should take place between them on a trawler in the North Sea. Rantzau said that he had been much impressed by the ease with which smuggling was carried on from the east coast of England and he thought SNOW would have no difficulty in obtaining the use of a trawler for this purpose. Rantzau would arrive either by submarine or aircraft and the real purpose of the meeting was to smuggle a new sub-agent, whom SNOW was to produce, into Germany, where he would undergo a thorough training in sabotage and espionage. During May 'this extraordinary project came to a head' and it became necessary for MI5 to produce upon SNOW's behalf both the trawler and the agent. The former was produced by arrangement with the Fisheries Board and the latter was discovered in the person of BISCUIT, a man who, 'after a prolonged career of petty larceny, dope smuggling and the confidence trick, had reformed and since acted as a capable and honest informer in criminal matters. He was accordingly introduced to SNOW, who can have been in no doubt but that BISCUIT was acting as an agent of this office. It is important to emphasise this point in view of what happened later and also because the case of SNOW and CHARLIE had previously been run upon the basis that neither knew that the other was controlled, though it is clear that after a while both of them must have guessed this fact'.[35] From this point on, MI5's faith in SNOW began to slip into agnosticism.

As the countdown to the intended rendezvous in the North Sea began, TAR Robertson took control of the mission. The potential prize of the DOCTOR's capture seemed to be within his grasp. Robertson went, on the morning of 18 May, to Richmond Park and met SNOW and BISCUIT to discuss at great length a suitable story for SNOW to tell the DOCTOR about BISCUIT, including his past history, his connection and friendship with SNOW. At the end of the meeting Robertson took SNOW on one side and asked him if he thought BISCUIT would be a suitable person to take. SNOW said that he thought BISCUIT would fill the bill admirably and that it was just as well that he was a greenhorn at this type of work. Later, however, while travelling in Robertson's car to Max Knight's flat, BISCUIT told the MI5 officer that he had had several talks with SNOW during the course of the day. The gist of the conversation was that BISCUIT had said that he would go on this trip and was willing to go into Germany for SNOW, but he (BISCUIT) wanted to know what sort of money he would be paid and whether his interests would be looked after. SNOW replied that BISCUIT need not worry a bit about this as the Germans would look after him 100 per cent and that they were all very fine people. SNOW added that he proposed to introduce BISCUIT to the Germans as a member of MI5 and mentioned Robertson's name. On BISCUIT saying that he thought this was extremely dangerous, SNOW said: 'You need not worry about that – they (meaning the Germans) know all about my connection with Robertson. They know exactly what I am doing.' He gave the same reply to BISCUIT when the latter asked him what answer he was to give if he was questioned on this point when he got to Germany. This, BISCUIT then told Robertson, had led him to conclude that SNOW was very pro-Nazi and was in actual fact working for the Germans and that he was being paid vast sums of money for being in touch with Robertson.

The seeds of doubt fell on fertile ground, for this seemed to ring true with Robertson's impression of SNOW: he recalled how, during the conversation the three of them had had in Richmond Park, he asked SNOW if he had any money which he could give to BISCUIT for settling up his affairs before leaving England. The MI5 officer had only 10 shillings with him but would give him some money if necessary. SNOW claimed that he was very short of money and only had £5 on him. Robertson noted: 'I had previously seen his notecase which was quite ½" thick' with money. Now he coupled this observation with a short conversation that SNOW and BISCUIT had in the Park and revealed by the latter: SNOW said to BISCUIT that he was not going to tell Robertson that he had money as he was anxious to get as much money out of him as possible; he ended the conversation by saying: 'Why shouldn't he pay, after all?' BISCUIT also told Robertson that SNOW had inferred that Robertson, as well as a good many others in MI5, were 'for it' as soon as the Germans landed in Britain. SNOW claimed that Robertson was earning at least £5,000 a year and that he pocketed the money, which his office was supposed to give to SNOW. Robertson noted: 'it is quite clear that SNOW is in earnest and is definitely dangerous'.

BISCUIT and Robertson went straight to Knight's flat to discuss the whole affair with him. BISCUIT was instructed to go on with the scheme and to act as though nothing had happened. He rang up SNOW – with both Knight and Robertson present – and told him that he had only been given £2 by Robertson who he thought 'was a pretty revolting sort of bloke'. SNOW agreed and asked BISCUIT to come round and see him straight away. Robertson arranged to see BISCUIT at 9.30 a.m. the next morning before he left, with SNOW, to catch the 11.10 a.m. train at King's Cross to Grimsby from where the maritime expedition to meet the DOCTOR was to depart on the trawler *Barbados*. From that morning meeting, Robertson emerged 'even more convinced that BISCUIT was telling the truth and that SNOW was double-crossing me. I went up to King's Cross to see them off and bid them farewell, but beforehand I had given BISCUIT instructions to get as much information out of SNOW as he possibly could on the journey up and on his trip in the trawler. I arranged with BISCUIT that he should ring me up that night from Grimsby if he could get away from SNOW.'

In the meantime, at a conference between Colonel Harker, Guy Liddell, Stopford and Robertson, it was decided that the *Barbados* should not on any account keep the rendezvous with the DOCTOR, but that the trawler should go out into the North Sea with SNOW and BISCUIT on board, do their fishing, and, at the appointed hour of the night, stand by at a place far removed from the correct one in order to make it appear to SNOW that everything was going according to plan so as to make him think that the DOCTOR had been unable to keep the rendezvous. It was decided that only the trawler captain and BISCUIT should be let into this scheme. In the evening BISCUIT rang Robertson up and said that all the way up in the train SNOW had been 'running down' Robertson and other officers in MI5 'and saying what a rotten organisation it was'. He had on him, apart from the information and photographs, which Robertson had also given him, an Important People Club List – from one of Kell's dinners held some years before – that should not have been in his possession. BISCUIT also claimed that SNOW had been making copious notes of everything that he saw from the carriage window on his way up to Grimsby in the train, such as particulars of aerodromes, power stations and the like, which he said he was going to hand over to the Germans. At this point it was decided by the MI5 officers 'that we should try and stage a "Venlo"' and try, if possible, to capture the DOCTOR alive. Arrangements were set in motion. The Admiralty suggested some sort of decoy ship, looking exactly like the *Barbados* in order to draw the DOCTOR and the enemy. The trawler was to be manned with naval ratings, carry depth charges and hand grenades, and, if possible, a wireless set. The plan was called Operation LAMP.[36] If Rantzau could not be captured, whatever ship he came in was to be sunk if possible.

Robertson, accompanied by Stopford, then made haste to the northeast whereon he was informed that a signal had been received from the *Barbados* saying that she was returning to Grimsby immediately with some important information. By the time the *Barbados* had landed, instructions had been given that none of the crew, including SNOW and BISCUIT should be allowed to leave the ship. The story that emerged of what happened was as follows: the *Barbados* had left Grimsby at about 5.30 a.m. on Monday morning. She got to the mouth of the passage to the North Sea, having passed through a minefield, when an aircraft of a monoplane type, coming from a westerly direction, circled very low round her and then left her again in a westerly direction. The machine, according to the captain of the *Barbados*, had red, white and blue markings vertically on the tail but he was unable to say whether it was a British machine as he had been unable to see the roundels on the fuselage or beneath the wings. He was shown the silhouettes of both British and German machines but could not recognise this machine among them. They had then proceeded out to the fishing ground and nothing happened until they got to a point roughly sixty miles from the rendezvous. This was about midnight and was still a number of days ahead of the rendezvous date. They had decided to do a trawl and had just put down the net when a seaplane seemed to appear from nowhere, flew over the ship very low, made a circle round her, shooting out green starlights from port, starboard, and rear and sending them Morse signals on their lamp to stop. The captain, who was the only one on board who saw it, BISCUIT and SNOW being below, reported the matter to BISCUIT, who gave instructions for the ship to put out her lights and depart speedily for home. On this being done, the seaplane left them and was not seen again.[37]

On the return to port, Robertson was handed a letter that had been removed from SNOW's person, while on board ship, and written before the *Barbados* had arrived at the rendezvous, to his partner Lily. This letter had clearly been written under a great strain and appeared quite genuine, as it had been made quite clear to SNOW that if he made a false step 'he would never see land again'. From members of the crew Robertson knew that SNOW 'had a pretty rough passage', but at the same time appeared to be most anxious to get hold of the DOCTOR either alive or dead 'and was willing to play the game as far as he possibly could'.[38] But BISCUIT was convinced this was a cover on the part of SNOW. He was of the opinion that they had been tailed all the way from Grimsby. Robertson's assessment was that: 'This to my mind is not very likely. However, it is quite possible that they [the Germans] had sent a machine out there for reconnaissance purposes to see whether the trawler was anywhere near the rendezvous. To my mind, the action which was taken was quite correct. They were not expecting to meet anyone that night and would naturally be rather scared at seeing a strange plane signalling to them.'

In case the DOCTOR showed up, Robertson decided to requisition the *Barbados*. Various details were fixed up such as wireless communications with destroyers that were known to be working in the vicinity. Robertson went with Stopford to H.M.S. *Corunia* and interviewed SNOW who was being held there in the naval prison: 'I took BISCUIT with me but in the first place kept him outside.'[39] 'To put it mildly,' he recorded, SNOW 'was in the most frightful mess, complaining of a duodenal ulcer and really looking desperately ill'.[40] Robertson asked SNOW a few questions relating to the voyage and to the various remarks which he had made to BISCUIT. 'I told him quite straight that I considered he was double-crossing me which he flatly denied. He said that he was never going to allow the meeting to take place and that he thought that BISCUIT was a German agent and was leading him into a trap. At a later stage I brought BISCUIT in and he again cross-examined him on the various points which I had raised previously.' Robertson asked SNOW why he had got a copy of the I.P. Club List and why he had notes relating to one or two points of interest which he had seen going up in the train to Grimsby. With regard to the I.P. Club list SNOW said that this had been given to him by his business partner – and MI5 nominee – Rolph who regarded Colonel Hinchley Cooke and Robertson as scoundrels; Rolph, as Robertson already knew, was very anxious to go over to Germany as an agent and was exceedingly hard up for money. When told by SNOW that Robertson would not agree to him going to Germany owing to the fact that he was a Jew, SNOW said Rolph had become very annoyed and produced papers to show that he was not a Jew. He then gave SNOW the I.P. Club list and told SNOW that he was, at all costs, to get from the Germans £2,000 which SNOW was then to hand over to him. With regard to the notes he had made during the train journey, SNOW reminded Robertson that he had previously told him that he could take notes on anything of interest which he saw either by the side of the road or by the railway in his travels.[41]

SNOW continued to deny emphatically that he was double-crossing the British and said that he had never given any particulars of anybody he had met connected with MI5 to the Germans. SNOW repeated that he was not certain of BISCUIT and thought that he was a German agent leading him into a trap; but, noted Robertson, 'he was quite unable to answer any question to the effect that, if he thought he was a German agent, why should he be taking him to Germany to act as a German agent and if he really thought this why didn't he tell us?' SNOW was questioned for over two hours but, for Robertson, only one thing of interest came from this interrogation. That was to the effect that SNOW seemed to have been 'living in a reign of terror' for some years from the Gestapo: when he was working for SIS in the early days of 1935 or 1936, he was commissioned by them to take a photograph of Kiel Harbour. This he did and got the photographs safely back to England. Some years after, when he met the DOCTOR, he was confronted with this act and on pain of death told Rantzau that he had done this for the British Secret Service.[42] The question before Robertson was what to do next. He decided to send SNOW back to sea in the *Barbardos*, this time accompanied by an armed crew of seventeen naval ratings; SNOW was warned that if there was any sign that he was double-crossing at the time of the rendezvous taking place, 'he would probably never come back to this country'; but, on the other hand, if he could be instrumental in unveiling and capturing the DOCTOR, 'I might consider his case again, but that in the meantime I was perfectly convinced, owing to various things which I had been told, that he was double-crossing me and that he had given my name already to the Germans.'

In truth, Robertson was confused as to what sort of game, if any, SNOW was playing. On reflection, he thought of SNOW: 'His mind is a very odd affair and it does not work on logical lines and the arguments which he put up for the things which he had said to BISCUIT were not exactly convincing but at the same time seemed to me to hold a certain amount of water.' Nevertheless, after this interview, Robertson saw Lieutenant Argles who was to command the *Barbados* and gave him final instructions for the voyage: namely that he was to take SNOW, but he was not to trust him for one moment and that if there was any sign of him double-crossing Argles at the rendezvous, 'he was immediately to take any action which he thought was suitable'. After going through the story again, with BISCUIT and Stopford, Robertson remained confused and confessed: 'I find it exceedingly difficult to make up my mind one way or another as to whether SNOW is in actual fact double-crossing me.'[43] The effort made to retrieve the situation by despatching the trawler with a naval crew to the correct position and time of the rendezvous yielded naught as there was no sign of any enemy aircraft or submarine. Fortunately, however, there was a fog and SNOW was subsequently able to represent to the DOCTOR, apparently with success, that he had been at the rendezvous at the right time and had missed Rantzau as a result of the fog.[44]

After returning to London, Stopford and Robertson both agreed that there was no possible chance of preferring a case against SNOW, as there was really very little evidence on which to base one. On Robertson's instructions SNOW was to send over a wireless message to the other side asking the reason why they had not made the rendezvous. SNOW at his last interrogation implored to be given one more chance, as he was quite confident that he could get the DOCTOR. His wireless message was answered but there was no message. While considering his next move, Robertson gave instructions for SNOW's telephone to be disconnected and for him to be placed under house arrest.[45] Finally, after discussion with Colonel Harker, a Detention Order under Regulation 18B should be issued against SNOW.[46]

But the final decision was to give SNOW the benefit of the doubt. MI5 accepted that BISCUIT had genuinely held the view that SNOW was working for the Germans and would undoubtedly reveal his position as a 'controlled' British agent as soon as he met the DOCTOR. 'SNOW on the other hand appears to have been, for reasons which we cannot analyse, under the impression that BISCUIT was a genuine German agent who would undoubtedly reveal his, SNOW's, ambiguous position' when their meeting with Rantzau took place. 'As a result of this he did everything in his power to convince BISCUIT that he was acting genuinely in the German interest, and thereby redoubled BISCUIT's suspicions. In this nightmare state of mind the two boarded the trawler and proceeded towards the rendezvous.' The follow up investigation into how SNOW had possession of the incriminating documents proved he was telling the truth with regard to this matter at least. When Rolph was questioned about supplying the documents to SNOW, 'his behaviour left no doubt of his guilt'. So, SNOW had told the truth regarding the IP Club List.

Even so 'there was, not unreasonably, some doubt as to SNOW's *bona fides*. These doubts were finally resolved in SNOW's favour, for it was clear that a great part of the trouble had had its origin in a genuine misunderstanding between SNOW and BISCUIT of each others motives and methods of work'. SNOW's case was continued as before and, since he had already told the DOCTOR in his wireless traffic that he had recruited a new sub-agent in the person of BISCUIT, it became necessary, since the meeting at sea had miscarried, to arrange some other means of contact. It was therefore agreed that BISCUIT should travel to Lisbon under the cover of a dealer in Portuguese wine. On the German side he had been instructed to put himself in touch with the hotel Duas Nacoes, Rua Victoria, which was entirely under the control of the Germans. BISCUIT arrived in Lisbon on 24 July 1940 and put up at the hotel as instructed. In Lisbon he had a short meeting with Rantzau who had travelled from Germany to see him, but passed most of his time in company with Hans Doebler, one of the principal resident German agents in Lisbon. The principal subject of conversation between BISCUIT and the DOCTOR was naturally the episode in the North Sea, which BISCUIT was apparently able to explain away by saying that SNOW had been at the rendezvous at the right time but had seen nothing. Rantzau confided to BISCUIT that, in his opinion, SNOW's work was falling off but that he had done excellent work in the past. He also told him that there was a South African waiting in Belgium to come to Britain, where he would be dropped by parachute as an assistant or sub-agent to SNOW. Lastly he asked that arrangements should be made in some suitable place where SNOW and BISCUIT could receive sabotage material dropped to them by parachute. BISCUIT returned to London on 21 August bringing with him a further wireless set for SNOW in a suitcase which he was apparently intended to smuggle through customs. He was also provided with a further questionnaire and microphotographs and some $3,000.[47] SNOW was still in business – at least for now.

2

'The Truth in the Shortest Possible Time'
Camp 020

Tin Eye

A key element of MI5's penetration of the Abwehrabteilung – the central intelligence organ of German naval, military and air intelligence espionage agencies – took place at the formidable sounding Camp 020. A suspected spy was likely to find himself here. In the description of Robin William George Stephens the atmosphere was intimidating. He was not allowed to sit down, but stood facing the British officers who had their backs to the window. The prisoner's file and property were on the table. A panel of four or five officers created the necessary impressive atmosphere[1] that was designed to be that of a General Court Martial. One officer interrogated. In no circumstances whatsoever might he be interrupted. Unless he issued an invitation no other officer was permitted to put any question whatever. The spy was only allowed to speak when spoken to. In the view of the Camp Commandant: 'Studious politeness, the courtesy of a chair, the friendliness of a cigarette, these things breed familiarity and confidence in a spy. Figuratively, a spy in war should be at the point of a bayonet.' This intimidating atmosphere was necessary because: 'The stake is high. It is the life of the spy against the security of a country. In roulette the odds are on the Bank; in contre-espionage the odds disappear. The long term policy gives way to the vital present.' It was necessary to find the motive of the spy: 'broadly, what manner of man is the spy? Is he a patriot, brave? Is he of the underworld, a subject of blackmail? Is he just a mercenary, who will sell a ship for the dollar, the piastre, the escudo, the franc? Is it possible to approach the problem in another way, are there national as distinct from individual characteristics?' Although many were motivated by higher ideas 'the patriots are few, and these brave fewer still'.[2] Once the interrogation had begun the objective was: 'Truth in the shortest possible time.'

> Some information in time is worth more than an encyclopaedia [sic] out of date.
> The length of a sound C[ounter]I[ntelligence] report is often in inverse ratio to the labour expended upon it.
> The ideal for a preliminary report is a signed confession. In itself it is a short report; it is a holding document; it is a stage in the

investigation from which the spy cannot retreat.
The penalty for espionage is death. If the spy tells the truth he may live. There is no guarantee; it is a hope, not more.
The quicker the spy realises that fundamental position the better.
Psychology and discipline should produce that result.
Arrest must be efficient. The less said the better. The quicker the handcuffs are slipped on the more pronounced is the effect of stark reality. The quicker ill fitting and shabby prison garb take the place of sartorial elegance the more profound and depressing is the effect.
No exceptions. No chivalry. No gossip. No cigarettes.
Incommunicado is the watchword.[3]

If everything else failed to produce a break, the prisoner would be consigned to one or other of two punishment cells, which was commonly described as the 'condemned cell'. These two cells were actually not much less comfortable than the ordinary cells and were the same size, but with windows higher above ground and they were colder in winter. But when a prisoner was put in one of these cells it was heavily implied in veiled terms that this was his last chance of coming clean. Surprisingly often this method proved successful and prisoners gave additional information in order to get transferred to pleasanter quarters. The address that was delivered to prisoners before being taken to, for example, Cell 14, was delivered by the Camp Commandant, 'Tin Eye' Stephens:

You will now be taken to Cell Fourteen.
In time of peace it was a padded cell., so protected that raving maniacs could not bash out their brains against the wall. Some recovered. Some committed suicide. Some died from natural causes.
The mortuary is conveniently opposite.
In time of war accommodation is short. Cell Fourteen is no longer a padded cell. Now there is no difference between that cell and any other cell. Perhaps it is remote, and cold and a little dark. That is all. But for some reason the sinister reputation persists.
Some spies believe in the supernatural. They say certain psychic elements are present. Some spies suffer from claustrophobia. Some spies have a guilty conscience and know no peace.
Results are interesting. Some spies have told the truth and been transferred. Some have committed suicide. Some have passed out

for the last time to their judicial hanging – their rich desert.
I shall not see you again. I do not know how long you will be
there. Petitions will be ignored. Only if you decide to tell the truth
will you be allowed to write. But just remember this, that we are
winning the war in spite of you – one man only – in captivity.
Maybe you are holding back information which is already in our
possession. Maybe you are more of a fool than a hero.
For the rest, you will be interested perhaps in the movements of
the sentry who will cover you every quarter of the hour. Perhaps
he comes to check. Perhaps he comes with food. Perhaps he
comes – to take you away – for the last time.

Stephens acknowledged that all of this was 'sheer unadulterated
melodrama', although it proved successful on many occasions.
Much depended upon delivery, atmosphere, timing – and not least
upon the personality of the interrogator: 'To use a phrase hackneyed
in melodrama – its not so much what you say but the way you say
it.' Effects, Stephens found, varied: 'A German lost his arrogance. A
Spaniard lost the glint of his dark and fiery eye. An Egyptian visibly
wasted. An Italian gesticulated wildly for writing materials within
the hour. A Frenchman lost his nerve and talked of the "cellule de
condamnés." An Iceland [sic] remained unmoved; between Cell
Fourteen and the land of desolation there was no contrast.' However,
danger lay in the finality of Cell Fourteen: if it failed then little hope
remained of a break. The lesson of Cell Fourteen lay in the exploitation
of a 'trivial circumstance' – the existence of an old padded cell. The
Intelligence Officer responsible asked himself this question: 'If I were
a captured spy, what would I hate most in my predicament?' Thus, to
Stephens, 'it became a matter of psychology – to say what would hurt
the mind most'. It was, however, a two-edged sword in cases where
prisoners did not respond to this treatment since they could not be
kept there indefinitely and some excuse had to be found to transfer
them to other cells.[4]

Stephens had a fearsome reputation as a temperamental
authoritarian; known as 'Tin Eye' on account of his wearing a
monocle, Stephens had a short fuse with regard to those he believed to
be working for the enemy although his immediate staff thought fondly
of him.[5] Stephens had been born to British parents in Egypt in 1900;
after being educated there he returned to Britain in 1912 to conclude
his studies at Dulwich College. He joined the Royal Military Academy
Woolwich, at age eighteen, later transferring to Quetta Cadet College
in India before finally joining the Indian Army; he served in five

campaigns on the North-West Frontier, took part in suppressing the Mahbar rebellion and was mentioned in despatches. After the Great War, Stephens appears to have been attached to the Indian Political Service. In September 1939 he joined MI5 with the rank of Captain. Field Marshall Birdwood, whom he had served under in India, was his sponsor.[6]

Stephens was the force behind the establishment of the effective interrogation complex for suspected spies that became Camp 020. From the beginning of the war, British nationals, suspected of subversive activities, and enemy aliens had been interned in large numbers and were interrogated by Stephens at various places, e.g. prisons, Scotland Yard, and in particular at the Oratory Schools in London, which were being used as an internment camp. In July 1940, Stephens complained to the Security Executive – which oversaw Home Security – of the inadequate facilities for interrogation at the Oratory Schools where prisoners were questioned in the officers' bedroom and mentioned the particular case of an internee called Schultz whose interrogation was delayed while one of the officers was changing his trousers.[7] Stephens was also concerned with the security of the internment camps. In one camp discipline was so lax that a wireless transmitter was found. In another he noted how visits to the dentist 'were a joy ride for the day, for the guards were corrupt and made drunk. One day there was an inevitable miscount and a party was returned as correct. Later, a prisoner returned unescorted and alone, and was refused admission to the camp as the numbers were officially correct'.[8]

An important step forward occurred when the suggestion that an Interrogation Centre should be set up on similar lines to that at Cockfosters (which was used for prisoners of war) was agreed by the Home Office. The Office of Works was authorised to allocate and equip a building for the purpose of holding and interrogating internees, mainly British nationals and enemy aliens, who could not be classified as prisoners of war. It was made clear that the internees should only be held for a limited period and must then be returned to their original place of detention. The Interrogation Centre was to function under MI5. Within a few days, Latchmere House, Ham Common, near Richmond was taken over as the most suitable of the sites proposed by the Ministry of Works, and Stephens, with his small staff, took possession of the building and grounds on 10 July 1940. At this time there were no precedents from the war of 1914–18 that could be followed. The Camp was, in the words of Major Sampson, (one of Stephen's Assistant Commandants), 'an entirely novel venture. There was no certain knowledge as to the methods which the enemy would employ or the magnitude of his effort'.[9] From this came a 'diet of Ham' – the description Stephens gave to the intelligence gleaned from the intake of prisoners; he added, cryptically but accurately, that: 'The story of Ham is stranger than fiction; indeed, as a work of fiction it would violate the probabilities.'[10]

At the beginning, all internees retained their own clothes, were allowed to correspond with their relatives and receive parcels within certain limits, and could have articles purchased for them with their own money. In time, however, these privileges were gradually stopped or brought within narrow bounds. Both in intelligence and administrative work it was necessary in many respects to proceed by trial and error, and early shortcomings were gradually made good. Latchmere House was selected for the site of Camp 020 since, having been used as a home for neurasthenic officers after the war of 1914–18, it already comprised an annexe consisting of some thirty cells which could easily be adapted for the detention of prisoners, while in addition the house and other buildings were roomy enough to provide accommodation for some half dozen Intelligence Officers, four or five guard officers and about a hundred troops, together with offices for the secretarial staff, and three or four interrogation rooms. The first internees arrived at the new Camp on 27 July 1940, by which time the necessary arrangements had been made for holding and interrogating them; listening apparatus was placed in a number of the cells and in the interrogation rooms.

The security of Camp 020 was always a concern. In the evening of 29 November 1940, Latchmere House received a direct hit during an air raid. Casualties were light, only one (a German prisoner) proving fatal but the material damage was considerable, and the work had to be carried on under great difficulties and in cramped conditions for many months. The officers' living quarters, the officers' mess, the interrogation rooms and the offices were seriously damaged. Repairs were started immediately and the opportunity was taken to provide additional accommodation for the rapidly increasing number of cases and the consequent increase in staff.[11] A second attack occurred in January 1941 when a lone German raider dropped a stick of four bombs over Ham again. As Stephens recalled: 'One bomb burst within two feet of a sentry box, and the sentry within, by a miracle, was unhurt. Unconcernedly he volunteered to continue his tour of duty. The only material damage was the loss by blast of one regimental cap badge. The Regimental Sergeant Major, of the Grenadier Guards, was by no means impressed. Indeed such was his rigid sense of the fitness of things that he duly laid a charge against the wretched sentry for being improperly dressed.'

Official speculation that this second attack was premeditated on the grounds that 'a recurring accident ceases to be an accident'[12] led to a decision, in the summer of 1941, that in case of emergency caused, for instance, by attempted invasion or further damage from air raids, a reserve camp should be made available. The site selected was Huntercombe Place, Nuffield, near Henley-on-Thames. Construction began in October 1941. This Camp, known as 020 R, was opened in January 1943, when thirty-two prisoners from Camp 020 were transferred there. The number of prisoners held at Camp 020 R finally rose to about seventy. Later, as the Allied invasion progressed after D-Day, plans were made to move over to the Continent. A camp was later opened at Diest, near Brussels, to which four Intelligence Officers from Camp 020 were detached. This was followed by the opening in August 1945 of a Camp at Bad Nenndorf, near Hanover. In July 1945, Camp 020 R was closed and the prisoners were brought back to Camp 020. Before the camp closed in the autumn of 1945, arrangements had been made to deport neutrals to their own countries, while the remaining Germans were placed at the disposal of 21 Army Group in Germany. By the middle of September 1945, the intake of internees at Camp 020 had been totalled as follows: 1940: 107; 1941: 55; 1942: 67; 1943: 65; 1944: 119; 1945: 57 (up to 14.9.45.); Total: 480.

The final joint intelligence establishment of Camp 020 and 020.R, was: one Commandant; one Assistant Commandant and twenty-five Intelligence Officers including Administrative Officers.

As in the previous world war, MI5 could only move against enemy agents or suspected persons by the use of emergency powers; for example suspects could be held for short periods under a 'refusal of leave to land' by an Immigration Officer or by a detention order by an Immigration Officer or other authorised officer under the Arrival from British and Foreign Territory Order; for long term cases under the Royal Prerogative in the case of enemy aliens; an order under Article 12(5A) of the Aliens Order or under Defence Regulation 18B in the rare case of British subjects; and DR.18A in the case of foreign nationals.[13] It was a fundamental principle of Camp 020 that, should any of those detained under emergency powers find themselves there, then no physical violence was to be use against them; in addition, prisoners' rations were never cut down as a punishment for offences. The only punishments imposed were the temporary deprivation of privileges, such as cigarettes and reading matter, and short terms of solitary confinement. On some occasions, however, individual Intelligence Officers took matters into their own hands: one officer, from MI9, who was present at the interrogation of one prisoner, TATE, took it upon himself to manhandle the prisoner. After an interrogation session one of the inquisitors, Malcolm Frost, wondered where his colleague, Colonel Alexander Scotland, had disappeared to. Frost found Scotland in TATE's cell. Guy Liddell recorded the story, as related to him, in his diary entry for 22 September 1940:

> He was hitting TATE in the jaw and I think got one back for himself. Frost stopped this incident without making a scene, and later told me what had happened. It was quite clear to me that we cannot have this sort of thing going on in our establishment. Apart from the moral aspect of the whole thing, I am quite convinced that these Gestapo methods do not pay off in the long run. We do not intend to have that particular military intelligence officer on the premises any more. I am told that Scotland turned up this morning with a syringe containing some drug or other, which it was thought would induce the prisoner to speak. Stephens told Scotland that he could not see TATE, who was not in a fit state to be interrogated. Actually there was nothing seriously wrong with TATE.

Such brutality was not needed anyway because the cracking of the German agents was not down to luck but due to the development and refinement of interrogation techniques, often through trial and error. Crucial, but not always possible, to the intelligence technique of the interrogators was preliminary information. By far the most important, and at the same time, reliable, source of preliminary information was intercepts of German Wireless Traffic through ISOS, since it represented actual service messages transmitted between various German offices. Another source of information, and one that was constantly growing in extent and importance, was that obtained from prisoners interned at Camp 020. Over time a vast amount of information covering every field of German espionage was assembled. By the end of the war, the 020 Registry contained a card index with over 100,000 cards of contacts and addresses including many thousands of personal descriptions and hundreds of photographs of agents and contacts. The prisoners themselves 'formed a sort of living reference library and there were many occasions when prisoners who had been in the camp as long as two or three years, were able to throw light on new cases or to identify photographs of German agents'.

The last and frequently a useful source of information was the prisoners' property. It was a matter of routine to examine all clothing and this was one of the reasons for stripping prisoners and providing them with prison clothes. Their own clothing was examined for makers' labels and tabs, which would give an indication of previous movements, and also for any articles, in particular S/W (secret writing) materials, which might be concealed in them. It was found that a spy 'will always try to carry everything in his head, and though German spies were always instructed to memorise all cover addresses, S/W formulae etc. many of them could not trust their memories, but resorted to some form of code for memorising them. Others again were careless and forgot to destroy incriminating scraps of paper.' One ingenious form of secret writing was given to the agent Jose Stevens who was detained at Trinidad when on his way to the Argentine. It consisted of rubbing one side of a sheet of paper with a blue copying pencil, placing the rubbed side downwards on the paper to receive the impression, in the manner of a carbon paper, and writing the message lightly through it. The only material required was a blue copying pencil that could be purchased anywhere. Towards the end of the war the Germans used small pellets stuck at the end of match sticks which could easily be concealed. The Portuguese agent, Ernesto Simoes, had impregnated material for use in developing S/W sewn into the lining of his coat. Kurt Brodersen had a pellet concealed inside the seam of a pair of plus fours and a further pellet inside a decayed tooth. Nikolay Hansen also had a pellet in a tooth and another stuck between his toes. The latter had come loose and disappeared when he took a bath.

Interrogators attempted, initially, to obtain a break by impressing the prisoner with the hopelessness of his own position 'and the omniscience and omnipotence of the British Secret Service'. The prisoner was told that he was in a prison for German spies, to which he had been brought on account of his own activities. He had been arrested not on mere suspicion but on definite evidence. It was pointed out that he was quite alone against the entire weight of the British authorities and had no access to his own authorities or to any outside advice. In some cases the obituary notices of spies already executed were shown to him in order still further to break down his morale. If the prisoner had been interrogated on landing or at the London Reception Centre, he might be told to forget any lies he had already told; this was his last opportunity to tell the truth. It might be pointed out to him that he was like a gambler who had played and lost, and it was, therefore, up to him to pay the penalty; the only way in which he could help himself was to tell the whole truth.

After an opening gambit somewhat on the above lines – which varied according to the type of prisoner and the information already available – some leading questions were put which tended to show the prisoner that the interrogators were not making vague accusations in the dark, but that they were informed about his previous movements and that any lies he told would be detected. It was essential as soon as possible to ascertain what relations the prisoner had left behind in German territory, since the Germans almost invariably threatened reprisals on them if an agent failed to carry out his mission or betrayed their trust.[14] A lot depended on the character of the men who were the interrogators. According to Stephens, the difficulty of setting out the requirements of a first class interrogator was more apparent than real. Interrogators, to him, were of two kinds. Firstly, there was the 'breaker', the man whose duty it was to reduce the spy to the stage of speaking, and of speaking at least some truth. He was 'a paragon, so to say, who is expected to overwhelm and disintegrate all opposition'. Secondly there was the investigator who, given the advantage of the break, 'must deal with the minutiae, check and counter-check, analyse, collate and report'. In Stephen's opinion the breaker was born and not made. First and foremost there had to be some inherent qualities: 'There must be an implacable hatred of the enemy.' From this was derived a certain aggressive approach, a disinclination to believe without independent corroboration and above all a relentless determination to break down the spy 'however hopeless the odds, however many the difficulties, however long the process may take'. It was an advantage if a man was bilingual; but this did not necessarily make him an Intelligence Officer and often a linguistic ability did not match with the qualities required to impress a particular spy:

> The peasant suspects the urbane man about town. The regular officer of the Wehrmacht does not respond to a man accustomed to the negotiations of trade... A spy will talk ships to a man who knows little ships; he will talk desert war with a man who understands the meaning of thirst; he will talk Latin logic with a man who had the patience of Job. Maybe he will not say much to a young man, however enthusiastic; perhaps he will be reticent with a socialite or a man about town. So much depends upon personality, upon mood, upon the man who can impress or cajole blow hot, blow cold, stand down at the psychological moment, without jealousy, in favour of another officer.[15]

If direct interrogation failed to obtain a break, there were other means that could be tried. Most prisoners responded to the initial, somewhat harsh form of interrogation, but a small minority did not. In these cases after this form had been tried, usually by the Commandant himself, the prisoner was in some cases interviewed in a friendly manner by a more junior officer who asked him to sit down, offered him a cigarette and professed sympathy for him, finishing off with the advice to tell the truth, in order to save further trouble. This method was surprisingly often successful. The use of camp agents or stool pigeons was a secondary method of obtaining information, which was occasionally used with success though it rarely led to a confession as the information could not be used without blowing the source.

Perhaps the most useful of these camp agents was Huysmans, a Belgian who arrived at the camp in May 1943. He was intelligent and well educated, spoke several languages fluently, and would have been a dangerous spy if he had not been caught. His wife had also been brought to Britain, for which he was grateful. Huysmans became an 'unconscious' stool pigeon, since no proposal to work for MI5 was ever put to him and he was never prompted in his dealings with other prisoners. He was put in with numerous difficult cases and his technique was always the same. Huysmans gave his own story in considerable detail, telling how he had at first denied all connection with the Germans but had been obliged to confess in view of the mass of evidence against him; the British Secret Service was all-powerful and knew everything and it was futile to struggle against it; moreover he, who had told the whole truth had been richly rewarded as his wife had been brought over and saved from the Germans and he had been allowed to receive messages from her. He strongly advised the other prisoner to follow his example. Huysmans had a persuasive manner and appeared to gain the confidence of his fellow inmates. Many of them responded by telling him their story; he discussed it with them and showed them the weak spots. A number of prisoners asked for associations with him and consulted him about the statements they were required to write. He showed a complete grasp of the cases which came to his notice, had a remarkable memory for details, and gave lucid written or verbal accounts of all the facts which he elicited. His most useful quality, however, was his capacity of persuading other prisoners to tell the whole truth and leave the result to 'the fairness of the British authorities'. There were many cases where a prisoner, after a severe interrogation in which he had been at a disadvantage but had not given way, was further weakened in his resistance by Huysmans 'good advice'.[16] Alternatively, confrontation between prisoners – playing one against the other – could be tried. But there were dangers. As Stephens noted, confrontation 'in theory, seems such an obvious and effective weapon. In practice, it is a most dangerous expedient which may well ruin the whole course of the investigation'.[17] If all else failed the suspect was despatched to Cell 14 or 15.

Knowing Your Enemy

Who and what constituted the German Secret Service, the Abwehrabteilung, or Abwehr (German for 'Defence'), that the Security Service found itself pitted against in the dark days of 1940? The Abwehr had a station in each military district called an Abwehrstelle or Ast that was sub-divided into Ast I (espionage); Ast II (sabotage); and Ast III (counter intelligence). In neutral countries Abwehr officers were attached to embassies or trade organisations called War Organisations or Kos (*Kriegsrganisationen*). But the alarming position of British Intelligence, in 1939–1940, was that it only had a limited knowledge of this enemy. One of the key roles played by Camp 020 was in allowing MI5 to piece together a typography of the German Secret Service and its espionage objectives in the United Kingdom. Basically, MI5 had no idea of the German espionage penetration in Britain from 1939 to 1940. Fortunately, there was none to speak of. But this changed after the fall of France. Over the following months MI5 compiled its analysis of the enemy intelligence machine from confessions made by German spies recently captured in Britain; from GC&CS; and from information already in the possession of the Security Service and SIS. The first attempt at understanding MI5's primary foe was based upon an analysis of the confessions of five captured spies: the unfortunate 'pre-invasion' agents Meier, Waldberg, van den Kiebroom, Pons and Goesta Caroli – a Swede who, it was noted, 'has a natural liking for the German people and belief in National Socialism. He is a brave man, prepared to face the full consequences of his action. The feeling that he was made a fool of by the German S[ecret].S[ervice]. has been mainly responsible for his full confession.'[18]

The first of the pre-invasion spies arrived, on 3 September 1940, at Dungeness in Kent. They were Josef Rudolf Waldberg, a German; and three Dutchmen – Karl Heinrich Cornelis Ernst Meier; Stoerd Pons and van den Kieboom. Meier and Waldberg had left Le Touquet via Boulogne in one fishing boat; Pons and Van den Kieboom departed in another. Both boats were towed by German minesweepers, under cover of night and mist to within one mile of the British coastline. The agents made it ashore in dinghies. Before making land Meier and Waldberg, alarmed by the presence of a British patrol vessel, jettisoned a weighted packet containing circular code and maps. Leaving their boat to be washed away by the receding tide, the two men carried ashore their radio transmitter, a parcel of food and personal belongings. The transmitter they buried, temporarily, in the sand; the food was placed in an empty boat drawn up on the beach. The two men took a few hours sleep against the wall of a house. Just before dawn they crept along an open stretch of ground with their retrieved equipment.

Meier, some hours later set off in the direction of Lydd in search of drink. He spoke good English and, in an inn, struck up a conversation with an Air Raid Warden. Meier – who Stephens described as somewhat 'ingenuously over-zealous' – soon began to make enquiries as to the disposition and number of British troops in the area. The warden – 'equally zealous, and more alert' – asked to see Meier's identity card. Meier 'became flustered'. He admitted that he had no such document; he was a refugee; then he unconsciously betrayed his companions by stating: 'We arrived last night.' After three hours of police questioning Meier confessed his mission and revealed Waldberg's location. Waldberg, in the meantime, had sent two wireless transmissions, in emergency code; he reported the spies' landing and then the fear that Meier had been arrested. Waldberg had just prepared a third message for transmission when he was arrested. As for Pons and Van den Kieboom they 'had been given even shorter shrift'. Upon landing they unpacked their transmitter and other equipment and began to take across the coastal road when a car containing two British officers pulled out and challenged van den Kieboom. While waiting to be handed over to the police he asked to be allowed to visit a lavatory and managed to rid himself of incriminating evidence such as a code, map and reagent for secret ink. Pons, busily engaged in unloading their equipment, 'somewhat innocently', approached a group of people standing nearby, claimed he was a Dutch refugee and asked where he might be. He was also handed over to the Police.

All four men were questioned at Seabrook police station and made confessions. By 6 September they had been admitted to Camp 020 where, 'already partially broken', it remained vital to extract from them their mission, recruitment and training and whether more agents might be on their way. The indication, assisted by the Orderly Officer's report on the men's demeanour in the course of his last inspection, was that Waldberg was the weak link: 'Thus the initial onslaught was against Waldberg,' stated Stephens. His disclosures, under interrogation, provided material to use against the other three. Meier and Pons 'spoke readily enough in their spleen against the shabby preparation of their adventure by the German Secret Service, a fact of which they were constantly and shrewdly reminded by their interrogators'. Van den Kieboom, 'who lived alternatively in hope and fear of an imminent German invasion' required 'less gentle persuasion' to part with his version of events. On 7 September he was instructed by interrogating officers to transmit a message to the Germans reporting that Pons had been shot and the rest of the party had gone into hiding for three days. On 24 October all four spies left Camp 020 for trial at the Old Bailey. Pons alone escaped the death sentence and execution: his plea that he had been forced into service for the Germans was accepted. He remained at Camps 020 and 020 R until the end of the war when he was deported to Holland.

The second batch of pre-invasion spies were discovered when, at 3.10 a.m., on 30 September 1940, a man and woman of 'foreign appearance' presented themselves at the Scottish railway station of Portgordon, saw that the station name was – as Stephens put it 'obliterated' – and enquired where they might be. They bought tickets to Forres. The stationmaster was suspicious: 'He didn't like their manner or their appearance; their clothes showed signs of exposure.' He reported their presence to the police who 'received them shortly afterwards'. The woman told the village policeman that she was Danish and her companion, who spoke no English, was Belgian. She claimed that they had recently arrived in Scotland from London on a visit. At the police station she retracted this statement. She now stated that she had sailed with her companion from Bergen twelve days before in a fishing boat. She gave as a reference Sonia, Duchesse de Chateau-Thierry of Dorset House, London. Stephenson noted that: 'History does not record whether the local police were impressed by the invocation of exotic nobility.' The police were too busy examining the strangers' luggage. The woman had a British identity card in the name of Vera Erichsen and £69 in Treasury notes.

The man had a Belgian passport in the name of Franziskus de Deeker; a British identity card and traveller's ration book with a Sussex Place, London address; and £327 10s in notes. 'Most embarrassing of all was the man's suitcase': it contained a wireless transmitter, a fully loaded revolver, a cardboard disc code, a list of British localities corresponding with the more important RAF aerodromes and some food. Shortly afterwards an inflated rubber dinghy capable of carrying four persons was discovered drifting towards Cluny Harbour. Enquiries were made to establish whether any other persons might have landed. At 6 p.m. it was reported that a suitcase that was damp and had particles of sand on it had been deposited at the Left Luggage Office at Waverly Station, Edinburgh. A porter stated that a man with a foreign accent had left it there and had said he would reclaim it later. When the man returned and produced the reclaim ticket he was surrounded by police officers. He attempted to resist but was overpowered as he tried to reach for a Mauser pistol in his pocket. On his person was found: a Swiss passport in the name of Werner Heinrich Waelti; a British identity card and traveller's ration book; £195 in notes and a railway ticket to London. The brief case contained a wireless transmitter and a disc code. Waelti, like de Deeker before him, 'professed to be hugely surprised at the revelation'.

Meanwhile, the woman Vera Erichsen, who had wavered under police interrogation, 'was obviously the weak link in the combination and the first attack was concentrated on her'. Another prisoner, unconnected with the new arrivals, provided information about her and the Abwehr in Brussels. When these facts were put to Erichsen she was clearly shaken as it appeared she had been under close and constant surveillance by the British in Brussels. She then admitted to recruitment by the Germans several years earlier and previous service for the Russians. Erichsen claimed to have married Hauptmann Dierks of Ast Hamburg, who had recently been killed in a car accident; de Deeker, a close friend of her husband, had been seriously injured in the accident. Little by little, in the following weeks, the interrogators put the story of the mission together. Waelti and de Deeker, however, refused to co-operate. Erichsen was 'clearly' trying to protect de Deeker but eventually 'slipped into a damning admission. She didn't know the exact purpose of his mission; at the same time she was to help him.' They were to find an address in Soho and then go out into the country and obtain information about aerodromes and troop dispositions. The reports would be transmitted to Germany by de Deeker. Erichsen also revealed that there was meant to be a fourth member of the party: a Norwegian, Gunnar Edvardsen, with a sabotage mission in the UK. He had a large trunkload of equipment and it was decided he should leave Norway later.

On 25 October a second group of German agents from Norway landed in Scotland. A police constable saw the three men of 'foreign appearance' and took them into custody: they were Gunnar Edvardsen, along with Legwald Lund and Otto Joost. The three men were transferred to Camp 020 on 28 October where Edvardsen's photograph was identified by Erichsen. Edvardsen was broken quite quickly and admitted recruitment in Norway in which he was to be assisted by Joost. Stephens remarked that: 'Theirs was a quaint mission. They were to race up and down the British highways on bicycles and cut telephone wires with specially insulated clippers.' Lund had separate orders to establish contact with some anonymous persons at the Scandinavian Seamen's Home in Glasgow. The bombing of Latchmere House, on 29 November, and the news, a few days later, that Waldberg, Meier and Van den Kieboom had been executed, 'appears to had its repercussions'. A Belgian seaman agent was enlisted as a stool pigeon and given access to de Deeker, to whom he confided that he was expecting repatriation shortly. De Deeker, 'whose nerves were probably on edge, took the bait'. On 5 December, he prepared a letter, in shorthand, addressed to a 'Spitzenberg' in Brussels. The address was passed to SIS and the letter to the School of Codes and Ciphers.

De Deeker, in the meantime, unexpectedly confessed to the camp Medical Officer, who was acting as the 'sympathetic and understanding link' over a period of time to gain the prisoner's confidence, that his real name was Karl Theo Druke and that he was a German national. The following day, SIS established that a German agent named Druke had resided at the address provided. The School of Codes and Ciphers revealed the contents of the letter; the writer, according to Stephenson, 'was either showing the first signs of mental derangement or was employing phraseology that had been conveyed for emergency use'. The letter confirmed that Spitzenberg was a German agent; the names of Druke's Abwehr contacts in Norway; and his loyalty to them. On 23 December, Druke 'officially' admitted his true identity to the Orderly Officer and acknowledged that he had been aware of the contents of his suitcase when arrested. He refused to give any further details. By now Erichsen had written to Druke urging him to reveal all 'for the sake of their unborn child'; she admitted to the MO that she was not pregnant but hoped that 'the little personal touch might sway her lover. It didn't' recorded Stephens. Druke and Waelti – who refused to confess – were committed to trial at the Old Bailey. Both men were found guilty, sentenced to death and hanged. Erichsen, whose real name was Schalburg, remained in detention.

From such interrogations, as MI5 pieced together a picture of the German Secret Service it found that all the captured agents seemed convinced that they were working for the German Army and not for the Gestapo. All the officers they had dealings with wore army uniforms, and they never saw anyone in Nazi uniforms. Agents intended for the UK appeared to pass at one time or another through a Brussels training centre. Caroli received most of his training during a five-week period in Hamburg, but even he received final instruction at Brussels. The others were trained almost entirely in Brussels, though for a period of about five days before their actual dispatch they were given some last minute instructions at the Chateau de Wimille, near Boulogne. Training included instruction in British military organisation and was mainly in the hands of a Dr. Kohler. Examination of all the spies indicated that the military instruction was extremely superficial. Thus, though they were expected to report on such military objectives as aerodromes, land mines and gun batteries, on examination they showed only a vague idea of the significant points to note. Instruction in W/T transmission by Morse code was up to a standard of 40–50 letters a minute and covered a period of about one month. This too was superficial and the agents could only claim an amateur knowledge of transmission technique. Some instruction was also given in secret inks, but the ones with which they were supplied were so simple in their application as to require little instruction: 'Not one of the spies can claim to be in any sense a trained agent. This may be due to the urgency of dispatching them to the UK in time to collaborate in military operations for invasion.'

Most of the German agents had been promised some financial or other assistance by their masters. Caroli worked to a written contract that was given him in Paris. On the German side a guarantee was given to him of four years free study in Germany or Sweden, or the equivalent in cash. Meier and Kieboom stated that they were not promised any definite reward, but were told that they would be well looked after on the completion of their jobs. While in the employ of the Germans, though before he was selected for the mission to England, Waldberg was paid at the rate of 400 marks a month while in Germany, 80 marks a week while in Belgium and 60 marks a week while in France. Promises of payment for his work in the UK were on the same indefinite basis as those of Kieboom, Meier and Pons. The preparation involved in preparing the spies was clearly amateurish. Caroli was landed in the UK by parachute: he was dropped from a height of 15,000 feet and as this was his first descent by parachute, the ripcord operated by means of a drop-cord from the aeroplane. He was unconscious on landing and was therefore not able to put through his first W/T call at the time specified, i.e. 2 a.m.–4 a.m. He was arrested at 5.30 p.m. on 6 September. MI5 noted:

The crudeness of the methods of entry into the UK by boats and parachute is obvious, but too much should not be made of this point as if the German S[ecret].S[ervice]. required their agents to start work immediately, they had no other means of dispatch and were, therefore, bound to take considerable chances. They seem to have been fully aware of the hazardous nature of the enterprise and for this reason created a false sense of security in the minds of their agents by over-optimistic accounts of the ease with which other German agents managed to go backwards and forwards to the UK. Moreover, they undertook to fetch any of the agents if they encountered difficulties. These promises were obviously part of the bluff necessary to keep the spirits of their men up to the point of readiness for action.[19]

By December 1940, the Security Service had added further to its knowledge of the German Secret Service via the use of double agents under the control of MI5 and SIS; and further information obtained from the interrogation of more captured German agents at Camp 020. With regard to the first source, MI5 and MI6 had two groups of double agents under their control. The first group, consisting of about seven agents, was in W/T communication with the Germans. The second group, consisting of about five agents, maintained communication by secret writing, the letters being despatched by airmail. MI5 regarded this as one of the most important techniques for counter-espionage work, enabling them to gain an insight into the personnel, methods and means of communication of the system working against them. With regard to the interrogations special care was taken in judging the value of information obtained by interrogation. Recent experience had shown that captured agents had 'all been supplied and rehearsed in a plausible story to account for themselves. Even when this has been broken down an agent may be prepared to confess only so much as he thinks will satisfy his interrogator for the moment. This has been a common reaction with the majority of the agents... and the reason is probably to be found in the fact that they believe in the imminence of a German invasion.' Nevertheless, this information was deemed of great importance.

Plans for the invasion of Britain and for aerial bombing had clearly necessitated an expansion in organisation and an intensification of effort in the sphere of German Secret Service work; the speed and scale on which these were undertaken produced a 'deterioration in execution and technique'. As a result, the British Intelligence Service, in contrast to the situation before September 1940, 'obtained what amounts to a bird's-eye view of a large part of the organisation working against England'. By December, the Security Service knew that the Heeresnachrichtendienst (henceforth referred to as ND), of which Admiral W. Canaris was the Chief, was run by the Oberkommando der Wehrmacht (OKW) – the German High Command of the Armed Forces – and had its Headquarters in the Reichkriegsministerium in Berlin. The special sphere of the ND was military information. Working parallel with the ND there appeared to be at least two other Secret Intelligence organisations, known as the Sonderdienst (SD) and the Innere Dienst (ID). The special sphere of the S.D. was political and economic information and it was probably under the direct control of the Reich Foreign Minister, Von Ribbentrop. The ID also interested itself in foreign politics, though probably from the propaganda point of view.

With the intelligence now gathered, MI5 could see that, from May 1940, what amounted to the complete transformation of the German Secret Service organisation in the Low Countries and in France occurred, with the creation of new and advanced bases for ND work against Britain. At the same time the 'older type' of German Secret Service work had been continuously directed against the British from bases in neutral countries, particularly in Portugal and Spain. It therefore seemed 'that we have in fact been witnessing the inevitable reorganisation consequent upon the displacement of the *Friedensnetz* or peace time organisation by the *Kriegsnetz* or wartime organisation'. The key to the new ND organisation in the Low Countries and in France was the creation of a whole series of new Abwehrstellen and sub-posts. In the early stages of the war, before the advance on the Western Front, ND W/T stations known to MI5 fell roughly into three groups: 1. Controlled from Hamburg and directed against England and British interests; 2. Controlled from Wiesbaden and directed against France and the Low Countries; 3. Controlled from Berlin and extending throughout Central Europe.

After the fall of France and the concentration of the German war machine against Britain, this system of regional division was put to a severe test; for while the Wiesbaden Group dwindled in volume and importance, the Hamburg Group was saddled with a quantity and variety of business for which it was apparently not sufficiently equipped, either in cyphers or in personnel. Thus, in the early summer of 1940 it was attempting to control agents wherever war against Britain was being waged – in Oslo, Bergen, the Baltic, the Gulf of Bothnia, the Channel ports, Britain, Ireland, Greece and the USA. Such overburdening of one control placed the whole sphere of ND activities against the UK in jeopardy. Consequently, through the summer of 1940 a complete redistribution of ND W/T control was carried out. Two new stelle, or stations, at Paris and Brest now took over a large proportion of the work previously controlled from Hamburg and, while keeping open their line to Hamburg, themselves controlled new stations at Le Havre, Cherbourg and Brussels. Meanwhile, Berlin Control extended its 'tentacles' westward to Brest and Paris, and assumed direct control over these two stations that Hamburg renounced. Thus Hamburg had, in the course of the summer, first monopolised the ND W/T communications for the war against Britain, then proved unequal to the strain, renounced it to the already existing and highly organised Berlin group and now had its primary sphere of interest, control of agents in Norway and the USA.

The whole machinery of the Gestapo, the Reich police, immigration authorities, employment and labour exchanges, shipping agencies, press and propaganda departments, had been placed at the disposal of the ND for recruiting purposes. Of the twenty-nine captured agents whose information was used by MI5, 75 per cent claimed that they were coerced into the service although, 'allowance must of course be made for the natural desire of a captured agent to excuse himself, and there is little doubt that some have told stories of coercion on the instructions of the ND itself. Nevertheless, some of them can justifiably claim this on account of former associations with political parties antagonistic to National Socialism'. Thus agents, such as the Norwegian seaman Legwald Lund, belonged to the Norwegian Labour Party, Pasoz-Diaz to a Communist syndicate in Spain and Robles was an International Brigadier. Where coercion was not necessary the ND made use of a great number and variety of 'talent-spotters'. A talent-spotter was usually a separate individual from the recruiter, and having decided on a potentially valuable recruit passed him on to the recruiter. A typical talent-spotter of the ND was Kurt Mirow of the Brussels and Hamburg stations. MI5 noted that the procedure of speedy selection or of coercion had 'certain obvious weaknesses on the psychological side. An agent who was coerced may be held in the service of the ND only so long as the influence by fear is still felt. Nor is there always the right inclination and enthusiasm for carrying out the work'. Realising these weaknesses the ND had developed two methods for meeting them. They attempted, by means of a signed contract and oath of allegiance, to bind their agents to them, while in order to influence their morale they employed officers whose special duty it was to study their agents from a psychological point of view and influence them in the right direction. The oath of allegiance was usually referred to as the *Eidgelöbnis* and ran as follows:'I bind myself to fulfil the commands of the Intelligence Service and am fully aware of the consequences if I do not fulfil them.'

At the moment this oath was taken the consequences (*folgen*) were graphically illustrated by the action of binding the eyes and firing a revolver at the head. The work of the special psychological officer was illustrated in the person of Dr. Schulz of the Hamburg station, who took care of the agent Goesta Caroli before he left on his mission to England. Schulz's technique was based on bluff. He made constant reference to the ease with which an agent's mission could be carried out and illustrated this by relating a series of graphic examples of the heroic exploits of some of the ND's most trusted agents. MI5 found that when an agent who had been coerced into the services of the ND was under arrest by enemy authorities, his reaction under interrogation would be governed by his experiences with the Germans. The Security Service found that one of the most profitable inducements to make such an agent confess was to convince him that he had been made a fool of by the ND and sent on an enterprise which he could never have hoped to carry out. From the longer-time spies – those with a track record of espionage activities – MI5 discovered that their general objectives were as follows: '1. Information concerning British aircraft production and production of aircraft armaments, together with the latest situation as to supplies from America; 2. Technical details concerning types of aircraft and their equipment. In this connection much interest is shown in the Beaufighter; 3. Detailed information concerning air raid damage, not so much from the point of view of targets hit as from the point of view of its effect on production; 4. Exact location of targets intended for attack by the German Air Force. Principal targets appear to be factories for aircraft or aircraft armaments; 5. Weather survey: The forecasting of English weather requires a vast network of W/T stations particularly to the west, and recent discoveries show that this is a particularly important responsibility of the Nachrichtendienst. It is presumably of considerable importance to the German Air Force, but it is also clearly significant for general operations against our shipping in the Atlantic; 6. Sabotage: The impression has been gained that it is only recently that the ND has concerned itself extensively with sabotage. At least six of the captured agents appear to have been intended for this purpose.'[20]

It was thanks to this ability to derive information from various sources that MI5 came up with an extraordinary strategy: to control the entire Abwher's espionage war against Britain. Even more extraordinarily, they executed the strategy successfully.

3

The End of an Era
Kell's Fall & Petrie's New Order 1940–1941

Breakdown

As Director of MI5, Major-General Sir Vernon Kell, was chauffeured around London in an Invicta bearing a blue pennant graced with a tortoise and the motto 'Safe but sure'.[1] But unsafe and unsure, however, might be the assessment that now applied to the Security Service. Kell at sixty-seven years of age was worn down by asthma and his advancing years [2] and the pace of counter-espionage investigation had slowed to that of a snail rather than that of a tortoise. With the collapse of French martial resistance and the scrambling of the defeated British Expeditionary Force back to England from the beaches of Dunkirk, a German invasion of the British Isles became a real possibility. Neville Chamberlain relinquished the premiership to be succeeded by Winston Churchill. The succession would cost Kell his job – for the Security Service literally broke down and was unable to carry out its functions.

The crisis had its origins before the war when the provisions of the Aliens Order 1920 had been enforced by Immigration Officers in accordance with the requirements of peacetime conditions; but to fulfill the requirements of security in wartime a staff of Field Security Police (FSP) were appointed under Security Control Officers (SCO) who were established at approved ports. At the same time an Exit Permit system was established and the Permit Office referred certain categories of cases to the Security Service for advice before granting a permit to British or neutral subjects. The large number of references to the Security Service in connection with travel permits was an important factor in overwhelming the Registry and contributed greatly to the chaos which resulted from other causes. One of these was that before the war, in order to enable the small Registry staff to cope with the rapidly increasing volume of work from 1936 onwards, a very large number of 'omnibus' files had been made in preference to a far larger number of subject files or personal files for individuals. It became apparent within the first three months of the war that, as a result of the enormous flood of new papers, the requirements of vetting, the references for Exit Permits and the demands of the Advisory Committee, 'the Registry was heading for an early breakdown'. It was frequently found that the same files were required simultaneously by several officers for several different purposes. Moreover, in the early stages of the war when there were only about half a dozen officers in B Division with any knowledge of the work or of the 'traces' on the files, the sectional officers were frequently unable to decide these questions themselves without reference to the handful of pre-war officers. As a result of these conditions large bundles of files frequently accumulated in many of the sections and the work of all sections was slowed down by demands for files in these accumulated bundles constantly received from other sections. And Registry staff were unable to obtain the files in order to put papers away in them and consequently masses of unfiled papers accumulated in the Registry. By Christmas 1939 'it was obvious that a serious breakdown had occurred. No action to remedy this was taken because of the difficulty of obtaining financial provision for sufficient additional staff, and the whole question of the organisation of the Service was left over for an examination by Lord Hankey which took place in March 1940'.[3]

Lord Hankey, now a Minister without Portfolio in the Government, inquired into SIS and MI5. His second report concerned the latter. Hankey found that one of the problems facing the Security Service was that it was 'somewhat isolated; rather a lost child'. It derived its funds from Secret Service Vote; the funds themselves were supplied to MI5 direct from the Foreign Office, which was formally responsible for their application. 'Here, however, the resemblance ends.' On the one hand, the Security Service was continually carrying out important duties in supplying information for the use of the Foreign Office, which in consequence took a close interest in its organisation, efficiency and even its methods of work. On the other hand, the Security Service rendered 'only slight service' to the Foreign Office. Its duties brought it into closer contact with the Service Departments and the Home Office: 'In other words, the Department (Foreign Office), which is responsible for Security Services supplies funds, is not the Department mainly interested in the organisation, efficiency and methods of work of the Security Service, and does not pretend to exercise any supervision over its activities.' This 'rather curious state of affairs', Hankey pointed out, arose from historical circumstances and in particular from the fact that in 1909, the Committee of Imperial Defence did not realise how divergent the functions of security were from those of foreign intelligence.

The title 'MI5', Hankey pointed out, added to the confusion as it gave the impression that the Security Service had a 'special relationship' with the War Office when, in fact, the Admiralty and the Air Ministry were just as much interested in security as the War Office: 'MI5', in fact, had been a title 'adopted largely for the purpose of "cover" or "camouflage"

for the activities which for a long time it was attempted to keep...
secret'. To remedy this, Kell wanted MI5 placed under the direction of a
Minister without departmental responsibilities; at the moment, Kell had
argued, if the Department that the Service advised rejected his advice,
there was no redress. Kell was opposed to being put under the Home
Office because he, and his senior colleagues, believed that a large part of
their work was with other Departments especially the Services. In fact,
they felt it inappropriate to be placed under any one Department. Kell
preferred that MI5 should be attached to the Committee of Imperial
Defence so that it would fall within the sphere of the Prime Minister.
Hankey, on the other hand, disagreed – in fact he thought that 'matters
should be left where they are', fearing that placing the Security Service
under the control of one Department would open up to scrutiny in
Parliament – at present it was immune from such inspection because the
Secret Service Vote was not subject to debate.[4]

And, far from reporting on the breakdown, Hankey referred in
'eulogistic term' to the efficiency of the Registry which he said he had
visited. 'This report not only failed to disclose the serious condition
of the Registry and the urgent need for further strengthening it, but,
while fairly exhaustive in certain respects, was somewhat superficial
in others' wrote a critical Jack Curry some years later. In particular
Hankey made no reference to the fact that MI5 had received no
information from SIS of any practical value about the organisation
of the German Secret Service which Section V and the Security Service
had jointly to combat; and this in spite of the fact that some eighteen
months previously the latter had informed Section V that the Abwehr
had established bases in Holland and Belgium to operate against
Britain and that SIS had established counter organisations in those
countries 'which had, however, been unable to obtain any information
of substantial value about their adversaries or the main organisation
behind them'. In one MI5 officer's view (Jack Curry), the point was
that Hankey ignored the dependence of the Security Service on Section
V in this respect; failed to make an adequate examination of the vital
nature of their functional relations and failed to bring out the fact that
both organisations had not been adequately staffed in peacetime to
enable them to prepare for the conditions of modem war – and as
a corollary to insist on the urgent need for giving them a chance to
develop on efficient lines.

Hankey 'failed to understand the responsibilities of the Security
Service for executive action' in combating the German Secret
Intelligence under the Oberkommando der Wehrmacht by denying
intelligence to the enemy, by the detection and prevention of espionage

and sabotage and by helping the fighting Services in active deception as a vital part of our military operations'. Furthermore, Lord Hankey did not mention the splitting up of the preventive functions between B and D Branches and the Deputy Director, although he described in some detail those functions as performed by Deputy Director Holt-Wilson and the Assistant Director (General Staff Branch) Colonel Allen, and he made no reference to the essentially preventive nature of the enquiries which at that time so fully occupied almost the whole of B Branch.

In Curry's view Hankey's report would have been of more immediate assistance to the Security Service in preventing the 'rot' from developing if he had emphasised the inadequacy of staff in B and D Branches and in the Registry at that time, and the urgent need for measures for recruiting competent personnel. The 'real position' was that not only had the Registry broken down through inadequate staff before the war and inadequate expansion after it, combined with a failure to heed the warning of H Branch in the previous war to the effect that a flood of paper was inevitable, but that there was no one under the Director who was responsible for all preventive action and preventive or security policy; and that B Branch was overwhelmed with an immense volume of investigation work of a mainly preventive nature. A contributory factor both to the breakdown of the Registry and the breakdown in the Security Service as a whole, was the volume of vetting, including vetting for Exit Permits. Early in the war this work reached unforseen proportions – the peak figure being nearly 8,200 cases per week in the quarter ending June 1940. This included vetting for numerous Departments, many of which suddenly became security minded as a result of the 'Fifth Column' scare after the fall of France. 'Sometimes almost Gilbertian proposals were made, such as a demand for the vetting of enemy aliens who were to be allowed to send parcels abroad. The mere weight of this work was a serious burden on the Registry, but it also had the effect of creating a situation in which officers were unable to pursue enquiries.'

In the first six months of the war, the head of B Branch's time was largely taken up with rendering personal assistance to Kell, and the duty of controlling and expanding the Branch fell to Guy Liddell as the Deputy Assistant Director of the Branch. B Branch, as the one which initiated all action aiming at detection and a large part of the action of a preventive nature, 'was the crucial part on which the efficiency of the whole depended'. But in the early stages of the war there were only about half a dozen officers with any experience of the work, 'and having worked at high pressure for a long period before the war they were

compelled to work for impossible long hours for the first twelve months
and more of the war, when nine to twelve hours a day for thirteen days a
fortnight was not uncommon for a large number of officers, secretaries
and Registry staff'. These long hours – 'all limitations of regular hours
were forgotten' – were done on the initiative of individuals and as a
result of a recognition of the urgent need of the situation, both in the
'Office' and outside it, at a time when the Government 'and the country
as a whole was indulging in the complacency which arose from the
conditions of the "phoney war".'

Thus in the early months of 1940 it fell to Liddell to attempt to
develop and expand B Branch, to co-ordinate the work of B Branch with
the security controls under D Branch and to cope with the problems
of the enemy alien. The Branch was expanding rapidly during these
months and this expansion was marked by an absence of co-ordinating
machinery within the Branch. The section under Lieutenant Colonel
Hinchley Cooke which had always dealt with German espionage
continued to be in the same isolated position which it had held for
some years. Certain other of the more experienced officers had been
set apart to deal with special cases at the beginning of the war but as
no special cases materialised they had drifted to other fields of activity
much as the general preventive enquiries mentioned.

It was 'obvious to everyone' that arrangements for the better
integration of these various activities were desirable, and at the
suggestion of Captain TAR Robertson a weekly meeting known as
the 'Lower Deck' meeting was organised under Curry. The purpose
of this meeting was to exchange information on B Branch matters,
i.e. on the results of the numerous current enquiries made by the B
Branch sections, the number of which had increased from the pre-war
half dozen to over twenty (some of which had several officers in them)
in the early months of 1940. The meeting 'served a useful purpose
in giving all the officers concerned a wider outlook and frequently
made it possible to co-ordinate enquiries which were being pursued
in isolation and would otherwise have remained isolated although
they were concerned with closely related subjects or individuals'. They
also produced an 'even more acute realisation than had previously
existed' of the need for developing the machinery specifically to deal
with the Abwehr, a detailed report on which was obtained from the
Czechs early in April 1940 as the result of a special liaison established
with them by an outside representative under the instructions of Dick
White and Curry.

The Czech information was important 'as it gave us our first real
knowledge of the organisation of the Abwehr and it helped to further

developments at which Captain Liddell had been aiming'. During the previous two or three months he had attempted to develop a plan to divide the work of B Branch into two parts, one under White to be primarily concerned with an active enquiry into the nature, organisation and methods of the German Intelligence System, and the other under Curry was to be concerned with the security or preventive investigations in which the greater part of B Branch was then involved. 'Full effect, however, was never given to this plan.' At the same time, attempts were made to set up nationality sections especially Dutch, Swiss and Swedish, the main object of which was to examine the possibilities of German agents coming to the United Kingdom from the countries concerned. The reason for this was the fact that it was known that the Germans had set up organisations in their Embassies in neutral countries for such purposes and that they had allies in the shape of sympathisers such as members of the Dutch Mussert Party. After the invasion of Norway on 9 April and Belgium and Holland on 10 May, the work of these sections was radically altered as they had to deal with swarms of refugees including British subjects and the subjects of other countries including, for instance, Spanish left-wing groups from France. The invasion and the fall of France 'inevitably had large repercussions on the work of the Security Service. It had to meet a situation for which it was unprepared.' As far as the refugees were concerned it was mainly met by obtaining the assistance of some personnel from SIS with local knowledge (e.g. Passport Control personnel) and by establishing liaison with the émigré Governments as they established themselves in London as well as with General de Gaulle's organisation representing France. The liaison with the Polish authorities led them to provide MI5 with a comprehensive statement of the use made by the Germans of their so-called 'Fifth Column' in the course of the invasion of Poland in September 1939.

By the time of the fall of France, the organisation of the Security Service as a whole 'was in a state which can only be described as chaotic'. In Curry's view this could not be disassociated from the fact that B Branch had no real knowledge of the German Secret Service organisations, that it was therefore compelled to assume that the Germans were in a position to run an efficient organisation for espionage, sabotage and, above all, for disintegration or 'Fifth Column' purposes, which it was unable to detect and against which it was unable to provide adequate preventive measures. Moreover, the policy of the Home Office in dealing with the problem of the enemy alien was governed by considerations other than those of security as the Security Service saw them. There was no machinery inside the Home

Office for the study and appreciation of intelligence dealing with the 'unprecedented phenomena of the totalitarian Nazi State'; and the Home Office, which had always dealt with individual cases on a purely ad hoc basis, was influenced in formulating a policy by the questions of MPs in the House of Commons. 'The M.P.s who asked questions on such matters were frequently those who were least representative of the opinion of the House and the officials of the Home Office were governed very largely by a desire to protect the Home Secretary from difficulties arising out of questions, however unrepresentative they might be.' The problems of security over the whole field of espionage, sabotage and the 'Fifth Column' fell on B Branch 'which was simultaneously attempting to evolve means of detecting German agents without any inside knowledge of the German organisation. At the same time the Registry system had broken down and the Service as a whole had found itself overwhelmed by the problems of expansion necessitated by the outbreak of war for which no adequate preparation had been made beforehand.'[5]

And the inadequacies of Hankey's report were seized upon in Whitehall. In his final paragraph, Hankey had written that MI5 continued, today, in its finest traditions of service to the State. This was not what many within Whitehall wanted to hear. As one official wrote to the Home Office: 'I feel rather strongly about the end paragraph. It is well known that there has been the enquiry and I would be afraid of the effect upon the staff if the result of the enquiry is to keep Kell in his present position. Moreover I feel sure that we are not getting the best out of Harker while he is being balanced by Kell.'[6] Kell's goose was well and truly cooked.

In June 1940, Churchill ordered Sir Horace Wilson, the Permanent Under-Secretary at the Treasury, to dismiss Kell, Director since its creation in 1909, and his deputy, Sir Eric Holt-Wilson. Brigadier 'Jasper' Harker was given temporary control of the Security Service with Charles Butler as his Deputy – although Harker did not last long in the top job. On Monday 10 June, Major General Kell wrote in his diary: 'I get the sack from Horace Wilson 1909–1940 Italy comes into the war against us. Dirty dogs.'[7]

The change did not come as a bolt from the blue. In fact it was the case that, during the first year of the war, as Jack Curry – the internal historian of MI5 – admitted, 'we had very little knowledge of the German Secret Service and were completely in the dark as to the extent of their espionage network in this country'. In reality – 'although we did not know it' – no effective German network existed in the United Kingdom at that time.[8] Despite this dire situation many within, MI5 were sad to see the old Director go; Guy Liddell, who now became Director B Division, recorded in his diary: 'The blow has fallen... I am terribly sorry for the Director General and his Deputy. It must be a frightful blow to them as being the pioneers of the whole show.'[9] It was.

Vernon and Constance Kell retired to the market town of Olney. They moved there, in September 1941, from their large Weybridge house, as their sons and daughter had now grown up and flown the nest. Sir Vernon had enrolled as a Special Constable at the local police station. Constance recalled how, in the spring of 1942:

> it was still very cold, we had had three years of quite unusually cold winters with constant snow and ice. We could keep very warm in the little house we lived in, but outside, it was piercingly cold, the more so as we were near the River Ouse. In good weather it was good fun to be so near, for we could carry down our fishing tackle and Vernon, like all good fisherman, always hoped to be successful, though that sluggish river gave very little chance of much sport. But in winter, our close proximity to the river made the cold more penetrating, and we would come back in the evening to sit gratefully by a blazing fire, and wait for the six o'clock news. Then Vernon would eagerly listen, hoping to hear something that would bring the longed for victory a little nearer, and I would realise what his unwilling inactivity meant to him.
>
> One day he went off as usual to the Police Station but returned early – he complained of a bad pain in his chest. He had caught cold which turned to pleurisy and pneumonia, and he did not recover.
>
> He had so eagerly looked forward to the time when at last the conquered and the conquerors would meet together on either side of a table, to work out something between them, that might lead to a lasting peace. This was the question, would it or could it, ever be a lasting peace? Vernon feared that the world must grow very much older in experience and wisdom, before this could be achieved.[10]

Rebirth

Under Churchill the Security Service was brought under greater ministerial scrutiny. A Security Executive was set up by the Cabinet in May, 1940, 'to consider questions relating to defence against the Fifth Column and to initiate action', under the chairmanship of Philip Lloyd-Cunliffe, first Earl of Swinton. Soon after its establishment, its functions were enlarged to cover the co-ordination of security measures generally, and to undertake the management of certain security organisations overseas. Swinton and his immediate successor, Duff Cooper, had personal responsibility for MI5 and SIS. The Chairman was assisted by two independent members without Departmental associations or responsibilities, the Right Honourable Isaac Foot (formerly Secretary for the Mines Department) and A.M. Wall (formerly General Secretary of the London Society of Compositors). The other members of the Executive were Departmental representatives who varied according to the subject under discussion. The staff of the Executive was originally headed by Sir Joseph Ball (formerly a member of the Security Service) and W.C. Crocker (a member of the firm of City solicitors of that name). They withdrew for other work early in 1941 and late in 1940 respectively. Sir Herbert Creedy (formerly Permanent Under-Secretary of State for War) joined the staff in August 1940 and was the Chairman from January 1944 until the dissolution of the organisation in July, 1945. Despite its title, the Security Executive had no executive functions apart from the management of the overseas organisations; it was for the Departments immediately concerned to take the operative action to give effect to its recommendations.[11]

On the relinquishment by Duff Cooper, of his position as Chairman of the Security Executive, Churchill decided to vary the arrangement whereby the holder of that position also exercised control over the Security Service. It was thought that while the full executive control of a Minister might no longer be necessary, it would still be useful for there to be some Minister to whom the Director General of the Security Service could look for guidance on matters of general policy and help in cases of special difficulty. Churchill decided that this Minister would, for the time being, be the Foreign Secretary, Anthony Eden. This would have the advantage of bringing under one Minister two branches of the Secret Service and avoid the necessity of spreading still further knowledge of secret activities. It was to be clearly understood, however, that this arrangement was a 'temporary wartime expedient only, and is personal to Mr Eden'. The question as to whether the Security Service should as a permanent arrangement, have a Minister directly or indirectly associated with it, and, if so, who that Minister should be, was reserved for later consideration.[12]

In 1940, morale within MI5 was at a low ebb. British retreat in the wake of the German advance in the West only compounded the situation for Guy Liddell who, on 22 May, confided to his diary: 'The last three days have been the worst I ever spent for some considerable time. The news has been so bad that it made me physically sick.'[13] It was clear that Churchill had little confidence in the Security Service. William Crocker was one of a number of people parachuted in to 'the Office'. This obvious lack of faith on the part of the new Government was dispiriting for many Security Service officers and Liddell was one of those who were seeking some direction. Instead, there was only confusion and muddle. On 27 August, Liddell found that Crocker had resigned: 'I gather he was not prepared to accept the position which we had to find for him but that the result was that he had retired not only from this office but from the Centre as well. Personally I am very sorry in a great many ways that this has happened, as I am sure that he could have done very useful work here. The real mistake is that he was pitch forked into this office on half-baked information of the situation. For this I am afraid he was to some extent to blame.'[14]

On 18 November, Liddell heard that Jane Sissmore, an officer with twenty years experience, had been sacked for insubordination towards, Harker, the Director: 'This is a very serious blow to us all. There is no doubt that she was completely on the wrong leg but somehow I feel that the incident should not have happened.' Liddell tried to see if anything could be done[15] and travelled down to Blenheim Palace to see Sissmore at the Bear Inn in Woodstock. He found her 'quite normal' and in fighting mood determined to put forward her views in high quarters. Liddell urged her to do nothing for the moment.[16] The following day he had a chat with Jasper Harker and Charles Butler. Liddell told the Director that although Sissmore had no technical right of appeal she certainly had a moral right of appeal in view of her long and devoted service. But Harker and Butler took the view that she had no right at all and that if the Director's authority was questioned in this matter he had no alternative but to resign. Both thought there was no possibility of her returning to MI5 even though she had tendered an apology. All was clearly not well within the Service. Butler, himself, later confessed to Liddell that he was very depressed 'and does not feel that he can stick it much longer'.[17]

By now Liddell also concluded that there had to be change at the top: he ruled himself out for the job of Director and thought Valentine Vivian, in SIS, would be by far the best choice.[18] When Butler was called by Lord Swinton to give him his views on the state of MI5, he recommended that the latter talk to Liddell 'but this did not go very well' with Swinton who said: 'You see, Guy thinks I'm a bloody shit.' Butler protested vehemently but without making much headway. Butler also mentioned to Swinton that Malcolm Frost

– also parachuted in to MI5 from the BBC – was a 'snake in the grass' neither loyal to the Security Service nor to Swinton himself. Swinton appeared worried by this.[19]

A meeting to clear the air finally took place between Liddell and Swinton, on 6 December. Liddell grasped the nettle first and announced 'that I should like to try and put something right. I had been told that he [Swinton] thought I was moved by certain personal feelings against him and I was in consequence obstructive. I wished to say that this was entirely untrue. I was only interested in doing my work as efficiently as possible and that I was very grateful to him for all he had done to put over my point of view with other departments.' Swinton seemed to accept this. Liddell then went on to speak about Malcolm Frost: 'I said that I could not see any peace in his office while he remained. He was obviously an intriguer first and foremost and was so regarded by everyone here.' Swinton did not demur but was anxious for Frost, for whose ability he evidently had regard, should not be isolated. He thought that after a talk with him, Frost would not misbehave himself again.

Liddell then went to address the position of Reg Horrocks, a management expert, who had been drafted in to sort out MI5's apparent dysfunctional structure. Liddell explained to Swinton that, while he had the very best personal relations with Horrocks 'I sometimes wondered whether he fully understood what he was trying to reorganise in our office.' The main purpose of Horrock's reorganisation plan was to create an active espionage section to which all cases of any importance should be thrown up. But Liddell 'did not think that this was a practical arrangement, and I gave the example of Russian espionage. I explained that various forms of information would be coming in and reference would be made to people and incidents which would only be known to someone who was making a close study of the Communist movement in this country and abroad. It was therefore imperative that any such case should be run by the Communist section and not by the active espionage section.' Swinton seemed to see the force of the argument.[20]

Indeed he did, for Swinton's next move was to appoint Sir David Petrie to inquire into the organisation of MI5 which was a pressing need. So far, the attempts to restructure the Service had only been even more damaging to morale. But Petrie had a long career in intelligence. He had joined the Indian Political Intelligence Bureau from the Indian police and had headed this organisation for seven years before being posted to Palestine. Now Petrie was recalled from the Middle East and left Cairo by air on 11 December 1940. Delays owing to engine trouble prevented him from reaching London before Sunday 22 December, and, with Christmas ensuing, he was kept from meeting Swinton until 30 December. But the intervening days Petrie devoted to 'desultory reading' of the minutes of proceedings of the Home Defence (Security) Executive and its subsidiary bodies, from which he 'derived a good deal of enlightenment as to the nature and extent of the task before one. This I was unable to set about properly until 1 January 1941.' Petrie's terms of reference were in the form of a note of instructions handed to him by Swinton on New Year's Eve:

> Sir David Petrie will review the system of Intelligence and administration in the Security Service. He is invited to pay particular attention to the selection and training of officers, the devolution of and responsibility for work in the Department, and the dissemination of information among the staff to insure that each officer carries out his particular work to the best advantage.
>
> He should also review the methods used to appraise information at its true value and to record such information and the value properly attaching thereto.
>
> He will recommend any alterations, which he considers, will improve the organisation and distribution of work within the Department, and the maintenance of the necessary contact between sections, having regard to the importance of maintaining an organisation, which will function continuously, and effectively despite the chances and casualties of war.
>
> The Director and his staff will afford Sir David every facility in his inquiry.

The appointment of Petrie proved inspired. Petrie set about his task with vigour, presenting his report to Swinton in February 1941. Owing to the great expansion of the Security Service, the multiplicity of its sections and sub-sections and the many-sided duties it performed, Petrie felt he had to address himself first to undertaking a 'ground-survey' of the machine in being, so that its different components would mean something more to him than a mere jumble of figures and symbols. He was in and out of MI5's two HQ's Wormwood Scrubs, and Blenheim Palace, where his second visit lasted for the better part of a week. Petrie talked freely to most of the principal officers concerned. This process, he found, had been 'rather lengthy and at times tedious for myself and, I fear, for others also; but it has brought me knowledge I could have acquired in no other fashion'.

Petrie had the further advantage of discussing the Security Service and its working with representatives of various kindred and overlapping departments, e.g. the Home Office, Scotland Yard, SIS and the three fighting Services, which gave him some idea of how the organisation was viewed by those who dealt with it from outside. In gathering this information Petrie 'was firmly convinced that my position must be that of a detached and independent investigator'.

Petrie felt himself bound by two special considerations: the first was the time factor, which he regarded as 'most urgently pressing, since I believe we stand on the brink of a period of great peril'. The second was the need for maintaining the service as a 'running machine. No re-organisation involving a considerable dislocation could justify itself in the present circumstances. Besides, I believe that manipulation rather than surgery is needed. For these reasons I have aimed at suggesting a working reorganisation which can begin to be put into effect forthwith.'

It appeared, to Petrie, that in pre-war days when the 'Office' was small, the Director and his officers generally knew of 'likely people' or got names from elsewhere. The idea was to catch persons with the requisite character and outlook and, if possible, with some experience. In those days there were very few posts to fill, and there were fixed financial limits. Training took place under the eye of a responsible officer and was acquired in the school of experience. There was nothing in the way of a regular 'course', though the War Office used to send some officers to receive instruction. Expansion on a modified scale had taken place at the time of the Munich agreement. But there was no reserve of officers, though the subject had been considered but not pursued. Superior officers at the outbreak of war numbered about eighty, and of these some fifty were added in the twelve months subsequent to Munich.

When the war broke out, Petrie discovered that each officer 'tore around' to rope in likely people; when they knew of none themselves, they asked their acquaintances. Occasionally recruits who were brought in knew of other 'possibles'. Various Ministries also contributed surplus staff. In much the same way, retired officers came to notice, and new people continued to be got by the same processes. With increased numbers, training had naturally been curtailed and lack of experience had produced some 'awkward results. If I am correctly informed, there have been cases in which recruits have been taken on by divisions (or sections) without so much as informing Administration. The "vetting" authority was often lower than the head of a Division and sometimes no record was kept of an engagement.' In most cases, perhaps in every case, newcomers were placed under old hands, or at least people with more experience than themselves. They were just 'thrown into it', no previous training being possible. 'At any rate, neither the Director nor even Administration were always consulted as regards fresh enrolments, and in some cases Administration only knew of new hands when they had been stopped by the police for having no entrance passes, or when a crowd of hungry people presented themselves for pay.'

Petrie understated the case when he concluded that the system of recruitment had been 'haphazard'. Having said that, he accepted that, when times were peaceful and the establishment was small, there was a good deal to commend it. The Director 'knew his own needs and it was within his compass to satisfy himself about every newcomer; at least, the same yard-stick was always applied'. The chief criticism Petrie heard levelled against the old system came from an officer who knew the department well and was far from unfriendly in his attitude. He considered that it resulted in selection being confined to those who were in social contact with the Director and his chief officers. That was to say, selection was made too much on personal qualifications and too little on business ones; and there was a tendency for the job to adapt itself to the individual, rather than the individual to the job. Moreover, one condition of service, liability to discharge at a month's notice, tended to narrow the circle of candidates to those out of work, and anyone with settled prospects and fixity of tenure could not lightly be invited to come over to service where conditions were so precarious.

Petrie found the system clearly ill-adapted to deal with a large intake required at short notice. The circle of guarantors widened not only to friends but to friends' friends, or even beyond. Thus the employer's knowledge of the newcomer was at the best second or third hand, or perhaps still more remote. With this diluted knowledge there inevitably came a diversity of standard, since many recruits were picked up direct by heads of sections, themselves new to their jobs, without any reference to Administration. In one case Petrie had seen, the head of a newly formed section recruited a person of no previous experience whom he wished to put in general charge of investigation, as he considered there was a great deal of disorganisation and inefficiency in the Security Service as a whole. This newcomer, on joining, found no work to do or directions how to do it; and when some cases began to come his way, he found them 'utterly trivial'. After two or three months he resigned in disgust. Petrie had no reason to think that this case, though not solitary, was in any way typical; on the contrary, much 'excellent material' had been obtained: 'but I quote it as illustrating the serious abuses that may creep in when rapid expansion is demanded and there is no central authority to assess qualifications and apply standards.' The remedy appeared, to Petrie, to be a very small standing committee headed by the Director or, with his authority, by the next senior officer, who would sit with the head of the division and the head of the section concerned.

The scale of this haphazard intake was revealed to Petrie when returns showed that there were now 234 officers, 386 secretaries and 11 clerks. It had also been brought to Petrie's notice that the head of a division who had a suitable candidate to bring forward might be left to fight out the battle of his emoluments or other conditions of employment. 'This is wrong. The head of a division does not "know the ropes", and he may well waste time that he should devote to more pressing work. These questions are the province of Administration, as are indeed recruitment and all cognate duties.' Clearly, the basic structure of MI5 was a mess when the duties of senior counter-intelligence officers were taken up in sorting out recruits' pay and conditions.

Petrie also found the Security Service's organisation of counter-espionage duties antiquated. Under a Director and three Deputy Directors, there were three main divisions, namely A, which dealt with Administration, Personnel and Finance; B, which handled security intelligence and investigations; and C and D, these being in reality the General Staff Branch, which, in collaboration with the Security Service proper, performed most of the original functions of MI5. The present layout was still that which existed in the years before the war. However, this had so swollen its dimensions that the Service 'can truthfully be said to have grown out of all recognition. When a great flood descends a river, it often spreads out... and quite obliterates the line of the banks. It is somewhat on this scale that expansion has taken place in the Security Service.' In pre-war days, reflected Petrie, the personal knowledge of the Director, or of one of his officers, was probably a good guide as to how far a candidate was suited for work in the Service. But at the time of the big expansion, not only were candidates brought in who were 'clean beyond the ken of the central authority', but whose sponsors must in many cases have been quite ignorant of the nature of the work which their nominees were expected to perform. In the circumstances, it was natural that many of the newcomers, not a few of them men of established position and repute in their own line of life, should tend to be of an individualistic outlook, 'not all of them the same shape as the empty holes in the Security Service into which they had to be pegged at short notice'. So, when a demand arose, as when some new aspect of an existing problem showed itself, a man was brought in and became a sub-section, with a separate label of his own. He was not absorbed in a larger section, where he might have been given better tuition and might have acquired more all round knowledge. 'Instead of being employed in a sizable field he was set to till his own allotment. This expansion, instead of being vertical in an organised sequence from top to bottom, has been as it were horizontal, thus impeding knowledge of the section as a whole and effective control from the top.' Many of the sub-sections could be described as outlying areas with a single inhabitant. The general impression of MI5's staff left on Petrie's mind was that:

as a body they are dispirited, or at least, not in good heart. They are not 'on their toes' as one would like to see people up against a tough job. I do not say this applies to every individual member... Nevertheless it is true of them as a body. I mention this as a fact, and I conceive this mentality to be in a great degree a reflection of the difficult times the department has recently gone through. The troubles encountered have been breakdown, disorganisation, delays bringing recriminations from outside, which, conjoined with other things, have served to engender a feeling among the staff that they were inadequate to the work, and were neither being led nor supported as they needed to be. Then many of them have been resentful of what they regard as interference 'from outside' over the head of the Director; they have thought that not only have the latter's hands been weakened, but that his authority vis-à-vis his own staff has been impaired, since he apparently had been adjudged by higher authority to be unequal to the control of his own organisation. Nor do they think that this so-called interference from outside has been either happy in conception or fortunate in result. I am not concerned here to say how far these views are justifiable – I am merely stating that I have found them to exist. That they are damaging to morale and, consequently, to efficiency can hardly be gainsaid. There are other contributory causes to the malaise, some of them beyond anyone's power to prevent. These have been the splitting of the office into two sections some 60 miles apart; difficulty of inter-communication; destruction by fire of a considerable part of the card index, and so on. Then there have been the change from town to country, life in billets, lack of amusements and amenities, all of which have done nothing to improve a depression of spirit arising out of the major causes I have just described.

The Registry was of such importance in the whole organisation, that it required special and detailed mention. It employed 246 women as against 386 for the whole of the rest of the Office, and it was still under strength. Petrie warned: 'If the Registry is bad nothing else can be good.' At present the Registry was undergoing reorganisation but the new system had not met with the approval of a number of senior officers who had experience of the old regime. Petrie found reason to believe that this fact had resulted in the new system not being as fully understood as it needed to be, and in denying it that co-operation from all hands which was necessary to give it a good start. Not only had this impeded progress but it had led to an antagonism between the Registry and certain parts of the Office, which cut at the roots of efficiency. 'The office blames the Registry for delay in producing papers, and the latter retaliates by accusing the sections of withholding papers peculiar to their own work and so preventing the Registry from completing its records. Thus the vicious circle is complete. The existence of this antagonism is unfortunately well known to the secretarial staff, and is conducive neither to high morale nor good discipline.'

Petrie felt it necessary for him to say a word about the two rival schools of thought in this dispute. The great merit of the old Registry, according to those who had experience of it, was that it was run largely on a 'section' basis. That was to say, the filing, indexing and referencing were done by some member of the staff who had a good knowledge of the work of the section concerned. The advantage claimed for this was that looking up could be done more intelligently, and so the 'girl in the Registry' who worked for a particular section always knew where wanted files or papers were to be found and could produce them at short notice. The upholders of the old method claimed that the present Registry was not, and could not be, capable of meeting the requirements of investigating officers because the essential features of the former system, were lacking; and, until these defects were made good, the present Registry could not function efficiently, even though it was operating perfectly within its present structure. Stated differently, the objectors considered that the Registry was too large and too mechanical in its operation; papers were returned to and could not be traced again if they were wanted back; while the over elaborate and cumbrous procedure resulted in delays which not only reflected on the reputation of the Office but brought the practical investigation of cases almost to a stand still. From the point of view of the staff employed in it, the work of the Registry was said to be of a 'deadly dullness and to be devoid of the element of personal interest which employees of former times developed in their work, and which enabled them to do it far more intelligently and expeditiously'. A mechanical apparatus had been substituted for an organisation relying on human personality and human knowledge.

In his previous report on the Security Service, Lord Hankey had written that some of the Government Departments 'when pressed on the point' stated that the Security Service was 'sometimes rather slow in answering queries' – a weakness which, he observed, was by no means confined to this Service. Some of those whom Petrie interviewed had been less hesitant, and had stated that delays were not merely occasional but constant and serious. Such witnesses had been free, but not indiscriminating, in their criticism, and they had never been carping. Hardly less common was the criticism that the fundamental weakness of the Service was want of control and direction from above. In a sense, complementary to the foregoing were animadversions on the lack, or at least the looseness, of organisation, which made it difficult for an outsider to know at what point he should make contact to obtain responsible and representative advice or opinion, or to institute effective action. In fairness to the Security Service, 'I must not omit to mention that most of the outside Departments spoke appreciatively of the high quality of the work done by some of its officers. This tribute I gladly endorse, as I have examined some work that has been wholly admirable and of high value to the State.'

Generally speaking, Petrie found that neither the position nor functions of MI5's Divisions were, or could be, in dispute. He was most concerned about the organisation of B Division: 'It is the very core and centre of the *raison d'etre* of the Department, and its duties are many-sided. It is not too much to say that the success of the working of the Service as a whole turns on the proper organisation of B division. Its duties are the most important in the whole office. In some respects, indeed, it is on account of B that other parts of the office have their being and do their work.' It followed, therefore, that whatever took up time and energy that ought to be devoted to investigation was something that B should be relieved of. The Division should command the best talent and experience that the Service possessed, and it had to be able to draw on the resources of all other divisions and sections.

The head of the Division had a deputy at Blenheim. They had the assistance of several Controlling Officers whose functions were to control and co-ordinate the work of the groups of sections and sub-sections assigned to each of them. In all, Petrie came across 29 different sections numbered from B1 to B29. This figure, however, gave little idea of the extent of the layout of the Division. Most of the sections were split up into sub-sections, some far more extensively than others.

Thus, B4 seemed to have 11 sub-sections, B7 had 11, B10 had 9, B17 had 4 and B24 had 10. As already mentioned a sub-section number in some cases was merely personal to the officer who ran it. However, whether applied to a sub-section or an individual, a separate label was used in each case. For instance, B4 was sub-divided into B4a 1, B4a 2 up to B4a 7, and then from B4b 1 to B4b 3: 'I cannot say exactly how many such labels exist, but at a rough computation there are between 70 and 80 in common use.'

The first impression Petrie got was that an organisation so highly segmented could scarcely be sound: 'It is patently loose and must be correspondingly difficult to control' in terms of not only supervision but instruction. From this standpoint alone the organisation was defective. The head of B Division was heavily overworked. His deputy at Blenheim was also a busy man. B Division employed no fewer than 133 of the total of the 234 officers now in the Service. Relief from what was unessential was clearly called for. Some of the defects of the existing highly sub-divided organisation were: '1. Multiplicity of sub-sections produces a collection of individuals rather than an organisation; 2. Sub-sections can and do work "blind", and there are many known instances of several sub-sections dealing with the same case unknown to each other; hence arise duplication and delay, with risk of grave prejudice to work; 3. Control and instruction are impeded, and not enough all-round knowledge is acquired; 4. Replies to outside departments are often sectional and unrepresentative; 5. Confusion is caused to the Registry and to outside correspondents, and there is delay in passing files; 6. Work in these narrow compartments is apt to stand still when the occupant of any one of them goes sick.'

Petrie warned: 'These defects are not imaginary; they have all, unless I am misinformed, shown themselves in actual working. In fact one or two pictures taken from inside reveal confusion and inefficiency to a disquieting degree.' He concluded that Alien Control, for example, could be removed completely from B Division without the slightest prejudice to the work of Investigation. Separation of Aliens would mean also the separation of internment problems, preparation of cases, appeals for release, internment camps and all matters connected therewith. Seamen and the control of them should also be cut away. Equally, Petrie could see no harm, but much good, in transferring to a new division or group everything connected with Communism, Fascism, Pacifist movements, Celtic and Nationalist organisations and the like.

Concerning the Registry, Petrie preferred the new system to the old. The latter, he believed, was bound to break down since the best human memory had finite limits, and would not stretch beyond a certain point. Apart from this, 'the loss of one well-stocked memory might in ordinary times be a serious one; in war-time a number of such losses might be calamitous'. In the matter of tracing files, there was nothing the human memory held that cannot be put down on paper, 'and I much prefer to rely on the latter'.

From the standpoint of morale, Petrie believed that a study of internal direction was:

> essential, if one is to diagnose with any certainty what the Security Service is suffering from and what remedies need to be applied. As in the domain of medicine, this diagnosis may have to be accompanied by some plain speaking. If I am found to be over-candid, I can only say I have had no desire to be so, and I am equally without any personal motive. In the circumstances of the day and hour, no one has any right to speak the truth as he sees it. The security of the country is at stake and there is no kind of consideration, personal or otherwise, that can be weighed in the scale against it.

It was clear that the main issue was a lack of leadership from the top:

> The complaint from all quarters, from within the Service as well as from without, has been clear and insistent against lack of direction and weakness of control. The language used to me has occasionally been embarrassing in its frankness. But the weight and unanimity of this testimony is such as to lead irresistibly to the conclusion that the main charge is established beyond doubt. The lack of a firm grip at the top seems to be felt everywhere. There is no authority, no galvanic current that permeates down through all the organisation from top to bottom, and makes itself felt even in the most outlying parts; and there has been no proper attempt at organisation. The word 'rabble' was used to me of the Service, and though I reject it as a gross overstatement, it at least contains the germ of the idea of a very loosely linked assemblage. There seems to be plenty of wheels, and good wheels at that, but they have never been properly assembled into a machine. The views of one or two outside persons of intelligence who have been connected with the department are of a devastating frankness on this point. Lack of organisation naturally leads to muddle and inefficiency, and there seems to have been a great deal of both. As in the case of the Registry, the Department has

had much against it. Sudden expansion was called for, there was no reserve, there had to be a change of Director, and from any quarters a formidable amount of new and extra work. These various factors, with expansion all the time continuing, made re-organisation difficult for the Director, even if he had had more time to give to it. But certain it is that, if control were lost at the time and for the reasons stated, it has never been regained.

Though the accuracy of complaints by the staff to what they regarded as 'interference from outside' did not concern Petrie, the idea it conveyed was clear enough: 'They have felt that things have been done from above over the Director's head, some of them things he would not have done except under order. Nor have all of these met with approval.' The introduction under outside authority of an entirely new Deputy Director was 'an unfortunate mistake. The evil that this man did lives after him'. He was invested with wide powers inside the Service while retaining his position on the staff of the Home Defence (Security) Executive, thus being at once under and over the Director. It was strongly felt that his intrusion into the organisation was done without regard for the needs and work of the Service or the feelings of the Staff. As the appointment was one for which the Director was not responsible:

it weakened his general position in his own domain, since the staff wrote him down as an ineffective defender of their work and position against interference from outside... The moral, in any case, is clear. The Director must be master in his own house. If he is not, he had better not be there. I am entirely of the opinion that direction and co-ordination from above are essential in the public interest and helpful to the Service itself, but the principle governing the policy of direction must be that of support and not of detailed control. The Director may be directed but he should not be deposed.

Petrie's observations and recommendations included:

1. Recruitment, which was formerly by selection, had 'recently become haphazard...' A small standing committee for recruitment should be established and presided over by the Director or his representative.
2. Administration's control should be re-established over recruitment, and all cognate matters... Training should include more frequent lectures or talks to staff.

3. The preparation of a new handbook of instructions should be undertaken as soon as possible, notwithstanding current work pressures.

4. Appraisement of information had been defective and could be much improved if senior officers noted systematically on cases and information coming before them.

5. Ironically the effect of the organisation's 'great expansion' since the outbreak of war was the feature of the existing organisation that required the most attention... it had produced a multiplicity of sub-sections, making knowledge and control of them from the centre difficult.

6. Staff were dispirited from a variety of causes such as breakdown, lack of direction, pressure of work, disorganisation, complaints of delay and alleged interference from outside.

7. There was a great need of a central Secretariat or Director's Office.

8. A fresh scrutiny should be undertaken of pay and grading of the female staff, both in the Registry and elsewhere.

9. The position of Regional Officers needed to be further examined to determine the best means of maintaining contact and control. This process should also be directed to securing a prompter disposal of Overseas business.

10. The work of Investigation was the most important in the whole office, and B. Division should be relieved of all that diverted either time or energy from it.

11. The existing organisation of B. Division was too loose for effective control, the head of the Division had too heavy a charge, and the many sub-sections have shown defects in working.

12. Alien control should be removed from B, which would maintain close liaison with a new Aliens division, which, in its turn, would refer to B any cases of importance. Internment cases, policy and camps should be transferred. Communism, Fascism and Right and Left Wing and Celtic Nationalist Movements should go over to another new division or group.

13. Skilled investigation should be carried out by B, with other Divisions collating information collected by them but not required for Investigation.

14. B Division (Investigation) should comprise B2, B5, B6, B9, B11, B13, B15, B18, B19, B22, B26, and B27. B9 should come to London. Press Section should remain with B. B8L other than for purely administrative duties, to be under B.

15. The Subversive Movement Division should include B1, B4, B7, and B21. B1 should remain a self-contained unit as at present.

16. The Aliens Control Division would then operate B3, B8, B10, B16, B17, B23, B24, and B29.

17. Changes were based on a principle of 'linking like with like and are purely evolutionary', aimed at better grouping and closer control. In the current 'inflated state of work' two new Divisions were preferable to one, and a Deputy Director was desirable to control all three. A 'comb-out' should be undertaken as necessary to ensure that knowledge and experience were used to best advantage.

18. Censored letters should go more directly to sections concerned... Agents required for special occasions should be drawn from general pool... The Security Service should have its own representation in the censorship, both in London and in important provincial centres.

19. The system on which the Registry is being re-organised appeared sound, though it was 'somewhat slow and cumbrous in working'. 'Certain expedients' could be adopted to simplify its processes and to make production of papers quicker.

20. There was a need for better knowledge of Registry both on part of its own staff and office generally. Some interchange could be possible.

21. No organisational change was needed in regard to C and D divisions.

22. The complaints of lack of direction and weakness of control should be regarded as established. Organisation has been defective and has played its part in this.

23. The staff had 'keenly resented' what they regarded as 'outside-interference', which had reacted adversely on morale as well as weakening the Director's position.

24. The feelings of 'soreness and despondency' felt by the Service when their advice is not accepted may be discounted as the responsibility 'rested elsewhere'.

25. The placing of the Service under a centrally placed Minister without Departmental responsibility should be entirely beneficial. The position of the Service should be left as it is. It seemed inadvisable ever to transfer it to a single Department, since it had 'to act as the agent of many, who probably would not agree to control by any single one of them.[21]

The War Office were delighted with the report particularly Petrie's suggestion that 'the whole organisation should be called "Security Service" and that the title "MI5" should be reserved entirely for the purely War Officer side... MI5 as a title was simply and solely used as nuisance value cover for the activities of Kell.'[22] Sir John Anderson, now Lord President, passed on Swinton's minute to the Prime Minister proposing that Petrie should be appointed to carry out the reforms.[23] Petrie, though, was not enthusiastic:

> My own idea would be to fill it with a man sufficiently young that it would still count for much to him in the making of his career. This is a strong and entirely legitimate incentive. Such a man would get better and better as time went on; one who is already past his best would probably deteriorate.
>
> Counting my active service of 36 years, I have spent practically 40 years out of England. I have been retired about 4 years. Since I returned to regular work in May last, I have been conscious that both my energy and memory are not what they were. I daresay they are still as good as in most men of my age (I shall be 62 in September) but I cannot disguise from myself that there has been a deterioration.
>
> Another point is that I have breathed in an Eastern atmosphere for so long that I am none too sure how I should get on with a purely English staff. Many are new to their jobs and need to be treated with more patience than I perhaps possess. I might be found wanting in the same way in my dealings with representatives of other departments.
>
> For these reasons I feel that you should carefully consider the desirability of appointing a younger man. Also, as you may be aware, I have left a post in the Middle East which it may not be easy to fill, and to which I would like to return.
>
> I do not wish to overstate things but I feel there is such weight in these considerations that I am bound to bring them before you. I am extremely adverse to involving you in any risk of being let down either by my failing to realise expectations or by buckling at the time of greatest need.[24]

Lord Swinton, though, was insistent and told the Lord President: 'In my opinion Sir David is the right man; I think he should be strongly impressed to undertake the task. You know better than I do the reputation he enjoyed in India.' He combined great 'Intelligence' experience with sound judgement. 'He is a strong man; and I don't think his energy has flagged. I find him receptive of ideas. He has, therefore, I think, the essential qualifications for the job. To all this is now added the full knowledge he has gained of the Service and its personnel; and he would be carrying out the reforms he has himself recommended. I need not stress the time factor: it is sufficiently present to all our minds.'[25] Anderson again pressed Petrie's appointment to the Prime Minister, pointing out to Mr Churchill that: 'he will take some persuading. He doesn't want the job and would prefer to return to the Near East. But I think we should insist. I doubt if otherwise we shall succeed in getting the required speedy restoration of an organisation that has sagged down very badly during a critical time'.[26] It would be the PM's power to persuade that decided the issue. On 1 March, Churchill saw Petrie at Chequers. They had, in the Prime Minister's words, 'a satisfactory talk', the result of which was that: 'He is quite ready to take charge of MI5'. Churchill told Anderson that Petrie 'may have some considerations to make as to being given reasonable discretion in the management of MI5 by Lord Swinton and his Committee... He strikes me as a very good man'. At the end of his minute to Anderson, the Prime Minister asked: 'What do you suggest should happen to Brigadier Harker who took over at a difficult time and has I suppose done his best?'[27]

Petrie wrote to Swinton so as to be clear about his new role as head of the Security Service and the corresponding relationship with the Security Executive, pointing out that the 'principle governing the policy of direction by superior authority must be that of support and not that of detailed control'. But the Cabinet minute of 19 July 1940, 'which entrusts you with the "executive control" of MI5 travels far beyond this, with results which... have not been entirely fortunate. What I have to suggest is that the Director should be given a free hand to do his own job. If he fails to do it properly he should be replaced. But no one should attempt to do his work for him.' The same applied the staff, who had been feeling that they too had ceased to enjoy the confidence of outside authority and consequently had lost some of their confidence in themselves. Hence: 'the practice I would like to see established is that superintendence and control of the Director should be general and not detailed; and, further, that it should be exercised through a single person (at present yourself) and not through any composite body, centre or organisation'. Petrie believed that these ideas were 'fundamentally sound, and the freedom I recommend is only such as I consider to be essential in the best interests of the work'.[28]

In his reply, Swinton was 'strongly of the opinion' that the 'Director should direct' and that he should have authority and responsibility for his work. He should enjoy this vis-à-vis his immediate superior and his own staff: 'I do not think the words "executive control"… happily express the relationship as I envisage it. Executive control imports the idea of managerial functions. That is not a position which I desire to occupy.' The 'proper relationship between myself and the Director is that between a Chairman and a Managing Director. General questions of policy should be decided by the Chairman in close consultation with Director. But policy issues in action; and the Director should have the executive responsibility for action. The Chairman must, of course, be properly informed of the activities of the Department and results. That is obviously necessary and is common form in any Ministry or Company'.

So far as the superintendence and control of the Director in relation to his Department were concerned, that control was intended, under the Cabinet decision, to be expressed by 'myself;' but it was not the function of the Security Executive to do this. At the same time the Security Service was a member, with other Departments, of the Security Executive; and any questions affecting the Security Service, in common with other Departments, came before the Executive. Swinton accepted that: 'In theory there may appear to be an anomaly in my dual position as independent Chairman of the Executive and the person in control of the Security Service' but in practice he felt that it worked well with other Departments. It worked because the two principles recognised and carried in practice were: '(1) that the Security Service is free in these matters to fight its own case and (2) that the Chairman acts in a judicial capacity with an open mind towards all views.'

And it would be for the Director of the Security Service and Swinton, as Chairman of the Executive, to decide together what matters arising in the Security Service were of such importance that they should be brought before the Executive. After discussing these matters with Petrie, Swinton was pleased to note that 'we are in complete agreement'.[29]

Petrie and Swinton saw Harker on 7 March to sort what his role would be now he was no longer Director. Harker expressed 'complete willingness' to stay on at a lower salary and to render whatever service he could. Petrie and Harker agreed that if either of them felt 'in the least bit embarrassed' by his retention, he might leave, or alternatively might be asked to leave by Petrie, 'without further question asked'. Since 10 March, when Petrie assumed his role – under a new title of 'Director General' – Harker's position was that Deputy Director General. For Petrie:

The advantages of keeping Harker on are easily stated. Apart from the question of organisation and control… there is no other side of the work on which I have not found Harker well and intelligently informed. For the better part of twenty years he directed investigation under Kell and acquitted himself so well as to be marked out as the most likely successor. He has a good knowledge of all the work of the Department, past and present, he is reputed to keep his end well at conferences, and is on good terms with a wide circle of officials in the many Departments with which the Security Service is brought into close relations.

There is yet another important consideration. The work of the Service... has expanded enormously. Pressure of mere routine work is constant and heavy. Much of it cannot be done for the Director by the heads of Divisions because none of them has the requisite all-round knowledge and outlook. It struck me as one of the grave defects in the present organisation (and this view finds wide acceptance outside) that the part, often a junior and inexperienced officer, has been too often allowed to speak for the whole. Even my three weeks' experience has satisfied me that it will be a big part of my job to direct, that is to keep the ship's head to the wind. I shall be handicapped in that if I allow myself to get 'snowed under' by routine, I need an alter ego who can take that off me. Harker is well equipped to do that.[30]

When Anderson informed the Prime Minister that all was going as well as they had hoped under Petrie's leadership, Churchill's scribbled comment was: 'Good.'[31]

Under Petrie, Regional Control was transferred from B Division to A Division in August 1941 when Petrie called a conference in connection with the regional organisation. He explained that the reasons for establishing Regional Security Liaison Officers (RSLO.s) were:

1. to bring the Security Service into closer touch with provincial Police Forces;
2. to reduce the accumulating amount of work at Head Office;
3. to expedite the treatment of reports and correspondence from Chief Constables;
4. to provide the basis of an organisation in case of invasion when Head Office might be cut off from provincial districts;
and that their principal functions were:
1. to deal with Chief Constables and their staffs on all matters concerning the Security Service (with certain specified exceptions, e.g. Communism);
2. to assist and advise those concerned in dealing with problems

of the arrest, search and interrogation of suspects of security interest;

3. to deal with individual cases locally where possible and to reduce the volume of enquiries sent to Head Office;

4. to collaborate with the naval, military and air force intelligence officers in the regions on all matters of mutual interest;

5. R.S.L.O.s should not normally make enquiries on their own, but should always act in this connection through the police.

Thus, by the summer of 1941 when the reorganisation of the Security Service was 'gradually put into effect the position of Regional Control and the RSLOs had crystalised and, after overcoming initial difficulties largely due to the flooding of the office with numerous denunciations and reports about suspected spies, the staff in the Regions had settled down to deal with its work on systematic lines'.[32]

Among the other changes Dick White was installed Assistant Director B Division, and other recruits were John Marriott (a young solicitor and Cambridge graduate) assigned to TAR Robertson as his deputy; Cyril Mills (from a circus family); and William Luke, (a young industrialist from Glasgow). Later they were joined by Christopher Harmer (again a solicitor and Cambridge friend of Marriott); Ian Wilson (also a solicitor); and Hugh Astor (an Oxford graduate declared medically unfit for military service on account of his lameness).[33] Many of the intake that flooded into the Security Service proved superb appointments; but the concept of vetting the intake was primitive: one of the functions of Kell's IP Club was to keep in touch with those who had been associated with MI5's work and, with the outbreak of war, it served a useful factor in the expansion of the Security Service.[34] But there was a least one cuckoo in Dick White's nest.

White initiated a number of innovations to maximise MI5's analysis of intelligence. He organised a group of B Division sections that were in contact with the German Secret Service, either through their communications or their agents, and evolved them into a central group under his direction. All intelligence, including from sources outside the Service, was assessed. White's innovation was to create a 'central mart', or exchange of information at daily meetings held in his room at 12 noon. At these meetings White co-ordinated the study of the enemy Secret Service organisations. He described these meetings as the B Division 'committee of action' and observed that, out of its daily discussions, emerged 'a consciousness of counter-espionage methods which had been lacking prior to their inauguration'. They became training grounds for counter-espionage specialists and White believed that it was hardly too much to say that they resulted in placing the Security Service in a predominant position in the counter-espionage field. While White co-ordinated the counter measures against the Germans, Liddell supervised and directed this work and, in addition, coordinated the working of B Division with the general security or preventative work of B and other Divisions.[35] Patricia McCullum, a secretary, described White's chairmanship as 'brilliant... Nanny would have said about Dick, "He's a deep one – always there if you wanted him.".' TAR Robertson, meanwhile, recalled that: 'Dick was never aggressive or vindictive' when mistakes occurred. White cultivated discussion – but always took the final decision.[36]

The reorganisation of MI5 coincided with a seismic breakthrough in Signal Intelligence (SIGINT). In August 1940 the Radio Security Service (RSS), also known as MI9, succeeded in intercepting Abwehr radio signals. By December the cryptographers of GC & CS, based at Bletchley Park, had cracked the main hand cipher used to encrypt the German signals. This SIGINT became known as Intelligence Service Oliver Stachey (ISOS) after the section head at Bletchley Park. In December 1941 another breakthrough occurred when the German machine cipher code was broken and this intelligence became known as Intelligence Service Knox (ISK) after the cryptographer 'Dilly' Knox.[37] The significance of this was that British Intelligence had the ability to read all Abwehr signals traffic for the remainder of the war; however, this did not mean that MI5 had access to all this material. There were a number of auxiliary sections of B Division that included sections dealing with subjects, neutral territories, liaison security, research and shadowing.

The Key B Division Sub-Sections.
1. Subject Sections
Neutral and Allied diplomatic representatives (part of B.1.B. Major Blunt)
Finance and currency enquiries (part of B.1.B. Sir Edward Reid)
Seamen and the personnel of airlines (B.1.L. Mr. Stopford)
Industry and Commerce (B.4.B. Mr. Craufurd)
Special Cases (B.1.C. Lord Rothschild and Mr. Hill)
2. Neutral Territories' Sections
Middle East (part of B.1.B. Mr. Kellar)
Spain, Portugal and South America (B.1.G. Lt.Colonel Brooman-White)
Ireland (B.1.H. Mr. C. Liddell)

3. Liaison Security Sections
Liaison with Censorship (B.3.A. Mr. Bird and B.3.D. Mr. Grogan)
Liaison with R.S.S. and with the B.B.C. (B.3.B. Mr. Hughes)
4. Security Sections
Lights and Pigeons (B.3.C. Fl.Lt. Walker)
Signals Security (B.3.E. Lt.Colonel Sclater)
5. Research Section
Information Section (B.I. Information Captain Gwyer and Mr. Bird
6. Shadowing Staff (B.6. Mr. Hunter).

Among the so-called subject sections the investigation of the activities of neutral and Allied diplomatic representatives (part of B1.B.) was one of the most important. It had long been realised that some of the neutral and Allied diplomatic missions in London were possible sources of leakage to the enemy about important political and military matters and an even more serious danger arose from the possibility that a German agent might be employed in one of these missions; 'and the event proved that this apprehension was well founded' in that the Germans employed agents in the Spanish and Portuguese Embassies throughout the war. In the early stages the responsibility for dealing with this problem had rested with each country section, but under the reorganisation scheme of 1941 most of the country sections were transferred from B to the newly created E Division. One of the more important country sections remained in B Division, i.e. that dealing with Spain and Portugal and South America. The Czechoslovak country section was in E, but B Division maintained special relations with the officers of the Czech Security Service in London. The Japanese section also remained in B Division. B Division officers felt that the problem of diplomatic missions should be studied as a whole and in March 1941 a special section was established for the purpose.[38] Under the reorganisation it became one of the B1.B. sub-sections under Major Anthony Blunt.

Blunt had been born at Holy Trinity vicarage, Bournemouth, Hampshire, in September 1907, the third and youngest son of the Reverend Stanley Vaughan Blunt (1870–1929) and his wife, Hilda Violet (1880–1969), daughter of Henry Master of the Madras civil service. His brothers, Wilfrid Jasper Walter Blunt (1901–1987) and Christopher Evelyn Blunt (1904–1987), were a teacher of art and a numismatist respectively. His mother's family were acquaintances of the future Queen Mary. As a child in Paris, where his father was the British embassy chaplain, Blunt acquired a lasting enthusiasm for French art and architecture, a passion encouraged by his eldest brother, Wilfrid, a future art master at Eton College. By the age of sixteen, at Marlborough College where with his best friend Louis MacNeice he was part of a group of rebellious young aesthetes, he was producing defences of modern art, much to the infuriation of the deeply conservative art teacher. In 1926 Blunt won a scholarship to Trinity College, Cambridge, graduating there with a second in part one of the mathematical tripos (1927) and a first in both parts (1928 and 1930) of the modern languages tripos (French and German). In 1932 he was elected a Fellow of the College on the strength of a dissertation on artistic theory in Italy and France during the Renaissance and seventeenth century; he remained there until 1937. By 1932 he was already writing for the *Cambridge Review* and within a year had become *The Spectator's* regular art critic, a position he held until 1938. While still an undergraduate, Blunt was invited to join the Apostles a secret, all male Cambridge debating society that regarded itself as constituting an elite. An influential minority of the society's members were, moreover, like Blunt himself, homosexual. In summer 1937 Blunt left Cambridge to work at the Warburg Institute in London, where he met a generation of Jewish émigré academics who greatly influenced his art history. Blunt was recruited into MI5 in 1940.[39] Blunt, and his colleagues, dealing with diplomatic missions, saw the problem of the sub-section they now comprised as being: '1. to collect material which was already available in other places, principally in SIS, but which was not reaching us; 2. to study diplomatic communications to and from London; 3. to evolve means of controlling neutral and Allied diplomats in this country so that they should be prevented from obtaining and transmitting information likely to be of value to the enemy and 4. to obtain the fullest possible information about the activities of diplomats by the placing of agents and by other special means.'

One of the first results of this undertaking was to emphasise what had long been known, i.e. that there was voluminous material in the possession of SIS which was of great interest to the Security Service but was not being passed to it. This material was: 1. BJs, i.e. deciphered diplomatic cables and telegrams and 2. Special Material, i.e. the recorded telephone conversations of diplomats in London.

In addition to these various methods of intercepting diplomatic communications steps were taken to obtain agents of the Security Service inside various diplomatic missions. These agents fell under four classes: diplomats, the personal contacts of diplomats, secretaries in missions and servants. Certain neutral diplomats were found who were so strongly anti-Fascist and anti-German that they were prepared to work for MI5. One of the useful functions served by diplomats and their contacts was to assist the Service in clearing up problems by obtaining information about individuals who for various reasons fell under suspicion. They were able to furnish not only filled in gaps in MI5's information but served as a check on possibly inaccurate information from other sources. The employment of servants was the work of a sub-section of Maxwell Knight's MS.

Some months before D-Day when restrictions of all kinds were being imposed on the British public and on foreigners in Britain it was realised that the most serious danger of leakage about the intended invasion was through diplomatic channels. On the advice of the Security Service, the Cabinet agreed to a total ban on diplomatic communications of all types from 15 March onwards. After this date no missions except the American and the Russian, were allowed to send cipher telegrams or uncensored diplomatic bags. These measures, which were effective, were justified not only on the principle that the use of diplomatic cipher was a concession and not a privilege, but from the security point of view by the information which had previously been obtained to show that some of the diplomatic missions constituted a real danger in this sense.

The section dealing with Spain, Portugal and South America, known as B1.G. first came into existence as a separate section when the Low Countries were overrun in 1940 and it became apparent that enemy intelligence operations against Britain were 'canalised through the Iberian Peninsula to an important extent'. The information available in MI5, on this subject, was 'extremely limited' and little had been done before the war apart from a number of enquiries about Spanish Falangists in Britain as part of the 'general "Right Wing" problem'. Some aspects of this had come to notice through contacts between BUF officials and Spanish Falangists, 'but in 1940 the question became more acute in view of the possibility that Spain and Spanish officials would adopt a more or less hostile attitude even if Spain did not come into the war against us'.

Unfortunately, MI5 'could not count on assistance from SIS' which the Security Service found 'was not in a position to render any useful assistance as their knowledge of the Spanish situation and of the organs of the German Intelligence which had been established in Spain and Portugal was deficient'. One of the first activities of B1.G 'was to assist in obtaining particulars of escape routes through Spain and full details of the system of documentation and control in force in the Peninsula with a view to helping to check the stories of individuals escaping from enemy occupied territory and Spanish seamen arriving here.' Close attention was also devoted to the Falange organisation and other

Spanish institutions in Britain. A preparation of lists of Spaniards to be interned in the event of war with Spain took up a lot of time in 1941 and early 1942 but 'was both an end in itself and a means of developing intelligence'.[40]

Since the invasion of the Low Countries, the neutral Iberian Peninsula had become the hothouse of espionage where the British and Germans vied for dominance against each other. It became the centre for German espionage against the UK. B1.G was concerned with these activities only in cases where Spanish and Portuguese subjects were involved and did not deal with Axis agents of other nationalities, even though they may have been recruited in, or despatched from, the Peninsula to Britain. A B1.G Intelligence Summary, from 1942, stated that, apart from seamen agents, Spanish espionage in the Britain had, 'as far as we know', been conducted almost entirely through the Embassy and representatives of the Spanish press 'who are in close touch with Embassy circles'. There was, at that time, no definite evidence that the Consuls in the provinces were directly involved in these activities, but there was 'good reason to suppose that their potentialities have not been overlooked' by the German Secret Service: 'Even if we are wrong in this assumption, and none of them have been recruited as conscious agents of the Axis, it is certain that they have nevertheless unwittingly provided information for the Germans. It is known that routine Consular reports, in common with other diplomatic documents which may be of interest to the enemy, are shown by certain officials in the Spanish Foreign Office to Axis agents in Madrid.' This was a leak which could not be blocked so long as the 'unscrupulous and violently pro-Axis' Serrano Suner continued to held the post of Foreign Secretary. It was, however, a point which merited some attention by RSLOs: 'If it comes to their notice that a Spanish Consul in their Region is on friendly terms with any important person who has confidential information in his possession, it is well worth getting in touch with Head Office and discussing the advisability of warning the man in question to be especially careful when talking to neutrals. Arrangements are also being made to pass across misinformation in certain selected cases.'

B1.G had no indications that the Spanish colony in the UK was engaged in serious espionage prior to the German invasion of the Low Countries, 'though ever since the Civil War the Franco supporters had been watching and reporting on the activities of the Republican groups' in Britain. In the spring of 1940, however, the Marquis de Murrieta was sent to Britain as a talent spotter by the Spanish General Staff. He recruited Miguel de Lojendio, who was at that time filling the dual role of Spanish Consul in London and Second Secretary at the Embassy, and entrusted him with the task of building up an espionage organisation. At a later date a Spanish diplomatic courier brought Lojendio money, secret inks and further instructions. Lojendio, who was a Basque, was a founder member of the Falangist Party. He was not, however, 'a man of very violent political views and is even known to have been mildly sympathetic towards the Basque Separatist refugees. There is no reason to believe that he was particularly anti-British; all our evidence is, in fact, to the contrary'. He was, however, 'conceited, frivolous and ambitious. From what we know of his character, it is reasonable to assume that he did not engage in espionage from any political motives, but undertook such work because it appealed to his sense of the dramatic, and also in the hope that he might thereby find a relatively easy path to fame and fortune. He was, as has been stated, recruited by a representative of the Spanish General Staff, and was ostensibly working for that organisation. As time went on, however, it became increasingly clear to him that he was in fact serving the interests of the Germans. When he realised this he was deeply distressed.'

B1.G's information about the extent and activities of the Lojendio organisation was 'rather limited'. It was known that he communicated in secret ink on the back of Consular reports which were forwarded to Spain in the diplomatic bag. He employed certain Falangist fruit merchants in London as sub-agents, and boasted that his network covered the whole country. This latter statement was 'probably based on the fact that he had access to the reports of all the provincial consulates, and could glean information from these sources. This may, in many instances, have merely duplicated information which the Germans would in any case have obtained through their more highly placed connections in the Spanish Foreign Office', but Lojendio would not have been aware of these arrangements in Madrid. Furthermore, there was a distinct possibility that one at least of the Consuls, the Count of Artaza, who was a relative of the Marquis de Murrieta, 'is directly connected with the espionage organisation'. Though there was no concrete evidence to support this view, Artaza was known to be violently anti-British and to have shown 'excessive zeal' in collecting information for his consular reports. He was formerly stationed at Newcastle and had now been moved to Cardiff. It was also believed that Lojendio made some use of his contacts with the Basque Separatists and with other Republicans whom he met through his Consular work: 'This point is particularly interesting. We know that officers of the German Intelligence Service in Madrid very much favoured the technique of using homesick and disillusioned Spanish "Reds" for espionage purposes and have boasted that such men did most effective work in France before that country was occupied. They state that Republican exiles, and in particular the more irresponsible elements such as former members of the Anarchist Groups, can be won over and controlled by the promise that if they will obey orders they can earn an absolution and remission of their past sins and will ultimately be allowed to return to their homes in Spain.'

In spite of 'what may appear from this account to be a rather imposing façade', B1.G was 'fairly confident' that the Lojendio organisation was in fact 'amateurish and relatively ineffectual'. Lojendio was 'lazy and temperamentally unsuited to the work. Moreover, he developed a strong distaste for its increasingly German flavour. We have an unconfirmed report that in the later stages he was even inventing information to save himself the trouble of collecting genuine material for his masters'. In August 1941, Lojendio was recalled to Spain as a result of denunciations charging him with 'political unreliability', and other offences including that of being in touch with British Intelligence. These denunciations were largely the work of a Spanish journalist Luis Calvo and a diplomat, Alcazar de Velasco, who was temporarily attached to the Embassy in London. As both these men were active German agents, MI5 had good reason to suppose that Lojendio was 'framed', and that the real reason for his fall was his neglect of his underground work.[41]

The 'outstanding development' in Section B1.G's work arose from an enquiry into the case of Miguel Piernavieja del Pozo, who proved to be a Spanish Secret Service agent working for the Abwehr organisation in the Peninsula.[42] In September 1940, while the Lojendio organisation was still active, a journalist called Piernavieja del Pozo, codenamed POGO by MI5, arrived in London. He claimed to have been sent as a 'special observer' for the Institute de Estudios Politicos, an organisation which could in some respects be compared to Chatham House, though it differed in being a political body controlled by the Falange Party. It soon became evident that Piernavieja's real mission was espionage on behalf of the Germans, with whom he communicated in secret ink. However, 'as he was a young, dissolute and irresponsible playboy, he soon found the girls at the Café de Paris more entertaining than spying, and proceeded to invest in them much of the money that had been entrusted to him for other purposes'.[43]

The key figure in MI5's penetration of the POGO ring was GW, SNOW's sub-agent. In October 1940, GW received a letter from a man on the paper of the Tuscan Hotel. The writer said that he met a friend of a Mr Kettering in Madrid and would very much like to see GW at the earliest possible moment. 'KETTERING' was a pre-arranged password between SNOW and Rantzau. It was changed to 'KETROCH' about three weeks before the arrival of the letter to GW.[44] GW met his contact, a Spaniard, and was given £3,500 in a tin of talcum powder. He was to report on factories in the west of England and on the Welsh Nationalist movement as well as working something up regarding sabotage. In the meantime, GW was asked to obtain an intermediary between himself and the Spaniard – who was POGO. Guy Liddell recorded that GW was 'very incensed at having the money taken away from him' and threatened to resign his service as an agent. J.H. Marriott managed to calm him down but Liddell concluded that GW was a 'rather unpleasant type who is obviously on the make'.

Embarrassingly for Sir Samuel Hoare, His Majesty's Ambassador to Madrid, the Spanish agent POGO had come to Britain under the auspices of the British Council and the personal recommendation of Hoare. On arrival in the UK, POGO told the immigration officer that he wanted Spain to enter the war and hoped that Germany would win! This, it seems, did not raise many suspicions. Liddell lamented: 'It seems a curious thing that our authorities should not be really wise to the fact that any member of the Falange, which is in fact a Spanish Nazi Party, must be right in the German camp.' POGO's address also appeared in the papers of Enrique Buena, a Spaniard who had been arrested by the police for taking the particulars of an air raid. The Police, 'thinking him a nitwit', released him.[45] So, when Liddell met with Lord Swinton, on 11 October, he reported the latest on the POGO case to the intrigued peer. Liddell then confronted Swinton, asking him what he wanted MI5 to report to him in the future 'as I had rather got the impression from our previous interview' that Swinton 'had no confidence in either myself or Dick White in far as the handling of this case was concerned'. Swinton was slightly embarrassed and protested he had every confidence in the way MI5 were handling the case 'but not in our desire to keep him informed'. Liddell stressed he had no wish to withhold information from him provided it went no further.[46]

Meanwhile, a telephone tap on Mrs Harris, POGO's girlfriend, produced a 'curious result': the many different methods of speaking that were adopted by her. Depending on whom she was speaking to, Mrs Harris employed a marked foreign accent, a slightly American accent, a Cockney accent and a comparatively educated and fluent English accent. When speaking to POGO on the phone, she 'appears to be a rather elderly woman with a poor command of the language, just as on other occasions she speaks fluently, quickly and with practically no accent at all'.[47] By early November, POGO had 'badly blotted his copy book by getting tight' and giving an indiscreet interview to the *Daily Express* during which he – again – said that he hoped Germany would win the war.[48] Not too long after this, an SIS agent, in touch with POGO, put forward the opinion that poor POGO was becoming more Anglophile on account of his treatment in Britain. POGO, it seemed, was rather upset by a Ministry of Information broadcast to Italy which attributed to him the view that although the Italian Air Force was good, the Italian infantry was hopeless. POGO accepted that he had said this but only when he was slightly drunk.[49] The same SIS agent was reporting that POGO had written to his chief in Spain stating that his stay in Britain had convinced him that 'Great Britain is invincible'.[50]

With POGO finally being manoeuvred into a position in which he might be exploited, the case began, in Liddell's words, to become 'rather difficult'. The Ministry of Information 'had told him he is no good and he had better go home' while the Spanish Embassy seemed to have come to the same conclusion. MI5 could not stop POGO being sent home without endangering the position of their agent, GW, and without causing an incident with the Spanish Government that the Foreign Office was anxious to avoid. The Service resorted to trying to get the British Council to smooth things over and then place the POGO case in the hands of Bill Cavendish-Bentwinck of the Joint Intelligence Committee (JIC) in order that he could be fed with 'interesting' Foreign Office news.[51] However, the damage was done and POGO was recalled to Spain in disgrace in February 1941, probably as a result of representations made by the German agent, Alcazar de Velasco, who had arrived in Britain in January of that year. Nevertheless, MI5 and B1G, through the contacts established by GW, had penetrated the Spanish espionage network – now under de Velasco's control – in London.

Alcazar de Velasco had come to London with the nominal title of Press Attaché – 'regardless of the fact that that post was already filled by a perfectly competent diplomat'. He took some steps to reorganise the Press Bureau at the Embassy, but stated 'fairly openly' in Spanish circles that the real purpose of his visit was to act as a personal observer for his friend Serrano Suner, the Spanish Foreign Minister. There was 'no doubt that he genuinely fulfilled this role and reported on the political reliability, from the Falangist point of view, of the Spanish diplomats and colony in the UK. The most important part of his mission, however, was to serve the interests of the German Secret Service, from whom he received substantial payments, and to whom he sent reports in secret ink via the diplomatic bag.' Alcazar was considered 'an extraordinary character' by B1.G. He enjoyed the friendship and support of the Spanish Foreign Secretary and appeared, in fact, to be Suner's 'favourite thug. He started life as a bootblack, made some money as a bullfighter, joined the Falange and soon rose to a position of authority as the result of several well-organised political murders. Finally he blossomed forth as a diplomat. While in London he was able, through his dynamic personality and sinister influence in Madrid, to terrorise and dominate the Spanish colony.'

Alcazar's first visit to Britain lasted just over a month. On his return to Spain, MI5 recommended that he should be declared *persona non grata*. This suggestion was not accepted 'for political reasons, but the Foreign Office undertook to adopt delaying tactics and we were hopeful that they would succeed in fending him off indefinitely. However, to our consternation, he arrived back in England on 17 July and remained here until September'.[52] Straight from the off, it was clear that Alcazar was POGO's superior and that he was working for Serrano Suner; the latter, as MI5 knew from Japanese BJs, [signals intercepts] had promised to pass on to the Japanese Minister in Madrid reports received from Spanish diplomatic representatives abroad. Eventually it was proved that Alcazar was the source of intelligence reports sent by the Japanese Minister in Madrid to Tokyo and that much of it was invented while some of it was based on the reports of another member of the Spanish Embassy 'who was in fact a double agent controlled by us'.

From these beginnings an elaborate counter-espionage network was developed 'which was very competently and successfully handled' by Lieutenant Colonel Brooman White and the other officers of B1.G; it 'afforded good grounds for assurance that the German efforts to obtain intelligence through officials of the Spanish Embassy in London were well covered'. Among other consequences 'of the elaborate Spanish intrigues on behalf of the enemy' was the arrest on 12 February 1942 of the Spanish journalist, Luis Calvo, on his arrival at Whitchurch aerodrome from Spain.[53] On Alcazar's departure he left 'as his *locum tenens*' Calvo who had been in Britain for a number of years as correspondent for one of the most important Madrid newspapers. He was 'not particularly' anti-British, nor was he an active member of the Falange Party. Calvo was, however, 'an unscrupulous opportunist with an eye to the main chance, and he no doubt hoped', that by working for Alcazar, he would not only earn a considerable amount of money but would also acquire valuable political backing in Spain. On 22 January 1942, he was summoned back to Madrid, ostensibly on press business, but actually in order to receive further instructions for espionage. On this visit Alcazar put him in direct touch with two members of the German Secret Service. He returned to Britain on 12 February and was arrested at the airport.[54]

GW, meanwhile, had approached Segundo, a porter at the Spanish Embassy, who had previously acted as a go-between between him and POGO. Through Segundo, GW was eventually introduced to Calvo, and from June 1941 until the latter's arrest, continued to see him periodically to receive money from him and to make to him reports which he had previously given to POGO. As far as MI5 could tell, Calvo did not at the time ('whatever he may have said after his arrest') entertain any suspicions about GW's bona fides 'and certainly forwarded his reports to his Spanish masters'.[55] Upon his arrest, Calvo was immediately sent to Camp 020, but the delicacy of the sources (GW, BJs, material 'and our agents in the Embassy') made interrogation difficult. One outcome of this arrest was an incident at the Spanish Embassy when the Duke of Alba examined the contents of all letters received, and this in turn led to difficulties in communication between the German agents among the Spanish officials and Alcazar in Madrid, all the details of which reached B1G through their network of agents. Through such sources B1.G. also learnt that the Germans recruited at least five journalists and a press attaché for espionage purposes through Alcazar.[56] There were indications that the Calvo arrest had caused 'considerable alarm and despondency' in Alcazar's circles in Madrid, and MI5 hoped, at the time, 'that it has given a fairly severe setback to espionage through Spanish channels in this country'. The Germans were probably, Brooman-White, speculated, 'further inconvenienced', by the 'providential death' of the Spanish Military Attaché, Colonel Barra, whom the Security Service had good reason to believe was also spying for the Axis.[57]

Not everyone within MI5 was as sanguine as Brooman-White: with the arrest of Calvo, 1942 began, in the words of MI5's John Masterman, 'with a major disaster', when GW was lost as an agent in February. The sheer scale of the Spanish espionage ring in Britain forced the Government into a position where it felt it had little option but to arrest Calvo as part of a plan to clear up the ring up. 'We dissented, of course, from the proposed action, but our protests did not prevail,' recalled Masterman. Calvo was arrested 'and GW's career as a double agent was ended. The loss to us was great, for he was by far the best channel we ever had for the transmission of documents, and his value in this respect might have been a growing asset. Moreover, his "elimination" placed others of our agents in danger and imposed a policy of extreme caution upon us. It is permissible to suggest that at a later stage, when the reputation of the double agent system was more firmly established and its uses better understood, our view would have prevailed. As things were we were compelled to make the best of a bad job and continue with a depleted team.' Fortunately MI5 were able to develop new cases 'which more than filled the gaps in the team'. Some of them were only of passing interest, while others presented new and interesting features.[58]

One of these was PEPPERMINT, a Catalan, who came from a prosperous middle-class family; his mother was English and his father was an agent for Kleinwort's bank. During the Spanish Civil War, PEPPERMINT was in Marseilles running an espionage organisation for Franco. Later, he was in business in Paris and did some odd jobs for the Spanish Embassy, gradually drifting more and more into the diplomatic world. He subsequently came to London and was employed for a time by the Spanish press services. On the outbreak of war he acted as diplomatic courier for the Spanish Embassy, later being appointed Press Attaché. PEPPERMINT's political sympathies were 'Monarchist and if anything pro-British, but he is weak, lazy and above all a terrible snob'.

In January 1941, and again in the following July, when de Velasco first visited Britain he 'acquired a fairly strong' hold over PEPPERMINT, both through his general intimidation of the Embassy personnel and through his knowledge that PEPPERMINT had 'temporarily' diverted some of the Press Bureau funds to his own use. Despite this, contact was actually made with PEPPERMINT in December 1941, when he gave MI5 full and accurate reports about two Spanish Republicans, Fernando Martinez Casabayo and Onofre Garcia Tirador, who had approached the Spanish Embassy offering extremely valuable information about SOE's training methods and Free French plans in return for permission to go back to Spain. Both these men were detained. It was at this time that PEPPERMINT also gave MI5 information about the espionage activities of del Pozo and Lojendio. In addition PEPPERMINT told the Security Service that he had himself been instructed by Alcazar while the latter was in Britain to report on the activities of the Spanish 'Reds', and also to send out general information about morale and the views of prominent British politicians. While telling MI5 about Onofre Garcia and Casabayo, PEPPERMINT had at the same time felt bound to send a report on them to Alcazar, and he was finally summoned to return to Spain at the same time as Calvo.

When he arrived in Madrid in January 1942 he was received by Alcazar 'with the utmost cordiality' and was told that all his expenses would be paid. That very evening he was invited to dinner with Alcazar. Calvo was also present. During the rest of his stay in Madrid, PEPPERMINT saw quite a lot of Calvo and met Alcazar several times. Nothing of major importance occurred until the afternoon of the day of his departure, when he called by appointment at Alcazar's house. He was immediately introduced by Alcazar to two Germans, who were later identified as Kuehlenthal and Friedrich Knappe. It was assumed that PEPPERMINT would do what he was told and the question of his willingness to work for the Germans was not even raised. PEPPERMINT spent about an hour in conversation with Alcazar and the two Germans. They said that statements about politics and morale in Britain were of no interest whatever. They wanted the location of large military units, the launching of ships, the location of new aerodromes, tempo of aircraft production, location and output of war factories and the general state of transport. PEPPERMINT was told that full particulars would be given him in the form of a written questionnaire that Alcazar would put in the Diplomatic Bag. PEPPERMINT was given instructions in the use of secret ink and also handed two pen nibs and two small wads of cotton wool. As regards the question of sub-agents, PEPPERMINT was largely left to his own devices, only being advised to frequent the London clubs, to use mercenaries as much as possible, and not to worry about expense.

On his arrival in London, PEPPERMINT reported his contact with the Germans to MI5 and agreed to work under its direction. On 5 March he sent his first letter in secret writing asking for further instructions in view of the Calvo incident. On 24 April he received instructions telling him to be very careful but to go ahead and obtain information on the subjects which he knew were of interest to the Germans. Between April and July, PEPPERMINT sent out a good deal of information and recruited certain semi-notional sub-agents – that was, these individuals really existed and were known casually to PEPPERMINT but they were only notionally collecting information for him. These contacts included a White Russian journalist, a member of the Home Guard and various journalists. The information sent had been largely of a political nature, but had included reports on the sailing of three convoys. ISOS revealed that this information had been received as the valuable report of a reliable agent.

At the beginning of July, PEPPERMINT received in another envelope, which escaped the censorship of the Ambassador, a further payment of £480 disguised as funds for the Press Office, and a handkerchief complete with instructions for developing the secret writing supposed to be on it. No trace of secret ink was revealed under treatment, and it was possible either that the handkerchief had been so carelessly handled before despatch as to destroy the writing, or that Villaverde, the First Secretary at the Embassy, who was 'a very able and active political intriguer', opened the envelope and substituted another handkerchief for the one with secret writing on it. In order to avoid arousing the Ambassador's suspicions by writing too often to Alcazar, PEPPERMINT sent his secret ink reports on the back of sheets of paper bearing press cuttings addressed to Carrete, the Foreign Ministry Censor in Madrid.

In September 1942, PEPPERMINT took the Bag out to Madrid. There he did not meet the Germans but dealt only with Alcazar, who expressed satisfaction with the espionage reports sent. 'He might well do so' noted MI5, for it was clear that by this date Alcazar had persuaded both Kuehlenthal and the Japanese Minister in Madrid, to whom he was also supplying espionage reports, that he controlled a considerable organisation in England, whereas in fact his only actual agent was PEPPERMINT. He added however that such information was only of interest to the Germans, and that PEPPERMINT should make every effort to obtain further details about the British attitude to a negotiated peace, as this was a vital Spanish interest.[59]

B1.G also covered the Portuguese Embassy in London which proved of little interest except for two cases. One of these, de Menezes, came to MI5's knowledge through intercepted Abwehr wireless messages. He was eventually arrested and confessed, was tried under the Treachery Act and sentenced to death, but the sentence was commuted at the request of the Portuguese Government. At the same time Sir Alexander Cadogan, of the Foreign Office, presented to the Portuguese Ambassador a detailed account of the German espionage network operating against Britain from Portugal. Faced with the scandal of a German agent employed in their own Embassy the Portuguese Government took action and arrested seventeen German agents, a result out of all proportion to the intrinsic importance of the case of Menezes, whose mission in the UK was of a very low level.

Ireland

The work of Section B1.H was dominated by the political relationship between the British and Irish Governments and the geographical position with special reference to the problem of the border between Eire and Northern Ireland. Although Northern Ireland was part of the United Kingdom this border was purely administrative and political – there were no physical barriers 'and as far as freedom of movement was concerned Ireland was in fact one country'. The Taoiseach, or Irish Prime Minister, Eamonn de Valera, had declared that Eire was neutral at the beginning of the War. This had enraged Churchill: the idea that a

Dominion of the British Commonwealth could decide whether or not it was at war was not a decision he believed Eire could make; as far as he was concerned when the King declared war all of his subjects were at war. The problem was that the Government of de Valera did not regard the population of Eire as British subjects. In 1937, Eire had become a *de facto* republic. And the Anglo-Irish Agreement of 1938 brought about the withdrawal of British garrisons from Eire ports that Britain had been entitled to retain under the Treaty of 1921. Strategically, this was a vital loss in the future Battle of the Atlantic.

Weighted against this, however, the pre-war improvement in Anglo-Irish relations between Britain and Eire had led to an exchange of information on defence plans between the British and Irish Governments. These in turn led, *inter alia*, to the establishment of a Security Service contact with Colonel Liam Archer of Irish Military Intelligence. As Jack Curry recalled: 'Perhaps the most important political factor was the policy of neutrality qualified by Mr de Valera's guarantee that his Government would not allow Eire to be used as a base for operations against this country. This guarantee was the only safeguard against a potentially dangerous consequence of the neutrality policy, namely that it might provide the enemy intelligence services with a very favourable situation for operating against us on ground, which they had had many years to prepare with many facilities for doing so.' At the time the guarantee was given it appeared to relate only to military operations, but in practice it was given a wider interpretation which included the possible activities of hostile intelligence services. The 'onus was thus placed on the Eire Government of satisfying the British Government that Eire was not being so used and provided the political justification for the development of the Dublin link (with Colonel Archer) and the putting into force by the Eireann authorities of various security measures which operated in favour of the British'. These measures, however, always stopped short of endangering neutrality by the internment of enemy nationals. The Irish civil and military authorities, 'hampered as they often were by their political superiors, lack of experience and inadequate means, did try, to the best of their ability, to watch and control the activities of enemy agents and their Eireann sympathisers'. In Northern Ireland the Royal Ulster Constabulary dealt with all enemy aliens without any reference to the Security Service apart from the fact that after 1938 they reported the presence and activities of certain Germans.

At the outbreak of war various controls were gradually established in Britain and in Eire.[60] But this developed slowly, and, as it did, it gave Guy Liddell a constant headache; for example, on 12 October 1939, he recorded in his diary: 'Eire neutrality rapidly becoming a farce.' A German submarine had sailed into Dingle Bay with the crew of a cargo steamer that had been torpedoed while two British aeroplanes landed in Kilmarnock; after the necessary repairs they were allowed to leave. A representative of the Civic Guard, the police, was said to have remarked: 'And who in the name of God are we supposed to be neutral against anyway?'[61] It was not until the early summer of 1940 that a trial scrutiny of Irish mail was authorised by the Cabinet Committee on leakage of information, although MI5 had asked for censorship in September 1939. The Irish coast watching service and their service for the interception of illicit wireless, which had been discussed before the war, also did not come into full operation until the summer of 1940.

A small number of Germans, from Britain, had left for Eire a few days before the outbreak of war. One of these, Werner Unland, carried on a correspondence in plain language code with an address in Denmark. MI5's Irish section and Irish Intelligence co-operated in keeping a watch on him until April 1941 when, as a result of his photograph being found in the possession of a German agent named Gunther Schutz, who arrived in Eire by parachute, he was interned. Early in 1940 another German, named Ernst Weber Drohl, came to the notice of the Irish authorities. His mission was to hand over a sum of money to the Irish Republican Army and he was believed to have accomplished it. The Irish authorities were unable to convict him of anything more serious than 'an illegal landing'. These cases, from MI5's perspective, illustrated the general attitude in Irish political and official circles 'which rendered the task of the Eireann Military Intelligence and our liaison with Colonel Archer more difficult'.

Two events led to a 'great change' in this attitude. The invasion of the Low Countries and the fall of France induced a sudden realisation by the people and Government of Eire that their country might be invaded; and in May 1940 a German agent named Hermann Goertz arrived by parachute with a mission to the IRA, a W/T set and 20,000 American dollars, which later were found in the house of an Irish accomplice, named Stephen Carol Held. The most important single item of this discovery, made on 23 May, was that of the papers connected with Goertz's mission, which involved plans for a joint German-IRA attack on Northern Ireland and arrangements for establishing secret wireless transmitters. Held was tried and sentenced to five years' penal servitude, but Goertz remained in hiding until November 1941.

On 15 May 1940, Guy Liddell and his brother, of the Irish section, had a meeting with Colonel Archer, the original purpose being to effect an improvement in the arrangements for the interception of illicit wireless in Eire. Colonel Archer, however, at once stressed the danger of a German airborne landing in Eire to which, he said, very little resistance could be offered. He guaranteed that the 'Fifth Column' in Eire would be dealt with, but could give no assurance that all enemy aliens would be interned. He urged that contracts for arms and equipment for Eire placed in Britain should be fulfilled and the possibility of Staff talks was discussed. The MI5 officers returned to London and gave an account of this meeting to Lord Hankey, Lord President of the Council. At a further meeting the next day with the Secretary of State for the Dominions, and Sir John Maffey, who was the British Representative in Dublin, reported that de Valera had expressed the same views as had Colonel Archer and that he had brought with him a list of Eire's unfulfilled contracts. The Security Service considered how, at the 'most critical moment' the good personal relations that had been established between the Liddells and Archer provided 'a friendly and unofficial channel' for co-operation between the two countries and were largely responsible for the subsequent despatch of a British Military Mission to Dublin, through which the General Officer Commanding Northern Ireland was able to work with the Irish Military Command and develop joint plans for defence in the event of a German invasion.

In the summer of 1939 the Irish Government had declared the IRA to be 'an unlawful organisation'. The Emergency Powers (Amendment) Act of June 1940 led to the arrest and internment of IRA leaders and members, leading to a close and valuable relationship between the Civic Guard and the RUC. In July 1941 an Eins Luft agent – an agent employed to obtain intelligence for the German Air Force – was dropped by parachute in Eire with a mission to make weather reports by wireless and to report on troops and shipping in Northern Ireland. He was an Irish agricultural labourer named Joseph Lenihan who had escaped from the Channel Islands and after being captured by the Germans had agreed to work as an agent (as an ultimate means of escape). The aircraft which brought him was not detected either over Eire or Northern Ireland and as an Irishman 'with a simple story of having been at sea, he aroused no suspicion'. He was only detected after he gave himself up.

What concerned MI5 most, during this period, were the dangers of a leakage through the German Legation in Dublin. In May 1941 Guy Liddell's brother met Colonel Archer in Dublin and discussed the question of wireless transmissions from the German Legation which was 'a constant source of anxiety'. In February 1942 the German battleships *Gneisenau* and *Scharnhorst* and the cruiser *Prinz Eugen* escaped up the English Channel. Advance weather information was vital to this and it was claimed in the press that this had been transmitted by W/T from the German Legation in Dublin. As a consequence of this adverse comment, the Irish Government warned the German Minister that it was known that messages had been sent by W/T from the Legation and that further transmissions would lead to the set being confiscated and might result in the breaking off of diplomatic relations. After this, no message was sent by the Legation W/T until the set was finally handed over on Christmas Eve 1943 at the request of the Irish Government. The German Foreign Office continued throughout the war to communicate with the Minister by wireless and, although he was requested to reply by wireless, he never did so. There was, however, 'always the danger that the German Minister would risk the consequences for the sake of passing on vital operational information in a crisis'. The transmission made would be known to MI5, through ISOS, 'but it could neither be read nor stopped'. The issue assumed importance at the time of the Allied landing in Morocco in November 1942.

From the beginning of 1943 onwards the contents of the German Foreign Office wireless messages to their Legation in Dublin had been made available to the Security Service 'and it was clear that so long as the W/T set remained in Dublin, it represented a grave threat to the security of future operations based on this country'. In November 1943 – with the invasion of France on the horizon – Liddell visited Colonel Bryan who had succeeded Colonel Liam Archer in Dublin. During his visit he was invited to stay the night with Lieutenant General McKenna, the Irish Chief of Staff, who, during a long talk, revealed the fact that the W/T set in the German Legation was a source of grave anxiety to the Irish as well, because it could give vital information about the expected landing on the Continent. McKenna, who had developed 'the most friendly relations' with General Franklyn, the GOC NI, also valued the good relations which had been established through Captain Liddell and Colonel Archer. Liddell considered that, 'though strictly loyal to the interests and policies of his political chiefs, General McKenna was sympathetic to the Allied cause. The General realised that if vital information reached the Germans through the Legation W/T set, it might mean the loss of thousands of lives and that if there should ever be a suspicion that a leakage of information had occurred in this way, the relations between Eire and Britain would, as he said, be put back a hundred years.' From information subsequently obtained from the German Foreign Office communications it appeared that, shortly after this interview, General McKenna must have suggested to the Taoiseach that he should take action by demanding that all foreign representatives in Dublin should surrender their wireless transmitting sets and 'thus prevent the undesirable consequences which, he had learnt, the British authorities were anxious to forestall'. De Valera informed the German Minister that he 'contemplated making this demand'.

The issue, though, came to a head with the arrival of two German parachute agents – both Irish nationals – dropped in Eire on 19 December and on the 21st. Ernest Walshe, the Irish Secretary of External Affairs, sent for the German Minister, informed him that the British and Americans had learnt of the agents' arrival and that the British Representative had seen the Taoiseach and demanded that the German Legation W/T set should be removed. The German Minister complained bitterly to the German Foreign Office about this and begged that no further agents should be sent. But, most importantly, the set was removed. As Jack Curry noted: 'The removal of the German Legation W/T set was of outstanding importance because it was the most dangerous channel of leakage and the circumstances in which it came about showed the very great value of the Security Service contact with the Eire authorities.'

As OVERLORD – the invasion of France – approached there was an intensification of all security measures. Churchill, on 2 February 1944 asked for the opinion of the Chiefs of Staff on the dangers of leakage of information about OVERLORD through the German and Japanese diplomatic representatives in Dublin, and stated that in his view a demand should be made by the United States and the British separately that 'the German and enemy Embassies should be sent away forthwith'. The Joint Intelligence Committee submitted a report on the dangers of leakage listing the pros and cons for expulsion. This was entirely based on a note prepared by Guy Liddell setting out these pros and cons, but clearly indicating that in the view of the Security Service there would be very little, if any, security advantage in the removal of the German Legation whose communications 'we then controlled.' If it were removed it might be replaced in the 'most critical period' by enemy agents with means of communication which it would take time to discover, 'all the more so as our relations with Eire would be so strained that it was at least doubtful whether we should continue to enjoy the assistance we had hitherto received in matters of this kind'. Nevertheless both the British and American Governments demanded the removal of the Axis Legations. De Valera refused.

In fact, the major threat to OVERLORD's security came from the Allies: the suspension of travel between Britain and Eire came into effect on 15 March 1944, 'but the effectiveness of this measure was largely stultified by the Service Departments at whose request it had been imposed. They continued to send men on leave to Eire, even when they belonged to well-known units of the Eighth Army' which had been brought back to Britain to take part in OVERLORD. In view of this the Home Office refused to cancel compassionate leave for civilians to Ireland, 'with the result that large numbers of persons, some of whom were well-informed, were able to avoid the travel ban'. An attempt was made by the Irish section to have this situation reviewed by the Home Defence Executive, but with no success owing to the lack of support by the Service Departments. Co-operation with the Irish authorities remained unaffected. A conference of British, American and Irish security officers took place in Dublin and the discussions covered the whole field, including the supervising of Axis Legations, Axis nationals and persons of pro-Axis sympathies in Eire; German airmen and seamen interned in Eire; neutral legations; watch at the Irish end of Eire/UK traffic; Irish censorship; the problem of the leakage of information from Northern Ireland and the intensification of the police watch on the Eire side of the border; the coast-watching service and the Irish Observer Corps; and the detection of illicit wireless and the control of authorised Irish Government wireless services.[62]

4

DOUBLE-CROSS

The Origins of the Double-Cross System

As the first German agents arrived, in autumn 1940, MI5 officer Jack Curry recalled that two options were open to the Security Service: 'One was to treat it as a simple security problem and to have every agent we could lay our hands on apprehended and executed; the other was to employ some at least of those caught as double agents and to let the Germans think that they were still at large and working for them.' The second course was adopted[1] but not without a fight. White and Liddell wanted to use German spies as double agents because 'Fortress Britain', believed White, 'should admit just as many double agents as MI5 wanted and needed'. But Churchill sought executions and wanted them made public; Lord Swinton, heading the Security Executive that oversaw home intelligence, forbade any negotiation by MI5 with a spy for his life.[2] So, when Swinton came to see Liddell and his colleagues, on 7 October, about recent spy cases it seems Churchill had been asking why some of the spies had not been shot. Liddell told Swinton that 'we understood that we had been given a more or less free hand to promise a man his life if we thought we were going to get information and that information was really by far the most important matter to be considered'. Swinton answered that MI5 had no authority to grant a man his life and quoted a minute as proof of this. On looking this up, it was found by MI5 that the minute 'was quite irrelevant'. It merely referred to the Director of Public Prosecutions's attitude in such cases which, according to Liddell, 'was that if we wished to prosecute we should not offer a man any inducement to talk'. Liddell pronounced himself ignorant of what Swinton's position, as head of the Security Executive, actually was: 'I have seen no charter, and all we know is that he appears to think he is head of MI5 and to some extent even of SIS.'[3] White recalled how 'there was anger' at the decision to execute captured spies; days on which a spy was executed saw a muted atmosphere in B Division. White was adamant: 'Intelligence should have precedence over blood-letting.'[4]

But the bloodletting continued. One enemy agent to meet his Maker that earned some of Tin Eye Stephens's hard earned respect was Josef Jakobs, a forty-three year old German, who was parachuted near to Romsey, Huntingdonshire, on the night of 31 January 1941. He lay in field with a broken ankle, draped by his parachute and surrounded by his equipment, until the following morning, unable to move. Jakobs, recorded Stephenson, had been 'boldly shy hitherto of betraying his presence, but by this time the physical hurt had become unbearable'. He drew a revolver and fired into the air to attract attention. Jakobs' 'moral strength probably stemmed from his patriotism. He had few other moral qualities'. He had started life as a dentist 'but had gone into decay' and had served a sentence of imprisonment in Switzerland following deals in counterfeit gold. Jakobs was 'manifestly unemployable as a double agent... There was no good reason why he should continue to live'. He was prosecuted under the Treachery Act and sentenced to death: 'He died at the Tower of London on 15 Aug 1941, a brave man. His last words directed the "Tommies" of the firing squad to shoot straight.'[5]

In the course of Jakob's interrogation, a description was obtained of another agent who was expected to arrive in the UK in the near future. Karl Richter, a twenty-nine year old Sudeten German, duly made landfall in a field near London Colney. Richter buried his espionage baggage in 'such frenzied haste that he included with it his emergency ration of salami and brown bread'. He went into hiding but 'three days of fearful cogitation on an empty stomach persuaded him that even if discretion were the better part of valour, food was the best part of well-being'. He walked into London Colney and up to Police Constable Scott, complaining of sickness due to lack of food and drink: PC Scott 'was not impressed into precipitate sympathy. He knew his drill.' He told Richter that 'he had better come along with him, young man, and the agent found himself under arrest'. After being admitted to Camp 020, Richter 'showed no anxiety to make a confession'. He was convinced that the Germans would soon launch a successful invasion and remarked 'that soon he would be sitting on the right side of the interrogation table'. The information derived from Jakobs was produced 'for his discomfort'; and when Jakobs, 'carefully groomed for his reluctant role', was brought into the room to confront Richter the latter 'slipped and began gradually to break'. Painstakingly, information was extracted from Richter, revealing where he had hidden his equipment, how he was recruited and what his mission was. Richter was convinced he would hang; Stephenson noted: 'He was not disappointed.'[6]

Eventually, though, Liddell and White won the day. Within B Division section B1.A had been given special responsibility for running double agents. It formed a Directorate, composed of Major TAR Robertson, Captain John Masterman and J.H. Marriott, which decided all matters of policy and dealt with relations with the operational and intelligence staffs of the fighting services and with other departments.[7] MI5 proposed to the Joint Intelligence Committee that 'a planning sub-committee shall be constituted to deal with questions arising from the use of double-cross agents and to make recommendations to the JIC'. This sub-committee would consist of, among others, representatives from SIS; Naval Intelligence; Military Intelligence; Home Forces Intelligence; the Home Defence Executive; and MI5. The Security Service would arrange for the meetings of the Committee and provide the secretariat.[8] MI5 drew up a 'Memorandum on the "Double Agent" System', dated 27 December 1940, for the JIC. It set out the case for bringing the ad hoc double agent system, that had been built up by MI5 and SIS under some formal control: at this moment in time the Security Service and SIS were experiencing 'considerable difficulty in keeping it in existence, mainly because the Service Departments (for obvious reasons) are chary of releasing sufficient information to the enemy for him to retain confidence in the agents. We submit, however, that it is possible to secure that the losses involved in releasing information are outweighed by the gains accruing from the successful working of the system.'

The memorandum pointed out that, during the 1914–18 war, the Postal Censorship and the British Intelligence Service abroad provided the bulk of the information for counter-espionage work. Postal communication had now ceased to play quite so important a part in espionage work, while, since the German conquest of the Continent, the British Secret Service operated under grave difficulties. In these circumstances the 'double agent' system had acquired a new and greater importance in counter-espionage work: 'It enables us to gain an insight into the personnel, methods, and means of communication of the German espionage organization in this country, while we are also led to the discovery of other agents supplied to the "double agent" as contacts. These at a chosen moment can be eliminated or brought under our control.' By building up a double agent organisation and establishing the enemy's confidence in it, 'we limit other enemy espionage activities. Incidentally, as the enemy is forced to run the system on a cash basis, funds are diverted which might otherwise be expended on enterprises not under our control.' Furthermore, when double agents carried out wireless transmission in cypher, 'the enemy is encouraged to believe in the security of his Secret Service cyphers. It is particularly important at the present time, when we are far advanced in the understanding of certain German cyphers, to retain these cyphers in use.' Messages from a whole network of German Secret Service wireless stations (used both for espionage and operations) 'have become comprehensible in the course of the last few months and MI5 and MI6 [SIS] have in consequence been enabled to build up a picture of the enemy organization on the Continent and to gain advance information of intended enterprises against this country'.

The most important part of the double-cross system, argued the memorandum, was its potential. If, and only if, confidence on the enemy's side had been established in a particular double agent it would ultimately provide the moment to mislead the enemy by false information regarding large-scale military operations by Britain. 'When such a moment arrives there should be no hesitation in sacrificing a "double agent" or group of "double agents" if important operational results are to be expected from the sacrifice.' The problem facing MI5 and SIS at this time was the reluctance of the Armed Services to allow accurate information to be used for intelligence purposes – in particular its transmission to the enemy in order to build up the credibility of double agents in the eyes of the Germans. But MI5 and SIS both emphasised 'that only by constant planning in advance and by the maintenance of an adequate flow of consistent and plausible reports to the enemy can the "double agent" system be kept in being and made available for effective use'. This policy, no doubt, involved the taking of certain risks, 'but we submit that the advantages, actual and prospective, which may be gained are sufficient justification for taking these risks'. At this time MI5 had two main groups of 'double agents' working from the UK. The first and more important was in wireless communication with the German Secret Service abroad. The second communicated by personal contact and by secret writing by air mail, mainly to the German organisation in Lisbon. There were also other agents working abroad:

> From our experience of these two systems we can say that most of the information required by the German Secret Service relates to air matters. Latterly, and doubtless in view of German air attacks, and the projected invasion of this country, the German Secret Service has been asking specific questions about the location of factories, military movements, air-raid damage and the like. Such questions raise the issue of risk to life and property versus Intelligence value in its most direct from. Are we really securing sufficient advantages to compensate for the information which we give to the enemy? The present problem is, in fact, to find a suitable plan which will ensure that we gain more (or with good fortune much more) on the swings than we lose on the roundabouts.

MI5 suggested that the double agents could be graded and developed in accordance with the importance attached to them. Subsidiary and less important agents could then be used on a short term basis with the expectation of their early eclipse and for the deliberate and immediate misleading of the enemy in matters of detail. The very few really important agents – especially those who had been in the confidence of the German Secret Service for some time – should be the ones entrusted with the handing over of such accurate information as could, after due consideration by the Service Departments, be released. These agents should be held in readiness and at the disposal of the Service Departments for a large-scale deception which could at a critical moment be of paramount operational importance.

Up to now the chief function of MI5 and SIS in this matter had been to provide the machinery with which to mislead the enemy and to invite the Service Departments to plan for its use. 'But there is a real danger that the "double agent" system which has been built up may be allowed to collapse because no adequate use is made of it. The present committee is convened to prevent this waste of effort. Its main objects are to co-ordinate suggestions from its members for making full use of the machinery provided; to construct plans developed from these suggestions; and, if necessary, to press for the putting of these plans into operation.'[9] This was approved and became the Twenty, or XX, Committee. The chairman of the XX Committee was MI5's John Masterman – Dick White's old tutor at Oxford. When he first arrived in the Office, Guy Liddell found the 'Oxford Don' a 'real tiger' although he, occasionally, went 'off the deep end' – as when he instructed D4 Branch to issue a circular that all Danzigers should be regarded as enemy aliens. This was in direct contradiction to the Foreign Office view. The 'necessary adjustments' had to be made.[10] On 30 September, the Oxford Don was 'deriving considerable satisfaction at ordering the internment of a complete (enemy alien) company of the White Horse Inn which turned up at one of our ports'. Masterman took the view that, as they had no means of support, 'they were better where they were' – interned. It then transpired that they were going to give performances at various air force depots. Liddell observed: 'If that is true they are certainly better where they are.'[11] Now, as chairman of the XX Committee, Masterman adopted a less excitable approach:

> My own part in all this was that of a 'back-room boy'. I had only occasional contact with some of the agents and had little say in the construction of their traffic (i.e. the messages which they sent), but I was a Chairman of the Committee (the Twenty Committee,

so called because in Roman numerals twenty is represented by a double-cross) which brought together the approving authorities, settled and combined the messages of the different agents, and decided how and where the agents were to be used. The first meeting of the Committee I shall not easily forget, for the fighting services as well as various departments all sent senior officers to represent them and I, a very junior officer, had the embarrassing duty of telling the members that I had orders to take the chair and preside over the meeting. It says much for the members of the Committee that this anomalous situation was accepted by all and caused no sort of difficulty – indeed the co-operation of many departments, the absence of red tape or protocol was, in my judgement, the solid basis on which the success of the double-cross system rested. I called the first meeting of the Committee for 16.00 hrs. on 2 January 1941 and made then a small but important decision, to wit that tea and a bun should always be provided for members. How utterly trivial! Nowadays such a decision can only provoke a contemptuous smile, but in the war years the case was otherwise. In days of acute shortage and of rationing the provision of buns was no easy task, yet by hook or crook (and mostly by crook) we never failed to provide them throughout the war years. Was this simple expedient one of the reasons why attendance at the Committee was nearly always a hundred per cent? The Twenty Committee held 226 meetings, the last on 10 May 1945 and only on one occasion was a vote taken; all other decisions were arrived at after discussion and without a vote.[12]

The XX Committee was technically a sub-committee of the 'W' Board which originally consisted of three Directors of Intelligence, C and Captain Liddell as the representative of the Security Service. To these were added Sir Findlater Stewart of the Home Defence Executive (Swinton's Committee) and Colonel Bevan of the London Controlling Section (which considered operational cover plans). The 'W' Board was created to co-ordinate the dissemination of false information but in practice it undertook the responsibility for the control of double agents, exercising that responsibility through the Twenty Committee. The XX Committee, in turn, acted as the clearing ground for information about the agents, approved traffic for them, discussed the policy adopted by B1.A in individual cases, passed on intelligence information gained from double agents to the proper quarters and indicated how the agents could best be used for the benefit of the department concerned. A 'cardinal prinicple never lost sight of' by the Security Service was that no information of any kind was passed to the Germans by wireless or letter unless it had the written approval of the competent authority i.e. of the Intelligence or Operational Staffs of the Services, of the Home Defence Executive or of the Foreign Office. At the same time MI5's B1.A always maintained the right to veto any information, which the Services wished to put over if it was considered that it might jeopardise the agent concerned. The position of B1.A with regard to the civil authorities was 'particularly difficult' as the running of double agents 'should be known to as few persons as possible'. A meeting of the 'W' Board with the Lord President of the Council, and subsequent discussions, led to Sir Findlater Stewart becoming the authority to whom B1.A applied for approval in the same way as they did to the Directors of Intelligence in questions affecting the fighting services.[13] While the XX Committee had to maintain a reasonable standard of German interest in the messages sent over by its double agents, there was always a danger of giving away a vital secret. 'It will readily be believed,' recalled Masterman, 'that the ultimate responsibility for allowing any message to pass to the enemy is a dangerous power. In communicating with the enemy almost from day to day in time of war we were playing with dynamite, and the game would have been impossible unless the "approving authorities" had been willing to assume this ultimate responsibility.'[14] The aim, in Jack Curry's words, was:

1.To control the German Intelligence system in this country. This was an end in itself because we felt that if we provided a reasonably satisfactory reporting system from this country the Germans would be satisfied and would not make excessive efforts to establish other agents. Naturally it was better for us to know what was being reported from this country than not to know. Even if a good deal of true information had to be given, we did at least know what information the Germans had and what they had not. Furthermore, we could not enjoy the other benefits on the deception side unless we had a fairly complete control of the German Intelligence system.

2. For the apprehending of other spies. This was the primary object of the system, but it became less and less important because, while ISOS, the SCOs, the LRC and Camp 020 were uncovering new agents as they arrived, the Abwehr showed signs of being satisfied with the intelligence they were receiving from those agents working under our control.

3. Code and cipher work. Apart from the original 'break' through the use of SNOW's traffic... the traffic of some of our later agents was found to be of great assistance to GC & CS in reading messages over an important part of the widespread Abwehr network.

4. Assistance to censorship. Information provided by letter-writing double agents in the form of cover addresses in neutral countries and types of secret ink used by enemy agents were communicated to Censorship, thus enabling them to keep in touch with German secret ink technique and developments, to discover the best re-agents and to put on the Watch Lists all over the world the addresses thus obtained.

5. To gain evidence of enemy intentions. The questionnaires and individual questions given to agents gradually built up a very complete picture of what the Germans wanted to know and therefore what their operational intentions were.

6. To gain knowledge of the personalities and methods of the German Intelligence Services, particularly of the Abwehr. This is self-explanatory.

7. To prevent enemy sabotage by controlling their saboteurs and this securing knowledge of their methods and equipment. One of the most remarkable aspects generally of the generally low standard of efficiency in the Abwehr during the war was the ineffectiveness, broadly speaking, of their sabotage in this country... We are satisfied that apart from the sabotage carried out under our control the Abwehr achieved practically nothing... of any importance.

8. To give misinformation to the enemy; in other words to take part in deception.

These were the aims and objects of the work of B1.A as they gradually developed throughout the war. The original – and fundamental – idea and the basic policy which governed all the rest was to control the German Intelligence agents in the UK in such a manner as to satisfy the Abwehr and thus to facilitate means of preventing them from establishing other agents not under British control both by making it appear to be unnecessary and by apprehending those who arrived. This was the policy conceived by Liddell and carried out by B Division under his direction. In order to achieve these objectives B1.A controlled a team of agents that, from the end of 1940 and during 1941, consisted of twenty-five agents. The twenty-five were controlled by case officers, the number of whom ordinarily did not exceed five. Each case officer was responsible for not more than one or two important agents and others who were of minor importance. The case officers were responsible for the penetration of the agent's wireless communication with the Abwehr and the well being and care of each agent and all matters concerned with him.

The double agent's traffic had to be run not as that of an individual but in accordance with plans and general conceptions co-ordinated by the directorate of the section. Extensive administrative arrangements were also necessary: a single wireless agent of enemy origin needed a house or a flat; a housekeeper to run the establishment; a wireless operator; and at least two guards. His living conditions had to be carefully arranged so that he did not attract attention and comment in the district where he lived. In the early days, the situation was complicated by the fact that B1.A had no means of knowing whether there were other uncontrolled agents whose reports to the Abwehr might contradict those arranged by MI5 or otherwise complicate the position of the controlled agent. The principle laid down and followed, as a result, was to instruct each case officer 'that he must, as far as possible, lead the life of each important agent; steep himself in the style and thoughts of the agent; make a careful psychological study of him and introduce into messages every sort of confirmatory detail which might convince the Germans that the agent was free and working for honestly for them'. If, for example, the Germans required a report on an aerodrome, the agent himself or an officer specifically detailed for the purpose was sent to that aerodrome to make a report, and such visits 'were always made on the assumption that the visitor was in fact a spy who would risk his neck if he were caught asking questions or finding his way into any place or area to which admission was not open'. Another important consideration was arranging for suitable answers to personal questions relating to the agents: when they were satisfactorily given 'they often proved a means of convincing the Germans that the agent was not under control'.[15] One of the first agents who fell under the direction of the Committee was, almost certainly, the most suave XX agent that MI5 ran during the war: SKOOT/TRICYCLE.

SKOOT

Dusko Popov, codename SKOOT by SIS, became a MI5/SIS double-cross agent as a result of a walk-in – literally walking in off the street and offering his services to the British. Popov was a Yugoslavian subject, born in 1912 at Titel. He was educated in France for six years and in Germany for two years (1935–37),[16] studying for the degree of Doctor in Law. He was inscribed at the University in Freiburg (Breisgrau), but stayed most of the time in Berlin. In the meantime, he also wrote political articles for the Yugoslav paper *Politika*. In Freiburg he was a member of a Club called the 'Deutsch-Auslandische Gesellschaft', which had a branch called the 'Anglo-American Society'. The President of both was Johann Jebsen, who despite his youth – he was only twenty-four to twenty-five in 1940 – 'possessed exceptional intelligence and was highly cultured'. He came from a very rich Hamburg family of high standing. The fates of both men would be intertwined as the war progressed. At that time SKOOT was convinced that Jebsen was strongly pro-British. The Club often held 'debating dinners' during which one member gave a political speech, on which the others afterwards gave their comments. There were also German members. In 1937, many speeches were attacks against democracy. During the debates, there was complete freedom of speech, except any utterances insulting to the Führer. Popov gave two speeches, trying to defend democracy. A few days after his second speech, he was arrested and imprisoned under various pretexts. Through the influence of the Yugoslav Foreign Office he regained his liberty, but was expelled from Germany in September 1937.

Popov went back to Yugoslavia, where he started work in collaboration with a solicitor, Dr Jaksich, in Dubrovnik. He was instructed to negotiate the exploitation of a concession to manufacture an explosive called Penta-Aertrite. The plant, necessary for the manufacture of this explosive, had to be imported from Germany, and he consequently often visited the German Legation in Belgrade. He was advised then to talk with a certain von Stein, a Secretary at that Legation. At the beginning of 1940, this man insinuated that Popov could do much more and better business with Germany, saying, 'You are well acquainted with Karlo Banac, the brother of Bozo Banac, and through this channel can get an easy entry into British circles.' Popov was a personal friend of Banac, whose brother Bozo was the richest man in Yugoslavia and a friend of the Duke of Kent. When Popov alluded to his expulsion from Germany, von Stein stated that they would willingly forgive and forget the past. Popov gave an evasive reply.

In the spring of 1940, Popov received a telegram from Jebsen, asking if he could be in Belgrade at a certain date, to talk about some very important business. He met Jebsen, who gave him a list of the German boats in neutral ports, mainly in the USA, and asked him if he would act as agent for the sale of these boats. He said that he could not sell these boats unless it was guaranteed that they would sail under neutral flags. However, continued Jebsen, no neutral country would buy them on those conditions, and he therefore suggested that Popov should sell them to the French or the British, 'as long as he, Jebsen, did not know anything about it'. Jebsen then left for Athens. Popov went with the list of ships to the British Legation, and saw a Mr Dow, who told him that it was very interesting but that he did not deal with such matters; but he would see to it that he would soon get into touch with somebody who did handle them. He told Popov to tell the Germans that he was willing to act for them. Popov was contacted by Fickis, a Passport Control Officer (the standard SIS cover), who told him that Jebsen's information was valueless, as anybody could get this from any newspaper. Jebsen was furious, and never gave any further information. Popov had to lend him 12 or 15,000 Dinars to cover his expenses, and he left.

On instructions given to him by Fickis, Popov informed his contact at the German Legation, Belgrade, that he was prepared to work for them and that he could secure information about Britain from a contact at the Yugoslav Diplomatic Legation in London. Popov was given three questionnaires by the Germans concerning British military, naval and air dispositions and armaments. The Germans suggested that Popov should go to London himself, which he agreed to do. Shortly before leaving in November 1940, Popov was visited by Jebsen who informed him that they were now 'both in the same service' and explained that he had accepted his employment with the Germans because it saved him from soldiering, of which he was very much afraid as he was a heavy sufferer of varicose veins; it was also a powerful help to him in his import and export business. He in his turn asked Popov how it was that he, being a democrat, was helping Germany; Popov replied that as his father and grandfather had never had need to work he did not see why he should always slave to exist and that he was also trying to get an easier living; he stated that the Germans had promised him 'very big positions' after the war. Jebsen thereupon advised him of the arrival of Major Ölschlager, one of the leaders of the Deutsche Wehrmacht Espionnage, who came to give Popov his instructions and to settle everything.[17]

Popov – now codenamed SKOOT – left Belgrade on 16 November 1940 by rail to Rome, where the arrived on the 18th. He then left for Lisbon and, from there, flew to England on 20 December and arrived at Whitchurch that evening. Having forewarned the British in Lisbon, on arrival Popov was met at Whitchurch by an MI5 officer and taken by car to the Savoy Hotel, London. On the 21st he was interviewed by

TAR Robertson, J.H. Marriott and Mr Bingham from MI5[18] to whom he told his story. SKOOT explained how he was verbally instructed to obtain the answers to the following questions:

> 1. He was to find out who were the people opposed to Churchill and who were working for peace with Germany, and was to ascertain how he could get into touch with them. What their contacts were and what also were their weaknesses, such as drink, money, etc. and what were their hopes. In other words he was to find out how best they could be approached.
> 2. Which type of bombing attack has the most effect on the morale of the population?
> 3. What kind of propaganda would now have the most effect on the people?
> 4. Which class of the population was most susceptible to propaganda and how could they best be approached?
> 5. He was to try and get into touch with the circle surrounding Vice Admiral Sir John Tovey, now C-in-C, Home Fleet.

In addition to actually obtaining the answers to the questionnaires supplied to him, his mission in Britain was, if possible, to make friends with some person of importance who could ensure for him, on a future visit, freedom of movement all over the country; and he was also to get into touch with a business house through which he could carry on an ordinary business correspondence with an address supplied to him by the Germans of a firm in Bilbao. On the back of these letters he would write his reports in invisible ink. Popov's present mission would only involve his being in the UK for a short time and he expressed the opinion that for a second visit he would receive instructions to obtain information about those matters which, from the reports of his present visit, appeared most likely to be ones about which he could get the best information. MI5 were impressed and concluded that: 'It is clear from this that [from] the answers to his present questionnaires we can direct him into whichever channels we think most profitable to us.' Bingham noted how Popov 'left an exceedingly favourable first impression upon all of us. His manner was absolutely frank and we all considered without question that he was telling the truth. He particularly impressed upon us that he desired no money from us and only stipulated that he should be allowed to go home as early as conveniently possible in January so that he might attend to his own business.'[19] In fact all Popov wanted was a guarantee that, if Yugoslavia was over-run, by the Germans, his entry to a British colony or Dominion should be facilitated.[20]

Having won the trust of his first contacts within MI5, it was necessary to provide SKOOT with a cover story. Commander Montagu, of Naval Intelligence and a member of the XX Committee, suggested that SKOOT merely report, this time, to the Germans that the information required was scattered all over England and/or was very carefully guarded: 'He could add that he has made his contacts (e.g. me!) and will be able to get some of the answers next time, or have got them ready by next time.' Montagu considered that it would be very difficult for anyone in SKOOT's position to have got anything more worthwhile in terms of the questionnaire during a first visit to Britain.[21] Montagu met SKOOT at the Savoy Hotel on New Years Day to put this suggestion to him; he 'found him a most charming person and I should be very surprised if he is not playing straight with us'. They found that the best link between them was sailing; Montagu therefore decided that they had been introduced by Mr Core-Lloyd of the Royal Ocean Racing Club 'who is the only one of my friends who has sailed down the coast. (C-Ll knows nothing of this)'.

Montagu and SKOOT then had a long chat about their 'business' together and the former gave him the name of 'Foster Brown' a Lieutenant Commander RN, as his contact with Admiral Tovey's staff: 'I told S that Foster-Brown had been in [a] Fleet signal officer [on the] Nelson and is now Liaising at the Admiralty for Tovey. The link with Brown is that I am encouraging S to bring his yacht Nina over to the Solent after the war and Brown had a convenient house at Warsash on the Hamble if S makes that river his base.' SKOOT was a little wary of the paucity of information that he was being given to take out as he had wanted to 'make a show' to impress his employers so as to gain their confidence: 'I think I was able to persuade him,' wrote Montagu, 'that he himself could not have got more on his first visit, and that his contact in the legation would not be likely to do or risk too much before he had met S who was only supposed to be an acquaintance and not a friend of his.' In consequence of this, SKOOT was grateful for the two pieces of information Montagu gave to him for the Germans: 'That almost every Atlantic Convoy is having an escort of one or more submarines and that it is intended to fit aircraft ot [on] most of the larger merchantmen. That it is not certain what type of aircraft but it may be torpedo-carrying. I am supposed to have let these facts drop in a moment of indiscretion.'

SKOOT then raised Jebsen's proposal for selling vessels: Montagu's initial response was it was impracticable although the matter was left for consideration. SKOOT and Montagu then retired to the bar of the Savoy 'where we were seen together discussing sailing and looking at photographs of my boat'. To support this background, and so that SKOOT would have something to show to his employers, Montagu sent him the following note: 'I much enjoyed meeting you again last night. Please do ring me as soon as you return to this country, as I am much looking forward to renewing our conversation. It is so nice in these troubled times to meet another who is as mad as I am about sailing! I hope that you... have a photo of "Nina" when you get back, as she sounds a grand boat; she must be brought over to the Solent after the war as I told you!'[22] After this, Marriott and Robertson also saw SKOOT the same day and gave him his final instructions before he returned to Lisbon. They went carefully through the whole of his questionnaire and told him to tell the following story to the Germans:

He is glad he came over here as he felt that his friend in the Yugo-Slav legation had not done all the work that he had expected him to do chiefly because having his own work in the Legation to do he had had little time to give to answering the questions and also he was very frightened being in a foreign country and doing anything which might rouse the suspicions of the authorities. He has, however, been able to obtain certain answers to the questions asked and SKOOT is to hand these over. He is also to say that he thinks it would be far better if he could come back to this country at a later date when he himself could set up contacts over here and find some better way to get answers to future questionnaires. He is to give them the names of all the people he has met over here and build up stories round them. He was allowed to keep a copy of the questions and answers which we gave him and has strict instructions from us that before going to the interview he is to destroy these papers and I think we can rely on him to do this. The only thing he is anxious about in connection with the questionnaire was how he would get this out of the country without being detected. I [Robertson] said I would arrange this for him with the S[ecurity].C[ontrol].O[fficer]. Bristol. He is also very anxious that he should be put in touch with one of our people in Lisbon to whom he can give future questionnaires for transmission to the UK and to whom he can go for advice. He is also anxious that when he applies for a seat on the 'plane to return to the UK arrangements will be made for him to obtain this without any delay. I instructed him to go to the Airways people in Lisbon on his arrival and put his name down for a seat in about three or four weeks time. With regard to the last five questions which he received in Lisbon just before coming to this country, he has been given carte blanche to answer these as he thinks fit. We gave him the names of Lords Brocket, Lymington and Londonderry of being of the opposition Party opposed to Mr. Churchill's war effort and that they are definitely members of the Party which would be prepared to accept peace terms with Germany at the moment.[23]

SKOOT left Britain for Portugal on 3 January 1941 and telephoned his German contact, Karsthoff, the day after his arrival, not from his hotel but from a public telephone box. Karsthoff gave him an appointment in the German Legation; there it was arranged that if Karsthoff called SKOOT and asked him to come 'to the legation' it would mean that SKOOT was to visit him in his villa outside Estorial. The day after SKOOT had seen him, Karsthoff went to Paris taking SKOOT's answers with him. When Karsthoff returned, about ten days later, SKOOT went to see him and others at the villa.[24] The Germans expressed themselves as being a little disappointed in the information which he had brought to them, pointing out that it was of too general a character;[25] yet, although, the Germans would have liked the answers to all their questions they did not expect to get all of them and told SKOOT that it would be better to answer a few questions in detail than answer all questions vaguely.[26] An interesting point arose during the discussion over an answer to a question dealing with air routes from Britain to Sweden and Portugal. Karsthoff compared SKOOT's answer with another answer that he had received from a separate source. Karsthoff said that this source was extremely good. When pressed a bit further by SKOOT as to who the source was, Karsthoff intimated that was one of the pilots from the Dutch airline, KLM, presumably doing the run between the UK and Lisbon. SKOOT noted this information to pass on to MI5 on his return to Britain.[27]

The Germans, it seemed, were especially interested in the London Underground shelters and wondered if any epidemics had developed and wanted to get a little more information on the Tubes. SKOOT's warning to MI5, as he was debriefed in England, was to watch out for the possibility of some bacteria or other which the Germans might try and spread in the Tube and which might possibly be brought into Britain by someone coming from abroad.[28] Meanwhile, the Germans had asked SKOOT if he would be prepared, after returning to England again for a few weeks, to pay a visit to the United States, in order to appoint an agent there who could pass information on to them in secret writing, and then to proceed to Egypt where he would remain as their agent in that country. SKOOT informed them that he was perfectly prepared to do this, and they then gave him a questionnaire which he was to memorise and, after taking notes on it, was to return to Britain and as far as possible obtain the answers. This questionnaire proved of great interest to the Service Intelligence Directors and MI5 subsequently provided SKOOT with a good deal of information that he later took back to Portugal. The questionnaire contained about fifty questions chiefly concerning the RAF and air force production.[29]

SKOOT landed in England again on 4 February, bringing with him the original questionnaire in German.[30] Apart from obtaining information, SKOOT was also expected to appoint a suitable agent who he could leave behind and who would pass on to the Germans further information from time to time. The original idea was that SKOOT should pretend to them that he had appointed someone in the Yugoslav Legation, although in fact the work would be carried on by one of MI5's nominees; but the Security Service now decided in view of Yugoslavia's position vis-a-vis Germany that it would be better for him to tell the Germans he had appointed a British subject instead. This work would be carried on by an ex-army officer, BALLOON. SKOOT was to tell the Germans that his Yugoslavian friend had in any case intended to obtain most of his information from BALLOON and that owing to the present international situation he was not prepared to appear in the matter himself and had therefore placed SKOOT in direct contact with him. MI5 also introduced SKOOT to GELATINE, a German woman who was employed in one of its sections and who before the outbreak of war was in touch with the German Secret Service representative in Britain. It was hoped to reintroduce her to the Germans through him. The objects then of SKOOT's visit to Britain, on behalf of the Germans, were as follows: '1. To take back as many answers as possible in detail to the questionnaire; 2. To send back by secret ink any information which he might obtain during his stay, if he considered it should be sent on at once; 3. To carry a package of secret ink...; 4. Before leaving this country to find someone, preferably his friend in the Yugoslav Legation to take over his job and write in secret ink information in answer to these questions which he himself was unable to answer; 5. To send a postcard in ordinary writing to one of the cover addresses in Lisbon giving a cover address to which letters could be sent.'[31]

To boost SKOOT's credibility with the Germans, the XX Committee, on 6 February, agreed that a plan of the East Coast Minefield barrier should be passed to the Germans, and that the channel for this should be SKOOT. The plan itself had been put up by Commander Montagu and the only thing that remained to be done was to discuss the means by which this plan could get into SKOOT's possession. This was discussed and agreed with SKOOT at lunch, on 8 February, and the plan to be adopted was put forward, as follows, by Montagu:

> Montagu being a Jew is anxious to have some sort of pass which will enable him in the event of a successful German invasion of this country to go free. He is a man who cannot be bought with money and this is the only way one can really get at him. He will indicate to SKOOT that the only terms on which he will part with plan are those stated above. This will mean that SKOOT will have to get in touch with Lisbon and inform them of his achievement by a letter in secret writing, and state the exact terms which are wanted.

It was considered that this plan would 'appeal to the German mentality enormously'.[32] SKOOT, during lunch with a MI5 officer at the Royal Automobile Club, mentioned his friend Jebson again; SKOOT was asked how it was that a young man with such an influential and wealthy father should be so short of money. SKOOT explained that the family assets were nearly all in ships which, at the present time, yielded little profit in Germany and thus, while the family capital had to be very large, their income had been seriously reduced as a result of the war. SKOOT's impression was: 'Jebsen is at heart pro-British but by force of circumstances a loyal German. He did not think it would be difficult for him to persuade Jebsen that he is fighting on the wrong side, especially if he could meet him in Madrid, provide him vivacious and beautiful feminine society and lose money to him at Poker.' It was noted that it 'may be considered desirable to enlarge on this theme' later. Following lunch, and over coffee, SKOOT hinted 'that a little high-class feminine society would be most acceptable'; his contact noted: 'I understand this little point is already being attended to.'[33] After his adventures, SKOOT, it seems, needed some recreational distractions – which were provided by the Security Service but also allowed it to keep an eye on him. On 8 February, Masterman and Robertson met with Major Lennox who introduced them to a Sergeant Lewis. Their chief concern was 'to procure from him suggestions as to possible female acquaintances of his who might be used as agents'. A woman was required 'purely and simply to entertain SKOOT and keep him out of mischief, and at the same time to keep us informed of the various curious associations which he is making in this country'.[34]

Not all MI5 officers were convinced by SKOOT. After lunching with SKOOT and Marriott at the RAF Club, W.E. Luke accompanied the men to Nell Gywn House where the Yugoslav wrote a letter in secret ink for the Germans[35] concerning his imaginary Jewish naval officer friend who had 'read of the atrocity stories of concentration camps' and sought a letter of safe conduct from Germans through SKOOT.[36] The letter also mentioned Commander Montagu's chart showing the gaps in the mined area off the east coast of England. SKOOT, having been shown the chart, would thus be able to describe it to the Germans and it was hoped that they would instruct someone in the UK to get in touch with Montagu, the password being 'Monsieur Saint Pierre'.[37] It was after this meeting that Luke expressed his doubts about SKOOT's *bona fides*:

> While performing this task [writing the letter], he [SKOOT] referred jocularly to his work on behalf of the Germans. Personally, I think he rather overdoes this and it is possible that he is play-acting. In fact I cannot help regarding him with a good deal of suspicion. He is supposed to be a wealthy man and yet has no particular preferences in the way of food and drink, being satisfied always to leave it to his host to choose the meal – probably this is due to his sparse knowledge of the English language. I have just the general feeling that he may be a most accomplished liar. In fact, if he was able to persuade the Germans that he has influential English connections, whereas the truth is that he only knows three rather insignificant people in the whole country, he must be a good liar. I think this sojourn in Glasgow may clear matters up a good deal.[38]

The 'sojourn in Glasgow' was a trip – mainly a vacation – undertaken around Scotland by SKOOT, accompanied by Luke; for the latter the journey north did clear matters up for, after spending a week almost exclusively in SKOOT's company, Luke wrote: 'I have come to the conclusion that he is quite definitely working for us and not for the Germans... Apart from admiring the scenery, he evinced no interest in the Gareloch where so many ships are congregated and made no effort to obtain information of any kind, nor did he ask any questions which could have any connection with espionage.' Luke also re-evaluated his opinion of SKOOT's material means; consequently the MI5 officer thought the Yugoslav should be used to pass authentic information to the enemy – which, of course, would then be rendered ineffective.[39] Luke also found that SKOOT was convinced that Great Britain would win the war within two years, due probably to Germany's moral and economic collapse;[40] as SKOOT wrote to the MI5 officer's half-brother, G.F. Luke:

> I shall be leaving London in a few days. It would be difficult for me to define the feeling I experience on leaving your brave country. However, it is with a heart filled with hope that I am leaving. On comparing the oppressive darkness of your existence in its commonplace and everyday aspects with the prodigious clearness of your minds, I can only conclude that it is the result of rule by sages. And wisdom has always been victorious. You, my dear Mr. Luke, are the classical example of this English calm. This moral health, so striking and so glorious, appears to be the effect of a superior and invisible power, something outside of man. Nevertheless, it is but the manifestation of the most powerful English weapon: 'to remain human'. When the time comes, it is this that will demolish Hitler's machine.[41]

By now W.E. Luke had clearly warmed to his subject, SKOOT's charm having worked its magic on the British Security Service as well as the Germans; in a briefing for SIS, Luke described SKOOT, who by now had been given a new designation – TRICYCLE - in the following terms:

> As to his personal character, he is intelligent, cultured but not energetic. He has obviously been brought up in an atmosphere of comfort and ease and has a first class European education. He does not drink much, and is naturally extremely discreet about his work, but it is doubtful if he would have been chosen by our organisation as a suitable agent as he is rather careless. He has personality and charm and would feel at home in society circles in any European or American capital, being much the usual type of international playboy. In peace time he spends a month or more of every year in Paris and he is very fond of the society of attractive women. During his last visit to Portugal he formed an attachment with a divorced French Marquise, Andree Pinta de la Roche, of whom we have no traces, and one night while in her company he struck an American journalist in Lisbon whose drunken absurdities offended his taste. He has shown no inclination to obtain information while he has been over here, and we have found him to be an ingenuous, cheerful and amusing young man of whose sincerity and loyalty we are perfectly satisfied.[42]

TRICYCLE, BALLOON & GELATINE

It was on 6 March that arrangements had been finalised between TRICYCLE and Luke with regard to GELATINE's introduction to the Germans. At this meeting it was emphasised that no connection should be placed between BALLOON and GELATINE. With this agreed TRICYCLE now headed off, once more, for Lisbon. On the evening he arrived, 15 March, TRICYCLE met Karsthoff, his secretary and another man in Karsthoff's villa. TRICYCLE recalled: 'I just announced that I was back and we arranged a meeting for next day at 6 o'clock at the villa when I brought all my papers.' Karsthoff read them through as much as he could. 'He always says he does not understand English but he read both the French and English papers which makes me think he does understand English,' noted TRICYCLE. On Tuesday 18 March, TRICYCLE went again to the villa to find the Germans had typed out all his answers to the questionnaire. By then they had had a cable from Berlin in which they were told that TRICYCLE was to go to Berlin or to meet some gentlemen from Berlin in Madrid. On 22 March he went to Madrid to meet a Mr Lenz ('they usually call him "Fruehling" as a nickname'). In Madrid, TRICYCLE was told that a cable had been received saying that Jebsen was going to come to see him. On 6 April, Jebsen arrived. He told TRICYCLE that a Dr. Warnecke and two other gentlemen, he called them 'specialists', were coming on the 9th and that he was to wait for them. Jebsen had been told to be 'very diplomatic with me so as to keep me friendly'. They told Jebsen that although they could use pressure on TRICYCLE by threatening to denounce him to the British they were not going to do it. Jebsen had the impression that his superiors in Germany thought Monatgu's chart was out of date. Karsthoff was very impressed with it though. Jebsen also told TRICYCLE that they would set free anyone of his family or friends in Yugoslavia that had been taken prisoner following the German invasion. TRICYCLE gave him his father's name. He also saw a cable from Berlin in which it said they – the Germans – should do everything to keep him working for them. In case he did not accept they should promise to take him back to Yugoslavia. But Jebsen warned TRICYCLE that they would not take him to Yugoslavia 'but would put me in a Kurort (spa)', where he would be well looked after but in fact be held prisoner.

On 9 April, Dr Warnecke arrived. TRICYCLE met him in the Hotel Ritz, and had a three and a half hour talk and met him several times later. TRICYCLE was asked what he felt about the offer to continue working for the Germans and he gave them his conditions: '1. Dubrovnik not to be Italian; 2. Nothing to happen to anyone of my family and 3. that the financial plan [for paying TRICYCLE] would continue as arranged.' Warnecke sent them to Berlin who 'promised everything'. Warnecke then gave TRICYCLE part of a questionnaire.

TRICYCLE, meantime, had explained the story of BALLOON to the Germans: 'That he was an officer, signed some cheques which were not met, gambling, drinking etc. That he feels very badly about it all as he is out of everything and that he hates them all. I told them that he wanted to become an officer again when war started but was turned down. I told them vaguely about his job but that he always spends more money than he has got. Their point of view was that that is my organisation and they don't mind with whom I work, though, of course, they want to know who it is. The chief thing is that the organisation functions.' Regarding GELATINE, TRICYCLE followed through the plan as arranged. He told Karsthoff first and he just said: 'Thank you, thank you.' TRICYCLE then told the same story to Warnecke who said the same thing but made notes. When TRICYCLE gave them the report about GELATINE, he told them both that he did not want to have anything to do with it as he was often in the same society as she was and she would not like to know that he knew and vice versa. GELATINE would sign communications 'Fritzi'. BALLOON would not send anything until he got money but he had been collecting information. BALLOON would sign himself 'Ivan II'.[43]

TRICYCLE arrived back in Britain on 30 April. His original intention had been to stay as short a time as possible in the UK in order to make arrangements for the payment of BALLOON and GELATINE, and ostensibly to carry further his negotiations with Commander Montagu and obtain a copy of the minefields chart. This simple programme was, however, 'complicated and protracted by the interminable difficulties and delays which always attend any attempt to obtain a visa for TRICYCLE.' Subsequently, messages were sent suggesting that TRICYCLE had talked further with Montagu, and was convinced of the genuineness and value of his chart. It was arranged that TRICYCLE should take back with him to Lisbon the following story:

Commander Montagu had acquired the chart while performing staff duties at Hull. Recently he had been transferred to the legal department where all instructions for the cancelling of previous orders passed through his hands. He was therefore in a position to be certain that the plan for the minefields had not been altered. He said, however, that dummy mines were extensively used to conceal the real channels through the minefields, and that it was therefore perfectly possible that the results of aerial reconnaissance should appear to contradict his information. However, he refused absolutely to go further in the matter without a safe-conduct signed by a high Army or Gestapo officer with whose name he was familiar.

Montagu was due to go to Belfast on 14 July on official business, and was willing to take the chart with him, as he knew that his papers would not be searched. If he received a telegram or letter by 1 July, signed 'St. Pierre' and containing the date '16th' or '17th', he would be at the Shelborne Hotel in Dublin on 16 or 17 July. He would there hand over the chart in exchange for the safe-conduct.[44]

The MI5 plan adopted for the payment of BALLOON and GELATINE was to interest the Germans in Plan MIDAS. This was an arrangement by which the Germans were induced to part with dollars at a low cost to the British Treasury. TRICYCLE was to represent to them that he had found a man who wished to acquire dollars in America, but was prevented from doing so by the British currency restrictions. This man was willing to buy up to £20,000 worth of dollars at a rate of not less than 2.25 dollars to the pound and preferably around 3 dollars. If $60,000 dollars were to be placed in his account in New York he would pay over £20,000 to any man named by TRICYCLE in London. The man selected to fill the role of 'currency dodger' was a theatrical agent. TRICYCLE was to explain to the Germans that this man was none too certain that Britain would win the war and as a Jew was in any case most anxious to be out of the country before a German invasion. For this reason he was intensely interested in providing himself with a nest egg of dollar bills in New York. TRICYCLE had arranged with him that as soon as he received the dollar bills he should send over a cable in an agreed code to the theatrical agent who would then pay over the sterling to his nominee in London. In the event, it turned out that the individual concerned was so nervous of associating himself with the scheme that it was impossible for him to play any active role in the affair. However, all that the scheme required was that TRICYCLE should possess his name and address, and be able, if necessary, to describe him. TRICYCLE was empowered in his dealings with the Germans to negotiate up to a maximum of £20,000, at a minimum rate of 2.25 dollars to the pound, he himself to keep 10 per cent of the resulting dollars. The flat rate between TRICYCLE and the 'currency dodger' was to be 2.50 dollars to the pound, anything in excess of this being divided evenly between them. The next point to be settled was the position of GELATINE and it was agreed that she should represent herself to the Germans as being able to supply them only with political information, and be of use as a contact with the 'higher class political circles in this country'. This was done for reasons of 'intrinsic plausibility' and also to keep her activities wholly separate from BALLOON. TRICYCLE wrote to Lisbon arranging that she should use the cover address of Maria Gonalves signing her communications 'Yvonne'. The BALLOON correspondence was also initiated at the same time.[45]

As far as the Germans were concerned, TRICYCLE was IVAN I and BALLOON was IVAN II; R or RALPH was the name by which the Germans knew the imaginary Yugoslav diplomat who was going to work for them at the beginning of the double-cross. BALLOON was only to have known TRICYCLE since his second trip to London. Formally, BALLOON was supposed to have done all the work for RALPH who then passed on the result to TRICYCLE: during his first visit to Britain, TRICYCLE 'obtained' certain information which he took back with him to Lisbon – it was BALLOON who was supposed to have obtained this, passing it on to RALPH who then passed it on to TRICYCLE. During his second visit to London, the imaginary RALPH 'informed' TRICYCLE that it would be easier to work in direct contact with BALLOON; thus for practically all the information TRICYCLE had obtained, the Germans had BALLOON to thank: being English he was able to travel around without much danger and it was with BALLOON that TRICYCLE was supposed to have travelled when he went to inspect aerodromes and the like, although BALLOON often travelled without him. It seemed that BALLOON would be paid $500 a month – and as he was told by MI5: 'this will be made in fairly frequent payments as you spend money easily and often lose in gambling. You have been borrowing money from Ralph for sometime and indeed this is what enabled him in the first place to recruit you'. BALLOON had also borrowed money from TRICYCLE. RALPH did practically nothing except provide BALLOON with political information from time to time. Although the Germans had pressed TRICYCLE, they knew nothing about RALPH: 'He is very much afraid of compromising himself with his own people and will therefore be unsuitable as a direct agent for the Germans.' TRICYCLE only retained him in his organisation because he knew about BALLOON and brought him into the service of the Germans. TRICYCLE had told the Germans that BALLOON was had volunteered to go to Lisbon, but that it had been difficult to obtain an exit permit. In order to have this it would be necessary for BALLOON to have a real reason to make the trip. In order to help him towards this end the Germans were going to employ one of their agents in the arms trade and would make a big offer to BALLOON with regard to sporting guns. The Security Service told BALLOON:

> As you know our present inclination is to avoid sending you there but if we should later decide to ask you to do so and you are willing to go you will have to be extremely careful. It seems that your best plan would be to occupy yourself with genuine business. While we have every confidence in you and feel that if you went there you would be more than equal to the occasion, it is only fair to point out that if anything should happen which would disclose to the Germans your true position and that of Popov, the repercussions on his family in Yugoslavia might be tragic.[46]

The Germans, however, swallowed the bait: TRICYCLE was given £300 for BALLOON and a further sum of around $2,000 for himself.[47]

In the meantime, on 16 May, Luke had discussed GELATINE's position with TRICYCLE and Max Knight, and the nature of her information was agreed between them. At a previous meeting, on 13 May, it had been decided that GELATINE should write a preliminary letter with ordinary ink which TRICYCLE would take over with him and that he would ask Karsthoff to send a memorandum, explaining to GELATINE what sort of information they would require from her. Once the correspondence had begun GELATINE was to write not more than one letter in ten days. It was confirmed that GELATINE should be run as a separate agent from BALLOON. In the meantime, however, TRICYCLE had already communicated with the Germans about GELATINE. He sent the following message, in secret ink, in a letter written by BALLOON on 8 May, ostensibly from 'Richard H. Keeping to Mr Paula Pinto da Lima' and dated 5 May 1941. The message was: 'Vu Friedl. Veut travallier. Ecrire adresse de Maria Gonzalves de Azevedo, signature Yvonne.' For some unknown reason GELATINE was now to sign her messages 'Yvonne' instead of 'Fritzi'. Masterman was concerned when he analysed this because it was always agreed that BALLOON and GELATINE were to be carefully segregated from one another; but by writing his message on one of BALLOON's letters TRICYCLE 'must have given the Germans the suspicion at least that he was not keeping the two cases properly apart, since he and BALLOON would be presumed to be writing in the same room and indeed on the same sheet of paper, and would therefore in all human probability talk to one another about what they were writing'.

GELATINE began to write letters in secret ink on 20 May, when she wrote two letters but these were later cancelled. The idea, apparently, was the letters were to be taken out by TRICYCLE. His departure, for Lisbon, was put off until 28 June and at the last moment it was decided that it was too dangerous for him to take GELATINE's letters with him and that they must be posted in the ordinary way. Three letters were accordingly sent. But GELATINE received no answer or acknowledgement at all from the Germans. Masterman presumed that the Germans no longer wanted to make contact with GELATINE; possibly they were always in doubt about her and in this case he concluded that their doubts might have been increased: '1. By the danger of tying her up with BALLOON through TRICYCLE using BALLOON's letter to communicate his news about GELATINE to the Germans. I feel strongly that this was a mistake; 2. By the change of signature which [must] have puzzled them as me; 3. By the delay on the part of GELATINE in writing her first letter. This would have been perfectly natural and explicable had not BALLOON been writing in secret ink during this period or if her first letter had been taken by TRICYCLE.'

Masterman now considered there was only a small chance of GELATINE being serviceable to MI5. He thought she should try once more, writing another letter saying that she had had no answer, no instructions, no money, no advice and that unless the Germans answered her speedily she would stop sending them letters of any kind, since loyal to Germany though she was, she did not wish to risk her neck unless she could be assured that she was doing something useful for the Fatherland. 'If no answer comes to this letter she should, in my opinion, simply cease to write and fade out from the picture.'[48]

W.E. Luke subsequently found out that it was TRICYCLE who had decided that GELATINE should write under the name of Yvonne and not Fritzi: '(a) because she is known to so many of her friends as Fritzi that her identity might be discovered if a letter written in secret writing were intercepted and (b) because the name is well in keeping with his own signature of Ivan.'

Luke did not agree that TRICYCLE's action in writing this short message in BALLOON's letter would cause the Germans to suspect that he was not keeping the two cases properly apart. It was too short a note to warrant a covering letter to itself at a time when cover addresses were being rather overworked and there was no reason why he should not have written it in the same room as BALLOON without letting him know the text. Nor did Luke believe that the delay in sending correspondence – which would have been explained by TRICYCLE to the Germans – would have prejudiced GELATINE in any way. It seemed to Luke that, from the very start, the Germans must have had doubts about GELATINE because of her 'relationship to a very high official' in the British Secret Service 'and I must say that if I had been aware of this relationship when GELATINE was recruited, I should have opposed the project of introducing her again to the Germans through the medium of an important and active double agent.' Another explanation was simply that the cover address provided to GELATINE was no longer effective.[49] Luke's consternation concerning GELATINE's 'relationship to a very high official' in the British Secret Service was because the individual concerned was none other than Sir Stewart Menzies, or C, the head of SIS!

SUMMER, RAINBOW & TATE

The next important incident in SNOW's career was the arrival of the parachutist Gosta Caroli, codename SUMMER, and the part that he played therein.[1] SUMMER was a Swede. Bespectacled and 1.75m, with brown eyes, dark hair and an oval face, he was born in Sweden in 1902. As a young man he had followed a number of trades and finally failed disastrously with a silver fox farm near Upsala. He had then wandered at large in Europe for some while, supporting himself as an itinerant artist and journalist. In this condition he fell in at the end of 1938 with a member of the Hamburg Stelle and was recruited by him for work in England.[2] SUMMER first came to Britain from Sweden in that year and stayed approximately four months. His stay was mostly in the Birmingham district to study English. SUMMER again returned to Britain, leaving for Sweden in August 1939. He was then apparently unemployed until March 1940, when he obtained a position as second steward on the ship *Matheinen* which travelled from Gothenberg to Norway and back to Sweden. This ship was sunk by a mine on 16 April, and those rescued were landed in Norway, from whence SUMMER returned to Sweden. He then obtained another position on the ship *Ludwigholfen* which travelled between Sweden and the port of Lubeck. During the various calls at Lubeck, SUMMER came into contact with a man who visited the boat on each occasion as a plain-clothes policeman, and always had a certain amount of discussion with SUMMER, supplying him with literature in Swedish enhancing the Nazi cause. SUMMER claimed during interrogation, subsequently, that he had approached his contact with a request that he should be allowed to join the German Army. He was then taken by a Dr Schultz to Hamburg and accommodated at the Hotel Reichahof. The following morning he was taken by Schultz to meet a Dr Haupt. SUMMER apparently made a favourable impression, and again expressed his desire to work for Germany, requesting in particular to be allowed to join the German Army: by this stage both SUMMER's parents were dead and a girl to whom he had been engaged for some time was dying of TB: 'He therefore imagined that as he had no responsibilities whatever, the life in the Germany Army would be very welcome.'

Dr Haupt informed him that Germany could use him on a special mission, to Britain, and 'undoubtedly flattered the man's vanity' describing the importance of this mission. To this effect, he was placed under the care of a man called Petersen who instructed him in Morse Code both for transmitting and receiving. He was also taken around to various aerodromes by a Hauptmann Bruns who instructed him in the appearance, size and anti-aircraft defence of aeroplanes so that, at a later date, he would be able to recognise them without difficulty. SUMMER was, in all, five weeks in Hamburg. After this he transferred to Paris where he received maps and signed a contract that stated that his reward for visiting Britain was to be four years' schooling in Sweden or Germany or, if he preferred, a cash equivalent. It was here also that he met the crew of three of the aeroplane which was to bring him to England. On 5 September 1940, SUMMER left Brussels by air and crossed the English coast at a great height. When over a point between Stratford and Banbury, he was dropped after some difficulty from a height of 15,000 ft. The rip cord was apparently operated by means of a drop cord from the aeroplane. SUMMER, it seems, had not been instructed regarding parachute descents and had never made a jump before this moment. He was unconscious on landing and was therefore not able to put through his signal at the time specified, i.e. 2 a.m.–4 a.m. in the morning. He was arrested by the police at 5.30 p.m. on 6 September, which was before his second time of transmission.

SUMMER was passed on to MI5 by Special Branch. He agreed to give MI5 all information in his possession and details of his code on condition that a colleague TATE, who was due to drop parachute by into England in the near future and with whom he had a rendezvous outside the 'Black Boy' public house at Northampton, should not be shot. Although he had only known TATE a very short time, i.e. since July, when he met him at the course of instruction he received in Morse, he apparently struck up a very strong friendship with the man, and suggested that the sense of danger brought them together. One of his Camp 020 interrogators was impressed enough by him to write: 'I would like to say that during interrogation [SUMMER] spoke in a very straightforward manner and sees himself as a martyr, saving his friend and if necessary, willingly facing death.'[3] Tin Eye Stephens, however, formed a different view. From the moment he met SUMMER until the time that he questioned him 'my suspicions had been aroused on numerous occasions by inconsistent stories which he himself told me'.[4]

At first things seemed to run smoothly. Under MI5 control SUMMER transmitted a cover story back to his masters: the Germans were told that SUMMER, who had injured himself slightly on landing, was still at large; they now believed he had spent the ten days after his arrival hiding in the open between Oxford and Buckingham. Then, as the weather was bad, SUMMER proposed to them that he find shelter for himself by posing as a Swedish refugee. The Germans vetoed this idea and instead instructed SNOW, by wireless, to make contact with SUMMER and arrange for his accommodation. The Germans were led to believe that, on 17 September, SNOW had despatched BISCUIT who met SUMMER by arrangement at the High Wycombe railway station. He then – imaginarily – took SUMMER with him to London, put him up in his flat and took steps to see that the false seaman's papers which he had brought with him were put into order. The Germans were also told, via SNOW's transmitter, that SUMMER had fallen ill as a result of his time in the open and was being nursed by BISCUIT. By 27 September the Germans had been informed that SUMMER had recovered and that as his papers were now in order he was ready to set out once more on his own. They gave instructions that he should be told to work the area covering London–Colchester–Southend. By 23 October, SUMMER was able to announce on his own transmitter that he had succeeded in establishing himself in lodgings to the south of Cambridge. There, as far as the Germans knew, he remained until the following January. There was no further contact between him and SNOW's organisation except that he had BISCUIT's address for use if necessary. At the end of January 1941 SUMMER's transmitter went suddenly off the air and the Germans were told, through SNOW, that BISCUIT had received a letter from him to the effect that he was under suspicion by the police and had taken advantage of his seamen's papers to cut and run. He had left his wireless set in the cloakroom at Cambridge station, whence on the Germans' instructions it was later retrieved by BISCUIT.[5]

In truth SUMMER had been installed, by MI5, in a house with a guard.[6] But he was a troubled man. SUMMER's unsuitability for double-cross work was soon demonstrated when he attempted suicide. As was seen before his arrival in England, SUMMER had found it impossible to find a regular job and settle down to it. Apparently he had been hoping to find some sort of work that would enable him to continue his education: on account of his age he feared that work as a farmer or a sailor would only result in his remaining as one or the other with no chance of promotion owing to his lack of education. As he grew older he realised that his chance of releasing his dream was becoming more remote. This continued to affect his state of mind. Now, SUMMER became terrified of the German Secret Service and of an invasion which, if it came, would see him 'try and make a beeline in the opposite direction as quickly as possible'. His attempted suicide appeared to be due to two reasons: the fact that his story – that he had not worked for Germany before and had only got into the

German Secret Service through trying to join the German Army – was discovered to be untrue; and, secondly, that Stephens had referred to 'this dirty' case – which made SUMMER think 'furiously that he was always getting innocent people into trouble and that if he was out of the way he could not continue to cause them harm. To his way of thinking this action would cancel out all the wrong he had done.' After the attempt to take his own life failed it seemed that SUMMER was coping better by 'becoming more resigned to things' and, while living from day to day, 'feels quite prepared to take the consequences'. His ambition after the war was, if possible, to go to Canada to try and make a fresh start.[7] But then, on 13 January 1941, SUMMER attacked his guard, Paulton, from behind, put a rope around his neck and tied him hand and foot, putting him on a sofa. He emptied the guard's pockets, went upstairs to collect some things and then left the house. Paulton, in the meantime, had noticed a knife on a table, which he was able to get to and cut himself free. He then contacted his superiors, including TAR Robertson, only to be startled to see SUMMER ride past the window on a motorcycle with a suitcase on one side of it and a twelve foot canvas canoe tied to the other. SUMMER later gave himself up to police, searching for him, at a railway station.[8] This was the real reason why SUMMER went off air. He was returned to Camp 020 for the duration of the war.[9]

Yet as far as MI5 was concerned, SUMMER had served his purpose in two ways: adding credibility, in German eyes, to the SNOW network; and paving the way for an altogether more reliable Double Agent – TATE, named after the musical hall comedian Harry Tate. But before coming to this agent, it is well to mention another agent acquired by MI5 at this time: RAINBOW. RAINBOW was born Bernie Kiener in London, the child of a German woman and a Portuguese surgeon, he was since naturalised as a British subject, who lived in the Rhondda valley. Shortly after RAINBOW's birth, his mother, who had come to England from Germany in 1906, married a German who kept a boarding house in London, and whose name RAINBOW bore. RAINBOW's step-father was interned on the outbreak of the 1914 war, and in 1916 his mother left Britain to return to Germany, taking RAINBOW with her. She returned to the family home at Schweidnitz, near Breslau, where she managed a small canteen, kept by her mother's sister. RAINBOW was educated at the local Oberrealschule, which he left at the age of eighteen, when he attended the Handelshochschule in Berlin for one year. During this year he was apprenticed to a Berlin branch of a Hamburg import firm and in 1934 he spent one year in Hamburg with this firm. In 1935, RAINBOW obtained a position with a firm, W. von Heidenheim, metal engravers, specialising in high precision work. RAINBOW worked with this firm in Berlin from 1935 to 1938, when the firm entered into some tentative arrangements with an English firm, the Betta Manufacturing Co., Enfield, who engaged in the same business, and RAINBOW was sent over to the English firm, arriving in April, 1938. He was to act as sort of liaison between the two firms, who were considering some kind of partnership, which was frustrated by the war. RAINBOW travelled to England on a British passport, which was issued to him in May 1937. This passport contained, however, no record of his exit from Germany or his arrival in England on this occasion. RAINBOW explained the absence of the former by the fact that he left before his Aufenthaltserlaubnis stamped on the passport had run out. In 1938 both the English and the German firms were working on armaments.

Shortly before leaving for Britain, RAINBOW had become engaged to his present wife, the daughter of a German mother and a Romanian Jew. This girl's brother left Germany before Hitler came to power and joined the French Army. RAINBOW expressed himself as ready to fight against the Nazis, but did not wish to see Germany destroyed, since that was the country where he was brought up and where he had friends. His political convictions were, MI5 noted, 'rather vague. Though not an admirer of the Weimar republic, he thinks some form of democracy desirable; in spite of his devotion to Germany (as distinguished from the Nazis) he states that he would remain loyal to this country so long as the war is being fought, even though there were a change of Government in Germany.'[10] RAINBOW described himself as '100 per cent Aryan German' and had been employed in a good position in German firm yet the authorities had refused to allow him to marry a girl whose ancestry had a Jewish 'taint'. This was why he left his employment and came over to Britain – to marry. This was to prove the key motivation in offering his services to MI5: unable to return to Germany, but with dual nationality proving no contradiction to him declaring he was loyal to Britain while still retaining his loyalty to Germany, he was 'out to down [the] Nazis by any means in his power', and would co-operate in any action MI5 considered desirable.[11] And what made RAINBOW interesting to MI5 was his contact with the German Secret Service derived entirely from his friend Gunther Schutz, with whom he was at school in Schweidnitz, and who came to Britain in June, 1938, 'to study'.

Later Schutz purported to work for a Hamburg firm of chemical manufacturers and shared an office in Queen Victoria Street with a man named Hardbottle, who also lived at the same house. RAINBOW described Schutz as a good looking adventurer, with no special Nazi convictions. RAINBOW stated that Schutz occasionally asked him questions about the locality, size and employees of prominent British firms and finally, just prior to the outbreak of war, before leaving for Germany, Schutz informed RAINBOW that he was employed under the cover of his business occupation as an agent by the Wehrkreiskommando in Hamburg and his chief was a Dr Praetorius, with whom he communicated through a Poste Restante in Berlin. His duties were to report the position of factories, number of employees, particulars of manufacture and the factories on which he was to concentrate were communicated to him in writing under the postage stamp of letters received from Berlin.[12] Schutz made it clear that, while he knew that the information sent in by him went to Praetorius at Hamburg, he himself had never had any personal contact with Praetorius, nor with any agents in Britain. He realised in fact that he was possibly one of a number, but that he himself played a very insignificant role, and that he had no contacts, nor was he acquainted with any other German Intelligence agents. He was under the impression that such information he had sent about various firms was probably required by the German authorities for the purposes of identification for eventual bombing attacks. Schutz conveyed the impression to RAINBOW that he did not relish the idea of being sent to fight on one of the fronts and would very much like to try to arrange a prolongation of his intelligence work; for that purpose he expressed a desire to maintain contact with RAINBOW, and hoped that he might possibly be able to work with him eventually. RAINBOW was of two minds whether to report this conversation to the authorities or not, but decided that Schutz would have no opportunity of getting back to Britain and the matter might be regarded as closed.[13]

But, on 23 January 1940, Schutz wrote from the Excelsior Hotel, Antwerp, to RAINBOW suggesting a meeting.[14] RAINBOW, who had previously refrained from denouncing Schutz on account of their friendship, now explained the position to the authorities, fearful lest he himself should come under suspicion. MI5 took over the case and it was then arranged that he should make the journey as requested. He left for Belgium on 4 February 1940 and returned a week later, having been given instructions regarding the work which he was to undertake in England by Dr Huckreide of Eins Wirtschaft Ost Hamburg, who had come specially to Belgium to meet RAINBOW. He was given a good invisible ink, a sum of money and a cover address. Instructions from the Germans were to be sent to him in the shape of microphotographs on full stops after the date in otherwise innocuous letters.

In April 1940 he paid a further short visit to Antwerp and received three more cover addresses.

RAINBOW's original mission was to report any developments in aviation and air defence, the effect of air raids and details of transport in the United Kingdom. He wrote several secret letters to one of his cover addresses along these lines, but by January 1941 he had received no fresh instructions from the Germans. Contact was, however, then renewed and in due course he received new cover addresses and small sums of money. His questionnaires by now related almost entirely to industrial and economic matters and were of a fairly high standard. His real and supposed position during 1941 was that of pianist in a dance band in Weston-super-Mare, but at the end of that year he received instructions from the Germans to obtain work in London, with a promise that if he did so they would not allow him to suffer financially. They agreed to pay him £1,000 for a year's work, and in December 1941 made this good to the extent of sending him £300 through another MI5 XX agent, TATE, and a further £500 by the same means in July 1942. In February 1942 RAINBOW obtained work with Gillette's factory, and this fact, together with that of his dual nationality, had furnished the Germans with a reason for his not having been called up into the Services.[15]

Returning to the case of TATE: he was born Wulf Schmidt of German parents on 7 November 1911 at Asbenraa in Schleswig, and automatically became a Danish citizen after the last war.[16] He was around five feet five inches, with blue eyes and light brown hair brushed back. Oval faced, well-built and freckled he spoke good 'Colonial English', Danish and German.[17] During his military service he became an officer in the Danish Cavalry, after which he spent the next few years studying agriculture in Europe and farming in the Argentine and Cameroons. His employment in Africa necessitated his becoming a member of a Danish branch of the National Socialist Party, a step that, as an ardent Nazi, he took without hesitation. At the end of December 1939 he managed to arrange that he should be sent back to Denmark from the Cameroons, and while passing through Germany was put in touch with Dr Scholz, of the Hamburg Abwehrstelle, who proposed various espionage missions to him. When TATE expressed his reluctance to perform this type of work Scholz brought pressure to bear on him on account of money that he had already accepted from the Germans. After an unfruitful intelligence mission in Denmark in the spring of 1940 – aimed, it should be noted against his own Danish forces – TATE was finally summoned to Hamburg for training in order that he could be sent to England as an agent of Eins Luft.

When his course of instruction in Morse and codes was completed he was sent to Brussels, where he waited about three weeks before leaving for England. In Hamburg, TATE's case was under the general control of the DOCTOR,[18] who was noticeable by his gold tooth and 'soft hands'.[19] TATE's actual case officer was Hauptmann Bruns,[20] (real name Bohckel – a 'typical Prussian officer' – who had been a flying officer in the last war)[21] who gave him his general training as a spy.[22]

It was at this point that TATE was introduced to SUMMER, about whom he had been told by Scholz, who had expressed the desire that the two should not become too friendly during their training together. They did, however, become good friends. As TATE and SUMMER had adjoining rooms at the Phoenix Hotel where they were staying, which were each fitted with a Morse buzzer, they were able to spend their evenings practising transmitting. As his departure for Britain drew near TATE was told that, in case of emergency he could get into touch with RAINBOW, whose address he was given; but he was to beware of being watched. The password for identifying RAINBOW was 'How is Mr O'Brien?' The reply was: 'Mr O'Brien is still in Guy's Hospital.' Several attempts at flying to England had by now been made, but it was not until 19 September that they were successful. TATE was dropped at Willingham, in Cambridgeshire. He landed undetected in the middle of an A.A. barrage and close to a searchlight battery. He made a bad landing owing to the wind and the weight of the equipment strapped on to him, hurting his hand and spraining his ankle. The next morning he hid his wireless gear and flying clothing, and went into the village to buy some aspirin and a watch, as his own had been damaged on landing. At 5 p.m. on 20 September, TATE was arrested through arousing the suspicions of a civilian who asked him for his identity card. He was carrying a British ration book and identity card, his own Danish passport and the sum of £136 in English notes and 250 dollars. TATE's arrival, of course, was not entirely unexpected by the British authorities, as SUMMER had agreed to give all the information in his possession on condition that TATE's life would be spared. As the two had made a private arrangement to meet at the 'Black Boy', the Northampton pub was watched on 20 September at the pre-arranged times; but during the afternoon TATE was identified as the man earlier arrested and the watch was therefore withdrawn.[23]

When he was brought to Camp 020 he was interrogated by Tin Eye Stephens. TATE began confidently – 'It seems I am to be treated as a spy. I am not so'[24] and stuck to his cover story that, having fought with a German soldier in Denmark, he had to flee the country and chartered a fishing boat to bring him to England where he intended to work as a newspaper reporter. He had arrived at West Hartlepool on 10 July, and had intended to put himself in touch with the Danish Consul in London. His ration book and identity card TATE claimed to have bought on the black market, in Birmingham, where he had spent three weeks.[25] He insisted that he had been at large for a total of forty-seven days, during which time he survived on food such as cake. He explained that he had hurt his hand and foot when he fell into a roadside ditch, in the process tearing some of his clothes. Stephens listened patiently but then asked: 'How much longer are you going on with this nonsense? Do you know what a man looks like whose hair has been growing for two and a half months?' TATE replied: 'It is different. My beard does not grow either.' Stephens countered: 'Another bad lie.' Stephens then asked about TATE's family and, on being informed that the suspect had a sister, inquired: 'Would you like us to inform her that you are going to be shot?' TATE replied in the affirmative and still did not crack. But Stephens was now growing weary of the joust; he told TATE:

> You know the whole of your story is a stack of lies. We know that. It's been proved. It is very badly told and does not fit in with anything. It is just a question of whether you intend to help yourself or not. We know a good deal about you, you see. Everything is consistent with your having fallen from a parachute a couple of days ago. Your clothes, in the first place are clean. Your hair has recently been cut. You probably hurt your hand and foot when you landed. You health is good, which means you have not been living on buns and chocolate for two months.

But still TATE refused to yield. Finally, Stephens delivered the *coup de grace*: he read out the relevant extracts from SUMMER's interrogation. 'At this juncture TATE realised that further opposition was useless.' TATE acknowledged that he had been sold by SUMMER: 'I see so. If you want shoot me. The man is a schwein.'[26] The next day brought the dramatic moment when Stephens offered to spare TATE's life if he would become a British agent:

> Q [Stephens]. I'm not going to keep you long. You can go to bed after this. I've gone through your case at great length with the officers who are mainly concerned with it and I'm satisfied that you've been speaking the truth, do you see?
> A [TATE]. Yes.
> Q. I respect you because you've got guts. I respected the way you

stood up to it yesterday. If we're talking in ordinary terms the scales are weighted against you – I had too much on you. I knew a lot about you –

A. Yes sir.

Q. But I say again that I respect you and the way you stood up to it and then in the end when I broke you, you told me you were going to speak the truth and you have spoken the truth... In many ways I am very much like yourself, I spent all my time out in the East and I suppose the question arises for you, as it does for me, as to what is going to happen at the end of the war. I like adventuring in South Arabia, India and Abyssinia and all over the place – probably you do too. You were asked a particular question this afternoon and I was rather struck by the answer. You say you like playing with danger, that's why you took this up, isn't it?

A. Yes.

Q. You were asked a question yesterday and you were asked the same question again today whether you were bound by any oath and as I understand it, you're not.

A. Yes, I am not bound by any oath.

Q. Now I've got no sentiment at all. You are a spy and you've been fairly caught as a spy. If I'd done the same thing as you've had the guts to do in Germany, I'd be shot, and that is your proper reward – you should be shot, but there are certain mitigating circumstances in this case and we've looked at it because we've tried to be just but at the same time we intend to be practical because that's stark business in war – you're following me?

A. I am following correct, yes.

Q. I am under no illusions whatever as to what Germany intends to do to this country and I hope Germany is under no illusions as to what we intend to do to her. It'll be a great day for me and for many of us if we can see Germany exterminated off the face of the earth and Germany feels exactly the same about Great Britain. The issue has been joined. There is no sentiment whatever about this – you have forfeited your life but there's one way of saving your life. You're not bound by any oath... I am going to ask you that question when I've given you sufficient time to answer it properly. I am a judge of character, if you say yes I may believe you but because of my extreme distrust of human nature at large I shall always check you – I shall always see that you don't doublecross me. Do you see?

A. Yes.

Q. If you doublecross, then it won't take long to finish you off. Do you understand?

A. I understand.

Q. There is adventure in it and there is danger in it. I am going to ask you very soon whether you will accept that offer and if you do I shall immediately put you upon check – I shall say I intend to send a message to Germany. As to whether I do or not has nothing to do with it. I shall get that message put by you into code and as it's a game, espionage, as war is a game... if we wish to use you for sending messages we shall come to you from time to time. You will be fairly treated. There are two senior Officers here – they will both tell you that if I say a thing like that I can be trusted. Well there's the issue.

A. Excuse, I must answer now?

Q. I think it's a good thing to answer now.

A. Yes. I'll do so.

Q. Well again I respect you because I think you've got guts – it needs guts to do that. Can you understand what I mean by guts. It means courage. I respect you because you've got courage to say that, do you see?

A. Yes.

Q. Because of that I am prepared to trust you and I'm going to check you – do you see the position?

A. Yes.

Q. Well then, with the leave of these two Officers you will go up to your room and you will be allowed a decent rest. We shall probably give you a message to write out into code and see how you do that... This is the first check. If that check is found correct then I think I can honestly say that your life is no longer in danger. Do you understand?

A. I understand.

Q. Now I don't want any hesitation from you at all – what is your answer?

A. Yes.

Q. You will?

A. Yes.

Q. Well done.[27]

TATE remained interned for some weeks, during which time, after several unsuccessful attempts, contact with the Germans was established and he informed them that he was safe but had been hurt on landing. Three days after first contact he received his first message from them. TATE was then moved to a house at Radlett in north-west London where he lived under the supervision of a full-time guard. He informed the Germans that he had obtained safe lodging in a house in Barnet and would now be able to devote his time to procuring information for them. TATE was allowed a certain amount of freedom at Radlett and small outings and parties were arranged for him from time to time; he did, however, grow increasingly resentful of constant supervision and, as the house was rather unsuitable, another one in the same district was found where conditions were easier. He was given a small allowance of up to £1 a week, and it was arranged for a regular sum to be invested in National Savings Certificates to be handed over to him at the end of the war on condition that he continued to work for MI5; the Security Service, however, were under no illusions 'that his new-found loyalty to this country would survive any severe strain'.[28] Nevertheless, TATE proved reliable. His mission for the Germans had been chiefly to transmit regular weather reports and detailed information about all matters concerning the RAF; of secondary importance were troop movements, morale and the food situation.[29]

As far as the Germans knew, TATE was a free agent, with no regular employment, who was chiefly concerned with a series of attempts to secure adequate payment. He had not been amply provided for when he arrived in Britain because, as Masterman noted, 'the Germans optimistically supposed that they would soon follow him to England'. As his money dwindled TATE was forced to beg for assistance and a series of attempts were made, by the Germans, to help him. He secured £100 by registered post through SNOW and entered into negotiations to receive money from RAINBOW to no avail. The Germans, as an alternative, came up with a plan to drop £500 for TATE by aircraft[30] with the drop point near Luton or Watford.

As the Germans became increasingly desperate to get funds to TATE, Tin Eye Stephens was told by TAR Robertson: 'It is hoped that in the new future we shall be able to provide you with another inmate. Provided everything goes well and according to plan, which it never does, we hope through the auspices of TATE to be able to affect the arrest of a courier who is being sent over to this country for the purpose of handing TATE a sum of money and a new crystal for his wireless set.' It had been decided that as soon as the meeting took place TATE should be arrested along with the courier. In taking this action 'we are reposing a certain amount of trust in TATE and I have indicated to him that I want his co-operation in this matter to the fullest extent. He has told me that he is quire prepared to play the game by us and not to give the show away and in this connection I am fully prepared to accept TATE's assurances. He has been told that he will be arrested and that it is his business to try and extract from his companion as much information as he possibly can with regard to his activities and so on.' As soon as the arrest was affected the two would be taken to Scotland Yard where they would be put into a room 'which will of course be specially prepared. This incidentally will serve as a check on both individuals... TATE, I am sure is quite prepared to act as stool pigeon, but I am most frightfully anxious that his presence in Ham [Camp 020] should only be known to a very limited number of inmates, as I propose that after he has done this job he shall be removed from there and if I am satisfied, be put under some form of honourable detention, for which I am now making arrangements.'[31]

But Robertson was to be disappointed and Stephens kept waiting for the planned drop – aptly at the Tate Gallery – failed to take place when the courier failed to appear. In order to force the Germans to send a courier, MI5 had to convince the enemy that their agent was facing destitution. On more than one occasion TATE had turned up to meet the courier but there no one had turned up. So, on 21 May, TATE complained to the Germans, via his transmitter: 'Once again I have met nobody. Now I should really like to know if you are playing the game with me or what is going on. I am desperate and have not even enough money to feed myself properly and can only anticipate the worst, but I will try and eke out to the next meeting and if nobody appears then I shall have to get away and cannot give you any guarantee as regards radio transmissions... Is it possible to drop money by air immediately? Expect your answer in detail by 11.30 hrs MEZ.'[32]

The Germans replied: 'In case, contrary to our expectations, the meeting today is not successful please do not lose your head as one of the things must succeed on or before the 25th... Nevertheless please give immediate answer tomorrow so that in case of necessity we will also prepare technically the dropping of money.'[33] TATE replied: 'Many thanks for message. It is at least something. I hope it is not only an "Aspirin" but that action will follow.'[34] The Germans reassured him: 'As always we are continuing to do our utmost to bring help. We will have further news this evening.'[35] The Germans reported that their courier – known to them as PHOENIX FRIEND – 'has not yet reported to us. He has probably taken a longer time to get to London. We have specially pointed out to him how urgently you require the money. You must stick to arranged meetings... without fail.'[36]

The Germans told TATE that they would attempt to get money to him, via the courier, who would meet him at the British Museum.

In addition to this the Germans devised another plan involving the Japanese Embassy delivering some money. TATE was told: 'You will wait on the 26th, 29th and 31st [May] at 16.00 hrs at the terminus of bus route no.11 at Victoria Station. You must enter this bus with a Japanese who carries "THE TIMES" and a book in left hand. You must wear a red tie and carry a newspaper and a book in left hand. After the fifth stop you both alight from the bus and continue by next bus of same route. You must sit or stand alongside the Japanese and ask him "Any special news. May I see the paper?" Thereupon the Japanese will give you the paper with an envelope in it. In case it is impossible to hand over you must leave bus with Japanese and follow him. In case no. 11 bus no longer runs please report another route number to us at once. Regret meeting cannot be earlier. Be precise in every detail as Japanese is very suspicious.'[37]

TATE replied: 'Many thanks for message' but 'Route no. 11 has not its terminus at Victoria Station. Therefore I propose route no. 16. Otherwise everything as suggested.' The Germans answered: 'Agree with no. 16 bus route with terminus at Victoria Station. We have asked our friends to do their utmost to make it successful on 26th.'[38] In case something went wrong with any of the elaborate arrangements, the Germans announced that: 'On night of 27th/28th we will drop near Chalton four birch tree branches each one metre long, each has money in the thick end. As a guide to you two 200 kilo bombs will be dropped near Luton in the direction of Chalton immediately after the bombs branches will be dropped which will probably drop 2 kilos further... In case meeting... is not successful please do not despair it is probably due to delay in transmission to our friend as it goes by a round about route.'[39] Given that the plans, to date, had all gone wrong the Germans offered a back up plan if everything went pear-shaped again: 'Chins up! In no circumstances give up. Should meeting not be successful tomorrow, go at once to the Japanese Naval Attaché at Japanese Embassy and ask for help. To make them receive you, give them an envelope with a note in it reading "I am friend Victoria Station bus number sixteen formerly eleven". We will help you whatever happens.'[40]

The Security Service arranged a plan with Special Branch to tail TATE to the British Museum and arrest any enemy courier who turned up. When TATE left his base, at the Piccadilly Hotel, at about 1.45 p.m. he was to be watched by two women police officers, who would also follow him when he left the Regent Palace Hotel at about 2.20 p.m. On leaving the Regents Palace Hotel by the side door he was to walk down Haymarket to the bottom into St James' Park, and then walk slowly to Hyde Park selecting a suitable spot where he would sit down and read. While he was there three or four people would watch him from a distance and would close in on anyone who contacted him. At about 4.15 p.m., TATE was to make his way to Marble Arch and at about 4.45 p.m. jump into a taxi and proceed to the British Museum. During his time in the taxi he was not be followed, but at the British Museum a party of police officers would be waiting for him there. At about 5.15 p.m., if no contact had been made at the British Museum, TATE was to leave by foot for the Piccadilly Hotel, arriving there at 5.45 p.m. and during this part of the trip he would again be followed. On entering the Piccadilly Hotel, Special Branch would cease tailing. Anyone who spoke to TATE was to be questioned and unless the explanation was obviously innocent he or she would be apprehended for enquiries to be made. It was to be left to the discretion of Special Branch officers as to whether or not an arrest would be made. If an arrest was made the suspect's home would immediately be searched if his address had been obtained. If any onlooker at Regents Palace should also appear as an onlooker at the British Museum, he was to be arrested on suspicion.[41]

But again no one turned up. And, by now, TATE had been informed by the Germans that the cash drop, by air, was off again: 'The aeroplane badly damaged taking off as the plane was specially adapted other plane cannot be used. We are very sorry we do not think plane will be ready before 29th.' After phoning Robertson, Luke agreed with TATE that the following message in reply might be sent:

> I do not believe any further in your goodwill and would never have thought that you would leave me in such a mess my confidence in you in strongly shaken what shall I do if nothing arrives on 29th I can't say but I am willing to go to any extremes. I have pawned everything and own nothing but what I stand up in. I am crazy with despair.[42]

With no courier it was left to the Japanese to get the money to TATE; unfortunately for MI5 this meant no arrest could be effected because of diplomatic immunity. A watch was kept on TATE and the contact from the Japanese Embassy was later identified as one of the Assistant Naval Attaches, Lieutenant Commander Mitinori Yosii. Yosii came to the no. 16 bus stop at Victoria Station about 4 p.m. but changed buses 'very badly' in Park Lane. He got out of the 16 bus at a traffic block, thinking it was a bus stop, and stood about for some time on the pavement while no less than three no.16 buses passed him. Having discovered his mistake he moved to a bus stop, and boarded the fourth no.16 bus which came past. In paying his fare on the second bus he dropped some money on the floor, which was retrieved by TATE, who after this had no difficulty in entering into conversation with him and asking for the loan of his newspaper. Yosii handed the paper over, and immediately left the bus, telling TATE that he could keep it. Inside the paper, wrapped up in paper, were two hundred £1 notes, all new. Yosii went straight back to the Japanese Naval Attaché's office at 30, Portland Square. Scotland Yard were able to get a film of Yosii and to follow him throughout.[43]

At last a delighted TATE was able to send a positive message over: 'Long live Japan and the yellow peril. I received with many thanks 200 potatoes as a first instalment. I take back all I said and now feel the reverse. The bus meeting was most successful. Now I will have a good "blind", eat plenty, and sleep at lot then I will go on a trip refreshed and full of energy to be able to give you good stuff.'[44] The Germans were delighted as well: 'The whole show is happy, with you, as everyone followed your fate and were anxious about you. Relax now after the terrible ordeal. We too will drink a toast to you.'[45]

It appeared that the Germans had planned to use two couriers for the money drop. It remained a mystery as to why one of them had failed to show up. The fate of the other courier MI5 knew all about: he was Karl Richter, the twenty-nine year old Sudeten German, who made landfall in a field near London Colney.[46]

But, before he went to meet his Maker, Richter claimed that he had been sent over to find out whether or not TATE was being controlled by the British. Richter also told MI5 that the Germans considered the information TATE had been passing over to be quite excellent, almost too good to be true. TATE, however, could not understand how the Germans could possibly suspect him and went over all his traffic to see whether he felt uneasy about any of the messages. He pointed out, however, that he had always been most careful about them and had sometimes criticised messages which MI5 had proposed sending and which he had thought might give the game away. Billy Luke recognised how: 'We have always seen his point and adopted his suggestion at least in a modified form except on one occasion, (message date 5 March) when we would not allow him to mention that several houses had been knocked down near the de Havilland works. He considered that as this information was of great interest to the Germans and the

damage was plainly visible from the air it was a mistake for us not
to pass it over.'

Luke found, after discussing the matter further, that TATE was
convinced that the Germans believed in him because: (a) their more
personal messages were friendly and sincere; (b) they sent a man over
to Britain at great risk to save his financial situation; and (c) they
finally paid him through the good offices of the Japanese Embassy
which they would never have done if they had had grave doubts
about his validity. TATE considered it likely that, having jumped
to the conclusion, the British controlled the TATE transmissions,
Richter was now trying to improve his own position by inventing a
story which, although quite untrue, might create the impression that
he was coming clean.[47]

Richter was hanged on 10 December 1941. MI5 were worried
as to how TATE would be react to being the key person involved
in a plan that was to lead to a man's execution. It fell to Billy
Luke to inform TATE that the person who was sent over by the
Germans to give him money would be hanged: 'I explained that he
had been captured very shortly after he had landed by parachute
on the 13th May and that apart from carrying a certain amount of
money for TATE and other agents he was also in possession of a
wireless set. Therefore he had landed in this country as a spy, had
been captured by the police and had to be prosecuted on these
lines. I told him that if his mission over here had simply been to
pay one of our controlled agents, the Intelligence Service would
had intervened and prevented the execution. I also told him that
his own conscience should be quite clear and that he should not
regard himself as having contributed in any way to this man's
death.' TATE was 'perfectly satisfied' with the explanation and
'profusely thanked' Luke for having warned him of the approaching
execution as he was convinced that the news would have been a
very severe shock to him if he had seen it for the first time in the
newspapers or had heard it without warning over the wireless.
Luke told TATE's watchers to be especially vigilant for the next
day or two but personally had no longer any anxiety about TATE's
reactions.[48]

As TATE was, in the early part of 1941 at this time notionally
unemployed – as far as the Germans were concerned – he was in a
position to travel about the country and answer their questions in
detail. From September 1941 the Germans expressed more and more
interest in agriculture and dairy farming, until in the summer of 1942
he was reporting chiefly on these matters, although in December

1941 he was exhorted to concentrate as much as possible on air force matters.[49]

In considering what to do with the case next, J.H. Marriott pointed out that TATE 'has been built up by us into a first class agent but on a low grade, i.e., the whole of his information is provided by himself and consists almost entirely of material which he can obtain by observation. For this reason it is impossible for him to put over any sort of operational and he is only capable of providing some sort of confirmatory evidence on rather a limited scale. For example, he could from observation, report that damage to aerodromes has been exceptionally heavy and so give general support to the major plan of drawing the enemy onto aerodrome targets. As matters stand therefore, the only use to which TATE can be put is the capture of other spies, and in using him we tend to supply the enemy with a very considerable amount of exceedingly useful information for which do not get much in return.' In order to remedy this situation it was agreed 'we must endeavour to promote TATE from a low to a high grade. It would be completely out of character to ensure this by suddenly providing him with highly placed contacts... and any suggestions that he had secured such contacts would, I think, at once arouse the enemy's suspicion.' He might, however, usefully be employed by the Germans mainly as a channel for transmitting information obtained by other agents in Britain with whom TATE himself would have very little connection.

Marriott thought that one way of getting the Germans to fall in with this plan would be for TATE to get himself into a position in which he found it impossible to devote his time to the task of obtaining information himself, and this could be reasonably fixed either by TATE pretending that he had become too nervous to do the work, or by his being compelled to undertake normal whole time employment either in industry or as a soldier. The story which he was supposed to have told about himself in Britain was that he was a British subject born and brought up in Denmark, who arrived as a refugee at the time of the German invasion. As a result, his age group would have registered for military service in about July of 1940, 'i.e., before he actually came here, and he must therefore be assumed, to reply to anybody who asked him why he is not in the army, that he did register in July, but that for some reason which he cannot explain, no step was taken to call him up, and that he has mislaid his certificate of having registered'. He could now say that as a result of a general comb-out, he had been required to have his medical examination and was therefore unlikely to be called up, but that he had been compelled to undertake whole time employment:

> He has managed to secure work on a neighbouring farm and although his is perfectly free to carry on with his transmissions in the evening, and may occasionally get a day off, it is now out of the question for him to undertake any journeys or to keep observations surrounding aerodromes. His own position he feels is absolutely secure, he has a first-class channel of communication and he is exceedingly anxious to carry on with his work. Have the Germans any really reliable person without a wireless set whom they would like to use his channel? If they have such a person and his discretion can be completely relied on, he himself would be willing to meet him and give him the benefit of his advice and experience as to the way he ought to go to work.

Marriott thought this plan 'might be acceptable to the Germans, more particularly if we approach it in rather a "cloak and dagger" spirit and insist upon the most elaborate cut-out arrangements between TATE and any persons who are to feed him with information'.[50]

As a result of a discussion between Robertson, Masterman, Marriott and Luke it was decided that TATE should send over a message informing the Germans that he had been forced to register for military service, and that his future activities would therefore necessarily be curtailed. The plan then called for him to send a second message stating that he had been successful in avoiding military service, but would have to do work of national importance on a farm. After outlining the scheme to him, Luke asked TATE to prepare a suitable message, or messages conveying a suitable story to the Germans. It was suggested that TATE should remain off the air until the information and the reply to the Germans questions on aerodromes in the Cambridge and Lincoln districts had been approved and was ready for transmission. He should then go over with his first crisis message, sending it all at one time. It was a long message, but TATE felt that he would get it off his chest as soon as he felt it was safe enough for him to do the transmission. He would then send information regarding the aerodromes, but after doing so for a day or two, he would go across with his second crisis message, after which he would continue sending the aerodrome information until it had been exhausted.[51]

On 12 September, after he had ostensibly returned from his visit to the North collecting information about certain aerodromes, TATE sent across the first crisis message at the 5.30 p.m. transmission time:

> Was caught in a police raid at Kings X Station. Police asked for Identity Cards of all travellers. On being asked whether I had yet registered for military service, I answered the truth – that is 'no', in order not to arouse suspicions by lying. They took the number of my Identity Card, my name, addresses, etc. I thought it wiser to give my real address to prevent closer investigation about the authenticity of my Identity Card, I was told to register at once otherwise I would be prosecuted. In order to prevent closer investigation, suspicion, or at the worst arrest and its accompanying investigations, there is nothing else to do but comply with their orders.

The reply came back on 13 September at 5.30 p.m. reading as follows:

> We are very anxious. Head up. Own safety first. Stop. Take into consideration the fact that you may be treated as a deserter as you have not followed the registration instructions. Further dangers are:– Personal particulars; parents; previous whereabouts... Consider whether it would not be better to disappear secretly from your lodgings... Possibly go to Northern Ireland for a time... In case of extreme urgency put an advertisement in THE TIMES every first of the month under Used Clothing Wanted, containing the words 'Dinner Jacket', Christian name of advertiser – William and address. Possibly you can make other proposals. Heartiest greetings. Hope you break arms and neck.

It should be noted that before receiving this message TATE had sent over some of the information about aerodromes which was supposed to have been collected before he was caught. On the morning of 16 September he transmitted:

> Today I intend to make a dangerous step. As this is most important for the future, please, only for today listen out at every full hour for 15 minutes. I ask for your utmost attention. If I do not come on I am 'in the soup'. Touch wood.

At 3 p.m. he informed the Germans that he would send them a message which he was coding, in an hour's time, and at 4 p.m. he sent the following:

> The following has happened. An acquaintance, the owner of a large farm with a modern dairy connected to it, who is of good family with important connections, the daughter of whom I was able to help out of an awkward situation, now recompenses me. After I had told him the story about my registration in highly coloured language and said the possibly unpleasant developments for me, he gave me a letter stating that I had been working for some time in his business and I had done him indispensable service and that my possible withdrawal would be irreplaceable to his firm and the nation. With this document I went to the local registration office and after showing it to them and first giving my explanation the official questioned me and asked my friend about my knowledge of agriculture, livestock, dairy work and farming machinery. As the officer was not very knowledgeable himself, it was easy for me to convince him of my first class qualifications. Contd.
>
> The consequence of this is that now, I, on one side, are no longer liable for military service as I am now busy on war work, but on the other side I must really enter in this firm at once as my friend's right-hand man; this of course is very inconvenient but is unavoidable and this must be understood by you for better or for worse. I am convinced that my friend, who possibly sees in me his future son-in-law will give me as much time and as free a hand as possible but the fact is that anyhow during the day I am tied and am unable to travel around. My opinion is that both for me and you it is worthwhile knowing that my position in this country is now stabilised and to a certain extent is justified, and I am almost safe regarding further enquiries but in spite of all this it is obvious that I must be very careful. My friend of course has not the slightest idea of my double life. Contd.
>
> I remain in my old living-place and can in future give the messages same as now. Of course I shall have to change my transmitting times in accordance with my working hours. You know I will use all my powers as far as possible for the sake of our cause but in future you must leave it to me and my intelligence how to do it and what to do. Finish.

In the middle of this message TATE gave the danger signal and went off the air for about three minutes before resuming transmission – the idea being that he was jittery. On 17 September at the afternoon transmission the Germans sent this message:

> Heartiest congratulations that everything has turned out so well. Nevertheless we recommend you to be on the alert and be careful. Break your legs and your neck.

Then on the morning of 18 September TATE said:

> Best thanks for messages. Am glad that the matter is settled and that you are not too disappointed. I personally feel much safe now and hope very soon to be useful again. Best greetings.

TATE told Billy Luke that he was 'quite satisfied that the Germans had swallowed the story'.[52] He was right. They had.

This represented a radical alteration in TATE's espionage career. In manoeuvring TATE in to agricultural employment MI5 had two main objects in view: (a) to restrict his freedom of movement and therefore his opportunities for obtaining information, since the latter had begun to reach a standard 'which was proving embarrassing', and (b) to induce the Germans to put other agents into touch with him 'since we believed that they would be unable to allow an agent with £20,000 and established W/T communication to remain virtually idle merely because he was unable to get information'. Nearly a year later, in August 1942, MI5 reviewed the case: with regard to the first object the Security Service had succeeded 'but in the second object we were, and have continued to be, wholly unsuccessful. No agent has been put in touch with TATE, nor has his traffic given any indication that the Germans are likely to put anybody in touch with him in the future.'

In these circumstances, if TATE was to play any part in a future deception plans, and in particular if he was to play the sort of high grade part to which he was entitled by virtue of the high degree of confidence which the Germans appeared to repose in him, it was necessary to consider once more improving his information. An examination of his traffic for the last ten months showed that, contrary to what might have been supposed, he had a surprisingly large number of sources of information of which, in J.H. Marriott's view, 'we have not taken sufficient account. Moreover the position which he is to be assumed to have occupied for the last year makes it reasonable for him to have some good contacts which can be developed. So far as the traffic is concerned, the following extracts relating to sources of information will show what I mean':

<u>1941</u>
30.9 Overheard in Savoy two... pilots
5.10 'Met an RAF Sergeant on leave.'
14.10 'Heard an RAF officer say – '(The context shows that TATE had been in personal conversation with the officer).
19.10 'Got into conversation with some Irish Guards.'
14.11 Overheard interesting conversation of two very high officers.
18.11 The first reference to MARY who works in 'a cipher department of one of the big ministries'.
23.11 Have been working my way slowly but surely in to the better circles in London... now matters well advanced.
25.11 'An RAF officer told me. '
18.12 Following rumour is current.
21.12 'Have heard that. (the information related to the position of A.A. Divisions and it is clear, therefore, that what he had heard had been the result of a conversation on the point).
29.12 'At Box Hill so and so is said to be the case.'
<u>1942</u>
2.1 Gives information about paratroop training in the Middle East.
11.1 'Overheard in a high class bar which I often visit.'
18.1 Have heard the parachute troops, etc.
22.1 A... Ferry Pilot told me.
28.1 Have heard that lately gliders have been active.
29.1 A naval Lieutenant told me.
1.2 Russian anti-tank plane is said, etc.
19.2 Mobile A.A. is said, etc.
26.2 Mobile A.A. is said, etc.
5.3 Heard from somebody about Wig Bay.
8.3 Heard from a good source (information about floating fortress off the east coast).
4.4 Introduced to a Norwegian ex-naval officer.
6.4 Overheard conversation of some naval officers.
19.4 MARY disclosed that she had been lent by her ministry to the Americans.
22.4 TATE received instructions to cultivate MARY and her circle of friends.

1.5 Heard that the railway line at Bath, etc.

8.5 Heard from MARY.

13.5 Met an officer from the RAF regiment.

31.5 MARY reports that.

19.6 Saw MARY yesterday.

22.7 MARY reports that.

28.7 TATE received instructions to make more use of MARY.

31.7 Had a party with MARY and met an American naval officer.

From all the foregoing it was quite clear that, as one might have expected, TATE had made a number of friends, presumably in London, with whom he could carry on conversations of more than a purely social character, and in many cases the sort of information which he gave must represent the result of quite a considerable number of meetings. In view of his good education and upbringing, and in view of the very solid background which he had from his farmer friend, 'it seems to me quite natural to assume that, as indeed he himself said as long ago as last November, he has acquired and been accepted by a wide circle of person whom he can meet by appointment. The only one that he has ever mentioned by name is MARY, of whom latterly he has been seeing a good deal, and I think that the time has come for us to furnish a number of his other friends with definite identities. In addition I think it would be quite reasonable for TATE by now to have been elected to some club since a club provides a perfectly normal and reasonable background for every conceivable sort of indiscretion on the part of well informed persons. The Junior Carlton suggest itself as a likely club. By now also one would expect TATE to have met one or two of the families living in his neighbourhood and it would not be surprising if some of the members of these were to prove to be persons working either in ministries, important war undertakings or at Lloyds.'[53] The building up of TATE, in this way, led to the formulation of Plan CARTER-PATERSON, the objects of which were: 1. to try to obtain a means to transmit documents etc to the Germans and 2. to convince the Germans that a portion of the minefield of the Faroes is more heavily mined than it is.

TATE was to send, on his W/T, messages to the following effect: that a 'Naval officer friend came to flat having arrived from mine laying expedition from Scotland. Stayed night and left unlocked bag in sitting room. In it were tracing of part of charts and pencil notes apparently for reports'. Preparation would be made ready to transmit the information 'if the Germans "bite"'.[54] And, of course they did; in fact they never wavered in their belief in TATE. After all they had already, in May 1941, rewarded TATE by arranging German naturalisation for him and awarding him the Iron Cross, lst and 2nd Class.[55]

6

The Fall of SNOW

By late 1940 there had been 'further interesting developments' in connection with the SNOW case and his sub-agents CHARLIE and GW. As early as the end of August 1940 the Germans had announced their intention of sending a wireless operator to assist CHARLIE in Manchester. A house was accordingly prepared for this man's reception in which was installed the transmitter which BISCUIT had brought back with him from Lisbon. In the end, however, this man, like the South African of whom BISCUIT had spoken previously, never arrived. Exactly 'what became of these two agents remains obscure', noted MI5; though according to SNOW's wireless traffic the South African was dropped at some time during the last week of August and CHARLIE's wireless operator on the night of the 15–16 December. So far as could be made out, both these men, if they were dropped, came down in the sea or at any rate in circumstances which left no trace of their arrival.

A similar misfortune appears to have overcome the three saboteurs whom the Germans suggested that they should send to assist GW in Swansea. Their impending arrival was first spoken of in July and thereafter continued to be referred to (though with some discrepancies as to the number of people involved) until 26 October, when the Germans announced that a man for Swansea would arrive in about a fortnight and would make contact with GW at the latter's address. No one did so but, on 12 November 1940, a little over a fortnight later, three Cubans – Robles, Martinez and Hechevarria – did arrive, overloaded with sabotage equipment, on the fishing smack *Josephine* at Fishguard. In the meanwhile, however, one actual emissary arrived in the person of the Spaniard del Pozo, who reached England on 27 September and, shortly after his arrival, addressed a letter to GW, in which he mentioned the password which had previously been agreed upon in connection with the men who were due to come to Swansea. When he heard this SNOW sent a wireless message asking for further details and was told that Del Pozo was a member of the COMMANDER's propaganda and sabotage organisation and was carrying money intended for SNOW. On 11 November a meeting took place between GW and del Pozo at which the latter handed over the sum of nearly £4,000. From then until the time of del Pozo's final departure at the beginning of February 1941, GW continued to have periodic meetings with him and even to pay him back sums of money in accordance with orders which SNOW received from Germany. GW also submitted to del Pozo detailed reports of his activities in Wales.

In the meantime SNOW himself, had been making arrangements with the Germans for a further meeting with the 'DOCTOR', this time to take place in Lisbon, and had undertaken to bring with him two further sub-agents or, as he preferred to say, 'side-kicks', one for instruction in Germany and one for a verbal consultation in Lisbon. On 15 February 1941, SNOW left by air for Lisbon, having been preceded a fortnight earlier by CELERY, one of the two 'side-kicks' referred to above. CELERY was an MI5 agent who had served during the last war in a branch of air intelligence 'but since then had shown a less satisfactory record and had been involved after his return to civil life in a number of dubious financial dealings. He was therefore able to represent to the Germans that he had a grudge against this country in as much as his record made it impossible for him to regain his commission in the air force. As he was an observant able man with a fluent knowledge of German he was regarded as being particularly suitable to undergo a course of training in Germany, from which we expected that he might bring back valuable information. Unfortunately these hopes were largely disappointed'. Instead, alarm bells began to ring again with regard to SNOW's loyalty. It led to the demise of SNOW's espionage career and his incarceration. Long after the SNOW case was liquidated, MI5 had to admit: 'We still do not know precisely what happened after SNOW arrived in Lisbon, but we can at least be certain that during his visit he compromised himself in some way with the Germans and that his career as a double agent came to an abrupt close.'[1]

In early April 1940, a Section B3 officer received a call from Special Branch concerning a British subject they had in detention at Richmond police station. The man, Walter Dicketts, from the East End of London, was arrested at Richmond South Railway Station by the CID officers of 'V' Division acting upon information forwarded by Special Branch, and had the following convictions recorded against him:

8-8-1921. Bound over in his own recognizances at Chesterfield Police Court for false pretences.
5-11-1921. Nine months and nine months (concurrent) at Central Criminal Court, London, for forgery.
16-10-1923. Bound over in his own recognizances at Central Criminal Court, London, for false pretences.
16-8-1925. Nine months imprisonment at Central Criminal Court, London for false pretences.

30-1-1925. Four months imprisonment and fined 500 francs (unreadable) chamber Tribunal of the Seine, France for swindling.
25-6-1930. Six months and six months (concurrent) and 6, 6 and six months (concurrent) at Marylebone Police court, London, for false (censored)... 18 months imprisonment at Hampshire assizes for obtaining money by false pretences.

Dicketts was again in trouble for trying to obtain money by false pretences. However, he stated that he wished to volunteer information of vital national importance. He described himself as a business agent who travelled extensively abroad, stating that he was educated at Southend-on-Sea High School and served in the Royal Naval Air Service and the Air Ministry Intelligence during the last war. Dicketts claimed that, around 16 March, 1940, while drinking in the 'Marlborough' Public House, Richmond, he casually entered into conversation with a man named Tom or Thomas Wilson whom Dicketts asserted was a German Secret Service agent. Dicketts claimed that he and his wife had befriended this German agent and his wife, with the former having lavished great hospitality and large sums of money on his newly found friends. Wilson had confided to Dicketts that he was 'the key man of the British Secret Service and that he is also the head of the German Secret Service in England'. Dicketts announced that he had visited Wilson's residence, which was watched over by a bodyguard of three, and where he had seen and heard a high powered transmitting and receiving wireless apparatus working. He also claimed to have been introduced to some business and Secret Service associates of Wilson and shown data and photographs of docks, airports and factories and details of British naval resources, presumably for the information of the German Secret Service. Wilson was supposed to have flown to Antwerp on 4 April, and was expected to return to England via Shoreham airport on 7 April where it was intended that Dicketts should meet him with his car at the aerodrome on his return. On hearing this Special Branch had communicated the information to MI5. Within a few hours, TAR Robertson had arrived at Richmond police station to interrogate Dicketts.[2]

B3 rang up the Deputy Chief Constable of Birmingham, Mr Johnson, in connection with the outstanding charges against Dicketts and told him, briefly, what had happened. MI5 were anxious, if possible, to get rid of Dicketts for some time and 'most anxious to try and prevent him from saying anything in the witness box in connection with the case of SNOW, which he might quite easily do in order to put in a plea of leniency'. Johnson assured MI5 he would do everything he could in order to prevent this form happening. At this stage, MI5's opinion of CELERY was that, 'although he is a rogue from a financial point of view and in other words a long firm fraud, he is loyal towards this country, his one motive being to try and get some sort of job in The Air Force' and in order to do this he saw his chance when he stumbled by luck across SNOW 'and his nest of German agents'.[3]

Dicketts now described, in more detail, his encounter with 'Mr Wilson'. On or about 15 March 1940, Dicketts was in the 'Marlborough' Public House, Friars Stile Road, Richmond, having a drink, when he got casually into conversation with a man – Mr Wilson. After a few minutes conversation he said to Dicketts: 'I can see that you have travelled a great deal' and he discussed at some length the countries in which Dicketts travelled and which he himself appeared to know intimately; the countries included America, Canada, France, Belgium, Holland and Germany. Shortly after, Wilson had a few drinks with him – 'for which he refused to let me pay – and he asked me to go with my wife to meet him at the public house that evening at 8 p.m. We spent the evening together and at 10 p.m. he invited us to play darts at his flat. We stayed at his flat until 1 a.m. the next morning during which time we consumed a considerable amount of liquor.' Before leaving the flat Wilson asked Dicketts to meet him again at the 'Marlborough'. He then told Dicketts he had very large available funds adding he was buying gold and diamonds as the pound was bound to fall in value. Wilson asked Dicketts what he did for a living; Dicketts replied that he was living on his very small means but that he had a proposed patent for ready-made mustard in tin containers similar to toothpaste. Wilson immediately said, 'That's an excellent idea and if my partner agrees I'll finance it.'

The following day Wilson apparently went to see his partner and upon meeting Dicketts he informed him that his partner was in full agreement and 'we would commence production of the patent just after Easter'. He also informed Dicketts that he had taken the trouble to lodge a provisional application at the Patent's Office. That evening Wilson took Dicketts and his wife out to the Richmond Theatre and then back to his flat for supper and drinks. After supper he took Dicketts into another room and told him he had taken 'a great liking to me and wanted my wife and I to accompany him on a five days motor trip to Devon and Bournemouth from Easter Thursday to the following Tuesday at his expense. I refused to go. He said, "Don't be silly, you can have whatever money you like from me".' Dicketts again refused and Wilson then suggested that they signed an agreement with regard to the mustard patent and advanced Dicketts some cash as a preliminary payment. 'Wilson signed the cash; Dicketts did not pass any remark as Wilson quietly said, pointing to the signature, 'I'll explain that another time.'

Dicketts and his wife went away with Wilson and his wife for five days during which they became very friendly and stayed at the Lansdowne Hotel, Bournemouth, The Castle Hotel, Dartmouth and the Boltons Hotel, Brixham. In each case Wilson signed the books and registration forms as 'T. Wilson'. On their return to London, Wilson asked Dicketts to visit his office in Sackville Street, West London, where he had a basement office run by his partner, a Swiss national and the late owner of Hatchetts Restaurant, Piccadilly. They discussed business but then Wilson informed Dicketts that it was impossible to proceed with the mustard patent as it was already on the market. This Dicketts knew to be untrue: 'I was very upset and he assured me that I had nothing to worry about as he could use me in other directions and money was no object.'

The following day, Wednesday 27 March, Wilson told Dicketts, in strictest confidence, that he was the key man in the British Secret Service; that the whole house where he lived belonged to him and that he had a bodyguard of three men living in the ground floor and basement flats. He then asked Dicketts what money he required to work for him, also instructing him to carry on normal business under his direction as a cover – not to alter his style of living; not to say a word to anyone; and not to move to any better address. Two days after this Wilson took Dicketts up to a locked top room at his address where he showed him a powerful receiving and transmitting wireless set. He tuned in to several countries including America and Germany and Italy: 'During this day he told me he knew all about me and I need not worry about anything.'

On Sunday 31 March, Dicketts and Wilson went out to celebrate the latter's fortieth birthday; Wilson paid all expenses. That night Wilson was very tired and the great amount of alcohol he had consumed somewhat overcame him. He told Dicketts that Germany was certain to win the war and that he and his wife were going to leave as soon as his work was completed in England; he also claimed he was 'Chief of the Secret Service over here' with unlimited resources. He then claimed that Germany was 'out for peace and that nationalities did not count'. Dicketts replied that any thinking man would sacrifice anything to stop the war.

Wilson told Dicketts that he was going to Germany on Thursday 4 April, and was importing batteries from Belgium to England, but he was going to drop it if he could get the necessary amounts of gin. 'He then asked me if I understood machine tools and heavy machinery.' On Wednesday morning, 3 April 1940, same day, Dicketts met Wilson at his house and they went together to Sackville Street, where Wilson told Dicketts to take a taxi, go to Victoria Street, and arrange to get some cheap whisky and gin which Wilson and his business partner were arranging to sell on, for a profit, using a printer to print new labels for the bottles. Dicketts left the office and:

[I] decided the time had come for me the get help from the British Secret Service and intended going to the Air Ministry to see Air Commodore Boyle, the Director of Intelligence with whom I had served in the Air Intelligence in the last war. While walking down Sackville Street, W, I noticed first one and then a second taxi draw out slowly. I therefore went into the Yorkshire Grey Hotel in Piccadilly, ordered a drink, came out, jumped into another taxi and told the driver '151 Victoria Street, via St James' Square, the Park and Palace Street' watching carefully through the back window. I saw two taxis following at intervals. To see if I could get a view of the occupants, I told my taxi to stop at the Phoenix in Palace Street. As he pulled up he said, 'You are being 'tailed' Guv'nor.' I thanked him and said I was on Government service.

After a five minute stay at the Phoenix, Dicketts re-entered the cab and went to 151 Victoria Street. After his interview there Dicketts walked out, crossed the road and into the Post Office 'when I noticed the taxi draw out. I stayed 5 minutes in the Post Office and realised it would be dangerous to go to the Air Ministry, so I jumped into another taxi and returned to Sackville Street, being followed all the way'. Dicketts informed Wilson 'that I had been followed – he was not worried until I mentioned two taxis – when he telephoned to a number, reported the fact and asked for a special watch to be kept. We walked out to the street, saw nothing suspicious... drove to Euston. He parked the car 160 yards from the station and I walked with him to the station buffet where he bought me a beer and a sandwich, gave me the keys of the car, told me to go back to it and wait' – while he met an agent from the North on the 1.50 p.m. train from Manchester. The agent was brought to the car by Wilson; he 'was obviously a German and appeared to be very scared. We went to the Sackville Street office and I was asked to leave the room for 10 minutes which I did. On my return I was admitted and saw on the table a large pile of photographic enlargements of apparently docks, airports and buildings, such as factories.

On the top of the photos was a roll of minute photographic film.' The photographs were put away and Wilson remarked, 'They are very good.' Wilson then gave Dicketts a paper and pencil and asked him to copy a thing sheet of paper which he had handed to him and which contained dates and details of approximate tonnages and maximum gun power. The list was then burned and Wilson took Dickett's list 'and that was the last I saw of it'.

Wilson then said he wanted a new photo enlarger which would cost £68. He took a roll of £1 notes from his pockets, gave the requisite money to the agent from the North and told Dicketts to take him in a taxi to the large photographic shop opposite Chappell's music shop in Bond Street. The agent went into the store by himself and Dicketts said he would get a drink. Dicketts stepped across to Chappell's, asked the manager for his private phone on Government business and contacted Air Ministry Intelligence. Air Commodore Boyle, whom Dicketts was trying to contact, was not in, 'but I was asked to state my business as I had said it was urgent. I replied that I could not speak on the phone, but would contact the next day.' Dicketts then bought two sheets of music for Wilson who was 'a keen but bad amateur pianist'. He then went across the road into the photographic store where the German was arranging to change his present enlarger for some money and a new one. While he was doing this, 'a tall man in a Burberry mackintosh was standing at the counter near the entrance focussing bay cameras in our direction and I am of the opinion that he was photographing us'.

Later that night Wilson warned Dicketts again of secrecy, gave him an open cheque for £10 (which his wife cashed the next morning) and instructed Dicketts to call for him at 8 a.m., Thursday 4 April, and go with him to Victoria and see him off on the 9.45 a.m. to Shoreham Aerodrome. Dicketts did so; Wilson did not talk in the train going up and said practically nothing on Victoria Station platform. Wilson carried one small attaché case. Just before the train left for Shoreham, he told Dicketts' to stay with my wife at his flat and look after his wife. He said he would notify her whether he was returning Sunday or Monday and might require me to meet him at Shoreham with the car. His last words were, 'If I am successful I shall be able to do anything I like. I'll give you instructions on my return and you will never have anything to worry about.' He had previously asked me to attend at Sackville Street at noon on the day he left, to meet a woman – I think her name was Mrs Thompson-Clarke, give him my impressions of her as he intended to put up the money for her to buy and run the Rialto Club in Rupert Street.'

After Wilson – whom Dicketts now knew was really Arthur Owens (SNOW) – left, Dicketts went to the Air Ministry. He was shown up to the Intelligence Department, but was told by Air Commodore Boyle's assistant that he was in conference and could not be seen. Dicketts then asked the assistant to put him in touch with the Secret Service, 'telling him that I thought I was in with the heart of the German Secret Service in this country. He asked me to come back in an hour and a half, see the Air Commodore and put the matter down on paper. I told him I was afraid to do this, but would call on Monday or Tuesday morning next when I expected to have full information re Owen's return and the other agents concerned. I then left him and on my way out met Air Commodore P.I.F. West, VC, an old friend of mine. I told him of the situation and he said, "I will mention it to Boyle and help you in any way I can to get back to the Service. If you bring this off you will be alright."

Dicketts then went to Sackville Street, and a few minutes later a very stout, tall, smart woman called and was introduced to him as Mrs Thomson-Clarke. She said Lady Gort and Jack Warner, the BBC performer, would open the club for her and that she could get society and naval and military people at once to join the club. She had a list of 100 ready. Dicketts then left to obtain forms for a wholesale wine and spirit licence and to carry on obtaining options on cheap whiskeys, gins, etc.

One evening Dicketts and SNOW returned to the latter's flat 'and as we past in the hall of the flat I heard radio signals from the floor above. Seeing that I noticed this he motioned to me to keep silent and said in a whisper, "They are working it tonight". He gave me the impression the messages were coming from Germany and that possibly a colleague was working in the wireless room. He had previously told me he was in constant wireless touch with Germany. He also said I had to be careful of my conversation in the sitting room of the flat as there was a Dictaphone record of all conversations made.' SNOW frequently said that the RAF successes reported 'are chiefly lies; the machines were not nearly so successful or as fast as the Germans; British pilots are refusing to go up and several officers have been court-martialled and shot; dissatisfaction is rife in the British Army in France and wealthy British people are sending their money out of the country as fast as they can; British currency is at the lowest value ever and will continue to fall, the dollar at the moment being 3.20; Hitler has Germany solidly behind him; stores, oils etc, were sufficient for 10 years at least; the German Army privates are being paid over £4 per week, and there is no doubt Germany will win the war.'[4]

Before Dicketts could make another move to contact the authorities they contacted him – by arresting him. For Dicketts had been correct in thinking he had been watched and tailed. The police had found out some of his details and checked a Passport Control circular which showed quite clearly that Dicketts had criminal records. It was after he had been arrested that Dicketts volunteered he had important information concerning national security in his possession with regard to a man he had recently been in touch with. MI5 were also informed. The authorities had been alerted to Dicketts for SNOW, once again, had demonstrated his inability to keep his mouth shut – an unfortunate trait in a spy. The authorities quickly established that, as far as his connection with SNOW was concerned, Dicketts 'was trying to obtain as much money from him as possible and was at the same time genuinely trying to find out as much about that matter as he could'.[5]

Fortunately Dicketts was let off with a £5 fine in Birmingham, so SNOW was not dragged into the case. Dicketts made his way back to London to pick up his wife. He went to SNOW's flat where 'there was a tremendous row but... ultimately' SNOW and Dicketts had 'become good friends again'. Dicketts was told by MI5 to remove himself at once from the flat and never return to the address again. Fortunately, Dicketts was under the impression that MI5 had assisted him considerably in letting him off with a £5 fine at Birmingham. Special Branch warned Dicketts not to mention, to anyone, what he now knew about SNOW. The Security Service, in the meantime, began to make enquires about seeing what could be done 'to influence the Air Ministry to give him some sort of job'.[6]

This was how Walter Dicketts was recruited as a XX agent by MI5. He was given the codename CELERY. In December 1940, CELERY was told by TAR Robertson that he should give his full attention to his new role – watching SNOW – for 'it was exceedingly important from every point of view that we should find out definitely whether SNOW is double-crossing us or not'. CELERY 'asked me if I had complete trust in him... to which I replied that I had'. CELERY warned that SNOW 'is very artful and is laying traps' to try and find out why CELERY had been put into touch with him. He also warned that SNOW was 'drinking very heavily, bottles of whisky disappearing like magic'. CELERY caught him one morning pouring out whisky into a tumbler at half past seven in the morning. SNOW, it seemed, was flush with money and was buying Lily a fur coat for Christmas valued at £1,500. Gradually, it was noted, 'the general atmosphere is improving' and CELERY 'is being accepted again into the bosom of the family. Apart from this he says that SNOW is an inveterate liar and lies even to his wife about everything. He is terrified of air raids and is bone idle.'[7]

By January 1941, CELERY was working under the instructions of SNOW – or so SNOW thought; in fact he was still reporting on SNOW to MI5. CELERY reported that SNOW was expecting news 'from the other side' with regard to the invasion of Britain and he was 'particularly anxious that their wives should not be left in this country without some adequate protection'. SNOW had made arrangements for them to be looked after in the event of an invasion when SNOW and CELERY were away and had given Lily a list of names of people with whom she could get into touch.[8]

CELERY was anxious that some sort of agreement should be drawn up between himself and MI5 which would give him some form of guarantee. It would ensure that, in the event of his being killed during any journey, his wife and child would be looked after. CELERY's idea was that MI5 should pay a sum of £3 10s a week for life or the equivalent which would amount to approximately £6,000. Brigadier Harker agreed to stand by him up to £2,000 while Dick White suggested that SIS be approached and asked to put up a similar sum. Captain Cowgill of SIS gave the initial agreement.

CELERY and SNOW were told by Robertson that, if it was at all possible to get information from Rantzau or anybody in Lisbon for that matter, about the impending invasion of Britain 'this would be of real assistance'. It would also be of great value 'if we could have any information relating to their secret weapons. We then had a long discussion of how SNOW could get CELERY to be taken into Germany for some training. I said that I was anxious for CELERY to go in as I thought his presence there would be of considerable assistance as he would be able to pick up a great deal of information.' SNOW was reassured that whatever happened to him during the time that he was away 'our obligation would be honoured as far as his wife and child were concerned'.[9] Robertson felt that few instructions could be given to CELERY, with regard to his visit to Lisbon, but he was told to be very careful and not to take anything with him which would arise the suspicions of the authorities there 'as they are getting very sticky'. He had a business cover that Robertson considered 'extremely good and quite adequate'. Robertson then handed him over to Cowgill and SIS.[10]

When it was known that SNOW and CELERY were returning by aeroplane from Lisbon, and would be arriving at Whitchurch on Tuesday 18 March, the Security Service arranged for both SNOW and CELERY to be searched thoroughly on arrival at the port; accordingly instructions were sent via D4 to the SCO Bristol, Major Stratton. Poole was also covered as also was Braunton. It was agreed that after they had passed through the controls they should be separated and interrogated separately at different places. Robertson prepared to leave London on Tuesday morning and proceed straight to the Regional Officer's office in Bristol accompanied by a representative of SIS. The party arrived in Bristol at about 2.15 p.m. and got into touch with Major Stratton's office, only to be told that the aeroplane, which had left Lisbon that morning, had had to return to Lisbon owing to bad weather conditions. The party decided to wait until the following day, in Bristol; but news was received at 11 a.m. the next day, that there would be no aeroplanes leaving Lisbon owing to the weather conditions. For various reasons, it was decided that the party should return to London. Finally, on Thursday morning, the news was received that weather conditions in Portugal were much better and that the aeroplane had in fact left Lisbon and that SNOW and CELERY were on board.[11]

When the plane touched down, Major Stratton, in accordance with a pre-arranged plan made with Robertson, visited the agents. SNOW was examined first by Stratton and stated that he had been to Portugal to purchase sardines. This was a complete contradiction of his story on departure, 'when he had told us that he was a manufacturer's agent. We asked SNOW why he had not obtained a Consular endorsement on his passport, particularly as he had been in close contact with the Consul in the course of his business. He could give no satisfactory explanation and we then asked him to produce all his documents and money. He declared £10 and various papers. We then told him that we were not satisfied and we regretted that we would have to examine him more thoroughly. On hearing this, SNOW asked to speak to us privately, without the Immigration Officer being present.' He then stated that he was employed by Major Robertson of MI5 and suggested that they should telephone to him. He had previously stated that he was travelling with CELERY who was his secretary, and he now added that CELERY was carrying some extremely important papers and that he could not understand why he had not been met at the airport.

An officer of the Bristol CID was then asked to search SNOW, and it was explained to him that it was impossible to obtain rapid communication with London, and as they had received no advice of his arrival, they had to safeguard themselves in view of his suspicious conduct. They promised to put a call through immediately, but in the meantime they would have to proceed with the search. SNOW was then stripped and thoroughly searched. He was carrying a large number of articles in his pockets, including £10,000 in notes. He also had two fountain pens in a leather case in his waistcoat pocket which he stated were very dangerous and contained explosives. All the contents of his pockets were placed into envelopes and sealed in his presence. A similar search was then carried out on his baggage and a large number of other alleged explosives were discovered. These articles were treated in a similar manner to the contents of his pockets.

CELERY was next examined and was 'very nervous and ill at ease'. Care was taken that he did not contact SNOW after the latter had been examined. CELERY stated that he was a manufacturing agent returning from Lisbon. He was also questioned concerning the absence of a Consular endorsement, 'and he also asked to speak to us privately. He then stated that he could not understand why we had not been advised of his arrival and that SNOW was working for him. This was a contradiction of SNOW's previous statement. We explained that we were far from satisfied with SNOW and that we very much regretted having to subject him to a similar treatment. We had told him that we had booked a telephone call to endeavour to confirm both their credentials.' CELERY was then searched and the contents of his pockets sealed up in a similar manner to SNOW. His baggage was also dealt with similarly.

At this point Major Robertson's MI5 officers, 'arrived' and CELERY who had resented the search was placated. Now that his *bona fides* had been established, CELERY was told about the explosives in SNOW's bag. CELERY was astonished to hear this information and said that he had no knowledge of it. CELERY also asked Major Stratton to communicate the following information to Robertson immediately: 'Three 12,000 ton transports leaving Elbe 28th probably early morning. Carrying troops to assemble in Netherlands. Troops were to assemble 26.3.41.' This information was passed on by Stratton. The MI5 officers present then took CELERY to London by car and took all the sealed belongings of both men with them. Stratton, accompanied by one of the officers, took SNOW to the Regional Commissioner's office where a car had been arranged to go to London.[12] The official interrogations then began.

According to CELERY, he arrived in Lisbon, on Friday 21 February and went direct as per instructions to the Metropol Hotel. There were no messages for him, and when he was registering the 'Little Man' – SNOW – arrived. This was by accident as he was going out. The Germans, it seemed, had given up on CELERY. But he was now taken to a house where he was introduced to the Doctor. His real name, apparently, was Jantzen. CELERY described him as 5ft 10in., broad, forty-six years-old, grey eyes, round face, perfect teeth, ash blond wavy hair, very thick, spoke English perfectly and colloquially with a strong middle-west American accent. The 'Little Man' had been drinking very heavily and the Doctor immediately poured CELERY out half a tumbler of whisky. The Doctor then brought in another man whom he introduced to CELERY as Senor Duarte, but whom he knew later to be Johan Dobler and who was 'the chief outside man' for the German Secret Service in Lisbon. The house was Dobler's house and he was living with a Portuguese girl of nineteen who was violently anti-British as her father was killed by a British car two years before and she had had no compensation. Dobler was a man of fifty-two, 6ft tall, had hair nearly grey, a pronounced nose but not hooked, slightly protruding teeth with a heavy gold setting in the left side of the upper denture. He had been serving in South America for many years and came back to Germany six months after the declaration of war. He was then sent to Lisbon as he spoke fluent Portuguese and Spanish – and English with a pronounced foreign accent.

The Doctor then said that he had been informed of CELERY's photographic memory and that he could be of great value to them if he was loyal and sincere. He would like CELERY to come to Germany for instruction and to see for himself how differently the people were governed and what great satisfaction there was there. CELERY expressed his willingness to go and the Doctor replied that he would arrange for CELERY to leave within forty-eight hours. They then got into Dobler's car, a grey Opel saloon, and drove to a house in Estoril which was, apparently, the Doctor's headquarters when he was in Lisbon. More whisky was produced and CELERY was interrogated by the Doctor on what he knew about the RAF's Beaufighter and infra-red detectors. CELERY told him that he was afraid that he should disappoint him 'as I had received no instructions before leaving England from the Little Man for the obvious reason that the Little Man was afraid to expose his hand to me until he was sure of me'. The Doctor accepted that this could not be helped but that they would give CELERY instructions as to what was required on his next visit.

The following morning, Saturday, CELERY went with 'Senor Duarte' to have his photograph taken and was taken to the German Embassy and introduced to von Kramer, the head of the German Service in Lisbon. He was about fifty, with a smooth face, small mouth and nose, partially shaved head, 5ft 11in. height, weight about 14 stone, blue eyes with 'rather a florid complexion'. His headquarters were in a house immediately behind the German Embassy and approached by the left hand gate of the Embassy garden. He arranged for CELERY to be sent to Germany on a Frenden–pass in the name of Walter Anton Denker of the same age and birthday as his own, his occupation being a merchant seaman and that he was a survivor from the *Siguerra Campos*. The Portuguese police 'were obviously' in German pay as CELERY's entry and exit visas were arranged the same day and his passport was handed to him on Monday morning. On Sunday, CELERY had a quieter day and went for a ride to Situbal with Dobler and his girl. He was gently reminded many times that 'my loyalty would be rewarded considerably but that if I was double crossing it would be unfortunate'.

On Monday, CELERY was informed that he must be at Estoril station at 6 a.m. on Thursday where he would be picked up by a dark Ford V8. He packed and said goodbye to the Little Man 'and then laid a trap for him. I told him that I was aware of certain secret information about aerodromes, the Beaufighter and the convoy routes. I said to him: "Shall I tell them all this immediately when I arrive in Hamburg or shall I keep something back so that you have information to give yourself?" He said: "No. On no account give any information of that kind. Tell them anything that you have been instructed to tell them but don't tell them these things that are likely to cause us loss of life." I was inclined to be suspicious of this as I thought he was safeguarding himself should we come back together and that he would probably notify the Germans so that they would question me on these matters when I arrived, and he would thus safeguard himself from the British point of view. However, the Germans asked none of these questions.'

The following morning CELERY was picked up at 6.30 a.m. by the black Ford V8. The driver introduced himself as yet another 'doctor' – Dr Hans Ruser. He was 5ft 10½in. in height, thirty-six years-old, 'had a swarthy complexion, slightly hooked nose and very bad discoloured teeth'. He was the Councillor to the German Embassy in Lisbon but did work for the Secret Service without the knowledge of his Minister. For the first half hour he coached CELERY in his behaviour at the Spanish-Portuguese frontier. Ruser was travelling as Embassy courier and consequently their bags or the car would not be touched: 'He was very nervous and asked me not to speak other than to say: Ja or Nein, and that he would go on talking all the time.' He told CELERY a little about himself, how he had done many favours for the Secret Service but it would probably lose him his position if it were known to the German Minister in Lisbon. He spoke fluent English with a strong American accent as he was in America from the age of five to fourteen. Apparently, he was very well connected. He was also 'violently anti-Nazi' and was not a member of the Party, and 'very pro-English' with relations in England to one of whom he gave CELERY a letter. For the second half an hour he was 'very cool and informed me quite bluntly that he did not like travelling with a traitor. I then informed him that in my opinion I was not a traitor as I had great admiration for the German system of Government and intense disagreement with my own and that I was prepared also on account of my Irish mother to go to any lengths to stop the war and I was certain Germany would win. He then changed his attitude entirely and agreed with me. He said that he hoped for the same thing himself as he was so fond of England and while being anti-Nazi in every way considered that Hitler was the saviour of Germany and could be the saviour of Europe. He also said that he was sure that Hitler was sincere in his desire for peace with England and had no territorial ambition in Europe other than Austria, Czechoslovakia and Poland.'

The two men were on very friendly terms by the time they reached the Portuguese frontier. Ruser was well known there and they were bowed through. The same thing happened at the Spanish frontier. They arrived in Madrid at 6.30 p.m. on Tuesday 25 February. On arrival they went to the German Embassy. CELERY was taken in and given a cocktail by Lieutenant Meyerduner, the Air Attaché. He was introduced to him as a repatriated German-American. CELERY's permit from Spain was then signed and he flew in the early morning on a Junkers 52 to Barcelona. In Barcelona, CELERY was taken to the Consulate and introduced to Dr Fischer who was travelling to Berlin the next day with his wife and the Baroness von Elten. Dr Fischer was Chancellor of the Embassy and the Consul was Waldheim 'who is violently pro-British and is in trouble with Germany'. Waldheim thought that Britain would win the war and hoped that Hitler will be assassinated. Twice Waldheim had been asked to return to Berlin and had refused on the grounds of ill-health. Ruser told CELERY that they did not wish to remove Waldheim from office while he was out of the country as he was very popular in Spain ('and Germany is _not_ popular'), particularly in Barcelona.

The following morning Dr Fischer called for CELERY at 6.30 a.m. and they went to the airport where seats were reserved in a 4-engine Heinkel. During the journey he became very friendly with Fischer and his wife, both of whom spoke fluent English and, while extremely pro-Hitler, were anxious to see the war over. They stopped at Lyon for refuelling and CELERY left the airport by himself and had a drink in a French café. They reached Stuttgart just after lunch and there Dr Fischer saw CELERY through passport control. CELERY reached Berlin – by himself – at about 4.30 p.m. and was just leaving for a hotel when he was greeted by an American who introduced himself as George Sinclair. The man's real name, as CELERY later discovered, was, in fact, Sessler. He was 6ft tall, dark wavy hair, 'good looking in a small featured way', good teeth and a four inch scar across his left cheek just under the eye (not a Schmiss). He was twenty-six years of age.[13]

CELERY was, initially, interrogated by Sessler – although the civilised nature of the 'interrogation' is illustrated by how CELERY then sat down for dinner with his interrogators. This, and subsequent interrogations, usually revolved around CELERY's record in the last war, what friends and contacts he possessed in Germany, and what he had been doing since 1930. On the fourth morning the DOCTOR himself appeared – having been away in Berlin – apologised for the interrogation and asked would CELERY be kind enough to go over the whole story with him again, as he had not been present. In the evening CELERY was again taken out to dinner as the Germans understood that he liked lobster and they thought he was a little tired. They asked him questions during dinner, which they had in a private room.

The following morning the interrogators were interested in air force matters. Dr Decker was the air expert. Standing about 5ft 6in., with an intensely pale face, protruding teeth and thick, ash coloured hair, 'he was violently anti-English, and showed great hostility' to CELERY. As he did not speak English very well, the interrogation was 'rather long'. CELERY explained again to the DOCTOR that not having had instruction from the Little Man he had very little information. Dr Decker showed 'extreme disbelief' at CELERY'S apparent ignorance, but the DOCTOR told him not to worry, as he realised that CELERY had had insufficient instruction. The next morning CELERY was informed that 'I had passed the test, and that they were prepared to trust me.' He was warned by Dr Schwartz to do nothing foolish, but that he could go about Hamburg unaccompanied. They suggested that they should take him round Hamburg to see the air raid damage, and the DOCTOR 'accordingly lent me his personal car, a black Wanderer and the latest model'. They then said that if CELERY got into any trouble he would be got out of it immediately, and that they would give him the telephone number of headquarters, to be mentioned only to the chief of police in any district if he happened to be arrested – they would then see that he was released immediately. CELERY toured Hamburg that morning, and was asked to direct the car himself. He saw very little air raid damage, the chief being two streets of houses in St Pauli, and a hospital on the other side of the Altona bridge.

CELERY was extremely disappointed at the lack of damage to Hamburg docks because although he was escorted on this occasion he had subsequent occasions of visiting the docks by himself and although the Germans repaired damage immediately and quickly they could not repair or disguise serious structural damage. In the evening

CELERY was taken out for a comprehensive tour of the dance halls and nightclubs of Hamburg. Starting with the Hofbrauhaus; dinner at a restaurant just behind the Alsterhaus 'well known and expensive'; then on to Igenier, Walhalla, Trichter and various small nightclubs. Although this was not a recognised day (as dancing was only permitted on Wednesday, Thursday and Saturdays) all these places were very nearly full, the major proportion being men in uniform and the hostesses of the various places. This night, as CELERY was left by Sessler at 4.45 p.m. to take a girl home, the agent was caught in a raid and was ordered by the police to go down to the air raid shelter under the Hauptbahnhof. In the shelter CELERY met three German staff officers and a junior officer. They talked with him, firstly in German and then in English, and finding out that he was a repatriated German-American 'asked me for my opinion on the Lease Lend Bill and the possibility of America coming into the war'. CELERY was purposely very vague and they did most of the talking. They informed him that the German territorial hold on Europe was so strong that the coming in of America would only serve to prolong the war and would not make any difference to the ultimate victory of Germany. Their opinion was that the war would end that year unless the American fleet helped convoy food and materials to England. CELERY stayed in the shelter until 7.20 p.m. and walked back to his hotel, arriving about 7.30 p.m.

The following morning the DOCTOR and Dr Decker arrived at 10 a.m. approximately with a complete book of the aerodromes of England. Each photograph had a page attached to it with an index of the 'most condensed information' of the buildings and personnel of the aerodromes. CELERY was asked to go through this in detail to see if he could supply any extra information that they had not already got. By now, he 'was getting very worried about this as I had continually to make the same excuse'. The DOCTOR, however, after spending two hours with him seemed convinced that CELERY had no knowledge but asked him to memorise certain factors and try and obtain the knowledge when he returned to England. Here Decker again showed his obvious disbelief and dislike and had an argument with the DOCTOR. The DOCTOR told him to mind his own business and to leave the room. The DOCTOR turned to CELERY and reassured him: 'Don't worry about this at all. I am looking after you and I am only responsible to Herman Göring. These people will all do as I tell them.'

CELERY was then asked to accompany the DOCTOR to dinner with his wife that evening explaining that he had booked seats at the Hansa Theatre. He arranged to send his chauffeur for 6.30 p.m., and told CELERY that he could have the afternoon off and have a tour around Hamburg by himself. The German laughed, and said, 'See if you can find any air raid damage, because I shall be most interested to know where it is.' The DOCTOR's car called for CELERY and he met the DOCTOR at the Ritz Bar, where he was introduced to the 'Baroness', his wife. CELERY was left during dinner to talk to her. She was a thin woman of about thirty-five, with a thin face and a thin, high bridged, hooked nose, and grey-green eyes. She dressed very well, was about 5ft 8in., and spoke very good English with a strong Bavarian accent. CELERY found her quite pro-British, hating the war, and was worried over her husband's work; the DOCTOR appeared devoted to her. In the box at the Hansa Theatre they talked of CELERY's wife and he was asked to bring her to Germany on his next visit, so that she would be safe from reprisals in England should CELERY be found out, or should the invasion suddenly take place.

The following evening was less high-brow. CELERY went out with Sessler to the Trichter and afterwards to the Young Nazi Political Club. They stayed there until 5.30 a.m., drinking and singing, by which time the entire club was in a state of drunkenness and quarrels. Some of them took great exception to CELERY, and wanted to fight, as he was an American. CELERY suggested to Sessler that they should fight their way out, but he said no, and then produced his police permit, called the ringleaders together, and warned them on concentration camps, and told them they were the worst kind of Germans. One man then called him a few filthy names, so Sessler, who was a first class boxer, hit him twice and knocked him out. 'We left the club in silence, and went home.'

The following morning CELERY was taken to meet Dr Gobbels's assistant at the Ministry of Propaganda. This man was about 5ft 10in., grey, very deaf, with many gold teeth. His eyes were hidden behind thick-lensed glasses; he had 'a medium complexion and a very boisterous disposition'. He was not introduced to CELERY by name, but did play him records of German parodies of 'We're Going to Hang Out the Washing on the Siegfreid Line', and gave him two pamphlets which he asked CELERY to present personally or send by post to Winston Churchill! Unsurprisingly, given his nocturnal activities, CELERY was feeling ill that afternoon, and went to bed, and stayed in by himself in the evening.

The following morning CELERY had his final interview with the DOCTOR, who informed him that he had been passed as their agent, and that he was leaving for Berlin the same day. He then had his photograph taken and a Diplomatic passport nominating CELERY as an Embassy Courier was produced. CELERY was sworn to secrecy about this, as it was done without the knowledge of the German Foreign Office.

CELERY travelled to Berlin by the afternoon express with Herr Sessler; a double suite had been reserved for them there at the Hotel Adlon. After another night drinking they came home at 5 a.m., and at 6 a.m. left for Templehof. At Templehof they had a reserved compartment on another 4-engined Heinkel which stopped at Stuttgart for passports and customs. They then proceeded to Lyons, Barcelona and Madrid without incident, except that Sessler became more and more friendly with CELERY, and said that he would like to get out of Germany and come to England. Sessler, it seemed, as well as being pro-British and pro-American was at loggerheads with all his department except the DOCTOR himself, of whom he was very fond.

They left Madrid and got to Valencia at eight in the morning on the Portuguese frontier. Travelling with them in their first class compartment was an English woman, repatriated from Marseilles. Her name was Mrs Marcelle Quenall, a slim ash blonde about 5ft 10in., twenty-eight years-old, extremely good looking 'with a regular small nose, regular teeth, medium mouth'. Sessler was very taken with her. He had a large bottle of Gordon's Gin and offered her a Gin Fizz. She replied that she would not drink with a German – the two men had been talking in German and in English with an American accent. The passport officials came into their compartment and seeing the Diplomatic passports and embassy bags passed them out with bows and no formality. Sessler then asked Mrs Quenall if she needed any money as she had been mentioning her terrible journey from Marseilles. She said: 'No, thank you.' But she had been studying CELERY intensely during the whole journey. They were met at the frontier by Dobler who had brought his Alicia with him.

The following evening CELERY was in the bar lounge of the Metropol in Lisbon and was talking to the Little Man and other people in obvious English when he turned round and saw Mrs Quenall listening to them. CELERY excused himself from his party and said he would be away for an hour or two. He then spoke to Mrs Quenall and asked her to have dinner with him. Rather reluctantly she agreed. CELERY took her outside into a car and then said: 'I am sorry to have to be unpleasant but I want your passport.' She was a little frightened. She said to him: 'I think you are obviously an Englishman.' He replied: 'It is none of your business, and since you are reliant on your stay here on your weekly allowance from the British Consul I would strongly advise you to forget everything you have seen or heard.'

CELERY then took all the details from her passport including the various foreign visas and asked her for a story of herself. She revealed she was a Belgian who was married to an Englishman and was now divorced from him. She had a French fiancé in Paris who was of military age and whom she was anxious to get out of the country to join the British forces. She asked for CELERY's help in this matter. CELERY took her to dinner and in the course of conversation she said to him: 'I am not a fool and I think you must be working for the British Secret Service on account of what I have seen in the train.' She further said: 'It is a service I would like to work for and I tried to do so in Paris, but my request went through a man who is not well liked and I was probably turned down for that reason.' She spoke fluent and colloquial English, French and German, all without accent; indeed her English was like an Englishwoman of birth and education as she had been at school in England. CELERY promised to forward her request and she gave him her word in return to ignore the whole episode. He eventually found that she was entirely without funds or baggage and living at a fourth rate hotel in the rua Douradoures, Hotel Franco. She was obviously ill and so CELERY got her a doctor, for she had a high temperature; he paid for fruit and medicine and gave her 200 Escudos. CELERY believed her to be sincere and thought she would be 'very valuable as she is attractive and accomplished'. CELERY saw her again before he left and found that she had been questioned about him by a Frenchman, called Regnault. CELERY found that she had kept her word as she only told Regnault – as he in turn told CELERY with surprise – 'that she was an old friend of mine with many years standing and knew me as a British commercial agent for export and import trades'. CELERY immediately asked Regnault about the Little Man and was told that he had been drunk consistently and very worried since CELERY left on his tour abroad. CELERY commented: 'I think you are making a very great mistake as I have been to Situbal, Badagos and Oporto.' But the Frenchmen replied: 'Who is this man [SNOW?]. He tells me that he is in the British Secret Service and can immediately give me lucrative employment.'

CELERY was not expecting anything like this; apparently the Little Man had been acting as mediator between an Englishman, called Patrick Nolan and his wife as the wife was contemplating running away with Regnault who was now complaining: 'He has taken my woman away from me after advising her to separate from her husband.' CELERY replied that he had 'never heard such nonsense in my life'. CELERY had already had been told that SNOW had been extremely ill 'and could only suppose that a man of his brilliant brain and business intelligence has also had Lisbon fever with his heavy drinking and has gone temporarily out of his mind'. CELERY convinced Regnault that this Secret Service story was rubbish and that he would try and persuade SNOW to help him further.

Shortly afterwards CELERY had a message to go to the Arcadia which was Lisbon's chief nightclub, to meet SNOW. CELERY found him there with two German dancing girls. SNOW was 'obviously very relieved' to see him, and CELERY was later informed by several people that 'he had worried himself to the point of a nervous breakdown about me during my absence'. They stayed in the Arcadia until 6 a.m. when SNOW informed CELERY that the two German girls were German agents whom he had to watch very carefully. One of the girls' names was Sophie and the other one was Ruth. Ruth informed CELERY that Lottie Schade whom he had previously met at the Arcadia had been worrying about him while he was away on business and had taken a great liking to him. She said: 'I must go and telephone Lottie and tell her you are back.' CELERY found Ruth good looking 'in a heavy Germanic way' with light natural red hair, broad flat nose, and large mouth with beautiful teeth. She spoke good English, French, Portuguese and Spanish. With a medium large figure, hard face, aged about thirty she had recently arrived in Lisbon from Tangiers where she and Sophie had been doing a 'Speciality Act' at the Casino Cabaret.

Sophie was a dark ash-blonde with an open face, high cheek bones, a very slightly hooked nose, slim waist but medium full figure. She looked twenty-eight but confessed to thirty-six and two children. She drank heavily and was drunk in CELERY's company; this gave him the information that although Lottie Schade 'was so simple and looked upon as the baby she was the chief of the troop' and that they had been ordered by the German Embassy to return for a time to Berlin. Later Lottie Schade arrived and monopolised CELERY. Lottie did not arrive until after Ruth was completely drunk and was furious with her. Lottie then stayed with CELERY until 5 o'clock and had been apparently informed of his activities as she gave him her address in Berlin and said: 'Should you be in Berlin while I am there, it may be a week or two you must write to me. If not, I will write to you in Lisbon when you come back.' None of this CELERY reported to the Little Man or to Dobler. These three girls had to leave, apparently, for Berlin because their work permit had been refused by the Portuguese Ministry of Labour. CELERY discovered, however, that this was not true as Ruth was staying in Paris and working with a man known as Monsieur Henry and would be in the Café Berry near the Ronde Point at the Champs Elysées every evening from 31 March between 4 p.m.

and 6 p.m. and would give information or assistance to anyone who said to her in any language: 'Hello, Ruth, I have not seen you for ten years.' Ruth told him this when she was very drunk and asked him to tell the Little Man as she thought CELERY was his secretary and believed him to be working with Dobler and knew Dobler to be the 'outside man' for the German Secret Service in Lisbon.

The following morning, Thursday or Friday, CELERY went with SNOW to the British Embassy by different routes and met there. CELERY told officials there that it was imperative that he should get back to England as quickly as possible on account of certain information that he had. He was asked where he had been and what he had to report but CELERY said that, regretfully, he had nothing to say. The official then said that he would get them off by the first available plane. That night was a repetition of the previous night at the Arcadia until 5 or half past in the morning.

By this stage the partying was taking its toll on SNOW. The Little Man was being nursed – 'as he was very obviously extremely ill' – by a Portuguese girl, called Madame Elisabeth Fernanda. She stayed with him in his room at the hotel and looked after him extremely well. To CELERY's 'almost certain knowledge there was no question of immorality as I had entered his room on many occasions and found her sitting fully dressed on the edge of his bed giving him cold towels and medicine or also holding his hand while he was asleep'. SNOW treated her lavishly and she paid all his bills for him, accounting to him for every Escudo and cutting down all the bills. He repaid her by buying new furniture for her parents and she came out in a car with SNOW and CELERY on the first and third morning to Cintra Aerodrome when they expected to leave. SNOW gave her about 1,000 Escudos a day apart from paying for her expenses.

On a Monday morning CELERY took his bag to the British Embassy, leaving by the back entrance of the hotel and making a detour by three taxis. He was certain that he was not followed. CELERY left his bag and was interviewed by appointment at 7 p.m. that evening by an SIS officer so that CELERY could unlock it in his presence as it was heavy and he did not know its contents. The papers therein were sealed in a foolscap envelope and they were addressed inside the bag to: T.A.R., Room 055, War Office. CELERY was later informed that he and SNOW were leaving from Cintra Aerodrome the next morning.

The night before CELERY left, he went down to Estoril with the Little Man as he had been invited to dine with Dr Ruser. CELERY took SNOW to Ruser's house for a drink but he was rather coldly received although invited to dinner. SNOW refused, however, and went back to the English bar to join Madame Fernanda. CELERY dined with Dr Ruser and his mother and they gave him a letter to post to their English relations. They asked CELERY to read it but he said: 'No, I will deliver it unread.' Dr Ruser then asked CELERY if he could save his case of valuable books in London, either if possible to have them sent to Lisbon or, failing this, to have them kept in safe custody until the end of the war. CELERY discovered that Ruser had a private recording machine in his house and had made records of all Churchill's speeches. The recording machine was in the lounge adjoining the hall 'and American bar' and could be switched on to record conversations. It was completely silent. CELERY was convinced that Ruser 'could be of great value to any of our people who are in difficulties as both he and his mother are sincere and lovers of England and the English and haters of the Nazi regime'.[14] By the time he returned to Britain, CELERY had been away, in Germany, for three weeks. So far, so good. Then SNOW, in his interrogation by MI5, delivered a bombshell: he had admitted to the DOCTOR that he was a British spy.

By his own account SNOW had met the DOCTOR on the evening of his first day in Lisbon and was accused by him of working under British control. SNOW knew, when he saw the DOCTOR's expression, that the 'game was up' and he admitted the charge. SNOW claimed that he had been detected some three months previously when British Intelligence 'walked in on him' at the beginning of December[15] and had since worked as a double agent for the British. The DOCTOR's response was to propose an elaborate scheme by which SNOW should return to England, still in the capacity of a double agent, but should indicate to the DOCTOR, by certain code words inserted into his traffic, what of it was true and what false. All this had occurred before CELERY's arrival in Lisbon, which was delayed by the ship on which he sailed being some days overdue.[16] But, just as alarmingly, if not more so, SNOW also claimed that he told CELERY that he had admitted to the Germans that they were both British agents and their cover was blown. If this were true then not only had SNOW betrayed MI5 but CELERY, who had not hinted at any anything along these lines, must be triple-crossing the Service and working as a German agent.

When J.H. Marriott began, on 31 March 1941, to interrogate SNOW he found that he had to work: 'having regard to the absolute inconsistency' between the accounts of CELERY and SNOW as to their reception by the DOCTOR, and to SNOW's 'complete inability to tell anything like a connected story'; therefore, he directed his attention only to an attempt to establish the three following points:

1. What happened when SNOW at his first meeting with the Doctor confessed that he was under our control we having 'walked in on him' at the beginning of December.

2. Whether he told CELERY exactly what had happened at his own first meeting with the Doctor, and if so when he had told him i.e. whether before or after CELERY's first meeting with the Doctor and if after that meeting whether before or after CELERY's first visit to Germany.

3. What (if any) story he and CELERY had concocted for Major Robertson's benefit as to their doings in Lisbon.

Whether Marriott would succeed in getting answers to any of these questions he thought it at least worthwhile to set out the reasons for their importance since the extent to which SNOW himself was able to give the answers would be the measure of his credibility as a witness on other matters connected with his visit:

1. If SNOW's account of his first meeting with the Doctor is accurate it is to my mind absolutely incredible that the Doctor should not have pursued the most exhaustive enquiries as to precisely what happened when the British Intelligence authorities walked in and caught him red handed, and yet according to SNOW this aspect of his case was only discussed at two meetings with the Doctor one lasting 2½ hours and the other lasting one hour. In 3½ hours therefore the Doctor had not only learnt the whole story about our discovery of, and turning round of, SNOW but he had weighed up the situation, decided that notwithstanding everything he could still use SNOW and given him £10,000 and a new code. The only material upon which the Doctor had to go was the fact that a number of men 'medium English people, thin faces and I think policemen among them' walked into SNOW's house, 'went right through it and the furniture', found the radio transmitter and the code, questioned SNOW for 'several hours' and eventually sent him back home to transmit with a man watching him. The Doctor was told that SNOW couldn't remember the names of any of the people who questioned him and that he had no idea of how we performed the remarkable feat of illicit wireless detection. SNOW's explanation of all this is that the Doctor 'trusts him 100%' and is prepared to rely on the mere statement by him that things are alright. This is found difficult to believe, but it is, I suppose, just possible.

2. SNOW's memory is so at fault over the question whether

and when he told CELERY of the Doctor's discovery of our connection with the party that I am forced to the conclusion that he is lying, and the only point of interest is the extent of the lie. The Doctor's discovery was an event of such tremendous importance that SNOW <u>must</u> remember when he told CELERY and any pretence that he does not remember can only be based on one of two things –

(a) The fact that he did not tell CELERY until after he met the Doctor or perhaps until after he came back from Germany, and that he is ashamed of this.

(b) The fact that the discovery was never made, that therefore he never told CELERY for the very good reason that there was nothing to tell him, and that the whole story has been invented by him.

If the answer is (a) he would surely now maintain that he told CELERY as soon as he arrived in Portugal. In fact even though his attention has been directed to the importance of this point he is on balance inclining to the story that he told CELERY <u>after</u> and not before the meeting. This story seems to me almost impossible.

That the answer is (b) it confirmed by the fact that SNOW saw our Air Attaché on 26.2.41. i.e. before CELERY went to Germany and yet said nothing about the Doctor's alarming discovery.

3. SNOW only produces the story that CELERY and he had an arrangement not to tell Major Robertson that the parties connection with us was known to the Doctor right at the end of his interrogation and then only after the idea was put into his head by me. If his story is true then CELERY and he <u>must</u> have come to some such arrangement and it would have been the first thing that he would have told us.

For all the above reasons the interrogator was 'satisfied that SNOW is lying and that he never disclosed to the DOCTOR his connections with us. I should add that his demeanour under interrogation conveys exactly the opposite impression and that he gives every appearance of speaking the truth, which indeed I feel he really thinks he is doing. I am more than ever convinced that SNOW's is a case not for the Security Service, but for a brain specialist.'[17]

Perhaps. Or maybe SNOW was telling the truth and CELERY was lying. When Ronnie Reed interrogated SNOW he was given the impression that SNOW had tried to double-cross CELERY – before CELERY arrived in Lisbon – but was thwarted because CELERY had already managed to double-cross SNOW first by, somehow, contacting the DOCTOR before his ship arrived in port. SNOW seemed to have formed this impression because it had been arranged, with the DOCTOR, that SNOW should go into Germany; but, after CELERY's arrival, this was cancelled and CELERY went alone. SNOW was not given any explanation. SNOW had heard from Duarte that CELERY had arrived at Lisbon on the Saturday evening, yet CELERY did not call and see SNOW at the hotel until Sunday afternoon. CELERY, however, told SNOW that he had called at the hotel in the evening only to be told that no one by the name of SNOW (Owens) was there, 'a quite impossible procedure'.

CELERY told SNOW that he had got to know one of the stewards, by the name of 'Burt', on the boat, and CELERY brought him ashore and introduced him to SNOW. SNOW wondered why he brought Burt ashore. Reed speculated as to whether a case of whisky, which CELERY had taken with him on the boat, had anything to do with bribing the ship's radio operator to inform the DOCTOR of the fact that SNOW was working for the British. Before CELERY's departure for Germany, SNOW claimed to have asked CELERY not to reveal all the convoy routes which he had obtained 'and to give them all the dope that he had with him'; but CELERY said that he would not. When CELERY returned from Germany his travelling companion told SNOW that CELERY need not continue to borrow money from him as CELERY had £450 with him. But CELERY only told SNOW that he had £200. SNOW also said that at the British Embassy he was told about a telegram which was intercepted by the British Secret Service and which had been sent by the German Intelligence saying that CELERY was 'their best man'. When CELERY was in Germany, SNOW asked Duarte to send a telegram to the DOCTOR saying 'It is essential that I come at once' but there was no reply. Reed believed SNOW wanted 'to make quite sure' that CELERY 'did not return, but was unable to do so'.

While SNOW and CELERY were away on their mission, an air mail registered letter was received at SNOW's home which was posted in Lisbon on or about 10 March (according to SNOW's partner Lily). It was addressed to either CELERY or his wife. The envelope was split and inside it was possible to see £10 in notes. Later, when Reed was in a car with CELERY's wife, Kay, going down to SNOW's home, he asked her if she had received the letter containing the money. She replied that 'she had done so but that the letter had been badly split' and inferred that it had been opened by Lily. Reed commented that it was a curious thing for a man in a foreign country – CELERY – to send £10 in notes to Kay as she was not hard up, but Kay explained that CELERY had told her, in the enclosed letter which came with it, that she was to send the money to someone else. When SNOW and Reed discussed this they agreed that this would have been an easy way for CELERY to get a message to a man in Britain at another address by having secret writing on the banknotes. Reed thought it significant that SNOW was going to be given some secret ink by the Germans but, when CELERY arrived, this arrangement was suddenly cancelled and SNOW heard no more about it. For good measure, SNOW also thought that CELERY should have appeared much more reluctant to go to Germany than he did and could only conclude that 'he was known in Germany very well'. SNOW claimed that CELERY was throwing his money about in Lisbon and buying clothes and presents. He was also 'a dope fiend taking a great quantity of Veronolin when returning on the plane and was very scared of flying, yet according to CELERY's previous history he was a great man in the RAF'.

By now SNOW was relating stories such as that concerning a mysterious man who visited CELERY, just before they left for Lisbon, and brought a note to the door at SNOW's home stating it was for CELERY and asking for an immediate reply. When questioned about this, Kay said the note was from a man who wanted CELERY to get him a commission in the RAF as a caterer but SNOW was 'very suspicious of this and does not believe it'. SNOW also wanted to know too why CELERY was taken around factories in Germany and stayed in such expensive hotels: 'He can only again conclude that CELERY is one of their men.' Then there was the tale SNOW told Reed about CELERY spending a lot of time with the proprietor of a pub, in his back room, one night 'and now wonders why'. The situation was not helped when Lily informed MI5 that she had gone through Kay's belongings – left in her room – and had read her diary, which had been left there as well as all her bills and all the other personal effects. The unfortunate thing was 'that in her diary she says she hates Lily! And that she is extremely worried about CELERY being with the Little Man'. SNOW remarked to Reed that CELERY was a very plausible man and that he believed MI5 was 'believing what he says rather than what I say and he is the biggest bloody liar I ever met'.[18]

Up until now it had been decided that CELERY should not, initially, be told about SNOW's confession. Soon, however, it was decided that the time had arrived when CELERY should be confronted with the fact that SNOW had given the game away to the DOCTOR before CELERY's arrival in Lisbon. The task fell to John Masterman who 'explained this extremely carefully to CELERY'. He set out his reasons for not disclosing this fact to CELERY beforehand, a fact which, after CELERY had realised the full implications, he agreed was the correct course to adopt and was in fact grateful that this information had been withheld from him. During the whole of this time another MI5 officer 'was watching CELERY most closely. My impression was that CELERY took this exceedingly calmly and in fact his first remark after Captain Masterman had finished was that he believed that SNOW was lying when he said that he had told the Doctor'. He was 'absolutely emphatic' that SNOW had never mentioned a word about this to him and never hesitated to say that if he had known he would not have gone into Germany.

The point was talked round at considerable length and among other things it was made quite clear to CELERY that it was apparent from the remarks which had been made by SNOW that he was exceedingly jealous of CELERY. Another point which emerged from the discussion was that SNOW, if in fact he had told the DOCTOR that British Intelligence knew all about his activities, was almost certainly sending CELERY to his death by allowing him to go into Germany. The group 'came to the conclusion that the reactions in SNOW's mind were that he could not even at the last moment bring himself to tell CELERY what he had done and that in all probability the Doctor had threatened him if he received any indication that SNOW had imparted his knowledge to CELERY. SNOW may also have realised that if he had told this fact to CELERY, CELERY would have refused to go into Germany which would of course have given the Doctor a clear indication that SNOW had broken his word. SNOW, being the little rascal that he is, preferred the security of his own neck to that of his friend CELERY.'[19]

CELERY was once more interrogated on 8 April. He was asked if he was clear what his instructions from Major Robertson had been once he embarked upon his mission to Lisbon. CELERY explained that the primary part of his mission was 'to clear up the Party so far as the Little Man was concerned, to use any means that I considered right adhering as closely as possible to the truth, take no risks. If I had to give any small information away I was to do so'. He was also to try and obtain information about submarines, shipyards, morale of the people, factories, etc. In order to check up on the Little Man the chief idea was to 'encourage him on anti-British lines. My plan has always been to be completely disgruntled with everything.' When asked if, before he left England, CELERY had reason to think SNOW would double-cross them, he replied:

A: Yes. And I was of the convinced opinion that he was double-crossing us.

Q: What reason had you?

A: His intense dislike of everybody in this department, his hurt pride, money was being kept from him, that they were pretending to rely on him and obviously checking up on him in another way. He suspected that I was doing it too.

Q: Did he show he suspected you?

A: Yes.

Q: Even before you left England, had he the impression that you had been put in as a spy on him?

A: Yes. He queried me bluntly on this. He said he knew, but that I was to look to him only as he was the only one that could see it through and he gradually came to trust me more and more and thought that I was gradually coming to his viewpoint. You know I had kept all Major Robertson's letters and I discussed with T.A.R. whether to let him see these letters to bear out my story and he agreed with me but said I was not to let them out of my possession. These letters the Little Man read to himself and to Lily and he said to me: 'I would not have believed it unless you have shown me these.' I again and again said how disgusting the treatment was and as these letters bore out the amount of money I had received – an average of £2 per week – Arthur said: 'I told them to give you all the money you wanted. It is my money and it is a scandalous thing that they have treated you like a pauper.'

Q: As you had planned this first part of your mission in your mind tactically, how did you think you could make your first approaches to the Doctor?

A: It had been agreed by T.A.R. and myself that as according to previous reports the Doctor was a heavy drinker, likes dirty stories, etc, that I should get to Lisbon before (censored) make a great play with the Doctor, go out and drink with him and try and supersede (censored) and, if necessary, sow doubts about (censored) in his mind and find out everything about him.

Q: Did you carry out this plan?

A: Yes. But I had to do it in an entirely different way because the Doctor was not the man he had been reported to be. He is like a very shrewd American middle-west businessman, speaks fluent English with a strong American accent, scarcely drinks at all and talks very little and carries a great deal of weight with his colleagues and he does command respect. I felt that had I attempted to sort of sell out my own country with him I would have got no trust, no confidence and no respect. He had had a build up of me before on account of certain experiences that you know of, of the last war, of what happened since and also my Irish mother. I led him to believe that I was not necessarily a monetary traitor but someone who had a definite hatred of this country and a pacifist angle. I did not pretend any fascist leanings. I am quite certain I had his respect. I met his wife and went out to dinner with them and he offered that I should take her out herself. He likes me.

Q: The broad outline of the Doctor's character is that he is a strong man rather violent who was respected?

A: I would call him a strong man but with much speaking character. He talks a lot, socially too, very much to the point and he won't be argued with from his colleagues and junior officers.[20]

After the morning's interrogation CELERY had been told that Masterman would call on him at 8.45 p.m. to take any further information which he might like to give as a result of the dual interrogations. When the Oxford Don called on him, CELERY handed him a long document of notes which he had made since the interrogation and which he wished to have placed on record. They then discussed the revelation made by SNOW and went over again some of CELERY's own theories and surmises. CELERY impressed upon Masterman that his whole object was to get back into one of the Services. For this he would make any sacrifices, and though he did not like the sort of work in which he was engaged, he would be perfectly prepared to go back to the other side if he had the confidence of the department and if MI5 wished him to do so. CELERY explained to Masterman that he was naturally somewhat chagrined to find that after completing what he regarded as a difficult and dangerous task, he was met with a good deal of suspicion, but Masterman believed he 'succeeded in making it clear to him that it was our duty to accept every statement from every agent with reserve and to check up on every detail that we could'. In fact, Masterman later thought 'it only fair to put on record that both in his interrogation and in every conversation that I have had with him since he arrived, he had been perfectly consistent in his statements, and though his memory is undoubtedly excellent I find it difficult to believe that he could repeat a story of this length and complexity on many occasions without introducing errors and contradictions, unless the story were substantially the truth'. Masterman's own conclusion was 'that though he was obviously dangerously impressed by German efficiency and may have toyed with the idea of involving himself too deeply on the German side, yet he has in the main behaved with loyalty and done his best for us'.[21]

In terms of whom MI5 believed, SNOW was losing support rapidly. To try and settle matters a confrontation between SNOW and CELERY was engineered. When the two men were brought together the Security Service 'wanted to make... quite clear... the seriousness of the position'. Therefore, the confrontation began with SNOW being asked to repeat exactly the nature of his warning to CELERY in Lisbon – that the Germans knew he was a British agent:

S[NOW]: CELERY knew exactly that the Doctor knew I was in touch with the British Intelligence before he left for Germany. That is right, isn't it?

C[ELERY]: I had gathered as much but I didn't know.

S: You didn't know?

C: You never told me anything about it. You never mentioned it to me.

S: You didn't know?

C: I have very grave suspicions but I didn't know.

S: You mean to tell me that you didn't know?

C: I am telling you. I have been told after working out my whole report that you informed me that you had blown the whole project to the Doctor [and] warned me accordingly. You never made any such statement. When did you speak it to me?

S: I believe I warned you when I saw you in the room.

C: You believe you did. I don't want to know what your beliefs are, I want to know exactly.

S: Do you remember me telling you in front of the Doctor? Remember this definitely, telling you in front of the Doctor that the Doctor knew everything about me in connection with the British Secret Service. Don't you remember you sitting there, the Doctor sitting there, me sitting on the bed with Dobler, and I said to you, 'The Doctor knows everything, you understand.' I definitely did.

C: I say that you didn't, and I am also informed that you warned me personally that you had blown the entire party to the Doctor, that your own advice to me when you tried the last two or three days when I was with you to assure me that you were the only person who could look after me, to put my whole trust in you and that you would see me back again as you had given your word of honour. You wavered on the last day and were obviously very nervous and you said to me on the pavement when I was getting into the taxi to go to Estoril station 'you are a very brave man, CELERY, don't go if you don't want to'…

S: Don't you remember a telephone call coming to my room from Dobler after we went to my room.

C: You telephoned.

S: I did not.

C: You made a call yourself. There may have been a call that came to you but you phoned yourself.

S: Not to Dobler.

C: Well I don't know who you phoned to.

S: Don't you remember me phoning down at your request to the bar for two Gin Fizzes because you said you felt so rotten? After that call came from Dobler[?]. Can't you get that clear[?]

C: Do you remember what he said on that telephone conversation?

S: He said to me, 'Do you know CELERY is in town?' and I said, 'Yes, he is just here, I have just met him.' 'Well,' he said, 'So is the Doctor in town. I shall want to see you right away.' The Doctor had waited over to see him. I said, 'Oh, that is lovely.' I said, 'When do you want to see us?' He said, 'Right away.' I said, 'Ok.'

[Question by Interrogator]: What were the Doctor's first words to you?

C: He spoke to SNOW who said, I think he said, 'He's turned up at last, we'd all given him up.' I and the Doctor said, 'SNOW has been terribly worried about you we are very glad to see you.' Is that right?

S: That's right.

[Q] Now when was this statement that you made to CELERY, to the effect that the Doctor knew everything.

S: Right then.

C: No statement of any such kind was made. If you made a statement of that kind the only thing I have to say is that you made it as an aside or a statement that I didn't hear. As far as I was concerned I knew nothing about it. If I had known anything about it I should never have gone into Germany.

S: Well, I said it alright.

C: And I'm quite convinced also that you were sure in your own mind that I didn't know the facts of the case because you refused to tell them to me and on the last night when I left you you very nearly persuaded me not to go. You were very worried and you

shook my hand half a dozen times and you told me what you
thought of me, that you would look after me, you were wavering
whether to tell me not to go or not in my opinion.
S: No I wasn't. I said you were a very brave man.
C: Well in that case you were sending me to my death because
you could have done nothing about it.
S: No, I wasn't.
C: That is my candid opinion. If I had known that the whole of
this was blown to the Doctor I should not have left.
S: CELERY, you knew perfectly.
C: I knew nothing at the time. I know you had relations with
the doctor and he knew a great deal about you but I had no
conceptional knowledge that he knew all about (censored) and
that you were controlled or anything like that at all. If I had done
I should not have gone.[22]

SNOW's fate as a XX agent had, probably, been sealed before this
confrontation – but the MI5 officers were clearly convinced by
CELERY's performance. Masterman wondered if SNOW had gone
over to the Germans 'a long time ago' in which case he was 'a major
traitor, who has always been working primarily for the Germans and
is now doing so more than ever'. Whatever the truth it seemed likely
that SNOW's behaviour in Lisbon 'was probably due mainly to the
consuming jealousy of CELERY. This hypothesis is to some extent
supported by the view of the specialist whom he saw today, who is
clearly of opinion that SNOW is extremely shrewd and sly, and by no
means so ill or so affected by drinking as he has led us to suppose'.
Whether in fact CELERY had told the truth about his adventures with
the Germans 'was to some extent independent of what SNOW says'. It
was clear that, whichever hypothesis was the correct one, SNOW, 'with
his extraordinary contradictions, vagueness, unreliability, complete
failure to carry out many of the tasks laid upon him in Lisbon, and
by his indiscretions in talking to undesirable persons there, cannot
be employed further on the old footing. It is therefore suggested that
he should transmit messages to the Germans to the effect that he is
becoming very ill, that his health is really broken and his nerve is gone.
He cannot continue any longer and must throw up the sponge'.[23]
    A conference was urgently convened. Attending were Guy Liddell,
Dick White, Robertson, Marriott and Masterman. There was nothing
for it except to agree that the only safe course was to assume that the
DOCTOR 'knew about our control of agents and that he probably
knew as much about it as SNOW or CELERY. On this assumption

SNOW can be of little if any further use to us', but the fact that the DOCTOR had given him £10,000 and the explosives showed that he wished himself to keep the party alive. 'The reason or reasons for this may be a wish to maintain his own prestige, a wish to use SNOW as paymaster or for contacts in the event of invasion and the belief that he can learn a great deal by studying information which we allow to go over, because it will tell him what we regard as unimportant and what we regard as important. The fact that he wishes to keep the party alive is a strong argument for closing down on it and it is also desirable that we should put the onus of ending it upon him.' SNOW was, therefore, to be informed 'that we propose to send a message... to the effect that his health and nerves have collapsed and that he must throw in his hand, he will also ask what he is to do with his transmitters and with his explosives'. The advantages gained from this course were that MI5 would be able to observe SNOW's reactions, 'which may help us to decide how far he has involved himself on the other side'; and that they should be able to watch the DOCTOR's reactions, 'since he must either himself break up the party by refusing to answer or send some sort of reply and instructions to SNOW. If SNOW accepts the decision without comment or a suggested alternative, we shall then tell him that we believe CELERY's story, that SNOW never warned him, which we regard as a foolish and treacherous act on SNOW's part. It is possible that this statement may elicit from SNOW further accusations and possible information about CELERY.' TATE meantime would go over with renewed and urgent requests for money, he 'will explain that he cannot send any valuable information because his money is running so short that he dare not spend it on travelling about to procure information. If he is not helped at once he must throw up the sponge'. Here again MI5 would be able to decide according to the DOCTOR's reply: what was to be done with TATE and the DOCTOR 'will have the responsibility (with the consequent loss of prestige to him) of breaking up the party'. Until these reactions could be assessed the MI5 officers decided that the future control of SNOW and CELERY was not to be finally decided on. There was general agreement that they would have to be kept under close supervision and that it might be necessary to shut SNOW up or alternatively to remove him from the country.[24]

SNOW's position was not helped, at the end of July 1941, by an ISOS interception of a message, by the DOCTOR, to Berlin. By now MI5 had learnt that 'Rantzau' was, in fact, really Major Ritter. In the message Ritter stated that SNOW, on 14 February, 'immediately informed me that his sub-agent CELERY who was coming by sea, was in his opinion suspect. I pressed SNOW strongly on this point, asking on what grounds he suspected CELERY, and why, if he did so, he had taken the risk of bringing him to Lisbon. SNOW replied that he had recently formed the impression, from a chance remark of CELERY's that he was acting in the interests of the British authorities. He added that he had not dared to break off his relationship with CELERY as to do so would have been regarded as a sign of guilt. He said that he had first met CELERY approximately ten weeks before.' This gave the impression that SNOW had volunteered the information.

Ritter had then told SNOW that he was not satisfied with his story and that he must, in his own interests, be absolutely honest with him: 'I explained to him that if, as he said, a British agent had been in touch with him for ten weeks, it was practically certain that the authorities already knew enough about his own case to arrest him immediately, on his return. It was, I said, obvious that they had only allowed him to go to Lisbon at all in order to gather final information against him through CELERY. Moreover, there was a grave question whether SNOW's sub-agents in South Wales and elsewhere... were not already implicated and perhaps under arrest. I told SNOW plainly that I should have to consider seriously if it would be safe for me to allow him to return to England, seeing how much he knew of my organisation and of me personally. I told him that he was wholly in my power and that I should have no difficulty in liquidating his case promptly in Lisbon.' SNOW was clearly 'very much frightened' by this threat.

While he was still in this 'amenable condition', Ritter pressed him with further questions and finally succeeded in extracting the following story from him: SNOW claimed that he had first met CELERY some ten weeks ago in a public house. He was certain that this meeting was purely accidental. In the course of conversation, CELERY, who was rather drunk, had confided to SNOW certain details of his previous career and the criminal record which prevented him from gaining his commission. He expressed himself as very angry and dissatisfied with the attitude of the authorities towards him. For this reason SNOW continued to cultivate his acquaintance, seeing in him a possible recruit. After a suitable interval, SNOW had made a tentative approach to CELERY. The latter accepted this so readily that SNOW's suspicions were aroused. He made careful enquiries about CELERY and discovered the following facts. What CELERY had said about his previous career was perfectly true, but he was now employed by the authorities as a counter-espionage agent. His duties were to hang about in bars and hotels in the London area and report to his superiors any suspicious persons that he met or conversations that he overheard. For this he received his expenses and a salary of thirty shillings a week.

He was not satisfied with this position and was looking round for some means to improve it.

SNOW then found himself in a serious predicament. If he broke off this acquaintance with CELERY there was every reason to think that the latter would report the slight suspicions which he had already formed to the authorities, since he would have nothing to gain by not doing so. The alternative was to continue the acquaintance, despite the obvious dangers which he would run by doing so. This SNOW considered the safest course. He was certain that he had not allowed CELERY to have any definite evidence against him or at most only the slightest. He did not believe that CELERY had yet made any report to his superiors, or would do so before he had a clear case to present. If he did his duty and simply reported his suspicions, he would gain nothing; whereas, if he waited until he was able to present a complete case, he stood a chance of being congratulated, though reproved for exceeding his instructions, and rewarded with the return of his commission. Moreover, SNOW had allowed him to see that he himself had plenty of money and to guess from what source it came. This had had a visible effect on CELERY, 'who is an extremely grasping man'. He also appeared genuinely impressed by what SNOW told him of the strength and efficiency of Germany. SNOW therefore formed the opinion that CELERY, despite his connection with the British authorities, could after all, if properly handled, be recruited by the Germans. What was wanted was that he should be thoroughly frightened, thoroughly impressed and offered a financial reward more valuable than the return of his commission. Having reached this conclusion, SNOW continued to encourage CELERY and suggested to him that he should go with him on his forthcoming visit to Lisbon. CELERY accepted SNOW's proposal that he should go to Lisbon, and was understood by the latter to have obtained his superiors' sanction by saying that, although he had to date obtained no evidence against SNOW himself, he suspected that this projected trip was not wholly for *bona fide* business purposes. Although SNOW told his story in a confused, disjointed and apparently reluctant manner, after listening to it and questioning him closely, Ritter 'was satisfied, particularly in view of my long acquaintance with him that he was telling the truth so far as he knew it'. The following immediate questions therefore arose: 1. Had SNOW assessed CELERY's position in the British organisation correctly? 2. Was SNOW right in saying that CELERY had so far given only negative reports to his superiors? 3. Was it certain that the British authorities had taken no action on these reports, despite their negative character? 4. Was SNOW right in saying that CELERY could be bought?

When CELERY arrived in Lisbon, Ritter saw him on the same day 'and my first impression of him coincided exactly with what SNOW had already told me. He had all the appearance of a crook and of a man who would do anything for money. He spoke often and convincingly of being in low water financially and being compelled to accept work which was below his real capabilities... This was my first impression of CELERY. Clearly, it could only be confirmed by careful interrogation and observation of CELERY over a period. This could only be done in Germany. Moreover, if it were confirmed, we should have to exert ourselves to the full to flatter, frighten and impress him. If it were not confirmed, it might be necessary to dispose of CELERY. For either of these purposes also Germany was the right place.' Thus, while there was no evidence here that SNOW had given the truth away regarding his recruitment to and tasks within the Security Service, he had clearly put CELERY in a position of some danger.

Fortunately, the interrogation of CELERY in Hamburg, the latter part of which Ritter was able to attend, 'went as well as could be expected. I satisfied myself, as nearly as one ever can in these matters, that the situation was substantially as SNOW had said.' Ritter therefore made financial arrangements with a view to confirming CELERY's loyalty to Germany 'and ensuring that he continued to keep his mouth shut about SNOW'. The basis of these arrangements was that CELERY should receive a few hundred pounds as an earnest of German goodwill and then be made dependent on SNOW for a much larger sum to be paid him in instalments. Obviously, CELERY would only receive this sum if SNOW remained at liberty for long enough to hand it to him, over a period at least of some weeks; but, thought Ritter, if CELERY postponed making a report to his superiors for such a period, he would find it exceedingly difficult to make one at all, since he would have no convincing explanation for his delay. This was the position when SNOW and CELERY returned to England together on 21 March. Ritter had by this time already left for the Near East and was therefore out of touch with the day to day developments of the case. On 24 April he received news from Hamburg that a message had come from SNOW to the effect that he was too ill to continue his work. 'This had an ominous sound, though there was as yet no reason to suppose it untrue.'

Then, on 1 June, Ritter received the surprising news that CELERY had arrived again in Lisbon, apparently alone. Ritter gave instructions that CELERY was to be treated with the greatest caution and suspicion. On the face of it, CELERY's behaviour was suspicious. SNOW's radio operator had been unable to contact him. Yet here, six weeks later, was CELERY arriving in Lisbon alone – 'a difficult even dangerous thing to do since, this time, he had no convenient excuse to offer his employers. This could only mean that he was wholly out of touch with SNOW, and his transmitter. Why should he allow himself to lose touch in this way, when if he were playing straight with us, he had so much to gain by continuing the acquaintance?' These suspicions were confirmed when CELERY refused to return to Hamburg and had made the alternative proposal that a German Secret Service representative should go back with him to England in order to sell the information which he possessed to the British, in return for which he was to receive a sum of money and a free passage to America. For Ritter, only two deductions could be made from this:

First, that our manoeuvres in Hamburg had been less successful than I had hoped and that CELERY was still acting in the British interest. Secondly, that he was probably a British agent of higher standing than we had previously supposed, since he had been allowed to undertake two independent missions. In these circumstances, it seemed more than likely that our whole previous view of SNOW's case had been mistaken. If CELERY were a trusted British agent, whose loyalty we had not succeeded in buying, it was certain that he had made a report on SNOW immediately on his return from Lisbon, if indeed he had not done so before. Either way, I was obliged to assume that SNOW's position as one of our agents was now known to the British. Evidently, since his transmitter had closed down, the British were not proposing to employ him as a controlled agent. Why they had not taken this opportunity could only be guessed – perhaps because they had not succeeded in extracting enough information from SNOW to make it possible. In any case, I could have no doubt on this hypothesis, that SNOW was in prison.

Ritter was now worried about the status of agents CHARLIE and GW:

for SNOW knows sufficient about both of them to procure their capture at any time. If SNOW is in prison their safety depends simply on his not breaking down under interrogation. But SNOW is an experienced agent and one, in my experience, abnormally difficult to interrogate. Moreover... the fact that the British have made no attempt so far to use SNOW's set suggests that they have obtained very little from him... it is safe to assume, since the set is still silent, that SNOW has not yet talked. For these reasons I am of the opinion that CHARLIE and GW are still undetected. From the former we have heard nothing as is natural since SNOW is his only link with us. The latter GW has now re-opened his line of communication through the Spanish channel. So far as can be judged from his traffic and from other reports he is free and not acting under control. The possibility that he is controlled does, however, remain and his reports are not therefore accepted except where they can be checked by those of another agent.[25]

What intercept from Most Secret Sources ISOS revealed to MI5 was that, despite major doubts regarding SNOW's position, the Germans still wanted to believe in his network. And the possibilities for deception remained. As did the mystery of SNOW's behaviour. One last attempt was made to get SNOW to reveal the truth in April 1942: John Gwyer interrogated him in prison albeit posing as someone from MI5 trying to go over the case for archival purposes; in this way, Gwyer was hoping that SNOW might reveal a little more. On the last morning that Gwyer was with him, SNOW said casually, *a propos* of something else: that he told the DOCTOR: 'that I didn't trust CELERY and thought he might be double-crossing. I said, "It's your business to find out. You take him to Berlin and cross-examine him and put him through it as much as you like." It was the only thing I could say.' Gwyer thought that: 'This may or may not have been a truer picture of what happened.'[26]

Most likely, it seemed, SNOW's actions in this regard were not premeditated: finding himself in a jam with Ritter he felt he had no alternative but to cast doubt upon someone else to save himself. But this still did not reveal if SNOW had been playing a longer, triple cross with MI5. SNOW, meantime, had been interned under at Stafford Gaol and had been laying plans to escape and make his way to Dublin.[27] Robertson and Masterman had interviewed Johan Kirk Boon a prisoner, at the prison on 13 August 1941 to hear the disclosures which he wished to make with regard to SNOW. Boon said that he thought that SNOW was the most important German spy in England. SNOW, it seems, had confided in Boon because he was a Dutch Fascist. He suggested that they should escape together and make for the German Legation in Dublin. Later, claimed SNOW, he would provide a submarine for Boon to go back to Holland. SNOW, it seemed, expected an invasion of Britain after the Eastern campaign and he spoke of long range guns which would be used to bombard

London. He did not suggest that he was unjustly imprisoned, admitted that there was plenty of evidence against him but that the Intelligence Service would be afraid of him and could do nothing. He said: 'I know too much for the important people in it.' But he mentioned no names. He expected later to be sent to Canada. SNOW, it seems, believed that in the case of invasion soldiers would come and shoot the prisoners and therefore he wanted to carry out the escape as soon as possible.[28]

Was SNOW, in the final analysis, a British or German agent? Perhaps he was neither. Masterman came up with another, and on the balance of probabilities, the most likely scenario:

> In this regard it is most important to remember that we are apt to think of a 'double agent' in a way different to that in which the double agent regards himself. We think of a double agent as a man who, though supposed to be an agent of Power A by that power, is in fact working in the interests and under the direction of Power B. But in fact the agent, especially if he has started work before the war, is often trying to do work for both A and B, and to draw emoluments from both.
>
> This seems to me to be probably true of SNOW. Perhaps he was 75 per cent. on our side, but I should need a lot of evidence to convince me that he has not played for both sides. It is always possible that he was paid money under another name and that this money waits for him in America. His later letters to Lily give some warrant for this view, as does his desire to be sent to Canada. We must not exclude the possibility that the DOCTOR regards him as a man who has been working at the same time for both sides and who could be bribed or frightened into doing his better work for the Germans.[29]

While one member of the SNOW household was attempting to escape from one of His Majesty's prisons, another was soon being accommodated at His Majesty's pleasure. On 1 August, SNOW's twenty-one year-old son – SNOW JUNIOR – had expressed a wish to see Robertson. As the Major was not available, he was interviewed by Captain Masterman at the Piccadilly Hotel. As a consequence of this interview, SNOW JUNIOR wrote the following letter to Robertson: 'I have information regarding the means which enable me to gain entrance and exit into occupied and enemy countries. Therefore I hereby offer my services to the State.' SNOW JUNIOR was interviewed by Robertson and Masterman on 6 August and volunteered the following information: some days before, he had arranged to meet his fiancée in Trafalgar Square. He arrived late and consequently was able to spend a short time only with his fiancée, who had to return to her work. He therefore lunched alone at the Mars Italian Restaurant, Frith Street, Soho. A man sat down opposite to him, and after about a quarter of an hour said to him, 'You are S.J.' This man appeared to know a great deal about him, and in a vague and allusive manner asked SNOW JUNIOR to join up with 'them' SNOW JUNIOR refused, and the man 'got nasty'.

From this 'very vague' approach, SNOW JUNIOR declared that he gathered that he had been invited to join the German espionage system, and that he could in consequence easily go to occupied territory, preferably France, or even to Germany itself, and there be of use to his country. He asserted 'many times' that the man made no definite statement or offer to him, but that he was quite sure what the proposal really was. It was pointed out to SNOW JUNIOR that he had no qualifications which fitted him for such a task; that he would never be trusted; that the safety of other persons would never be risked in his hands; and that he grossly over-estimated his own potentialities and capabilities. There seemed no obvious way at all in which he could be of any assistance.

SNOW JUNIOR had insisted throughout his interview that his whole conduct was dictated by his wish to improve the position of his father, and that he was prepared to take any risks to secure this end. When it was represented to him that his father's case was quite independent to his, and that he apparently had nothing to offer except this very unconvincing story of a contact with a supposed German agent, who might, for all he had told Robertson and Masterman, only be trying to gain his assistance in some illegal or criminal enterprise, SNOW JUNIOR became piqued, and incautiously suggested that the Germans would probably wish to contact him and would know a good deal about him, and that he was quite certain that this was a German espionage approach. He then rashly admitted that he had himself done something for the Germans which would encourage them to seek his assistance. 'He evidently wished to remove the impression that we did not believe his story, and at the same time to exaggerate his own importance and possibly thus to secure well paid employment for himself.' SNOW JUNIOR claimed that in the summer just before the war he had mapped the aerodromes of South London, mentioning especially Biggin Hill and Kenley, for the Germans. Having made this admission, 'he realised that he had committed a blunder of tactics', and he refused to say what he had done with the plans after he had made them. The sentence: 'He refused to say what he did with the plans after he had made them, because he was afraid that if he replied the answer would do harm to his father,' was written down and read to him slowly many times. He agreed that it was a correct statement. It was pointed out to him that, if he persisted in his refusal, only the worst interpretation for himself and his father could be placed upon his behaviour.

After a long delay, SNOW JUNIOR finally admitted to Robertson and Masterman that he sent the plans to the Auerbach Battery Company, Hamburg, which he knew to be a cover address for the German Intelligence HQ in Hamburg. He obtained this address from his father. He addressed the packet to himself at one post office in London, collected it and re-mailed it to Hamburg. SNOW JUNIOR declared that he did this on his own initiative, and that his father was angry when he was told about it after the package had been sent. He thought that his father 'would swing over to Germany at the beginning of the war, though he now considered him to be entirely pro-British'. SNOW JUNIOR had sent over the plans out of a sense of adventure, and he had received no payment; but a message had been sent over the radio to say that the Germans were very pleased with what had been done. He therefore believed that this present approach was the result of this previous act of his. He had helped his father with the radio transmissions, but had had no dealings with the Germans after this act.[30] MI5's response was inevitable but seemingly not what SNOW JUNIOR had expected: they concluded that he knew enough about his father's recent activities to be able to establish communication with the German Secret Service and 'He is consequently potentially very dangerous.' In March 1941 the Home Secretary had already signed a detention order in respect of SNOW JUNIOR for execution in the event of invasion. It was now decided that the detention order should be served at once.[31] Which it was.

In the end, despite all the concern the consequences of the breakdown of SNOW's organisation were not quite so serious as had at first been anticipated. SNOW's revelations had apparently had no adverse effect upon TATE, 'though logically they should have done' since he had made a payment to him. Similarly GW was able to re-open his contact with the Germans or at least with the organisation of Alcazar de Velasco, which passed on its information direct to the Germans and was eventually introduced to Luis Calvo, and from June 1941 until the latter's arrest continued to see him periodically to receive money from him and to make to him reports which he had previously given to del Pozo. 'As far as we can tell' Calvo 'did not at the time (whatever he may have said after his arrest) entertain any suspicions about GW's bona fides and certainly forwarded his reports to his Spanish masters. It is, however, still not clear whether this must necessarily be taken to mean that in the Germans' eyes at any rate GW 'was not for some mysterious reason compromised by the overthrow of SNOW'.

With the arrest of Calvo in March 1942 'the SNOW case in all its many ramifications came finally to an end. Although his own career had ended more or less disastrously SNOW's case had not been by any means unprofitable to us. He had given us at the beginning of the war information which formed the basis of our knowledge of the Hamburg Stelle and which was of considerable value at the time when that Stelle was the one principally concerned with work against this country.' Similarly he had through BISCUIT and latterly through CELERY provided valuable information about the German organisation in Lisbon. 'It is true no doubt that without SNOW's assistance we should nevertheless have detected all the agents whom we did detect,' with the possible exception of Mrs Krafft, 'but still the part which SNOW played in these early cases, both directly in the way of making payments to other agents and indirectly in that he provided the information upon which the Germans constructed their false papers, shows that he was then regarded as the linchpin of the Abwehr organisation in England. Consequently we were able by a study of his case to form an impression of the Abwehr's methods of working which has been of incomparable value since.'[32]

7

MUTT & JEFF;
HAMLET, PUPPET & MULLET

On 7 April 1941 two young Norwegians landed by rubber boat at Pennan, Banffshire, Scotland. At the earliest opportunity they gave themselves up to the local police, explaining that they had been landed by a German seaplane on the Moray Firth, whence they had rowed ashore. They went on to say that they had been sent over by the Germans as spies and saboteurs, for which purpose they were equipped with one wireless transmitter, code, sabotage material and formulae for further sabotage material. They maintained, however, that as their real sympathies lay with the Allies, they placed themselves completely at the disposal of the British authorities. They were then brought to Camp 020 but later released under MI5 control and installed in a house in North London for XX purposes and given the codenames MUTT and JEFF.[1]

MUTT was John Moe. He was born in London in 1919 of an English mother and a Norwegian father. About a year after his birth his parents returned to Norway where his father established himself in a women's hairdressing business in Oslo. During this period he made more than one visit to England in order to visit his grandparents. In June 1939 he came to England on a rather longer visit and, until the outbreak of war, worked at Max Factor's studio in Denham learning the business of a make-up artist. After his return to Norway, Moe continued to work in his father's business and was also employed at the J.A.R. Film Studios near Oslo. He was not called up for military service. By the end of July 1940 a few months after the German invasion of Norway, Moe found himself virtually unemployed since his father was doing little business and his employment at the film studios had come to an end. At this juncture Moe for the first time met Tor Glad – JEFF – when a certain Eilif Hammeroe, whom Moe had known previously, introduced the two to each other casually in a restaurant.

At the time when he met Moe, Glad was already employed in the German censorship bureau in Oslo. He was a 'pure' Norwegian, born in 1916 at Bostun near Oslo. After leaving school he had found himself employment as a clerk in a number of firms, 'to none of whom he apparently gave satisfaction', since, as his record showed, he never held any one position for more than two or three months. In September 1939 he again became unemployed. At this point Glad was introduced by some friends of his to a Dr Benecke of the German Legation. Benecke, hearing that Glad was out of work, offered him temporary employment as a counter-espionage agent. His duties were to investigate the alleged activities of certain British agents in Christiansand, Stavanger and Haugesund. Glad accepted this proposal without hesitation and was not conscious of any disloyalty to his own country in doing so.[2] Glad, or JEFF, was emphatic that he was not commissioned to report on the movement of Norwegian troops, shipping or aircraft, and that his job in no way constituted working against his own country. JEFF insisted to MI5 that he did not take the job seriously, 'and states that he was neutral in his attitude towards the Anglo-German conflict'. His whole explanation of the affair, however, was 'confused, and it is difficult to ascertain from the records what his precise motives were'. Whatever they were, he undertook the mission and did indeed visit the places stipulated, but claimed that he merely spent the money, some Kr.200 he received as expenses, and returned without carrying out Benecke's orders. On his return he had nothing to report, which angered Benecke, and JEFF was told that he was of little use to the Germans.[3]

In November 1939, after being paid off by Benecke, JEFF entered as a volunteer the cadet school at Akershus Fort near Oslo. He was still there when the German invasion came. His unit was mobilised and took part in the general retreat of the Norwegian forces towards the north, finally surrendering at Gausdal. JEFF was first sent as a prisoner to Lillehammer but presently released. He was almost immediately contacted there by Benecke who, 'despite what should have been an unsatisfactory experience of him before', offered him further employment, this time spying in Trondheim on those Norwegians who were attempting to escape to the north to rejoin the King's Forces. This proposal JEFF also accepted without hesitation, although his country was then at war and he was still technically a soldier since he had not yet been discharged from the army. His work in Trondheim over, JEFF returned to Oslo and was interviewed there by Major Oelsner who had by then apparently taken Dr Benecke's place. Through him he obtained a post in the German censorship office and started work there in May 1940.

About three days later the meeting between MUTT & JEFF took place. JEFF suggested to MUTT that he should obtain a position in the censorship office and 'for the better furtherance of this design' they both decided to join the Norwegian National Socialist Party – 'an organisation less notorious and more down-at-heel than the National Sjamling' but of the same Nazi leanings. On 29 July 1940, MUTT joined JEFF in the censorship office and the two worked there together until the beginning of October when MUTT was dismissed. The reason seems to have been that he had been involved in stealing a copy of the censorship black-list which he had then passed on (or so he said) to a certain Rantzau Baltzersen, a friend of his father's, whom he understood to be in touch with the Norwegian Government in exile in Britain. MUTT came under suspicion, as the result of this episode though nothing was proved against him but JEFF, though he said that he was also involved, was apparently able to clear himself and continued in his employment. By the end of December, however, he had tired of censorship and approached Major Oelsner with the suggestion that he should be sent to Britain as an agent. This proposal was accepted (despite what JEFF alleged to have been his previous bad record) and he was then introduced to Carl Andersen, who told him that he must have a companion for the expedition; JEFF thereupon proposed MUTT.

On 8 April 1941, after a number of alternative plans had been discussed and discarded, MUTT & JEFF left by seaplane from Stavanger, equipped with one wireless set between the two of them. They were landed by rubber boat on the west coast of Scotland early on the following morning. Their instructions were to sabotage certain, not too clearly defined, objectives in Scotland and to report by wireless on civilian morale and troop movements. There was also some suggestion that they should find their way to London and there seek employment, JEFF in the Norwegian forces and MUTT in the Norwegian Government. It seems to have been anticipated that in this event they would bury their transmitter and thereafter fulfil the role of propagandists and Fifth Columnists. Finally – though this was by no means clear – it seems also to have been suggested that JEFF should seek to penetrate either SIS or the Norwegian Secret Service and return to Norway in the capacity of an agent: 'There has always remained some suspicion that this may in fact have been the principal object of the whole expedition' noted MI5.[4]

After careful consideration by B1.A officers a favourable impression was formed of MUTT: 'He is fairly intelligent, frank and open, but appears to be gullible and rather too ready to trust other people with little question. He is vain and probably indiscreet, but there is little or nothing in MUTT's story to show that he had any German connections or sympathies prior to his application for a job in the German Censorship Department.' Perhaps the only unsatisfactory part of MUTT's case was the fact that the Germans, in spite of having dismissed him from the Censorship, and in spite of knowing that he was half-English, accepted him in their service for the purpose of espionage in Britain; but, 'In the absence however of further evidence and taking the case as a whole I think MUTT's reliability must be accepted.' The case of JEFF 'is very different'. In the first place he had confessed to working for the Germans in Norway both before and during the war. As, however, his activities on these two occasions:

> do not constitute an offence against this country, and as we can produce no real evidence to prove that in his subsequent behaviour he acted in bad faith against this country, the case against him is one which after the war will not really concern us. It must be obvious however, although JEFF does not appear to realise this, that his case is, and will be, of absorbing interest to the Norwegians, and furthermore that the case against him should be fairly simple. Briefly, it seems to me that the charge is that while his country was at war and his fellow-countrymen were still fighting in the north, JEFF, a Norwegian soldier, entered into the service of the enemy. He will doubtless defend this by giving the motives for his action, and, as an example of his good faith, his subsequent offer to work for the British Secret Service. From what I know of the official Norwegian attitude towards people of this type I have a feeling that his defence will be inadequate.

His motives were 'obscure, his excuses weak', and when he maintained that he made no effort to carry out the mission for which he was appointed by the Germans in June 1940, 'one wonders why, for a period of some five to six weeks he was paid at the rate of Kr.125 a week. He amplifies his excuses by emphasising that so far from carrying out his mission he even went to the extent of warning several loyal Norwegians from discussing their plans for escaping to Narvik. The question which arises then, is why did the Germans, knowing that he had failed in this mission, seek to employ him again? Why, unless JEFF was a man of proved competence and pro-German sympathies, was he given two further opportunities to work for the Germans?' The general impression formed was 'that this man had done more work for the Germans than he has admitted'; it was also deemed significant that at his first interrogation he omitted entirely to admit working for Dr Benecke prior to the invasion of Norway. The possibility that JEFF's real mission was one of penetration, with MUTT as the unwitting cover, was considered. The danger did exist but MI5 thought that 'perhaps the risk in employing him was no more than is normally contingent to double-cross work. It was, however, wisely decided at the outset that if JEFF were to be used at all it should be for a limited period only.' The immediate task after the decision to employ MUTT & JEFF was to transmit to the 'other side' a plausible and reassuring story of their activities over in Britain. The following, therefore, was finally decided upon by MI5 as the story MUTT & JEFF would tell the Germans.

On reaching shore from the seaplane they immediately buried their radio and after having made sure that they had not been observed they set off on their bicycles in a westerly direction until they arrived in some woods south of Banff where they deposited their bicycles and luggage. MUTT went into Banff to buy food and newspapers and on his return they both read in the press that a faculty at Edinburgh University for foreign students was going to be founded and they thereupon decided that if they were questioned they would pretend to be students at this University. At dusk they returned to the point where they had landed, unearthed the wireless set and then proceeded to cycle south-east to Aberdeen. Eventually they found lodgings in a farm house where they stayed for two or three days. During their stay there they went into Aberdeen to see if they could obtain incendiary materials but when the chemist demanded authority for these purchases they decided not to pursue the matter. They then attempted to find permanent lodgings but as the landlady told them that she had to register all the particulars of her lodgers with the police and that she would require their ration books and identity cards when they moved in, they cut short the interview. As their position was becoming difficult they decided to get in touch with the other side and ask for instructions.

The next day, 11 April, they left the farmhouse and cycled to Aberdeen and after buying food on the way they spent the night in some woods near Blackburn. They then tried to get the wireless set working but as soon as they started, a searchlight exposed nearby revealed that they were very near a military camp. They therefore decided that the attempt to work as under-cover agents was far too dangerous and that they would give themselves up. The next morning, therefore, they put their heads together and after due consideration decided that they would first destroy everything incriminating and then work out a cast-iron story to tell when they surrendered. The former they did, and the story they arranged to tell the British was as follows: they would give all the details of their lives up to the time when JEFF left the Censorship, concealing, however, his association with Dr Benecke and the work he did for him. The shortage of employment in Norway would explain the reason for his taking up work with the Censorship. Immediately, however, on his arrival at that office he saw the opportunity of working against the Germans and, with this in mind, got his friend MUTT a job there in order to help him. JEFF left the Censorship about Christmas time and both he and MUTT then decided to try to escape to Britain as volunteers for the Free Norwegian Forces. Both received from their respective parents enough money to finance such a venture; MUTT's portion included a quantity of English currency. After a certain amount of careful investigation they eventually approached a man called Sorensen whom they supposed to be pro-British and, after giving him a guarantee of Kr.300, received instructions from him to travel to Haugesund and contact the owner of a certain fishing smack. They left Oslo about the beginning of April equipped with the necessary border passport and duly met the fisherman. Both men memorised the descriptions of Sorensen, the fisherman and the description of the ship. On the afternoon of 9 April they set off with the fisherman and two of the crew and on 14 April, after an uneventful journey, sighted the coast of Scotland and were rowed ashore in a lifeboat.

Having decided upon this story they buried the transmitter, revolvers, ration books and, with the exception of £25, all their money. They also destroyed any of the photographs that might have incriminated them. As so many people in that area of Scotland had seen them they decided to go further south and find a suitable notional landing place before they gave themselves up. They therefore cycled towards Dundee and decided upon a spot near Lunan Bay. Their scheme was then to go to Manchester, visit MUTT's grandfather, and tell him their story, relying on his influence to save them from many unnecessary complications. On 13 April, therefore, they took the train from Arbroath to Edinburgh and then boarded the Manchester train there. Unfortunately, however, shortly before crossing the Forth Bridge, inspectors came round to examine tickets and identity cards and as MUTT & JEFF were unable to produce the latter they were forced to give themselves up there and then. After being taken under police escort to Edinburgh and being searched and questioned there they were escorted to London.

On arrival in London they were taken to the Patriotic Schools where interrogations of Aliens took place and where it was soon found out that MUTT had been born in Britain. He was therefore removed to Pentonville Prison where he managed to satisfy the authorities with his story and was released on 16 April. JEFF, in the meantime, had been found to possess a small Swastika badge and was therefore under suspicion. It was not without the greatest difficulty that in the end he succeeded in convincing the authorities that his invented story was true. Eventually he was released on 25 April. MUTT, by now, had visited his grandfather in Manchester but, as he had not been received in a very friendly fashion, he left almost immediately and went up to Aberdeen. There he collected the wireless set and returned to London where he took lodgings. On 25 April he was joined by JEFF and, after spending two days settling down, they began trying to contact the other side.[5] The story sent over to the Germans was that MUTT had been released on the basis of his English relations guaranteeing his good behaviour and, later, JEFF on MUTT's guarantee. MUTT had obtained employment as a hairdresser and JEFF as a translator and clerk attached (somewhat vaguely) to the Norwegian Government. His duties were connected with the landing and interrogation of Norwegian refugees and in this capacity he presently left London for Aberdeen.[6]

The Germans believed the story. In actual fact, MUTT & JEFF were for the time being housed at 35 Crespigny Road, Hendon in London. To begin with, their liberty was restricted and they were constantly watched by three members of the Force Security Police (FSP). In addition their conversation was 'covered' for a period of eight weeks. These security measures were intended to last until such time as it was decided that the operation as a whole, and the two principals in particular, were satisfactory. The first contact made with the other side was on 29 April 1941. But then, suddenly, the atmosphere surrounding the XX seemed to change. On 8 May, the Germans sent a message to the effect that MUTT and JEFF were in danger as they were suspected of working for the Germans. They were advised to take great care, to hide their set and if possible make their next transmission on 1 June. MI5 feared that their XX operation had been compromised. The four explanations for this message which immediately suggested themselves to the Security Service were: '1. That the names of MUTT & JEFF had been mentioned in Norwegian Government circles as possible suspects and this information had got back to Norway; 2. That some British agent in Norway had reported MUTT & JEFF to the British authorities and that the Germans had either caught the agent in question or intercepted the message; 3. That the Germans by inference drawn from MUTT's and JEFF's statements thought that they were both under suspicion; 4. That the Germans suspected that MUTT & JEFF were working for us, and that this latest message was an attempt to confirm this.'

Any one, or any combination of these four explanations was plausible, and until further information came into MI5's hands, the whole plan in general, and the traffic in particular, would have to be based on the assumption that the Germans *did* suspect them. MI5 came up with a plan to try and reassure the Germans. The following story was sent over: 1. That JEFF left London almost immediately after the receipt of the last message, but before doing so he and MUTT hid their wireless set. As a further precaution they decided that it was unwise for them to correspond and that they would merely send postcards from time to time stating that they were all right; 2. That JEFF should send a post-card stating that he was stationed at Aberdeen; 3. That MUTT should transmit on 1 June, 1941, expressing surprise at the last message, and asking for particulars. He should also state that JEFF was safely placed in a new job in Aberdeen.

This plan was carried out, but on 4 June the other side reported that the danger they had suspected appeared to be over, and normal traffic was then resumed.

As MUTT & JEFF had now received identity cards and ration books, it was possible for them to travel and it was decided to separate them, sending JEFF to Carlisle and retaining MUTT in the London area. The reason for doing this was that if they were double-crossing MI5 and had some secret arrangement between them, then the knowledge that they were to be separated for some time would, in all probability, result in their deciding future policy. The conversations were 'covered', therefore, but nothing of an incriminating nature was overheard. JEFF was duly taken to Carlisle where he stayed with, and was under the watchful eye of, the FSP. MUTT remained at Crespigny Road. At this stage the state of the case was 'far from satisfactory' from MI5's perspective. On the one hand the circumstances in which MUTT & JEFF were recruited and trained, their previous history and indiscretions in Oslo, the time they had been in Britain without communicating and the 'fantastic story' they had told the Germans to cover this up, 'made it appear improbable that the Germans would believe them'. Added to this was the warning message, which showed that the Germans themselves might be nervous about the case being compromised. On the other hand the case did present a wireless channel to the enemy and it was felt that it should not be ignored. It was decided, therefore, that MUTT & JEFF should be operated on a short term basis and that 'we should go all out to push over a deception. To a great extent this would accurately have described our attitude at almost any period of the case. The history of the MUTT & JEFF case from this time onwards is a series of deception or other plans designed to push over one more deception before blowing the case. For over two years these deceptions built up rather than blew the case.'

Plan OMNIBUS/Plan PYRAMID

The first deception effort mounted by MI5 was Plan OMNIBUS/Plan PYRAMID. According to the story sent over to the Germans, JEFF was supposed to be doing important work for the Examination Authorities in Aberdeen investigating refugees. At the time, a large number of refugees were arriving, in Britain, from Norway in fishing boats, and it was thought that any information on this topic would be likely to interest the Germans. A plan was therefore put forward by B1A in consultation with the authorities at the London Reception Centre – Plan PYRAMID – the object of which was to make it appear that an escape organisation existed in Norway and that Norwegians who were helped out of the country by this organisation stamped their papers with a little red triangle. It so happened that at the same time British military authorities were anxious to provide cover for a projected operation and wished to indicate a possible attack against southern Norway, south of Stavanger. A whole series of messages were accordingly worked out to mislead the Germans on these two points, and the threat to southern Norway was of sufficient importance to bring in several other agents later, when the plan therefore received the name Plan OMNIBUS. It was thought that if JEFF were to get a lot of vital information of this sort he must also necessarily have a certain amount of information about the names of Norwegians who had escaped and their boats and so on, and with the help of SIS a certain amount of information on these lines was included in JEFF's radio traffic. In the eyes of the Germans he came down especially from Aberdeen to send this information. The information sent over by JEFF was, according to Most Secret Sources (ISOS intercepts), well received by the Germans and MI5 had 'almost conclusive evidence' that it was taken seriously, although this information did not come to light for some time.

In order to gather supporting material for Plan OMNIBUS, MUTT & JEFF were each sent with an FSP Sergeant to different parts of Scotland. JEFF went to Aberdeen but, in attempting to obtain information from a soldier in a public house there, he 'behaved very stupidly' and as a result both he and the FSP Sergeant were arrested by the police as suspicious characters. This incident brought the case of JEFF to a head. He was recalled from Aberdeen and reprimanded but it was obvious, as a later incident when he broke curfew regulations showed, 'that he was not going to be an easy person to control and that there was really no way of dealing with him in between complete liberty or complete internment'. The decision was then made to intern him. His past record, and particularly his work for the Germans before his present mission, was considered to be ample justification for his internment and it was thought that if the Germans could be informed that he had been posted far away (Iceland was in fact decided upon) there might be a good chance of continuing the case with MUTT alone, who was considered to be reliable. JEFF was accordingly interned in Camp WX, on the Isle of Man, on 15 August 1941.[7]

For the Germans, however, another story had to be concocted. This was that JEFF had remained in Aberdeen (with occasional visits to London when on leave) until the middle of August when he fell into difficulties again and was arrested but released after further questioning. He was then handed over to the Norwegian military authorities and in the following month despatched by them to Iceland, where to his extreme annoyance he found himself enrolled in the Pioneer Corps. He later 'returned' to Britain but his future – 'even upon an imaginary plane' – remained obscure. During the whole of his absence from Britain he was, of course, out of communication both with the Germans and with MUTT, who remained in London with the transmitter. He continued his imaginary work as a hairdresser until December 1941, when he was called up for military service and entered first an AA unit but later transferred to the FSP, underwent a course at Matlock and was now in a depot at Winchester awaiting a posting. As with JEFF, MUTT's life during this period was entirely a figment of MI5's vivid imagination. MUTT's relations with the Germans during this time had remained reasonably good, except for one period, during October 1941, when he lost wireless communication with them for more than a month. This was thought to have been deliberate upon their part and to suggest a lack of confidence in him.[8]

Plan GUY FAWKES

In an attempt to reassure the Germans, MI5 came up with Plan GUY FAWKES. MUTT & JEFF were considered by the Germans to be, primarily, sabotage agents, and although the Germans at the outset had been content to receive their reports, after a few months they started to press for acts of sabotage. Up to October, when radio communication with the Germans was broken, neither MUTT nor JEFF had engaged in any act of – imaginary – sabotage. It was therefore obvious to MI5 that if the case were to be kept going a faked act of sabotage would have to be committed, and the decision was therefore, reluctantly, made to attempt an explosion in a food store. A site known as No.5 Buffer Depot, in Wealdstone, was chosen. This was in use by the Ministry of Food as a flour store and two incendiary bombs were placed in these premises on 9 November 1941. The Commissioner of the Metropolitan

Police was informed that this act of sabotage was being committed, and the Divisional Superintendent accompanied the party who actually placed the bomb. He in turn nominated one policeman who was in attendance at the flour store in order to ward off any strangers who might turn up. The act of sabotage was committed in the early hours of the morning: a car took an FSP sergeant, Sergeant Cole, to the flour store and he climbed over the gate and placed two incendiary bombs in a pile of timber. As soon as the incendiaries ignited the party drove off. Unfortunately, a reserve police sergeant happened to pass by between the placing of the incendiary bombs and the time they ignited, and he not only surprised the party but was also in a position to warn the Fire Brigade immediately. The local CID were then called in and discovered parts of the incendiary bombs which they identified correctly as being Special Operations Executive (SOE) material. This led to a 'very delicate situation' in connection with the enquiry being made by Scotland Yard. Ultimately, however, the enquiry died out.[9]

So, MUTT was able to announce that he had carried out some successful sabotage and to offer confirmation of this from what had appeared in the press. Whether because this restored the Germans' confidence in him or for some other reason, wireless contact was presently restored. MUTT transmitted satisfactorily as before, though of course, as he was – as far as the Germans were concerned – now in the army he was only able to send infrequent messages. The important fact was that he 'now appears to stand well with the Germans'. JEFF, meanwhile, was languishing (after an attempted hunger-strike) in Liverpool Gaol.[10]

The XX Portfolio Expands

Slowly, MI5 began to build a formidable array of XX agents. One, DRAGONFLY, was born in London, of German parents who had been in Britain since 1885. In 1923 he returned with his family to Germany and followed a variety of trades, each for a short period only. Around 1934 he was married to a Dutch woman, and in 1939 they went to live with her parents in Holland. There, DRAGONFLY set himself up in business marketing a German toilet product named Trixale. His 'somewhat shady business dealings' in connection with this activity made it necessary for him to make frequent visits to Germany from the last of which he returned rather hurriedly at the end of August 1939, leaving all his furniture and goods in Cologne. A few months later, ostensibly in order to help him retrieve his furniture, his sister in Germany put him in touch with an unimportant member of the German Secret Service, who made various proposals to DRAGONFLY, all of which the latter reported to the British and Dutch authorities, thereafter refusing to take any further part in the matter.

A short while afterwards his sister wrote explaining that she had now met another member of the German Secret Service, von Carstaedt, who had expressed interest in DRAGONFLY and hoped to be able to arrange a meeting with him. At the end of April 1940 his sister visited DRAGONFLY in Holland bringing with her a secret ink and a message from von Carstaedt to the effect that he was about to come to Holland himself to give further instructions to DRAGONFLY. At this, DRAGONFLY took fright and fled to England with his wife. There he was interrogated, and it appeared that he was telling the truth at any rate in so far as the main points of his story were concerned. Accordingly it was agreed that he should accept the proposal, previously put forward by the Germans through DRAGONFLY's sister, that he should meet them in Lisbon, which he eventually did at the end of October 1940 under a suitable business cover. In Lisbon he was contacted by Carl Otto Merckel (alias Mathews), Leiter Eins Wirtschaft, Lisbon, by whom he was introduced to Major Kliemann (alias Dr Kielbug), a leading member of Eins Luft Paris, whom DRAGONFLY believed to be von Carstaedt. He was given a certain amount of training in wireless and codes and returned to England on 3 January 1941 with a considerable sum of money, a cover address and a wireless set disguised as a portable gramophone.

His actual position in Britain had been that he lived in North-West London with his wife and two children, and reluctantly found himself work in a factory after turning down various offers of employment which MI5 had obtained for him. The Germans believed him to be employed by the Food Office, and he told them that he had not been called up for military service on account of an old injury to his ankle. During the latter part of 1942, DRAGONFLY was notionally transferred to the Worthing Food Office, but he told the Germans in 1943 that he was back in London. Effective wireless communication between DRAGONFLY and the Germans was established on 17 March 1941 and continued satisfactorily, his transmitter being operated by one of MI5's own men. His original instructions were to report in general on anything that might be of interest to the Germans, with particular reference to aircraft production and the RAF. The information which he provided for the Germans chiefly consisted of regular weather reports and the results of his own personal observation of aerodromes and troop movements. He only received a few questions of any special significance, and his traffic to a great extent consisted of discussions about his payment, a matter which caused the Germans much difficulty. They suggested several methods of getting money to him, only one of which, a commercial deal concerned with the sale of the European rights of Trixsale, proved successful, making DRAGONFLY richer by £1,000.

FATHER was a Belgian in his early thirties, who was formerly a well known pilot in the Belgian Air Force. After the capitulation of Belgium and France, he returned to Brussels, where he was recruited by the Germans to go to America, obtain employment in an aircraft factory, and send back technical information on aircraft production. He was trained in W/T operating and in secret writing. He was to buy his W/T set in America. The Abwehr officer with whom FATHER was principally in touch and who controlled his case, was Rademacher. Rademacher and another Abwehr officer escorted FATHER as far as Barcelona, where he was left in the care of the local Abwehrstelle with instructions to obtain for himself a visa for the United States. As he found it impossible to do this he came instead to Britain, in June 1941, as a volunteer for the RAF, having informed the Germans of his change of plan. He reported full details about his case as soon as he arrived in Lisbon and offered to work for the British as a double agent. The instructions he received from the Germans were vague and consisted principally of trying to steal a plane and flying over to Occupied Europe. He had later, however, received detailed instructions for work once the Germans started communicating with him.

The Security Service regarded FATHER as trustworthy. He refused payment for his work as he regarded this as incompatible with his position as an officer. He consistently told the truth about his position, with the result that his real and supposed position was that of a serving officer in the RAF. FATHER started communicating with the Germans by secret writing, asking for instructions and contacts. For several months they appeared to take no interest in him. In November 1941, however, DRAGONFLY received a message telling him to write a letter to FATHER (in the latter's own name) and arrange a meeting with him. This meeting took place a week later, but on further instructions from the Germans, FATHER and DRAGONFLY were no longer allowed to come face to face but only to telephone each other. In these later conversations DRAGONFLY informed FATHER that he would be called at certain times by radio by the Germans. This resulted in a one way wireless communication, the Germans sending two messages each week on two occasions every morning, which FATHER was supposed to be picking up on a fairly good broadcast receiver. FATHER also continued his secret writing.

In March 1942, FATHER was again instructed by the Germans to steal and fly to occupied territory a night fighter of the latest type, but managed to stave off a definite reply. Meanwhile, independent evidence established that for a considerable period the Germans regarded FATHER as an agent of the utmost importance. In August, FATHER suggested that he would be of more value to the Germans if he had a wireless transmitter, and arrangements were made throughout the winter with the object of this being dropped by parachute. But, by 1943, the Security Service had received information that suggested the Germans 'are suspicious at the least of FATHER and the case at the moment, therefore, is in rather a confused state'.[11]

In May 1942, THE WEASEL 'fell into our hands, and it appeared likely that he would be a valuable addition, for he had been trained in secret writing and W/T and was a man of experience and intelligence'.[12] THE WEASEL, formally a doctor in Belgium until 1930 and then in the Belgian Congo until 1937, returned to Europe because of failing health to join the Compagnie Maritime Belge as a ship's doctor and was still serving in that capacity at the outbreak of war. In June 1940 he found himself on board the Belgian vessel SS *Thysville*, which was then lying in Lisbon. The Germans endeavoured, through their consul, to persuade the crew of this ship to return to Belgium and in the negotiations, which followed, THE WEASEL 'appears to have played a rather discreditable part and to have endeavoured to persuade a number of members of the crew to accede to the German proposals'. He returned to Belgium in September 1940. In October 1940, THE WEASEL, who was then in Antwerp, was approached and asked if he would take service as a German agent with the object, as it later appeared, of returning to the Belgian Congo and sending reports from there of a general political and economic nature. After a short period of hesitation THE WEASEL accepted and, between October and July of the following year, received instruction in secret writing and W/T in Bremen and in Antwerp. Towards the end of August 1941, THE WEASEL, who was now accompanied by his wife, reached Lisbon where he remained for several months attempting to obtain his visa for the Congo. THE WEASEL was finally advised by the Belgian Legation that it would be necessary for him to go to the Congo via London in order that he might there put himself at the disposal of the Belgian authorities. The Germans encouraged him to follow this course and provided him with a further questionnaire, mainly of a naval type, which he was to endeavour to answer while in Britain.

THE WEASEL finally arrived in Britain with his wife on 5 May 1942. He was immediately arrested and put in detention. Under MI5 control he wrote to the Germans that, after having been regarded with some suspicion on his first arrival, he presently managed to clear himself; he had not, however, been able to obtain a visa for the Congo but had taken instead a post as a doctor in a hospital at Hull. He invited the Germans to provided him with a Post Box number in Lisbon to which he could write (he was already provided with secret ink). The Germans provided him with a cover address to which THE WEASEL subsequently wrote further letters but he did not succeed in eliciting any response from the Germans who appeared to abandon interest in his case. The Security Service speculated that the reason for this may well have been that his mission in Britain 'was always regarded by them only as a preface to his real work in the Belgian Congo, with the result that, as it now appears that he will remain permanently in England, their original motive in running his case has disappeared'.

In June 1941 another promising case, that of CARROT, a Luxembourger, also failed to develop, owing partly to complications over his dealings with the Deuxième Bureau, and WASHOUT, whose father was employed as a night-watchman in the British Embassy at Lisbon. WASHOUT, 'a person of no great intelligence', was a mechanic by trade but had had a varied career, which included service with Franco's Foreign Legion during the Spanish Civil War. He was recruited by the Germans in Lisbon. WASHOUT himself was instructed to report upon troop dispositions in Britain and also to obtain, if possible a position in an aircraft factory and to report upon British aircraft production. For this purpose he was provided with secret ink and two cover addresses in Lisbon. WASHOUT arrived in England in June 1942 and was immediately arrested. He remained in detention until the following September but represented to the Germans in his letters that he was employed as a mechanic in a garage in Clapham. After his release, his real and supposed occupation became that of night watchman in an East London clothing factory. Unfortunately, WASHOUT 'was always ill-suited both by temperament and ability to the role of secret agent'. His case, had, however, served one purpose, in that his letters were used by SIS as the basis for protests to the Portuguese Government about the operations of German agents in Lisbon.[13]

HAMLET, MULLET and PUPPET

'Much more interesting and important' was the case of HAMLET and the other agents connected with him.[14] MI5's connection with HAMLET was made through MULLET, a British subject born in Belgium. He was educated in Belgium and in Paris, and had been in business in Belgium most of his life. In the words of one MI5 officer: 'He is in many ways more Belgian than English.' His wife, was a member of a well known Belgian family. When the war extended to Belgium in May 1940, MULLET rendered certain services as a guide and interpreter to the British Army. He had previously attempted to join the army as a volunteer but the Military Attaché in Brussels had told him that there was at that time no opportunity of his being trained for military service if he came over to England. In these circumstances, MULLET and his wife and children left Belgium on 16 May 1940, and lived in Unoccupied France until August 1941 when they left for Britain via Lisbon – MULLET having finally succeeded in persuading a medical tribunal that he was unfit for military service and so could be legitimately repatriated under the terms of the Armistice.

MULLET was in Lisbon from 30 September until 24 November, 1941, waiting for seats on the aeroplane for himself, his wife and children. About 15 October, MULLET received a telephone call from a man who was a close friend of a cousin of MULLET's mother. MULLET accordingly invited the man to dinner, during the course of which the latter, apart from dealing with the family business, mentioned that he had met in the train on the way to Lisbon a very friendly German whose children were in England; he had therefore suggested that MULLET might take over to the children certain property which their father was anxious to send them. For this reason, the friend of the family said, the German was anxious to make his acquaintance. MULLET, after obtaining the approval of the British and Belgian authorities in Lisbon, agreed to this suggestion and a few days later was invited to dinner at the Palacio Hotel, Estoril, by a man who was later given the codename HAMLET by the British.

After this introduction MULLET dined with HAMLET about twenty-five times in the course of the next six weeks. Usually present were the man who had introduced them and another Belgian called Tyssen, who was then resident in Portugal where he owned or managed a coalmine. In the course of these conversations it appeared that the man who introduced the Briton to the German was no casual acquaintance of HAMLET, as had been alleged, but his secretary; further, though a Belgian, he was 'more pro-German than the Germans'. It also appeared that Tyssen had got into some trouble with the authorities in Occupied Belgium and that HAMLET had arranged permission for him to travel to Portugal, as a result of which Tyssen was permanently indebted to the latter.

HAMLET told MULLET that he was a German-Austrian, 100 per cent Catholic and very anti-semitic; his conduct and conversation showed that he was 'very conscious of his social and intellectual superiority to the majority of his fellow human beings, and very overbearing to his inferiors'. He had served in the Austrian Air Force in the last war, reaching the rank of captain, and after that had resumed his profession as a chemical engineer. He had a business of his own in Brussels where he employed sixteen chemists working under his direction, and was apparently a man of considerable importance as he had recently travelled in Germany and was treated with deference by many officials. HAMLET explained to MULLET that he had been in England in the early days of the war and had a business associate in the UK. HAMLET first asked MULLET if he would bring some diamonds over to his two children who had been living in England since before the war, where they had been sent for the purpose of their education; he offered to pay MULLET's air passage if the latter could leave for England immediately. At a later stage he asked for the diamonds back, stated that he had arranged to send his children £100 through New York, and asked MULLET to bring certain gold-plated articles to the children instead. In addition, HAMLET's conversation dealt principally with two other topics, business and peace propaganda.

HAMLET explained that he had come to Portugal to form two Portuguese companies, a holding company and an operating company, for the exploitation of certain patents. His representative in Portugal was a Portuguese of Dutch extraction. The patents of which HAMLET principally spoke were a lemonade powder, a degreasing fluid, and a bandage. HAMLET suggested that MULLET should be appointed as his representative in Britain with the object of exploiting his patents in that country, and proposed to give him a power of attorney with this object in mind. MULLET declined this proposal on the advice of British officials in Lisbon. HAMLET nevertheless told him to think it over and suggested that he should get in touch with his representatives in England or Belgium if he wished to go ahead with the business proposals. MULLET noted that when discussing the development of his business interests in England HAMLET was always very careful not to be overheard and impressed on MULLET the necessity for keeping this secret from the Germans; he had no objection, however, to MULLET keeping the British authorities fully informed.

During their meetings, HAMLET also talked to MULLET at length about politics and the war. He represented himself as a member of the old German officer class who was in favour of the Nazi philosophy in so far as it was anti-Jewish and anti-democratic, but opposed to its interference with business. He believed that England and Germany were the two greatest nations in the world, and that their common interest was to live at peace and strengthen their position against their common enemies which were the United States, Russia, France and Japan. He referred in general terms to the desirability of Germany making peace with England, which he said could be done without any loss of face because German military honour had been vindicated in Russia. He urged MULLET to repeat his views to people whom he met in England. MULLET remembered him saying with great emphasis: 'When you get to England tell them that these are the views of the real leaders of Germany.' MULLET noted with surprise that HAMLET never hesitated to express these views in public or to be seen by members of the German colony and legation in Lisbon holding such conversations with an Englishman. While wishing to preserve secrecy about his commercial proposals he took no such precautions with regard to his political views.

When MULLET came to Britain at the end of November 1941 he reported fully on his relations with HAMLET in Lisbon. He had been careful to keep the British authorities in Lisbon informed of this contact and had done so with HAMLET's knowledge and approval. When his story was considered an attempt was made to assess what lay behind HAMLET's talk. Three possible explanations were considered by MI5: 1. That HAMLET's motives were purely commercial, that he was an able businessman who was trying to develop his business interests to the maximum possible extent in Portugal and England as well as in enemy occupied territory, and that his views on politics and the war were purely personal; 2. That HAMLET had some mission from the German authorities to put out peace feelers; 3. That HAMLET was engaged in espionage and was using his business as a cover and his peace talk to sugar the pill.

It was felt that 1. was unlikely to be the whole explanation of his activities because if he had no official connections it was unlikely that he would have had the influence to talk so freely about the war in public with an Englishman. It was also felt that 3. was unlikely because he had made no real effort to use his acquaintance with MULLET for purposes of espionage. While no great confidence could be felt that 2. was the true explanation, it was nevertheless felt that HAMLET must have some official backing, and that he was probably at the same time trying to develop his own business interests and carry on some officially inspired peace propaganda: therefore, the case warranted further investigation, and it was accordingly decided that MULLET should get in touch with the HAMLET children in Britain, and that the commercial utility of the degreasing patent should be examined with the idea of sending MULLET back to Lisbon, ostensibly to purchase the patent rights if it seemed of interest, but in reality to find out who was behind HAMLET in his peace aims. A subsidiary contingent object was to cause discord between HAMLET's 'real leaders of Germany' and the German Government.

In accordance with this decision MULLET got in touch with HAMLET's children – one of whom who had come to Britain as a domestic servant but was then (in December 1941) serving as a probationer nurse. Her brother was working in Leicester. It appeared from MULLET's contact with HAMLET's children that they were pleasant and well-educated young people of noticeably Jewish appearance, who had evidently come to Britain as refugees, the daughter having only described herself as a domestic servant for the purposes of obtaining a visa. HAMLET's business 'representative' in Britain was interviewed in due course but it appeared that this gentleman, who now held a Commission in the navy, knew very little about HAMLET and had merely given him an introduction at the request of a mutual business acquaintance. The attempts to investigate the commercial possibilities of the degreasing fluid were not very successful as the documents containing details of the specification had been lost; from what MULLET was able to tell MI5 from memory it did not appear probable that this invention was one of which the British would wish to make use in wartime. Nevertheless it was decided that MULLET should endeavour to obtain further information in order to keep up the HAMLET connection. He accordingly wrote a letter to HAMLET on 18 March 1942, referring to his previous conversations with HAMLET and asking for further particulars of the patent. A telegraphic reply was received from on 24 May, reading: 'Impossible poursuivre negociations sans nouvelles mon correspondant.' As HAMLET had returned to Belgium shortly before MULLET left Portugal for the United Kingdom, it appeared that he was still away and the case therefore appeared dead, or at least moribund.

As MULLET had now been hanging around practically unemployed for nearly six months after having come over to join the Armed Forces, steps were taken to let him fulfil this object. In fact he was taken on by SOE but after a fortnight's training he was released from their employment as not entirely suitable, and he then joined the army in the ordinary way as a private and started his primary training. But then, on 17 June, MULLET received a letter from Lisbon. This came from HAMLET, who stated that he had returned to Lisbon and that he was taking out a Portuguese patent for a product and that he had certain samples with him and was expecting other samples and other particulars which MULLET had asked for in his letter. He said that he did not expect to remain there long but spoke of the possibility of seeing MULLET in Lisbon again if he were able to return at a later date. MULLET replied in a non-committal way saying that he would be glad to hear when HAMLET would be in Lisbon again, and on 20 July received a telegram asking him to start applying for his passport immediately. Before he complied with this request MI5 felt it was desirable to obtain some further indication as to whether HAMLET wished to resume discussions only about business or about his peace propaganda as well. MULLET's reply was accordingly non committal in tone but indicated that the friends on whose assistance he counted in order to be able to make the journey, would be more interested in helping him if they had some indication that HAMLET had other proposals to put forward. The reply was received from HAMLET himself on 9 August, stating: 'Everything ready for (blank) and others suggestion (blank). Very interesting your friends.'

Preparations were accordingly made for MULLET to leave for Lisbon as soon as possible, which he did during the last week of August. He went out with instructions which covered both the commercial and political sides of the case. As his mission was ostensibly to do with business he was supplied with a number of letters representing correspondence with the Ministry of Food about degreasing fluid or fatless soap, in which the Ministry expressed interest in the patent and asked for further particulars of its specification and manufacture. On the political side MULLET was supplied with a story about various contacts which he had notionally made in the City with prominent business men who were interested in HAMLET's political ideas about the identity of interests between Britain and Germany, and the desirability of an early peace. 'Armed with this bait' MULLET left for Lisbon on 26 August 1942, it being expected that he and HAMLET would each endeavour to discover the undisclosed principal behind the other, and hoped that MULLET would be the more successful of the two. MULLET was in Lisbon from 28 August to 10 September 1942. During this time he was in touch with HAMLET almost daily and often spent the greater part of the day with him.

In the course of their conversations HAMLET made some 'very interesting revelations' to MULLET. He said that MULLET, having seen his children, must now realise who he was, and that he had good grounds for hating the Nazis because he had suffered so much at their hands: HAMLET revealed that he was Jewish. And, in addition to being a Jew himself, he had been imprisoned at their hands and lost his property in Austria before starting his business in Belgium. He explained that his chief desires now were to revenge himself on the

Nazis and help his children, but that at heart he was a good German and a good European and therefore believed that the only way all these objects could be achieved was for the German Army to kick out the Nazis and make peace. He had come to Lisbon to start a bureau for obtaining information about Britain and the United States, which he was going to use to convince the responsible leaders of the German Army that they had lost the war, and that it was in their interest to accept the Allies' peace terms. The information that he obtained would go direct to Admiral Canaris, whom he described as the Head of the German Intelligence, one of the most powerful men in Germany and the real leader of the army, who was also in close touch with Hitler, by whom all his reports were seen. If the Allies were prepared to pass him information – possibly exaggerated – showing the overwhelming strength of Britain and the United States, he could pass the information through Canaris to the German High Command and to Hitler, with the object of convincing them that they had nothing to gain by going on fighting. He claimed that since MULLET's last visit to Lisbon he had become a first class agent of the German Intelligence Service, and was reporting direct to Canaris using the German Diplomatic Bag from Lisbon, through Korft, the Commercial Attaché in that city. No one in Lisbon, however, had any control over him. He was using his cover as an agent to develop his business activities, and also to try in his own way to bring the war to an end as quickly as possible. He emphasised that he wanted MULLET to act quickly in getting information about British and American production, and said that he could give MULLET secret ink with which the latter could write letters which the British censors would never discover. Alternatively and preferably, if the British Government would agree to supply information, MULLET could use the Diplomatic Bag and send communications to HAMLET through the British Military attaché in Lisbon. HAMLET emphasised that he was not an ordinary spy trying to get military information about new weapons and things of that sort, but was more interested in the larger issues of production, morale and politics. He wanted MULLET to get in touch with one or two men very highly placed and mentioned the Foreign Secretary, Anthony Eden, or someone in his immediate entourage.

HAMLET told MULLET that one of his friends who shared his views was a Colonel on the staff of General von Falkenhausen – essentially the ruler of Occupied Belgium – in Brussels. It was this Colonel, with whom he was in close contact, who gave him his instructions and had been responsible for getting him appointed as a first class agent. He would not give MULLET the name of this Colonel but said that he could come down to Lisbon if necessary. He also showed MULLET an extract from a typewritten letter in German, which contained instructions from the Colonel to get his commercial information service working in England and South America as quickly as possible. Another of his friends in Brussels, he said, was an Austrian – codenamed by MI5 as PUPPET – who had lived in Belgium since 1933; he was not only anti-Nazi but also anti-German and in favour of the restoration of Austria. PUPPET was a personal friend of von Falkenhausen – MULLET was able to obtain independent confirmation of this later. HAMLET said that PUPPET and he had the same ideals and wanted to get rid of the Nazis, and he believed that von Falkenhausen shared his ideas, disliked the Gestapo and the Gestapo system, and realised that Germany had lost the war.

HAMLET also questioned MULLET about the food situation in Britain, and was so impressed by what MULLET told him that he asked for a written report on this subject. MULLET, after taking instructions, complied with this request, and HAMLET stated that this report would go through to Canaris and Hitler and amount to one instalment of the picture which HAMLET wished to build up of an invincible Britain. In return, HAMLET gave to MULLET, as a proof of his good faith, a copy of an official report on the oil industry in Belgium, for which he said the British authorities would be prepared to pay £1,000. This was subsequently passed by SIS to the Ministry of Economic Warfare, who considered it a most valuable document. As HAMLET was leaving Lisbon shortly before MULLET was due to return to Britain, it was arranged that the latter should communicate with Mrs Ida Spitz, a Viennese Jewess who hated the Nazis, and had resided in Portugal since 1936. An *en clair* code was to be employed and MULLET was to telegraph stating that: 'Acid Lemonsecco' had, or had not been, successful, by which he would indicate whether or not his efforts to interest the British authorities in HAMLET's proposals were successful. HAMLET said goodbye to MULLET on the evening of 9 September, and practically his last words to MULLET were: 'Whatever happens to me my children are cared for now. If I disappear they need not worry – they have enough money to live on.'

After MULLET had returned to England on 10 September, a full report on the results of his mission was prepared and the HAMLET case was again reviewed by MI5.[15] Among those reviewing the case was Chris Harmer. After hearing and considering MULLET's story, in Harmer's view no consideration of the MULLET case was possible without an adequate appreciation of HAMLET's background:

It must always be borne in mind that this man is an Austrian Jew with a Russian mother, and that since the advent of the Nazis to power he has been wandering from one country to another in Europe until finally he has found his way to Brussels. We know that he was put in a concentration camp, but only for a very short period, and the possibility must not be overlooked of this having been, as in other cases we know about, a cover for some sinister activity later on. The fact that, even if we accept in full his account of his ill treatment at the hands of the Nazis, he has managed to recover his position and become once again a prosperous man, shows that he is intelligent and, in all the circumstances, cunning. Therefore in my view, however genuine HAMLET's views and actions seemed to a man like MULLET, they should always be regarded as part of a cleverly designed scheme to achieve some definite purpose.

Having said this, in Harmer's opinion, HAMLET's statements were in substance correct. The evidence tended to show that HAMLET was not engaged in espionage, but had some unofficial backing for the views he put forward with regard to peace. HAMLET had confirmed to MULLET that this was in fact the position. HAMLET said further that since he last saw MULLET he had been appointed a German agent, and a certain amount of confirmatory evidence was obtainable on this point from Most Secret Sources, 'in that we never had any record of HAMLET in these sources before recent times'. On the main set-up of HAMLET's story: 'I am of the opinion that he has told MULLET in substance the truth.'

However, in Harmer's view, 'there are various matters of detail upon which HAMLET has not told MULLET the truth or the whole truth'. Thus Harmer could not accept HAMLET's statement that the reason he wanted information for Canaris was so that the latter could be persuaded that Germany would lose the war. Harmer thought it more probable that the reason HAMLET wanted to send information to Canaris was to build up his position as an agent in the latter's eyes. 'I do not think either that we should accept wholly HAMLET's statement that he is a first class agent, or the story about the Colonel.' In sum there appeared to be three possibilities with regard to the story told by HAMLET to MULLET. They were:

1. That HAMLET is speaking the whole truth and nothing but the truth. For reasons indicated… and also because of HAMLET's background as an intriguer and scheming man, I do not think we can accept this conclusion.

2. That everything HAMLET said to MULLET was said on the orders of the Germans. In other words, that HAMLET was sent down to Lisbon by the Germans, who realised from MULLET's letters that British Intelligence was behind his visit on an analogous kind of mission. This is a conclusion which one is very tempted to make on the facts of the case, but, in order to make it, it is necessary, I think, to decide what would be the Germans' objective. A possible objective would be that they wished to prevent the Allies in the west from taking any military action in the near future by convincing them that German morale was very low and that the war could be won by intensive bombing raids. In this way they might hope to make us hesitate, and thus gain valuable time. Against this, HAMLET impressed on MULLET that the Dieppe raid was a great success and that he thought that the Allies would have no difficulty in landing in Europe, and moreover the Germans would have need of more men to keep peace in the occupied countries than to fight battles against the Allied armies. His fear about a second front was not from a military point of view, but because of the tremendous destruction which it would cause in Western Europe.

Had HAMLET, therefore, been sent down with an objective such as I have outlined above, I do not think that he would have expressed these views about a second front.

A second objective might be to try to inveigle some responsible British official down to Lisbon to talk peace with HAMLET's Colonel, and then play on us the sort of trick we hoped to play on them, namely, to let the Russians or Americans know about it with a view to causing friction between the Allies. This might be a possible objective, but in that event – and indeed on any other basis than the second front one – I cannot see that HAMLET could have been given authority to tell MULLET that German morale was very low and to emphasise the paramount necessity of bombing Germany. We know from our own activities that it is an impossibility to be allowed to put forward views of this sort. Therefore, if HAMLET had been sent down on an analogous mission to MULLET, I think we would be entitled to expect that he would have emphasised the futility of carrying out bombing raids and that German morale in spite of such raids was high.

In my view, therefore, alternative 2. cannot be accepted either.

3. That HAMLET is playing a game entirely for himself. This is the view that I take of the case. I think it quite probable

that with MULLET's letters he has bluffed certain responsible German leaders into appointing him an agent in Lisbon, and that he has made promises to his German masters that through his relations in America and Britain and contacts in business circles throughout the world he will be able to render them a very valuable service as an information bureau. I think that having done this he has set up his office with the intention of running a glorious racket whereby he starts companies abroad to exploit his various processes; that in the course of this business he obtains valuable information which he transmits to the Germans; and that he spends the war in comfort in Lisbon and finishes up one of the most powerful industrialists in Europe, all the time sitting pretty with both sides.

For instance, should any of his tricks become known to the Germans, he will explain them away by saying that this type of conduct or remark is necessary in order to enable him to obtain the valuable information. Similarly, so far as the British are concerned, he discloses his work for the Germans, but offers to double-cross them. I think that his tactics in this case i.e. to ask for information to make CANARIS come down on the peace side of the fence, are probably unique to the MULLET case, and that he would probably vary his approach so far as other people are concerned. In short, I think that HAMLET is playing a very risky and clever game, and he may very well succeed. A good example of the way he behaves is that of his getting three influential Portuguese on to the Board of his Company and giving them large blocks of shares so that the Portuguese authorities would give him a visa more readily.

HAMLET, Harmer had good reason to believe, was an Abwehr official, 'and I think MULLET's story confirms it. I think that he will make every effort to run his information bureau successfully, even to the extent of making up information if he does not receive it from his contacts.' In view of the opinion expressed above that HAMLET was running a racket and that that was his technique with his various customers, 'I think that his peace talks should be taken with a considerable grain of salt. On the other hand, I would expect his business affairs to be completely genuine and of great value. If his talks about the political situation in Germany and the possibilities of peace are analysed, it will be seen that they represent at the best very little more than his own personal opinions. I think we should therefore not pay too much attention to the peace side of the talks.'

Harmer thought that HAMLET's affection for his children was genuine, 'and this is probably the one really constant factor in his life outside his own personal interests'.[16]

Harmer's assessment impressed TAR Robertson who considered that great credit was due to Harmer for the way in which he extracted the information from MULLET, 'who is not an easy customer to deal with when it comes to getting a story on paper'. He thought, also, that MULLET himself was to be congratulated for the way in which he had carried out his mission. Yet TAR, in contrast to Harmer, was 'very much inclined to think that we have got to accept the story at its face value and not to lay too much emphasis on any one particular aspect of the case'. He agreed with Masterman, who had pointed out that HAMLET was a man who was obviously going to build himself up as much as possible in the eyes of a man like MULLET; at the same time, 'I am rather inclined to think that, although the business side of HAMLET discussions with MULLET is probably genuine, Harmer's construction of this side of the case is probably a little too strong. I think there is a distinct possibility that the rift between the army and the party is becoming more apparent and the thing that strikes me most forcibly in the whole report is the fact that HAMLET should say that he would like information from this country about past happenings but that in order to convince his military masters, this information should be exaggerated.' Robertson felt that if HAMLET was endeavouring to get information out of MULLET for purely espionage purposes, he would surely lay stress on the fact that this information should be as accurate as possible. Another point which he considered significant was the way in which HAMLET viewed 'the American problem. He does not seem to bother to hide his dislike for the United States'.[17]

Masterman, in turn, acknowledged the 'special difficulties' in forming a balanced judgement on this case. When the case began it seemed possible that it was nothing but a commercial business, 'and the fact that it has proved to have an interesting political and espionage side carries with it a danger of accepting too readily the value of it to us'. HAMLET's obvious tendency to exaggerate his own importance and his own power, together with his equally obvious and natural desire to do the best that he could for himself and his family, 'are on the other hand likely to predispose one to dismiss him as a fraud or simply a self-seeker'. A further difficulty was that British Intelligence, at this stage at any rate, could not speak or listen to HAMLET himself, but had to take all their evidence filtered through MULLET. For all these reasons 'an unprejudiced judgement is difficult'. Masterman, however, was inclined to think that HAMLET was genuine, and that the case had great possibilities – 'though rather for other Departments than for us'; by this he meant with regard to possible peace feelers from the Germans. Masterman thought the matter of dates important: at MULLET's earlier meetings with HAMLET, in October/November 1941, the conversation, 'or that part of it in which we are interested', was confined to two subjects – business and the possibilities of peace negotiations. No attempt was made to arrange for MULLET to send over information, and no sort of questionnaire was given to him. This bore out HAMLET's own statement that he had become an important agent *since* the earlier meetings. But it also bore out his contention that he now required information for the reasons which he had given i.e. to convince wavering Germans of high position that Germany must lose the war in the long run, and that the army should therefore seize power in order to make a peace, for he put forward the 'peace proposals' at the first meetings when he did *not* want information. 'I therefore regard his political proposals as a genuine statement of his views and his hopes, and not as a cunning screen put out to cover his quest for information.' Masterman did not think that 'we need worry' about the suggestion made by Harmer that HAMLET might be 'intending to drive a wedge between us and the Russians by luring us into peace negotiations and then announcing them. Such negotiations can always be disavowed, and it is always open to us to tell our allies that we are in fact trying to find out how much division there is between the Party and the Army, in order to make use of it.' And, for HAMLET to stress the weakness of German morale 'runs clean contrary to all German propaganda'. Masterman was more sceptical when it came to HAMLET's account of his relationship with Canaris, which did not ring true.

Masterman therefore came to the conclusion that the most probable explanation was that HAMLET and his story were genuine: 'I believe that his first object (of which he has made no secret) is to secure his own position and the future of himself and his children, but that his second object is, as he states, to convince waverers of the need for the Army chiefs to gain power in order to bring about a speedy peace.' MI5 had to guard themselves 'constantly against accepting the facile and erroneous view' that because HAMLET was a Jew with a shrewd eye to the main chance, he was therefore 'necessarily incapable of having other motives in acting as he does'. In Masterman's general estimate of HAMLET, he was guided to a great extent by MULLET's own appreciation of him. MULLET 'is in my opinion a shrewd and entirely honest man with good training and sound basic ideas. It is commendable in him that he is chiefly anxious now to get back to his army training and not to be involved instead in what may be quite lucrative business. He is not a very good reporter, but he is an excellent observer, and he has quite clear cut impressions which he retails without hesitation if a direct question is put to him.' His conviction that HAMLET was genuine 'impresses me'.

What now had to be decided was the action to be taken. The uses to which the case could be put depended mainly upon the line which 'we are taking with regard to the possible split between the Party and the Army in Germany'. In a report the Polish Assistant Military Attaché in Lisbon had argued: 'I think quite truly, that this can be encouraged in two ways, (1) by not frightening the German national with "revenge" and "punishment" motives (whatever we really intend to do), and (2) by persuading the German nation of the limitless strength and power of the Allies.' If this was their policy, the case might well be used to further it; but obviously the decision as to method would have to be taken by authorities outside MI5. It might, for example, be considered advisable to supply HAMLET with exactly the sort of information which he himself suggested; it might, on the other hand, be thought better to send some one out to Lisbon to contact him and if possible to get the affair on a higher level, or at any rate to test out MULLET's estimate of him.

As a result of these assessments a conference was held at which it was decided that that MULLET should be sent to Lisbon once more. He would be going to find out if there was any substance in HAMLET's 1941 talks, 'so that we could decide on his return whether to follow up the case or not'. The Security Service was taking the case along in the hope that it might be useful to other Departments, particularly the Foreign Office. But it also seemed that the case had its espionage side which might be of equal importance with the other, especially because of the alleged connection with Canaris. Masterman recommended that all the papers should be handed to Major Foley, who was C's representative on the XX Committee.[18] SIS were, indeed, interested and Foley was assigned the task of accompanying MULLET back to Lisbon. MI5 issued the latter with his instructions:

1. You are travelling out to Lisbon with Major Foley. You will take instructions from him during the journey as to the supposed relationship between you and the method to be employed for contacting one another in Lisbon.
2. Your prime task in Lisbon will be to bring together HAMLET and Major Foley (under a name which he will indicate to you). The method of doing this will be laid down by Major Foley.

3. In the meantime you will tell HAMLET the story set out on the attached paper. After HAMLET and Major Foley have met you will act under the instructions of the latter.

4. You will hand to HAMLET reports on Non Food Commodities, Morale and Production, as well as certain menus bearing on the Food Report already sent.

5. In your commercial transactions with [HAMLET] and his associates you will endeavour to get such extension to the Power of Attorney and other agreements in your favour as will ensure a continuation of the commercial relationship as cover for possible future contact. You should not, however, indicate to them too optimistic an outlook in this respect. You can, if necessary, at your discretion, reveal to HAMLET that your commercial conversations are primarily a cover for the other discussions.

6. Generally with regard to your return and further developments you will act in accordance with HAMLET's instructions. You will not contact anyone else in Lisbon without his authority.[19]

MULLET returned to Lisbon on 15 December in the company of Major Foley (or MAJOR X as he was also referred to) with instructions to explain that he was now in direct contact with British Intelligence. Major Foley had several interviews with HAMLET and his associate, PUPPET. From these it emerged that he had set up the 'Kolberg Organisation' as a cover for collecting information, which he wished to do in the manner most conducive to an Allied victory. But, of course, the Germans thought that HAMLET was their man and, as such, working for the Brussels Stelle of the Abwehr under Major Bergman (whose real name was Brinkhaus) the Chief of Eins Heer in Brussels. HAMLET had originally come to Lisbon to establish, under genuine business cover, the 'Kolberg Organisation', an espionage service directed – as far the Germans thought – against Britain and the Western Hemisphere, working independently of the Lisbon Stelle, and in direct touch with Brussels through diplomatic bag. Korff, the Commercial Secretary in the German Legation in Lisbon, was the intermediary. Berlin agreed to the establishment of this new organisation because they were dissatisfied with Lisbon's work and wished to establish a channel under commercial cover in case diplomatic cover became unworkable owing to an Allied occupation of Portugal.

Bergman, according to HAMLET, was a man who belonged to a family interested in the textile trade but was a professional soldier who had lost money on horses. He had nothing to do with General von Falkenhausen in Brussels, but HAMLET took advantage of his financial difficulties to interest him in his business by giving him shares in his companies. When the partnership was well established HAMLET had suggested that he should be given facilities to go to Lisbon to establish his organisation there, and Bergman had agreed to obtain the necessary authority. HAMLET, through the 'Kolberg Organisation', had by the end of 1942 established six imaginary sub-agents who were all Poles, about whose names and departure from Lisbon HAMLET had somehow managed to find out. One of these sub-agents was notionally in England and the remainder in America. By extensive reading of newspapers and magazines and by picking the brains of persons whom he met in Lisbon, HAMLET had forwarded to Bergman seventy-three reports up to 13 January 1943. These reports had evidently been well thought of by Bergman who had told HAMLET, for his information, that one or two items had been observed independently in the press. The material sent on had included five reports supplied by MULLET himself. It seemed that Bergman was most anxious that the 'Kolberg Organisation' should remain independent of the Lisbon Stelle and that he was trying to establish a wireless station of his own, with the idea of taking over the whole German Intelligence Service in Portugal in the event of an Allied occupation of the country. Indeed, Bergman described the Lisbon Stelle as their 'competitors'.

PUPPET, HAMLET's accomplice, was in fact a member of Nest Cologne, to whom he was known as V-Mann (German secret agent) FUERST, by arrangement with whom he also worked for Eins Heer, Brussels, under the pseudonym of Famulus. With this background PUPPET was an ideal ally to build up HAMLET's position in the eyes of his Abwehr masters, as indeed he appears to have done successfully, while becoming at the same time privy to all HAMLET's secrets.[20] PUPPET, was an Austrian whose mother was a member of the old Austrian nobility. He had been schooled in Dresden before travelling to the United States to learn the lumber business. From 1931–1942 he was an office manager, sales manager and later a managing director of a company in Brussels. Between 10 May–10 July 1940, however, PUPPET was deported to France as an enemy alien. There he volunteered to join the French Foreign Legion, but before his actual enlistment was arranged, the French armistice took place and he was released. From July 1940–November 1942 he lived in Brussels. Before the German invasion of Belgium he had succeeded in transferring most of the company's liquid assets to the United States. In autumn 1940 PUPPET became friendly with General von Falkenhausen, the Military Governor of Belgium, on an introduction from his father who was a fellow art student of the General's in their youth. He became an intimate friend of von Falkenhausen and spent numerous weekends with the General at the Chateau de Seneffe, and was a member of his small circle of poker playing friends.

At the end of January 1942, HAMLET met PUPPET at a dinner party in Brussels. PUPPET was about to visit Portugal in an attempt to obtain fatty acids for his business in Belgium, a project in which HAMLET, having just returned from Portugal might be able to assist him. A business connection between the two subsequently developed. In the middle of February, PUPPET made the journey to Portugal in quest of raw materials for his factory, but met with little success. Before leaving he was asked by a man called Herm to report any economic intelligence which he could obtain on his journey, but received no special training as an agent. It had been Herm who had introduced PUPPET to HAMLET. Herm was described by PUPPET as a captain, aged between forty-five and fifty, a cultivated man and a good musician, whom PUPPET believed to have been a member of the Abwehr for a number of years.

After PUPPET's return to Brussels, his friendship with HAMLET developed. HAMLET knew that PUPPET was on friendly terms with von Falkenhausen and was quick to take advantage of the opportunity thus presented. In April or May, Bergmann gave a dinner party at which were present Herm, HAMLET and PUPPET; on this occasion it was suggested and agreed that PUPPET should join the Kolberg Organisation. Herm told PUPPET privately that if he did so and went to Lisbon he must send all economic information from Portugal to him through the German Legation in Lisbon. From the beginning HAMLET got on well with Bergmann, but was distrusted by Herm, who was bitterly anti-semitic. PUPPET on the other hand disliked Bergmann 'whom he regards as stupid', but got on well with Herm 'whom he regards as an intelligent and cultivated man'. Herm made it clear to PUPPET that he did not trust HAMLET and PUPPET was in effect given the job of checking up on HAMLET's reliability. Bergmann on the other hand always believed in HAMLET. By this time also PUPPET had won HAMLET's confidence and the latter had elaborated his programme to the effect that the better elements in Germany must turn out the Nazis in the hopes of getting a compromised peace.

Now, after meeting with MULLET and Foley – known as MAJOR X in Lisbon – HAMLET proposed that he should come to England in furtherance of his scheme but, on Foley's rejection of this idea, it was suggested that PUPPET should come instead. This idea was approved on both the British and German sides and a conference was held in Biarritz at the end of January between representatives of the Brussels Abwehrstelle and KO Lisbon to settle the details. It was decided that PUPPET should come to England under the commercial cover afforded by MULLET's agency of the Portuguese company and should send to Lisbon in secret ink information collected from a notional Polish agent already established there and possibly from other agents, whom he should recruit himself. At a previous meeting in Estoril at which MULLET was interviewed, an attempt was made to check that HAMLET and PUPPET were not being endangered by a double game on MULLET's part. It was apparently decided as a result of this meeting that MULLET was an honest business man who was not working for the British Intelligence but had been imposed upon by the wily HAMLET.[21]

HAMLET wanted MI5 to supply him with information for his work, 'but made the rather startling suggestion that all the information which we should give him should be information which would indicate the strength of Great Britain, particularly with regard to the bombing of Germany, in order that the hands of those opposing Hitler should be strengthened'. Clearly, then, 'the case offered great opportunity for political warfare, for it provided a channel whereby we could be reasonably sure that information about our power and resources would reach the right quarters in Germany'.[22] Unfortunately, it also became apparent that the 'impression or assumption that HAMLET represented a Peace Party, or a group of German officers and others who were weakening in their determination to continue the war and were thinking of sounding us about a compromise on an anti Nazi basis, is wrong'. HAMLET asserted, and his statements were confirmed independently by PUPPET, that General von Falkenhausen, Colonel von Harbou and many officers on the Governor's staff and in the Armed forces of the Reich, were convinced that Germany had lost this war when she failed to invade England; 'but these men did not send HAMLET to Lisbon to negotiate'. The truth was that he was not in direct touch with von Falkenhausen or von Harbou. The General, Foley had learnt, was 'most exclusive and would not receive a Jew. He does not automatically receive even German officers.' It was, however, true that, until fairly, recently the General and his entourage openly criticised the Party and the Führer's conduct of operations. But the dismissal of high officers in the Reich and the appointment of a Nazi official to the Governor's staff 'had a sudden sobering effect. They have harnessed their tongues'. Foley assumed that officers and politicians throughout the Reich 'have also become more discreet and that if there is any inclination in the army to plot against Hitler, it will be done without running lines to any one outside, unless they are very sure in advance of the contacts that are to be met. They will not send a man out on to neutral highways to look for them.'

HAMLET was merely the representative of the Abwehrstelle at Brussels and in particular of Major Bergmann. It interested Foley to know whether Bergmann had approached HAMLET or HAMLET Bergmann, and in either case what had determined Bergmann to back HAMLET, to trust him and to press for permission to employ him in spite of the prohibition against the use of Jews without the explicit sanction of Himmler. HAMLET, after all, was 'not a small agent controlled by an immediate chief but the controlling person in an organisation outside Germany. Both questions are closely connected with the personalities of the two men'. HAMLET was:

> a typical example of the extremely clever and well educated merchant banker who flourished in Central Europe and who made large fortunes at home and larger ones when they emigrated to Western Europe and the Western Hemisphere. They had great contempt for the brains of the aristocratic officer class. He studied law; so did his father, grandfather and great grandfather. He is proud that four generations of HAMLETs have been doctors of law. He has always been rich. The Nazis broke him and dispersed his family. He went to Brussels, the Nazis caught up. He has, according to his statement, been in prison twice, but not in a concentration camp. He was an officer in the air arm of the Austrian Army in the last war. He was Austrian Intelligence officer at Trieste for six months. In Brussels he was trapped again, he developed an all absorbing desire to revenge himself, or as he understates it, to settle his account with the Nazis.

HAMLET's plan of attack and revenge was based on his knowledge of the state of the German military mind, which thought defeat inevitable. He would further depress their minds and weaken their fighting spirit by emphasising to the actual and potential strength of the allied nations. He felt he was clever enough to serve up acceptable reports received theoretically, from agents, but in fact gathered from open sources such as newspapers. 'It must not be forgotten that he has the greatest contempt for their intelligence.' Foley thought it wise to build up HAMLET's organisation by making the Germans think that he had succeeded in placing a first class agent – PUPPET – in England: 'The more they valued his work the easier it would be for him to double back on them in our interest.' This was 'the ideal type of double-cross agent as it avoids the flaw in the French system when the agent was allowed access to both countries. HAMLET can only give the Germans what we give him through PUPPET. Revenge is the best motive.' And, of course, the Germans 'will pay for the whole service'.[23]

The HAMLET case, though, presented clear difficulties for MI5 in terms of what exactly the XX should be used for. The continuation of the HAMLET case with PUPPET operating in Britain as a double-agent under MI5's control and reporting to HAMLET in Lisbon appeared to one Security Service officer, A.H. Robertson to have the advantage that, unlike any of the other double-agents now functioning in Britain, 'the "spy-master" as well as the spy would be acting under our control and in our interests'. It appeared to be the case that the 'ordinary "spy-master" is always very anxious to justify the agent to his superiors, and reluctant to believe that he is working as a double-cross; nevertheless in this case the "spy-master" will not only have the ordinary incentive to justify the good faith of his agent but will know that in all probability his life will be forfeit if the true position of the agent is discovered, because he will himself be not only an accomplice but the instigator of the double-cross'. So long as MI5 believed in HAMLET's good faith, 'as in my opinion we must do, there are the strongest reasons for supposing that the double-cross will operate successfully'. Potentially the greatest value of running the HAMLET case, in Robertson's opinion, was 'its possible post-occupational use in Portugal. We know that Berlin is anxious for HAMLET to have independent means of communication. (Special Sources). According to HAMLET this is because the Germans are anxious for him to continue operations in Portugal under commercial cover in the event of an Allied occupation of Portugal. Should this occur, it would be of the greatest value to have a German Intelligence Service already organised and operating in the country under our control'.

Against this, Robertson pointed out that the very fact of the 'spy-master' being an accomplice in the deception increased the danger, though not the likelihood, of the truth being discovered. By this Robertson meant that though HAMLET had a far greater interest than the ordinary 'spy-master' in preserving a belief in the honesty of the agent, 'there is nevertheless a possibility that his guilty knowledge might betray him, particularly if an enquiry into the case is held in Brussels or Berlin and he is summoned to it and cross-examined'.

For this reason MI5 should be particularly careful to keep a check on HAMLET's movements. 'Unfortunately,' warned Robertson, 'it appears that too many people may be, or may become privy to the secret.' It was unclear, for example, whether or not Bergmann – and others – were either aware of HAMLET's true position or were prepared to come over to the British side under his guidance;[24] there was even one report – from a German Secret Service agent working for the British – ARTIST – that: 'Brussels know that PUPPET is controlled by the British, but pretend not to.' ARTIST originally stated that he was asked to take on the running of this case, but was advised by KO Portugal 'not to touch it with a barge pole, as neither Berlin nor the Lisbon organisation had any faith in PUPPET'.[25] The result of all this was, ultimately, the sense of a lost opportunity; certainly, this was what Masterman felt:

> As a double-cross case HAMLET, MULLET, and PUPPET represented a highly attractive proposition and in some ways a unique opportunity. For purposes of information MULLET and PUPPET could be supplied by us and could pass their information to HAMLET under an elaborate business cover. This business cover was the branch of HAMLET's Portuguese company which was established in this country (and which compelled B.l.A to embark on considerable business activities connected with soaps, impregnated paper, and degreasing patents, as well as lemonade powder). The unique opportunity was that HAMLET, who was really himself a double-cross agent, was actually a member of the Abwehr, and we could therefore be sure that our information reached its goal and that it would in all probability be believed.
>
> There were, however, certain drawbacks, which prevented us from drawing a proper dividend from the case. In the first place, the opportunities which it offered to other departments made us chary of using the case fully for our own ends; secondly, HAMLET'S own motives were for a long time suspect, and he was not built up as he should have been by an adequate supply of information in the early days; and thirdly, we were unable to get as much information about him from other sources as we did in the case of other agents. As a result, full advantage was not taken of the opportunities presented, though some advantage was reaped from it at a later stage.[26]

8

Enter BRUTUS

In the autumn 'more recruits were added'.[1] JOSEF was a Russian of about thirty years of age, who was trained as a GPU agent and since 1934 had worked intermittently as a seaman, principally in Yugoslavia, Holland and Spain during the Spanish Civil War. He was a Communist, fairly well educated, knew a number of languages, and was 'undoubtedly clever and astute'. He first came to MI5's notice in 1941 in connection with some sabotage incidents on the Dutch SS *Parklaan*, which were never satisfactorily explained. He was detained in the Oratory Schools from March 1941 to August 1942, where he became friendly with Matsumoto, the former Honorary Press Attaché to the Japanese Embassy, about whom he reported to the Officer-in-Charge. After his release he went to Lisbon as a seaman and on MI5's instructions called at the Japanese Legation, introducing himself as a friend of Matsumoto's, a course which the latter had suggested during their internment. JOSEF visited the Japanese in Lisbon on at least three separate occasions: 'He has been seen by the Assistant Naval, Military and Press Attachés, also by two European sabotage experts, who were working with the Japanese in Lisbon and are believed to be Hungarians. On his last visit he took with him some information relating to shipping and marine construction on the Clyde; and the outlines of a plan for sabotage in the Glasgow docks.'[2] However, JOSEF and other seamen agents of the same kind were never an entirely satisfactory part of the XX system. As Masterman recalled: 'It is true that they established a useful link by personal contact with the Germans and Japanese at Lisbon, but in the nature of things they could not be properly controlled. However reliable we might consider such an agent, and however carefully he might be coached, it still remained true that a seafaring man might well, when questioned, give away a great deal, particularly about convoys, which we desired to suppress. Nor, again, could we be at all certain that he would accurately convey to the enemy the misinformation which we had given him. In fact, as much harm as good might well be done by a seaman agent of this kind.'[3]

GWLADYS was a young Welshman, educated at secondary schools and at Oxford where he read modern languages and took a war degree after one year's residence. As an undergraduate he interested himself in politics, having previously joined the Labour League of Youth and the Young Communist League. He ceased to be a member of the latter on the outbreak of war. He spoke Norwegian, French and Spanish, and had some knowledge of Italian, Portuguese, German and Swedish. On leaving Oxford in 1940 he went to sea, preferring a seaman's life to military service, and for two years was in a variety of Norwegian and Swedish ships, being torpedoed in June 1940. In September 1942, he applied to the Merchant Navy Reserve Pool for release in order to undergo training as a radio operator. This letter was shown to one of MI5's Port Officers and he was duly recruited to work as an agent.

In November 1942, at MI5's instigation, GWLADYS joined the Welsh Nationalist Party and became familiar with their organisation and policy, on which he duly reported. In December he signed on the Panamian SS *Gaizka*, which sailed between Port Talbot in South Wales, Lisbon and Dublin, with instructions to pose as a Welsh Nationalist. On her return from this voyage in January, he reported that when he was in Dublin, he got into touch with Edward Murphy, who was the organising secretary of the Pan-Celtic Union, an organisation which was trying to promote a united front between the Irish, Scottish and Welsh Nationalists against the common enemy of English domination and British Imperialism. Murphy also wished to bring into his united front the Breton Nationalists. GWLADYS played his Welsh Nationalist role 'with such effect' that he was requested by Murphy to act as a courier for taking copies of the Pan-Celtic Union manifesto to the Scottish, Welsh and Breton Nationalists, in explaining the objects and ideals of the Union and, generally, in organising the common front. GWLADYS duly got into touch with the Welsh and Scottish Nationalists, whose reception of Murphy's Union however was rather lukewarm.

The chief interest in GWLADYS' mission was the proposed link with the Breton Nationalists, because it was known from independent sources that there existed before the war a certain liaison between the Breton and Irish Nationalists, that the Germans had since the occupation of France subsidised the Bretons, that Murphy had quoted this fact with approval, and that the Abwehr had caused enquiries to be made in Brittany as to whether these links could be re-established. 'It therefore seemed interesting to arrange that they should be re-established through a channel which operated under our control.' GWLADYS was accordingly sent to Lisbon as a member of a crew which was being sent out to bring back to Britain a trawler which had just been built in Portugal. Arrangements were made with SIS that GWLADYS should be put in touch with a Portuguese who was working for the Germans as a contact man for British seamen in Lisbon under the direction of SIS.

This arrangement worked satisfactorily and GWLADYS was introduced by SIS's contact Kuno Weltzien, a German business man in Lisbon, who acted as an agent on behalf of Hans Bendixen the Leiter Eins of K.O. Portugal. Weltzien expressed great interest in GWLADYS' story and offered to send Murphy's manifesto to the Breton Nationalists through the German diplomatic bag. He also interrogated GWLADYS in a rather superficial manner about the ship on which he had sailed, the cargo she had carried and the nature of the preparations which were being made in England for the opening of a Second Front. SIS's contact was later able to provide certain information about the internal squabbles of the Eins M. organisation in Portugal, and in particular the disputes between Kuno Weltzien, Ernst Schmidt, another principal agent of Bendixen's, since arrested and another German named Kramm. In assessing the case MI5 had to warn: 'Approving authorities... that GWLADYS is [a] seaman agent, who passes his information orally. In consequence it cannot be guaranteed that any traffic approved for him will reach the Germans in exactly the form in which it is given to him.'[4]

In October, BRONX established herself with MI5 as a 'very competent letterwriting agent'.[5] BRONX was the daughter of a Peruvian diplomat, who was formerly in Vichy and then in Madrid. She lived for several years before the war in Paris and in the south of France, and came to Britain in September 1939. She was 'a typical member of the cosmopolitan "smart set"'. She accomplished a successful mission to France for the British in July–October 1942, but on her return stated that she had been in touch with the enemy intelligence service, who had asked her to report on industrial affairs, and had given her two cover addresses in Unoccupied France to which she was to write in the secret ink with which they provided her. BRONX was promised a salary of £100 a month, or more if she required it, to be paid to her London bank through Switzerland, and purporting to be part of a divorce settlement from her husband. Since her return, she had been writing fairly regularly, giving low grade industrial information and political chatter. At the end of January 1943 she was given a new cover address in Lisbon, to replace two in former Unoccupied France. Apart from this, 'the other side showed no interest in her'.[6]

'Another valuable addition' was LIPSTICK, a Catalan much concerned with the Catalan Separatist movement.[7] During the Civil War, LIPSTICK, who had already received training as a chemist, served on the Republican side as a technician, attached to the Ministry of National Defence. During this period he was able to render certain services to a Dr Xamorro, who was introduced to him in Barcelona by a friend, and for whom he obtained work in the local Government laboratory. After Franco's entry into Barcelona, Xamorro revealed to LIPSTICK that he was in fact a captain in the Civil Guard, and therefore 'well in with the new regime'. It was probable, though not certain, that Xamorro had in fact been acting in Barcelona as an agent of France. In return for his past kindness Xamorro arranged for LIPSTICK's papers to be put in order, with the result that the latter, although an ex-officer in the Republican Army, escaped imprisonment.

After the Civil War, LIPSTICK continued to study chemistry at the University of Barcelona, and subsequently became the director of a factory in Barcelona manufacturing plastic and synthetic materials. During the same period he did his military service again in the capacity of a technician. At about this time LIPSTICK joined the Union Democratica, of which his father had been a member since before the Civil War. In this way he came into contact with Juan Cornudella, the leader in Barcelona of the Frente Nacional de Catalun, a combination of all the Catalan democratic parties. Cornudella and LIPSTICK discussed together the possibility of the latter's coming to Britain, at least partly with the object of getting into touch with the Catalan movement in exile there, with whom Cornudella had been unable to communicate for a considerable period. With this object in view LIPSTICK approached in March 1942, Karl Erich Kuhlmann, a German whom he had met at the Barcelona Tennis Club, and who represented himself as a person of influence in Spanish Government circles. Kuhlmann, who was in fact an agent of Ast Berlin, agreed to help LIPSTICK, and introduced him to Carlos Mode. Mode, alias Don Carlos, was an official of the German Abwehrstelle in Barcelona. He agreed to help LIPSTICK to obtain a passport, but at their second or third meeting revealed to him that the condition of his assistance was that LIPSTICK should act as a German agent in England. LIPSTICK agreed, and Mode then introduced him to Luis de la Reguerra alias Don Gonzalo, who thereafter took general charge of LIPSTICK's case.

In April, LIPSTICK and Reguerra went together to Madrid in order that the former might obtain the necessary papers for his journey. On the day after his arrival there LIPSTICK visited the British Embassy and recounted his whole story to Major Lovelock, the Military Attache, and invited his assistance. Thereafter followed the 'usual period of vexatious delays', which in LIPSTICK's case continued until the end of October, when at length he was finally granted his British visa. During this period LIPSTICK lived either in Madrid or Barcelona, and was in constant touch with the Germans. At the same time he reported his dealings with them in detail to Major Lovelock, or later to the Passport Control Officer (SIS) to whom his case was passed on.

In July, LIPSTICK returned to Madrid after a short visit to Barcelona. He had previously been told by Reguerra that he would be approached there by a man named Christian, who would in the future handle his affairs while he was in Madrid. Christian turned out to be Ewald Christian Paschkes, a man with whom LIPSTICK had previously been acquainted in Barcelona, 'and whom we know to occupy the position of personal assistant to von Wenkstern, of KO Spain.' LIPSTICK and Paschkes got on very well together, and in fact during the rest of his time in Madrid, LIPSTICK usually stayed with Paschkes at the pension where the latter lived together with a number of members of the German Embassy staff.

Finally, at the beginning of October it appeared that the various problems connected with LIPSTICK's papers had been overcome, and he was therefore given instruction by the Germans in secret writing, and in the nature of the mission which he was to fulfil in England. The lessons in secret writing were given him in Barcelona by Lanschk, alias Don Alfonso, and familiar to MI5 from other cases. The instruction consisted originally of writing with a silver nitrate pencil, but after LIPSTICK had protested that this was an inferior and easily detectable ink a Heinrich match was provided, of the same type as that given to TRICYCLE and other agents. LIPSTICK's general instructions were given him in Madric by Paschkes. He was told to report on troop dispositions in England, fortifications on the south coast, and on all the details which he could acquire of army Co-operation Command of the RAF, in particular of such units of it as were stationed in the north of England and Scotland. Certain other items concerned with aviation spirit and details of the new service gas mask were later added by Reguerra in Barcelona. Finally LIPSTICK was provided with a questionnaire in the form of micro-photographs attached to his passport.

On 25 October, LIPSTICK left by air for Lisbon. He had previously been told by Paschkes that the arrangements for his reception there would be in the hands of Paschkes's brother Roland Paschkes (alias Silva), whom MI5 knew to be an agent of KO Spain attached to the German organisation in Portugal. LIPSTICK was told that Roland Paschkes would make arrangements for him to be met and provided with money, and a microscope, which he was to use for the purpose of reading further communications sent to him in the form of micro-photographs. LIPSTICK did not, in fact, actually meet Roland Paschkes in Lisbon, but on 29 October an emissary of his called upon him at his hotel in Lisbon and gave him the money, a microscope and also some developer for secret writing in the form of impregnated cotton wool, concealed in some wooden shoe-trees. The money consisted of £12 British and 23,000 escudos.

Armed with all this material LIPSTICK arrived in London on 2 November. He was taken in the ordinary way to the Patriotic Schools for interrogation, but abstracted from there on the following day and accommodated by MI5 in a flat of his own.[8] The 'weak point in the case', noted Masterman, 'was that his own first interest was to further the Catalan movement rather than to assist us'.[9]

After his arrival in Britain, LIPSTICK's career was 'comparatively uneventful'. He regularly communicated with the Germans at the six cover addresses in Madrid, Barcelona and Lisbon with which he was provided by the Germans, and had received acknowledgements and answers from them. In pursuance of his original purpose in coming to England, LIPSTICK brought with him letters from Cornudella to the Catalan movement in London, which he has delivered. For the rest, acting upon instructions from MI5, he had 'been careful to move mainly, or wholly, in Falangist circles, although we have arranged that he should have a private contact with Batista y Roca, a member of the Catalan organisation'. A 'slight interruption in the smooth progress of his career' occurred when MI5 discovered that he was the cousin of Miguel Ribas, an SIS agent, who was also in touch with the XX agent PENGUIN. Ribas wrote to LIPSTICK requesting him to deliver a message to PENGUIN, and in fact the two met on several occasions. MI5 took steps, in view of PENGUIN's 'notorious indiscretion', to see that the two did not meet again. The only other difficulty was occasioned by the fact that three of LIPSTICK's cover addresses had, or should have, been compromised by the arrest of two other British agents.

PENGUIN, the agent who had caused this difficulty, was born in London, in 1905, of British parents, educated in England, France and Italy, and spoke the languages of these countries fluently. She had three children, but was separated from her husband in 1937, when she went to live in France. After the outbreak of war, she held various positions with the French Red Cross until, in June 1941, they told her they could no longer employ her. She managed to obtain visas for Spain and Portugal and arrived in Lisbon in October 1941. Through friends whom she made in Lisbon she was introduced to a German named Werner Schielbald, who proposed that on her return to England she should devote her energies to spreading peace propaganda for Germany. On the instructions of SOE, to whose representative she had reported her association with the Germans, PENGUIN appeared to fall in with these proposals, but refused to carry any propaganda material back with her to England. It was accordingly arranged that someone should contact her in Britain on Schielbald's behalf. She arrived in the UK on 14 March 1942, and at the end of May received a postcard from Schielbald inviting her to write to him. She had by this time written several letters to a Portuguese friend of hers in contact in Lisbon with the Germans, complaining indirectly that she had heard nothing from Schielbald. In view of this friend's status as an SIS agent, the communication between him and PENGUIN was discontinued, but PENGUIN wrote again explaining that she was now employed by the Censorship (a purely imaginary job) and was therefore in a position to correspond easily with him. At the end of August, Schielbald replied that his friend was 'crazy' to get in touch with her, and suggested that PENGUIN should go to Lisbon. PENGUIN replied that this was impossible and she could not understand why his friend found it difficult to contact her. At the end of December a plan for opening communication with Schielbald through the postal 'rebut' service was put into operation, but no response was received from the Germans.[10]

In November 1942, WATCHDOG was landed from a U-boat in Canada together with a wireless set and an extensive questionnaire. This move on the part of the Germans threatened an extension of MI5's 'activities to other parts of the world, but in fact the case did not develop very satisfactorily'.[11] WATCHDOG was a German who, after leaving school in 1922, joined a Freikorps, and in the following year became a member of the Nazi Party. Thereafter he worked for a short while as a volunteer on a National Socialist newspaper in East Prussia. In 1925 he took up flying and held various posts as a commercial pilot. In 1927 he joined the Reichswehr, and under cover of the normal duties of a Reichswehr officer, gave flying instruction. Three years later he abruptly gave up this post and emigrated to Canada for reasons which remained unclear. He remained in Canada until 1933, during which time he obtained 'miscellaneous employment of no very remunerative type'. He also married, and it was probable that his decision to leave Canada in 1933 was the result of his having quarrelled with his wife and of his being therefore unable to live any longer on her money. WATCHDOG then returned to Europe and enlisted in the French Foreign Legion, with whom he served until the end of 1938. He was then discharged and made his way back to Germany, where, by his own account, he was almost immediately interned, as he said all returning Foreign Legionaries were. After a short while he was released upon condition of his joining the German Army.

From this point onwards WATCHDOG's story was 'obscure'. He gave a long account of his association with the Brandenburg Regiment in its early days, and of his service with them during the Dutch and Belgian campaigns. He alleged that in the early part of 1941 he was transferred together with units of the Brandenburg Regiment, to Libya, where he was attached to Rommel's forces. He also stated that at the end of 1941 he was transferred to Brussels in the capacity of an Abwehr officer attached to Abteilung III. He described how, in August 1942, he quarrelled with his superior officers in Brussels, with the result that he was offered the choice of a concentration camp or serving overseas as an agent. He chose the latter alternative, with the result that on the morning of 26 September 1942 he was embarked at Kiel in a submarine, which conveyed him across the Atlantic and landed him upon the coast of Canada on 9 September. He was put ashore in naval uniform with a wireless set and instructions to report by wireless in accordance with an extensive questionnaire embracing information about military, naval, air force and industrial matters. This, at least is what WATCHDOG claimed. By 1943, though, the Security Service was able to declare:

We are now in a position to state that almost the whole of the foregoing story is false. It is true that WATCHDOG was landed in Canada at the time, in the circumstances and probably with the mission described. It appears, however, that everything else which he has said about his career between leaving the Foreign Legion and arriving in Canada is in some degree or another fabrication. WATCHDOG himself has, we understand, now withdrawn his early story in favour of a fresh one in which he speaks of having served in Casablanca during the early part of the war as a saboteur, and of having subsequently been attached to the Abwehr organisation which worked under cover of the Kontroll Inspektorat Afrika. Details of this revised story are not yet to hand, and until it has been studied it is not possible to form any clear appreciation of the real nature of WATCHDOG's case. All that can be said at the moment is that he is an agent, probably run jointly by Ast Brussels and Ast Hamburg, and that he has a mission to perform in Canada of approximately the type he has described.[12]

BRUTUS

Roman Czerniawski – codename BRUTUS – was the kind of man whose character can best be summed up in the reply that MOUSTIQUE (his mistress) received from her friends after he had made 'a most unorthodox proposal' of marriage to her: 'Ah, but you must remember that he is a super-man, and super-men are always eccentric.' Born at Plust, Poland in 1910, he served for ten years as a pilot with the First Regiment of Aviation stationed near Warsaw 'and earned the reputation of being one of their ace fighter pilots'. In 1938 he went to the Staff College at Warsaw, after which he was employed at the Air Ministry. He was 5ft 6in., of medium build with an oval, clean shaven face; his head was described as 'large in proportion to his body'. With a fairly 'youthful complexion, slightly Jewish appearance' his chief characteristics were that he spoke 'very quickly' and was 'always smiling'.

Czerniawski had charisma. And he was a decorated war hero. He was decorated with the Polish Croix de Guerre and two bars, 1939; the French Croix de Guerre, 1940; and the Virtuti Militari 1941, the Polish equivalent of the Victoria Cross. Czerniawski was a Polish Air Force officer who fought in the war in Poland and later escaped to Paris where he was taken prisoner for a day or two but escaped and went to Unoccupied France where he set up an intelligence organisation; his codename was WALENTY. Mathilde Lucie Carré, alias VICTOIRE, was his second-in-command of this resistance network known as the INTERALLIÉ.[13] On 17 September 1940, Carré was in Toulouse where she had arrived, with some friends, in the general retreat from Northern France. From May 1940 she had been working as a Red Cross nurse at various emergency stations near the front, from which her unit had been successfully evacuated. When she reached Paris she had been instructed to go to Bordeaux, but was unable to reach it. The armistice found her at Toulouse. After dinner, on 17 September, she was accosted by a Polish officer, who had been sitting at the next table to her at dinner. He turned out to be a captain in the Polish Air Force and a fighter pilot. He started a conversation with her and asked her to give him French lessons as his French was not very good. They met the next day in a café, discovered they were both restless with nothing to do, but determined to carry on the struggle against Germany somehow. Thus began Mathilde Lucie Carré's friendship with WALENTY. Thereafter she and WALENTY saw a lot of each other, found they had much in common and soon became lovers.

On his return from a two day journey, WALENTY began to receive visits from a number of his compatriots and he asked Carré to make a trip with him to Lyons, Limoges and Vichy on 15 October 1940. She accepted and was glad to have the opportunity of taking her mind of the departure of Jean, an old friend of hers who was then her lover.

On their return to Toulouse, WALENTY revealed to her that he was, in fact, a Polish Intelligence officer engaged in intelligence work in Vichy and that he now had the authority of the Polish Government in exile to become chief of staff and colonel of this organisation. He invited her to join his organisation. Carré jumped at the chance. She became VICTOIRE. Both of them arranged to live together in Paris; they cover was that WALENTY was VICTOIRE's cousin and his French was bad because he, and his parents, had always lived abroad.[14]

INTERALLIÉ was the first large resistance organisation to be established in France; it was, indeed, Britain's sole regular source of information from France during this period. In addition to regular courier services to England, Czerniawski had under his control four W/Ts in Paris, which transmitted a mass of information from the whole of France, and which enabled Allied intelligence to build up a complete picture of the German Order of Battle in that country.

Czerniawski, it was agreed by his admirers in Britain, 'showed himself to be a man of great daring and initiative' and had contacts among both Vichy and Gestapo authorities, and was also able to produce false documentation. He himself crossed the demarcation line between Occupied and Unoccupied France illegally upon eighteen occasions and with false documents upon twelve occasions. He was the first agent to leave Occupied France by air, arriving in Britain in October 1941, when he was received by General Sikorski of the Free Polish Forces and decorated with the Virtuti Militari. He returned to France a fortnight later, but owing to the treachery of a member of the organisation he was arrested on the 18 November 1941, and further denunciations by the same agent led to the arrest of some sixty Allied agents.[15] Then, in February 1942, VICTOIRE escaped from German captivity and arrived in Britain. Even more dramatically, Czerniawski also escaped from the Germans, made his way south to Madrid and subsequently to Gibraltar in October 1942. He arrived in Britain in the same month. But, perhaps unsurprisingly, not everything was as it first seemed.

On 27 June 1942, MI5 decided to intern her. Chris Harmer dealt with the case. During her stay in Britain, VICTOIRE had been associated with SIS, SOE and MI5: 'She has conceived, principally out of jealousy, a violent dislike to some of the officers she met in SOE which has resulted in her believing that that organisation is opposed to her interests.' Initially she had been welcomed by British Intelligence; but as MI5 dug more and more into her background in France they became more and more suspicious.

VICTOIRE was born in 1908 at Creuset, Sanoe et Loire, France. Little was known of her previous history. She maintained that she received no formal education until she was about fourteen when she went to Paris to the Lycee. After leaving school she lived in Paris where studied nursing. She also took up writing and secretarial work as a profession. About 1932 or 1933, she married and went to live with her husband in Morocco. It was believed that he had some sort of official appointment there and that she lived for most of the six years of her married life there. She returned to France, permanently, shortly before the war, when she separated from her husband and decided to divorce him. WALENTY employed various sub-agents (almost all of them Frenchmen) dealing with the whole of occupied France in clearly defined sectors and sending in periodical reports. He had at least three wireless operators and three different sets located in separate apartments in Paris and his transmissions functioned with regularity. A courier service was also in place, through Brittany by fishing smack, and during the year he operated there were several air operations in regard to sending and collecting agents. WALENTY himself was collected by air and brought back to England in October 1941. VICTOIRE was, for a short time, WALENTY's mistress but 'he apparently tired of her' – and for the rest of the time the relationship was exclusively of a professional nature. She acted as secretary in preparing reports and messages as well as recruiting sub-agents: many of these sub-agents were people known personally to her from before the war. Her attitude was described by one of the wireless operators as 'being very correct in her work'. But Harmer noted: 'In her private life there is no doubt that her behaviour was anything but correct and although she maintains that she never mixes personal relationships with her work on principle, this is not borne out by independent statements and it appears that she was mixed up in love affairs and intrigues with a good many of the organisation.'

By the time the Germans rolled up his organisation, WALENTY was living with another girl, whose code name was VIOLETTE, whom he had previously known in Strasbourg; she was 'a lady of great charm'. Although VIOLETTE originally had no importance in the organisation, she quickly – because she was living in the house of the chief – became WALENTY's *de facto* second-in-command. When WALENTY travelled to England, in October 1941, there was intense personal rivalry between VICTOIRE and VIOLETTE. On the one hand, VICTOIRE had been there from the beginning and had, to all intents and purposes, been second-in-command; on the other hand, VIOLETTE was on much better relations with the wireless operators and also with an agent – known as ADAM – sent over by SIS (who were by this time running the organisation in conjunction with the Poles) to look after affairs while WALENTY was in England. VIOLETTE was in the position of censoring anything that VICTOIRE prepared to be sent over to England during WALENTY's absence and, concluded Harmer, 'It is not difficult to imagine the rivalry and jealousy that existed between these two, not only for personal but for business reasons.'

On 18 November 1941, at 5 a.m., the Germans arrived at WALENTY's apartment and arrested him and VIOLETTE. He was living in a flat on the first floor; his principal wireless station was located in the flat above this. The two wireless operators therein heard the arrests taking place and several shots fired – they managed to escape out of the windows and over the roofs. From that point on the Germans began rounding up all the sub-agents from information given, either voluntarily or under duress, and from captured documents. Finally, the Germans scooped in about 100 agents. But they continued to work the wireless transmitter and they were assisted by several members of the organisation – the principal one of whom was VICTOIRE.

VICTOIRE had admitted that she collaborated with the Germans 'to the greatest possible extent' from 18 November. Harmer admitted that there was no evidence to suggest that she had worked for them prior to her arrest on that day. She claimed that she had no option but to collaborate because they found some incriminating evidence in her diary that made it impossible for her to save the various sub-agents she betrayed. Whether true or not, Harmer pointed out: 'Although one cannot say for certain that any particular agent would not have been arrested if VICTOIRE had not given them away, yet she was instrumental in securing the arrest of a great many of the sub-agents. Moreover she worked with the Germans in connection with the messages via the transmitter in such a way as to deceive the British and Polish Services, who were receiving these messages. Further, she shared with them in the proceeds of certain funds which were sent from England to finance the organisation. The story told by the Germans via the transmitter was that although WALENTY himself had been taken, the wireless station and several of the agents had been saved.' The principal member of the German Service with whom VICTOIRE collaborated was a Gestapo officer named Bleicher. She later became his mistress.

At the end of December 1941, she came into contact, through her lawyer, with an important SOE agent, Pierre de Crevoisier de Vomécourt, codename LUCAS, who had an organisation there but was in difficulties because of his slow means of communication. VICTOIRE's lawyer knew that she had facilities for sending wireless messages through to London and, accordingly, brought the two of them together. LUCAS asked VICTOIRE if he could use her channel of communication and send through urgent messages to London, which he did. VICTOIRE then presented these messages to the Germans. They revealed to them that LUCAS was a very important agent who was working to fuse all British organisations in France under his leadership.

VICTOIRE always maintained that she was accompanied to the first meeting with LUCAS by Gestapo agents and had no option but to betray him. 'This is believed not to be the fact,' noted Harmer. 'To my mind it is reasonably certain that she betrayed LUCAS voluntarily and thereby obtained the maximum amount of confidence possible from the Germans.' LUCAS had been trying to make arrangements to get to Britain but two attempts, by air, to get him out failed – after having been sent via VICTOIRE's German controlled transmitter. Finally, it was agreed that he would be picked up by a sea operation.

By now LUCAS had realised that VICTOIRE was working for the Germans. He confronted her. She admitted the fact. LUCAS offered her the chance to work with him in outwitting the Germans. Why she agreed to this was not clear although, given the 'intense personal hatred' she now felt towards Bleicher, 'it seems possible that it was due to some personal reason connected with him'. VICTOIRE now became LUCAS's mistress and, from that moment on, had appeared to work, honestly, against the Germans. LUCAS accordingly suggested that she should accompany him back to England; she put this proposal to the Germans, who referred it to Berlin, where, after a certain amount of discussion, they agreed. This indicated the trust they placed in her. The sea operation was only successful at the third attempt: it was believed that the Germans intercepted the first attempt and shot two SOE wireless operators sent over to assist LUCAS at his request: 'It was obvious then, that at this time the British had not made up their minds definitely that the VICTOIRE transmitter in Paris was being controlled by the Germans as they would not have sacrificed two men if they had this information.'[16]

Czerniawski, meanwhile arrived in the United Kingdom from Gibraltar on 2 October, 1942. On arrival Czerniawski was exhaustively examined by the Polish Intelligence Service and completed a series of reports setting out in great detail his account of (a) the reasons for the break up of INTERALLIE, (b) his interrogation and treatment in prison, and (c) his escape and subsequent journey to Britain. After this he was presented with reports on interrogations of VICTOIRE and MAURICE (the former W/T operator of INTERALLIE, who escaped on 18 November, 1941, and reached England in May 1942) and of other agents formerly belonging to, or connected with, INTERALLIE. He was given in addition the memoirs of VICTOIRE.

As a result of all Czerniawski's reports since his arrival, it was possible to piece together a consistent story which added certain details but in the main, and in every important particular, confirmed what was already known as to the break up of INTERALLIE. With regard to his interrogation and treatment by the Gestapo, 'he presented a surprising picture of an important agent left practically without serious interrogation for eight months and treated severely but without brutality. His account of his escape and subsequent journey was amazing but on the whole appeared to be credible, so far as he was concerned'. A number of factors, however, caused Colonel Gano, the Chief of the Polish Secret Service, to refuse to accept it 'in toto'. A preliminary interpretation of all the facts was that the Germans, 'having imbued WALENTY with suitable propaganda, had helped him to escape, without his knowledge, in the hopes that his escape might result in the weakening of the Polish effort on the Allied side and in the opening of the door of collaboration'. WALENTY was not examined by the British, but a full interrogation was arranged to start on 23 November. But, just before this was to happen, on 20 November, Czerniawski delivered a shocking confession. He asked to see Colonel Gano and presented him with a manuscript book entitled 'The Great Game', in which he set out the true facts of his escape from prison.[17] Czerniawski recalled how:

> On the day of my arrival [in Britain] I stated that I should have further reports to make in a month's time. I explained the delay by the necessity of first making sure of certain facts... Today the period which I had set myself for this task is up and therefore I am making my further report. All my statements heretofore have dealt with the 'past'; this report will deal with the 'present' and the 'future' – i.e. it constitutes at the same time a plan of action, which has great chances of realisation... Before drawing up the present report I have done all in my power to facilitate the realisation of the plans I am about to submit. During my preparation I was faced with two alternatives: to risk my so-called 'personal position' in order to secure real chances for the realisation of my plans or to jeopardise my plans by safeguarding my own person. I chose the first. I realised that I should be unable to start to put my plans into operation so long as I had not secured by my own efforts and in an entirely natural manner my return to a normal private and official existence.

I estimated that this would take me approximately one month. And, indeed, my position today allows me to take this report and to submit it under conditions, which guarantee its execution.[18]

He revealed that while in the hands of the Germans he consented to return to Britain as a secret agent, that his escape was deliberately staged by them and that he was provided with crystals (hidden in his shoes) for constructing a W/T set and instructions with regard to W/T communication and codes and given a mission which involved sending back, either in W/T messages, or by means of landing a plane on a disused airfield in Northern France, information on military matters, and the attempt to mobilise the Poles in Great Britain as a Fifth Column to work on behalf of the Axis. In his book he set out his reasons for not revealing his true story earlier, 'which are that he deliberately created a smoke screen to be circulated round the departments concerned (he being convinced that the Germans have well placed agents in official quarters), behind which he could tell his true story to his Chief.' He also offered to work a W/T set against the Germans in order to deceive them, this being 'the great game', and demanded a revolver to shoot himself if his request were refused and he was found to have failed in his military duty.[19] His written account finished with the following flourish:

IF I HAVE ACTED WRONG
IN ORGANISING THE 'GREAT GAME'
THE NEWS THAT I HAVE PERISHED IN AN AIR
ACCIDENT
WILL SAVE MY FAMILY AND MY COLLEAGUES.[20]

After reading through what he had written, what could only have been an astonished Colonel Gano, informed Czerniawski that he had not carried out his military duty in that he had withheld this vital information for so long, and that in any event he had failed as an Intelligence Officer in that he had not convinced anybody as to the complete accuracy of the story so far told by him. Colonel Gano then reported the matter to Commander Dunderdale, of SIS, and it was in turn reported to MI5. Colonel Gano subsequently told Czerniawski in Chris Harmer's presence that he must reveal the full story to him. Harmer therefore commenced an interrogation on 23 November.[21]

Czerniawski, or WALENTY, as MI5 referred to him at this stage, began his interrogation with Harmer by describing the man who arrested him – he resembled a person known to the Security Service, from VICTOIRE's account, as Bleicher.[22] He was known to MI5 'as a man of great ability and ingenuity and a specialist in running double agents. He was also a man of great personal ambition'.[23] WALENTY was taken to the Feld Gendarmerie where he experienced the only act of brutality – at the hands of the Duty Officer. On recounting this incident later to another German officer, Major Ische, the latter replied that the officer in question would have been severely punished had this been known at the time. WALENTY, having given his particulars, he received no interrogation during the first few days except that described by him at the hands of a Naval Commander, from whose description appeared to have been the same man as the 'Colonel' who came to visit VICTOIRE on one occasion.

On 27 November, WALENTY was visited by VIOLETTE; according to him the opening move by the Germans to recruit him as their agent was made by VIOLETTE. WALENTY described in his original report her coming to see him with a German officer named Borchers, being left alone for half an hour and how he made her answer questions about what had happened to the various agents of INTERALLIE. At the beginning of his talk with VIOLETTE and again at the end, however, she raised the question of collaboration with the Germans, saying that they were anxious above all to obtain his assistance and that he ought to accept and try and save himself. VIOLETTE represented the Germans' proposal to be that WALENTY should collaborate in technical matters and as a specialist on army intelligence matters. He replied to VIOLETTE that any sort of collaboration would entail giving away the names of comrades which he was not prepared in any circumstances to do. VIOLETTE replied that they would not ask any of these questions and urged him to accept, saying that she had thought it over a great deal.

After Borchers returned he indulged in some 'clumsy propaganda', asking WALENTY why he had worked so well for the Jews and the British. Borchers then retired with VIOLETTE, leaving WALENTY to think it over. He decided that he could not escape but decided to put into operation a new plan; he claimed that he was farsighted enough to realise that he must not accept any proposition immediately but only over a period of time. After his conversation with VIOLETTE and after 'long meditations' WALENTY claimed:

I reached the conclusion that her plans had a fair chance of success and that if I should prove a match to the Germans in the matter of nervous resistance, I would win the game... I arrived at the following conclusions:

I would continue to refuse to supply any data about mine or other organisations as well as any data whatever concerning my personnel; such an attitude might even strengthen my position;

With regard to Polish and British military secrets – I had nothing to betray, not even unconsciously, as I had no information on the subject – so that I would not be running any risks in that respect;

By stressing the fact that I was working for the Polish and not for the British Government, I might plant the suggestion that they might reckon on my collaboration if they offered me work for Poland (!) based on German collaboration (!) I thought that they might be impressed if I gave them to understand that in my opinion England was leading us, Poles, up the garden path.

As I was fully aware that the Germans would not believe my too sudden ideological 'conversion' I decided to present a long resistance and to put forward great demands. I realised fully that I would only win the 'great game' if I could match my nerves against theirs.[24]

WALENTY therefore wrote out a letter addressed to Stulpnagel, the OC of German forces in France, in which he set out his position as a Polish officer and many things also about the position of Poland, pointing out that the assurances given by Britain were insufficient and all Poland's sacrifices were in vain and only if Germany gave suitable assurances to Poland as to her position in the new Europe would any form of collaboration be possible. Two days later when Borchers and Bleicher returned they asked him if he accepted the suggestion of collaboration, and he handed them a letter he had written and said that he declined:

I carried out my duty as a soldier during the war in Poland as a fighter for the rights of the Polish Nation. I continued this struggle during the war in France, now I am continuing the struggle in the ranks of the Polish Army allied with England.

In all three cases I have done everything possible merely for the good of my Nation. No collaboration which might be proposed to me could come about unless I was convinced that I was working for the good of the Polish Nation.

I consider that in the New Europe all the nationality problems ought to be solved. The Polish Nation represented by thirty million Poles cannot disappear and this will obviously be one of the questions to be solved by the Germans after the war. If the

German nation has amongst its plans the reconstruction of the rights of the Polish Nation, in this case alone discussions about my collaboration could take place.

Even in this case all conversations could only take place with an officer of the General Staff who knows these problems and who is authorised to discuss them with me.[25]

According to WALENTY: 'It was in that spirit... when the German captain again renewed his proposals... that... I informed him of my views and stated that any discussion on the subject would only be possible with an officer authorised to discuss these matters... He insisted, however, that I should show my "good will" by giving the Germans some details they needed. I replied (simulating indignation) that if they thought me capable of treason, surely they could not reckon on any loyal collaboration on my part in the future.... The officer was taken aback and did not insist any longer.' Borchers then gave him a semi-Nazi salute and departed.

When, during the next two months, 'no one came to see me, I understood that the "war of nerves" had begun'. But, eventually, during March, WALENTY was interviewed by a Colonel of the General Staff attended by an ADC in the rank of Lieutenant. Upon WALENTY entering the room, in reply to his bow, they gave the military salute. Their behaviour during the interrogation was 'tactful'. WALENTY did not feel well during this interrogation: 'I was cold and unshaven, hungry, and on that particular day in an exceptionally bad temper... ' But this conversation 'proved to be the turning point in the history of the new affair'. After stating that he was acquainted with details concerning WALENTY's military work in France and that he was aware of his visit to England, the Colonel 'informed me that the purpose of this interrogation was to discover the state of mind in the Polish Army and, in particular, among the leading circles in the Army. He stressed the point that he would leave me a free hand in answering and that he would not exert pressure to obtain the replies.' After this short introduction the Colonel put forward the following questions:

Question: What is the state of mind in Polish Units?
Reply: I did not come in touch with Polish Army Units during my visit in England.
Question: What is the state of mind among the leading circles?
Reply: The Polish leading circles are doing their utmost for the restitution of the rights of our Nation. Under present circumstances only an alliance with Great Britain offers these

possibilities... In my opinion the establishment of any 'platform' for arriving at an understanding with the German nation is impossible so long as the present German methods of treating the Poles prevail.

Question: I admit that the methods of treating the Poles have been more than harsh. The Poles, however, are an obstacle to our realization of our great conception of a unified Europe. In principle no one can deny the greatness of our conception in the light of historical perspective. No large plans or conceptions can be realized – without sacrifice. The German nation has already made many sacrifices up to the present other nations too will have to sacrifice certain things now and in the future and give up some of their privileges /e.g. full sovereignty/ for the good of the commonwealth. Unfortunately, the exalted individualism of the European nations renders the realization of a uniform programme impossible without pressure and leadership i.e. without sacrifice. In particular the Polish Government and the Polish Nation under its influence – a young and dynamic nation – refuses to grasp this. It is a pity that this dynamic power is not being exploited in collaboration on realizing our programme. Are the Polish leading circles aware of this situation?

Reply: These circles are wondering on what grounds the German government thinks itself entitled to impose its will on other nations.

Question: In order to enable you to understand my meaning and to facilitate your answer let me remind you that, once upon a time, Rome, disposing of much smaller technical possibilities, succeeded in organizing Europe and advancing the development of her civilization by several centuries. At present, the German nation, aware of its dynamic propensities and of the advantage of possessing a man of Hitler's stature, has undertaken to realize a programme which had existed in the minds of many, but appeared impracticable. Under planned leadership the economic, social and cultural issues of Europe will be normalized shortly. The realization of this programme by evolution would have taken many centuries. Moreover by organizing Europe we shall counteract the yellow peril, which is bound to arise in the future. Do the Poles realize they are jeopardising this programme and their own position. It can not be doubted that all nationalist problems will be solved after the conclusion of the war and that all nations will form separate states within the framework of future Europe. We do not deny the rights of the Polish Nation, but

we ask its cooperation as we do with regard to other peoples…
You, Poles, are in the habit of shedding your own blood for other
peoples' causes… Now, instead of rising to the opportunity and
joining your dynamic power with our efforts at realizing our
programme, you have tied yourselves on the one hand with
'capitalist-Jewish' England, and, on the other, with 'Communist-
Bolshevik' Russia. Neither one nor the other will do anything
for you as far as your full sovereignty is concerned, even if they
should win the war, because the first will not be in a position to
do it and the others will not be willing to do it. By joining us you
will contribute to the realization of our programme to advance
Europe by several centuries in one leap, and at the same time you
will help to strengthen her against aggression from Asia. Did you
not sense whether these factors are not being considered by the
leading Polish circles.

Reply: I stressed in my reply the fact that I was only a soldier
carrying out orders received, that I was not in the habit of
commenting upon political matters and finally, that in view of the
attitude of the German authorities to Polish affairs, all comments
were excluded a priori.

After concluding the interview 'by means of a few banal questions
concerning my life in prison' which was 'far from enviable', the Colonel
left the room with his ADC after saluting. The Colonel left WALENTY
some paper and a pencil and asked him to write down his views on the
subject: 'In complying, I stated that I was fully prepared to undertake
such a mission, on condition that I should be entrusted with a distinct
mission and proposals for my Government. I stressed that under no
circumstances can they expect me to work against my countrymen (I
felt this argument was creating rather a good impression – and that
was all I wished to achieve).'

A fortnight or so later he had the first of two interviews with a
Commandant who was known to MI5 as Major Ische and described
by VICTOIRE. During the first interview Ische gave WALENTY a
long propaganda talk in which he never referred to INTERALLIÉ
but spoke instead of Germany's mission in Europe, maintaining that
economically and politically Poland should come within Germany's
orbit and they could not hope for anything from Britain or Russia.
A great deal of the talk was anti-Communist but there was no anti-
Semitism. Ische spoke enthusiastically of a United States of Europe.
No suggestion was made about a mission. WALENTY claimed that he
'pretended to agree' with what Ische said.

From this time forward WALENTY was given specially selected German newspapers (prior to this he had obtained a certain amount of information as to how the war was going from torn up newspapers issued as toilet paper). Then, after another lapse of a fortnight or more, Ische returned and repeated his propaganda talk. This time, however, he added that if WALENTY thought as he did, he could render a great service by working as a specialist on information and particularly by going to England as an agent, or directing someone else who was going. Ische added that if such a mission should succeed, all his comrades would be released, and left him a pencil, paper and an envelope addressed to 'BUREAU IC' and told him to write down all he could about this suggestion, put it in the envelope and hand it to the guard. WALENTY claimed:

> These arguments were undoubtedly well calculated. but they also fitted in well with my plans
> He asked me that, <u>if it should prove possible</u>, I should persuade one or more 'chiefs' of Polish Organisations in France to collaborate with them. This was, for me, a 'blind spot', but as he did not insist on this point I did not take it unduly to heart.
> At that time my estimate of the position was as follows: I had already outlasted the Germans in the 'war of nerves' and did not, even now, feel their intellectual superiority over me; I might therefore count on escape – and this time the Germans themselves were going to help me in it!
> I must continue to 'bargain' with them, in order not to lose my prestige and their confidence in me;
> by playing up the argument 'they cannot wish to work with a traitor' I might entirely avoid any investigations on the subject of Polish Organisations in France;
> By pretending that I believed their propaganda arguments and their good intentions with regard to Poland (Oh German naivete!) I must convince them that I really believed that the future of Poland lay in German hands... that the British would do nothing for us... etc – just as though I had really swallowed their propaganda.
> Ultimately I reached the conclusion that the time had come for me to take the initiative.[26]

WALENTY then sat down and wrote what he described 'as one of the best efforts of his life':

Having reflected for a long time in prison, I have arrived at certain conclusions which are the following.

That Poland is in the German sphere of influence.

That England, who knows that she is not capable of giving aid direct or indirect to Poland, has nevertheless given on two occasions false promises, once before the start of the war in 1939, the second after the war in France.

Whatever collaboration Poland might have with Great Britain would be merely to help the selfish aims of Great Britain.

That after the war, if the Allies win it, Russia would be in a position to decide the New Order in Eastern Europe and Poland would thus be under the heels of the barbarians and Communists in Russia. In these circumstances England would not be able to help and Russia on the contrary would do us harm.

That all things considered, the best solution would be to come under the cultural protection of Germany, since German culture is preferable to barbarian culture.

That Germany in constructing a new Europe would be forced to create the possibility of life for all the nations which form this Europe.

That the military collaboration of the Poles would be a great help to the Germans in achieving and speeding up the realisation of their programme, and that this military collaboration would be much appreciated by the Germans.

That collaboration in the sphere of military information and in the sphere of the Fifth Column would also give good results.

That in the sphere of military information they would be in touch with a well organised service in England, since at this time they could have good information not only from England but also from America, Canada, North Africa and Russia.

That in the sphere of Fifth Column politics they could rely not only on the collaboration of certain persons in the army, but what is more important on the Fifth column ready at the moment that Germany attacks England.

That a direct collaboration between the Germans and certain Polish organisations working in Europe would not necessarily be excluded.

That according to my considered opinion the result of all these conclusions would be the acceleration of the end of the war and the realisation of a New Order in Europe.[27]

The result of this statement was 'fantastic'.[28] Immediately on receipt of WALENTY's proposal he was interviewed by the Colonel. The Colonel was accompanied by Ische. The Colonel said he was very pleased that he thought as he did and in his present state of mind it would be possible to discuss how best he could render them a service:

> Colonel: Do you think that even if certain mistakes have been made with regard to certain agents who have worked for us, which mistakes should give rise to mistrust in England... your mission would be possible or would it be more difficult?
>
> WALENTY: If I appear to escape from prison, don't you think I will get away with it?
>
> Colonel: You have proved that you know how to work. As a guarantee we have your family in our power and your comrades in prison. We have also VIOLETTE here, and you know she did a lot for you. Are you prepared to leave these people as a guarantee of your good faith?
>
> WALENTY: If I work for you, it will be for ideological reasons and there will be no need of reprisals.
>
> Colonel: You will be required to sign a declaration that these people are held as guarantee for you. What help will you need over there?
>
> WALENTY: I have no requests to make in this respect because you know I would not work for money.
>
> Colonel: If you need it later, you can count on us.
>
> WALENTY: If I agree to work for you it is not to get out of prison but for ideological reasons.

They then proceeded to discuss details. The Colonel stated that WALENTY's mission to Britain would be twofold. First of all he would be required to give information, in order of importance, relating to the production of aeroplanes and tanks in Britain, Canada and the United States; movements of large units of troops; and the Order of Battle in Britain (although the answer to this question was stated to be of minor importance as the Germans were receiving reports about it from 'other sources'). WALENTY's second task was to examine the possibility of creating a Fifth Column amongst the Poles in Britain which should include possible subversive propaganda and sabotage. They then discussed the question of means of communication and the Colonel enquired whether a radio link would be possible. WALENTY replied that he had already thought this out and had decided that it would be easy to arrange something. He mentioned in the first place the name of a 'mythical' friend, a radio engineer with whom WALENTY had spoken on his last visit to Britain. If he failed, however, there was an 'officer friend' who had lived near him in Poland on whom he could count, and he was a specialist in these matters. He also added that he had been able to manage to construct three sets in Paris and the situation was, without any doubt, easier in England. WALENTY suggested, in addition, that it might be possible to deliver packages by aeroplane. He said he could obtain the assistance of some friend who flew over occupied territory every day. The Colonel said he would have to consult the Luftwaffe. Both the Colonel and Ische appeared to be highly pleased at the success of the interview and the former, after about an hour, brought it to a close in saying that Ische would be in charge of all details and would see him again.

After another fortnight or so, Ische returned and referred to the question of delivery of packages by aeroplane, saying that he had consulted the Luftwaffe but had received no reply. WALENTY complained about having to stay in prison so long and Ische excused this on the grounds that there were many things to arrange. He said he was trying to arrange for WALENTY to escape from the prison hospital and asked him to be patient. It was during this period (i.e. from the previous interview onwards) that WALENTY started to receive Red Cross parcels and gradually started to regain some of his strength.

About 26 July 1942, Ische arrived to see WALENTY and told him that he had thought the matter over and that it would not be advisable after all to arrange the escape from hospital 'because it would be necessary to let too many people into the secret'. WALENTY was not given any details as to how his escape should in fact be arranged. He then heard nothing more until 29 July, when two NCOs arrived at about 1 p.m., and he was told to put his shoes on. They drove into Paris and when they were near the Rue de la Faisanderie they appeared not to know the way and attempted to ask the way from a gendarme. Their French, however, was so bad that WALENTY himself asked to see the card on which the address to which they were going was written down, and himself enquired the way. The actual address was 5/7 Rue Dufrenoy.

WALENTY arrived about 1.30 p.m. and was shown into a room on the ground floor. They then discussed WALENTY's supposed story of his escape. The Staff Colonel, who had seen WALENTY in prison, was also present at this interview (dressed, however, in civilian clothes), and he gave WALENTY a tablet of chocolate. He told him he was very pleased to see him out of prison and that he was now free and could rest and could arrange for his departure from Paris to the free zone (Vichy). The question of documents was discussed and Ische left during the interview and returned later with one set of false papers, to be used by WALENTY, and 10,000 francs. WALENTY was also given some loose ration coupons and a certain amount of small change in order to enable him to go to the barber and have a shave.

The final interview with the Germans was on 15 August. WALENTY had previously suggested to the Germans, in order to build up their confidence in him, that somebody might accompany him to the Unoccupied Zone and be at hand in case of any trouble. The Colonel said that Bleicher would go with him, and he intervened at this stage to ask where they should meet. WALENTY said that he would go first to Vichy and then to Lyon, and that he would stay in the latter town at the Hotel de Bordeaux. He said that it would be inadvisable for Bleicher to stay there as well, but he must go each day at a certain time to the Restaurant Brasserie Georges where WALENTY would turn up if he had anything important to report. They then discussed what WALENTY should do after leaving occupied France, and it was arranged that three weeks after the Germans assumed WALENTY to have left the Continent they would start calling by W/T. The Germans gave him ration cards for unoccupied France but no new identity card, nor any money above the 10,000 francs which they had given him on the day of his leaving prison. They did, though, ask him whether he would have need of any more money and he refused.

Just before the interview ended, WALENTY was shown a German document which, according to his recollection, was an acknowledgement by him that, acting on the dictates of his conscience, he was starting to work for the National Socialist State and in a military capacity. The document also acknowledged that he was undertaking the mission voluntarily, and that if he failed in his duty the Germans would be entitled to take reprisals. WALENTY signed the document and returned it. He was then saluted in a military fashion and they then shook hands with him and wished him good luck. He was instructed to make his own way out of the Occupied Zone.

WALENTY left Paris on the morning of 16 August from the Gare de Lyon. He crossed the frontier at Paray-le-Monial. Two or three days later, he met Bleicher at Lyon, in the cafe specified, and gave him a note saying that everything had gone all right. He left the next morning. On his way to the station he gave a note to the porter at the Grand Hotel, saying that he had to go immediately. In this note, 'which is described in his own account, he asked Bleicher to give his regards to everybody' and ended by saying 'Long live Hitler, the great creator of New Europe.'

Now it had to be ascertained, by MI5, if WALENTY was telling the truth. Right now WALENTY was not, exactly, popular, among the Free Poles in Britain. As Chris Harmer noted, in his assessment of the case, the admission by WALENTY, a month after his arrival, that he had been given a mission by the Germans was a 'bombshell', particularly for the Polish Deuxieme Bureau. It was particularly unfortunate because the officers put in charge of the case by Colonel Gano had expressed their findings that WALENTY was honest, and their personal reputations were involved. Now there was a tendency on the part of these officers (one of whom at least missed promotion because he had been fooled by WALENTY) 'to go to the opposite extreme and assume that WALENTY was wholly bad'. Colonel Gano accordingly decided that in connection solely with WALENTY's conduct as an officer it was necessary to have a Military Court of Inquiry to go into the question of his escape. It was a rule of Polish military law that any escaped prisoner had to go before a Court of Inquiry. The Court consisted of Colonel Mayer (previously a high official of the Polish Deuxième Bureau and at that time head of the Polish Intelligence School in Glasgow), Major Zychon (Colonel Gano's deputy and who had been in charge of the preliminary investigation of the case) and Major Zarembski who was a personal friend of WALENTY (and with whom WALENTY had collaborated to some degree in France). Captain Plocek of the Deuxieme Bureau was Secretary to the Commission. In the end, the Commission suggested that WALENTY's explanation be accepted as sufficient, but they expressed their opinion that he should be severely reprimanded for jeopardising several persons, including an officer from a neighbouring post, by his behaviour. They also expressed the opinion that WALENTY should be severely reprimanded because he did not report the whole matter to his superiors immediately on his arrival. Crucially, they expressed the opinion that the affair initiated by WALENTY should be continued and then made a cover award accepting WALENTY's explanation of his escape.

But was WALENTY – or had he been – a German agent? It fell to Harmer to try and untangle the evidence. At this stage VICTOIRE, who had betrayed WALENTY's network, was still working as a contact between the British and the Germans. Harmer had to take note of how VICTOIRE, in her memoirs, claimed that the Germans had told her that WALENTY had suggested he should return to England to mobilise Poland as an ally of Germany as a *voluntary* gesture on his part; and that the Germans were suggesting to the British, in the VICTOIRE radio messages, between March and June 1942, that it was possible to arrange the escape of WALENTY from prison and were trying to extract from the British his 'test civil'. Both these factors might suggest that WALENTY was 'unsound'.

With regard to the first point, Harmer had to admit that much of what VICTOIRE had written was correct: 'In fact my view is that it is all accurate except where the circumstances are to her disadvantage when she twists them round. In this case I believe she has recorded exactly what the Germans told her.' She remarked that WALENTY's original suggestion amused the Germans and that they had sent an officer disguised as a Staff Officer to see him. 'The last part they probably made up for VICTOIRE's benefit,' concluded Harmer. Had, however, the suggestion for collaboration come from them, as WALENTY stated, 'I cannot conceive any German Intelligence Officer revealing this story to VICTOIRE, or even if reasons then existed for doing so (they did not at that time know of course that she was coming to England) that they would have then allowed him to come after they assumed (as we know they did) that she was in prison and would probably have revealed the story.'

Another relevant point was that, during his first interrogation of him, Harmer was definite that WALENTY had interpreted VIOLETTE's suggestion of collaboration on behalf of the Germans as an invitation to come to Britain on a mission of some sort. 'I pressed him on this and his answer was clear. Nevertheless on returning to the subject again two days later, to make sure I was not mistaken he withdrew this and said she only suggested collaboration on technical questions, that is collaboration in continuing the INTERALLIÉ affair. I find it impossible to accept the possibility that the Germans, nine days after breaking up INTERALLIÉ, could have made any suggestion to its chief which could be interpreted as an invitation to go on a mission to England. WALENTY, in my view, realised this himself and consequently withdrew this point. I think probably VIOLETTE's suggestion to WALENTY was merely that he should collaborate in giving away his comrades on condition that his life was spared. I think also that, to his credit, he refused. His first account of this interview, on the whole strikes me as being the correct version.'

With regard to the Germans' messages about arranging the escape of WALENTY from prison, 'We took the view that this was a clumsy effort on their part to extract money from us. We never solved the question why they kept on asking for the true name, date and place of birth of WALENTY... we are justified in assuming, I think, that the Germans had not realised that VICTOIRE had betrayed them. It may be, therefore, that they were at this stage trying to check up on WALENTY to see what hold they could get on him. Although it is difficult to draw a very definite inference from this, I think on the whole this points more to an approach by WALENTY than an approach to him.' In addition there were various points which caused Harmer to think that WALENTY was 'holding a good deal back'. Among these were:

> WALENTY, a trained Intelligence Officer, is unable to remember the fictitious name he gave to the Germans of his friend who would construct the W/T set. This seems to be inconsistent with his story that he was carrying out a carefully worked out plan to fool the Germans... He failed to find out the name of any German official. This is rather surprising in view of their friendliness to him towards the end. It suggests the possibility that for some reason he cannot admit to having found out their names himself and consequently relies on VICTOIRE for his source... His accounts of his movements after leaving... on the day of his arrest are very hazy. If it is true that he walked the distance he says he did, I think that he must have left prison a very much stronger man than he admits.

The result of these points, and also the general impression he gave, caused Harmer to think that the true story of his recruitment was still to come. What, then, were WALENTY's motives in holding back his real story? Harmer attempted to fathom this out. WALENTY's explanation of this was that he intended all along to reveal the truth, that the only chance of his being able to prevent his betrayal getting back to the Germans was to create a 'smoke screen' by telling the false story, which would then be circulated in Polish and British circles. This explanation, 'coming from an ordinary individual, might well be doubted'. But, conceded Harmer, WALENTY might have been scared by the length of his interrogation by the Poles when he arrived in Britain (he had been questioned for a month and had not started his interrogation at the hands of the British) or by reading VICTOIRE's memoirs and wondering what else she knew (the memoirs were given to him on 3 November and he started to write the 'true account' on 10 November). Above all he may have been struck by the realisation that the Germans had not carried out the underlying assumption of his mission, namely that the war against Russia would be concluded by the autumn, and he had therefore decided not to carry it into effect. However, on arrival in Britain, he told Colonel Gano that he would have something important to tell him in a month's time. 'The last point is of major importance. Without it WALENTY's explanation would be very hard to accept. As it is his explanation is not so extraordinary having regard to his feeling of self importance, which would cause him to think that his story would be the only topic of interest in official circles, and his dramatic sense which would cause him to make the of handing over his book "The Great Game" as startling as possible. The greatest difficulty is in understanding the delay.' Putting WALENTY in his worst perspective from a security aspect, Harmer suggested the following possibility:

WALENTY in prison is visited by VIOLETTE who tells him that VICTOIRE has given everything away and that he should save himself by helping the Germans. WALENTY refuses, but since a firing squad does not fit in with his grandiose and dramatic ideas of his own destiny, he evolves the idea of writing to the Germans suggesting that in return for generous terms he will raise the Polish Nation on the side of Germany. In pursuance of this idea, he resorts to his most effective method of expressing himself, namely a written document which he transmits to the Germans, applying for a visit by an officer in the General Staff. This he does not immediately after VIOLETTE's visit (as he now states) but later on during December (as VICTOIRE states). Nothing happens and no notice is taken of him until March when, [with] VICTOIRE safely out of the way,... formal interrogations [start] (this is confirmed by VICTOIRE). He then repeats his ideas of collaboration. In the meantime he has grown weaker physically and mentally and is falling a prey to Axis propaganda. Moreover, the treatment he has received from the Germans is not so bad as he had thought and this is bringing him together with them to a certain degree. After the departure of VICTOIRE to England, his writing starts to be considered by the Germans and taken more seriously and they send either a German Staff Colonel, or someone disguised as such, to see him and pretend to take him seriously... towards the end of March, what WALENTY originally intended to be primarily a means of escape has begun to be taken seriously by both himself and the Germans. As his condition gets lower, so his credibility of propaganda and his idea of grandeur become greater. The Germans meanwhile seriously start to consider sending him on his mission to try and split the Poles from the Allies. To realise such a mission will be a gamble and as a guarantee they must have some hold over WALENTY. They therefore decide to apply to London in their messages for details of his true name so that they may be certain of having his family in their power to guarantee the carrying out of his mission. They think over possible reasons for asking for these details and hit upon the idea of saying that his escape may be possible on payment of a large sum. If this succeeds, it will give them everything they want, namely the details about WALENTY, a credible explanation of his escape and return to England, and a large sum of money to line their pockets. Thereafter WALENTY's treatment starts to improve, his food gets better and he continues to submit writings which strike at the Germans' weakest point, i.e. their conceit. Their confidence in him therefore grows and when later he suggests that he might also act as a spy for them, they take this suggestion also seriously and send the Staff Colonel to visit him again. They keep him in prison until June 29th but he is receiving better treatment all the time and is reasonably strong by the time he leaves. He himself meanwhile really thinks there may be a possibility of fixing up an arrangement between Poland and Germany, which belief is based all the time on the assumption, so often stated to him, that the Germans will conclude the war against Russia in the Autumn... On arrival in Great Britain he is in a difficulty... he has been told by the Germans that VICTOIRE is probably in prison and she may have given certain details away. To cover himself, therefore, he tells his Chief that he will have something important to say in a month's time and decides in the meantime to explore himself the possibilities of carrying out his mission. During the month of October it becomes evident that the Germans will not finish the war in the East this year. He finds that so far from wanting collaboration, the Polish official circles here are determined to continue the fight against Germany. He finds moreover that his story is not accepted without question, but that it is extensively investigated and that in addition to his own Service, the British intend to go into it and, above all, as his health and strength and sense of judgement return he realises that as a loyal and patriotic Pole, it is impossible for him to carry out his mission. With a dramatic gesture, therefore, he presents his book to his Chief.

Whatever the truth, MI5 could still exploit WALENTY, argued Harmer: 'If my conclusion is accepted that WALENTY has now told the truth about his mission, even if he is holding something back about the rest of the story there is no reason why we should not open up his transmitter and work it on our behalf.' While it would probably be impossible to send over military information of a high a standard, his mission to raise a Fifth Column gave such a wide scope that, with imagination, 'and above all with his very original mind, we might possibly confuse and deceive the Germans on the question of European politics to a remarkable extent'. So, with regard to the disposal of WALENTY, Harmer recommended:

1. If WALENTY is regarded as a self confessed spy, a case could be made out for his arrest and detention. The worst interpretation which I could make of his story is, however, not sufficient to make me recommend such a course. After the very great service which he rendered to his country and to Britain in 1940/1941, it would need in my view overwhelming evidence that he had worked, or intended to work, against this country before we would be justified in imprisoning him. That evidence has not been forthcoming. Even if WALENTY were genuinely mislead by German propaganda in prison, I think there are in his case extenuating circumstances and it cannot be denied that in the end he revealed his mission voluntarily and not under hostile interrogation. My first recommendation, therefore, is that WALENTY should be allowed his liberty for the time being.
2. On the other hand he has certainly not behaved in a current fashion and his own Chief has told him that his conduct from a military point of view, in withholding his true story, is inexcusable. His error becomes greater, if my conclusion is accepted that he has not yet revealed the true circumstances of his recruitment. I therefore recommend that Colonel Gano be invited formally to give him a severe reprimand and to refuse his entry into the active ranks of the Polish Airforce for at any rate a limited period, and to give him some minor administrative job for the time being, and also that Colonel Gano be invited to order him to reveal the further details which he is now holding back.
3. That in collaboration with WALENTY, we start calling [to the Germans] in order to establish W/T contact with Paris. In this connection we know that Paris are already calling him.[29]

This aptly illustrates the problems MI5 faced in trying to establish an agent's *bone fides*. Indeed, J.H. Marriott considered Harmers report such a 'masterly' one 'that I hesitate to criticise it in any way'. But it seemed to him that, from a strictly B1.A point of view, 'we are not very much concerned with the reliability of WALENTY, except in so far as his reliability has any bearing upon the question whether the Germans are likely to place reliance upon messages transmitted by him.

Purely as a personal opinion', however, Marriott felt that WALENTY had been rather more truthful than Harmer suggested. 'He seems to me to have made out a very good case for concealing his true story for as long as he did. Secondly, I do not share Harmer's doubts about the accuracy of WALENTY's story of his recruitment … Harmer's view about VICTOIRE's veracity may well be correct, but I should have thought that the application of Harmer's test could produce a totally different explanation of VICTOIRE's statement that she had heard from the Germans that WALENTY had volunteered to work for them. VICTOIRE knew that she had acted discreditably throughout, and she may have thought that her offence would be regarded as much less serious if we were told that even WALENTY himself had offered to work for the Germans. I think it is quite possible that VICTOIRE invented this altogether.'

As far as Marriott could see, the only concern of B1.A was the question whether WALENTY's wireless transmitter could, and should, be used. So far as the first part of the question was concerned: 'We know that the Germans are calling WALENTY: presumably therefore contact can be easily established. With regard to the second part I am by no means so clear. The objectives to be gained by running double agents are numerous, but there is surely one over-riding objective, namely to delude the enemy to his undoing. Indeed the whole essence of a double agent is the fact that his ostensible master is deluded into the belief that he is operating as a free agent. If we operate WALENTY successfully the Germans will labour under this delusion, but I am not at all sure that they will thereby suffer any particular disadvantage, and I am afraid that the balance of disadvantage will be on our side.'

What the Germans would first of all believe was that the turning round of enemy agents was a practical proposition, and that this afforded a good way of getting agents into Britain. Sooner or later this belief, 'which appears already to be dangerously widespread, will be shared by SIS and SOE agents. It seems to me that in the interests of both those two services it ought very soon to be made absolutely clear to them that we are never going to tolerate any person who has worked for our service agreeing in any circumstances to work for the Germans'. Secondly, with regard to his mission to recruit a Polish Fifth Column, 'I cannot for the life of me see how this can possibly do us any good. I should have thought that the last thing we wanted the Germans to believe was that there was, or could be, such a thing as a Fifth Column amongst any of the exiled governments.' Thirdly, the Germans had to suppose that, if WALENTY was believed at all by the British, he would be regarded as a most important man, and would accordingly, in view of his vast experience, be employed in a highly confidential position. The information that he could get would therefore be of the highest grade. 'I doubt very much whether the provision of misinformation on this level is within our powers under the present arrangements. It is, incidentally, curious to my mind that the Germans should have given WALENTY the instructions which he has reported. WALENTY is an Intelligence Officer, and one would have expected his first assignment would have been information about Polish organisations working on the Continent.' The other objections to running the case were sufficiently obvious to Marriott in view of the fact that, 'as I see it, it will be necessary to collaborate completely with the Poles. This I am sure will meet with disapproval from the Twenty Committee. Moreover I think that it is important not to over-estimate the importance of the case. The Germans have really lost nothing by letting WALENTY go, for they had cleaned up the whole of his organisation, and the only thing left to them would have been the doubtful satisfaction of executing WALENTY himself.'[30]

But Marriott was overruled and the XX Committee decided that WALENTY should be run as a double agent, at any rate for the time being, and this decision was communicated to Colonel Gano and Commander Dunderdale of SIS on 17 December 1942. WALENTY was given a new codename: BRUTUS. To cover the possibility that BRUTUS had another mission, and also because the revelation that he had accepted a mission for the Germans 'made it appear that he was a very much more sinister individual than had been expected', it was decided to keep BRUTUS under the closest watch with a telephone check and a HOW applied for so that his correspondence could be watched. The checks revealed nothing of importance.

It was also decided, as Harmer recommended, that it would be unwise to let BRUTUS rejoin the Polish Air Force and fly. Colonel Gano originally proposed to try and get him a job in the Military Attache's office in London. This was because he considered that it would be unwise to have a man known to be a German agent working in the Deuxieme Bureau, not for security reasons, but if it ever leaked out it would have been a means of levelling criticism against him, Colonel Gano, not only on the part of rival officers of the Polish Headquarters, but also, for example, by the Russians. However, on reconsideration Gano decided after all to employ BRUTUS in the Deuxieme Bureau, and he received a position in the section studying the Italian Army. There was also, at this time, a change in BRUTUS's personal life: Mademoiselle Deschamps, alias MOUSTIQUE, had escaped from the Occupied Zone at the time of the arrest of the BRUTUS organisation in Paris, and she reached the UK shortly before he did. She thereupon started to live with BRUTUS and had been his mistress ever since. At the beginning of December 1942, BRUTUS started to call with a wireless set constructed for him by MI5. He established contact with the Germans on 20 December 1942.

The BRUTUS case was considered, again, by the XX Committee on 31 December. The Committee, after hearing an explanation by TAR Robertson, took the view that the case should not proceed any further without the approval of the 'W' Board, on the grounds that it was necessary to give the Poles full information about the case, and that some of the members of the Board were always sensitive about the passing of information to officers of Allied countries. The 'W' Board was therefore convened and duly considered the case: it decided that it should proceed on the understanding that the Poles would not wish to be supplied with copies of the W/T traffic, and that they were not allowed to discover that other cases were being run. The Board also decided that so far as possible the BRUTUS case should not be used for operational deceptions, and if it became too difficult it could be closed down. The Board further stated that they had no objection to the case being used for the purpose of attempting to improve the treatment meted out to the Poles by the Germans. The Foreign Office also, in agreeing to the case being run, was of the opinion that the Poles should be let in fully. From this time onwards the Poles were not supplied with traffic, although Colonel Gano was shown 'interesting messages'. He showed no desire to pry into the details of the case, although there was some concern that this might have been due to the fact that the Poles had BRUTUS's code and could monitor and read all his messages.

BRUTUS's principal mission for the Germans was to report on aircraft production. Nevertheless, he started off in, January 1943, giving the Germans details of the Polish Armed Forces, followed with general information and an appreciation of the political situation so far as carrying out his mission was concerned. BRUTUS stated, in effect, that unless the Germans were prepared to improve the condition of the Polish population, and in the absence of German victories on the Eastern Front, it was impossible to raise a Fifth Column of Poles in Britain. In March, 1943 he paid a visit to Scotland and prepared an 'exceedingly good report' on the situation there, which was largely passed and sent over in the first half of April. The great number of messages passed was used by MI5 as a reason for asking the Germans to send him an operator and some money, and they agreed in principle and asked for BRUTUS's advice. He proposed that they should drop the operator and the money by parachute.

BRUTUS then proceeded to send over a very lengthy report on the south coast. On 4 June 1943 the Germans said that they would not parachute an operator but would send money. Having agreed to the place proposed by BRUTUS, namely the Wash region, they subsequently, on the eve of his departure there in June, said that it was too near London. Meanwhile, BRUTUS had himself done a tour of South-Eastern Command and had turned in another 'exceedingly good' report which formed the basis of many further messages. In regard, however, to his political mission, messages were always much more difficult to provide. The Russians having broken off relations with Poland, it was obvious that German propaganda was being very successful and BRUTUS's 'obvious course, had he been in truth an agent', would have been to encourage them in their propaganda. 'As we could not obviously do this, we have had to hedge to a very large degree' so MI5 indicated that he was in indirect contact with the people who were directing Polish underground newspapers critical of the exiled Government. In fact, BRUTUS was up to his neck in the internal politics of the exiled Poles and his activities threw the entire XX case into jeopardy.

Before the crisis erupted, though, BRUTUS's case officer had an opportunity to analyse the agent's traffic to the Germans and search for evidence that he had been turned by the enemy. For Harmer the evidence that came to light appeared to confirm that BRUTUS had told the truth about his mission. One question 'which was slightly disturbing' was that it turned out that the code given to BRUTUS by the Germans was very similar to the code captured from a British agent. 'This might have pointed to the fact that the Germans intended BRUTUS to give himself up and offer himself as a double agent since, if such were their intentions, they would not be compromising a code.' An expert opinion on this from SIS, dated Christmas Eve 1942, stated: 'Similar they certainly are; both are double transposition, and both have keys based on memorised phrases, but BRUTUS' code has the extra complication of (a) a special indicator system, and (b) the use of dummy letters. While it is perfectly clear that [the British agent] PELLETIER's code is a simple modification of the original British Service code, the differences of BRUTUS' code are such that it would not be automatically compromised by the possession of PELLETIER's code.'

This expert opinion appeared to support, if anything, the belief that BRUTUS's mission was a true one, and the subsequent traffic to a large extent bore this out. There were also various ISOS references that put the issue, for all practical purposes, beyond doubt.

Thus, on 7 May 1943, BRUTUS reported on the arrest of another agent, CARELESS. It was hoped by this message to get a reaction on Most Secret Sources because BRUTUS's message was so worded that it should suggest to the Germans that another double agent, GARBO, was in danger, and thereby cause them to communicate with Madrid and warn them. Actually they did not do this, but on 21 May, Berlin informed Madrid that Paris had reported that the English had arrested someone with the same surname as CARELESS. There was no qualification to suggest that the source was not a genuine one. Later BRUTUS was described in German signals as a 'hitherto very valuable wireless agent'. Harmer was convinced that this evidence was enough to 'prove almost conclusively that... they believed him to be a perfectly genuine agent'. A number of BRUTUS's questions had also appeared in Most Secret Sources, which was consistent with the questions being genuine and BRUTUS being regarded as a reliable agent. Harmer was clear: 'It can be stated, therefore, almost certainly that BRUTUS did not have a triple-cross mission.'

With regard to the question of his part in his recruitment by the Germans, one or two small points had indicated that Harmer's original conclusions, as to BRUTUS's reliability, was correct. One of the code phrases used by BRUTUS consisted of the words 'Londres est en Angleterre'. Whenever BRUTUS wrote the word 'Londres', he left out the final 's', and when he wrote out the details of his code the word appeared as 'Londre'. The first message received from the Germans to BRUTUS was coded on this phrase, and the mistake was pointed out to BRUTUS, upon which he said that it was his mistake and that as the Germans had chosen the phrase they would code up with the final 's'. Nevertheless, the message was found to be coded with 'Londre' without the 's', and all messages based on this phrase had been similarly coded ever since: 'This implies either that the Germans made the mistake or, more likely, that BRUTUS himself chose the code phrase. In the latter case it is not only obvious that he was not speaking the truth, but also it implies that he took a greater part in preparing the details of his mission than he has admitted.' Finally, the fact that BRUTUS had become embroiled in Polish politics, based largely on extreme anti-Bolshevism, appeared to Harmer, to be consistent with his being really actuated by anti-Russian sentiments. It indicated that BRUTUS's activity in this connection, however much it showed anti-Russian sentiments, did not involve any pro-German and direct anti-Allied activity. As a result, therefore, of a year's working of the case, and over a year's watch, Harmer declared that 'the original conclusions in my view stand, namely that BRUTUS told the truth about his mission, but that the circumstances of his recruitment have not been entirely divulged by him'.[31]

9

CARELESS Whispers

GARBO

On 2 April 1942, ISOS intercepted the following message from Madrid to Berlin:

> Agent (V-Mann) 372 of Stelle FELIPE reports from Liverpool on 26/3 the sailing from Liverpool of a convoy of 15 ships including 9 freighters, course BASTA (Gibraltar) and probably going on to Malta, possible intermediate port LISA (Lisbon). Composition: 1 collier 2,000 tons, 1 tanker 2,000 tons, 5 freighters 5,000 tons with following cargo: 2 freighter tanker 2,000 tons, 5 freighters 5,000 to 10,000 tons with following cargo: 2 freighter with A.A. ammunition and war material, 3 freighters with food; 1 further freighter 5,000 tons with Air Force technical personnel bound for Malta, 1 freighter 1,500 tons with hospital supplies and ambulances, other freighters with cargo of war material. Route of voyage Liverpool, possible LISA, BASTA, Malta according to statement of master of Greek freighter New Hellas now sailing for England.

This was the first indication of the existence of Station Felipe V-Mann 372, apparently a German agent operating from Liverpool. The fact that the information was being re-transmitted to Berlin seven days after the date of the report in Liverpool indicated that the Liverpool agent had some special means of communication: the time lapse was too short for the information to have been passed by ordinary air mail and yet too slow for W/T. The information was checked by MI5 and though a great number of convoys had sailed from Liverpool around this date none could be found which fitted exactly with this description. As MI5 officer Tommy Harris recorded: 'The report was sufficiently substantial and plausible to leave the impression that it had been the work of an inaccurate reporter. The message seemed plausible enough to Berlin who immediately flashed out the signal of alert to Mediterranean outposts.'

The German agent who had sent the message – V-Mann 372 – was Juan Pujol, the son of a Spanish industrialist. Pujol had received a Catholic education in Spain up to the age of fifteen. His father, a man of moderate means, died in 1933 when Pujol was twenty-one years of age but left his family well provided for. Pujol ventured into the manufacturing business with his elder brother. He was a cinema proprietor and later owned a road transport business. Shortly before the Spanish Civil War he sold out his interest in his business to his elder brother. A few months later, the factory on which Pujol family depended for their livelihood was commandeered by the workers and with the outbreak of the Civil War, Pujol was called up for service in the Republican Army. Pujol decided that he would not fight on the side of a Government 'which was unable to maintain order and permitted the injustices which were being perpetrated against the Roman Catholic church and the Spanish constitution'. In August 1936, he went into hiding in the house of some friends and did not leave the house or venture into the streets for nearly two years. On seventeen occasions the house received a routine search by the police. On the eighteenth occasion, in April 1938, he was discovered and arrested together with other male members of the household. For nineteen days he was held incommunicado in a prison cell. A woman prisoner, who was having an affair with one of the warders, managed to arrange for a party to escape. Pujol was one of forty-nine who got away. He again went into hiding until he managed to acquire some false identity papers. In possession of these documents he enlisted, voluntarily, in the services of the Republican Army with intent to desert to the Franco side. After a short training he was put into a Communications Company and sent to the Front as the time of the Franco counter-attack following the Ebro offensive.

In September, 1938, 'at the risk of his life' he crossed to the Franco side. After a period in a concentration camp and following interrogations by the Franco authorities, he was enlisted in the Franco Army. After two months leave in Burgos he was posted to the Teruel Front in January, 1939. On 13 February Tarragona fell. 'There were great celebrations' but an incident then occurred which, it appeared, convinced Pujol that the Falange were 'endeavouring to dominate Franco Spain, with the same despotic intolerance, as the Communists had tried to dominate Republican Spain'. For expressing his sympathy with the Monarchy, Pujol was struck in the face by his Colonel and imprisoned. Although after a few days 'he engineered his release through intervention'... he was permanently left with the knowledge that Spain, under Fascism, was as intolerable as it would have been under Communism'.

After the Spanish Civil War ended, he returned to Burgos where he met his future wife. In October, after his demobilisation, he went to live at her home town and in April 1940, they were married in Madrid. 'He soon discovered that unless one was in sympathy with the Party there was little opening for a young man in Spain.' He went to Lisbon 'where he found conditions little better' and in November planned to go to the United States with his wife, or at least to explore the possibilities of getting there.

But in February 1941, Pujol called on the German Embassy in Madrid and asked to be put in touch with the department dealing with 'secret affairs'. He was interviewed by the Chancellor, Herr Heidelburg to whom he declared that he was prepared to work for Germany in any type of work in which they considered he could be useful. Pujol volunteered to go to Lisbon to operate as an informant for the Germans there. And, if they could suggest a method of reaching Britain, 'he would willingly go for them'. Pujol gave his alias as Senor Lopez and provided a telephone number where he could be reached by the Germans. After not hearing anything for ten days, he telephoned the Embassy and was given the message that somebody would be calling on Senor Lopez in due course. Three days later he again telephoned the Embassy for news. Pujol was told that someone would call on him that afternoon. The visitor was a Spaniard serving as a contact man for the Germans. He took note of Pujol's background, including his service during the Spanish Civil War, and promised to make contact again in the near future. Two weeks went past without news. Pujol again telephoned the Embassy and pressed for an interview with the Chancellor which was granted the same afternoon. The Chancellor told him that his idea to go to Lisbon had been rejected as 'uninteresting'. But, he was told that, providing he could 'put up a project for going to England they would be interested'. It was left to Pujol, not only to work out a plan, but to a find suitable cover and make the travel arrangements as well.

After ten days Pujol once again telephoned the Embassy – this time, not to complain, but to say that he had something important to communicate. He was told that he would receive a visit from someone that evening. The visitor was a man named Lang (alias Emilio). Pujol told him that he had recently been in contact with a friend of his, a secret police agent employed on the investigation of contraband currency transactions. Pujol described how when he was last in Lisbon he had happened to meet a British subject called Dalamal whom, he stated, was trying to negotiate the exchange of some five million pesetas into sterling. Dalamal had returned to Britain without accomplishing his mission. Pujol explained how, in matters of this sort, Spanish secret police agents operated on the basis of commission: if the transaction was intercepted and the five million pesetas confiscated, the police officer responsible for the case would receive a substantial commission on this sum. This particular police officer, Pujol said, had offered to split his commission with him if he would be willing to go to Britain to continue the investigations and secure Dalamal's confidence. Pujol had accepted the invitation – but only if he were sent to Britain, officially, by the Spanish security police as a Government official. Pujol 'tested' Emilio and asked whether the Germans would be prepared to help him to get a visa should he be sent to Britain as an agent of the Spanish Seguridad. Emilio, however, replied that he thought the proposition complicated and absurd. He thought that it would be much better and simpler if Pujol could get himself a job as a correspondent of a Spanish newspaper and went to Britain under this sort of cover. Emilio left his telephone number and told Pujol to ring him if he could arrange this.

Pujol then went to go to the British Consulate where he applied for a visa but was told that it was not likely to be forthcoming. A few days later he rang Emilio and when they met he told him of his visit to the Consulate and the difficulties he anticipated. Emilio revealed that he was already aware of Pujol's visit to the Consulate since his movements were being watched. Emilio recommended that Pujol go to Lisbon where he would find the possibilities were greater both for getting press work and for getting a visa. Pujol agreed to this proposal and, after an examination of his passport, by Emilio, he was told to try to obtain a Spanish exit permit and a Portuguese entry visa. Emilio gave Pujol 1,000 pesetas for his expenses and on 26 April 1941, Pujol left Madrid for Lisbon.

On arrival in Lisbon, Pujol called at the British Consulate where he put in a formal application for a visa to the UK. He then returned to Madrid and called at the German Embassy. Emilio was away and for the first time Pujol met Fritz Knappe-Rately, operating under the alias 'Federico', who was joined, shortly, by Kuehlanthal, whose alias was Carlos. At first, Pujol was given a cold reception, by the Germans; told that they were 'extremely busy'; that his visit was inconvenient; and that in no circumstances should he call at the Embassy in future. But, before leaving, Pujol managed to 'whet their appetite' by saying that he had ascertained from the British Consulate in Lisbon that he would be granted a visa to go to England. He also took this opportunity of handing Federico his telephone number should further contact be desired.

The next day Federico telephoned. He wanted to meet and, when they did so, Pujol was asked to go over his story and plan for going to Britain on behalf of the Spanish Seguridad.

Pujol told Federico that his Seguridad agent was a man called Varela, attached to the Spanish Embassy in Lisbon whom he had met by chance on several occasions. Varela worked closely with the Portuguese international police and his job was that of Security Officer at the Spanish Embassy in Lisbon. Federico asked if Pujol knew Dalamal well and where he was at present. Pujol replied that he did, and that he was in England. He proposed to follow him there. The five million pesetas which he claimed were owned by Dalamal were in Tangiers. Pujol was convinced that he could persuade Dalamal to handle the transaction on his behalf and that he was anxious, therefore, to undertake the mission for the Spanish Seguridad since he would profit to the extent of 25 per cent of this amount if he could persuade Dalamal to allow him to handle the transaction with the result that the funds would be confiscated by the Seguridad. Varela would receive a similar percentage of the sum confiscated which was the reason for his inducing the Seguridad to facilitate Pujol in going to Britain on their behalf. Pujol stressed urgency of the matter lest Dalamal negotiate through some other channel over which Pujol would have no control. Pujol also revealed to Federico that Varela was trying to get him a diplomatic passport for Britain and to arrange for him to be sent to the Spanish Embassy in London as an Honorary Attache there. Varela, he pointed out, was a member of the Plantilla, or professional police, and therefore paid by salary; as such he was not entitled to any form of commission. In introducing Pujol as an outside agent for the Dalamal case he had done so because he knew that Pujol would give him half of his commission. If this were discovered Varela would be dismissed and so Pujol's chances of going to Britain ended. It was essential, therefore, in their mutual interest that Federico should treat this confidence with the greatest secrecy.

Three days later the two met again, this time at Federcio's suggestion, to discuss whether Pujol had received any news from Varela. Now it seemed that the Germans were keener. Federico explained that they naturally had to be extremely careful. He confided to Pujol that there had been the case of an agent whom they had taken on and, after paying him monies, they discovered that his project was a myth. He did not, therefore, wish to be caught a second time. Pujol then received a telegram from Lisbon stating: 'You must come here urgently. The affair has been arranged. Signed: VARELA'. As soon as the telegram arrived with the Lisbon post mark Pujol contacted Federico who read the telegram and put it in his pocket. The next afternoon they met again. Federico said he had been instructed to tell Pujol to leave immediately for Lisbon to see Varela in connection with his telegram. He gave Pujol 500 pesetas and told him how he could get more money in Lisbon should he run short of funds. Pujol then went to Lisbon and made contact with Federico's people there, from whom he got additional funds. Pujol then returned to Madrid to tell Federico that he had seen Varela who had given him instructions for making contact with the Seguridad where his final arrangements would be made. He said that Varela had already laid on all the preliminary arrangements through the Diplomatic Bag to the Seguridad in Madrid. The Seguridad had agreed that Pujol should work directly under Varela on the Dalamal case. His passport and final instructions, Pujol said, would be issued to him personally by the Seguridad. Pujol was going, that day, for his instructions and they arranged to meet the following afternoon when Federico was told everything had gone according to plan and, the whole affair now settled, Pujol was to return the following day to collect his passport.

Early the next morning Pujol telephoned Federico 'in an excited state insisting on an urgent meeting which could not wait'. Federico, 'alarmed and furious', agreed to meet him five minutes later at the cafe opposite the offices of the Seguridad. Pujol had, he said, received his diplomatic passport and the only thing now missing was the stamp of the Spanish Foreign Office. Pujol explained that he had only two minutes to spare. He said that he had called Federico in order to be able to satisfy him that he now had the passport and was about to leave. There was a messenger and car waiting outside the Seguridad doors opposite where they were sitting, to accompany Pujol with the passport to the Foreign Office where it had to be stamped. From there it would be sent to the Spanish Embassy in Lisbon by Diplomatic Bag. Pujol was to pick it up on his arrival in Lisbon, where he would travel on his ordinary passport. This, he explained, was the only moment he would actually have the document in his possession to show him. He was therefore anxious for Federico to take the opportunity of seeing it with his own eyes so that any remaining doubts as to his genuineness should be dispelled. Pujol then produced the document and, looking round to see that no one was watching, he opened it under the table, giving Federico a chance to inspect it. He immediately folded it up again and put it back in his pocket.

Federico 'was greatly impressed, called him a good fellow, and patted him on the back'.

That night Pujol reported to Federico that everything had gone well at the Foreign Office. Federico said that Pujol should delay his departure for a few days, pending the arrival of instructions from Germany. Pujol replied that in that case he would have to telegraph Varela at the Spanish Embassy in Lisbon to make some excuse for the delay. He drafted out a telegram saying: 'In a few days I will leave for Lisbon, Signed: JUAN.' After this the 'sole anxiety' of the Germans was to give Pujol 'some sort of rapid training so as to be able to take advantage of his visit to England under diplomatic cover'. When they next met, Pujol impressed on Federico the necessity, in their mutual interest, of keeping the secret about Varela and his contact with the Seguridad. He warned Federico that any leakage through him would ruin his cover in Britain. Federico promised, so far as the Germans were concerned, that what Pujol had told them would for ever remain a 'dead secret'. He left Pujol four questionnaires which he was instructed to study. Within a few days Pujol had been trained in secret writing and the questionnaires had been substituted by miniature reproductions which he could study 'at his leisure' and conceal on his person when he left Spain.

Federico then boasted that he envied Pujol going on this mission 'because it was not dangerous and was only a job of collecting information as an observer and did not entail the theft of documents or dangerous exploits'. To reassure Pujol, Federcio told him that Luis Calvo, correspondent of the ABC in London was working for them. He also suggested that in case of need Pujol could use the Spanish Diplomatic Bag, as they could arrange for him to be given facilities in this way through one of the Service Attaches. Pujol, however, said he did not wish to know the names or particulars of anyone they were using. He did not expect them to disclose his name to others. He said he preferred to operate alone and the results would prove which of their agents was the best. At this 'final farewell' Kuehlanthal 'put in an appearance' and gave Pujol his last instructions. In Britain he was to get as much information as possible and try to recruit sub-agents whom he could leave behind when he had to return. He was given cover addresses and money and a warning that he should be careful not to underestimate the British as they were a formidable enemy. He warned Pujol that he should not anticipate a quick German victory as he was personally of the opinion that it would be a very long war. He said that the questionnaires were only to serve him as a guide since all information was of interest. Arrangements were made to make his wife and child an allowance while he was in England. Pujol then left Madrid to join his wife.

On 19 July 1941, Pujol wrote his first secret ink letter to the Germans explaining that he had left for Britain, on 12 August and was staying with a Spaniard who was recommended to him in Lisbon:

> This gentleman has put me in touch with an official of the Air Line Company which runs the service England – Portugal. I put forward urgent reasons for sending letters to my wife which he has promised to post in Lisbon without their passing through British Censorship. He charges a dollar per letter. I am assured by the Spaniard, who also sends correspondence to Spain by this method that delivery will be safe and quick. When you receive this, write immediately so that I will have a check on the security and rapidity of this route to guide me for future correspondence. Reply to the name of Dionicio FERNANDEZ (For J.P.) Poste Restante, Lisbon. This gentleman will hand your letter to the English Air Line official.

Pujol did not write again until he received a reply to this letter which reached him some two weeks later, signed by Federico Knappe, in which he said: 'I received your letter of the 24th. The method of communication is good and the letter developed well. We await with interest further news. Do not forget to number your letters. Your wife is well and cared for. Kindest regards and good luck.' By 17 August, Pujol was able to report that, by cultivating friendships with people in sympathy with the Axis, he had recruited a Portuguese named Carvalho, a resident of Newport, Monmouthshire, whom he had instructed to watch, and report on, the Bristol Channel area, and take note of the shipping and the import and export of war materials. Furthermore, he stated he had recruited a Swiss subject named Gerbbers a resident of Bootle, Liverpool, whom he had instructed to cover 'that important district'. In the same letter he asked for a special ink for intercommunication between agents. In this third letter, to the Germans, Pujol gave information about the arrival of convoys in the Clyde. He stated that, on arrival off the coast of Scotland, the convoys dispersed all over Britain and smaller ships, mostly of 2,000 tons or less, were used in these convoys, firstly so that the smaller British ports could be used for disembarkation after the convoys had dispersed, and, secondly, because they provided a smaller target against submarine attack and smaller losses when hits were scored by the enemy.

One of the letters to the Germans was delivered by Pujol's wife. The cover text read as a normal letter from husband to wife but adding a postscript that as soon as she received the letter she was to proceed from Lugo to Madrid without delay and there telephone a number which he gave her and ask to speak to Don Federico and arrange to meet him in Madrid where she should simply hand over the letter to him. When contacted by Mrs Pujol, Federico accepted the invitation to meet her. But, before handing over the letter she read Federico the postscript saying that she considered it very strange that her husband should make such a peculiar request as to pass on to an unknown friend of his a personal letter which could be of no interest whatever to anyone but herself. Federico, 'anxious to get possession of the letter', explained that he was a very close personal friend of Mr Pujol and that he had not heard from him since he had left for Britain 'and made the unconvincing excuse' that he thought Pujol was anxious to let him know in this way that he was well and safe in England. But Mrs Pujol then told Federico that his remark considerably increased her suspicions about her husband since he had told her when he left that he was proceeding to Ireland. Federico now informed her that he had gone to Britain while the letter, she noted, had been mailed in Lisbon. She 'became highly excited and said that she was convinced that her husband had run off with a woman' and that Federico 'was an accomplice in his escapade. The unfortunate man was at a loss to know how to answer, but he succeeded in extracting the letter from her, promising to meet her again that afternoon when he hoped to be in a position to dispel her suspicions.'

Federico returned in the afternoon with the secret text of the letter developed. 'No doubt, having been given approval by his chiefs, he showed her the letter and said that he had to confess that her husband had gone to England on a secret mission for the German Government.' At this point Mrs Pujol began 'to throw a fit' and expressed her worries that he would be caught by the British police and executed. Poor Federico tried to convince her that he was immune from danger: he had gone there with diplomatic cover and had already started to engage in most valuable work which she should not interrupt. She said that she could not understand how he could be of use to them when he did not even speak any English to which Federico answered that to have produced results without knowledge of the language of the country in which he was operating was an added proof of Juan's ability. To pacify Mrs. Pujol, Federico offered her a job in the German Embassy in Madrid, or money to live at a luxury hotel, but she refused these offers, insisting that she wanted to return to her family in Lugo.

She gave Federico a photograph of her child, making him promise to forward it to her husband whom she feared would never see his child again, 'and on this sentimental note they parted'. After this experience Federico sent a letter to Pujol saying that 'he should not send any further letters via Lugo'. He had also, by this time, written to Pujol to say that his stay in Britain would have to be a prolonged one and that under no circumstances was he to return without their permission. This disappointed Pujol for it meant that he would have to 'invent more reports to forward to his masters'. For Juan Pujol was not in Britain spying on behalf of the Germans. He was in Lisbon and had never been to Britain at all. He had made the whole thing up – the Dalama case; his relationship with Varela; his diplomatic cover – everything was a figment of Pujol's imagination. And he had done it all on his own with no help from the British[1] – in fact, quite the opposite.

Far from being a German agent, Pujol wanted, desperately, to be a British one. But the British, or rather SIS, told him to go away every time he secretly approached them. In doing so the British almost lost a man who would become one of the greatest double agents in History. In truth, in 1940, after he returned to Madrid, Pujol had taken the decision to leave Spain until the Franco regime had been overthrown – but he had also come to the conclusion that the prospects of a change of government in Spain were dependent on a British victory in the war. Years later, when granted a private audience with the Duke of Edinburgh at Buckingham Palace, His Royal Highness asked Pujol, after he had told him of his wartime exploits: 'Why were you, a Spaniard, so keen to help the British during the Second World War?' It was a question he been asked before:

> The answer lies in my beliefs; the same beliefs that my father instilled into me during my childhood, beliefs which urged me to fight against all tyranny and oppression. I have never borne, nor indeed do I bear now, any grudge against the German people. In fact, I have always admired their industry and their love of tradition. They suffered a crushing defeat in 1918 and no one was there to give them a helping hand. They had been deeply humiliated and left with no friends to comfort them. It was at this point, at this decisive moment when the lack on the part of their neighbours left them scorned and offended, that an ambitious man being – a maniac, an inhuman brute – arose and cajoled them with his empty verbosity. He made them believe in what was not believable, in what was irrational, unlikely, impossible and inadmissible, namely the strength of the Prussian army and

the greatness of the German people. Both these notions were
decisive in bringing about that stubborn arrogance which fuelled
the Nazi leader's provocative talk. How could the German people
have fallen victim to such stratagems? What sophistries and
snares had those devious despotic rabble-rousers used to enable
them to indoctrinate the minds of intelligent and resourceful
Germans so successfully?

The man's name was Adolf Hitler; his doctrine, Mein Kampf.
Hitler hated the political parties of the Left and those which
supported the Habsburgs. His greatest spite though, he reserved
for the Jewish people, whom he managed to exterminate by
the most perverse, malignant and evil means ever witnessed in
history. Many millions were his victims and their deaths were
upon his conscience. Mankind would not tolerate such Satanic
splendour. Nor would I. That was why I fought against in justice
and iniquity with the only weapons at my disposal.[2]

Pujol had been aware of what was happening in Germany before the
war. But despite censorship, word eventually spread to Spain: 'My
humanist convictions would not allow me to turn blind eye to the
enormous suffering that was being unleashed by this psychopath Hitler
and his band of acolytes... But what could I do to arrest such excess?
Little, very little... In my hours of loneliness I would be tormented by
odd pieces of information and graphic details which merged in my
imagination into a confused and horrible nightmare. Unable to express
my feelings, I yearned for justice from the medley of tangled ideas and
fantasies going round and round in my head, a plan slowly began to
take shape. I must do something, something practical; I must make my
contribution towards the good of humanity.'[3]

It occurred to Pujol that with his background, having deserted from
the Republicans to Franco, 'it would not be difficult for him to get a
job in either Germany or Italy. Once there he would be able to serve
British interests'. He discussed with his wife the idea of offering his
services to the British. 'She approved' and, after making their plans she
called, in January 1941, at the British Consulate in Madrid. She was
granted an interview and told the story that she knew of a man who
was willing to work for the British and was prepared to go either to
Germany or to Italy to conduct espionage on behalf of Britain. The
Consular official replied that he 'was not interested in this sort of
proposition'. When Pujol was told the result of his wife's visit to the
Consulate 'he decided that he would at least show us that if we were
not willing to engage in espionage against the Germans, the Germans

did not feel the same way about us'. It was his desire 'to endeavour to obtain evidence in proof of this belief' that spurred Pujol to approach the Germans.

Thus he concocted a plan to fool the Germans. The diplomatic passport that Pujol had shown to Federico – and claimed that he received from Varela, his police contact – was a fake. After Pujol had visited the British Consulate, in Lisbon, to obtain a visa to visit Britain he had then set about obtaining a false Spanish diplomatic passport, calling on a firm of engravers in Lisbon and asking them to make him a die. With this in his possession Pujol then called on a small printer to whom he said he was an employee of the Spanish Embassy in Lisbon and offered to bring him the Embassy's printing. He would, 'of course, expect a commission'. As a 'trial' he wished the printer to set up some proofs for a Spanish diplomatic passport on which the Embassy would judge the quality of his work. Pujol had made a sketch of the layout of the document and produced what he purported to be the Embassy seal. After choosing, with great care, the types to be used and the quality of the paper, he arranged to call back in a few days to collect the proofs. With the document in his possession, his photograph affixed, and his name inserted as the bearer, he returned to Madrid to entice the Germans into believing he had received the diplomatic passport from Varela, – a real policeman but not in reality linked to the story Pujol had told the Germans.

Even the telegram from Varela was a fake. Pujol, after he had met Federico for the second time, had, on his return home, thought out a deception to convince Federico that he was genuine. On his first journey to Lisbon, Pujol had met in the hotel there, a Spaniard, with whom he had become friendly, named Dionicio Fernandez. Pujol decided that Fernandez 'should unwittingly be made to play a role in his set up'. He telephoned Fernandez in Lisbon and asked his assistance 'in a purely personal matter. Pujol said he was anxious to get back to Lisbon but that he was prevented from doing so by his wife who suspected that he had a girl friend there'. Pujol said it would be a very great favour if Fernandez would send him a telegram for him to show to his wife. He then dictated the telegram that convinced Federico that Pujol was for real: the 'You must come here urgently. The affair has been arranged' telegram. And the café meeting with Federico, where Pujol had shown him the (forged) passport and told him he had a car waiting to rush him to the Foreign Office in order to have the passport stamped, was staged. Prior to the meeting, Pujol had taken the precaution of getting the son of the owner of the pension where he was staying to wait for him at the door of the office of the Seguridad where he also had a taxi waiting. Having shown Federico the document he said that it was safer that they should not leave together, volunteering that he should go first. He got up, walked over to the doors of the Seguridad where he was picked up by the young man who was supposed to be his escort. They got into the waiting taxi and 'asked in a loud voice to be driven to the Foreign Office'. They, of course, did not go to the Foreign Office. The final act, at this stage, in convincing the Germans he was genuine was the telegram Pujol sent to Varela at the Spanish Embassy in Lisbon to make some excuse for the delay in meeting him. Pujol, it will be recalled, drafted out a telegram saying: 'In a few days I will leave for Lisbon, Signed: JUAN.' But, pretending he was in a hurry, he had handed the draft to Federico asking if he would be good enough to send it off for him. Thus, Federico, 'had not only seen and confiscated' Pujol's telegram which purported to come from Varela, but he had also despatched Pujol's reply to him. 'Any doubts which the Germans might have had' in Pujol 'had now been for ever dispelled'.

When in Lisbon, Pujol had had another go at convincing the British to take him on as their agent. He tried, and failed, to get an interview at the British Embassy there. He 'promptly realised he would have to play for time and evolved a new plan through which he hoped to get further evidence of German espionage activities against the British'. Pujol contacted his Spanish friend, Dionicio Fernandez, and told him that he was 'embroiled in a love affair with someone in Madrid with whom he wished to be able to carry on correspondence without the knowledge of his wife'. Pujol asked whether, in order to make this possible, Fernandez would mind his using his name at the Poste Restante in Lisbon for the purpose of receiving letters from the woman in Madrid. Fernandez agreed. Pujol used this address for corresponding with the Germans.

As soon as correspondence with the Germans was in his possession, believing that he now had more than sufficient evidence to interest the British, he called again at the British Embassy in Lisbon, and 'after difficulty' he was interviewed by someone in the office of the Military Attaché to whom he explained the purpose of his visit. Pujol volunteered to produce, not only the secret inks used by the Germans for espionage communications, but also the questionnaires which they distributed to their agents. He explained the personal danger to which he had exposed himself in making contact and that, after handing over the material which he had promised, he would never be able to return to Spain. It would likewise be dangerous for him to remain in Portugal. He therefore proposed that in exchange for the information which he was prepared to supply he should be assisted to get to the USA.

The British official said that he would have to take advice in this matter and suggested that Pujol should return some other time. Pujol pointed out that it was extremely dangerous for him to keep visiting the Embassy. It was eventually arranged that the Embassy official should meet Pujol at the English Bar at Estoril at 7 p.m. the following evening with another Englishman who would accompany him to discuss the matter with Pujol. He kept the appointment but no one appeared. Pujol was 'extremely annoyed' but returned the following day to the Embassy to make a final appeal. He was interviewed by the same official who explained his failure to appear at the appointment by saying that he had been unable to get hold of the other man whom he had hoped to bring along. Eventually, after a lengthy discussion, Pujol left the Embassy 'in disgust, convinced that there was no one there at all interested in Intelligence matters' and decided that if he were ever to make a successful approach to the British he would have to go back to Madrid.

Pujol then decided that he would have to cover up the story which he had told Federico about Dalamal and the illegal currency transactions which he was supposed to be investigating in London. There was a risk that the Germans might check up on this. Pujol therefore called on Varela who immediately asked for an explanation of the 'curious telegram' which Pujol had sent him some weeks previously to announce his arrival. Pujol told him the story of the imaginary Dalamal and his illegal trafficking in pesetas and claimed that he had come to Lisbon specially to discuss this with him. Varela replied that there was nothing to be done about this unless Dalamal one day set foot in Spain. The interview 'had at least served its purpose' since if ever Federico should confront Varela he would get confirmation that Varela knew about Dalamal and had discussed him with Pujol. 'Any variation in the stories would be accounted for as subterfuge' on the part of Varela.

Towards the middle of August 1941, Pujol realised 'that if he were to get out of the very compromising situation in which he now found himself, and was to make contact with the British it might take a considerable time, and in order to safeguard himself and the successes which he had already achieved he would have to continue to send secret letters'. But he was 'confronted with the difficulty that he did not speak a word of English, he had never been to England and whatever information he passed to the Germans would, therefore, have to be imaginary with the result that he would soon be discovered. He therefore decided to comply with the instructions which he had received in Madrid to collect a network of agents'. Having 'recruited' his network the information 'which he would pass over he could always attribute to one or other of his imaginary agents. If an item were one day found to be false he could blame the agent responsible and liquidate him, and thus he hoped to safeguard his channel of communication for a longer period than might otherwise be possible.'

This brings us to the meeting between Mrs Pujol and Federico which had a purpose that was twofold. In the first place Pujol had decided to go to Madrid to contact the British Embassy there 'with the forlorn hope that they might receive him more sympathetically than he had been received by the British in Lisbon', and secondly he planned to allow his wife to make contact with Federico in Madrid in order that she should be able to discover from him whether or not Juan 'had so far successfully deceived the enemy about his mission as a secret agent in England'. At first Pujol and his wife went to Madrid: 'This time he was armed with the name of a Secretary to the British Embassy in Madrid which had been given to him by a friend.' He called at the Embassy and asked to see Mr Thompson but was told that Thompson 'was about to leave on a journey and that he should come back some days later. This he was unable to do because he realised that it would be far too dangerous to hang about in Madrid' when, of course, he was supposed to be in Britain. Mrs Pujol was then sent to the unfortunate Federico. By now Pujol had constructed his imaginary espionage material with the aid of the following which he bought in Lisbon: A map of Great Britain; a Blue Guide to England; a Portuguese publication entitled 'The British Fleet' and an English/French Vocabulary of Military terms.

He used a number of reference books and magazines in the Lisbon library in which he found advertisements which supplied the names and addresses of shipbuilding firms and factories. Pujol would introduce some of these into his secret communications to the Germans 'and produce remarkably good effects'. He used the Blue Guide for allocating the position of camps, training centres etc., which he would usually situate within woods with plenty of camouflage. The reports would often be accompanied by drawn plans. The book on the British Fleet was used to describe warships although Pujol was reluctant to name destroyers in case they should have been known by the Germans to have been sunk. British newsreels and extracts from the press were used to construct reports although, sometimes, Pujol would just make the whole thing up. As Tommy Harris, his future MI5 case officer, wrote: 'It is not so strange, however, that the Germans should have believed these purely imaginary reports since it was not until we had had an opportunity to thoroughly investigate GARBO [Pujol] in this country that we were able to induce the British Services Departments to believe that GARBO had never before been in the UK and that he had created his reports only through his fertile imagination and astuteness. On the other hand on careful examination of his letters composed alone one saw clear indications that he was not conversant with the habits of this country. A passage from one of his letters which is worthy of quotation is the following: "There are men here (in Glasgow) who would do anything for a litre of wine." It was not, in fact, until he came here [Britain] that he realised that it was not the custom of English labourers to drink their bottle of wine as they do in Spain.'

His expense account, rendered in November 1941 to the Germans, was another example of how he deceived the Germans:

Railway journey expenses: £.s.d
1. Southampton – London: 0.17.04.
2. London – Cardiff: 0.66.06.
3. Cardiff – London: 0.66.06.
4. London – Liverpool: 0.43.04.
5. Liverpool – Glasgow: 0.42.11.
6. Glasgow – London: 0.87.10.
7. London – Liverpool: 0.43.04.
8. Liverpool – London: 0.43.04.

He obtained the fares from a railway guide but he did not risk totalling these strange sums as he was not certain how to convert pence into shillings or shillings into pounds, 'therefore, he said in his letter that he would send a statement of the balance of his account in his next letter. From then on he rendered his accounts in dollars, the currency in which he was paid and which he understood.'

The second letter received from the Germans asked Pujol for publications by the Institute of Statistics of Oxford. He called at the British Propaganda Department in Lisbon, and, claiming that he was a 'student of statistics', asked if they would write over to England on his behalf and obtain pamphlets for him. The British Propaganda Department 'was most obliging, and within a short time handed them to him gratis!' Now he had the problem of sending them to Spain. Pujol believed the Germans would suspect him if he pretended that he had sent them to Lisbon by the imaginary airways official. He therefore wrote to them claiming that he had handed them to a Swiss friend of Gerbers, 'my agent at Bootle', who was returning to Switzerland by sea via Portugal. Pujol then wrote to the Germans instructing them to send a representative, whose connection with the German Secret Service should not be known, to collect the books from the Swiss against a letter of authorisation for delivery which he enclosed. Pujol next went to a detective agency in Lisbon and hired a man to put up at a hotel in Lisbon in the assumed name of Mr Mayer, to impersonate the imaginary Swiss traveller. This name, and the address of the hotel, he had already given to the Germans as the name and address in Lisbon 'of the good man who was facilitating the delivery of the books'. After some delay the books were finally collected by the Germans, though contact between the German messenger and the Portuguese detective, alias Mayer, was never made. The Germans were, however, in a position to be able to check that the man did appear to exist and had resided at the address given by Pujol.

Pujol was soon able to tell the Germans that he had 'recruited' a third sub-agent, this time a Venezuelan, 'a character of some financial standing' whom he claimed had been educated at the University of Glasgow, and who was to operate in Scotland. Pujol's motive behind this recruitment became apparent when, soon afterwards, the new agent produced a brother who was about to return to Venezuela, where Pujol 'envisaged he would be able to assist the Germans by setting up a refuelling base for German submarines operating in the Caribbean near his property at Camana'. Unfortunately the Germans 'did not fall for this.'

Towards the end of October 1941, Mrs Pujol wrote to her husband to ask if he would go to fetch her as she wanted to rejoin him in Portugal. En route he stopped in Madrid where he succeeded in making contact with Mr Thompson at the British Embassy. Pujol took with him the miniature photographic questionnaires which he had been given by the Germans but he was still unable to convince Thompson that he was genuine. Partly, this was because Pujol was using an alias at the interview and refused to disclose his real identity until given assurance that the British were interested in his information and would undertake to protect him for having double-crossed the Germans: Pujol, it seems, 'was always suspicious that the Germans had an agent in our Embassy. It is indeed a pity that note of the questionnaires was not taken at that time. Had they been examined and exploited it is possible that valuable intelligence might have been gained, in particular with regard to the forthcoming Japanese war. The questions were certainly significant.'

By now Pujol felt that, if he persisted further, it would only result in the Embassy staff starting a check up on him which, 'if inadequately handled, would have resulted in blowing him. He gained the impression that the person with whom he was dealing was not accustomed to handling matters of this delicate nature and reluctantly decided to abandon hope and collect his wife to return with her to Lisbon.' It was after this that his wife, realising Pujol's 'bitter disappointment decided, without his knowledge, to enter into negotiations with the Americans'. She called at the American Embassy in Lisbon where she made contact with Rousseau, the Assistant Naval Attaché. 'She said that she knew a man whom she had reason to believe was a German spy who had a room at the Pension where she was staying. She said she had seen him in possession of what appeared to be unusual documents relating to military affairs, and she pretended she was trying to get further information about his activities which she would eventually pass to the Americans.' The meetings with Rousseau broke down, eventually, due to his having to go to Madrid on a visit.

Further complication arose when Pujol's friend, Dionicio Fernandez, had to leave Lisbon for Spain for family reasons, and thus he deprived Pujol of his only cover address. To provide a new one Pujol went to a bank in Lisbon and rented a safe deposit box in the name of Mr Joseph Smith Jones 'and forthwith wrote to the Germans giving them the brief instructions that they should, in future, send all letters and monies to Mr Joseph SMITH JONES – J.P. and he furnished them with the box number and the name and address of the Bank. He added that 'this gentleman would receive the letters addressed for him and that the initials 'J.P.' which followed the name of SMITH JONES should not be omitted' since they indicated that the letters were for Pujol. This cover address operated from September 1941, until the end of the war with Germany. Tommy Harris thought it 'undoubtedly the weakest link in the whole of the GARBO case through which it could have been blown at any moment had the Germans taken the trouble to investigate. Fortunately they never did so. That they did not do so is not so strange as it as first appears, for they had to realise, that from their point of view, an investigation of this nature might easily have led to the blowing of their agent GARBO'. The Germans, however, 'appeared to have had implicit confidence in the security of this address and the notional courier who was responsible for smuggling the letters by air from England to Lisbon, and we were unable, even to the end, to persuade them to allow us to discontinue this channel for correspondence'.

By November 1941, Pujol's 'patience and endurance reached its limits and in despair he made application to the Brazilian authorities in Lisbon to immigrate with his wife and child to Brazil'. His wife, 'realising that to have been forced to abandon his project would have had a very harmful and lasting effect' on Pujol who was 'a man of great pride and character, tried to force the issue with the Americans'.

She again made contact with Rousseau, who had now returned from Madrid, and promised to bring him evidence to expose the spy about whom she had previously told him. 'The methods she employed give some idea of her ingenuity.' As the Americans had not yet entered into the war 'she decided her spy should be engaged in activities against the USA if she were to make them take notice of her. She opened her negotiations by offering to sell the information for $200,000. The high price was hoped to induce greater interest. She eventually produced the information without any financial consideration. In the first place she produced a secret ink letter written in French, a language which she did not know'. She brought with her a bottle of developer which she claimed she had seen used by the spy and proceeded to develop the secret text which read on the following lines:

Agent 172 of Chicago reports that both he and his Detroit agents are awaiting your orders as they now have everything ready to commence sabotage in all the agreed factories at a moments notice.

The letter had in fact been written by Mrs Pujol in the ink which had shortly before been supplied by the Germans for inter-communication between Pujol's imaginary agents. She had chosen to write in French since she realised that Rousseau 'knew she was unable to speak this language and thus it would tend to convince him of the genuineness of the letter. In order to get the French text she called on a French friend of hers and asked if she would be good enough to draft a telegram for her, pretending that she was sending a telegram on behalf of her husband who was a writer and who was temporarily away from Lisbon.' The telegram read:

LECLERC FILS of Paris reports that both he and his Madrid agents are awaiting your orders as they now have everything ready to commence publication in all the agreed journals at a moments notice.

By changing the words LECLERC, PARIS, MADRID, PUBLICATION and JOURNALS she was able to produce the above spy report threatening sabotage. Promising to endeavour to obtain further evidence of the spy's guilt, a meeting between Mrs Pujol, Rousseau and a third party was arranged. Rousseau's 'companion at this meeting was a rather cynical Englishman' who was introduced to Mrs Pujol as a member of the British Intelligence Service. Mrs Pujol brought with her one of the miniature photographic questionnaires, a bottle of secret ink and a secret ink letter from Federico as well as the developer. The Englishman 'unfortunately adopted the attitude' from the beginning of the interview that he regarded Mrs Pujol 'as an adventuress and that being a man of considerable experience he did not propose to allow himself to be taken in. He spoke perfect Spanish and proceeded to be offensive' to Mrs Pujol 'to the extent that she left the interview without showing the material she had brought with her. To crown the Englishman's offensive attitude, on her getting up to leave, he brought from his pocket 20 escudos which he put on the table, saying: "Here you are. Take this for your trouble and your fare".'

All this had occurred without Juan's knowledge. Tommy Harris reflected how: 'there is no doubt that had he learnt about this incident at the time the case would have been irrevocably lost'. Fortunately, the 'harm created was repaired' by Rousseau who apologised for the incident, and eventually Mrs. Pujol confided that the so-called spy was in fact her husband. It was not, however, until 15 January 1942, that Pujol had an opportunity of explaining his whole situation to Rousseau. Finally, in the middle of March, Pujol was introduced to a member of SIS in Lisbon to whom he repeated his story. Pujol's case only came to the notice of MI5 on 22 February 1942 when the Passport Control Officer Lisbon (SIS's cover there) who happened to be on a visit to London, asked, in the course of conversation, whether Apartado 1099, Madrid, was a genuine German cover address since he was interested in a case in Lisbon in which this address had occurred. It happened that this same address, provided by the Germans, was also in use by a double-agent run by MI5. The Security Service pressed that for Pujol to be brought to Britain at the earliest opportunity 'as it was clear that he could not hope to continue his present career indefinitely without discovery unless he was given every assistance. It seemed a miracle that he had survived so long.'

Pujol was finally smuggled out of Portugal on 10 April arriving in the UK on 24 April. He had left Lisbon on the understanding that he would be allowed to return to his wife within a month, but he immediately volunteered to carry out any order MI5 gave him 'on the condition that if we requested him to continue to double-cross the Germans under our guidance we should arrange for his wife and child to be brought over here as soon as possible'.[4] In accepting MI5's offer, he had to place himself in the hands of the British. It was daunting for him:

> I had to trust that the British would indeed get me to London
> from Gibraltar, but did not know how, when or in what capacity

I would travel there and couldn't help wondering what treatment the British would have in store for me on arrival... All I had to do was to board the ship... the captain had precise instructions what to do with me when we reached Gibraltar: he was to hand mc over to two officers, who would provide me with money and find me somewhere to stay.

My legs were shaking as I walked up the gangway past the Portuguese policeman at the top... I went down to the crew's mess; so far all the arrangements for my departure from Portugal had been faultless, which increased my confidence. Sometime after supper, when I was lying on my bunk, I heard the bang and rattle of the engines as the ship slipped her moorings. Early next morning one of the crew tapped me on the shoulder and made signs for me to follow him to the mess for breakfast. Afterwards he signalled for me to follow him up on deck for a breath of fresh air. It was a beautiful day; we seemed to be sailing twelve miles or so off the Portuguese coast, gently cruising along in convoy with three other merchantmen. The fresh air did me good, for I had found it rather claustrophobic shut down below and had not much cared for the smell which made me feel sick. At about ten o'clock an alarm went off, everybody raced to action stations and a sailor threw a life-jacket at my feet indicating that I should put it on. Were we in danger? Had they spotted an enemy submarine or a plane? Then I realized that this was not a genuine emergency, just a practice drill.

We coasted along the shore for twenty-four hours and then, very early the next morning, I heard the ship's engines stop. When I went on deck I found the Rock of Gibraltar towering overhead. At about 8 a.m., a small boat approached and two officers stepped on board. The captain sent a sailor to bring me to his cabin and there introduced me to the two officers who both spoke Spanish: one said he was a port official and the other that he had been instructed by London to look after me. I took leave of the captain and followed them into the small boat; we landed and walked unchallenged through the passport police check and customs and headed straight for a restaurant. Over a large English breakfast I was informed by one of the officers that there was a room at my disposal for my own exclusive use and that I could come and go as I pleased. He then handed me a wad of sterling notes and suggested that I buy some clothes as he knew I had brought no luggage whatsoever with me, not even a change of clothes. He ended by telling me that I might have to wait for two or three days before getting a plane for London as I would be travelling on an unscheduled flight... Two days later I left Gibraltar in an extremely uncomfortable military plane which had no seats, just long benches, which made me think that it was meant for transporting paratroopers. There were two other passengers, but we were never introduced nor did we speak to each other throughout the long eight-hour journey. They were carrying mail so were probably diplomats or special couriers.

In order to avoid German fighter planes, we headed far out into the Atlantic and so did not reach Plymouth until late afternoon, when we arrived tired and hungry as all we had had during the flight was tea. I don't think I've ever drunk so much tea in all my life as I did during that long cold journey, not even during the London Blitz when we used to spend hours on end in underground shelters. I must have had more than twenty cups in a desperate attempt to keep myself warm. I caught a glimpse of Plymouth from the plane and was suddenly acutely aware that I was away from home and about to enter an alien land. Would the English be friendly towards me? Would they believe my story about the tussles I had had with their embassies in Lisbon and Madrid, which showed how inefficiently these places were being run? Would they understand my motives for all that I had done and honestly believe that I wished to work for the good of mankind?

I thought about the city states of Ancient Greece, of Cleisthenes' Athens, of Pericles and the beginnings of democracy. I reiterated to myself my firm belief that individuals should have a say in their own government and knew that I had been right to put all my efforts into upholding such a doctrine. I entered England full of restless anticipation. What would my future hold?

My first recollection of England on that calm clear day in April 1942, as I walked down the steps of the plane, was of the terrible cold – cold outside and icy fear inside. At the bottom of the steps stood two officers from MI5, who would shape my destiny. The one who introduced himself as Mr Grey didn't speak a word of Spanish; I didn't say anything to him in my faltering English. The other, Tomas Harris, spoke Spanish like a native.[5]

Tomas Harris, of B1.G, now became Pujol's case officer. He was a gifted artist, born in 1908, who had transferred to MI5 from the Special Operations Executive which specialised in sabotage in German occupied territories. Harris had joined SOE on the recommendation of one Guy Burgess. Harris as an accomplished artist, had won the Trevelyan-Goodall Scholarship to the Slade School of Fine Art at London University – when he was just fifteen years old. He had been educated in Spain, where his mother had been born, with the result that Harris spoke Spanish. After attending the Slade, he had spent a year at the British Academy in Rome studying painting and sculpture. Harris's father, Lionel, was an English Jew and a renowned Mayfair art dealer. His Spanish Art Galleries concentrated on the sale of the work of Velázquez, Goya and El Greco, and in 1930 Tomas joined his father's business. Tomas, or Tommy, Harris was also a sculptor and sometimes worked in ceramics, stained glass, tapestry and engraving. As well as Tomas, Lionel Harris had three daughters, Conchita, Enriquetta and Violetta – who followed their brother into the Security Service as a Spanish-speaking officer serving in B1.A. Late in 1941, after Brooman-White transferred to SIS to run Section V's Iberian section, Harris was appointed to succeed him as head of B1.G.[6] Together, Pujol and Harris forged a close and profitable working relationship. The former recalled:

> From the moment I set foot in England in 1942 until I left after the war, I gained great pleasure from the beauty, of the countryside, from the lush greenness of London's gardens and from the great variety of trees which lined the streets and filled the parks. I arrived in April, when the country was just about to appear at its best, the days were getting longer and the sun, the little sun that there is at that time of year, came peeping though the cloudy skies, welcoming me with its warmth and friendliness to a land which was to be a most hospitable host: a land which received me with open arms and often made me feel extremely happy, especially when it allowed me to associate myself with its joys and sorrows.
>
> Although it was April, I found England cold. The day after my arrival I asked Tommy Harris if he would come with me to help me buy some warm clothes, but that had to wait. First I had to undergo a long and detailed interrogation. Mr Grey led the cross-examination, with Harris interpreting. My English was not just poor, it was almost non-existent, so they suggested, that I should, as a matter of priority, have some lessons so that I could learn the basics of the language of Shakespeare. However, I thought it much more important to make immediate contact with the Germans, sending them some really useful information, for I had been silent for some weeks, Three days later, after consulting

various sections of MI5, I sent the Abwehr a juicy letter which, for the first time, included some true information about England… Tommy Harris and I concentrated hard on drawing up a short-term and a long-term programme of action.

Tommy Harris had endeared himself to me right from the start, not just from the firm way he had shaken my hand, but because he had also put his arm round my shoulders in a gesture of protection and friendship. We soon began to confide in each other and I always trusted him completely: my trust was never misplaced.

Together we invented the role of GARBO, a creation that afforded us both great pleasure… Tommy… always dressed impeccably in an elegant sports jacket which he wore with a most distinctive air. He smoked like a chimney and the fingers of his right hand were almost chestnut coloured as he never put out a cigarette until it was about to burn him.[8]

By this time MI5 had already begun to suspect that Pujol, now codenamed GARBO, was identical with the unidentified V-Mann 372 who had appeared on ISOS as the author of the 'famous' Malta convoy report. The advisability of using GARBO as a double-agent was put up to the XX Committee who, at that time, with the exception of the Admiralty and SIS representatives, did not have access to ISOS material. The majority of the members of the XX Committee, through not having access to this material, and the GARBO story to date 'being so incredible, were not at all satisfied as to his authenticity or of the advisability of using him'. It was over this issue that it was finally decided that the members of the XX Committee should be given access to ISOS material.

As GARBO was debriefed, MI5 built up, from this and other sources, a picture of his German Control. The GARBO case was handled on behalf of the Germans by Karl Erich Kuehlanthal, former Military Attache in Paris. He was of partly Jewish origin and was, for a while, regarded with suspicion by the SD and the Abwehr. His 'partly non-Aryan' origin was said to have prevented him from entering the army but as he was well connected in Spain and a protégé of Admiral Canaris, 'his role as Abwehr representative in Madrid was assured'. Kuehlanthal was legally 'created an Aryan' at the instigation of his Stelle in Madrid in 1941. He was described as a 'very efficient, ambitious and dangerous man with an enormous capacity for work. His efficiency and capacity for work have been proved'. Some of the other agents recruited by Kuehlanthal included THE SNARK, CARELESS and PEPPERMINT.

By the summer of 1942, MI5 had, through GARBO, 'begun to swamp
the Germans with information, mis-information and problems'.
Whether MI5's 'ever increasing activities were beginning to satisfy'
Kuehlanthal's 'enormous appetite for work or not is hard to say' but
it appeared that from that time Kuehlanthal 'made no further attempt
to send more agents to the United Kingdom'. And MI5 endeavoured
to report 'as much confusing bulk as possible and, in the absence of
another objective, to increase our network of notional agents'. The
Security Service, in Tommy Harris's words, asked for Kuehlanthal's
collaboration, through GARBO, 'and we were given it. As a keen and
efficient officer he did everything in his power to supply GARBO with
cyphers, secret inks and addresses of the highest grade to ensure his
greater security. He was always forthcoming with considerable funds
to cover GARBO's expenses in England.'

And MI5 'strived to gain' Kuehlanthal's 'ever increasing confidence
in GARBO. We played up to what we believed to be the German
understanding of Spanish psychology as they appear to have conceived
it through their association with Falangist Spain. We endeavoured to
maintain the initiative throughout the running of the case, keeping one
step ahead of the opposition in order to be able to direct the course
of the case on the lines best suited to our plans'. Kuehlanthal was
encouraged to regard GARBO as 'a quixotic, temperamental genius,
whom he learned to be cautious not to offend. He came to regard
GARBO as a fanatic, prepared to risk his life for the Fascist cause.
His characteristic German lack of sense of humour, in such serious
circumstances as these, blinded him to the absurdities of the story we
were unfolding. Instead he was patient and confident in the ultimate
success of his protege.'

And, facing Kuehlanthal, was his opposite number, in MI5, Tommy
Harris who 'had one great advantage' the German did not: through
ISOS 'it was possible to confirm German reactions to our work'.
The fact that the 'team' of Kuehlanthal, GARBO and Harris was
maintained over the entire period of the case permitted 'a consistency
in style and planning. It allowed us gradually to build up the character'
of GARBO in Kuehlanthal's eyes. From MI5's point of view 'it gave
us an opportunity to discover the strength and weaknesses of our
opponent'. Just as Kuehlanthal 'found the pressure of the GARBO
work increasing and becoming a full time job, we too, in forcing the
pace, began to find our hands full'. From the summer of 1943, the
GARBO case became more than a full time job for three members of
MI5 to manage the routine running and planning of the case. Gradually
the Germans 'were persuaded to accept GARBO's verbose style until

they, themselves, became infected by it'. Their communications became longer, more explicit and more frequent. 'From their first telegraphic message in secret writing consisting of a few lines, they were worked up to the climax of sending us no less than twenty-four foolscap pages of secret text in one letter. It is true to say that whenever they have been encouraged by us to exert themselves in this way the contents of their longer letters, which occasionally arrived, were always of very considerable counter-espionage value.'

And, had it 'not been for the fact that we were able to judge the German reactions to GARBO through Most Secret Sources there is little doubt that the case would not have been exploited so extravagantly. In fact it is somewhat doubtful whether we would have believed the already incredible story with which GARBO presented us on his first making contact had it not been that MSS [Most Secret Sources/ISOS] provided us with conclusive evidence that the essential of his story was true, and furthermore that the Germans believed him to be operating in England on their behalf.' Not only, therefore, did ISOS 'provide us with conclusive evidence as to the degree of success with which GARBO was meeting in Madrid but it also allowed us to control the accuracy with which his reports were being forwarded to Berlin and the degree of importance which Headquarters in Berlin attached to them. Thus it became apparent that the Madrid control had implicit trust in GARBO's reports and that Berlin was beginning to recognise the important work which was being accomplished by the Stelle in Madrid.' In fact this Stelle 'had become our mouthpiece' and the problem was no longer one of building up GARBO in the eyes of Stelle but of building up the Stelle in the eyes of the Abwehr, Berlin. 'If we were to enhance the Abwehr in the eyes of the OKW it was essential to maintain a high standard of reports. If the OKW could be made to trust and rely on Abwehr reports, then it was inevitable that the GARBO network would provide an invaluable channel through which he would be able to deceive the enemy.' And, so it proved, for it was through ISOS that MI5 learnt that Himmler, shortly after becoming chief of the German Intelligence Services, sent a personal message of appreciation to the Stelle in Madrid for the work achieved by his network in Britain.[10] Although they could not know it at the time, MI5's recruitment of GARBO was to prove one of the intelligence masterstrokes of the Second World War. As Masterman wrote: 'If in the double-cross world SNOW was the W.G. Grace of the early period, then GARBO was certainly the Bradman of the later years.'[11]

CARELESS

The same could not be said of the XX agent CARELESS. He was a Pole that 'reliable information' pointed to having been born in Kronstadt in 1914, although he was reported to have said on one occasion that his documents were all wrong and that he was really born in 1910. He was an only child and both his parents were alive and in Scotland. His father before the last war was trained in a naval college at St. Petersburg, and during it served as a Russian U-boat commander in the Baltic. After the war the family went to Warsaw; from 1923 to 1926 they were in Grodno, and from 1926 to 1936 they lived in Warsaw again, the father being the head of Polish Army institution equivalent to the Royal Military Arsenal, Woolwich. CARELESS attended High School in Warsaw and went to the College for Political Sciences in 1933. In 1935–1936 he did his military service at Demblin. He was trained as an airman and reached the standard of liaison pilot. He then got a job as secretary to a man named Struminski, an arms dealer who was supplying the Red Government in Spain. In this capacity he spent five or six weeks in Valencia at the end of 1936. He subsequently got a job with another engineering firm, for whom he travelled fairly widely in Poland in 1938. In 1938 he married Barbara whom he later divorced. MI5 considered him 'dissolute, mendacious and temperamental'.

In August 1939 CARELESS was mobilised into the training squadron of the 1st Air Force Regiment at Warsaw as a 'reserve aspirant' and he subsequently served as a liaison pilot. On 15 September he was shot down by the Germans in the neighbourhood of Zloczow. He managed to get away to Tarnopol and on the collapse of the Polish Army he crossed the frontier to Cernauti. He was treated in the Jewish Hospital there and, though the Romanians had taken all his papers, he managed to get on to Bucharest where the Polish Consulate took him in hand, and he was subsequently enabled to travel to France via Yugoslavia and Italy. In France he was sent to hospital at Val de Grace and remained there for several weeks. He claimed that on his discharge from hospital he was posted to the Polish camp at Coetquidan but was given no special duties. What was clear was 'that he gave himself up to a life of drink and dissipation and spent most of his time in Paris'. He there fell in love with a Comtesse Deym Kronacker. CARELESS had a wound on his hip 'which he generally attributes to the occasion when he was shot down in Poland, but under interrogation at Camp 020 in August 1941 he admitted that it was the result of his attempt to commit suicide when the Comtesse rejected his advances'. Thereafter he was in hospital again, and on discharge was transferred to an infantry regiment, though he saw no active service with it.

With the French collapse, CARELESS retreated to Bayonne, Lourdes and Marseilles, where he arrived about 25 August 1940. Here he got into touch with his father, who he found had been put in charge of a Red Cross Camp for Polish relief near Nimes. He also found his mother, who was living at a Convent called Bois Fleuri at Pont Vivant. Having been put in funds by his father, CARELESS 'restarted his life of dissipation' and acquired as his mistress a woman who went under the name of Nadine Orsat. He 'gadded' about Unoccupied France with her for some time, but quarrelled with her in November. She then accused him of fraudulently converting some securities of hers and the result was that he was imprisoned for three months. At the beginning of March 1941 he was released provisionally and, on the advice of his father, he decided to go to Perpignan. In order to avoid identification, in case he should be picked up again by the Police, he destroyed his passport and got a seven day permit from a sergeant. He removed the name of the man to whom it had been made out and substituted the name 'Clarc Korab', which he claimed was an alias of his own invention. Arriving in Perpignan in the second week of March he registered at the Grand Hotel under the name of Korab and 're-embarked on his life of dissipation'. In about a fortnight's time he had run out of money and returned to Marseilles where he collected some more from his father. He finally left Marseilles on 28 March 1941 in the company with four Frenchmen, with whom he travelled to Toulouse, Tour de Caroll, Carcassonne and Bourg Madame. From there they crossed the frontier into Spain.

They went on foot to Barcelona. On the way the four Frenchmen were arrested but CARELESS, who had lagged behind them through foot soreness, was able to hide in a wood. He reached Barcelona safely about the middle of April and went to an address which had been given him by a Spanish woman whom he had met on the train between Toulouse and Tour de Caroll. Next day CARELESS called at the Polish Consulate and saw Madame Morbitzer. He told her his story and apparently persuaded her to help him although he had no papers to prove it. She fixed him up with new identity papers and money. CARELESS claimed that he spent most of his time and money in Barcelona trying to arrange a secret route by which Poles could travel from there to Madrid. Whether this was 'true or not, it is clear that he allowed himself to be recruited as a German agent'. He was accosted one day in a cafe by a man called Munk who claimed to be a Yugoslav and to have fought for Franco in the Civil War. They became friendly and Munk suggested that CARELESS could make some money by working for the Germans. CARELESS agreed, and immediately asked for something on account. Munk said he could not advance money himself, but introduced CARELESS to Herr Muller of the German Consulate. Muller told CARELESS to report to Colonel von Bruck at the German Embassy in Madrid.

During his previous visit to Spain, in 1936, CARELESS had made some friends among Republican Spaniards. These people now helped him to get to Madrid by a 'somewhat devious route'. He arrived towards the end of May and reported to Lieutenant Zagorski at the Polish Consulate. He claimed that he gave Zagorski the details of the route from Barcelona supplied by his Republican friends. Within a few hours of his arrival CARELESS went to the German Embassy and saw Colonel von Bruck. Bruck seemed to know all about him. He gave him 200 pesetas, had him photographed from three different angles, and handed him over to the care of – GARBO's – 'Federico' his assistant. Under Federico's direction he was trained as a German agent in order to be sent to Britain.

Federico began by giving CARELESS 1,000 pesetas for his immediate needs and 75 dollars (which were not to be spent in Spain) for future emergencies. He also dictated a long questionnaire which CARELESS was to learn by heart and which related to all aspects of the supply of aeroplanes from America to Britain. CARELESS told Federico that as soon as he got to Britain he would try to get a job as an Atlantic ferry pilot. He was to write his reports in secret ink. Payment for his services would be made to CARELESS via America and Federico asked CARELESS to suggest the name of someone from whom he could pretend to be receiving money. CARELESS named the Comtesse Deym Kronacker whom he said he might pass off as his aunt. CARELESS was instructed in secret writing. He was to write on one side of the paper only. He could sign his letters either as 'Eduardo' or in his cover name of Clarc Korab, which he had already disclosed to Federico, or in any other name which he chose. Incoming letters were to be developed by soaking in a solution of soda crystals. CARELESS remained in Madrid for about five weeks and saw Federico four or five times, besides ringing him up fairly often. He led his usual life of dissipation and soon got rid of the 1,000 pesetas supplied by Federico. One night he tried to change $20 (being part of the $75 which Federico had given him) at a night club called the Conga to which Federico had introduced him. This transaction immediately came to the ears of Federico, who gave CARELESS an extra 200 pesetas with which to redeem the $20 bill, since it was illegal to change American money in Madrid. Nevertheless CARELESS did get some friends of his to cash $40 for him and therefore had only $35 left when he left Madrid.

All this time it would seem that CARELESS was being officially supported and provided with lodging by the Polish Consulate. He never told them anything about his relations with Federico. Nevertheless, they suspected him, since his 'riotous manner of living' and his unexplained possession of dollars which he tried to change in various quarters attracted attention. They decided to send him on to Lisbon and keep him under observation when he got there. In due course CARELESS heard that he was to leave Madrid on 5 June 1941. He immediately rang up Federico and made an appointment to meet him. 'Probably his object was to get a further payment before he left.' However, Federico told him that if he had information to communicate from Lisbon, or if he wanted money while he was there, he should get in touch with one, Merckel, at the German Embassy. Federico also took away and tore up the questionnaire about aeroplanes which CARELESS was by now supposed to have memorised, but CARELESS had already noted down most of the material points on the back of an identity certificate issued to him by the Polish Consulate.

CARELESS was taken with four other Poles by taxi from Madrid to Badajoz. Thence they walked across the frontier under the guidance of a Spanish smuggler, and once they were well inside Portugal they were picked up by another taxi which took them on to Lisbon. They arrived on 7 June and stayed for two or three nights at a pension run by the Polish Consulate for Polish subjects escaping through Spain and Portugal to Britain. Two days after his arrival CARELESS called at the Polish Consulate and there bumped into a Jewish friend of his named Jan Muhlstein alias John Mills, whom he had met previously in France and who had crossed into Spain shortly before he did. Muhlstein introduced him to two other Polish Jews named Edward Balsam and Abraham Jacob Sukiennik. CARELESS soon became on intimate terms with these three men and within a few days he was sharing a lodging with Balsam and Sukiennik in the Rua Santa Marta. MI5 observed later: 'We now know that CARELESS' meeting with these men was not accidental.' His arrival in Lisbon had been preceded by a report from Madrid that he was suspected of having entered into relations with the Germans, with the result that Jaworski, the head of the evacuation department of the Polish Legation, instructed Muhlstein to see that CARELESS was watched and Muhlstein selected Balsam and Sukiennik for this purpose.

After a few days, CARELESS ran out of money and, according to his own story, he rang up the German Legation and got an appointment to see Merckel, to whom he introduced himself as Eduardo. Merckel had obviously heard about him and readily gave him 3,500 escudos.

CARELESS had 'a good time with his new friends' on this money and rang up Merckel on various occasions to ask for more. After a while he wrote to Federico at one of the cover addresses he had been provided with, asking that Merckel should be instructed to pay him some more and saying that he expected to leave for Britain shortly. Receiving no reply, CARELESS sent a telegram to Federico asking if the 'letters' had been received, and finally received a telegram himself saying that an answer awaited him at the Legation. It was not clear, however, whether CARELESS succeeded in getting any more money out of Merckel simply on the strength on this correspondence.

'What is clear is that at one time or another, drunk or sober', CARELESS disclosed a great part of what he was doing and had been doing to Sukiennik (who probably passed on the news to Balsam), and that, on 28 June, CARELESS took Sukiennik with him to the German Embassy and introduced him to Merckel as 'Lieutenant Kieljeszek', supposed to be an official of the Polish Legation who was badly in need of money. On this occasion Merckel gave Sukiennik 2,500 escudos. According to CARELESS this payment was merely to relieve Sukiennik's financial position while, at the same time, giving Merckel a hold over one who, he thought, would be in a position thereafter to supply useful information. A few hours later CARELESS, Sukiennik, Balsam and Muhlstein all left Lisbon together on the SS *Avoceta*.

On 21 June, a week before he left Lisbon, CARELESS gave a signed statement to in which he set out his life history in brief and the adventures of his journey from Marseilles to Lisbon in considerable detail. In this statement there was no mention whatever of his contact with the Germans in Barcelona, Madrid or Lisbon. On the contrary, the statement ended by explaining that CARELESS had received extra financial help 'through the good offices of relatives of my wife', Messrs. Deym Kronacker, 'who are at present in Atlanta, USA'. CARELESS had arranged with Federico to use this name as an imaginary channel for receiving money.

On arrival at Gibraltar CARELESS gave Balsam two letters to post. One was to his family and one was to one of the cover addresses supplied by Federico. In this letter CARELESS asked for money to be sent to him c/o the Polish Consulate in London. At Gibraltar, CARELESS and his companions were transferred to the SS *Scythia*, which sailed about 6 July 1941 and arrived in the Clyde on the 13th. On 10 July, in the course of the voyage, CARELESS made a confession to a British officer. Although short, the statement covered all the essential points, mentioning CARELESS's contacts with Munk in Barcelona, Bruck and Federico in Madrid and Merckel in Lisbon.

It contained a summary of the questionnaire, a description of the secret ink processes, the arrangement for the receipt of money from the USA through the use of the name of Comtesse Deym Kronacker, the cover name of Korab and the two cover addresses in Madrid. 'Not content with this confession' CARELESS also confided his contact with the Germans to Mrs Graves, a British lady of French extraction with whom he became friendly in the course of the voyage.

'Unfortunately for CARELESS his arrival in England, like his arrival in Portugal, was anticipated by the Polish Intelligence Service.' Before he landed MI5 had already received from them a denunciation based upon the reports of Muhlstein, Balsam and Sukiennik.

The case made against CARELESS by these informants was, in substance, that he had allowed himself to be recruited as an espionage agent by the Germans, that he had received money, secret ink and cover addresses from them, that his confession on board the *Scythia* had been made only as an insurance against possible detection so that he could work for both sides and earn double wages, and that he had omitted from this confession the most material fact of all – namely, that he had already sold valuable information to the Germans in the shape of a detailed account of the escape route used by the Poles for evacuating their nationals from France through Spain into Portugal.

'Obviously the whole substance of the case depended upon his allegation about the escape route,' noted MI5. The remainder of the charges against CARELESS, 'in so far as they were not vague or trivial', amounted to little more than CARELESS had himself admitted. 'What was interesting about them was their wealth of reasonably accurate detail,' which showed how completely (whether he realised or not) CARELESS had let Balsam and Sukiennik into his confidence. They were fully informed, for instance, about his method of secret writing, his contact with Federico and the cover addresses he was to use. It was evident that Balsam and Sukiennik had 'not merely heard CARELESS's story from his own lips but had taken every opportunity when he was drunk or asleep of going through his pockets and reading his notes'.

The gravity of the charge against CARELESS was such that, after a short time at the Patriotic and at Brixton Prison Hospital where he had to be treated for VD, he was removed to Camp 020, where the allegations made by Balsam and Sukiennik were carefully examined. The original accusation as set out in written statements given to the Poles by Balsam and Sukiennik on 16 and 17 July 1941 was that, on 26 or 27 June, CARELESS decided that he and Sukiennik should prepare a report on the Polish escape route and sell it to the Germans. CARELESS therefore dictated a detailed story to Sukiennik, who took it down on his typewriter in draft form and made a fair copy later. The fair copy was given by Sukiennik to Balsam on the morning of 27 July with instructions to pass it to Jaworski, and CARELESS himself gave Balsam the original draft on the evening of the same day. How CARELESS recovered these documents, or either of them, was unclear. However, CARELESS had the fair copy back in his possession by the following morning when Sukiennik claimed to have met CARELESS at the Cafe Bijou, received the document from him and gone with them by taxi to the German Legation. Merckel apparently interviewed them in the garden and CARELESS introduced Sukiennik as 'Lieutenant Kieljeszek' who was supposed to be Colonel Maly's right hand man at the Polish Legation but who was in need of funds. CARELESS then asked Sukiennik to produce the report on the escape route, informing Merckel that it had been stolen from the Polish Legation and would have to be replaced before twelve noon. Merckel took it away to be photographed and returned it to Sukiennik shortly afterwards, at the same time paying him 2,500 escudos and paying CARELESS 1,500.

On 14 August, Balsam and Sukiennik were interrogated at the Patriotic Schools. At these interrogations they both maintained that the original draft of the report was taken down by Sukiennik, not on a typewriter but in his own handwriting, and that he made a fair copy on the typewriter later. The document was said to have borne what purported to be Colonel Maly's signature. In his written statement Sukiennik had said that CARELESS must have forged this, but under interrogation he said that CARELESS asked Balsam, in his presence to forge it. Balsam, on the other hand, maintained that it was already signed when he first saw it. Sukiennik said that on their return from the visit to Merckel, CARELESS asked him to tear up the report which Merckel had photographed and throw it down the lavatory, which Sukiennik did. Balsam said that he had both the original draft and the typed copy in his possession for about twenty-five minutes. During this time he copied part of the typed fair copy, and later on he gave the original draft and his own partial copy to Jaworski. Jaworski found the original draft illegible and told Balsam to make a fair copy during the voyage to Gibraltar and to hand it to a Captain Krajewski, who would meet him there. Krajewski did not turn up, so Balsam delivered his fair copy to Polish Intelligence when he got to London, having thrown away Sukiennik's original during the voyage. There were 'various other obscurities and inconsistencies in these stories', but three points stood out:

> 1. It was not suggested that there had ever been any copy of this report in CARELESS's own handwriting, and, according to

BALSAM's final explanation, the only handwritten copy now in existence was written by himself; 2. Neither BALSAM nor SUKIENNIK made the smallest effort to prevent CARELESS from selling this document to the Germans, but rather abetted him; 3. BALSAM made no serious effort to bring the affair to the notice of JAWORSKI until the morning of the 28th when, as he knew, CARELESS and SUKIENNIK were already on their way to see MERCKEL.

The 'profoundly unsatisfactory character' of their denunciations led to the arrest and detention at Camp 020 of Muhlstein, Balsam and Sukiennik on 15, 16 and 17 September 1941 respectively. Muhlstein was released after a fortnight since it appeared that he had no evidence to give other than what he had heard from the other two. Balsam and Sukiennik were kept there. At an early stage the Poles had informed MI5 that Sukiennik belonged, in their opinion, to the 'doubtful type of people ready to sell their own mothers for money'. Muhlstein they had described as a 'crook on a large-scale. suspected of shady dealings'. They seemed to have had more confidence in Balsam, but since he was a close friend of Sukiennik's and was selected as a confidential agent by Muhlstein 'there was no reason to assume that he, also, was not a crook'. Anyhow, after a few days at Camp 020 Balsam and Sukiennik started accusing each other of being liars, and in a written statement of 23 October Balsam retracted his previous accusations to the extent of declaring that he never at any time saw the escape route document or any copy of it in CARELESS's possession, and added that it was only on the voyage from Lisbon that Sukiennik had told him of his visit to the German Legation with CARELESS. A few days later Balsam withdrew substantially the whole of his remaining allegations against CARELESS, saying that they had only been based on what he had heard from Muhlstein and Sukiennik.

On 13 November, MI5 at last received from the Poles a photograph of the handwritten statement said to have been given to them by Balsam. This 'undoubtedly purported to be a fairly detailed description of the escape route', but since it was not in CARELESS's handwriting 'it did not appear to carry the case against him any further. Apart from his dissolute habits and general lack of responsibility the only point which could properly be held against CARELESS was that, having been tentatively recruited by the Germans in Barcelona and definitely taken on by them in Madrid, and having received money from them both in Madrid and in Lisbon, he had never said a word about his contacts with the Germans to the Polish authorities at either of the last two places. This was indeed a strong point, and it has never been convincingly explained.' No doubt it was somewhat weakened by the written confession which he made on board the *Scythia*, but at the same time it seemed probable that CARELESS must by then have realised that, since he had taken Balsam and Sukiennik so far into his confidence already, the story was bound to leak out sooner or later and that he had better confess to somebody for his own protection. The conclusion MI5 reached was that CARELESS was 'first and foremost a rogue and a spendthrift, who had amused himself by getting money out of the Germans and who probably hoped to get some out of us as well, but that there was not sufficient evidence that he ever intended to act as a traitor'. He was released from Camp 020 on 3 December 1941.

Meanwhile MI5 had already been making CARELESS write to his cover addresses in Madrid in anticipation of the possibility that his character might be cleared. His first letter, written from the Patriotic Schools on 20 July, merely announced his safe arrival. It was signed 'Clarc Korab' and gave his address as 25 Redcliffe, Old Brompton Road, SW5 (the address, in fact, belonged to a member of the Schools staff). During his five months' detention at Camp 020 he wrote five secret letters giving a certain amount of useful information and explaining that, though he had little chance of being accepted for the RAF, he hoped to join the balloon barrage. In his sixth secret letter, written soon after his release, he said that he had done so and thereafter, throughout the whole of his career as a double-agent, he was notionally working in the balloon barrage. Meanwhile, he had received incoming secret letters Nos. 1, 3 and 4 (No.2 never arrived). These showed that the Germans were on the whole satisfied, and contained a substantial questionnaire largely about AA defences.

For the first month of his liberty, CARELESS was lodged in rooms in Chiswick under the supervision of Sergeant Annet of the FSP. He had been 'landed' on condition that he joined the Polish Forces. His first desire was to join a Polish squadron of the RAF 'but his health, his character and the nature of the work he was doing for us combined to put this out of the question'. His enlistment in the Polish Army would almost certainly have involved his being posted to Scotland, where he would have been difficult to get at. Moreover, in spite of his clearance from Camp 020, the Poles were not thought likely to take kindly to CARELESS; 'nor did he take very kindly to them'. For all these reasons it was considered preferable to enlist CARELESS as a special case in the Pioneer Corps of the British Army; but: 'It now appears probable that this decision was unwise, though it is hard to see what better one could have been taken at the time since it was soon obvious, after CARELESS' release from Camp 020, that a life of reasonably strict discipline was essential if he was not to be constantly in trouble.' Before CARELESS was enlisted, MI5 received a formal declaration from the Poles, dated 23 December, that CARELESS 'will no longer be considered guilty of the charge brought against him unless you have reason to change your opinion of him'. This declaration from the Poles was to have potentially serious consequences for CARELESS.

On 7 January 1942, CARELESS went to Ilfracombe and joined the Pioneer Corps. Even before he joined, CARELESS had objected to the Pioneers, on the ground that the company which he would have to join was composed largely of Germans and Austrians. 'In this he was of course correct, and throughout the whole of his military career, which lasted for ten months, this point was a source of real and increasing grievance to him, a grievance which was exacerbated by the fact that he considered his status in the Polish Air Force in 1939–1940 to have been that of an officer or officer-cadet, whereas in the Pioneers he was only a private.' After a few weeks training at Ilfracombe he was posted to No. 229 Company at Codford, near Warminster, and thereafter he was moved around from one camp to another from time to time, but was always somewhere in Wiltshire. It soon became clear that it was 'evidently a mistake to suppose that the discipline of the Pioneer Corps would have an improving effect upon CARELESS'.

On 2 February he telephoned to MI5's Mr Martin (really C.B. Mills) at the War Office that he was in London on forty-eight hour leave. He asked for an interview and told Martin that he had just heard that his father had died in Marseilles and that he was therefore going to see the Polish authorities and a solicitor. The story of his father's death was untrue and five days later CARELESS was still in London, absent without leave. He was arrested by the police and sent back to his unit. On 17 March he went to Salisbury and sent a telegram to himself purporting to come from Martin and summoning him to London for an interview. He showed this to his CO in the hope of getting leave. The forgery was detected and CARELESS received fourteen days detention. Sometime in March 1942, probably just before this incident, CARELESS spent a week with a woman at the George Hotel, Amesbury, absenting himself from barracks every night. He left his bill unpaid, though Martin forced him to make a part payment some months later. On 27 June he was again absent without leave in London. In July he went into hospital at Basingstoke as his old wound was giving him trouble. While there he bought a pair of slippers for 5/11d, for which sum he received a receipt. On 28 July he appeared unexpectedly in London and was seen by MI5's Mr. Horlock (in reality C.P. Harvey) as Martin's deputy. In the course of the interview CARELESS produced the receipt, which he had altered so as to read £5.5.11, and asked to be repaid this amount, which he said he had spent on dental treatment with the approval of Martin. He was given the money, which was subsequently deducted from his emoluments. Throughout the period under review, CARELESS 'was generally in drink or with women, or both, whenever he had the chance'. Nevertheless, MI5 admitted that it was only fair to add that he continued his correspondence with Federico under Martin's direction, 'not only with willingness but with enthusiasm', and on several occasions provided traffic or suggestions for traffic himself. 'There was and is no reason to suppose that he was not genuinely anxious to help us and mislead the Germans.'

All the time, however, he was protesting against the Pioneer Corps and the Germans he was forced to serve with. On 4 March he asked to be transferred to the Polish Army. On 28 March he asked for a transfer to a combatant unit, saying that he would not be answerable for his conduct if it were refused. In May he made efforts to get transferred to the Airborne Division, and shortly afterwards he renewed his application for transfer to the Polish Army. On 8 July he wrote to Martin to say that he had now made six applications for transfer and that he refused to work for MI5 any more unless it were granted. Martin agreed to help him and negotiations were reopened with the Poles – who were at the Rubens Hotel. One reason for MI5 assisting CARELESS to transfer to the Polish Forces at this stage was that his father and mother had recently got out of Unoccupied France and were now in Lisbon waiting for a passage to Britain. Although CARELESS had been in correspondence with them for some time he had not told them that he was in the British Army, and it was obviously going to be rather difficult to explain to them why he was serving with the Pioneers. It was therefore hoped, 'rather faintly', that CARELESS might be transferred to the Polish Forces before his parents arrived. Even if this could not be arranged he could perhaps allay suspicion by telling them that he did not like the regime at Polish headquarters when he first came to Britain and therefore had asked to be allowed to join the British Army, but that there had now been changes in personnel at Polish HQ and he was therefore arranging a transfer. In fact, his parents arrived on 4 August and were cleared on the 15th.

It was CARELESS's attempt to transfer to the Polish Forces that 'resulted in his undoing'. On 4 August he attended at the Rubens Hotel for an interview, but the interview 'did not go very well'. CARELESS began by saying that he was prepared to join the Polish Forces on certain conditions: such as, that he was given the rank which he had held in 1939–1940. His Polish interrogator soon made it clear to him that the Poles were not themselves asking for him and that he would be accepted, if at all, on their own conditions. He also asked CARELESS some searching questions about his past career which CARELESS did not answer very satisfactorily. However, it was arranged that CARELESS should attend for a further interview. He did so on 18 August, when it was arranged that he should come again at 3.30 p.m. on Friday, the 21st. On Saturday, the 22nd, MI5 received a telephone message from the Rubens Hotel to say that when CARELESS arrived on Friday 'he was in liquor' and he was therefore told to go away and return the following morning. On the Saturday he failed to turn up at all. 'Naturally the Poles were extremely annoyed.'

Nevertheless, Martin managed to arrange another interview for CARELESS, which he himself attended, on 2 September. CARELESS was then interrogated again by a Polish officer and gave a signed statement outlining briefly the history of his contact with the Germans in Barcelona, Madrid and Lisbon. CARELESS was also interrogated about the escape route to Portugal. He was then told to withdraw and, as soon as he had left, the Polish Officer told Martin flatly that CARELESS was regarded as a spy. He produced a handwritten description of the escape route, which turned out to be none other than the same document mentioned before, though Martin did not recognise it at that moment. The officer said that he now had abundant specimens of CARELESS's handwriting, that he himself was a handwriting expert, and that he had no doubt that the escape route document had been written by CARELESS. This suggestion had never previously been made by anyone. The officer added that if CARELESS were taken into the Polish Forces he would be arrested and imprisoned as soon as he had put on Polish uniform. Next day, Martin – or rather Mills – went to Camp 020 to look at the photograph of the document now resurrected by the Poles. Martin and Tin Eye Stephens had no difficulty whatever in satisfying themselves that this document was not in CARELESS's writing but in Balsam's. Martin returned at once to the Rubens with samples of Balsam's writing and told the Polish officer that he was clearly mistaken. The officer said that, whether this was so or not, he still regarded CARELESS as fit only for a Court Martial. He had formed a 'thoroughly bad opinion' of him at the first interrogation, 'a worse one' when CARELESS turned up drunk for his second interview, 'and an even worse one' when he failed to turn up at all for his third interview. It was finally arranged that on his next visit to London, CARELESS should be taken for the last time to the Rubens, and should be told by the Poles 'exactly what they thought of him'. He would then be handed over to Martin who would inform him that the next time he misbehaved he would be locked up again or even handed

over to the Poles. On 21 September, CARELESS got one day's leave
to visit London for this interview. Unfortunately, the Polish officer
was ill and the interview could not take place. CARELESS 'thereupon
decided to give himself some extra leave' and, although giving Martin
the impression that he was returning to his unit the same evening, he
sent a wire to his CO to say that he would be away until the 23rd.
Apparently he had a new CO and succeeded in talking himself out of
trouble when he returned.

On 6 October, MI5 were informed that CARELESS had been
absent without leave since 28 September, and on 8 October he rang
up Martin, disclosed the fact that he was in London and offered an
interview only on terms that he was not handed over to the Police. At
this interview CARELESS said that he had been up to Scotland to see
his father (who had been posted to Falkirk at the end of August). It
appeared that CARELESS had by now become 'thoroughly suspicious'
of the Poles at the Rubens Hotel and he claimed to have found out:
first, that the officer who was to have seen him on 21 September
did not really go sick at all, but was only delaying the interview for
'some sinister motive', and secondly that the Poles were conducting
some enquiry in Scotland into the affairs of his father. He told Martin
that for these reasons he had taken his father into his confidence and
told him everything. He promised to return to Marlborough the same
evening, give himself up and take his punishment. He did not do so,
however, until 14 October, by which time he had been posted as a
deserter. When finally apprehended he was found to be suffering from
VD and was therefore sent to a military hospital under escort.

Since CARELESS, on his own showing, 'had now betrayed our
confidence to his father and since, on any showing, he was too dissolute
to be trusted any longer', it was decided that the only practicable
course was to 'lock him up for the remainder of the war'. Accordingly
a Detention Order under Article 12(5a) of the Aliens Order was
obtained, and on 24 October CARELESS was transferred from military
custody to the hospital at Brixton Prison. Meanwhile, the necessary
steps were taken to discharge him from the army, and his discharge
became effective on 6 November. On 26 October, CARELESS tried to
commit suicide in Brixton Prison by strangling himself with his belt.
He left behind a letter for Martin in which he 'solemnly affirmed that
he detested the Germans and had never acted as a traitor', and repeated
his complaints about having been made to serve among Germans in the
Pioneer Corps. CARELESS apparently did himself no physical harm
by this attempt and, having recovered from his other complaint, he
was at last put back into Camp 020 on 3 November for the remainder

of the war. As soon as he arrived there CARELESS wrote another letter to Martin, saying that in spite of all that had happened he was willing and indeed anxious to continue with his W/T traffic as hitherto, since his only desire was to help to defeat the Germans. He did, in fact, write a secret letter on about 10 November, two more on or about 2 December, and two more on 31 December. On this last occasion he was 'argumentative, disgruntled and tearful, and required a little persuasion before he would consent to write'. On 8 January 1943 he was interviewed for the purpose of making experiments with a new method of secret writing which had just been proposed by Federico. On this occasion he began by refusing to write at all, and 'a full half hour's persuasion' was necessary. On 15 January he finally refused to write any more, 'and no amount of persuasion or intimidation' could induce him to change his mind. He 'never receded from this decision and his case has thus come to an ignominious and inconvenient end'. On 13 February 1943, the Security Service wrote to the Polish Security Service to say that 'we had now completely changed our opinion of CARELESS, who had proved most unsatisfactory, and to request them to re-enter his name on the list of persons to be tried by Polish Court Martial after the war'. They replied that they had done so.[11]

Unwittingly MI5 had now put CARELESS's life on the line. Sometime before CARELESS's arrival in the UK, on 13 July 1941, the Poles had sent MI5 a report from the Chief of their Agency 'P' in Lisbon, saying that CARELESS's contact with the Germans had been established beyond doubt since he had made a report to them on the Polish escape route across Spain. In a further document dated 'London, 16.7.41' the Poles informed the Security Service that, on the evidence of Sukiennik, Muhlstein and Balsam: 'The punishment to which he is liable... is the death sentence. ' On 12 December, B1.A wrote to the Poles saying that, in view of the fact that the chief witnesses in the case Balsam and Sukiennik, 'have proved themselves to be liars of the worst kind' MI5 were satisfied that 'there is no case against' CARELESS 'and we have no justification for holding him any longer. We should therefore be grateful if you would give us an assurance that on the strength of our statement you consider [CARELESS] cleared of the original grave charge brought against him incurring the sentence of death in accordance with Polish military law.' On 23 December, the Poles replied that 'in accordance with your request, [CARELESS] will no longer be considered guilty of the charge brought against him, unless you have reason to change your opinion of him'. Then, on 13 February 1942, MI5 had written to the Poles, referring to this former correspondence and saying, 'The officers dealing with [CARELESS] have now completely changed their opinion of this man who has proved most unsatisfactory. I am informing you of this with a request that, in view of this, [CARELESS's] name may be re-entered in the list of persons to be tried by Polish Court Martial after the war.' In March the Poles thanked MI5 and said that this had been done. But then C.P. Harvey suddenly realised:

> It appears to me that the natural inference to be drawn from this correspondence is that we have now finally concluded that CARELESS did sell the escape route to the Germans, and are willing that the Poles should deal with him after the war on that basis. From what we know of the Poles it is almost certain that they will put this interpretation on our letter. At the very least, they will use it as an additional piece of evidence to prove that CARELESS was all along acting as a spy and a traitor.
>
> Whatever may be CARELESS' other faults (and he has many) I am not aware that anyone who has investigated his case has felt that the evidence established affirmatively the general proposition that he was ever a real spy. As to the particular allegation that he sold the escape route to the Germans, the evidence taken as a whole is entirely in CARELESS' favour and no fresh evidence has come to light...

MI5, Harvey realised, had exposed CARELESS to possible execution for treason. The 'real case' against CARELESS, as it seemed to Harvey, appeared to be that he undoubtedly received money from the Germans in Madrid and Lisbon and espionage instructions in Madrid, and that at no time before his arrival in the UK did he tell the Polish authorities anything about it: 'This in itself probably constitutes an offence for which he can be Court Martialed. But the Poles are not satisfied with this. It is only too clear from the files that, having found out from other sources that CARELESS was in contact with the Germans, they leapt to the conclusion that CARELESS was a real traitor and as soon as he arrived in Lisbon they set about collecting the evidence to prove it. The subsequent history of the case suggests most strongly that, being unable to find any cogent genuine evidence on this point, they determined to manufacture some. If this view is accepted, it would obviously be very wrong for this Office to assist them, and if (as I think) we have inadvertently done so by our letter... we should now take steps to correct the false impression we have given.' Since it would 'probably be somewhat embarrassing for us to take any such step, and since the opinion expressed above is merely my own', Harvey set out his reasons for thinking that the Polish case against CARELESS was 'not a genuine one'.

> The essence of the charge had already been described: the 'Chief of Agency P' set out verbatim what he said was the extract from the escape route document which Balsam made with his own hand and which he himself received from Balsam. He also indicated that in the course of the voyage Balsam would be making a complete copy. Sooner or later, therefore, one would have expected the Poles to produce to MI5 in London (a) the original in Balsam's writing of the excerpt quoted by 'Agency P', and (b) a longer document, also in Balsam's writing (or possibly typed), which included the whole of (a). In fact the only document they have ever produced contains no passage which even remotely resembles the passage quoted by 'Agency P'.

The document in question was apparently written on the paper of the Hotel Tivoli, Lisbon: it was 'manifestly' in Balsam's handwriting but it did not mention the names of Zagorski or the Hotel Perdrix or the Calle dos Hornos, all of which appeared in the extract quoted by the 'Chief of Agency P'. This point (which did not appear to have been noticed until now) 'is to my mind so crucial that until it is explained – and it is hard to see how it can be – it cannot be held that the case against CARELESS has been set on its legs at all. However, the matter does not rest here. Let us assume that somehow or other the document produced can be reconciled with the charge made by the 'Chief of Agency P'. What then?'

Obviously it was necessary to connect this document, in some way, with CARELESS. The only admitted fact in the whole case about the escape route was that, on the morning of 28 June 1941, CARELESS and Sukiennik went together to the German Legation in Lisbon, saw Merckel and got money out of him. This was the only occasion on which it was suggested that the document could have been handed over. The evidence required was, therefore: (a) that CARELESS prepared, or helped to prepare, this document sometime before that date, and (b) that it was handed over on that date in his presence (which ex hypothesis depended on the evidence of Sukiennik alone). The 'striking difficulty' about establishing point (a) was that, although Balsam and Sukiennik lived with CARELESS and were able at various times to abstract and copy the documents he carried about with him, not a single note or memorandum about escape routes in CARELESS's writing was ever found. On the contrary, the first rough draft was said to have been made by Sukiennik at CARELESS's dictation. Sukiennik's first statement, on 17 July 1941 said that, on 27 June, 'he came to me and dictated the report to me. I typed it on my typewriter in draft form and made a fair copy of it later.' Interrogated at the Patriotic Schools on 14 August, Sukiennik said that the first draft was made in his own handwriting and only the fair copy was typed. Balsam agreed that these were the documents which he was shown and from which he made the partial extract.

So far, CARELESS's connection with these documents depended solely on the word of Sukiennik. Balsam, however, strengthened the case by saying in his original statement of 16 July that CARELESS: 'himself gave me the original of this report on Friday evening'. In a subsequent statement of 24 July he said that, on 27 June 1941, CARELESS 'gave me his report to read. The original was typewritten.' Interrogated on 14 August 1941, he said that Sukiennik first gave him a copy in his own handwriting, but twenty minutes later CARELESS brought him a typewritten copy of the same document. On 23 October, Balsam 'exploded the whole case' in a written statement made at Camp 020 in which he said Sukiennik 'gave me the copy and later he showed me the original. In order to make my statement quite clear I must add the following': that when Sukiennik 'gave me the copy and showed me the original [CARELESS] was not present, and I have not seen either the copy or the original in [CARELESS's] possession'.

Harvey concluded that: 'We are thus left with nothing' but the evidence of Sukiennik to show that CARELESS ever had anything to do with the preparation of the document, or that any such document was sold to the Germans. But, even on his own showing, Sukiennik went out of his way to destroy the value of his own evidence. According to him, there were two important points about the document shown to Merckel: (1) that it bore a forgery of Colonel Maly's signature, and (2) that it had the words 'Secret and Personal' written on it in CARELESS's own handwriting. There were 'the wildest contradictions about the signature'. In his statement of 17 July, Sukiennik said, 'I did not notice when [CARELESS] faked this signature, but without doubt the signature was a fake because I myself typed the report.' But, on 14 August he said that CARELESS, in his presence, asked Balsam to forge it. Balsam also said, on the 14th that when he first saw the document it was signed with a name which he could not read, though in his previous statements of 16 and 24 July he never mentioned the signature at all. One would have thought, commented Harvey, that this original, which was actually photographed by Merckel and which bore a forged signature and a heading in CARELESS's handwriting, was the one piece of evidence which it was vital for Sukiennik to preserve. 'However, he says that on his return from the German Legation he destroyed it at CARELESS's request!' Sukiennik 'has thus deliberately left himself with no evidence against CARELESS but his own word. In this connection it is worth remarking that at the very outset he was described by the 'Chief of Agency P' as a man who "deserved to be called a crook" and who "belongs to the doubtful type of people, ready to sell their own mothers for money".' It was to be remembered that Sukiennik was employed by Jaworski, through Muhlstein, for the specific purpose of producing evidence against CARELESS. The only conclusions Harvey could draw were either that there never was any document which was passed to Merckel on 28 August 1942, or that, if there was, it was of so spurious a character that Sukiennik was ashamed to produce it afterwards. Before parting with Sukiennik's evidence, Harvey thought it was worth remarking that it was Muhlstein – also described by the 'Agency P' as 'a crook on a large-scale' – who, at Jaworski's instigation set Sukiennik to collect evidence against CARELESS. Since he had been in Camp 020 Sukiennik had repeatedly stated that Muhlstein told him and Balsam that they were at liberty to get as much money as they could out of the Germans with CARELESS's assistance, and keep it for themselves – 'an invitation to fabricate evidence if ever there was one'.

Finally, Harvey could not help remarking on 'the complete lack of scruple with which the Poles have presented the case'. Two examples he quoted: (a) the dossier which they supplied to MI5, in October 1941, included a statement by a Second Lieutenant Rajchel which showed that CARELESS's father was at 'all material times' a German spy, and that CARELESS was working with him for the Germans long before he ever got into Spain. Nevertheless, CARELESS's father now held an appointment with the Polish Forces and; (b) on 2 September 1942, the Poles, for the first time, made the accusation that the escape route document in their possession was in CARELESS's handwriting and that a handwriting expert would vouch for it. The only document they had ever produced was 'manifestly not' in CARELESS's writing. When Cyril Mills pointed this out to them 'they had the effrontery to say that it made no difference and that CARELESS was a spy anyway! Quite obviously they do not care what they say so long as it blackens CARELESS.'[12] In the end, of course, MI5's efforts to spare CARELESS the death penalty were not needed for there would be no restoration of the Polish state in exile to power – Stalin would see to that.

ZIGZAG Drops In

While Tommy Harris forged an admiring relationship with GARBO, this did not extend to the latter's wife. He recorded: 'In contrast with her husband, Mrs GARBO was a hysterical, spoilt and selfish woman.' Having said that, Harris also acknowledged that she was 'intelligent and astute and probably entered into her husband's work because it was dangerous and exciting'. Mrs GARBO had only agreed to her husband coming to Britain after being assured by SIS that he would only be absent from Lisbon for three to four weeks. But MI5 decided that his case could only be run satisfactorily by his remaining in Britain, and that this would not be safe unless his wife came over to join him. 'When she was told to leave for England she put up strong opposition and it was not without difficulty that she was convinced to come here.' It did not help matters that her journey to Britain was the first she had ever made outside the Peninsula. On her arrival, 'domestic household complications immediately set in and it was only after several months of domestic upheaval that we managed to find her a house where she could run her home without interference from this Office'. At the time this move was made, GARBO assured Harris that 'we would no longer be put to worry over their household domestic difficulties, and this undertaking was fulfilled to the best of his ability'.

Unfortunately, Mrs GARBO 'at first found it difficult to adapt herself to the English way of living'; neither had she been able to learn the language. GARBO very carefully supervised her contacts and took every possible precaution to avoid her mixing with Spaniards, or any other aliens in the UK, through whom there might have been the slightest possibility of the Germans being able to check up on their activities. 'All these causes intensified the already acute homesickness from which Mrs GARBO had been suffering ever since her arrival here. Her desire to return to her country, and in particular to see her mother, had driven her to behave at times as if she were unbalanced.' For many months she begged Harris to make arrangements for her to return to her home town, even for a week. As she was 'a highly emotional and neurotic woman... we never definitely disillusioned her in her hopes that she might be allowed to see her mother before the termination of the war, neither did we, on the other hand, give her any reason to believe that we would accede to her request'. As her state worsened she became desperate and 'she threatened to take action which would spoil the work and leave her free to return'. There were, as a result, 'many tense moments which existed from time to time in the GARBO domestic set up', recalled Harris.

One of these developed after Mrs GARBO and her husband became friendly with a Spanish family in London, Mr and Mrs Guerra, with whom they had occasionally dined. The Guerras invited the GARBOs to attend a dinner at the Spanish Club at which all the Spanish Embassy personnel were to be present. Mrs GARBO was very keen to go but GARBO refused to allow her to do so, explaining that it might endanger his work if he were known to be in contact with members of the Spanish Embassy, particularly as he had told the Germans that he was now out of these circles. He explained to her that it was always possible that someone in the Spanish Embassy might be in touch with the Germans and that any contact with the Embassy would therefore be most dangerous. Harris recorded how: 'Apart from her disappointment at this decision, it gave her the idea that if her husband were anxious for her to keep away from the Embassy a threat to visit the Embassy would frighten us into paying attention to her request. It appears that the husband and wife quarrelled rather violently over this, and later Mrs GARBO threatened him that she was going to tell us that she intended calling at the Embassy to disclose the work he was doing for us. The row happened on the evening of the 21.6.43. After this threat he left the house to telephone from a public call box to warn us that if his wife should telephone and be offensive in any way we should ignore her remarks as she was in a highly excited frame of mind.' That evening Mrs GARBO telephoned Harris and said:

> I am telling you for the last time that if at this time to-morrow you haven't got me my papers all ready for me to leave the country immediately – because I don't want to live five minutes longer with my husband – I will go to the Spanish Embassy. As you can suppose going to the Spanish Embassy may cost me my life – you understand, it will cost me my life – so telling you that I am telling you everything as I haven't got any further with threats even if they kill me I am going to the Spanish Embassy. I know very well what to do and say to annoy you and my husband I shall have the satisfaction that I have spoilt everything. Do you understand? I don't want to live another day in England.

While 'we were not unaccustomed to such outbreaks, the present crisis seemed particularly serious'. GARBO was rather embarrassed when told that evening of what had transpired, though he expressed his view that he, personally, was convinced that she would not carry out her threat. It, nevertheless, 'seemed clear that he was somewhat hesitant to take full responsibility for her actions, being aware that she was in a desperate state'. Harris and his agent discussed the matter at some length and GARBO recommended that, in order to tide matters, 'we should telephone his wife the following morning, after receiving his signal that he was no longer in the house, to say that we would give her the answer to her question at 7 o'clock that evening and that meanwhile she should give her husband the message that the Head of Section wished to interview him in town as soon as possible'. Harris further agreed with GARBO that a watch should be kept on the Spanish Embassy 'and that should she approach it we would detain her'.

The following morning Mrs GARBO was called by telephone in accordance with the plan arranged with GARBO the previous night. That afternoon, Harris met GARBO who, having given the whole matter his careful consideration, put forward a rather drastic plan which was subsequently put into operation. He took full responsibility for all possible reactions which his plan might produce on his wife, and expressed confidence that, providing it was properly carried out it would produce a good effect on her. It was agreed, before putting the plan into operation, 'that we should enter into it on the understanding that it would be directed by GARBO, and that if the reactions were not as we had anticipated, we would be prepared to modify it in accordance with any special request which GARBO might make'. The plan was as follows: GARBO wrote a short note to his wife to tell her that he had been detained, and requesting her to hand to the bearer his 'toilet requirements and pyjamas'. Shortly after 6 p.m. the note was delivered to Mrs GARBO by CID officers. After a 'hysterical outburst she refused to accede to her husband's request for clothing'. Meanwhile, her first reaction had been, as GARBO had hoped, to telephone Harris. She was in tears when she got through and pleaded that her husband had always been loyal to Britain and 'would willingly sacrifice his life for our cause'. It was therefore inconceivable that he should have been arrested. 'This gave us the opening we had anticipated to be able to tell her our story.'

Harris explained that when he had met GARBO that afternoon and he had been taken before the chief, the latter had expressed his absolute willingness to give Mrs GARBO her papers to return to Spain, but had said that he wished GARBO and the children to return there with her. Before doing so, however, he instructed GARBO to write a letter making some excuse to the Germans for discontinuing his work.

GARBO, at this stage, she was told, 'became offensive to our chief', stating that they had made a contract with him which he intended to see should not be broken. Even if they had approved that she should return to Spain they could not force him also to do so. Rather than write the letter they requested, he would first go to prison. He asked the reasons for their request for the letter. They replied that they needed it to protect their interest against a betrayal by his wife in Spain such as she had threatened in Britain. Mrs GARBO was told that when the word 'betrayal' was mentioned by the chief, GARBO completely lost his temper 'and had behaved so violently that his immediate arrest had been necessary on disciplinary grounds'.

Mrs GARBO replied to this by saying she thought that her husband had behaved just as she would have expected him to do. She said that after the sacrifices he had made, and her knowledge that his whole life was wrapped up in his work, she could well understand that he would rather go to prison than sign the letter MI5 had asked for. She said also that she was convinced he had behaved in this way to avoid the blame for all that had happened falling on her. 'The conversation ended.'

Having reflected for a little while, Mrs GARBO telephoned Harris again, 'this time in a more offensive mood', threatening to leave the house with the two children and make a disappearance. A little later GARBO's wireless operator telephoned to say that Mrs GARBO had telephoned him, 'apparently in a desperate state', asking him to come round within half an hour. He arrived at her house a little after eight to find her sitting in the kitchen with all the gas taps turned on. For some time after his arrival she was incoherent. She again attempted suicide later that evening. Harris thought: 'There was a 90 per cent chance that she was play acting. There existed a 10 per cent chance of an accident. To avoid any risk of an accident arrangements were made for someone to stay the night at her house.' The next day, at her request, she was interviewed. She pleaded that it was she who had been at fault and that if her husband could be pardoned she promised she would never again interfere with his work, or behave badly, or ask to return to Spain. She signed a statement to this effect. By this time she was 'extremely nervous and had been weeping incessantly for hours on end, and though she was left with the feeling that the matter was serious, the interview had given her hope that a solution to her troubles would soon be found'. She was told that she would be allowed to see her husband in detention that afternoon, and that a car would call for her at 4 p.m.

Under escort she was taken to Kew Bridge, and at 4.30 p.m. transferred to Camp 020, blindfolded. Her husband was brought to her dressed in Camp 020 clothing and unshaven. He first of all asked her to tell him on her word of honour whether or not she had been to the Embassy. She swore that not only had she not been there, but that she had never intended going, and only used this threat to force MI5 to pay more serious attention to her request. She promised him that if only he were released from prison, she would help him in every way to continue with his work with even greater zeal than before. She would never ask again to go back to Spain and leave him in Britain. She said she thought he had been quite right in refusing to allow the British to break their contract with him. She told him how she had been interviewed that morning and of her signing a confession, taking all the blame on herself. She said she was optimistic that something would soon be done for him, and therefore she had decided not to bring him the parcel of clothes which she had prepared. She was hopeful that he would not be detained very long. He told her that he was coming up before a tribunal the following morning and that since she had not been to the Embassy he had a plan which he thought would convince his judges that she had never intended going there. She left Camp 020 'more composed, but still weeping'. The following morning she was told she would be interviewed by a chief of the Service at the Hotel Victoria, Northumberland Avenue. At that interview she was told in brief that her husband had been before the tribunal that morning which had recommended that he should be allowed to continue his work. She was warned against a repetition of her recent behaviour. She returned home 'very chastened' to await her husband's arrival. He returned to his home that evening. Reviewing the situation afterwards, Harris considered:

This episode was not without interest in assessing the qualities of GARBO and his wife. We learnt that she had never intended to carry out her threats, and even had she crossed the threshold of the Spanish Embassy she would never have discussed there anything to do with her husband's work. She had only made the threat in order to cause us to pay greater attention to her request. This confirms that the conclusion which GARBO had drawn before putting the plan into operation had been correct. It gave us further evidence of the implicit confidence which GARBO placed in us, for him to have allowed us to put into operation a plan which, had it failed, would have ruined for ever his matrimonial life. It showed us the degree to which he was prepared to co-operate in order to ensure that his work should continue uninterrupted. The extraordinary ingenuity with which he conceived and carried through this plan saved a situation which might otherwise have been intolerable... It should be added that Mrs. GARBO gave us no parallel trouble thereafter.[1]

ZIGZAG

On 7 January 1943, Tin Eye Stephens wrote: 'The story of many a spy is commonplace and drab. It would not pass muster in fiction. The subject is a failure in life and those who train him do not appreciate he must fail in espionage as he fails in everything else. The motive is sordid. Fear is present. Patriotism is absent. Silence is not the equipment of a brave man, rather is it a reaction to a dread of consequence. High adventure means just nothing at all.' However, the story of Edward Chapman, the spy of the German Secret Service who landed by parachute in the night of 15/16 December 1942 in Cambridgeshire, was 'different. In fiction it would be rejected as improbable. The subject is a crook, but as a crook he is by no means a failure'. His career in crime had been 'progressive', from army desertion to indecency, from women to blackmail, from robbery to the blowing of safes. Latterly his rewards had been large 'and no doubt he despises himself for his petty beginnings. Today there is no trace of sodomy and gone is any predilection for living on women on the fringe of society.' The man, essentially vain, had grown in stature and, in his own estimation, 'is something of a prince of the underworld. He has no scruples and will stop at nothing. He plays for high stakes and would have the world know it. He makes no bargain with society and money is a means to an end. Of fear he knows nothing, and while patriotism is not a positive virtue he certainly has a deep rooted hatred of the Hun'. In a word, adventure to Chapman 'is the breath of life. Given adventure he has the courage to achieve the unbelievable. Discretion is not his strong suit, yet paradoxically his very recklessness is his stand-by. Today he is a German parachute spy; tomorrow perhaps he will undertake a desperate hazard as an active agent-double, the stake for which is his life. Without adventure he would rebel; in the ultimate he will have recourse again to crime in search of the unusual'.[2]

Coming from Stephens this was praise indeed. So who was Edward Chapman or, as he became for MI5, ZIGZAG? He was born at Burnup Hill, near Newcastle, County Durham. He attended school in Sunderland before spending two years as an apprentice electrical engineer. In 1932 he enlisted in the 2nd Battalion The Coldstream Guards. He was not a model soldier. In August 1933 he deserted and received eighty-four days detention as punishment. Three months later he was dismissed from the Service. From 1933 to 1939, apart from occasional work as a film extra, Chapman earned his living by blackmail and robbery. In 1936 he married a German subject, Vera Freidberg; divorce proceedings were begun against him in 1939 but, being in prison, he never heard the outcome of the case. During 1935, 1936 and 1939, Chapman served various sentences for stealing; obtaining money by false pretences; being found on enclosed premises for an unlawful purpose; offences against public decency in Hyde Park; and obtaining credit by false pretence. In March 1939, when due to appear at Edinburgh on a house-breaking charge, he broke bail and fled to Jersey. In the same month he was charged at the Jersey Royal Court for burglary and received two years hard labour. In July of that year he escaped from HM Prison Jersey, was re-arrested in London and finally sentenced to twelve months' imprisonment in Jersey, to run concurrently with the previous sentence.[3]

Thus Chapman was in prison when the German occupation of the Channel Islands began; he served his full sentence and was released in September 1941. He went to stay with a friend and his wife. The men discussed ways of getting off the island; they came up with the idea of offering their services to the German Secret Service with the aim of being sent to the UK and thus escaping. After making the offer to the Germans both men found themselves under arrest, charged with sabotage. Within an hour of their arrest, Chapman and his friend found themselves on a boat and were told if they resisted they would be shot. They were transferred to Fort Romanville, near Le Rourget. This was a camp for hostages. Chapman was held here, with his friend, from November 1941 until April 1942. They were the only Britons in the camp. All the inmates had been charged with either espionage or sabotage against the German Army. But, in January 1942, Chapman received a visit from several members of the German Secret Service. They were only interested in Chapman not his friend. The Germans asked Chapman if he was prepared to be trained by them for work in England. Chapman agreed and an order was made for his release. He was then transferred to Nantes for the beginning of his training.[4]

Chapman's controller was Dr Graumann – who was in fact Rittmeister von Grening who had taken over command of the Nantes dienstelle in March 1942. He had previously served on the Eastern Front as a Staff Officer attached to Oberkommando 4 Heeresgruppe Mitte. It was through ISOS that MI5 knew his real identity; they also knew who were the other officials connected to the Nantes dienstelle – in fact, thanks to SIGINT they had monitored ZIGZAG's entire training programme: they followed the training of an agent – 'the

Englishman' – referred in the traffic as FRITZCEHN through wireless training to his first parachute jump – revealed by the fact that the agent needed dental treatment afterwards.[5] Of course, at the time, the British had no idea of the true identity of FRITZCHEN; but thanks to ISOS interceptions MI5 expected that, before 9 October, a German agent – 'Agent X' – would be dropped by parachute. He was almost certainly of British nationality and possibly from the Channel Island of Jersey. They believed him to be under 30, about six foot tall and certainly with a canine tooth, if not more, replaced by a false tooth. Agent X would be in possession of two identity cards – one showing him to be an Irishman resident in England and another showing him to be an Englishman resident in England. One or both might be green; one or both the names might be Chapman.[6] The operation to intercept and arrest the agent was codenamed NIGHTCAP. Colonel Stanford was the Security Service representative at RAF Fighter Command, Stanmore, tasked with following incoming enemy aircraft and identifying, if possible, the aeroplane containing Agent X: if Stanford received information from Section V SIS, Fighter Command would commence their search for incoming aircraft. After this, Dick White was to be informed that NIGHTCAP was on. If SIS could provide the location of the drop the relevant Chief Constable would be alerted.[7]

For unknown reasons the expected October drop did not occur. Then, on 16 December, at 1.48 a.m., Sergeant Joseph Vail, of Littleport police station, Ely, received an air raid alert warning. At 3.45 a.m., Vail was informed by Sergeant Hutchings that he had received a call from Apes Hall Farm. Vail and Hutchings arrived at the farm at 4.30 a.m. There they were met by George Convine, the farm foreman and his wife Martha. When the policemen entered the living room they found a man in civilian clothes who came out and met them with hand outstretched. He seemed pleased to see them although a little agitated. He spoke in perfect English. On going into the living room the man produced a fully loaded automatic pistol and said: 'I expect the first thing you want is this.' He unloaded the magazine and handed the pistol to Vail. The policeman asked the stranger where had he come from; he replied: 'France, I want to get in touch with the British Intelligence Service, it is a case for them, I'm afraid I can't tell you much.' The man was handed over to other policemen from Ely at 5.45 a.m.

The police learnt what had transpired prior to their arrival: Mrs Convine had been in bed during the air raid alert. She heard what she assumed to be a German plane circling overhead. Some time after the all clear she heard someone knocking on the door. Mrs Convine awakened her husband and got out of bed. She called from the window: 'Who is it?' A man's voice replied: 'A British airman had an accident.' Mrs Convine went downstairs and let him in. Her husband was lighting the lamp. She noticed the man's face had blood on it. He said: 'I want to speak to the Police at once.' She let him use the phone; after a time she asked him where his plane was. The man replied: 'Across the field.' Later he said he had parachuted out of a plane. Mrs Convine recalled that: 'I thought I heard a "Jerry".' The man answered that this was a cover plane 'for ours'. She remembered that the man was very polite.[8]

After being handed over to the Security Service, the first inclination was to use Chapman for XX purposes. But then Chapman's long criminal record was discovered, so a decision was made to send him to Camp 020 for custody and examination overnight. Robin Stephens decided that time, was of the essence and began a general interrogation, leaving detail for investigation if and when opportunity recurred. He found that the Germans had been training Chapman as a high grade saboteur and spy: 'For once in a way it must be conceded the German Secret Service did their work well. In Nantes they had the wisdom to accept this crook as an equal in an officers' mess. They pandered to his vanity, granted him liberty and treated him with respect. In the end he became something of a hero, for he won a wager for the Mess by worming his way into a well guarded arsenal and placed there a dummy package of explosive, wholly unobserved.' On his departure for England he was seen off by members of the mess and the Chief of the Stelle promised champagne all round on receipt of a message from Chapman which would herald the success of his mission. The Germans, however, 'made two fatal mistakes'. In the first place they had searched him before departure as a last vital check on his good faith, yet in the hurry of the moment thrust into his hand English banknotes bound in a German bank wrapper which proved conclusively that Germany was the country of origin. When Stephens told Chapman that wrapper might cost him his neck, 'his respect for the British Secret Service in relation to the German Secret Service was established in our favour'. In the second place when searching for the motive of surrender on arrival in Britain, Stephens asked Chapman whether the Germans were aware of the hazard to him, for not only was he known to the police but also to associate thieves 'among whom honour is a quality unknown'. Chapman replied he had made this plain to Graumann, and had asked for America as an alternative venue. Then with some bitterness he added Graumann had laughed, saying a criminal was the type of man who was of service, for he would never dare to betray them. 'There lies the blackmail,' and the beginning of Chapman's 'hatred for the Boches who otherwise have treated him well, and there lives the reason for his surrender on arrival in England, notwithstanding the risk of penal servitude for crimes at present untried'.[9]

But Stephen's initial assessment of Chapman was not quite on the ball. Chapman proved a more complex character, torn by conflicting emotions that meant that MI5 never really knew where his ultimate loyalty lay. But Chapman was also remarkable in that he was quite open about this. From the very first contact he had with the Germans he set out to try and mass together a series of facts, places, dates and so on that he thought would be a task 'fairly formidable even for one of your trained experts'. Chapman's German was slight, his French even less – two languages essential for this work. But Chapman studied French until he mastered it, even learning the slang. He also learned to understand German and to carry out any simple conversation in it. Then, for nearly nine months, Chapman listened intently to every conversation that he could hear; he opened drawers containing many documents and poured over dictionaries to try and – only half – understand them. Chapman even bored very small holes from the bathroom to the room of Dr Graupmann – 'a man very much my friend'. And this last statement was the key one to understanding his state of mind. He outlined his torment in a letter to Stephens:

> Sir, one does not expect gratitude from one's own country – but allow me to draw your attention to two facts. For thirteen months now I have lived under German Rule. During this time even while undergoing detention I was treated with strict fairness and friendliness... I made many friends – people who I respect and who I think came to like me – unfortunately for them and for me... Several times I was disgusted with myself – much more than I can ever explain. I sometimes wondered deeply which was the greatest, love of one's country or love of one's friends. On one side you may draw the picture for yourself. Here am I outcast from my own country – a criminal – a man who never had any friends in England suddenly befriended and shown kindness and for the first time treated like a normal human being. Don't think I am asking for any now it's a little late – On the other side this strange thing patriotism. I laugh a little cynically when I think of it sometimes. I have fought the fight and my country won (why I can't explain). I wish like hell there had been no war – I begin to wish I had never started this affair. To spy and cheat on one's friends is not nice it's dirty... However, I started this affair and I will finish it.[10]

This won him respect from his interrogators. Stephens found Chapman candid during questioning. There were few discrepancies in his material that could be checked and the consensus of opinion among the Camp 020 officers was that they were natural inexactitudes: 'Motive is a streak of hatred for the Hun coupled with a sense of adventure... He is possessed of courage and nerve.' Stephens's opinion was that Chapman should be used for double-cross purposes and that Camp 020 was no place from which he could be used.[11]

As a study in counter-espionage Stephens found Chapman 'a case of undoubted fascination. The war issue whether the man can be used as an active agent-double is one of exceptional difficulty. In 90 per cent of the cases which come to Camp 020 I am opposed to this course for they are the rabble of the universe, their treachery is not matched by their courage and a further mission is foredoomed to failure. In the remaining 10 per cent of the cases, the risk is considerable, but then so long as there is a chance of success I think the risk should be taken, for otherwise nothing constructive can be done.' But for Chapman 'only one thing is certain, the greater the adventure the greater is the chance of success'.[12]

Chapman was released into the supervised care of two members of the Field Security Police who were given a standard letter stating that the bearer was engaged on special duties for the War Office and was accompanied by Edward Simpson, whose photograph was annexed. It was particularly requested that 'no questions as to the identity or activities' of Simpson should be addressed to the bearer.[13] Simpson, of course, was Chapman. The FSP were told that there was no reason to doubt Simpson's loyalty and they were not to regard themselves as his guards nor were they responsible for 'the custody of his body'. Their first function was to act as his chaperones and 'act as a screen between him and the outside world'. Simpson was therefore never to be left alone, either day or night, although they were to make this as little irksome as possible for him. Despite not being under guard, Simpson was, nevertheless, to obey their orders absolutely and, if at any time he attempted to disobey these orders, the FSP men were authorised to 'compel their acceptance and if necessary for this purpose you are authorised to place him under restraint'. Their second main duty was to endeavour to obtain Simpson's confidence and to assist him to recall and record every single detail of his association with the Germans.[14] Before long 'Simpson' had been given his new codename: ZIGZAG.

The stories which began to emerge from ZIGZAG about his former profession unnerved some of his MI5 controllers. He told his FSP minders how he escaped from prison in Jersey, stole a car, lost it, found another the door of which he forced. He was about to drive away when the irate owner appeared. ZIGZAG said: 'We had a bit of a scuffle and I threw him over a wall.' Towards the end of his freedom he was cornered on a beach at Jersey by three policemen in plain clothes. They asked him if he would go with them quietly but he told them they had better take him. There was a fight in which ZIGZAG enlisted the aid of the other people on the beach by claiming he was a policeman and the other men were attacking him. There followed a 'free for all' in which several people were hurt during which ZIGZAG eluded capture until unformed officers arrived.[15] R.T. Reed, his MI5 case officer, became alarmed as ZIGZAG began to reveal more crimes – of which the police were unaware, such as the 'humorous' entry into a pawnbrokers at Grimsby when he cut through five floors of a house and blew six safes with gelignite; and the breaking into a fur store in the West End by disguising himself as a Metropolitan Water Board inspector and knocking down two walls of a Jewish financier's flat. The financier was later imprisoned for three months for complicity in the crime because ZIGZAG and his friend, Darry (a Burmese crook currently serving seven years) had promised the occupier of the premises considerable financial reward for 'cooking' the amount of damage which had been done to the flat. Reed urgently sought a ruling as to whether MI5 should tell Special Branch about these new adventures 'or whether we should keep it entirely to ourselves but have it on record. I think the latter course is probably preferable'.[16]

Details continued to emerge. His 'instructor' was Jimmy Hunt 'whom ZIGZAG describes as one of the best cracksmen in London'. He did his first 'job' with Jimmy Hunt at 'Isobel's' Branch in Harrogate where they stole some furs. ZIGZAG recalled that throughout the operation he was shivering with fear and was unable to assist. On one of the co-operative wholesale society jobs, when he and his mob arrived, they found another gang had been there before them and had ripped open the safe. ZIGZAG also did a few 'smash and grab' jobs. One of them was in or near Oxford Street where the gang were immediately pursued by the Police. They were in a Bentley and made their way to Baker Street where they crashed some traffic lights and smashed into a taxi. The whole gang made their get away in the side streets. Apparently a crowd gathered round the scene of the accident and a man whom ZIGZAG described as a 'snive', in other words a small time local thief, put his hand on the radiator of the Bentley. The police naturally found this man's finger prints, arrested him, and he was eventually identified by the taxi driver and by one of the assistants at the shop where the robbery had taken place. Although this man had taken no part whatever in the operation, he was given five years. Reed noted, on this occasion, that: 'I think we ought to keep these things on record in case we ever want to use them.'[17]

ZIGZAG's original mission for the Germans had been to sabotage the power house of the De Havilland aircraft works at Hatfield. He was then to return to occupied territory by one of three methods: 1. To obtain a berth on a ship going to Lisbon and to make contact at his cover address with the password 'Juli Albert'; 2. To escape to Eire and contact 'their people' about whom he would be told over his radio transmitter; 3. To be picked up by a submarine somewhere off the coast of Great Britain, but this method would only be used in the event of failure of the other two.

Before leaving France, ZIGZAG had said that he would try and obtain contact for the first time on his transmitter on Friday morning, 18 December 1942. He did not, however, transmit to them until Sunday morning, 20 December when he said he had arrived and was well, with friends. In France, ZIGZAG had tested his transmitter for many months with a large number of stations and had only experienced a little difficulty in maintaining consistent communication, so that on arrival in Britain he thought that he would be able to transmit with the same ease as he did while he was training in France. The Germans had told him that, if difficulty should be experienced, they would, if necessary, construct a special station to receive him and that MORRIS (one of the best of the operators at Paris) would take a special set down to the coast of France in order to ensure the communication.

Under MI5 instruction, ZIGZAG sent a message to say that he had been to see the De Havilland Aircraft Factory at Hatfield and had made reconnaissance there: 'This factory is referred to in the messages as "WALTER". It could also be called "THOMAS".' Walter Thomas was the name of his constant companion during his training, who spoke extremely good English and who had revealed to ZIGZAG that he had many years ago been a student at Southampton.[18]

In fact Ronnie Reed, his case officer, and ZIGZAG had visited the factory at Hatfield, on 7 January 1943, to inspect the boiler house which had been suggested as the best building for sabotaging. ZIGZAG and Reed, after considerable discussion, came to the following conclusion: 'We should send over one morning a message saying that ZIGZAG intended to carry out his sabotage of the building that evening. This should not be done, but the following morning another message should be sent that it had been found impossible to do so as there were too many guards and that the sabotage would be attempted the next evening. This would give us an opportunity of seeing whether the enemy sent a reconnaissance aircraft over on the evening that we say the sabotage is to be attempted.' If a reconnaissance aircraft was not sent, camouflage was to be erected over the roof of the boiler house and on the side of it which faced the roadway. A large amount of rubble and brick was to be deposited around the boiler house and, if possible, one or two old armatures placed in the immediate vicinity as if an explosion had taken place and to appear as if these had been hurled from the main machine room. This would do away with the necessity for informing any large number of people that sabotage had been attempted, as excuses could be made that repairs were taking place to the roof of the boiler house, 'and if enquiries are considerable the information to be gained by the works people will take so many forms that they will find it difficult to arrive at the correct conclusion'. If, on the other hand, a reconnaissance aircraft was sent over it would be necessary to stage a fire on the roof of the boiler house or on the waste ground on either side of it. This could also be done by placing asbestos sheets on the roof and sprinkling on them incendiary material. Unfortunately this would mean that the fire and subsequent camouflage 'will appear very queer, and it will be obvious to the works people that we are pretending that sabotage has taken place'.[19]

In the end arrangements were made to obtain the tracks of any aircraft which should approach de Havillands on the night selected for the sabotage, but it was considered inadvisable to arrange for a fire to take place at the factory when the sabotage was supposed to occur as, if there were enemy planes in the vicinity, this might indicate the vulnerable points to them and thus invite a bombing attack. In order to cover the talk that the erection of camouflage would almost certainly cause amongst the factory employees it was decided to spread the story that the tarpaulins and wooden constructions which would be erected at the real and notional sub-station sites had been put there for the purpose of camouflage for high altitude photography. It was arranged for a British aircraft to take photographs of the sabotage on the morning after it was supposed to occur, and to lend truth to the story told to the factory employees. Camouflage experts arrived at dusk on the night of 29 January and, in a few hours, had strewn the courtyard of the real sub-station with debris and erected dummy transformers at the notional sub-station site. An attempt was made to get a paragraph put in the *Times* reporting that a factory explosion had taken place in the London area, but the editor found it impossible to publish information which was 'entirely' untrue; MI5's Press Section eventually succeeded in having a paragraph published in the 5 a.m. edition of the *Daily Express* which went to Lisbon on 1 February.[20]

On 28 January a message was sent by ZIGZAG to say that 'WALTER' would definitely be sabotaged on Friday night, 29 January, and that he was taking as his objectives the sub-stations. On 30 January ZIGZAG sent a message to say that 'WALTER' had been 'blown' in two places and that it was important that he should return immediately to France. After a congratulatory message on 3 February, ZIGZAG received a request from the Germans to give information on the newspaper publicity that the sabotage had received and that they required to know from him what would be the best way for him to return, as it was difficult for them to make the arrangements for him not knowing the exact state of affairs in Britain. They promised to do all they could for him. On 4 February ZIGZAG asked if the Germans could pick him up by submarine or speed-boat and, for the first time, said that he was trying to obtain ship's papers to enable him to return by sea. He said that a newspaper report about the explosion appeared in the *Daily Express* on the back page on 1 February. MI5 presumed this planted newspaper report to be in the possession of the Germans. The report was headed 'Factory Explosion' and said: 'Investigations are being made into the case of an explosion at a factory on the outskirts of London. It is understood that the damage was slight and there was no loss of life.' On 8 February, ZIGZAG was told that it was impossible for him to be picked up by submarine and that the only way left for his return would be the 'normal' way as a ship's passenger to Lisbon. After a further request by the enemy to give details of any newspapers which printed information about the sabotage at De Havillands, a message was sent, by ZIGZAG, on 11 February to say that the two sub-stations had been 'blown' with 60 lbs of gelignite which was placed under the transformers. He had since heard that they were completely destroyed and that great damage was done. He had seen no newspaper reports, except perhaps a mention of the sabotage on the back page of the *Daily Express* of 1 February headed 'Factory Explosion'.[21]

As ZIGZAG was very keen to bring his friend Jimmy Hunt into the story it was decided that he should maintain, on return to enemy territory, that Hunt had sabotaged one of the sites while he had attacked the other. A great deal of the whole of the ZIGZAG cover story hinged on Hunt, and the Germans could confirm that Hunt was known to have criminal convictions and to be a person of the type with whom ZIGZAG would associate from his criminal record; this was available to them in Jersey.[22] Things had, so far, 'gone very smoothly for the whole project and we decided that it would be necessary to introduce some upset into his notional position over here. We arranged, therefore, to close down his transmission one morning by giving a series of the letter 'P', which was supposed to indicate to the operators in the reply stations that ZIGZAG suspected the police were in the vicinity.' On 10 February, and shortly after this previous occurrence, he sent a message to say that it was dangerous to continue transmitting, that things were getting awkward. ZIGZAG pointed out that he had some important documents and that the production of false papers to enable him to return by ship was a very difficult business.[23] According to the cover story that ZIGZAG intended to tell on his return to occupied Europe he was supposed to have contacted Jimmy Hunt and offered him, in return for Hunt's assistance, the sum of £15,000 and the aid of the German Government in escaping from the UK. Notionally, therefore, Hunt was taking a considerable interest in the radio traffic, and when the message was received saying that it was impossible for the enemy to pick ZIGZAG up by submarine, and it was obvious that no assistance in this matter was forthcoming, it was assumed that Hunt would doubtless be somewhat annoyed. By becoming ZIGZAG's accomplice he was liable to the death penalty, and he had assumed responsibility and danger for apparently no reward. Hunt would insist upon returning with ZIGZAG and obtaining this money. As Reed noted: 'The arrangements at this end appeared still to be going well and to have worked without very much difficulty. A disaster on a small scale, it was felt, would have provided some realism.' The story was that Hunt was wanted for various criminal offences, and it was agreed that he should be notionally arrested on suspicion of possessing explosives. This would confirm ZIGZAG's cover story regarding the method by which he obtained his explosives and would also eliminate Hunt from the return journey to Lisbon.[24]

On 12 February ZIGZAG sent a message to say that he had seen a chance to return to Lisbon and hoped that the Germans would make sure everything was ready for him there. On this same day a small paragraph appeared in the *Evening Standard* headed: 'Gelignite Enquiries', which stated: 'A man was questioned at Shepherds Bush Police Station last night in connection with the possession of gelignite.' On 13 February a message was sent by ZIGZAG saying: 'Jimmy arrested. See Evening Standard February 12th Front Page. Closing transmitter at once. Will try and get to Lisbon. FRITZ.' MI5 believed that it should now be clear to the Germans that things had not gone well and that ZIGZAG was in considerable danger owing to the arrest of his friend. The Security Service decided that no further transmissions were to be made on ZIGZAG's transmitter unless an urgent message was received from the control station asking him to come on the air.[25] The transmitter was not operated again, in spite of the fact that the reply station continued calling each day. In the intercepted words of the Paris stelle, it would be 'absolutely inexcusable' not to listen for ZIGZAG in case he should wish to contact them. Despite the elaborate subterfuge ISOS showed that the German reaction to this was disappointing, for, 'owing to interference or stupidity', they had not heard ZIGZAG's 'danger' signal and had assumed that he had closed down in the normal way. As Reed remarked, after making such careful arrangements for ZIGZAG to indicate that the police 'were on his track they had failed him in practice'.[26]

By now the XX Committee, which controlled all XX agents, had realised that an early decision as to the future of this case had to be taken. The opinion of experienced police officers who were familiar with ZIGZAG's criminal career 'was that he would always be a criminal, and that there was no reasonable expectation that he would abandon his criminal career. Furthermore ZIGZAG himself made no secret of the fact that as soon as he again found suitable opportunities he would, partly from choice and partly from necessity, again resume his normal activities'. On this score alone, therefore ZIGZAG 'is a difficult man for us to handle, since we may expect tiresome brushes with the police which, even though they can be dealt with, may nevertheless compromise his position, and he will also be a potential danger and nuisance to the community in his criminal capacity'. It was also relevant that the Security Service was, as matters stood, compounding two felonies at least of which it had notice, and a great many more which it had reasonable grounds for believing to have been committed. 'It is true that in the circumstances this is perhaps a technical point, but it is one whose solution may necessitate the disclosure of the true facts to more people than is, in the circumstances, desirable.'

B1.A also had to contend with ZIGZAG's temperament and character. He was undoubtedly a man with a deep-seated liking for adventure, movement and activity: 'It is our view that this is more likely to be the cause, rather than the effect, of his criminal career. If this view is correct it is felt that it is extremely improbable that his dislike of an uneventful life can be subordinated to an appeal to his patriotism. His own wish is that he should return to France, and that he should there commit acts of sabotage in the British interest, and he has even suggested that he should assassinate Hitler.' He had said, in terms, that he had no wish to proceed on a sabotage mission to America for the Germans. 'In our opinion he would not be content merely with supplying information to us. So much the less would he be content to live the cloistered life of a double agent in this country, who was merely operating a transmitter and going through the motions of committing controlled acts of sabotage. He is already insisting upon being allowed to meet a woman with whom he was formerly associated, and we feel that it is only a matter of time before he asks to be allowed to contact some of his old associates. If this request is made and refused there is no doubt, in our view, but that he will take the law into his own hands. From every personal point of view, therefore, we consider that ZIGZAG should be dispatched from this country.'

The recommendation was that ZIGZAG should return to France by shipping him as a seaman to Lisbon. His cover would be that his act of sabotage, though successful, had resulted in a hue and cry for him, and that he was in consequence compelled to escape from the country. MI5 still had to settle the matter of what ZIGZAG should do after his return to France. He was, himself, extremely keen to indulge in sabotage, 'and it is not impossible that whatever instructions he is given he will nevertheless pursue his own course'. In order to afford him the maximum security it was suggested that he should be told that he was to go back as a counter-espionage agent, whose task was the acquisition of information about the Abwehr, but that he should not look for military information and should not attempt to communicate information of any kind until the British next got into contact with him. He was also to be told to accept any mission offered him by the Germans, and to take the first opportunity available to him of contacting the British or Allied authorities outside Occupied territory.[27]

As ZIGZAG prepared the ground for his departure to Lisbon, Reed reflected, in March 1943, on his charge: 'The case of ZIGZAG has not yet ended. Indeed, time may well prove that it has only just begun.' Reed, like others in the Security Service, retained the fear that, on his return to enemy territory, ZIGZAG would be persuaded, or even forced, to reveal his association with British Intelligence and therefore be in a position to give the enemy whatever information he had gleaned by observation and during conversations; the primary concern, therefore, was the protection of ISOS and the planting, upon ZIGZAG, of false information regarding the capabilities of the British interception organisation to pick up and decode radio messages or intercept and track down any other agents who might be in Britain. Reed's instinct, however, told him that, for now at least, ZIGZAG would remain loyal to the British. This, he felt, had more to do with the radio message from the Germans stating 'impossible pick you up by submarine' which only confirmed what had hitherto been suspected, and went some way to persuading ZIGZAG that the enemy were not over anxious to pay him the £15,000 they had promised him for the De Havilland job.

But what seemed clear to Reed and the Committee, was that this risk had to be taken, given that it was improbable that ZIGZAG could be run as a long-term agent: 'Being by nature an active and adventurous man, abhorring all restraints, he would soon have found odious the constant restrictions upon his liberty and this, together with the very great difficulties of running a long term <u>sabotage</u> agent, presented us with two courses of action. Either we could run him as long as possible and try to prevent him from "going bad" on us (an unenviable and practically an impossible task), or he could be sent back to the enemy to accumulate more information and carry out other plans.'

The chance the XX Committee were taking in sending him back appeared, to Reed, worth it because the prospects opened up by ZIGZAG's return were impressive. 'He maintains that he can embark upon any number of schemes, and it is true that the treatment and care that were lavished on him while in the hands of the enemy give some substance to this statement. He says that he will be allowed to tour Germany as a reward for his endeavours; that he will be able to take up a position in the Dienststelle at Paris, Nantes or Angers; that he could go on another sabotage mission to the United States, or, if his cards are played properly, return to this country with a band of saboteurs for large-scale operations... He believes he could also set up an organisation in France on fifth-column lines which would be intended to stay behind in the event of an Allied invasion. Obviously if he were to obtain control of such an organisation the value to the Allied cause would be immense.' Whether or not such an outcome was realistic seems to have been ignored; Reed, like others within the Service, had clearly fallen under Chapman's spell and seemed to want to believe it was possible. Reed found ZIGZAG:

a most absorbing person. Reckless and impetuous, moody and sentimental, ZIGZAG becomes on acquaintance an extraordinarily likeable character. It is difficult for anyone who has been associated with him for any continuous period to describe him in an unbiased and dispassionate way. Those who have been with him for any length of time will confirm that it was difficult to credit that the man had a despicable past. His crimes of burglary and fraud, his association with 'moral degenerates', and his description as a 'dangerous criminal' by Scotland Yard, was difficult to reconcile with his more recent behaviour. True, small actions like the disappearance of a pair of scissors and a nail file which he had coveted for a time, and his unexplained entry into the case officer's room at the hotel for the purpose of ordering himself dinner and beer, would give rise to some speculation concerning his covetousness and resource.

The fact remains that ZIGZAG submitted to authority, when it was shown to be not unreasonable. His only reaction to a disappointment was to stay in his room for a day, without eating, and go to bed. He was full of stories of his criminal ventures and dispensed the details to an admiring audience with pride and, at times, with some exaggeration.

His love of newspaper publicity was apparent time and time again, and it was continually necessary to explain to him that, though the exploits in which he was notionally engaged would admittedly have been given a 'good press', paper shortage and the currency of a major world war had reduced the amount of interest that the public were considered to show in such matters...

So far ZIGZAG had been honest with his hosts. His demeanour under his first interrogation at Camp 020 was reported as having been frank and straightforward, and it was true that, though his observation may at times have been poor: 'His sincerity in reporting details could hardly be doubted in view of the considerable checks on them, both from other informants and especially from Most Secret Sources [ISOS].' There was, however, an unfortunate trait from which he suffered which, until it was understood, gave rise to the contrary impression: 'ZIGZAG is quite unable to remember times or dates. For example, during an interrogation on his cover story before return to enemy territory he was quite unable to remember what he had done on Christmas day, only six weeks before, in spite of the fact that all that was required for the purposes of the story here was the truth. It is also recorded that, when cross questioned by the Gestapo in France at one time, a subsequent check upon his information showed that he was ten years adrift. Indeed, he was firmly resolved for some days to prosecute the Jersey police for illegal detention, as the only chronology which he could produce for his detention there made it appear that he had served eight months too long in jail.' And, when it became obvious to him that much of the first week or two of his stay with MI5 would be spent in expanding previous information he had given, 'the evening inactivity became odious to ZIGZAG and his inherent boisterousness and vitality soon turned to the path of the inevitable feminine relaxation'. Reed noted that such a reaction was not entirely unforeseen, for advance information had been gathered from ISOS that he was prone to 'undesirable emotional activity'. Many attempts were made to 'sublimate these emotions and direct his energy into more profitable channels'. The speedy production of a questionnaire for his return to France, the construction of ingenious gadgets for sabotage, and the collecting of information of military value, were some of the measures adopted. 'All, however, were but temporary solutions and only caused ZIGZAG to become more restless and venturesome.'

But then, recorded Reed, something changed: 'It is often extraordinary how obvious a course of action seems after it has been taken... the introduction of a specific woman into the case overcame nearly all of this difficulty and re-orientated the whole picture of his emotional problems and his attitude to life.' From April to December 1938 ZIGZAG had lived, as man and wife, with a young woman named Freda Stevenson White at Shepherds Bush. Shortly after he was imprisoned by the Jersey authorities Freda wrote to ZIGZAG saying that he had become a father and that they had a baby daughter. ZIGZAG was unable to reply and Freda's letters to him became increasingly vexed and eventually stopped. The child was now about three and a half years old and shortly after his release from Camp 020, ZIGZAG asked to be allowed to see both Freda and his daughter. Enquiries were made and it was found that Freda was living at Southend-on-Sea, Essex and that she had married but was not living with her husband. She had been making enquiries of the police to trace ZIGZAG, and it was thought that this was in connection with an application for a maintenance allowance.

Since ZIGZAG 'had a criminal record of some distinction' and charges were still outstanding against him which would probably account for a not inconsiderable period of time in prison, MI5 considered it to be unwise for him to see this woman as, if she bore any malice and realised that ZIGZAG was back in Britain, she would probably go to the police and cause an embarrassing situation. 'We therefore refused his request for an immediate reunion and asked him to wait until just before he returned to enemy occupied territory. This refusal had a very bad effect and ZIGZAG became truculent and moody. In this frame of mind he might easily have gone bad on us when he returned and revealed to the enemy his association with us. Even if this did not happen he would probably have been unwilling to carry out any of our instructions and would have acted entirely upon impulse and his own fancies.' Against this, Reed noted that ZIGZAG would have had to explain to the Germans why he had not used the emergency code given – five 'F's' – right from the start of the transmissions. ZIGZAG would have to admit that he had been caught immediately on landing and there would have been no excuse for not including these letters.

During this 'truculent period', ZIGZAG insisted that he was under no obligation to the British authorities and did not wish to return to enemy territory acting under British instructions but to carry out some 'personal' plans of his own. It took some time to extract the nature of these plans, but after exercising considerable patience with him he said that he wanted to return to assassinate Hitler! Dr Graumann had been impressed by ZIGZAG's apparent admiration of all things Nazi and had promised that one day he should be allowed to attend a meeting in Berlin when Hitler was expected to be present. 'It was on this vague promise that ZIGZAG was setting his hopes. When it was suggested that such action as he contemplated was hardly likely to succeed and would, if either successful or abortive, mean a speedy end to his own life, he retorted: "I know. But what a way out!" To depart thus in a blaze of glory, with his name prominently featured throughout the world's press, and to be immortalised in history books for all time – this would crown his final gesture.'

But the entry of Freda White 'represented a turning point in the attitude of ZIGZAG to his work'. In 1941 Freda had married a man called Butchart; but after three months they had parted with mutual disaffection and they continued to live apart. ZIGZAG's divorce had meanwhile been made absolute, and on this 'combination of happy circumstances ZIGZAG has resolved that, on his return to Britain, he would marry Freda as soon as she could obtain a divorce'. Reed noted that: 'This resolution provides a strong incentive for him to return to Allied territory.'[28] As if to prove this point, Chapman desired that all his financial rewards from the Germans should be devoted to his daughter and her mother and to ensure that his daughter should benefit from a good education. He had already given £350 to two officers of B1.A who arranged for Freda to be paid £5 per week from this sum until it was exhausted. ZIGZAG hoped that this arrangement could be made to her indefinitely. To ensure this he was going to try and send some of the money he was to receive from the Germans upon his return to France. If he was to die while on a mission he wanted the British to fulfil his contract with the Germans – £15,000 to be divided equally between Freda and their daughter. ZIGZAG, incidently, was convinced the Germans would pay him. The problem, as another MI5 officer, L.G. Marshall, pointed out, was that ZIGZAG 'did not realise the impracticability of the British authorities being able to extract fulfilment of his contract with the Germans'. Against this, MI5 felt honour bound to arrange something for him: Chapman had volunteered very valuable information that, had MI5 not had access to ISOS, would have been of 'inestimable value'. Furthermore, it was clear that if his *bone fides* was suspected by the Germans and he was subjected to rigorous interrogation 'he will pay with his life'. Against this MI5 could not be absolutely certain that ZIGZAG 'once returned to his friends in Nantes' would remain 100 per cent loyal to the British. In the end the recommendation was to make a substantial payment to ZIGZAG on the basis of his value and loyalty – particularly since the Germans had been particularly generous to him up until now.[29]

ZIGZAG took his first steps towards returning to Occupied Europe when he and Reed left Euston at 10.35 a.m. on Saturday 27 February 1943, and arrived at Liverpool at 3.10 p.m. ZIGZAG would be travelling on board the *City of Lancaster* under an assumed, but real, identity: that of a convicted felon, Hugh Anson. The main difficulty would be in coping with the interrogation, of the Field Security Police and of the members of the crew before the ship set sail. After considerable discussion, it was decided that ZIGZAG's story should be that he, as Anson, spent the last five years in Lewes Gaol and that he had been released on Ticket of Leave, had come to Liverpool and had reported to the Police, after having been offered a job by the Prisoners' Aid Society. This would cover the FSP interrogation on board ship, and if they were to query the Liverpool Police, MI5 could arrange that they would confirm that Hugh Anson had reported to them from London. The first evening in Liverpool was spent in going over the whole of ZIGZAG's cover story to make quite sure that he had everything clear.[30] On board ship ZIGZAG was to tell his companions that he had served a prison sentence and had been told, on release, that he could either go into the Merchant Navy or be allowed to join the Armed Forces. He had been given the job with the assistance of the Prisoner's Aid Society and was trying to 'make good'.[31]

On the following Monday it was agreed that ZIGZAG should be placed on the *Lancaster* as assistant steward. This would excite no suspicion on board the ship as the Chief Steward would be only too pleased to receive additional help. All of this involved the co-operation of senior members of the port authorities. The next step was to make sure the real Hugh Anson was not going to show up: he was thought to have had his last conviction in Preston in July 1941. Reed travelled to Preston police headquarters to confirm this – and other information: he was told that Anson was at present serving in the RAF at Aberdeen, and was expected to leave there in about three weeks when it was thought that he was going home to be married. When Reed returned to his hotel room he found that ZIGZAG had, in some way, managed to obtain entry and was reclining on the bed awaiting dinner which he had ordered on by telephone (together with a number of bottles of beer). ZIGZAG, it emerged, had apparently already been introduced the skipper of the *City of Lancaster*. ZIGZAG was just a little disturbed that the Master of the ship – Captain Kearon – was an Irishman, 'but I reassured him on this point' noted Reed.

The next day, Reed met with Captain Kearon and told him of ZIGZAG's mission. Reed impressed upon him that ZIGZAG's life was from now on in the Captain's hands and that it was absolutely essential that no word of ZIGZAG's mission should become known to any of the crew. ZIGZAG intended to desert in Lisbon and he should be reported to the authorities as a deserter in the same way that all other members of crews who did similar things would be reported. Kearon was given a sealed envelope and asked him to keep it in his safe so that on arrival at Lisbon he, the Captain, would cut the string and destroy the OHMS (On His Majesty's Service) envelope and give ZIGZAG an inner envelope and a revolver. The Captain stated that he had seen ZIGZAG that morning and had got the impression that ZIGZAG was very willing and that no suspicion whatsoever was attached to him. The Captain impressed Reed as being discreet 'and I feel he will co-operate fully'.[32] Thus, ZIGZAG left Liverpool on the 5th March, travelling as Assistant Steward in the name of Hugh Anson on board the *City of Lancaster*. As he sailed for Lisbon he also took with him fourteen sheets of ordinary writing paper, on which intelligence information, supplied by MI5, had been written in secret ink.[33]

It was on the morning of 21 March that information was received by MI5 that focused everyone's attention on the issue of ZIGZAG's loyalty. Commander Montagu of Naval Intelligence telephoned to draw the Security Service's attention to a reference from ISOS which appeared to indicate that ZIGZAG was planning, with the Germans, to commit an act of sabotage against the ship in which he had travelled to Lisbon. Throughout the afternoon discussions took place between Dick White, Commander Montagu, Major Masterman, Reed, D.I. Wilson, and by telephone, with SIS. From this MI5 concluded:

> It was apparent that our objectives must be:
> 1. To protect the ship from sabotage.
> 2. To preserve Most Secret Sources.
> 3. If this could be done at the same time as achieving 1 and 2, not to interrupt ZIGZAG's mission, unless he was, or it seemed probable that he was, double-crossing us.

During the afternoon information was received that Berlin had approved the sabotage proposals suggested by the Abwher in Lisbon.

It seemed probable, though not perhaps altogether certain, that ZIGZAG was either the author of the suggestion or that the suggestion had been communicated to him. If ZIGZAG were really intending to commit the act, then it was essential that he should be brought back under arrest. If he was merely pretending to commit this act, either at his own suggestion because he thought it 'would build him up' in the eyes of the Germans, or because the Germans suggested it and he did not see how to refuse, there were four possibilities:

1. That ZIGZAG would merely dispose of the sabotage material in a harmless way without informing anyone.
2. That ZIGZAG would inform the Master but that neither he nor the Master would inform any British authority in Lisbon for fear of prejudicing ZIGZAG.
3. That either from ZIGZAG or through the Master information of the Germans attempt would be given to the British authorities in Lisbon.
4. That ZIGZAG would, through the Master, endeavour to communicate details of the plot to us on the Master's return to England.

It was clear to MI5 that: 'Whatever view we took of ZIGZAG's character and patriotism we could not run the risk of taking it for granted that he would not, in fact, commit the sabotage.'[34]

Reed was despatched to Lisbon, arriving on 23 March, to try and ascertain what the true state of affairs was. There he met with Mr Jarvis of SIS who told Reed that Captain Kearon had been interviewed but denied emphatically that 'Hugh Anson', who had jumped ship, had anything to do with British Intelligence – as far as he was concerned. Kearon had, furthermore, denied that he had been told anything about Anson. Reed explained that Kearon was probably denying all knowledge of ZIGZAG because he had been told by the MI5 officer that he should tell 'absolutely no one' about the intelligence and that once they left Liverpool, ZIGZAG's life would thereafter be in his hands. Reed, passing under the name of Mr Johnston, met with Kearon at the Royal British Club – recognition between the two was immediate. Captain Kearon explained that ZIGZAG had given him a bomb, disguised as a piece of coal. It was now deposited in the Captain's safe on board ship. Kearon, understandably was keen to get the bomb off his ship.

After being filled in by Kearon on what he knew about ZIGZAG's movements, Reed had to address the issue of the bomb's disposal. Although ZIGZAG had said that the explosive in the coal was worked by a detonator that became active under the application of heat, it was possible the Germans might have planted explosive apparatus which was activated by an acid delay. Jarvis pointed out that 'it would be most unfortunate' if an explosion were to take place in the plane during Reed's return journey home 'both for the plane, the political consequences and myself'. It was arranged, therefore, that the explosive coal should be placed in a heavy iron box, to deaden the force of the explosion should one occur, and sent to Gibraltar in the care of Captain Kearon where arrangements would be made for dealing with it there.[35]

By now Chapman was far from Lisbon. When the *Lancaster* docked there, ZIGZAG went ashore with some of the crew and, while taking a drink with them, slipped away to find his Abwher contact to whom he was to give the password 'Joli ALBERT'. He went to the address he had been given only to find no contact there except a woman who opened the door but knew nothing about his code word. However, she put him on to his contact by telephone; but he did not know anything about the code word either. They agreed to meet anyway. He returned the next day to be greeted by two men who took notes of his story. The following day he was introduced to Dr Baumann.[36] After establishing contact, ZIGZAG returned to the *Lancaster* and offered the captain his revolver – which he had taken with him in case there was trouble – as a present. ZIGZAG and Kearon then made arrangements for a fight to take place on board ship in which ZIGZAG would be involved. Knives were accordingly drawn in the stewards' pantry between ZIGZAG and another steward. No substantial injury was sustained by either party; later ZIGZAG started another fight with a second steward which was fought by Marques of Queensbury rules only to be terminated by the steward butting ZIGZAG in the face and causing one of his eyes to swell slightly. ZIGZAG considered that such an injury to his face would give confirmation of his story to the Germans that he had a rough passage at the hands of his companions on board ship.[37]

In due course Baumann, whom ZIGZAG was visiting each day, announced that permission had been granted by Berlin to carry out an act of sabotage on the *Lancaster*. He handed ZIGZAG two coal-bombs. These he was to place among the coal in the ship's bunkers in such a position that they would be soon used. The explosion would occur instantly after their introduction to the furnace. Returning in the early hours to his ship, the bombs secreted on his person, ZIGZAG found a sailor occupying his bunk. When he ordered the man out a fight took place when, 'encumbered by the awkward position of the black luggage he was carrying', ZIGZAG received a black eye and cut lip. Having disposed of the sailor, ZIGZAG, when serving the Captain early morning tea, took the opportunity of handing over the bombs to him for safe keeping. He asked the Master to take the bombs back to England and pass them to the authorities in London. Kearon was, at first, alarmed and wished to start at once for Britain. He was persuaded, however, to carry on his usual routine and act as if nothing had happened. After reporting to Kearon, later in the morning, ZIGZAG left the ship. He rang up Baumann and informed him that he placed the bombs but had an accident, mentioning his fight with the sailor. Baumann, believing ZIGZAG to be in danger, decided to get him away from Lisbon as quickly as possible. By 11 a.m. a plane was made available to take him to Madrid.[38] ZIGZAG was aware that the fact the ship would not be sunk would eventually come to the knowledge of the Germans in due course with possible fatal results to himself. Nevertheless, he thought that the value to the British of getting examples of the devices used by the Germans justified the risk to himself.[39]

The British now knew that ZIGZAG had not betrayed them. A plan – DAMP SQUID 1 – was devised to convince the Germans that ZIGZAG's sabotage mission had been a success. It was hoped that ZIGZAG's bomb would arrive in the UK – being removed perhaps in Gibraltar – before the *City of Lancaster* did, so that its form and functions could be confirmed. When the ship docked in the UK, Reed was to board the ship in the guise of a Customs official, Customs themselves having been informed. Reed was to contact the ship's Master and obtain his permission to plant a 'bomb', provided by B1.C – MI5's anti-sabotage unit – in one of the ship's bunkers although not the one from which the coal would normally be taken. The bomb was to be brought on board in an attaché case, by Reed, and having obtained the Master's approval he was to pass it to Customs official 'X'. 'X', having previously been at MI5 for tuition in working the bomb, was to proceed and 'examine' the bunker for contraband. He was then to place the bomb in the bunker, start the fuse and retire making certain that no one entered the room until after the explosion. The delay would be approximately three minutes between starting the fuse and the explosion. Upon hearing the explosion, Customs official 'X' was to fall down and pretend that he had hurt his arm which would be bandaged up by Kearon. All members of the crew were to be interrogated from the point of view of them being responsible for causing the explosion and the possibility of a bomb having been put on board at the last port of call, or the port before that.[40] A copy of the bomb, after examination in Gibraltar, had been prepared by Baron

Victor Rothschild of B1.C. To do this he employed Lieutenant Colonel L.J.C. Wood, of the Royal Engineers and the Experimental Station of the War Office, who informed Rothschild: 'Herewith your three toys: one for you to try for yourself – not in a house! The other two for your friend to play with.' Wood emphasised that the 'toy is rather fragile and will probably break if dropped'. Reassuringly, there was 'no danger of it going off'.[41] His Lordship replied: 'Looking forward to one of the biggest bangs in history (I refer to the one after Damp Squib).'[42]

Plan DAMP SQUID 1, however, was not set in stone and flexibility dictated the need for an alternative option. The Germans had shown the greatest interest in the *Lancaster* and were anxious to discover if the act of sabotage actually took place and whether it was successful or not. It seemed that the only satisfactory way of convincing the Germans of ZIGZAG's reliability and his competence would be by staging an actual explosion on board and making sure that an account of this explosion ultimately reached them.

The problem, however, was that it seemed impossible to have a bogus explosion on board during the voyage since such an explosion would not deceive the crew or else would be too dangerous and harmful. Owing to the length of time that had elapsed 'it would be too dangerous a coincidence' to stage the explosion just when the *Lancaster* docked in the UK. In addition it was thought undesirable to take a new set of people into MI5's confidence as would be necessary if an explosion were to be arranged at port. In consequence it was proposed that all members of the crew would be questioned separately. The result of the enquiry would be that all the members of the crew 'would feel convinced that some curious incident had happened during the voyage, of which he, however, was uniformed'. When the *Lancaster* next touched at Lisbon, German sub-agents would certainly try and get in touch with members of the crew. 'They will succeed in two or three cases; but they cannot question the crew closely, and will only elicit from them garbled and differing accounts of what happened. The only certain thing is that these low sub-agents will get the impression (probably in most cases from some intoxicated seaman) that something curious had happened on the voyage because there was a formidable enquiry when the ship returned to the UK. This is all that is necessary to get across to the Germans in order to build up ZIGZAG.'[43]

On 23 April, St George's Day, Reed arrived in Glasgow, where the *Lancaster* was to dock. There he consulted with the SCO, Major Brown, and his deputy, Captain Simpson. They discussed the options – either conducting a search of the ship, interrogating the crew and discovering the unexploded device; or exploding the dummy bomb on board. It was thought, however, that this coincidence of an explosion as the ship was searched was so unlikely a coincidence as to arouse considerable suspicion. The *Lancaster* arrived at Rothesay Dock at 4 p.m. She was then boarded by the SCO's party in the normal way. A quarter of an hour later, Reed and Brown went on board. Everyone played their parts as if the unfolding drama was real. Captain Kearon was asked if he had anything to report about his trip: he replied that there had been no crew changes except for a man called Anson who had deserted in Lisbon. The interrogation of the crew then began, paying particular attention to any information concerning Anson. The interrogations lasted until 5.30 p.m. At this point Major Brown reported to the Captain that a result of an examination of Anson's belongings had revealed certain incriminating papers and that, as a consequence of reports concerning the actions of this man while on board, it was considered necessary to conduct a thorough rummage of the ship; the Captain's permission was asked for and granted. Captain Kearon appeared surprised but sent for the Chief Engineer and Chief Steward and asked them to give Brown every assistance.

A thorough search of the ship was made and a number of men were detailed to search the coal bunkers and told to report immediately if they should encounter any suspicious objects. The search continued until 8.45 p.m. when Major Brown returned to the Captain's cabin holding an object in his hand that looked like a lump of coal. He reported that Lieutenant Whitley, one of his staff, had found this object on one of the side bunkers and that it certainly contained explosive material as there was a slight hole in the side of the coal which had been damaged and probably contained a detonator. The search was called off and the crew were allowed to go ashore if they wished to do so. The Chief Engineer was called to Kearon's cabin and was told about the discovery. The hope that the rumour mill would then start was confirmed when, later, a member of the local Security Control Officer staff boarded the *Algerian* and was informed that its crew had heard that some sabotage equipment had been found on board the *Lancaster*.[44] Even the Prime Minister was following the dramatic events that were unfolding in the ZIGZAG case. Churchill showed 'considerable interest' in the case and Duff Cooper, the head of the Security Executive (overseeing intelligence matters) wanted TAR Robertson to let him know if and when contact was re-established with ZIGZAG.[45] The deception worked. ZIGZAG's prestige was enhanced and his position protected.

BRUTUS is Arrested

In the meantime another of MI5's flamboyant XX agents was busy getting himself into trouble. On 17 June 1943, Chris Harmer received a message that Colonel Gano, of the Polish Secret Service, wished to see him extremely urgently as a very grave and urgent matter had arisen in connection with the BRUTUS case. Harmer went to see him straight away and was informed that a warrant had been issued for the arrest of BRUTUS as he had been found to be responsible in some degree for the publication of an illegal Polish newspaper. Gano had at that time in his office the Captain of Gendarmerie of the Polish Air Force who was charged with the execution of the warrant. Gano was in rather an excited state and annoyed and upset by this development. He said that he had wanted to see Harmer in order that he might be present, if necessary, while BRUTUS's flat was searched, so that MI5 might extract any papers relating to his XX activities. At that moment none of the Poles knew where BRUTUS was but Harmer was in a position to tell them that he knew. BRUTUS was in fact working his transmitter.

By now, in addition to the Polish Air Force Captain, Squadron Leader Chaney of the Air Ministry, Captain Derbyshire, and two Special Branch Officers were now present in Harmer's company. Harmer ascertained from Captain Derbyshire that a warrant had been set in motion after Squadron Leader Chaney had received information from his contact in the Polish Air Force that they were on the track of an illegal pamphlet that was being circulated by certain dissident circles within the Polish Air Force. He was given the names of various officers, five in all, who were implicated and against whom the Poles were issuing warrants. He was asked to co-operate in obtaining search warrants in order that their apartments might be searched. Chaney communicated with Derbyshire, who made the arrangements through Special Branch. Unfortunately, BRUTUS's name as transmitted to Derbyshire was spelt wrongly, so it was not until Harmer met Derbyshire that he realised that this particular officer was identical with BRUTUS. BRUTUS was arrested after his return from lunch; the assembled party took him down to his flat searched it, and found there a duplicator and copies of the current edition of 'In Defence of our Comrades', all ready to be sent out. Derbyshire asked BRUTUS what had caused him to do this, and he replied that any patriotic Pole would have done likewise. Squadron Leader Chaney asked him where the typewriter used was but BRUTUS refused to tell him.

Gano's fears about the whole affair were based, first, on the fact that it would put him in an awkward position that one of his officers should have been implicated; and, second, he was terrified lest BRUTUS should try and justify and defend himself by saying that he had done it in order to help 'Le grand jeu' – The Great Game – and claim that he had been given authority to act in this way. Gano saw BRUTUS for a few minutes on his arrest and reminded him that the security of his work was of paramount importance and must not be revealed to anybody in any circumstances, even to any Court Martial. With the searching of BRUTUS's flat, Gano became visibly relieved and almost cheerful about the whole affair, saying that it had turned out to be a thing of little importance and he had feared it would be much more grave: the pamphlet contained violent attacks on nearly all the senior officers of the Polish Air Force, and would probably be dealt with on the basis of an air force Court Martial for breach of discipline, and not for political offences such as treachery or mutiny.

But BRUTUS's arrest caused a problem for MI5 in terms of contact with the Germans. Harmer urgently sought an interview with his agent and, fortunately, was granted one by the Judge of the Court Martial. His only purpose was to arrange the text of a message that could be then sent over by W/T to the Germans. The message cooked up by Harmer and BRUTUS stated:

> My collaborators in the field of the newspaper ALARM [an underground Polish Army journal] are being searched for by the police. I foresee my arrest as very probable. I am going to hide my set and all compromising documents. I am hoping for the best but the situation is very dangerous. In the future listen only every Sunday, even if you have to go on for a long time.

Another W/T operator imitated BRUTUS and sent this message, on 18 June, so far as Harmer could gather with complete success. The substitute operator was confident of a good imitation as BRUTUS 'is very easy to imitate, because he is a very bad operator and commits very distinctive faults'. The message was seen and approved by Gano, and he and Harmer jointly came to the conclusion that it was the only course they could take 'since it would enable us, if BRUTUS is imprisoned, to close down, leaving the Germans to think that he served them faithfully and was caught. On the other hand, if the whole affair is over in a week or two, it gives an explanation which could be verified by the Germans if they had any means of enquiry over here.'

At Harmer's interview with BRUTUS, the latter apologised for the harm he had done to the 'Great Game'. He said it was the only thing he regretted, and apart from that his conscience was clear. He had seen the Polish Air Force mis-managed in peace time and the same officers were now in control in Britain. It was the duty of somebody to expose this, and he was the only person in a position to do so. He was quite certain the Court would justify his action and the whole affair would be over in a few weeks. All MI5 could do now await developments.[46]

As the facts began to emerge, it seemed to Harmer that, from the moment BRUTUS arrived and set up an establishment at 41 Redcliffe Square, he was having meetings of his compatriots, who were largely air force officers, to discuss matters of current interest. At the beginning, these meetings appeared to be principally to discuss the preparation of BRUTUS's treatise on the organisation of an efficient network of agents on the Continent. His relations with a good many officers of the Polish Deuxieme Bureau were, of course, 'very bad, not only because he had held back his true story and made fools of them', but also because at the Commission afterwards which enquired into his conduct he was 'very roughly' handled by Major Zychon. In addition to this, he 'not unnaturally threw his weight' about in the Deuxieme Bureau 'and gave himself airs' about his experiences in the field. Added to all this was the fact that 'he is a vain and conceited man' and, moreover, a man who had spent a considerable period of the war in exciting activities and now found himself doing a largely academic job. The result of this, except for a few of the younger officers and Colonel Gano who had gone to great lengths to remain loyal to BRUTUS, was that 'he got at loggerheads' with all the other officers in the Polish Deuxieme Bureau. The mutual antipathy was increased by the fact that when Colonel Gano came to study his recommendations for the network of agents in Europe, it was found that it was a 'totally impracticable scheme and, however nice it looked on paper, it would be impossible to realise'. BRUTUS 'did not like being told this'.

It was apparent from the start that BRUTUS was involved in minor intrigues in the Deuxième Bureau, and it appeared, in the light of subsequent events, that BRUTUS 'must have also started intriguing' in the affairs of the Polish Air Force in the spring of 1943. In the spring there occurred a rupture of Russian/Polish relations, due to the discovery at Katyn of thousands of corpses of Polish officers murdered by the Soviets and the publication of the details on German radio. Concurrently with the political aspect was the opposition among the Polish Air Force in Britain to the then Inspector General, General Ujejski. The younger members of the Polish Air Force were strongly opposed to this man, not only because he had held the office since several years before the war, but also because he had never been a pilot and owed his position to political intrigue in Poland in peacetime. As was 'so eloquently stated' in the pamphlet subsequently written by BRUTUS, Ujejski graduated to the Air office 'through the captive balloon section'.

Then, on 22 December 1942, the 25th anniversary of the Red Army, there was a reception at the Soviet Embassy which was attended by General Ujejski. This was resented by various leading Polish pilots, among them Squadron Leader Poziomek who, with certain of his colleagues, addressed a protest to the President of Poland, and this, contrary to military law, was passed to him direct and not through the usual channels. This protest was a dramatically phrased document about 'dishonour to Polish uniform', and violently anti-Russian. General Ujejski found out about the letter and had the Polish airmen responsible imprisoned for breach of military discipline. This caused intense indignation amongst the junior officers of the air force, and particulars were publicised in various underground pamphlets circulating amongst the Polish Forces, amongst them a journal circulating in the Polish Army 'Alarm', which was thought to be a successor of, or connected with, a previous anti-Russian underground pamphlet called 'Walka' which had been exposed and closed down. 'Alarm', which was also circulating in the Polish Army, closed down voluntarily. It appeared that BRUTUS then got together certain of his friends, purchased a duplicating machine and produced many copies of a pamphlet entitled 'In defence of our colleagues', which 'exposed' the whole history of the Ujejski/ Poziomek affair and set out a short biography of General Ujejski, 'which on any showing is tantamount to the gravest military indiscipline, and which is tainted throughout with violent anti-Russian sentiments'. In some way the Security Department of the Polish Air Force got to hear that this pamphlet was being published, and on 17 June 1943, BRUTUS was arrested. BRUTUS was held in detention by the Poles first of all in London, and afterwards sent to Scotland, where he remained in custody for six weeks. From there he wrote a series of letters to MOUSTIQUE, which were of no importance in themselves, 'but which demonstrate a desire to dramatise himself and his life and a capacity for exhibitionism which almost suggests the first signs of delusions of grandeur'.

BRUTUS was released on 24 July by the Polish military authorities, pending Court Martial. His release was probably due to various factors, principally the sudden death of General Sikorski and the appointment of General Sosnkowski as Commander in Chief. The latter was apparently anxious to have as little bitterness as possible in the Polish Forces, and was, in addition, himself reputed to be anti-Russian.

Shortly after taking over he retired General Ujejski and substituted a new Air Staff, including BRUTUS's friend Poziomek, who became deputy Chief of Staff. 'From that time onwards BRUTUS's Court Martial appeared to all intents and purposes to have been a farce.' On the one hand it was impossible to interfere with the course of justice once it had been set in motion and the court martial had to proceed; on the other hand the Supreme Military and Air Force authorities were 'obviously anxious to hush the whole matter up as much as possible'. From a XX point of view, the case had been discontinued until he was released from prison, when a message was sent on 22 August, in which BRUTUS reported his arrest, detention in Scotland and his release.[47]

On 19 August, Harmer had seen BRUTUS and settled the message to be sent the Germans on 22 August. It was, in Harmer's opinion, 'a bit long-winded, but he is in any event long-winded and if we cut it down I think we could only do so at the expense of clarity'. In it BRUTUS informed the Germans of the following:

> The 20th June arrested in the clandestine anti-Russian affair. Detained in Scotland. After enquiry finished freed the 24th July. Liberty to stay in London. Await trial during September. Foresee light punishment and probably after the war. Fear I am being watched at present. Until the end of the trial too dangerous to transmit but could write if you gave me immediately an address in Lisbon and the best method of secret ink. Will listen each Sunday at mid-day London time for reply. Send message blind, repeating it twice. I regret difficulties. Morale good. Am hopeful. Greetings.

After agreeing the message, the conversation turned to the Pole's Court Martial. Harmer asked BRUTUS whether he had any news. He said that he thought it might be a few weeks yet before the actual trial, but he did not anticipate a severe sentence as the other aviators involved had received fairly nominal sentences, some of them only to operate after the war. BRUTUS then asked Harmer what he recommended him to do about his Court Martial. Harmer replied that he could not give him any advice in an official capacity, but as a private individual it seemed to him that his position was clear: according to BRUTUS, General Ujejski was being relieved of his post and, therefore, BRUTUS's objective as stated by him had been achieved. In these circumstances it seemed to Harmer to be an act of folly on BRUTUS's part to try and justify at his Court Martial everything that he had done: 'I said it seemed to me that he would stand a much better chance of being treated leniently if he appeared at the Court and expressed regret. If, on the other hand, he tried to justify his attack on General Ujejski, he would put the Judges in the impossible position of either having to find that General Ujejski had been guilty of dereliction in his duty as Inspector General of the Polish Forces, or of justifying the General, which would imply a severe sentence on BRUTUS.'

BRUTUS, Harmer thought, was impressed by this argument and said that if the accusation against him, which he had not yet received, merely accused him of indiscipline he would throw his carefully prepared justification into the fire and admit that he had acted irregularly. If, on the other hand, it accused him of more serious offences, then he would have to reconsider the matter. 'He referred to the matter again as we were walking away from our meeting, and it is obvious I think that I have given him something to think about. Altogether he was in a much more reasonable frame of mind. I drummed in to him on this occasion, and shall continue to do so whenever possible, that the work he is doing for us is of the utmost importance if it is worth doing at all, and that it is essential that he refrains from other forms of activity.'

Despite all the problems he had caused MI5, Harmer made an argument to his superiors for reopening the BRUTUS case: 'In doing so I will try and analyse the evidence as objectively as possible, but I am bound to be influenced to some degree by the fact that BRUTUS is potentially the best case, in my view, that I have been given to run.' As the Case Officer concerned, Harmer felt justified in saying: 'If I can run the case until Christmas, I can present you with a very good channel.' The advantages seemed to him to be the following:

1. All the evidence of fact which we have goes to show that BRUTUS is believed, more so, so far as I can see, than other agents whom we build up with great care and attention.

2. The messages received show that BRUTUS is getting questions on the same level as GARBO, i.e. if the channel is believed it is a high-grade one.

3. It is a wireless link and a link with Paris, and of all our circuits my own view is that the Paris one should be the best for our purposes. In this respect I think BRUTUS, if he could ever be established, might even be a better wireless link than GARBO. This is not on the question of reliability but on the geographical position to which he works.

4. We might turn the case into a money-making concern. When we broke off communication, the possibility of their sending him

over some money looked promising. I think we could well do with this money.

5. BRUTUS may quite easily be built up by the circumstances of his arrest and imprisonment.

If, however, the decision to re-open the case 'is against me, I put forward the following very tentatively as an alternative. I suggest that we use the station as a channel of communication between the British and German Intelligence Services. That is to say that we lead off with a message somewhat as follows: "We have caught your man. It was clever of you to recruit him, but we know everything now. We think he is a little mad, and so we are not going to shoot him. We will, however, communicate with you from time to time to discuss matters of mutual interest." After that my idea would be to use the channel as a mixture of propaganda and an effort to bribe or cajole an officer of the Abwehr either to discuss general matters or come over here, with the idea of getting information out of him or deceiving him.'[48]

BRUTUS was kept waiting until the end of November 1943 before the Court Martial proceedings actually started; meanwhile he was given a job in the Planning Office at Polish Headquarters. He continued to hold meetings at his house, and these meetings continued to discuss political affairs. He, in addition, 'declined to give any promise that he will not interfere in Polish internal affairs, explaining that it is impossible in the Polish Forces to divorce politics from military matters, that the two are intermingled and that if any interest was taken in the country's affairs it was necessary also to interfere in military matters'.

Finally the Court Martial started on 26 November and finished on 9 December. BRUTUS was condemned to fortress imprisonment for two months, from which the six weeks in prison in Scotland were to be deducted, leaving a fortnight's further imprisonment, which was deferred until after the war. The position, therefore, was that BRUTUS had received a nominal punishment only for his admitted military indiscipline. Harmer's assessment was that BRUTUS 'has probably come out of it a little tinpot hero in the eyes of his fellow Polish airmen'. The young airmen had been placated by a complete reorganisation of the Staff of the Polish Air Force, and it was understood that, as a result of further Polish intrigue, Colonel Gano and Major Zychon were both retiring from the Polish Deuxieme Bureau and were being replaced by officers brought from the Middle East. BRUTUS, meanwhile, was still working in the Planning Office 'and his personal position would appear to be better than his conduct warrants'.[49] As it turned out Harmer would but be one of thousands who would be glad that BRUTUS, for all his faults, was the man he was.

Turf War
MI5's Battle with SIS Over ISOS

The SIS department responsible for counter-intelligence was Section V, a unit at one time headed by Valentine Vivian – the son of Comley Vivian, the Victorian portrait painter – who had been recruited from the Indian police in 1923.[1] Shortly before the outbreak of war, Vivian recruited Felix Cowgill, Deputy Commissioner of the Special Branch in Calcutta. Cowgill had served in the Indian police from 1923 where he had conducted a detailed study of Communism in India and written a significant account of the subversive threat from that source, in 1933. Cowgill took up his new post, in London, in February 1939[2] and went on to reorganise Section V along geographical sections: an individual case officer became an expert on the enemy's activities in a certain theatre by being assigned geographical regions.[3] This was entirely different from the subject basis that MI5 had utilised to organise its counter-espionage cases. Of more importance was that Cowgill's intelligence background convinced him of a fundamental principle: that advance information of an enemy's intention was of little value unless security was watertight.[4] A turf war developed between MI5 and SIS over Cowgill's desire to have sole responsibility for the security of ISOS and for controlling its use; and, at the same time, his desire to confine the Security Service to any action and to the recording of intelligence within the three-mile territorial limit of the United Kingdom and any other British territory. This gave rise to a long drawn out controversy which was also marked by the failure of SIS – in the Security Service's view – to maintain adequate records for counter-espionage action outside British territorial limits – which then had consequences inside the United Kingdom. The obvious example of this conflict was Cowgill's restrictions concerning the intercepted ISOS material. And MI5 were desperate to secure greater access to ISOS because it:

1. It led to the identification and arrest of spies.
2. It filled in – in the course of time – a large and detailed background picture of the Abwehr and SD [Sicherheitsdienst or Nazi Security Service] organisations, their methods of working, their technique of espionage, their cover addresses, their secret inks, the identity of their officers and relations with other parts of the German military machine.

3. It supplied information regarding the technique of sabotage, especially against British shipping, and thereby assisted in the development of counter-measures by the Security Service.

4. It provided a valuable means of checking the elaborate and complicated working of an extensive ring of double agents manipulated by the Security Service.

5. It provided information of operational value, e.g. the formation or assembly of Abwehr Commandos before and in the neighbourhood of a projected German advance.

6. It provided political information e.g. the nature and extent of Spanish collaboration with the Germans.

7. It provided valuable material concerning the German organisation and its detailed working which was used with good effect in order to obtain information during the course of interrogation.

A second point was that ISOS material allowed MI5 to instigate the arrest of enemy agents in British territory, on the high seas, or for the purpose of interrogating suspected agents. MI5's view was that Cowgill's 'excess of security by isolation' not only served no useful purpose 'but should not have occurred' because all the different parts of the intelligence organisation existed in order to achieve the same objective: the arrest of enemy agents and the compilation, and use for that purpose, of all relevant intelligence. For MI5 the restriction of ISOS access increased the risk of a failure to act in matters of Security Service responsibility, such as the prevention of sabotage in 'the mistaken aim of ensuring an impossible degree of security', which was impossible because Security Service action was often based on wireless interception and necessarily became known to many hundreds of people in the Security Service, in SIS and in the intelligence and operational staffs of the armies in the field. Thus the 'practical value and use of ISOS material was marred by a failure to co-ordinate the machinery dealing with it'.

So, for example, a small fraction of the wireless of the RSHA Intelligence Service (the Reichsicherheitshautamt or Nazi Party Security Agency) was intercepted in 1940 and 1941, but 'at the instance of Colonel Cowgill this suddenly stopped'; and in June 1941, 'after it had been withheld for some time,' MI5 came to hear 'unofficially' that there were references on it to an attempt by the SD to arrange for British telephone directories to be smuggled out to them through Japanese diplomatic channels. Copies of these messages were only obtained, after a considerable delay, and as a result of a request to Section V for information. When a general request was for the whole series was made, Section V replied that it was of no counter-espionage interest and they had adequate machinery for passing on any material of a counter-espionage nature. 'In fact,' noted Jack Curry, 'it was of the greatest interest and importance.' For the Security Service the event proved that the machinery in Section V was 'not adequate at that time, and for a long time afterwards' to formulate a proper appreciation of this SD material which 'as a result of inadequate knowledge about Nazi Germany they did not understand'. Such was the lack of information coming from SIS that B Division were, at this time, even ignorant that the letters 'SD' in ISOS material stood for Sicherheitsdienst, the Nazi Security Service: 'At the instance of Section V they had interpreted them as representing an unexplained "Sicherheitsdienst".' It was only when the facts came to the notice of the Security Service's Research section that MI5 discovered the importance of the SD. This was in early 1942.

Cowgill also decided that the MI5 interrogators, based at Camp 020, should not be allowed the undisguised text of intercepted messages relating to agents or suspects whom they were interrogating; instead only blanketed versions were to be provided. It was only after a great deal of argument, and subject to the restriction that Guy Liddell should personally decide on the appropriate arrangements in each case, that Cowgill waived his objection. And it was only as a result of 'a slip on the part of someone in Section V' that it was discovered, in April 1942, that GC & CS had been instructed to withhold certain ISOS messages that were believed, 'very often mistakenly', to refer to British agents in the field. By the time these facts were disclosed it 'came out' that more than a hundred messages had been withheld from MI5, some of which directly concerned double agents who were operating under Security Service control. In spite of the 'obvious importance' of these facts it was only after protracted negotiations that it was agreed that this type of message – known as ISBA – should be supplied to B Division 'and then only on the unreasonable and useless proviso that they should be received and kept personally by the Director'.

The difficulties between Cowgill and MI5 manifested themselves in virtually all areas of contact. In May 1941 arrangements were made for a fortnightly meeting of a joint committee to be composed of Section V and Security Service officers to consider the technical aspects of RSS's radio interception work. Cowgill aimed at confining the discussions to these technical aspects and to the question of regulating the priority of the various ISOS services. But, as 'was inevitable', the intelligence content of the messages formed the basis of discussion and many members of the Committee were persuaded that the representatives of the Intelligence Directorates of the Services who received the ISOS material as well as representatives of GC & CS ought to attend the meetings. They were also convinced that the terms of reference should be extended to deal with any aspect of the problems arising from the interception including questions of their intelligence content. SIS opposed this and attempted to have the Committee closed down on the ground that it had outlived its usefulness in spite of the fact that all of its members, with the exception of Cowgill, were agreed that the terms of reference and the membership should be extended. With the assistance of Mr Reilly, of the Foreign Office – and also at that time the personal assistant to C – a decision was obtained, in 1943, on the lines desired by MI5.

Over time, MI5 officers formed the opinion that the ISOS material could only be properly exploited as the result of analysis by experts who were in a position to make a complete study of the whole material including a large quantity of undeciphered material. A body of qualified experts existed in SIS's Section VW under Major Trevor-Roper assisted by Palmer of the Intelligence Section of GC & CS. According to Jack Curry, however, Cowgill, 'had a different opinion' and regarded these experts as 'unreliable' on the ground that they made mistakes by basing themselves on the internal evidence of the texts without access to other sources of information. His view was contested on the ground that what was required was to integrate the evidence obtained by an analysis of the texts with information available from other sources. Cowgill then claimed that the personnel of Section V were 'the experts in the interpretation of this material and the proper staff to decide questions of making use of it conjunction with other information'. MI5's view, however, was that Section V was handicapped by the fact that they were divided into subsections on a geographical basis and studied the material after dividing it into corresponding geographical groupings with the result that their 'inexpert and more or less isolated subsections' were unable to understand much of the material or to see it as a whole as could be done by experts in VW. The Security Service pressed for the extension of VW's role because it was convinced of the value of their analyses. As a result the subsection was ultimately separated from Section V and in 1943 became a separate department of SIS directly responsible to C with the title of RIS.[5]

But this was after the heads of MI5 and SIS went head to head in a bitter turf war in 1942 concerning a Security Service suggestion that its B Division should merge with Section V. On 7 April, Sir David Petrie despatched a letter to Sir Stewart Menzies, informing him 'that once again relations are not very happy' between Section V and MI5. 'Something,' wrote Petrie, 'will have to be done.' The DG suggested that, instead of something palliative: 'We... look a little deeper and see if we can't overcome the root cause of the trouble.' As a beginning, Petrie asked if C would like to come and see him for a preliminary talk.[6] C and the DG met three days later to discuss the crisis. A memorandum on closer SIS–MI5 co-operation was subsequently drawn up by the Security Service and presented to Menzies with, explained Petrie, 'the single purpose of doing better a most important job, which is a joint responsibility for both of us, and a heavy one at that, since the stake is no less than the whole of national security'. Petrie emphasised that MI5 approached the question purely on its merits and one of organisation and efficiency with any discussion conducted 'in an atmosphere free of the slightest taint of personalities'.[7]

MI5's general case for the merging of Section V and B Division was on the basis that the German 'did not recognise our artificial divisions of home and foreign but operates without regard to geographical or other boundaries'. The responsibility for meeting 'this attack', from whatever quarter directed, 'rests on the Security Service'. And MI5 needed as complete a picture as possible of the enemy machine, including its centres of activity, methods, communications, and personnel: 'If it is to meet the attack, it must know all it can of the forces mastering to deliver it, and of their plans and intentions.' But the existing system led to considerable conflict of opinion as to how far the material available could be used practically. The simplest method of securing 'unified control' would be that SIS should no longer handle counter-espionage as a subject. 'It should act as a getting agency for counter-espionage, as it does for operational intelligence. At present we use two hands not directed by a single body, and the one does not always know what the other is doing.' The whole of the counter-espionage effort was in danger because of the tendency to 'bottle' or withhold information on the grounds that it was the concern of one department but not of the other. This could be a 'recipe for defeat' with the German Secret Service allowed to work its will unrestricted 'with the risk it may win the [intelligence] war while we continue to pile up material instead of using what we now know to paralyse and defeat the enemy forces'. MI5 declared that the collection of counter-espionage had 'one paramount object: to defend the UK, British possessions overseas and the British Armed Forces from the activities of the German Secret Service'.[8]

In his reply Menzies stated that it was 'unnatural' that MI5 should wish to assume a responsibility of the nature of which 'it has no detailed knowledge, and which the department as a whole is unadapted by experience or training to fulfil'. For C, one of the central and primary factors governing Secret Service work in foreign countries was that it could only be directed safely and effectively by an organisation having, on the one hand, a detailed knowledge of the subjects of investigation and, on the other, an equally close knowledge of the local conditions governing 'our work abroad and an even closer knowledge of our foreign organisations, their potentialities, their strengths and their defects'. If the object of Petrie's proposal was to avoid duplication 'it could only do so at the cost of stultification'. For, having transferred Section V to MI5, 'I should either have to rebuild Section V *de novo*, thereby doubling any duplication' or 'submit to being turned into a post-office'. Menzies could hardly believe that Petrie's long experience of administration would commend to the DG such a state of affairs.

Menzies also rejected the case for the amalgamation of SIS and MI5 on the grounds for which this had been rejected previously – in 1927 and 1931 i.e. that the whole outlook and technique of the two organisations were fundamentally different (the former collecting information by covert means in foreign countries generally against the laws of those countries and the latter engaged in preventative security work on British soil) and 'unadapted to unified control'. C, thus, did not want to waste time over details 'if the fundamental principles are unsound and impracticable'. Menzies also refused to relinquish, as Director of GC & CS, any responsibility for the any portion of its output or that Section V should receive orders from any department outside his control. And, as for the dangers and inconvenience of separation: 'I cannot but feel that they have been exaggerated.' All of C's experience had shown that the separation of operatives from their records had far greater dangers and inconveniences that the separation of one set of operatives from another. It was precisely this factor that persuaded C to locate his central registry and Section V in close proximity to each other. Petrie's proposal to sub-divide C's records would be 'quite impracticable' because all records had to be available to SIS's sections. After examining everything, Menzies concluded: 'I do not feel inclined to agree that Axis espionage is, like Peace, one and indivisible.'[9]

Petrie's reply was blunt. He was disappointed that C did not admit any inadequacy of the present order or any readiness to consider ways and means of improvement. C's earlier responses had led Petrie to expect something 'more constructive'. Taking one point mentioned by Menzies, Petrie pointed out that while it was true that German espionage activities were directed against the USA and USSR, the DG

asked of C: 'Do you seriously argue that it is a primary function of SIS
to protect those countries from the activities of enemy agents or that
your obligation to them is on all fours with that to the British Empire?'
Surely SIS's primary purpose was to protect British interests and British
possessions everywhere. Until a year before, observed Petrie, Section V
consisted of only a handful of officers 'and was in very deep water'.
To put it on a proper footing, C had to had to draw, considerably,
on MI5 staff: 'Are we to accept it then that they alone are capable of
handling the products of C[ounter]E[spionage] intelligence by some
esoteric method outside of our comprehension and experience?' It
was a fact that SIS and the Special Operations Executive had been, for
months, suffering serious losses of agents on the Continent because
both agencies were being penetrated by the Germans: 'If this is a fact,
as I have good reason to believe it is, is it not one that needs to be
candidly admitted and faced up to? You have no umbrella over you
on the counter-espionage side – the ships have been without "fighter
protection."' It would seem then that 'a close day-to-day study of all
relevant material available' must still be 'leaving something wanting
and that counter-espionage intelligence does not just automatically
emerge as a by-product of the other kinds of activity'. In fact, Petrie
told Menzies: 'You are not producing enough CE material because of
"operational" claims, and you are falling down over "operational"
because of your neglect of CE, so that the vicious circle is complete.'

Petrie also hoped 'it has been made clear to you that it has been no
part of our proposal to turn you into a mere post office, any more than
you are now a post office in respect of information supplied to the
fighting services'. As for C's allusion to the different outlooks of SIS
and MI5, Petrie pointed out that it was just that difference of outlook
which made effective co-operation difficult: 'If, for example, your
people in Lisbon had not been lacking in the Security outlook, they
would have handled a certain recent case very differently. The case...
was spoilt by their failure to appreciate anything of what constitutes
legal evidence in the UK. Again an officer of yours was anything but
a good witness in a Treachery Act trial that has just concluded.' Petrie
asked if it was not a fact that, thanks to XX agents and interrogation
at Camp 020 'we are able to tell you rather more than about the
enemy's intelligence organisation all over the world than you can tell
us?' As a sting in the tail, Petrie added: 'I am not, of course, including
ISOS, which is a product of neither of us.' Petrie wanted CE material
handled as were XX agents abroad through the Twenty Committee
on which both MI5 and SIS were represented: the separate handling
of intelligence was 'only likely to blow the whole system sky-high'.

The root cause of the problems remained the 'basic unreality of our attempted division between Section V and B Division'. Petrie finished off by warning that if, as seemed likely, 'we are both going to stand our ground' the correspondence should be submitted to Lord Swinton.[10]

On 28 June, Menzies replied to Petrie: 'The letters you and I have exchanged have certainly cleared the air, and if I may say so have allowed us to blow off a little steam. They have not really got to the root of the matter, which is the only way that we can tackle this.' After giving 'very careful thought during the last week or two to the whole matter', and having had the benefit of discussing it with many of his principal assistants ('and not least of all with you yourself in our informal talk recently'), C had to admit: 'I find that there is no doubt whatever that the general basis of your original proposals is logical, and that you and I should immediately do something to implement a development which must be to the National advantage. You may, therefore, take it that I accept in principle the argument that there should be a single unified body responsible for studying the activities of the enemy Secret Services and for co-ordinating and directing action to counter them.'

Menzies therefore suggested the establishment of a new unified Department of Counter-Espionage (DOCE), which would be jointly subordinate to both MI5 and SIS. 'It would thus be jointly responsible to you and myself.' This Department would study enemy espionage activities throughout the world, drawing its information from all sources. In addition to the DOCE, Menzies would set up in his HQ a Contre-espionage circulating section which would be responsible for all communications with SIS stations and agents on CE matters. Similarly, the general direction of all CE representatives and agents in foreign countries should rest with SIS and not with DOCE. The training of agents for work abroad would also be exclusively the task of SIS. The circulating section, and not DOCE, would be responsible for obtaining decisions on the use to be made, in communications abroad, of ISOS and other GC & CS material and all other secretly intercepted information. C told Petrie: 'I realise that direct access to GC & CS on this point, was an important part of your scheme, but my view remains that the best judges of what use can safely be made of most secret material in communications abroad are the people who are directly in touch with the stations abroad and, therefore, familiar with conditions at those stations, ie SIS officers, rather than the GC & CS officers.'

In addition to this, SIS would remain responsible for all communications with its representatives, stations and agents on

Contre-espionage as on other matters, and for all codes, transmission questions etc. The SIS Central Registry would remain as and where it was, but all its records would be available to DOCE. DOCE would be situated outside London at St Albans. Its Head and Director would be Valentine Vivian, with Dick White and Major Cowgill as his co-ordinate Assistant Directors. Part of C's present Section V would move to London to become the new Circulating Section V. The main body would remain at St Albans and be joined by a suitable MI5 contingent to form DOCE:

> I think that the above forms a workable scheme. I have, of course, only attempted to set out the main lines, and many details would have to be filled in. I suggest that when you have had time to consider it, you and I should meet for a preliminary discussion, and if we reach agreement in principle, we should then set up a small Joint Committee to work out the details... I think that I should add a word of warning that even when some such re-organisation has been carried through, it may well remain true that the volume of CE Intelligence available is less than desirable. I appreciate the force of your point about 'fighter protection' and the vicious circle which arises out of the competition between 'operational' and CE Intelligence, but the difficulty of expanding the amount of CE Intelligence is a very real one. Under existing conditions, it may well prove impossible to obtain more CE information without sacrificing other information which is vitally urgent. Nor is it possible to strengthen, at will, CE personnel abroad. In foreign countries, the problem of cover is a serious one; eg in Spain, it is impossible to add to the existing staffs of HM Embassy and Consulates. This difficulty is, as you will appreciate, accentuated by the cover necessary for SOE work. Nevertheless, I am always considering steps to strengthen the staffs of my representatives abroad on the CE side.[11]

At about the same time Lord Swinton came up with his own document laying down general principles establishing the necessity of 'a joint intelligence and joint planning body of the two services charged with the reception, appreciation and distribution of CE Intelligence and responsible to C and the Director General of the Security Service jointly'. After assessing Swinton's document as the basis for any reorganisation which might have to be carried out between B Division and Section V, Dick White warned his Director General that was 'important to understand its implications very clearly. The proposal is that instead of the present Section V there should be a joint body for the "reception, appreciation and distribution of CE Intelligence".' This appeared to mean that the body was not envisaged as one possessing executive – i.e. decision-making – powers but purely as a group for the study and analysis of all available CE material from SIS sources and responsible for its distribution. White thought this was brought out in the Swinton document by the use of the phrase 'prevention of espionage' instead of 'detection of espionage'. There was, to White's mind, 'no doubt, therefore, that the document does not envisage a merging together in one section of the executive functions of Section V and B Division'.

White also considered the weaknesses of C's proposals as lying in the fact that he had not made clear whether he intended DOCE to represent a merging of executive functions or 'simply a joint study group with certain planning and directing functions of a general kind added to it – ie the Swinton plan. It would appear that he intends the former... If this is so, his application of those sound and solid principles is very disappointing... We asked for, and he... agrees to, "a single unified body responsible for studying the activities of the enemy's Secret Service and co-ordinating and directing action to counter it". I am afraid I think only lip service has been paid in C's letter to this principle.' It was most important to realise that the new 'circulating section', to be established in SIS and situated at their HQ in Broadway, was to possess all the 'really important functions' of the former Section V. This was explicitly stated by C., who had listed the following functions as reserved for the new 'circulating sections':

1. General direction of all CE representatives and agents in foreign countries.
2. Training of representatives and agents for work abroad.
3. Ultimate control of the use of ISOS and of GC & CS material.
4. Maintenance of all communication with foreign stations.

Where, therefore, does DOCE come in? Its presumed functions must be as follows:

1. Reception of all CE information, its study and analysis.
2. Power to request action abroad through Circulating Section.
3. Power to request action at home through MI5.

Set side by side in this manner... DOCE emerges from C's letter as little more than a joint study and analysis section whose power for action is at one removed from the executive machine.

The first question to decide, therefore, was whether the new joint section was to have executive powers or not: 'If I interpret the Swinton document correctly, it is scarcely conceived as an executive body. Whether C conceives it as such or not hardly matters, for he has already removed from its sphere and back into SIS the vital functions of control and direction of CE work abroad which are to be vested in his new "circulating section".' It was clear, to White, therefore, that DOCE would offer no answer to the kind of difficulties MI5 experienced over the double-cross cases 'where we have been kept in the dark'.

One thing, White thought, must be emphasised at the outset and in all further discussions, and that was that if 'Mr White and a suitable contingent from MI5 – which must, I think, mean the B1 sections I at present control – are to be the MI5 half of a joint section, if we are to continue the functions which we at present perform, we cannot possibly be moved to Glenalmond, St Albans.' In any case, it appeared to White 'far more important to be in the vicinity of the new "circulating section" at Broadway than to be in the neighbourhood of the SIS Registry at Glenalmond. It must not be forgotten that we have functions to perform for outside departments here in London, that we control the R[oyal]P[atriotic]S[chools for interrogation of aliens] and 020 and must be near them, that we run agents – a considerable number and rather important ones – and that in all these respects the present Section V has nothing which makes it correspondingly important for them to be in London. Even so, they made in my opinion a fundamental error in isolating themselves at Glenalmond.' To bring C's proposals into the realm of practical intelligence work: 'We must finally ask this direct question: what functions are envisaged for the rump of B Branch presumably under Liddell, reinforced by the rejects from Glenalmond...? Either they must take over the executive functions formerly performed by myself and the B1 sections, in which case we become pure students, or else they can have but a minor part to play in the work of counter-espionage.'

To sum up White's impressions of C's proposals, it appeared that Menzies had begun by accepting the principle of 'a single unified direction and control of CE work', but ended by creating three bodies in place of two. The principle of a third and joint section was conceded by the Swinton memorandum, and it was important therefore to be clear whether it was intended by this a planning staff reviewing all the available information but with no executive powers – ie, a small picked body from B Division and Section V – or an executive body. If the latter, 'such a section should be created here in London'.[12] In response MI5 came up with the following:

HEADS OF MI5 PROPOSALS

The Joint Section should be in London, preferably at 58, St James's Street [Broadway]

At the present stage the Joint Section should have no single head but should consist of two Assistant Directors – one from MI6 responsible to CSS [Menzies] through Colonel Vivian... and the other from MI5 responsible to DGSS [Petrie] through Director B and to CSS through Colonel Vivian.

Coordination in the work of B Division and of the Joint Section should be secured by means of a Standing Committee consisting of two heads from each side meeting, say, once a week.

The Joint Section should be staffed by picked representatives of the sub-sections of the present Section V and picked representatives from any of the sections of B Division.

The organisation of the Joint Section should be based on territorial sub-sections in roughly the manner of the present Section V. The organisation of B Division should not incorporate territorial sub-sections, but subject sections and sections for investigation.

The Liaison Section at Broadway should be as small as possible and facilities for transmission of Joint Section communications to stations overseas should be as direct as it is possible to make them.

From the commencement of work in the Joint Section work on records in this section should be handled by the MI5 Registry. Those records from the Section V era now handled at St Albans should be available to the Joint Section for action and for copying where necessary.

A meeting was held to discuss these proposals on Wednesday 22 July. Alongside the DGSS and CSS were their key subordinates: Brigadier Harker, Captain Liddell, Major Cowgill and Dick White. The first problem considered was that of the location of the proposed Joint Section. Menzies stated that, in his opinion, the new Joint Section must be situated in close proximity to the SIS Registry. C explained that SIS and Section V were so bound up with their Registry, in St Albans, that if the new Joint Section were to be located in London, he would have to recreate another Section V near their Registry. All incoming telegrams went to the SIS Registry to be joined to previous papers, while 'advance copies' were sent to the appropriate sections. At its present location Section V got priority of access to SIS files. Telegrams were coming in all through the day and very often all through the night, and by 10.30 a.m. Section V were receiving telephone enquiries from C himself and other sections of SIS. In the view of C and Major Cowgill, it was absolutely essential for the speedy handling of SIS business that this arrangement should continue. They felt that even the delay of approximately one hour entailed by having the papers sent from the SIS Registry to London would adversely affect the work of the Service Section.[13]

In reply, Liddell suggested that some system could be devised to overcome this difficulty. He pointed out that the MI5 Central Registry was situated even further away from London than the SIS Registry and that now there was no appreciable delay in receipt of files at MI5 London Office. This was the case although one Division of MI5 alone had to deal with some 10,000 vetting enquiries per week, and a very large number of files were in constant use in all Divisions. Liddell also reminded the meeting that a small Registry was maintained in the MI5 London Office of files and documents of a Most Secret character particularly related to counter-espionage work. He added that the policy in the MI5 Registry had been to split the number of files as much as possible. He suggested that some scheme could be devised by which separate files were maintained in the SIS Registry for matters of counter-espionage interest.

Cowgill, however, felt that this arrangement could not be carried out as telegrams which were relevant to Section V work were very often also relevant to the work of other sections of SIS. In his opinion, any system which entailed the SIS Central Registry receiving less material would be extremely detrimental to the work of SIS abroad. In their answer the MI5 representatives, on the other hand, felt sure that some system could be devised to overcome this difficulty, and pointed out that when files were sent to the Joint Section in London they would be brought very close to the London Office of SIS. Cowgill countered that, before the SIS Registry was moved, Section V officers had been left at the original headquarters of the Registry to deal with enquiries from MI5 and elsewhere. It was his experience that this system did not work.

Petrie then asked the meeting to consider the difficulties which would be entailed from the point of view of taking immediate action on material received if the Joint Section were located outside London. White said that when consideration had to be given to the question of immediate action, the Admiralty, the Foreign Office, the Home Office and the Ministry of Economic Warfare were becoming more and more interested from various points of view. The MI5 case for locating the Joint Section in London was based upon their view that the Joint

Section and B Division were two halves of what was in reality a single service and were doing complementary work. MI5 felt that to separate them geographically would be to prevent that continual exchange of ideas and experience without which either side would ultimately be impoverished. White stressed the fact that there was a difference between case work, as understood by B Division, and the handling of intelligence which would be carried on in the Joint Section, and that each was essential to the other. He further pointed out that if the Joint Section were to be located away from London it would be at once necessary to duplicate part of its machinery in London for the benefit of the case workers, who could not be entirely separated from original evidence or the main pool of CE Intelligence maintained by the Joint Section.

In answer to this, Cowgill said that since 80 per cent of the work done in the Joint Section would be of no direct concern either to the UK or British possessions overseas, he felt that the point made by White was not an important one. Questioned further upon this issue, he explained that 80 per cent of the work done at present in Section V covered enquiries made in foreign countries, which did not lead to action, or else was action taken against enemy agents proceeding from one piece of foreign territory to another. In this latter sense they served the Foreign Office and there were many other ways in which they served Departments other than MI5. For these reasons he contended that the Joint Section and B Division work would not be so complementary as White now thought. In answer to a suggestion that the material for dealing with sixty-five cases of enemy agents had come from sources available to both Section V and MI5, Cowgill said that for those sixty-five cases Section V might have had to examine some 300 cases. The meeting could reach no agreement on the question of location.

C then suggested that a compromise should be considered by which some B Division officers should be sent to Section V. Petrie and C were in agreement that if this proposal were accepted, it would be clearly understood by both organisations that such officers would be under joint control. White felt that during such an experimental period it would be necessary for MI5 to maintain their existing B Division machinery. C said that the position really was that both organisations were hesitant about upsetting their present delicate machinery. Eventually it was agreed that a party of B officers, to include if possible, White, should go to Section V for a period of about ten days, in order to acquaint themselves with the day to day work of that Section, and so be in a better position to understand the point of view expressed by the SIS representatives at the meeting.[14]

Before White had a chance to report back from his visit to St Albans, Petrie ordered a study into to the number of spies captured as a result of SIS information; compiled by H.P. Milo, it confirmed MI5's prejudices regarding the deficiencies of SIS. Given the special status of ISOS, Milo decided that it 'has not been treated as "SIS information"':

> I would venture to make the following observations as to what has emerged from this analysis:
> 1. The most striking fact is that in only one single case – namely that of DE JAEGER – has a spy been captured as a result of a denunciation by an SIS agent. Even in this case the achievement is not entirely free from blemish as the methods employed were of a highly questionable 'agent provocateur' character.
> 2. Hardly less striking is the thoroughly unreliable character of denunciations by SIS agents. In no less than 8 cases have such denunciations proved entirely without substance and in the cases of LITTLE and STILLWELL they resulted in gross injustice to the persons in question, and the outcome can only be described as disastrous to everybody concerned.
> 3. In the majority of cases where SIS have been given the credit for a capture their services have taken the form of identifying characters or enterprises referred to by cover names on the ISOS. In many cases this function could have been performed equally well and expeditiously by consular enquiries.
>   The schedule may be summarised as follows:
> SIS have been responsible for the capture of 16 agents out of a total of 87.
> In only one case has a capture been attributable to an SIS agent, and in 9 of the cases for which SIS have been given credit the original information has been derived from ISOS.
> In 5 of the 16 cases SIS have made contact abroad with persons anxious to double-cross the Germans, and in one of the 16 we discovered that a woman employed by SIS was in fact double-crossing them with the enemy.
> Out of the grand total of 87, 20 of the agents have ISOS to thank for their captivity.[15]

In the meantime, Dick White had travelled to St Albans. Cowgill, as White recognised, gave him every facility for enquiring into the work of Section V, and issued instructions in advance of his visit that officers whom he questioned could answer on all points with perfect frankness. This being the case, White reported that there were a good many officers in Section V who agreed with him in believing that a Joint Section should be located in London. There were also a good many – 'and these notably the best' – who were very keen on the idea of a Joint Section. With regard to the question of personnel, White found that Section V was, in certain of its sub-sections, under-staffed and in others commanded insufficient ability: 'But in general I was much better impressed than I expected to be with the quality of the officers and the work they are doing. They lack nothing in keenness and for many of them their hours of work are almost impossibly long. I think they all suffer from the parochial atmosphere that has undoubtedly developed in this country house Intelligence Centre. They should get about more and mix with their opposite numbers in other departments.'[16]

While Liddell had a great deal of sympathy for White's view that there was 'a big job to be done in the foreign field which is not adequately covered and that we are likely to suffer if some improvement is not effected, I feel bound to say that I view with grave apprehension the formation of a new directorate operating in a different building under a head with a dual responsibility'.[17] One of the examples behind this was what MI5 found in relation to SIS activities – or rather lack of – with regard to counter-espionage activities in Switzerland:

> There is virtually nothing to be said in regard to this section which is in fact not a section at all but merely an additional task performed by Major Ferguson on a side line... It is of course ironical that this territory which by geography and tradition is in the obvious danger spot of Europe should in effect be a terra incognita for the purpose of Section V. Such communication as does exist for Section V purposes takes place by bag with all the consequent delays. Of this fact, a case in which we are sharing, affords eloquent testimony and the results are correspondingly depressing.[18]

Furthermore, Liddell pointed out to the DG that the scheme put forward by SIS purported to be on a parity basis. But the blue-print of the organisation seemed to be heavily weighted on the side of SIS, while much of the responsibility for the work done 'must ultimately rest on the shoulders of the Security Service'. It seemed that the head of the Joint Section 'is still to retain his position as a representative of SIS, and it is suggested that he should have under him two assistant directors from SIS. Our contribution is to consist of one assistant director and ten or twelve of our best workers from B Division.

Our assistant director who will only have right of appeal to you through the director... is to be responsible for the Middle East, Balkans, W Africa, the UK and the Empire, and will have no direct say in matters affecting the Americas, Europe, Iberia, Scandinavia or the Baltic, which will come within the province of the SIS assistant directors.'

On the basis of the draft charter for the Joint Counter-Espionage Intelligence Planning Centre put forward by C there was 'an implied suggestion that C's interests and responsibilities for counter-espionage matters generally are equal to our own'. Personally, Liddell could see only four interests which affected the offensive espionage work of SIS:

1. the right to veto any operations abroad which may jeopardise the offensive organisation and thus hamper C in his efforts to obtain information for the Foreign Office, the Fighting Services and other departments which he serves.
2. the desirability of obtaining as much information about the German Intelligence Service in the areas in which he operates in order that his agents may work with less risk of discovery. This is sometimes referred to as the provision of an umbrella. It may be said that this umbrella is just as necessary to SOE as it is to SIS.
3. safeguarding of certain sources of information which, though primarily of interest to those dealing with counter-espionage, are also of interest to the Services.
4. prevention of damage by Axis agents to British interests in neutral countries.
... Apart from the above interests, the main purpose of counter-espionage is to prevent the penetration of British territory by German agents, and it would seem inevitable that this major responsibility must lie ultimately with the head of the Security Service.

For Liddell, C's proposals envisaged the setting up of a separate directorate, with its own funds, and with a dual responsibility to C and the Director General Security Service. This organisation was to be the recipient of all available information regarding the German intelligence system throughout the world; it would plan counter-action both at home and abroad and issue the necessary directives to those concerned. Cowgill agreed that this envisaged the direction of XX agents by the proposed Directorate. If the scheme put forward by C was to be carried to its logical conclusion, the body in possession of all the facts and with the authority to plan and give directions would absorb the whole of B Division. This brought Liddell to the 'logical conclusion' that the only real solution of the problem was the amalgamation of B Division and Section V under the control of DGSS 'who must bear the major responsibility for counter-espionage. I should have thought that C's interests would have been perfectly well covered by putting into the amalgamated organisation such representation as he thought fit to ensure that his interests were safeguarded... One must inevitably swallow the other.' In the meantime, Liddell was 'opposed to the formation of anything in the nature of a new directorate with dual responsibilities'.[19]

The position of the Security Service now hardened as Petrie backed Liddell and informed C of MI5's plan 'for complete amalgamation by taking over all Section V, which we... feel to be the right solution'. This was a step beyond the disputes of the 22 July meeting where 'the big point which impeded further progress was location'. This still remained a core division and Petrie 'urged that it was time we ended a system under which there was no unified view of the subject or planned direction of activity'. He suggested 'taking over Section V, so that action should rest with us and production abroad with you, both based on an integrated picture'. Not surprisingly C 'disapproved'. But, for Petrie the problem remained 'of the principal objection we take to St Albans, namely that it is too remote and out-of-touch. If Section V experiences that disability, so would the Joint Section' – where SIS wanted it to be sited: 'If remoteness is a handicap in the field of "Production", would it be any less in that of "Action"? Conversely, if location in London is going to help the one, so it will the other. If you could have the working end of Section V in London, just as we have to do in the case of our own organisation, close liaison with them would, I feel sure, be a definite step towards what we aim at. We each have a country office and our HQ in London. Surely the latter is the right place for a Joint Section. I cannot well contemplate the opening up of an additional supply line to St Albans or the establishment there of a third section of my office.' Petrie informed C that: 'I have just seen your representative from Cairo,' who confirmed 'that there the most complete concord prevails' – between SIS and MI5 – 'just because they work in close physical contact and are engaged on what they regard as a common task. If that can be done in Cairo, can we not allow things a chance of working themselves out on the same lines here?' But, as C would not yield, Petrie lamented that it

'will be with a sense of real disappointment' that he would have
to inform Lord Swinton and Sir John Anderson that 'we have been
unable to make any headway'.[20]

12

DREADNOUGHT & ARTIST

TRICYCLE in AMERICA

On his arrival – after considerable visa difficulties – in the still neutral US, TRICYCLE was in possession of a large sum in dollars that included those which he had been given by the Germans as a result of Plan MIDAS. He duly handed over to the British $40,000 less $2,000 commission he had paid to Karsthoff and less $4,620 which he was allowed to keep to compensate him for private business losses he sustained while in Portugal. A cable was sent to him in the name of 'Sand' from London, mentioning a mythical Samuel Sand in New York to whom, so far as the Germans were concerned, he was supposed to pay over the MIDAS dollars. TRICYCLE's stay in America, observed MI5, 'was not, on the whole, a happy one'. There was insufficient co-operation between the FBI and SIS and practically no consultation with MI5: 'It is clear in retrospect,' wrote Ian Wilson, an MI5 officer closely involved in the case, 'that it was a mistake to pass over to the United States an agent whose case was interlocked with that of other agents in England.' Not only had he left BALLOON and GELATINE behind him in Britain but Plan MIDAS associated him with another Double-Cross agent, TATE, who in turn associated him with other agents.

The objective of the FBI in running double agents appeared to be that they should get their double agent into contact with genuine agents, whom they could arrest and have tried in the full light of publicity. They tried hard to get the Germans to put couriers in touch with TRICYCLE; as Wilson stated: 'From our point of view it is fortunate that they failed, because it would have been extremely embarrassing for us if they had caught a courier and wanted to use TRICYCLE as a witness.' The absence of powers of detention in the United States or of holding without trial those concerned in espionage 'would have made it extremely difficult for the FBI to handle any genuine agent who was put in touch with TRICYCLE without blowing TRICYCLE'. Personal relationships between the FBI and TRICYCLE 'were not good'. He did not resent the fact that he had been checked up pretty thoroughly by MI5 on his arrival in Britain, but he objected to the further checking up and suspicious attitude of the FBI on his arrival in the States. In particular TRICYCLE complained of inadequately concealed microphones wherever he went. He was apparently asked by the FBI at an early stage what he wanted to get out of them for his services. This wounded his pride. The fact that the Germans then failed to pay him what they had promised, meant he had to borrow money first from the FBI and later from SIS, which caused him some embarrassment. As TRICYCLE had, at the outset, large sums of money at his disposal and was left almost completely unoccupied, as he was only occasionally consulted about his case this 'tempted him into idle and extravagant habits'. He did not appear to have taken sufficient interest in his radio traffic on the few occasions he was consulted. No proper steps were taken to provide him with a reasonable cover for his presence in the United States. He left Britain with a letter from Sir Walter Monkton that indicated that he had some mission to report on the effect of British propaganda on the Yugoslav speaking population in the US; but this was not followed up. The British Ministry of Information in the States knew nothing about him, with the result that the Yugoslav colony in the country were inclined to think that TRICYCLE was working for someone, though whether the Germans or the British was not quite clear: 'Throughout his stay in the United States he lived the life of a play-boy, and his only useful activity seems to have been that he took a course of flying lessons.' When his own money and the money he got from the Germans had run out, TRICYCLE drew upon certain funds he had and really belonged to his Yugoslav banker friends and clients, the Bailonis: 'He had perhaps some excuse for this in as much as they probably owed him greater sums in Yugoslavia. He seeks to excuse this extravagance on the grounds that he had to acquire suitable social contacts from whom he would be supposed to obtain information. The excuse is a bad one as he obtains no information himself and the contacts upon which he spent his money... are not of interest to a spy as such. In all he managed to spend some $80,000 in fourteen months. He took an expensive penthouse on Park Avenue, which was expensively done up by interior decorators, he bought a large car, in the winter he went skiing at Sun Valley, Idaho, and he took a country house. Towards the end, after he had been given a good talking to, he checked his expenditure to some extent, although not sufficiently.'

In November 1941, TRICYCLE went to Rio de Janeiro on the instructions of the Germans in Lisbon. This was to enable him to hand over certain documents that he had obtained about the American Army. His German contacts there told him to establish a radio transmitter upon his return; it in fact was operated by the FBI from a point on Long Island some forty miles outside New York. Contact was established with the Germans on 1 February 1942. TRICYCLE had not trained as an operator and was supposed to have found a disaffected Croat to do the transmitting for him while he himself did the coding. The set required a long aerial which it would not have been easy to conceal; but it was assumed by the Germans that TRICYCLE had the set erected at a house on Long Island where the aerial could be concealed by trees. Information was transmitted fairly regularly until July 1942 when, owing to the Germans failing to pay him, the radio operator 'went on strike'. Although the Germans failed to pay TRICYCLE for the last three and a half months he spent in the States there was good evidence that they tried hard to get a further $10,000 to him. This non-payment proved an advantage because it provided TRICYCLE with a ready-made explanation of his failure to get much information towards the end of his stay – this was as a result of the FBI handing TRICYCLE back to MI5 and ceasing to obtain information comparable to that which he had previously been transmitting. When he finally left for Lisbon on 12 October 1942, TRICYCLE was carrying a genuine diplomatic bag which had been obtained from the Yugoslav Minister in Washington for the Legation in Lisbon. This, in fact, only contained letters of a rather personal nature to members of the Legation staff. He also carried a dummy bag prepared for him and addressed to the Yugoslav delegation in London. This contained his papers for the Germans. The contents were photographs of a naval conference, of an aero engine mentioned in his traffic, and his own notes on information to give verbally. The photographs had been prepared by the FBI. It was decided that TRICYCLE should take the attitude with the Germans that he had at all times worked for what he was paid and not for any other motive. He had ceased to try, therefore, to get information after June 1942 and what he had got was merely dinner table indiscretions. He had seen no reason why he should spend borrowed money on buying secret information for the Germans.

Up until the middle of March 1942 there had been no indication that the Germans suspected TRICYCLE. Later in the month there were indications that the Germans had begun to recognise for the first time the possibility that he might be a double agent. This suspicion seemed to have originated with Eins Luft. In May these suspicions seemed to have grown and for some time no questions on air matters were given to TRICYCLE. His immediate chiefs in Lisbon, however, refused to accept the Eins Luft suspicions.[1] On 21 March it was 'reliably reported' that the Germans in Berlin considered that a question which they had put to TRICYCLE was a trick question to test whether he was under British control or not: 'They were inclined to think that he was.' The question was whether TRICYCLE wanted his salary to be paid to his family or to be paid to him in New York. Inquiries were made in New York and it was found that TRICYCLE had already been asked this question on 13 March and had replied to it on 18 March.

TRICYCLE gave a non-committal reply. MI5 considered that: 'Neither the FBI nor our representative... consider that this non-committal reply has done TRICYCLE any harm. We do not know whether the Germans are satisfied or not.'[2]

An ISOS intercepted teleprint of 8 May added to the confusion. It referred to a message from Berlin to Rio, dated 20 March, which stated that Berlin suspected TRICYCLE of working for both sides and recommended extreme caution when dealing with the matter.[3] Of those MI5 and SIS figures involved in the case, Flight Lieutenant Charles Cholmondeley thought it 'desirable that we should salve what we can from the wreck. For this purpose it must be taken for granted that we cannot continue the case as heretofore since it will be impossible for us to decide whether or not our information is being believed.' The alternative was, therefore, to try and supply the enemy with the relevant facts that would confirm in their minds what they would like to believe. The only positive interpretation that Cholmondeley could put on things was that, since BALLOON had been introduced to them by TRICYCLE and provided accurate information, it could be assumed that the German case officers running the TRIBAGE organisation – the term for TRICYCLE's group of agents – 'must be very loath to reach the conclusion that they have been led up the garden path from the very start and will certainly review the case to try and establish from what date the case went wrong. A further spur will be added to their labours since the conclusions will undoubtedly reflect on their own efficiency and hence their pride will receive a severe shock'.[4]

The position of the case was discussed between Major Cowgill and Major Foley of SIS and Marriott, Masterman and Wilson from B1.A. It was agreed that future policy must depend on the correct interpretation to be placed upon the message which gave rise to the teleprint of 8 May 1942. It transpired that the SIS report on the teleprint of 8 May was an 'inaccurate report' and the SIS statement that Berlin had 'definitely' decided that both TRICYCLE and BALLOON had been under British control since the former arrived in America was 'were far more definite than the facts justified'. In the first place the reference in this context should have been to TRICYCLE only and not to TRICYCLE and BALLOON. Secondly, it appeared that the true picture was that those dealing with German airforce intelligence maters had reasons for suspecting that TRICYCLE had become a controlled agent rather than that they had decided that this was the case. The intentions of SIS were to continue and in fact improve the TRICYCLE traffic with a view to dispersing those suspicions and they were averse to the immediate adoption of a policy which made TRICYCLE irretrievably a blown agent and which also caused BALLOON to become blown in the near future. SIS emphasised the fact that the members of the German service responsible for running TRICYCLE and BALLOON would fight hard to persuade Berlin that they were still genuine German agents. Masterman, on the other hand, stressed – if the Germans had in fact either already concluded or were going in future to conclude that TRICYCLE was blown – taking all possible action to ensure that they would not come to the conclusion that TRICYCLE and BALLOON had been controlled from the beginning. In the end it was decided that TRICYCLE should, for the time being, proceed with his traffic as before and, if possible, improve it; and that BALLOON should write further letters, as before, and, in all probability, not write for a fortnight or two. If he were to run as blown agent, a period of silence while 'he was broken' would be desirable and if he was to be continued as a genuine agent the silence could be explained by illness or even left unexplained, leaving it to be assumed that a letter had been caught in the Censorship.[5]

On 16 May, TAR Robertson informed Major Foley of information from the Germans referring to an agent: 'I do not think it at all probable that this refers to TRICYCLE, but it is I think interesting to see how quickly and vigorously the Germans rise in defence of an agent.' but Robertson also warned that: 'Unless we see, in the near future, some similar local reaction in favour of TRICYCLE, I think he conclusion we shall have to draw is that the situation is a good deal more serious than we had hoped was the case.'[6] In the end the crisis appeared to have passed with Lisbon's faith winning over Berlin's doubts. But, by now it was clear, in D.I. Wilson's view that, 'TRICYCLE is not doing much good in the USA. From our point of view it is clearly a disadvantage to have him there.' He suggested that SIS might discuss with the FBI the possibility of the return of TRICYCLE to the UK.[7]

This is what had led to TRICYCLE being recalled to Europe. He was once again sent to Lisbon on Wednesday, 14 October 1942. On Wednesday 21 October, TRICYCLE left Lisbon for Britain. There TRICYCLE reported that he had only met Karsthoff at the first two meetings. TRICYCLE was of the opinion that all personal doubts which might have existed in the Germans' minds about him were dissolved at this first meeting. They discussed the work in America, and Karsthoff immediately expressed great interest in the radio operator. TRICYCLE explained that he had met him in a pub in 45th Street West frequented by sailors and Yugoslavs. He was an excellent radio expert, but inclined to exaggerate his capabilities in other directions. He worked well as long as he was well paid, but was difficult about money and very grasping. He did not know the code and had not been told what TRICYCLE was doing, though he had probably guessed. On one occasion, so TRICYCLE declared, the operator had asked what was being sent over and had been shown the message because it was a message asking for money. Karsthoff then asked if this man could work for someone other than TRICYCLE, but TRICYCLE replied that he did not believe that they could send anybody else to work with this man. The suggestion was made that the radio operator might have been caught, but the Germans agreed in rejecting this hypothesis, since TRICYCLE in that case would not have returned to them. The actual information that TRICYCLE gave the Germans about America did not appear to have interested them particularly. He gave them the papers that had been sent over in the Diplomatic Bag and explained what these things meant at one of the later interviews. The Germans asked few questions themselves about America. They looked at the letter that he had taken from Sir Walter Monckton, but did not read it carefully as it was not shown to them until after their suspicions had been (in TRICYCLE's view) already cleared up.

From the interviews that he had TRICYCLE considered German morale was 'pretty bad'. From this evidence, Masterman, in London, concluded that the Germans continued to believe in BALLOON, though they were dissatisfied with his actual letter-writing. As for GELATINE, TRICYCLE was told by the Germans: 'Do not see her too much. You cannot avoid seeing her socially but as you never discussed business with her you must not do it now.' TRICYCLE was told by another officer, in front of Karsthoff, that the latter was a very good friend to TRICYCLE, but added: 'Berlin are stupid fellows. They are sitting at desks making statistics and can't put themselves into your or my position and do not realise the difficulties of being without money. Therefore please work hard, or we shall all have trouble here, and you will see we shall be able to give you big bonuses.' Masterman concluded that the struggles over money, together with these remarks, seemed to support the view that Karsthoff had defended TRICYCLE as his agent. He did accuse TRICYCLE of 'living like a prince in America', but TRICYCLE explained eloquently the necessity for his extravagant way of living, and alleged that Kartshoff admitted that his point of view was reasonable.[8]

That was in October 1942. Since TRICYCLE returned to Britain his case carried on without any striking developments. Up to the end of March 1943 he had written, or was supposed to have written, twenty-five letters, each containing one, two or three pages of secret text. By January 1943 TRICYLE was beginning to get a 'bit restless' as he felt that it should be possible to make better use if his relationship with the Germans than merely including a few odd pieces of mis-information in his letters to them. His proposals were that cover should be arranged for him to visit a neutral country for the purposes of: '1. Re-establishing personal contact with Johnny JEBSEN, from whom TRICYCLE believes he could obtain information of value to us in view of the close personal relationship between them; 2. To try and contact TRICYCLE's elder brother with a view to arranging a nucleus of dependable persons in Yugoslavia who might be of great use to the cause of the United Nations in the event of an invasion of that country; 3. So that he could meet his younger brother outside Occupied Europe and arrange to keep him outside.'

As far as his old friend Jebsen was concerned, TRICYCLE was confident that his character was such that if and when he realised Germany was going to lose the war he would be only too willing to reinsure himself with the victors by doing all he could 'notwithstanding that this involved ratting on his own country'. According to TRICYCLE, Jebsen was 'amoral, has never been pro-Nazi and has no loyalty to anyone except himself'. Jebsen, he believed, knew that TRICYCLE was not assisting the Germans for any ideological reasons but only in the hope of material gain; it would therefore be relatively easy for TRICYCLE to approach Jebsen on the lines that they were both businessmen out for what they could get and that the prospects of German success being now vastly different to what they were when Jebsen persuaded TRICYCLE to act for the Germans, 'they should consider reinsuring their respective positions against the prospect of Germany losing the war'. TRICYCLE would say that he had good contact with the Yugoslavs and British and was sure that if later it became obvious that Germany was losing he could arrange for Jebsen to receive favourable treatment and not suffer the punishment, which no doubt he deserved, provided that he had something worthwhile to sell to the British authorities. TRICYCLE would not, in the first instance, ask for information but try and persuade Jebsen to collect information so that at a later stage he would have no difficulty in obtaining full details of the personnel of the Abwehr and its agents in many countries. In view of the fact that the channels that the British could provide for deceptive purposes were not being greatly used by the Services, MI5 decided to try and carry out TRICYCLE's proposals.[9] By a remarkable coincidence Jebsen and TRICYCLE's elder brother in Yugoslavia – in complete ignorance of his proposals – had already began working together.

DREADNOUGHT

TRICYCLE'S elder brother was Dr Ivo Popov. When news began to filter out of Yugoslavia that there was an attempt to send out German agents that would, in fact act as Double-Cross agents for the British, neither MI5 or SIS knew for sure the identities of the men behind the endeavour; they merely knew of a mysterious 'X' (who was Popov) and a 'Stohrman'[10] who turned out to be Jebsen. The British had their suspicions but eventually gave Popov the codename DREADNOUGHT; by now they had been referring to Jebsen in communications as ARTIST.

DREADNOUGHT was born at Titel, Yugoslavia, in 1910. He was educated in France and Italy, as well as in Yugoslavia, and qualified as a physician. Prior to the invasion of Yugoslavia he had a good private practice as a doctor in Dubrovnik and also interested himself in medical research. He took no part in politics. At the time of the invasion of Yugoslavia he was called up as a reserve officer, and when the Yugoslav Army capitulated in April 1941, he was serving as an officer near the Albanian frontier. He fled to the mountains, but the local situation in that area made it impossible for him to remain long in hiding there, and he gave himself up as a prisoner-of-war to the Italians. Shortly afterwards he escaped from the Italians and made his own way to Dubrovnik. He quickly learned that his name was on the Ustasha Black List, and that an uncle of his had been shot by the pro-Nazi Ustasha. DREADNOUGHT therefore made arrangements to evacuate his wife and child with other relations and friends to the island of Mljet, where there was less disorder than in Dubrovnik, while he himself fled to Belgrade, where his family had a house and his father and TRICYCLE had many business interests.

Shortly after DREADNOUGHT arrived in Belgrade, the persecution of Serbs in Dalmatia by the Ustasha increased, so that not only persons on the black list of the Ustasha were in danger. Through a Russian, Count Avalov, he was able to bribe certain German officials to provide the necessary papers to enable his wife and child and parents to follow him to Belgrade, where they arrived in September 1941. During October 1941, a German girl came to see DREADNOUGHT in Belgrade. DREADNOUGHT found out later that she was Fraulein Liste, a secretary in the Abwehr office in Belgrade; she was the niece of General Keitel and the mistress of von Lasser of the Abwehr. Fraulein Liste told DREADNOUGHT that she had met a German friend in Berlin who was interested in DREADNOUGHT's family, and wanted his address in case he could help the family. She asked DREADNOUGHT whether there was any help he needed, but 'he treated her rather coldly' and declined German help. The German friend's name was not mentioned, but a week later ARTIST came to see DREADNOUGHT.

DREADNOUGHT knew ARTIST by name as a friend of his brother TRICYCLE from student days. At this time DREADNOUGHT had no idea that TRICYCLE was supposed to be working for the Abwehr. He knew that TRICYCLE had had some contact with the British in Belgrade before the invasion of Yugoslavia, but he was not aware of the nature of the contact. He also knew that TRICYCLE and ARTIST had participated in many commercial ventures together. ARTIST told DREADNOUGHT that he had come to Belgrade to give DREADNOUGHT personal news of TRICYCLE, which ARTIST pretended to have received through a Swedish diplomat. ARTIST at once stated that he was anti-Nazi, and consulted DREADNOUGHT as a doctor for advice as to the best means of avoiding military service. DREADNOUGHT advised ARTIST to simulate jaundice. ARTIST talked at length in a very anti-Nazi strain. DREADNOUGHT was careful in his first conversation, but gradually let ARTIST see that he was 'anti-German'. ARTIST asked what DREADNOUGHT's intentions were, and DREADNOUGHT said that he wished first of all to safeguard his family, and then he himself would go to the mountains to fight against the Germans. ARTIST argued that DREADNOUGHT could attack the Germans without necessarily going to the mountains to fight. ARTIST told of an anti-Nazi group, of which he was a member, and which consisted of young men with large business and financial interests and anti-Nazi views. The group were fighting in Germany itself and throughout Europe to keep finance and industry in private hands and to cause the breakdown of the planned economic system that it was the Nazi Party's policy to create. This group at that time seemed to expect a German victory, and was not in fact opposed to a German victory so long as it was not a Nazi victory, but they considered a Nazi victory in the war as even less to be desired than a German defeat. The group were not closely organised but the members, who used the password 'SENI', assisted each other in transactions calculated to further the interests of the individuals concerned at the expense of the Reich and to disrupt the centralised economic organisations. ARTIST suggested that DREADNOUGHT should help this German economic group in their fight. ARTIST's proposition was roughly as follows:

> You, as a Serb, are fighting Nazism. I and my friends, who know that controlled economy is the ruin of Germany, are also fighting Nazism. You have the chance of looking after your family's business interests by carrying on businesses in accordance with

our advice, in such a manner as to sabotage the Nazi control of industry in Europe and, by so doing, you can help in the fight against Nazism more effectively than as a single soldier fighting in the mountains.

Because of his supposed jaundice, ARTIST stayed in Belgrade for six weeks, during which time he and DREADNOUGHT became much more intimate: ARTIST explained to DREADNOUGHT that one of the means by which his financial group obtained influence and contrived to retain freedom to conduct their financial affairs instead of being called up, was by working for the German Intelligence Service. By now DREADNOUGHT had accepted ARTIST's proposition, gradually revived some of the businesses which had been controlled by his family, and began to acquire other businesses, all of which were run with the object of preventing the Germans, so far as possible, from deriving economic benefits from their occupation of Yugoslavia.[11] DREADNOUGHT's family, for example, controlled a factory in Belgrade which made boot polish. After the German occupation the sole permitted customer for this factory was the German Army. DREADNOUGHT, on his own initiative, caused the formula for the polish to be varied so that instead of preserving boots the polish accelerated the tendency of the leather to crack. Again, when the Germans brought to Belgrade, for sorting, such factory machinery and raw materials as they were able to seize on the occupation of Yugoslavia and Greece – for example the contents of the munitions factory at Obilicevo – DREADNOUGHT made it his business to see that as little as possible of this material reached Germany. The handling of much of this material was entrusted to the German firm of Ferro Wolff in Belgrade. Many of the officials of the firm could be and were corrupted to certify as useless and sell locally on the black market machinery that was urgently required in Germany. DREADNOUGHT persuaded this firm to employ Yugoslavs who would assist in keeping as much as possible out of German hands. DREADNOUGHT also became intimate with Toeppen, who was head of the organisation entrusted with obtaining the maximum of supplies from all occupied territories. Toeppen spent several days a month at Belgrade living in DREADNOUGHT's house. Through Toeppen's influence, DREADNOUGHT became the trusted agent of the Ueberwachungstelle in Belgrade. This office was supposed to stop the black market. In fact, the Germans found it impossible to do this and the Ueberwachungstelle endeavoured to operate the black market to the German advantage, as it was only by buying secretly on the black market that the Germans could get at many types of goods available in the Balkans. DREADNOUGHT bought and sold goods on the black market, nominally for the account of the Stelle, but actually in such a manner as to ensure that the Germans obtained as little as possible that was of real value to them, and that as much as possible disappeared from their reach.[12]

ARTIST had also made another proposition to DREADNOUGHT. He told DREADNOUGHT that he could strengthen his own position and that of ARTIST and his friends if he could help them find suitable individuals for the German Intelligence Service to send abroad as agents. At the outset ARTIST made it clear that it did not much matter to him whether or not these agents should work once they got abroad. DREADNOUGHT, who still knew nothing of TRICYCLE's activities, agreed to try and find some agents for ARTIST and the Abwehr, as DREADNOUGHT could see that there would be advantages in the fight against Germany if the Germans could be persuaded to send out as agents, individuals who would double-cross them.[13] DREADNOUGHT introduced to ARTIST and the German Intelligence Service, three Yugoslavs known to MI5 as VELOCIPEDE, THE WORM and METEOR. All three were accepted and trained by the Germans, and all three had agreed with DREADNOUGHT before being introduced to the Germans that their purpose in accepting German instructions was to double-cross the Germans with British aid. DREADNOUGHT and ARTIST kept the case of METEOR separate from that of THE WORM and VELOCIPEDE.[14]

It was about the end of 1941, or January of 1942, that DREADNOUGHT had selected VELOCIPEDE as a suitable agent. ARTIST had told DREADNOUGHT that two agents were required. DREADNOUGHT himself was not at that time in touch with General Mihailovic, the Serbian resistance fighter, but VELOCIPEDE was in touch with him so DREADNOUGHT asked VELOCIPEDE to select the second agent. VELOCIPEDE proposed his cousin, THE WORM, for the job.[15] The Germans mismanaged the arrangements for the escape of all these agents from occupied territory. VELOCIPEDE was sent out eastwards by the Germans, who ran into difficulties arranging his cover for getting into Turkey, but they ultimately overcame these difficulties and VELOCIPEDE arrived in Cairo and offered his services to the British there. It was decided that it would look suspicious if all this group of agents were to appear to the Germans to carry out their missions successfully, and no attempt was therefore made to use VELOCIPEDE as a Special Agent.[16] The Germans assisted THE WORM to reach Switzerland by May 1942, but were baffled by the problem of sending him on from Switzerland to the UK, and he did not reach Spain for another year. He had given to the British full particulars of his mission on arrival in Switzerland, and when he did ultimately reach Britain he carried on a secret ink correspondence with the Germans under MI5's direction.

METEOR was supposed, by the Germans, to find his own means of escape through Salonika and the Greek Islands. This broke down and METEOR was arrested by the Gestapo in Salonika; he was rescued from prison by the Abwehr, and early in 1943 reached Britain through Spain with, noted MI5, 'an ingenious cover story which, as far as we know, is unique'. His cover story was to disclose that he had been sent out as a German agent and to hand over a secret ink and a cover address to the British. The Germans had also given him another and better secret ink and cover addresses which he was not intended to disclose. METEOR in fact disclosed both sets of German instructions.[17] When interrogated by MI5, METEOR declined at first, on DREADNOUGHT's advice, to reveal the identity of DREADNOUGHT or the real name of ARTIST. Most Secret Sources enabled METEOR's story to be fully checked and MI5 were convinced that it was in fact TRICYCLE's brother who had introduced METEOR to the Abwehr. 'We therefore put METEOR in immediate touch with TRICYCLE, to the delight of both of them, and TRICYCLE assisted us in overcoming METEOR's reluctance to appearing to carry out both parts of his instructions from the Germans; that is to say by writing one set of letters known to be under our control and a separate set of letters supposed to be those of a genuine German agent.'[18] After being left in TRICYCLE's care, METEOR had asked him a few questions to make sure that he was in fact the brother of Dr Ivo Popov and then explained that the doctor had asked him to get in touch with TRICYCLE as soon as he could and to take TRICYCLE's advice on how much he could tell British Intelligence about his brother's activities without endangering his brother or his organisation.

On 26 April, TRICYCLE and METEOR had lunch with Ian Wilson and they confirmed that MI5 had been right in its assumption that 'X' was TRICYCLE's brother and that 'Stohrman' was Jebsen. METEOR stated that he wished to take an active part in fighting and was not keen to engage in double or triple-cross work although he accepted the fact that it might desirable in order to protect TRICYCLE's brother that some correspondence should be carried on, at least for a short time.[19] B1.A interpreted METEOR's mission as a German vote of confidence in TRICYCLE.[20] METEOR then carried on, under MI5's direction, a lengthy correspondence with the Germans, which was of particular value to the Admiralty as METEOR was a naval officer and could plausibly pass the Germans deceptive naval information.[21]

Sometime after METEOR's arrival, THE WORM made it to the UK after his year's hold-up in Switzerland. THE WORM had last met DREADNOUGHT (dressed up as a Sonderführer major) in Paris in May 1943.[22] By this stage it had occurred to DREADNOUGHT that TRICYCLE might be working as a German agent. DREADNOUGHT had asked ARTIST if that was the case, and for the first time learned that TRICYCLE was a German agent. DREADNOUGHT felt absolutely confident, although he naturally had no proof and at this stage could not confide enough in ARTIST to discuss the matter, that TRICYCLE must be working for the Germans on British instructions. It was in case TRICYCLE was acting on his own without British authority that DREADNOUGHT had decided to tell the agents he was sending out that when they got in touch with the British Intelligence, they were not to mention DREADNOUGHT's own name or that of TRICYCLE until they had got in touch with TRICYCLE himself, although they were to tell the British everything else.[23] In fact the whole story was given away by THE WORM, to MI5, before he met TRICYCLE. THE WORM reported that ARTIST had shown indications of being prepared to pass information to the British, and that DREADNOUGHT, with the connivance of ARTIST, was indulging in many types of economic sabotage against the Germans.[24]

In connection with the recruiting and training of these agents, ARTIST had put DREADNOUGHT in touch with von Lasser of Ast. Belgrade; later DREADNOUGHT got in touch with Munzinger, Thoering and other officers from Eins Heer, Berlin. The Abwehr took the line that the agents were not willing to work against Yugoslavia or against any of their fellow countrymen who continued to fight the Germans, but that they had no objection to helping the Germans against the British. Their alleged motive was to ensure future good relations between Yugoslavia and Germany within the New European Order and which the agents appeared to accept as the only alternative to Communism. They, apparently, did not expect immediate large financial rewards, but they did expect that at the end of the war the Abwehr would arrange that DREADNOUGHT and the agents who were being sent abroad would receive lucrative commercial positions and contracts. The Abwehr officials, who were themselves anti-Nazi, took it for granted that any anti-Communist European would be willing to help the German war effort, in order to save his own country from Communism. By this time it had become clear to DREADNOUGHT that what ARTIST wanted was that he should be able to claim the credit for getting these agents successfully to Britain, but that ARTIST himself did not care in the least whether they worked for the Germans, or against the Germans, or did not work at all once they got there. ARTIST explained that of a hundred agents that the Abwehr tried to send to Britain, only ten were likely to reach there, and of those ten only one was likely to work.

Through ARTIST and the agents he had introduced, DREADNOUGHT got to know many Abwehr officials in Belgrade, or who came from Berlin to Belgrade. He did everything possible to get on good terms with them so that he could use their influence to assist his own underground activities in Belgrade. All German officials arriving in Belgrade found it difficult to buy what they wanted, because even if they had money in Germany they could not get permission to spend it in Yugoslavia, where it was possible, if one had sufficient money, to buy many articles of food, clothing etc., on the black market. DREADNOUGHT obtained many things for these officers on the black market, being willing to accept promises of payment in marks in Germany for what he obtained. He supplied benefits originally to von Lasser, Munzinger and Thoering and later to Kohutek, Sensburg, Sommerfield, Martl and particularly to Toplak. Because of the personal advantages which DREADNOUGHT was able to obtain from his black market connections for these officials, he had much more contact with them than was really required in connection with his supposed duties to the Abwehr of recruiting these agents and assisting in arranging for their journeys to Britain. The agents were technically controlled by Berlin and in particular by Munzinger, and not by Belgrade; so, for many purposes, DREADNOUGHT himself rather than Belgrade provided the link between Berlin and the agents. Berlin instructed the local officials in Belgrade that if DREADNOUGHT asked for anything they could do it for him if they thought fit without having in every case to refer back to Berlin for authority.[25]

ARTIST

By the beginning of April 1943, TRICYCLE was continuing to complain that he ought to be doing something more active than sitting in London writing letters at MI5's dictation. A plan had been submitted for him to regain personal contact with the Germans, by a journey to the Middle East and Turkey, but fell through.[26] When Wilson saw TRICYCLE in late April he found him very depressed about his own position vis-à-vis his Yugoslav compatriots: 'They do not of course realise what work he is really doing and are apt to despise him, (a) because he does not appear to doing any active job of value in the war and, (b) because they think he is much too British.' Wilson reminded him that the risk to TRICYCLE's family would be far too great if the Yugoslavs generally were told what he was really doing. Unfortunately, noted Wilson, when asked to be more specific as to what more active part he could play in the war 'he becomes rather wild and not very constructive'. His suggestions varied from his becoming a pilot, his being dropped by parachute to General Mihailovic, or his undertaking the organisation of supplies for Mihailovic. Wilson felt it 'easy to sympathise with TRICYCLE's view that he is not doing enough... merely... once a week writing a letter. It is not easy to convince him of the value and necessity of such operations'.[27] On 29 April, Colonel TAR Robertson, Major Masterman and Wilson visited TRICYCLE at his request. Roberson suggested that there were now three options for TRICYCLE:

1. That TRICYCLE should undertake some Intelligence work of a more active, ambitious and dangerous character.
2. That his double-cross work should continue as before, that is by writing letters from London, but that he should have some separate and more active part in the war effort.
3. That his letter writing etc should be brought to an end and that he should undertake some entirely different work.

All concerned expressed the view that the first course was preferable if a suitable scheme could be worked out. TRICYCLE stressed that he was ready to take almost any risks to achieve anything that would be really useful.[28]

In MI5.'s view the main value of another journey to Lisbon was the information that TRICYCLE could obtain from ARTIST. Since their student days together, ARTIST had been anti-Nazi and at least since the first German summer offensive against Russia had been halted ARTIST had been convinced that Germany had lost the war and he became prepared to do all he could to finish the war as soon as possible. It was clear from the histories of THE WORM, METEOR and VELOCIPEDE that, at least since early 1942, ARTIST had been co-operating with DREADNOUGHT in anti-German activities. ARTIST also talked freely to TRICYCLE about the position in Germany, and about Abwehr organisation, personalities and activities. MI5 were 'in a position to check a large part of the voluminous reports that TRICYCLE made to us on the latter subject and there is no doubt of their accuracy'. Although TRICYCLE's curiosity on these subjects 'could only be accounted for in one way', neither TRICYCLE nor

ARTIST openly admitted his position to the other. To quote from TRICYCLE's own report on his return:

> In spite of not having told (ARTIST) that I am working for the British I am absolutely sure that he knows it, although he has not said so to me. The way he talks to me and his whole behaviour shows this very clearly. I never wanted to tell him for the simple reason that I am afraid that (ARTIST) after that would not give me any more information about the German Intelligence Service, if only for the reason that he would not like me to think him a traitor... (ARTIST) said that there are two types of people in the office in Berlin; Nazis, who are damned idiots; and reactionaries. The Nazis are too stupid to question my genuineness. The others might I think that I was not genuine, but it would be absolutely against their interests to let this be known or to discuss it.

ARTIST, though, was living in some fear of the Gestapo and was being protected from the Gestapo by the Abwehr. The Gestapo were not suspicious of ARTIST's real anti-Nazi activities but he had fallen foul of them apparently over some currency transactions in which he had originally participated with the Gestapo but which he denounced when he found that the £5 notes which were being passed were forgeries, the profits on which were being pocketed by Gestapo officials. Some of the officials had lost their positions, but the survivors among them were keen to get their revenge on ARTIST and he feared that they had sufficient power to seize him if he returned to Germany. As a result, ARTIST came up with a suggestion, which was approved by the Abwehr. TRICYCLE was to tell the Yugoslavs in London that he had met in Lisbon an old friend of his (ARTIST) who, afraid of the consequences of Germany losing the war, wanted to get on good terms with an Allied Government. He was, therefore, willing to ingratiate himself with the Allies by using the influence that his official position gave him in assisting some Yugoslav prisoners of war to escape. He was willing to obtain passports for ten or twelve Yugoslavs of TRICYCLE's choice in return for an understanding that when he felt the time had come to desert the Germans he would be given assistance, and when the war was over would be allowed to live and work in Yugoslavia. This was to be the official plan which TRICYCLE was at liberty to mention to the Yugoslavs or the British. ARTIST also settled with TRICYCLE certain code telegrams which would indicate if ARTIST was in acute physical danger; in which case TRICYCLE was to try and arrange for ARTIST to be evacuated. In this way the Germans thought they would be sending double agents into Britain whereas, in fact, through their selection by ARTIST and TRICYCLE the agents would in fact be pro-Allied and working against the Germans.

Soon, however, 'a substantial change took place in the position of ARTIST'. When TRICYCLE left Lisbon, ARTIST went to Madrid where he had various conversations with JUNIOR, 'a hanger on of the Abwehr', who reported information to SIS. JUNIOR confirmed that ARTIST was in trouble with the Gestapo which prevented him from returning to Germany as there was doubt whether the Abwehr could fully protect him there. JUNIOR met ARTIST through one Moldenhauer, son of a former German minister, and partly Jewish, who worked, mainly in Madrid, for I Wi. Brussels. Moldenhauer seemed to be one of a number of anti-Nazis who had avoided active participation in the war by undertaking service with the Abwehr 'that they make no effort to carry out conscientiously'. JUNIOR learnt and reported that ARTIST had agents in Britain, 'one of whom was a rich Serb he had recently met in Lisbon'. On 22 September an enquiry from ARTIST reached SIS in Madrid through JUNIOR and a Swiss businessman, Oswald, used for contacting JUNIOR. At first it was thought that ARTIST was thinking that a superior had overheard some conversations that would brand ARTIST as a traitor in German eyes; ARTIST apparently was now requesting immediate evacuation to the UK. Later, when direct contact was established with ARTIST it became clear he was not in quite such a panic as had first been believed, but was afraid that he was becoming suspected by the Abwehr, and that they had already voiced suspicions of TRICYCLE in Lisbon, and were making accusations to Berlin against both TRICYCLE and ARTIST. ARTIST was not seeking immediate evacuation, but was trying to ascertain if the British would evacuate him if his position with the Germans became untenable. ARTIST made it clear that he was sincere in his desire to preserve his own and protect TRICYCLE's cover by declining an offer of immediate sanctuary in the British Embassy. The main grounds of his fears were telegrams ARTIST had received from various friends in Germany warning him not to return.

Before he made direct contact with the British, ARTIST, observed Ian Wilson, 'was rash enough to expose his position' to his friend Moldenhauer 'by an act that might well have proved fatal'. By this act, Moldenhauer, 'had he been a loyal German', would have been bound to disclose the true position of ARTIST and his supposed agents to the Germans. To cover his evacuation, had it taken place, ARTIST proposed to fake his suicide, leaving an explanatory letter behind him to be transmitted to his chiefs Munkinger and Thoering in Berlin through Rohescheidt, the head of Abteilung III in Madrid. He prepared this letter in the presence of Moldenhauer, so that Moldenhauer could be a witness of his intentions to commit suicide. Although ARTIST later told Moldenhauer that his difficulties had been overcome and he was remaining in his previous position, it was 'inevitable' that Moldenhauer should learn that ARTIST was betraying Germany. ARTIST excused himself on the grounds that he was sufficiently confident of Moldenhauer's anti-Nazism and discretion to be sure that he would never betray ARTIST or refer to the matter if, as happened, evacuation proved unnecessary. Events to a large extent justified this confidence as it was clear that Moldenhauer did not denounce ARTIST to the Germans; and having failed to do so at the time it was almost impossible for him to do so convincingly many months later. But Moldenhauer did make some reference at the time to ARTIST's actions to a girlfriend of his, who also reported to SIS: 'so there was clearly a serious danger' that Moldenhauer, 'by indiscretion if not deliberately, might blow the whole matter'.

In due course the suicide letter was handed over by ARTIST to SIS. It alleged that ARTIST was driven to suicide by conflict of loyalty to Germany on the one hand and to his old friend TRICYCLE. It also stated how TRICYCLE having been said to have confessed to ARTIST in Lisbon, under pledge of secrecy and after having extracted the names of ARTIST's other agents, had in recent months been turned round by the British. The letter elaborated this theme in a manner that ARTIST claimed would have protected DREADNOUGHT's position in Yugoslavia and would have enabled the British to continue to use METEOR as a controlled agent even though the other agents with whose recruitment ARTIST had been concerned would have been blown. 'This may have been ARTIST's intention but it is difficult to believe that it would have succeeded or that the whole of his plan for a faked suicide was other than a piece of extreme foolishness brought about by excess of nervous strain,' noted Wilson in his assessment. ARTIST, in the meantime, sent a letter to TRICYCLE through SIS which provided evidence that he had all along been aware that the Yugoslavs he had sent out would double-cross the Germans; and 'we have plenty of impeccable evidence to show that he deliberately concealed this from the Abwehr as no doubt his own exemption from military service depended on his appearing to be responsible for genuine and useful Abwehr agents'.

The crisis through which ARTIST had passed in Madrid forced him into the open as a conscious informant for SIS/MI5. From this time onwards he provided a mass of useful information that 'can be checked to satisfy us of its very high standard'. The information now being given by ARTIST, pointed out Wilson, 'was in some respects highly embarrassing. He gave us certain details which might well have assisted us in capturing GARBO had we not already controlled him'. Attempts were made, both in the early contacts with ARTIST in Madrid and subsequently, to prevent ARTIST from realising what other agents MI5 might control. 'But as time went on it must have become increasingly clear to him, from the fact that agents of whose activities he has given us some evidence continue to operate, that we control those agents. It was a matter for serious thought whether we ought not to evacuate ARTIST as a "reference library" and wind up the TRICYCLE group of cases rather than run the risk of leaving him at large in the Peninsula with grounds to suspect that other agents were under control.'[29]

But this was not a decision reached without serious concerns being expressed by Wilson's colleagues. Hugh Astor intervened – although the 'fate of ARTIST is not really my concern' – because of the direct bearing it had on the running of other double-cross agents. He argued that, if ARTIST was assumed to be a reliable informant in Abwehr circles, the information he could provide fell into two categories: (a) the information which was already in his possession relating to Abwehr activities in the Balkans and German internal matters and (b) counter-espionage information relating to Abwehr activities in the Peninsula. MI5/SIS had three controlled agents operating here: LIPSTICK, GARBO and TREASURE; Astor feared that it would ultimately become obvious to ARTIST that these agents were not working for the Germans but for the British. 'Thus the fortunes of some of our most valued agents will be entirely dependent on the whims of a German whom we know to be brilliantly clever, but unscrupulous and dishonest, and who may turn over his knowledge to the Germans, either [of] his own volition or though force of circumstances.' According to his own story, ARTIST was now in great danger from the Gestapo and liable to suspicion by the Abwehr. If he was interrogated by the Gestapo and compromised British agents: 'The sudden loss of a large number of B1.A agents would in itself be a serious blow, but it would be far more serious if this loss occurred after the agents had embarked upon the implementation of the OVERLORD deception plan, since it would enable the Abwehr to read their traffic in the opposite sense. For these reasons I submit that under no circumstances should ARTIST be allowed to remain in the Peninsula.' To Astor's mind the sole function of a B1.A agent at the present time was to play a part in the deception plan and 'in my view any agent who is unable to fulfil this role is unworthy of preservation'. Astor wanted ARTIST brought to Britain so as to 'interrogate him at leisure'.[30] Tomas Harris, running GARBO, concurred on all points with Astor.[31] Ian Wilson, however, found himself 'in complete disagreement' with Harris and Astor and warned of the 'losses we would incur by taking action to avoid a risk, the magnitude of which is clearly a matter of opinion':

1. While getting the benefit of ARTIST's present knowledge, we lose all chance of using an agent within the enemy Intelligence to obtain further information which we desire.

2. We force ourselves to bring to an end the cases of TRICYCLE, BALLOON, GELATINE, METEOR and The WORM.

3. We render it impossible for us to start using VELOCIPEDE or the two agents introduced by TRICYCLE's brother, one of whom at least is now undergoing wireless and other training.

4. In my view, if it is logical to say that in view of such knowledge as ARTIST may now have or may acquire it is impossible to use any agent of whom he has knowledge for any deceptive purposes, it is at least as logical to say that if we evacuate ARTIST and blow him to the Germans it would be impossible to use TATE and MUTT & JEFF thereafter. ARTIST must know TATE put through Plan MIDAS, and the Germans, if we are to treat them with any power of thought at all, must assume that if we get our hands on ARTIST, and through him on TRICYCLE, we will obtain sufficient evidence to trace TATE, and through him, MUTT & JEFF.

5. While on a matter of this magnitude we must presumably disregard the personal issue of TRICYCLE's brother and other persons in enemy or enemy occupied countries who may be involved, we will almost certainly put an end to the activities of TRICYCLE's brother in Yugoslavia the importance of which we have insufficient evidence to assess fully, though clearly they are beneficial to the Allied cause.

Wilson denied that it followed that the position in future depended upon the 'whims' of ARTIST or that he was correctly described as unscrupulous and dishonest: 'Although he may be unscrupulous and dishonest towards the present German Government, [he] has not only been taking care to protect the double agents of whom he has knowledge, but has been deliberately sending out agents with the knowledge that they would double-cross, and has supported TRICYCLE's brother in his anti-German activities on other lines.'[32] In assessing ARTIST, Wilson observed:

ARTIST's motives in co-operating with the British are highly complex but would seem to include the following factors: the influence of DREADNOUGHT, who by all accounts has a dominating personality with which he impresses all who come in contact with him; a genuine dislike of Nazism, of which TRICYCLE can give some evidence dating from before the war; a belief in the British political system; a conviction dating at least from the failure of the first German offensive against Russia, that Germany had lost the war; a fear of Communism in Germany, which can only in his view be avoided by increased English influence in Western Europe; a contempt for the inefficiency and corruption in the Abwehr, on which he had played for so long to prevent his having to join the Army; the realisation that his own future as a big business man depended on the restoration of normal trading activities in Europe, which he thought would only be possible after an Anglo-American victory; and a desire to reinsure himself.

No doubt ARTIST is acting mainly out of self interest but of a clear-sighted and long-term character which, to a man of his undoubted intelligence, seems likely to prevent him from trying to deceive us on any matter where he is liable to be found out after the war to have deceived us.

ARTIST was born at Hamburg of Danish parents. All four grandparents were Danish. When ARTIST was twelve years old his father became a naturalised German and ARTIST acquired German nationality at the same time. He states that as a youth he was inevitably caught up in the Nazi movement but lost all regard for the party when as a University student he began to think for himself and made friends with other students from other countries.

ARTIST has not suggested that he should receive any financial rewards for his co-operation with us. Conditionally on our being satisfied, when we have full information after the war, that ARTIST has assisted us to the best of his ability we have assured him that, should he so desire it, we will use our best endeavours to assist him in regaining Danish nationality; that so far as practicable he would have freedom of travel for business purposes after the war and that, assuming the account he had given us of his part in the dealings in forged notes was accurate, he would be protected in any charges that might arise after the war against those responsible for the dealings. ARTIST was also assured that if any genuine German agents, (not being British subjects), were caught exclusively on reports given by him, the death penalty would not be exacted, and that should anything happen to him we would do our best to look after his wife's interests. ARTIST did not ask for financial provision for his wife as he had already taken steps to look after her financial future.

Wilson's arguments won through and 'it was decided that the advantages to be gained by going on with the TRICYCLE/ARTIST organisation outweighed this risk'.[33] Only time would tell if he was right – or a catastrophic mistake had been made.

13

Turn of the Tide
Preparing to Liberate Europe 1942–1944

By 1942 what became known as the 'Turn of the Tide' had occurred: with the Red Army delivering a massive defeat to the Germans at Stalingrad, Montgomery's defeat of the Afrika Corps at El Alamein and Anglo-American landings in North Africa, the Allies, in the West, began to consider the invasion of France. The Security Service was destined to play a crucial part in the strategic deception of the Germans.

The road to this historic use of intelligence began modestly when the Operations Section of MI5 was first formed in the autumn of 1940 as part of the newly constituted W Division. Major General Lakin was in charge of it and he had under him a number of liaison officers. The Operations Section's original charter was 'to receive Secret information, particularly in regard to operations, from the fighting services, through these liaison officers, and to examine communications with this object; also to test the security of Service establishments in which special work of operational value was being undertaken'. This proved a 'somewhat vague' charter and, as the original Operations Section did not have many of the necessary contacts and almost nobody outside the Service knew what its role was supposed to be, the results were 'not entirely satisfactory'.

For instance, MI5 were already fully represented on the Inter-Services Security Board (ISSB) by Major Lennox, one of the Operations Section liaison officers sent, to hold a watching brief for W Division.[1] The ISSB came into being early in 1940 as a sub-committee of the JIC. The Board met daily until VE Day (8 May 1945) and thereafter three times a week, plus ad hoc meetings for specific purposes. In its early days the Board was responsible for deception planning and implementation, in addition to its main function of operational security, and notable instances of this were in connection with the landings in Norway and the invasion of Madagascar. Later, however, the London Controlling Section (LCS) came into being and the deception functions of the Board were undertaken by the Controlling Officer and his staff. There remained, however, useful liaison between LCS and the Board, the Controlling Officer having a permanent representative on the Board and himself attending meetings on subjects of particular interest to him.[2] In the beginning, though, Major Lennox was not a member of the

ISSB and 'somewhat naturally' that body objected to passing on highly secret information to a non-member, and to duplicating, apparently, the work in so far as the Security Service was concerned.

During the first few months of its existence, MI5's Operations Section 'tried to get wind' of forthcoming operations or secret tests, and 'when it was lucky enough to do so, it sent an officer to find out further details on the spot. This obviously did not lead very far.' When plans were being made for secret operations, including secret exercises and tests, MI5 was 'apt to be left in the dark' if it had no direct and trusted link with the people concerned. Yet one of the roles of the Security Service was to safeguard these very secrets and see that information about them did not reach the enemy. If a leak was suspected 'it was clearly very difficult to deal with it if the Security Service did not know whether the matter which was alleged to have been leaked was true or false'. It was felt that there must be some direct link between the people responsible for deception plans and the two wings of the Secret Service, which could both help greatly in implementing such schemes.

In the summer of 1941 the Operations Section was reconstituted[3] by Sir David Petrie, working directly under himself, and under the charge of Major Lennox. The Section acted as a liaison between the Fighting Services and the Security Service on all matters affecting operations, the word 'operations' being used in its broadest sense. The objects for of the section were as follows: '1. To give early warning to the Security Service of intended operations, exercises, secret tests and experiments etc., so that suitable special Security measures may be taken by the Security Service; 2. To indicate to the Security Service the areas in which, because of special operations etc., enemy agents may seek to obtain information; 3. In connection with any intended operation, to see that information of operational value, which may become known to the Security Service or SIS, is passed quickly and suitably to the Service or Department concerned; 4. To implement where possible, through the Security Service and SIS, cover plans, and through them to take any necessary action intended to mislead the enemy; 5. To indicate to the Service or Department concerned with an operation, targets or objectives of interest to the Security Service and SIS, and in this connection to arrange for expert help and advice with regard to these targets and objectives; 6. To keep the Director General of the Security Service fully in the picture as regards intended operations, future plans and Service news generally.

With regard to all operational information of a highly secret nature, it was agreed, at a meeting between Petrie and the Directors of Intelligence, that Lennox should have full access to all relevant information available, and should convey it personally to the Director General. It would then be the responsibility of the Director General to pass on, through Lennox, to the various divisions and sections in the Security Service, only as much of the information as was considered necessary for the work to be carried out efficiently. Lennox became a full member of the Inter-Services Security Board, and Major Cass, who in turn joined the Operations Section, had been on the staff of the Board. This meant that Lennox, or Cass acting as his deputy, would be able to attend all meetings of the Board.[4]

By now 'Combined Operations', using its own craft and men, had begun carrying out raids which were planned in the greatest secrecy and the details of which were seldom known to anyone outside that headquarters. The Admiralty, War Office, Air Ministry and SIS were also engaged on secret operations which were often not known to each other or to Combined Operations. A request was therefore made from various quarters that MI5's Operations Section should undertake the responsibility of seeing that clashes did not take place. This was 'perhaps a strange duty for a section of the Security Service, but was in fact perfectly logical in the circumstances'. Nor was it a particularly difficult responsibility, so long as the Operations Section could be certain of keeping itself fully informed. A secret map was prepared and kept in a locked cupboard, showing exactly where all future operations were planned and, clearly, if two operations were not planned in or near the same place, there could be no clash.

The Operations Section also undertook the preparation of a weekly secret Project List. This List showed, in geographical order, all projected secret operations throughout Europe and Africa, which were planned or known about in Britain. Three copies only were made, one was delivered each Monday to 'C', and one to Air Commodore Boyle of SOE, for their personal use and information, and the third was retained in the Operations Section for use within MI5. These Project Lists were produced weekly right up to the end of the war in Europe. The war in the Far East was only covered as regarded major plans and operations. Also, it was found and agreed that it was impossible to cover fully such things as the normal bombing operations against the Continent, liable as they were to be changed or cancelled at the last moment, but as far as it was practicable, any air operations which might clash with something else were listed. B Division also found it convenient and useful to ask the Section to advise as to the truth and importance of operational material disclosed in Most Secret Sources. This became almost a daily duty of the Section.

Finally, at the request of the War Cabinet Offices, the Operations Section became responsible for advising on and applying special security measures for the journeys of VIPs outside Great Britain. A special drill was laid on, by Section D4 of MI5, for the journeys of less important VIPs, and in this the Operations Section took little part, except when it was able to advise when any doubt arose. In nearly every case the Section knew why the journey was being made 'and obviously quite a number of people were inclined to think that they were entitled to VIP treatment when in fact this was not necessary'. Also, the Section could advise D4 just what particular aspect of the journey it was desirable to conceal. It was, however, with regard to the journeys of the two important VIPs, His Majesty the King and the Prime Minister, that the Section took a more active part. It became its duty to have a representative present at the various meetings at which the Prime Minister's journeys were planned and discussed, so as to give security advice.

Later, many of the security arrangements were actually made and implemented by the Section. It also had the responsibility of watching Security Service and SIS sources for any leakage about such journeys, particularly from enemy sources, and of reporting such occurrences in time through the proper channels. Care had to be taken that the duties of the Section in this connection did not interfere with the recognised responsibilities of the police and other authorities. A 'good deal of tact was sometimes necessary'. Gradually this work increased, particularly with regard to the Prime Minster's journeys, 'until it may almost be said that he and his missions did not leave the country without having been seen off by the Operations Section'. On the occasions of the Yalta and Potsdam Conferences the Operations Section was asked to go even further. Major Boddington of the Section accompanied the delegation to Yalta as Security Officer for the Conference. He was responsible for collaborating with the Russians and Americans on aspects of security. At Potsdam security was the responsibility of 21 Army Group, to which Major Boddington was lent, but he was in personal security charge of the Conference itself and the buildings which housed it, again collaborating with the Russians and Americans. Among the tasks MI5's Operations Section was involved were the following:

OPERATIONS
26.12.41 – ASCOT & BRACELET – Raid on Bodo and Lofoten Islands.
27.12.41 – ARCHERY – Raid on Malloy and Vaagso.
27.2.42 – BITING – Raid on Brunevald.
28.3.42 – HARIOT – Raid on St Nazaire.

4.4.42 – MYRMIDON – Plans for raid on Bayonne, later abandoned.

21.4.42– ABERCROMBIE – Raid on N and S of Hardelot Beaches.

4.5.42 – IRONCLAD – Invasion of Madagascar.

1.7.42 – BARRICADE – Attempted raid on Barfleur.

August 42 – -JUBILEE – Raid on Dieppe.

20.9.42 – MUSKETOON – Raid on Haugvik Aluminium Works.

2.11.42 – TORCH – Invasion of N.Africa.

1.1.43 – BACKCHAT – Attempted raid on the Cherbourg Peninsula.

23.1.43 – CARTOON – Raid on Alderney.

Aug/Sep 43 – ALACRITY – Occupation of the Azores.

June 43 – HUSKY – Invasion of Sicily, leading to the invasion of Italy.

6.6.44 – OVERLORD/NEPTUNE – Invasion of France.

VIP JOURNEYS

TRIDENT – 5.5.43 – PM and Chiefs of Staff... from Glasgow to New York (Washington Conference).

LOADER – 11.6.43 – HM The King from Northolt to Algiers.

QUADRANT – 5.8.43 – PM., Chiefs of Staff and large ministerial party... from Glasgow to Canada (Quebec Conference).

SEXTANT – 12.11.43 – PM and Chiefs of Staff in HMS Renown and London from Plymouth to Middle East for 'Big 3' conference (Teheran).

OCTAGON – 5.9.44 – PM., Chiefs of Staff and large ministerial party in... from Glasgow to Halifax to meet the President of the USA (Quebec).

TOLSTOY – 7.10.44 – PM, CIGS., Foreign Secretary and Staffs from Northolt to Moscow to visit Stalin.

ARGONAUT – 30.1.45 – PM., Chiefs of Staff and large ministerial party to the Crimea. VIPs by air and the remainder in HMT Franconia (Yalta).

TERMINAL – 15.7.45-3.8.45 – PM., Chiefs of Staff and large ministerial party to and from Potsdam, mostly by air.

SECRET TRIALS & TESTS

POPLIN – Sonic Warfare.

TOURIST – Jet-propelled aircraft.

CDL – (Canal Defence Lights). Dazzle searchlight on tanks.

DD Tanks – (Duplex Drive). Swimming tanks.

HIGHBALL – Bouncing bomb for use against capital ships, dams,

etc. Including UPKEEP, BASEBALL and LOWBALL, smaller
bouncers; GROUSE-SHOOTING, bouncer in tunnel; OXTAIL,
HIGHBALL against Japanese Fleet; SPEEDEE American code-
word for HIGHBALL.
MULBERRY – Including PHOENIX, BOMBARDON,
WHALES, HIPPOS and RHINOS. GOOSEBERRIES US codename. Artificial harbour.[5]

The evolution of strategic deception, leading to OVERLORD (the
invasion of Europe) might be said to have begun with Operation
COCKADE, an elaborate camouflage and deception scheme extending
over the whole summer of 1943, the aim of which was to pin the
Germans down in the West and keeping alive the expectation of large-
scale cross-Channel operations in 1943. This would include at least
one amphibious feint with the object of bringing on an air battle,
employing the RAF and US 8th Air Force. Operation STARKEY
– part of COCKADE – was in fact the 'amphibious feint'. The official
definition of STARKEY was 'an amphibious feint to force the GAF
[German Air Force] to engage in intensive fighting over a period of
about fourteen days by building up a threat of an imminent large-
scale British landing in the Pas de Calais area'. Operation WADHAM
– also part of COCKADE – was a purely deceptive operation to give
the impression of preparations for a large-scale American landing
in Brittany (Brest Peninsula) towards the end of September 1943,
involving U.S. forces from the UK. In conjunction with STARKEY,
this was intended to pin down German reserves in France and the
Low Countries. Operation TINDALL completed the COCKADE
picture, being a purely deceptive operation designed to pin German
forces in Norway by giving the impression of preparations for a major
British operation about mid-September for the capture of the port
and airfields of Stavanger. While it was not thought that the Germans
could be persuaded to reinforce Norway at the expense of the West, it
was important that the Arctic-trained troops stationed there should
be pinned down by threatened attack and not used to reinforce the
Russian front. The threat was maintained until mid-November 1943.[6]
MI5's role in STARKEY was to carry out Exercise HARLEQUIN:
to assess the potential for security leakages. The Operations Section,
under Major Boddington, found the initial security implications
'alarming to say the least': as a result of an extensive tour of the south-
east and south coasts from the Thames estuary to Southampton, MI5
(Ops) 'have come to the conclusion that owing to the complete lack of
co-ordination of security it would have been the simplest matter, had

the men been briefed, for an agent to have obtained an almost complete picture of the whole operation'. Boddington warned that the lessons for future invasion plans and assault operations meant: 'It must be clearly appreciated we can only expect to keep from the enemy primarily WHERE and secondly WHEN we are going to attack, plus strength of force, and to achieve this there must be at the earliest possible stage a co-ordinated plan of security under one central body. That body must have complete authority and must be accepted by all services.' Already there had been leakages, such as with Operation TORCH; therefore: 'We further emphasise the necessity to ensure that all concerned fully realise the penalties of any breach of security whatsoever, and that these penalties will be inflicted irrespective of rank.' Among the primary duties of any central body would be to ensure that all security personnel knew where their particular duties began and where they ended. Liaison with the police through the Regional Officers was of vital importance. It was essential that the Chief Constables were taken into the confidence of the Co-ordinating Body more fully and at an earlier stage that heretofore. From a general security point of view the size and date of closing of restricted areas, road controls and system of passes were the four main problems. These points could only be settled in conjunction with the Chief Constables concerned, Regional Officers, MI5 and the General Staff, Officers of the Forces involved, plus Movement Control. In the actual embarkation area the sole responsibility to the Body for security would rest with Movement Control advised by representatives of MI5 in conjunction with their Port SCOs. To do this effectively, special areas in close proximity to beaches, for example, should be evacuated to a depth and width to be decided upon locally.[7]

Towards the end of December 1943, Plan BODYGUARD, the overall deception policy for the war, against Germany was submitted by the Controlling Officer of the War Cabinet which directed the policy to be adopted up to the D-Day of OVERLORD. In brief it dictated that the enemy should be induced to believe: 1. The bombing by Allied air forces would be continued and increased in the hope that it might bring about a total German collapse without necessity for an amphibious invasion; 2. The Allies were in readiness to occupy and maintain order in any western European countries from which the Germans might decide, through a serious weakening, to withdraw, utilising the troops in the UK yet untrained for assault operation; 3. An attack on northern Norway, to be concerted with the Russians, would be launched in the spring; 4. No large-scale cross-Channel operation would be possible until the late summer; 5. Owing to shortage of manpower it had been impossible to maintain all formations at full strength; 6. Some of the US Divisions arriving in the UK had not yet completed their training; 7. Some personnel from Anglo-American formations in the Mediterranean were being returned to the UK for training inexperienced formations; 8. The supply of invasion craft was not up to schedule. etc., etc.

These points were all intended to make the Germans believe that the Allied state of preparedness for the cross-Channel invasion was not far advanced 'and in consequence they would draw the conclusion that the attack was planned to take place considerably later than the real target date.' All these points were brought out in the messages transmitted by the GARBO network during the first months of 1944:[8] as Tommy Harris, GARBO's case officer, recalled, the success of the OVERLORD operation depended on the speedier build up of Allied forces in the bridgehead, in the initial stages, than the enemy could anticipate or contain. 'It seemed likely that the enemy would be able to draw upon its superior and mobile reserves at a greater speed than we, in carrying out the most hazardous of all amphibious operations, could hope to land large formations and their supplies.' In a 'less magnificently conceived plan, the enemy would logically be expected to draw upon their reserves, and with great speed, supply the already well established defending forces with unlimited reinforcements, with the inevitable result, that the attacking forces would be thrown back into the sea before they had time to establish a substantial bridgehead'. From this picture, as Harris explained, two essentials emerged:

> 1. The enemy would have to be taken by surprise as to the target area. (A fundamentally difficult problem in view of the gigantic preparations which could not concealed from them); 2. The nature of the undertaking must be concealed from the enemy. (This was dependent on the enemy being led to believe that the invasion would be launched in at least two stages.)[9]

In February 1943, acting on a general directive from the London Controlling Section, the saff responsible for deception plans, Home Forces, had begun to construct an imaginary Order of Battle. It was agreed that the deception plan must combine the reports of MI5's XX agents, the necessary W/T traffic purporting to emanate from and concern the bogus formations as well as camouflage and dummies which would deceive the enemy's aerial reconnaissance. By the winter of 1943–1944 this W/T cover was available and the creation of the false Order of Battle began to develop.[10] Prior to D-Day there were two independent plans which had to be implemented: FORTITUDE (NORTH), a threatened attack against Norway, to be carried out by an imaginary Fourth British Army and FORTITUDE (SOUTH) a threatened attack against the Pas de Calais, to be carried out by an imaginary First US Army Group, known as FUSAG.

FORTITUDE (NORTH) was principally concerned with naval deception and was worked out in considerable detail on lines similar to Operation STARKEY. A large transport fleet was to assemble off the east coast of Scotland. The Planners, believing that the German naval staff would realise that port facilities in the east coast of Scotland were inadequate for the requirements of an operation of the scale of FORTITUDE (NORTH), decided to route the transport fleet north around Scotland to the Clyde. In fact it continued on its journey south, to the real invasion bases but it was reported, by GARBO, as having put into the Clyde to join up with the (imaginary) battle fleet; meanwhile it was reported by his (imaginary) Agent No. 3 as exercising there. Formations under command of the (imaginary) Fourth British Army were then reported as assembling at camps in the Glasgow vicinity. The plan culminated on D-1.[11]

FORTITUDE (SOUTH) involved the creation, through the medium of MI5's agents, two Army Groups, one real (the 21st Army Group) and one imaginary or notional (the 1st US Army Group or FUSAG). When the 21st Army Group went overseas – to France – FUSAG would be left in England consisting of the US 3rd Army (a real one) and the British 4th Army (a notional one). In the final stage when the real US 3rd Army had gone overseas on about D+3, FUSAG would be left with only imaginary formations, these being eventually the 14th US Army and the 4th British Army. The object of this plan was to induce in the German General Staff the belief that the invasion of Normandy was a diversionary move and that the real attack was to come in the Pas de Calais area.[12]

As Roger Hesketh – one of its architects – noted, in his report on FORTITUDE, it was important to take into account the workings of the German Intelligence Service, 'without whose co-operation the double-cross system in the United Kingdom could not have existed'. The German Intelligence Service suffered, Hesketh observed, to some extent from the dual control which 'affected the whole German conduct of the war and which arose from the struggle for supremacy between the fighting services and the Party'. So far as espionage was concerned, the matter was temporarily settled by a 'gentleman's agreement' arrived at in 1939 between Heydrich, 'the Party man' and head of the RSHA

(Reichssicherheits-Haupt-Amt) and Canaris, the head of the Abwehr, whereby the latter was left in sole charge of the German spy system. As Himmler's power increased the Secret Intelligence Branch of the RSHA known as Amt VI, in spite of the agreement of 1939, began to run its own spies. But 'it displayed a singular ineptitude in the art of espionage; it put its agents in touch with each other and in other ways broke the most elementary rules'. The Abwehr 'at least proved itself capable of administering a large network of British-controlled agents in the United Kingdom'. The RSHA 'could not even do that'. All the spies that MI5 used in FORTITUDE were Abwehr agents. In spite of this, the Abwehr was 'now suffering eclipse on the home front'.

In the spring of 1944, Canaris was dismissed, being replaced by Hansen, and on 1 June, five days before OVERLORD, the whole Abwehr was taken over by the RSHA. This 'might have been a very serious thing for deception, and it caused a good deal of anxiety, in Allied circles, at the time'. In the event, however: 'It turned out to be a gain rather than a loss. Although all the Abwehr chiefs were swept away, the machine was preserved, a course which the RSHA could in fact hardly avoid as it had nothing to put in its place.' Now Schellenberg, the head of Amt VI, who replaced Hansen after the attempted assassination of Hitler, was a 'more influential man' than any of his Abwehr predecessors 'and for him to claim possession of our controlled agents could be nothing but an added strength to the Allied cause'. There was some fear of the 'new broom' when Amt VI took control. It was thought that they would 'submit the easy-going Abwehr organisation to a close scrutiny, in which case we might have some difficulty in preventing our channels from falling under suspicion'. As it turned out, however, the RSHA 'preferred to let well alone'. The Abwehr had also purported to glean information about what was going on in Britain:

> from an equally spurious type of spy. Certain individuals, residing in neutral capitals, having persuaded the Abwehr that they controlled networks of agents operating in the United Kingdom, were able, by the exercise of ingenuity and imagination, to supply the Germans with a constant stream of intelligence which had little foundation in truth. They do not usually appear to have been actuated by any feeling of hostility towards the Central Powers, nor by a wish to help the Allied cause, but were moved either by a desire for personal gain or to avoid the inconvenience and hardship of active service... To us they were always a nuisance and often a real danger. Sometimes, by intelligent guesswork, they

came alarmingly near to the truth, at other times they talked such nonsense that they lowered the credibility of agents in general in the eyes of the military commanders, but unfortunately seldom went quite far enough to discredit themselves.

Messages sent, by MI5 agents, to the Germans were worked out and approved by means of daily meetings between the Special Means officer at Supreme Headquarters Allied Expeditionary Force (SHAEF) and the Case Officers affected. On one or two occasions of particular importance the agent himself joined in the consultations. To provide a constant flow of information on military subjects, through G.H.Q., Home Forces, all the Field Security Sections in the United Kingdom were told to put themselves in the position of a German spy and to send in a fortnightly report of observations which, in their opinion, would have helped a spy to draw conclusions about the invasion. The real object, however, was to give MI5's controlled agents 'something to say. We could pick items from these reports which had all the attributes of realism because they had in fact been seen. B.1.A. also employed an officer with a motor-car, who could supply local colour about places which the agents had visited in imagination only.[13]

It was as a result of the preparation and execution of OVERLORD than MI5 finally got the integrated Counter Intelligence (CI) system that had soured relations between the Service and SIS in 1942 – and thereafter. When the plans for the invasion of Normandy were being prepared, Dick White acted in the capacity of an adviser on counter-espionage to the staff responsible for planning the organisation. Eventually the American Army system was adopted, the organisation at SHAEF headquarters comprising G-2 Operational Intelligence and G-2 Counter-Intelligence (G-2 CI and G-2 CI) equivalent to the British formations of GSI(A) and GSI(B). G-2 CI under the direction of White was responsible for discharging, within the zones of military operations, the same functions as were discharged by the Security Service inside the United Kingdom, that was to say, all the functions of security and counter-espionage. In particular they were responsible for the arrest of enemy agents whether left behind by the Germans as they retreated or subsequently despatched by them to penetrate behind the Allied lines.

At the end of 1943 and at the beginning of 1944 a suggestion was put forward for the formation of a Central Counter Intelligence Bureau which was to be responsible for collecting and analysing, for the benefit of Counter Intelligence Staffs with Allied Army Groups and

Armies, all relevant intelligence about the German Intelligence Service and its agents. It was realised that OSS, the American Special Service, and the Security Service and SIS, the two British Services, between them possessed almost all the information that existed anywhere about the German Intelligence Services (the Abwehr and the Sipo and SD) and that they were the only organisations that had personnel properly trained to deal with this subject. The problem, therefore, was to devise some means by which all this information could be made available to the Counter Intelligence Staff in a satisfactory form. Difficulties arose because of objections raised by SIS – again, in MI5's view, 'from the special position claimed by Cowgill, as the head of Section V, for his organisation'. Once again, Cowgill claimed that intelligence concerning persons outside the three-mile limit of the UK was the concern of Section V but not of the Security Service; and that he was therefore entitled to withhold it at his discretion. His attitude 'obstructed the comprehensive study of the enemy organisations and the collation of intelligence about them at any point as a centre. It had the effect that when the Allies landed on the Continent there was no focal point through which G-2 CI could receive and transmit intelligence derived from ISOS, Camp 020, their own interrogations and other sources. The machinery was diffused instead of being centralised'.

The failure to find a solution dominated the relations between MI5 and SIS during 1943 and 1944, 'with adverse effects on the efficiency of both of them'. An agreement was made to set up a joint organisation comprising the sub-sections of OSS and SIS dealing with France and the Low Countries to perform all the functions of the Security Service for the purposes of the G-2 CI formations – but with MI5 excluded. This new organisation was established under the name of the 'War Room' and under the joint direction of the Western European sections of OSS and Section V. A Security Service officer was attached as a liaison officer to whom all matters concerning MI5 were referred and from whom information from Security Service records was received. French representatives were attached for a similar purpose. But it became apparent, in the early autumn of 1944, that this organisation was not satisfactory. 'It did not furnish the necessary focal point for the centralisation of intelligence. On the contrary it represented a renewed attempt to place that point in Section V (instead of in the Security Service) with inadequate machinery and without the necessary staff of trained personnel.' So, from October 1944, negotiations were carried on between the G-2 CI sub-division of SHAEF and OSS, the Security Service and SIS for the purpose of setting up a new body of experts to inform and advise the CI Staffs in the SHAEF area about the organisation, operations and personalities of German Intelligence.

It was only, in February 1945, that it was finally agreed that a new organisation to be known as the SHAEF G-2 Counter Intelligence War Room should be created under the direction of MI5's TAR Robertson, with an American Deputy, Mr Blum. OSS, SIS and the Security Service (referred to as the Special Services) agreed to place at the disposal of SHAEF the personnel and records required for the purpose. It was not until 1 March 1945 that this new machine came into effective operation. It lasted until the end of July 1945 and created 'a single organ through which all the relevant and available information and advice from OSS, the Security Service and SIS could be furnished to Counter Intelligence Staffs in the field'.[14] Finally, the Security Service, in its battle with SIS, had been proved right, albeit very late in the day.

The Return of BRUTUS

Chris Harmer had never given up on BRUTUS. Neither, it seemed, had the Germans. They had replied to his message of 20 August 1943 – drawn up with Harmer – informing them of his arrest and court martial. In it BRUTUS had stated that he thought it, in the circumstances, too dangerous to transmit, but asked for an address and a method of secret writing and asked further that the Germans should send their reply blind. On 29 August the Germans replied with the address, but unfortunately as appeared from subsequent messages sent on 5 September, they hedged on the question of supplying secret ink. This appeared to be consistent with an 'understandable' suspicion of BRUTUS in the peculiar circumstances of his arrest and release. The main object of getting the address was to be able to write and show that it was BRUTUS himself who was operating the case. To carry this out, a postcard was sent, to the address given, on 10 September, and this had since been followed by a further postcard and also a letter to VIOLETTE on 9 November. For some time no information was sent except an account of BRUTUS's arrest, in which he told more or less the full story. On 7 November the Germans sent a message from which it appeared that they were still suspicious to some degree of BRUTUS, to which he replied on 11 November that he had supposed, wrongly, that his difficulties interested them as well as other information. He then proceeded to start a report on the south-east coast which was only completed at the end of the year. After BRUTUS's release the case had come up for review, and it was decided to continue it but, as a precaution against BRUTUS 'starting some other activity', to interpose a radio operator as soon as possible. A favourable moment appeared to have arisen when BRUTUS was about three quarters of the way through his long report on the South-east coast region. The Germans then appeared to have regained confidence in him, and the operator accordingly started on Christmas Day and seemed to have been accepted. His cover name was CHOPIN, and he was supposed to have been recently retired from the Polish Air Force, to be in receipt only of a small pension and to be working principally for the ideological motives, having lost his family in Russia. In the message received just before Christmas, the Germans expressed their great appreciation of BRUTUS's work.

On the last day of 1943, Harmer made a plea to take the BRUTUS case further. His decision to do would prove inspired. Harmer argued that, in his opinion, BRUTUS's present position, 'at the worst, is merely that of a member of a subversive movement inside an allied government. In my view we can never guarantee that he will not intrigue and get into trouble, but we are justified in assuming that he will not act directly as a German agent without our knowledge and authority.' Harmer hoped, however, that the reorganisation of the Polish Air Force and the retirement of the former chiefs of the Deuxieme Bureau that had occurred would be enough to 'keep him quiet, at any rate until the war over here becomes sufficiently exciting to occupy his thoughts and activities'. The 'real problem', believed Harmer, was that of his future career. BRUTUS stated that he had possibilities either of going to America at the end of January 1944 for a three-months staff course, or of being nominated for one of the eight staff-liaison jobs which the Air Ministry had offered the Polish Air Force, or of doing a refresher course in aeroplanes or of remaining in his present office. So far as the British authorities were concerned, Harmer considered that their security interests in the circumstances could be adequately safeguarded by refusing him permission to go back to flying duties. Insofar as the interests of the case were concerned, 'I also consider that it would be inadvisable to let BRUTUS leave the country... To sum up; it is not considered that BRUTUS represents a serious security danger to the country, though he represents a real danger to the Poles, and he can be a great nuisance to us insofar as the case is concerned if he gets into trouble again.' As to the running of BRUTUS as a XX agent, Harmer felt that the bar, imposed in 1942, 'against operational deception makes the case a trial or a complete waste of time'. But it now appeared to be an appropriate time now to review the situation 'and see whether it is worth making application to have the bar against deception raised, or alternatively deciding whether the case is worth continuing'. Harmer pointed out that:

there is almost incontrovertible evidence that BRUTUS was regarded by the Germans as being a reliable agent... and if all other things are equal it is believed that the BRUTUS case could be developed as an effective means of deceiving the enemy... It is submitted... that once they have accepted him and regarded him as an important agent, they are unlikely to go back on their judgement unless an entirely new factor in the situation arises... In all the circumstances, therefore, it is submitted that a case should be made out in an attempt to have the ban on the use of the case for deception lifted, either in whole or in part. If the ban could be lifted the opportunities for using this case for deception are very great.

It was not until February 1944, 'as nothing untoward had occurred and in view of the great potentialities of the case', that the decision not to use BRUTUS for operational deception was reversed and in March BRUTUS joined the FORTITUDE team.

The 'Move to Concentration'

Once the composition of the imaginary FUSAG had been determined and locations fixed, MI5's XX agents proceeded with the task of building up the fictitious Order of Battle and of preparing for the false move to concentration of forces for the imaginary invasion of the Pas de Calais. The disposition of the agents was the first consideration. It had for long been known that travel restrictions would be imposed in the embarkation areas. It was important that the movements of GARBO's imaginary agents should not be hampered by security measures, and it was to meet such a situation that his (imaginary) Agent Seven's (imaginary) sub-agents had been recruited in December 1943, the idea being that they should be sent to places on the south and south-east coasts early in the New Year and so acquire a resident's qualification before the visitors' ban was imposed. Thus on 18 February – in Letter No. 16 to the Germans and despatched to Lisbon on 19 February with eight other letters in a tin of curry powder – GARBO informed the Germans that he was sending Sub-Agent 7 (2) to Dover, 7 (4) to Brighton, 7 (5) to Exeter and 7 (7) to Harwich. Under the original arrangement agent 7 (5) was to have been placed in Southampton and agent 7 (6) in Exeter. On reflection Tommy Harris 'decided that it would be dangerous to put anyone in Southampton because he might see too much'. That area could if necessary be covered by periodical visits. Under the revised arrangement 7 (6) was to remain in South Wales, his place in Exeter being taken by 7 (5). And, of course none of these agents existed except in the mind of the Germans.

Madrid, in a letter from the Germans in Lisbon dated 3 April and received 22 April 1944, 'showed itself to be favourably impressed' by the progress which Seven's new organisation was making: 'I have taken note with great interest of what you have told me in your letters about the amplification of your network, and the numerous messages which you have sent during the last few weeks have demonstrated to me that you have been absolutely right in your idea of nominating the old collaborators as sub-agents of their networks. In particular, the network of Seven appears to be the one which is giving the best results.' Meanwhile GARBO had been conducting 'tests' upon his agents. Of 7 (2) he was able to report, to the Germans, on 7 March: 'Dover. I was able to confirm last Sunday the accuracy of the recent report sent by 7 (2) from Dover. I am, therefore, able to classify him in future as a good reporter.' Of 7 (4) in the same message: 'With regard to the military report, it is completely accurate so that we can catalogue this collaborator as being good.' Of 7 (7) he said: 'I consider this first report of this collaborator fairly good as he tries to get details from which one is able to appreciate the interest he takes in explaining what he has seen.'

It was then, as Roger Hesketh recalled, that: 'No one was quicker to appreciate the full implications of the new situation than GARBO's case officer,' Tommy Harris. In a memorandum dated 4 May, which outlined in detail the part to be played by the GARBO network during the coming weeks, Harris concluded with the proposal that forty-eight hours after the invasion had begun, GARBO should state that since last communicating he had given careful consideration to all the developments of the last two months and that, after consulting with his agents, he had arrived at the conclusion that the present large-scale attack in Normandy was only one prong of the Second Front to be carried out from Britain. The strategic importance of the attack was that of drawing reserves to the assault area in order that the second assault force should be able to make a comparatively unopposed advance along their direct route to Berlin: 'GARBO will then proceed to compare the logic of this analysis with the build-up of reserve forces, as will have become apparent from his agents' reports to that date, laying particular stress on those divisions still in the FORTITUDE area. He will end his message requesting that this report should be passed to Berlin together with his strong recommendation that they should guard against falling into this British trap by moving into the threatened area reserves which must be held available to hold and counter the second blow when delivered.' The plan Harris had come up with, if believed by the Germans, could tilt the balance of the forces engaged around Normandy by pinning German armour in the Calais area to await a non-existent landing there. But, suddenly, a crisis broke that threatened the entire MI5's entire network of XX agents involved in FORTITUDE.

The ARTIST Crisis

When TRICYCLE had his latest meeting with his German controllers in Lisbon at the beginning of March 1944, he received, according to his own account, 'a rather cold reception'. But, on the following day, when the contents of his material brought over from Britain had been telegraphed to Berlin and their comments had been obtained: 'The atmosphere changed to one of trust and confidence. He gained the clear impression that his reports had been well received by the higher authorities.' It seems that the key factor in bolstering TRICYCLE's position was the role played by his old friend ARTIST. Some further light was thrown upon these events by an interview which took place on 28 April between ARTIST and the SIS representative in Lisbon. ARTIST reported that German faith had been restored in TRICYCLE after ARTIST 'complained to TRICYCLE that he was not earning his keep. TRICYCLE then decided to collect material himself, and the result has been his last report' – it was so good that everyone was now in entire agreement that it was 'inconceivable that the British should have deliberately fed it'. SIS reported that: 'From ARTIST's point of view, the outcome is a complete triumph' and he was sure that whatever happened the Germans would 'never reverse decisions so categorically expressed'. To crown it all, ARTIST was awarded the 'Kriegsverdienstkreuz, 1st Class', an honour shared by no one in Lisbon. Thus, as Hesketh later recorded: 'To all appearances ARTIST's credit could hardly had stood higher. In reality, though neither he nor we knew it, disaster lay very near.'[15]

By April 1944, ARTIST was well aware that his position was precarious because of his previous financial dealings. He placed some faith in Brandes, an Abwher officer, who seemed to be looking after his interests. From ISOS intercepts MI5 were aware that, on 18 April, Brandes reported that ARTIST had told him he saw a clear trap when he was asked to attend a conference in Biarritz and that he was certain this entailed his immediate arrest. ARTIST was supposed to have told others that he was unable to travel to Biarritz as this would be an illegal crossing of the frontier and incompatible with his cover. In the meantime, also on 18 April, ARTIST had a meeting with SIS during which he was warned not to trust Brandes but the only ground that they could give him for this advice – they could not reveal Most Secret

Sources – was that British Intelligence did not have faith in previous reports from ARTIST when his source had been Brandes. ARTIST replied that Brandes's position was weak because he had difficulty in explaining why his 'mythical agents' could not be produced: Brandes had, in fact, invented a number of agents he was running to curry favour in Berlin. By 25 April, ARTIST went on to state that further investigations of TRICYCLE were being made and that a series of further tests were likely: the first of these had been the instruction to ARTIST to go to Biarritz. ARTIST was confident that Brandes would, as far as he was able, keep ARTIST warned of future tests. On 19 April, another German officer, Schreiber, insisted ARTIST go to Biarritz. MI5, however, maintained that this was a bluff. ARTIST duly packed his bags and made arrangements for the trip. On the 20th however, Schreiber, told ARTIST, at the last minute, that Berlin had decided against ARTIST going. In the meantime ARTIST had handed over $50,000 to SIS, of $75,000 allocated by the Abwher to TRICYCLE, keeping $25,000 – as arranged – for himself.[16]

On 25 April it had been reported in London that ARTIST seemed 'somewhat over sanguine in believing that the Groupe III check-up on himself and TRICYCLE was at an end'. The trouble, it now seemed, was not the General Staff nor Groupe I but that Groupe III, having given their opinion that TRICYCLE was not reliable, 'are now unwilling to admit themselves wrong'. Schreiber had gone to Madrid to discuss the matter further but ARTIST was confident that the former would uphold TRICYCLE before his critics.[17] In fact it seemed to ARTIST that Brandes was in more trouble than him: he reported that there was a chance of Brandes being recalled because of his failure to produce his agents. Brandes had told ARTIST the he was worried that TRICYCLE should be so good an agent the he would report the date and place of the invasion and thus prolong the war. ARTIST was convinced that Brandes was not trying to trap him, with this statement, into any admission but acted as though Brandes was so trying and therefore always reacted to the suggestion 'as a good German should'.[18]

Then, suddenly, on 29 April, ARTIST disappeared. Most Secret Sources intercepts indicated that ARTIST had been forcibly removed from Lisbon by Schreiber. On 30 May, Schreiber reported from Madrid to Berlin that he was going to Biarritz at once bypassing the Abwehr in Madrid or the SD. The 'luggage' he was carrying would be handed over in Biarritz to be sent on to Berlin. Subsequent messages made it clear that the undertaking on which Schreiber was engaged consisted of taking ARTIST to Biarritz: 'This had clearly been done in great secrecy and without the knowledge of other members of the

Abwehr in Lisbon.' On 3 May the SD in Lisbon reported that ARTIST had not returned to his house since the 29th and his whereabouts were unknown. The British were quite clear that ARTIST's troubles stemmed from reports against him made by the man he trusted, Brandes, whose 'motives are unlikely to be those of a patriotic German as he has no scruples in submitting to the Abwehr invented reports from notional agents'. Although it was too early to come to a clear and definite opinion, the general tenor of the intercepts seemed to be that the Abwehr were afraid that ARTIST was intending to go over to the British or to cause TRICYCLE's radio messages to be interrupted rather than suspect that ARTIST was already a traitor to Germany or that TRICYCLE was a controlled agent.[19] On 8 May there was a further – corrupt – message from Lisbon to Berlin that twice referred to people by the initials J and M. 'J' seemed to be ARTIST but the identity of 'M' was unclear.[20]

The disappearance of ARTIST, because he was aware in varying degrees of the British double-cross agents, had, potentially, enormous consequences for the deception plan for the invasion of Europe – Plan FORTITUDE. In spite of the danger, Major Masterman was inclined to the view that the agents should continue to operate without change. If indications and messages on ISOS were to show that TRICYCLE was blown and the other agents were under suspicion: 'We can change our policy... i.e. we can attempt by diversity of messages to create confusion in the enemy's mind even though we have to abandon the hope of getting a complete cover plan over to the enemy. This would, admittedly be a "second best", but it would not be bad.' If the conclusion was that, after a time, practically all the agents were in fact blown: 'We could take the extreme step and abandon all efforts at deception and... deny all information to the enemy closing down all agents... In my view even this, though less advantageous to us... would still leave us in a fairly strong position. The enemy, faced by the sudden collapse of our controlled agents, would... be effectively deprived of all information from agents at a time when he needs it most, and would have to prepare himself in the dark to meet any eventually.' The danger that the enemy would be able, having discovered the agents had been controlled, to deduce the cover plan 'seems to me greatly over-rated' given that most of the double-cross reports to the Germans 'have been factual and at least 75 per cent true'. This time factor alone convinced Masterman that 'we ought not to close down the agents, however suspect, until at the earliest shortly before D-Day'. Masterman, therefore, recommended:

1. That we continue to run the TRICYCLE traffic in the same style as before and with as little change as possible – but that no FORTITUDE deception is put over on it.

2. That the other agents continue for the time being exactly as at present.

3. That if we get information that the situation has deteriorated, the agents are used to fill the Germans with confusion instead of passing over a complete cover plan.

4. That if and only if the blowing of TRICYCLE and GARBO is certain, we close down all agents shortly before D-Day and deny all information to the enemy.[21]

But GARBO's controller, Tomas Harris, remained worried. He pointed out that the ISOS intercepts had seemed to confirm ARTIST's impression that Schreiber was his ally and was fighting his battles against the suspicions of the High Command, the Abwher and the SD, whereas Schreiber was in fact the man chosen to carry out his apparent kidnapping. Since ARTIST, in the opinion of MI5, had little doubt that the Spanish network in the UK was controlled by them: 'GARBO is therefore in the position of being able to carry out or blow FORTITUDE... without there being any likelihood of our getting warning on M[ost]S[ecret]S[ources] that he has been denounced by ARTIST.'[22] The danger, if the Germans broke ARTIST and discovered the network of double-cross agents, was brought home by an analysis of B1.A weekly traffic reports, from March 1943 to April 1944, undertaken by a military expert. The analysis, in the main part, drew the following conclusions:

1. Agents have been at pains to make no definite forecast as to the date when operations are likely to be launched.

2. There is a strong likelihood that invasion operations will be launched in the Mediterranean theatre at the same time as the main attack.

3. An attack on Norway, possibly of a diversionary character, is to be expected any time in May prior to the main attack.

4. It is suggested that the initial landings will be made against Belgium and the Pas de Calais area.

This assessment of approximately twelve months traffic was made by one officer, working normal office hours, in approximately two weeks. If the GARBO plan for implementation of FORTITUDE were put into operation and he was compromised at any time up to D-3 days the enemy could, within twenty-four hours, analyse the entire B1.A traffic for the two months leading up to his compromise and would be able to draw the clear conclusion that:

1. The cover plan threat is against the Pas de Calais area
2. We wish the enemy to believe that the assault will be two-pronged.

Such a discovery by the enemy, if made at any time up to D+3 days would, according to the Chief of Staff's appreciation, be 'catastrophic'.[23]

ARTIST's disappearance effectively ended the TRICYCLE network's participation in FORTITUDE: one XX agent connected with the network – FREAK – had been transmitting material that had become increasingly deceptive. Early in May, it was confirmed that ARTIST had been taken back to Germany; from early in May the traffic transmitted through FREAK's radio ceased to be highly deceptive for fear of endangering the cover plan for invasion. In the middle of May, a message was received in Britain originating from Mihailovic circles in Yugoslavia suggesting that before his escape FREAK had had contact with the Germans. It was known that the Germans knew that such a report had been made in Yugoslavia. As it was impracticable to continue with high grade traffic, at the same time avoiding the risk of compromising the cover plan, it was decided to make this denunciation of FREAK an excuse for suspending transmissions. TRICYCLE wrote a secret letter to the Germans explaining that, because of this denunciation, certain enquiries were in progress against FREAK, and for that reason they had temporarily hidden the wireless set. The transmitter was, therefore, not on the air from 18 May.[24] By now TRICYCLE was aware that ARTIST had been missing from his house since 29 April and that the longer his absence lasted the more likely it seemed to be that he had, 'by trick or force', been taken back to Germany. TRICYCLE realised that as long as British Intelligence was uncertain as to whether or not the Germans had found out that he was a controlled agent no use could be made of his radio traffic. He suggested that if MI5 'have no better means of ascertaining the position he would be prepared to be dropped in Yugoslavia by parachute to try and make contact with DREADNOUGHT'.[25] The burden of FORTITUDE now rested upon others' shoulders.

Back in Yugoslavia events were conspiring against DREADNOUGHT too. On his return to Belgrade at the beginning of April 1944, he found that a Sonder-Kommission of the SD was at work in Belgrade investigating charges of corruption, which was rife among all German officials in Belgrade. Although the corruption was probably worst among SS and SD officials, the Kommission took every care not to notice their misdoings but concentrated on the alleged misdoings of Wehrmacht officers and other officials who were not Party members. This Kommission consisted of Schaeffer, who had been head of Abwehr III in Belgrade which had, by this time, been taken over by the SD. Altogether about forty Wehrmacht officers were arrested in Belgrade by this Kommission, and seventeen of them were shot. Early in April, DREADNOUGHT was called before the Sonder-Kommission and questioned mainly about financial dealings he had had with Toeppen, and to a lesser extent with ARTIST. DREADNOUGHT refused to answer, on the grounds that he was doing secret work for the Abwehr and was not authorised to discuss his activities. He was arrested and taken to a Gestapo prison where he was beaten; but later he was taken to an officers' prison where his treatment was somewhat better. He was kept here for a week, and continually questioned by members of the Kommission, and questioned on one occasion for seventeen hours at a stretch. Questions were always about financial matters, primarily with ARTIST. After about a week, DREADNOUGHT was released by orders coming to the Kommission from Berlin, which he believed to have been obtained through the influence of his Abwehr friends. The Abwehr I officials in Belgrade were in fairly regular contact with DREADNOUGHT during May and early June 1944, but almost entirely for the purpose of requesting DREADNOUGHT not to mention to the Kommission that he had from time to time given them money, food or other assistance. They had a strong personal interest in assisting DREADNOUGHT to clear himself with the Kommission.

On 13 June 1944, DREADNOUGHT was again called to the Gestapo offices where an SS Colonel from Berlin, who had interrogated him before, told him to consider himself under arrest. He gave as the reason for this that information DREADNOUGHT had given about the paying of a bribe had been incorrect. DREADNOUGHT denied all knowledge of this and was temporarily released. He left immediately for General Mihailovic's headquarters. After his flight from Belgrade, DREADNOUGHT sent a letter to his family telling them that he had been called suddenly to Berlin; this was for his family to produce in case they were questioned by the Gestapo. He also wrote a long letter of explanation to his Abwehr contacts, explaining that he had been forced to flee from the Gestapo as he could not put up with any more attacks upon himself by the Gestapo, although these were no doubt due to a misunderstanding by them of the work which he was doing for the Abwehr. DREADNOUGHT emphasised that if he were arrested by the Gestapo and this became known to TRICYCLE, the latter would obviously stop work and that DREADNOUGHT, therefore, in his own interests as well as in the interests of the Abwehr, was going to keep away from the Gestapo. He would, however, be ready to come back to Belgrade and work again when the Abwehr could assure him that he was no longer liable to persecution by the SD. In order to conceal the fact that he was going to Britain, DREADNOUGHT left his typewriter and a number of sheets of paper signed with his German cover name, PAULA, with a Mihailovic intelligence officer who would, from time to time, send letters to make it appear that DREADNOUGHT was still in the mountains.

On arrival at Mihailovic mountain headquarters, DREADNOUGHT had a wireless message sent out which was picked up in Bari on 7 July, and which was addressed to Ian Wilson by name. This message did not, however, reach anyone who could appreciate its contents until 31 July, when London was consulted and Bari were instructed to evacuate DREADNOUGHT at the same time as they were evacuating over 200 American airmen who had baled out over Yugoslavia and were being looked after by the Mihailovic organisation. No message, however, was sent through to Mihailovic headquarters confirming that the British wished DREADNOUGHT to be evacuated; but on 9 August, DREADNOUGHT managed to get himself taken up in one of the aeroplanes which was collecting the Americans, and arrived in Bari, from where he was sent on as quickly as possible to London. He arrived in London on 15 August, travelling under the name of Fredrag Ivanovic. To protect DREADNOUGHT's family in Belgrade, and to avoid all risk of leakage to the Germans about his movements he continued to live under that alias. DREADNOUGHT was not aware, until he was informed by the British at Bari, that ARTIST had disappeared from Lisbon. DREADNOUGHT then recalled that, when on his way to Lisbon at the beginning of March 1944, he was given a message by a woman who met him in Vienna and said she was the daughter of Munzinger, telling him that Munzinger would contact him in the train but he was to appear not to recognise him. They sat opposite each other in the restaurant car, pretending to be strangers, but on leaving the restaurant car Munzinger drew DREADNOUGHT into a lavatory and told DREADNOUGHT to tell ARTIST not to go into any German Consulate or into occupied territory as the SD were laying a trap for him. DREADNOUGHT presumed that this related to the old Gestapo charges against ARTIST. Munzinger also asked DREADNOUGHT for assistance in covering a financial transaction of his own which he was afraid might be the subject of enquiry by the SD.[26] Unfortunately it was all to no avail. DREADNOUGHT had escaped but the fate of ARTIST remained a mystery.

14

Finest Hour
The Liberation of Europe 1944-1945

By the middle of May, the bulk of the reports concerning the move to concentration were in Germans hands – sent over by MI5's controlled agents. At this stage the Germans 'had, as it were, been given all the pieces belonging to the puzzle, but not the key which would explain how to fit them together'. For the agents who had been posted to observe the recent troop movements, while they were well qualified to identify single formations and even to say what corps some division belonged to, 'were hardly of high enough standing to learn about the grouping of senior formations or to discover their operational tasks'. For this 'someone with more exalted connections would be needed'. GARBO's 'friends' Agent J (5) at the Ministry for War and Agent 4 (3) at the American headquarters in London, had, 'to a certain degree', been able to fulfil such a role. On 10 May, for example, GARBO gave the following account of a conversation he had had with his American sergeant friend: '4 (3) said that the Second Front would open as soon as the two Army Groups destined for operation were ready. One of these, the 21 Army Group, is under Montgomery. The other, the First Army Group, is provisionally under the orders of Bradley. The American troops which are expected here will enter the latter Army Group. He assured me that Eisenhower would give a very important task to the American Army Group.' But MI5 'now required a more continuous view of planning at the higher level'.

FREAK, being a military attaché, would have been in a position to supply intelligence of this kind, and he had on 21 April informed the enemy that the Canadians in south-east England were to be grouped with Americans and not with British, and that an American corps would be brought under the Canadian Army, but 'both he and TRICYCLE were now *hors de combat*'. It was therefore decided to give BRUTUS an appointment at the Headquarters of FUSAG, the imaginary army group. 'Here he would be able to weld together into a connected whole, the heterogeneous reports sent in by the "ground observers."'.[1] A plan was formulated to cover BRUTUS during the period 27 May–15 June to support 'FORTITUDE' (SOUTH) by reporting:

1. FUSAG Order of Battle.
2. Preparedness of FUSAG for operations overseas.

3. Air exercise in KENT which indicates 'FORTITUDE' target area.

In order to fulfil these tasks it was decided to post him to the imaginary FUSAG on 27 May. His appointment 'should be such as to give him access to such information as we require him to pass on and to no more. It should also remove him physically from CHOPIN and the transmitting set so that we can limit the number of messages sent to suit our purpose'. For these reasons it was considered that he should not work at the Main HQ at Wentworth on the one hand, nor in London on the other.

The cover story was that a small section had been set up under FUSAG with the object of recruiting Poles in the FUSAG theatre of operations and forming them into army and air force units. This section was under the command of an American Colonel and had Polish Army and Air Force officers attached to it. It was located at Staines. It would be necessary for the Head of the section, accompanied by Polish military and air officers, to visit US formations before they went overseas in order to make the necessary arrangements. This story 'should prevent BRUTUS from learning too much; it will keep him away from his transmitter; it will help to indicate the target area as there are many Poles working in the French coalfields near LILLE and, by the order in which FUSAG formations are visited, it will help to indicate the order in which these formations will go overseas'.

As Polish Liaison Officers were being attached to 21 Army Group it was considered plausible to suggest that they were also being attached to FUSAG; however, if BRUTUS were posted notionally to FUSAG just before D-Day, it would be necessary to explain the efficient continuation of the service – i.e. that his espionage work for the Germans – after that date. If that could be explained 'he would be in an excellent position to report on the Order of Battle and operational intentions of FUSAG'. The plan 'considered that his recent marriage to MOUSTIQUE provides the basis for such an explanation'.

BRUTUS was to pay a notional visit to Scotland between 12 and 15 May, to enable him to continue implementing 'FORTITUDE' (NORTH). He would also inform the Germans about his marriage to MOUSTIQUE and tell them 'that she has been helping him for a considerable time'. He would also mention the possibility of his being given an operational liaison job. On his return from Scotland, BRUTUS would announce his nomination to post in FUSAG, to join up about a month before D-Day and announce his intention to leave MOUSTIQUE in charge of the service, if he had to leave London or go overseas. This was to be implemented if necessary by putting a notional MOUSTIQUE on the air to the Germans. MOUSTIQUE was also to present BRUTUS with a Free French officer sub-agent who was going overseas. Then:

> On D-5 BRUTUS to report his posting to FUSAG and to hand over to MOUSTIQUE...
>
> On D-3 BRUTUS to report through MOUSTIQUE: (a) Commander and Order of Battle of FUSAG (b) that D-Day is a fairly long way off...
>
> From D-Day to D+10 BRUTUS, through MOUSTIQUE: (a) to complete Order of Battle of FUSAG (b) to report separate operational role of FUSAG against NORTHERN FRANCE and BELGIUM...
>
> On D+10 BRUTUS, through MOUSTIQUE: to report that 1 Polish Armd. Div. has been attached to FUSAG...
>
> From D+10 onwards BRUTUS, through MOUSTIQUE: (a) to report preparations for move to embarkation areas of FUSAG formations (b) forthcoming move south to advanced base of 316 (Pol) Squadron.
>
> Later, according to developments,... to explain away failure to carry out PAS DE CALAIS operation.
>
> If... BRUTUS appears still to be believed, MOUSTIQUE: (a) to send reports from sub-agent in FRANCE (b) to report BRUTUS himself in FRANCE.[2]

The story for the Germans was, therefore, that a small section had been set up under FUSAG with the object of recruiting Poles who worked in the German occupied territory. On 18 May, BRUTUS announced his new appointment, via traffic, to the Germans and on the 25th reported that the posting was to take effect on the 27th. The Germans were cock-a-hoop: 'All my congratulations on your post. It is a pity that you will not be able to stay in London.' All the 'anticipated difficulties attaching to such an appointment were experienced by BRUTUS'. On 10 June he complained: 'I have had to ask CHOPIN to come to Staines to collect the news. Difficult to leave this locality to come to London,' and on the following day: 'With regard to FUSAG, it is difficult for me to penetrate the Operations Room because my personal relations are still weak' and because of security restrictions.

The Germans, by now, were also being groomed to accept the information to be sent over by GARBO: 'Form was already beginning to tell among the sub-agents of Seven.' While Agents 7 (2), 7 (4) and

7 (7) 'were improving their reputations daily', 7 (3), 7 (5) and 7 (6) 'were falling by the wayside'. 7 (3) having finished her preliminary training at Mill Hill, had been sent about the middle of the month to a camp near Newbury, where she had already passed an examination in Hindustani. 'She thinks that she will be sent to India,' GARBO informed the Germans. This enabled her to be ruled out of involvement in the deception plan. 7 (5) 'had never taken kindly to espionage. His nervous disposition unfitted him for the work. In his very first message, despatched on 19 April from Taunton, he confessed that he had found it impossible to establish himself in the protected zone'. On 17 May he wrote from Exeter: 'I entered this prohibited area where vigilance is extremely strict. I do not see any possibility of remaining here owing to the continual demands for documentation which up to the moment I have been able to evade.' On 2 June he ran into trouble. A message reached GARBO through 7 (6) in Swansea, which revealed that 7 (5) had been arrested for being in Exeter without permission. 'No doubt his guilty looks had betrayed him.' He was sentenced to one month's imprisonment. GARBO informed the Germans on 2 June: 'Apparently there is no indication that any suspicion exists regarding the mission with which he was entrusted by me and that it was only a routine case for not having complied with the present restrictions.' With 7 (5)'s retirement from the scene 'we were relieved of the ungrateful task of having to send military reports from Devonshire'.

For the 'sake of realism' GARBO and Tommy Harris thought that at least one of the sub-agents should prove to be a complete failure. This role was allotted to 7 (6), who lived in South Wales, an area upon which FORTITUDE was not dependent for reports. 'I received a long letter from 7 (6),' wrote GARBO on 28 April, 'with reports, the majority of which were stupid. We can therefore discount the ability of this agent as an informant in spite of the repeated instructions given. His usefulness is nil.'

It was felt that 'for an agent of his stature' an appointment should be found which would enable GARBO to 'penetrate more deeply into the inner councils of those who were directing the Allied war effort'. In February, GARBO had 'stolen' from the office of J (3) the specimen of a pamphlet which was to be dropped in France in the event of the Germans' voluntary withdrawal from that country. Describing this exploit as 'a master stroke', Madrid had added: 'Very important facts can be obtained in that Ministry since they prepare all the propaganda for the countries in which they are interested for their projected offensive.' Thus an 'opening had already been made by the Germans themselves'. The head of the Spanish section at the Ministry of

Information was on a visit to Madrid at the beginning of May. GARBO had already led the enemy to suspect that this individual was no other than J (3). On 2 May GARBO 'casually threw out the observation': 'J (3) has left England.' It was 'fairly certain' that the Germans would connect this remark with the Ministry official's visit to Spain.

Then, at the insistence of MI5, this official was requested to return to Britain and arrived home at the middle of the month. On 22 May GARBO reported: 'Result of interview today with J (3). He returned from Madrid for reasons connected with propaganda preparations for the Second Front. He proposed that I should help him, offering good remuneration for work which I could do at home. I accepted provisionally, telling him that I wished to consult my wife, in order to allow time to receive approval from you since it concerns work for the enemy which I would only accept as a sacrifice to be compensated by getting important information.' The Germans in Madrid 'took the bait' on 23 May: 'Have studied carefully the question of J (3). Am of the opinion that you should accept the offer, as apart from his being able to facilitate good information, this work assists your cover in every respect.' The latter was an advantage which not even GARBO and Harris had thought of. On 24 May GARBO was able to say that he had accepted the proposition and had been made to sign the Official Secrets Act: 'I attach much importance to this because I learnt that only people who may get to learn details which may compromise secret plans are obliged to sign this.'

The aim of giving GARBO an appointment at the Ministry of Information was in order that he should gain access to the Allied propaganda directives. By reading these 'in reverse', he would learn the Allies' intentions. 'Thus, supposing that, after the invasion had begun, these directives placed an emphatic veto on all speculation as to the possibility of a second Allied landing, it would be reasonable to suppose that such a landing was intended.' GARBO's new appointment, and the greatly increased volume of traffic now passing between London and Madrid made it essential for him to find personal assistants to relieve him of a part of the burden which he carried as head of the organisation. In the middle of May, therefore, the widow of Agent Two, the agent who had died at Bootle in 1942, was called in to help with the enciphering, while GARBO's deputy, Agent Three, was summoned from Scotland and assumed responsibility for collecting all messages and arranging for their despatch.

On the evening of 5 June a small party consisting of GARBO, Harris, the wireless operator, the head of B1A and the Special Means Office at SHAEF, converged in a villa in the north of London, where GARBO's wireless transmitter was installed. At three o'clock in the morning a message was encoded, and the operator called Madrid. Madrid failed to reply. The call was repeated at intervals, but without result. At first this failure to attract the attention of the Germans 'caused some consternation. The invasion fleet was already approaching the French coast, and in a short time the landings would take place. It seemed as if we were to forego the benefits which would accrue from an advance report.' On reflection, however: 'It seemed possible to turn the situation to our advantage, for since we now knew that the Germans would not receive the message until after the landing had occurred, we could strengthen the wording and still claim that GARBO had received it several hours before the troops landed.' In fact the message did not go off until 8 a.m., by which time the imaginary GARBO was on his way to work at the Ministry of Information 'oblivious of Madrid's negligence'. The message, transmitted on the morning of D-Day, reported that Agent Four, had hastened to London with two American deserters. Four had been unable to contact GARBO, by telephone, because only official calls were being accepted. He therefore journeyed, clandestinely, to London in order to report personally: 'He states that he wrote me three days ago, announcing anew the distribution of cold rations and vomit bags, &c., to the 3rd Canadian Division. This letter has not yet reached me due to the delay in the mails. Today he says that, after the 3rd Canadian Division had left, Americans came in, rumours having reached him that the 3rd Canadian Division had embarked. The American troops which are now in the camp belong to the First US Army. The two Americans who escaped with him through fear of embarking.' The reference to the distribution of vomit bags was to convey the message that the invasion was underway: 'Thus we may picture GARBO leaving for his office on the morning of 6th June, congratulating himself on having been able to give his masters advance information of the great landing in France.'[3]

At this point it is perhaps appropriate to recap on the situation that MI5 had presented to the Germans by D-Day: 21 Army Group with the 1st US Army and the 2nd British Army were going overseas to France. The Anglo-American threat to Norway 'was off.' But new American formations were being landed in the United Kingdom. Both the Army Group in the field, in France, and the Army Group in England, remained under the Supreme Command of SHAEF to co-ordinate the overall invasion. As far as the Germans knew, the imaginary FUSAG which remained in Britain now threatened a second cross-Channel assault of even greater proportions which would be launched against the Pas de Calais. But, as Tommy Harris pointed out, the attack was not made to appear imminent for three reasons:

1. The greater the postponement, the longer we would be able to retain German reserves in the Pas de Calais area.
2. The enemy would be bound to realize the time required to cope with the transport problem which a second large-scale landing would involve.
3. We would be expected to require the use of landing craft which were employed in the Normandy assault.

The imaginary FUSAG, supposedly under General Patton's command, had grown in strength by the incorporation of formations hitherto included in the (imaginary) 4th British Army which moved from Scotland at intervals during June and July to take up new headquarters in Sussex. An (imaginary) 14th US Army composed of newly arrived US troops had been created and incorporated in FUSAG. 'Thus, for a short period, during which our armies established themselves successfully and firmly in the Cherbourg Peninsula an increased threat to the Pas de Calais area was maintained by the four Armies now represented as being in the southern half of England': 1st Canadian Army; 3rd US Army; notional 4th British Army and notional 14th US Army.

As time went on, MI5 gave the Germans the impression there were numerous indications of reinforcements for FUSAG which left it apparently stronger on D+45 than it was on D-Day. Meanwhile formations from the 1st Canadian and 3rd US Armies were rapidly being transferred to the battle area in France. A complete black out on all information about these moves was carefully and successfully maintained. MI5 agents continued to report them as still in the United Kingdom until such time as the forces in question were likely to become engaged in operations, and be identified by the enemy. Having built up the strength of Allied Forces by the creation of imaginary formations, it was the role of MI5 agents during PHASE II of FORTITUDE to tell the following story:

1. The landing in the Cherbourg Peninsula by 21st Army Group should be considered as a one-prong thrust of a two-pronged operation.
2. The first landing was primarily a large-scale diversionary assault intended to draw German reserves to the battle area.
3. As soon as German reserves had thus been drawn away from the Pas de Calais area, the major landing would be made there to

provide the shortest road to Berlin, and, at the same time, dispose of the V weapon sites.

4. FUSAG, assault divisions, were already fully trained and prepared for operations.

5. Airborne forces were training for a new operation.

6. Numerous marshalling areas had been located within the sealed areas on the east and south-east coasts.

7. Assault craft (dummies) were assembling in eastern and south-eastern ports.

GARBO's phantom network continued to play a key role in support of PHASE II of FORTITUDE. On the evening of D-Day, Agent No. 3(3) communicated that while a state of alarm still existed in the Clyde and Glasgow area the troop transports had not yet departed neither had the troops embarked. This was hoped to maintain the threat against Norway. GARBO himself reported that, immediately on learning the news that the invasion had started, he went to the Ministry of Information to find it in a chaotic state. All Departments, he said, had been handed copies of a special directive issued in connection with the recent offensive. The official attitude to be adopted by the Ministry was that: 1. The offensive was a further important step in the Allied concentric attack against the fortress of Europe; 2. It was of the utmost importance that the enemy should be kept in the dark as to our future intentions; 3. Care must be taken to avoid any reference to further attacks and diversions; 4. Speculation regarding alternative assault areas must be avoided; 5. The importance of the present assault and its decisive effect on the course of the war should be clearly stated.

A copy of the fake directive was printed and forwarded to the Germans. As Harris explained: 'By reading this directive in the reverse, as we had previously indicated they should, the conclusion which they were intended to draw was that there were to be one or more operations to follow which the British were trying to conceal from the enemy.' GARBO reported to the Germans that he had summoned all his agents to London for a conference. This was to enable MI5 'to prepare to be able to put over the big deception story'.

On D+3, GARBO sent over what Harris called 'the most important report of his career'. By now GARBO had transmitted the entire substance of Plan FORTITUDE for which the whole organisation had been building up for so long. The report, as far as the Germans were concerned, was compiled from the information obtained at the conference with all his agents. GARBO requested that this information should be submitted urgently to the German High Command.

The report set out, in a concentrated form, a summary of the information which MI5 had been transmitting for the last two months.[4] At seven minutes past midnight on 9 June, GARBO began to send what Hesketh called his 'great message', the transmission continuing without a break until nine minutes past two in the morning. Having announced that agents 7 (2), 7 (4) and 7 (7) had arrived in London and delivered their reports, GARBO proceeded to give a full list of all major formations, real and fictitious, in Sussex, Kent and East Anglia. Following closely on the lines recommended by Tommy Harris, a month before, the message concluded:

> From the reports mentioned it is perfectly clear that the present attack is a large-scale operation but diversionary in character for the purpose of establishing a strong bridgehead in order to draw the maximum of our reserves to the area of operation and to retain them there so as to be able to strike a blow somewhere else with assured success. I never like to give my opinion unless I have strong reasons to justify my assurances, but the fact that these concentrations which are in the East and South East of the Island are now inactive means that they must be held in reserve to be employed in the other large-scale operations. The constant aerial bombardment which the area of the Pas de Calais has suffered and the strategic disposition of these forces give reason to suspect an attack in that region of France which, at the same time, offers the shortest route for the final objective of their illusions, which is to say, Berlin. This advance could be covered by a constant hammering from the air since the bases would be near the field of battle and they would come in behind our forces which are fighting at the present moment with the enemy disembarked in the West of France. From J (5) I learnt yesterday that there were seventy-five divisions in this country before the present assault commenced. Supposing they should use a maximum of twenty to twenty-five divisions, they would be left with some fifty divisions with which to attempt a second blow. I trust you will submit urgently all these reports and studies to our High Command since moments may be decisive in these times and before taking a false step, through lack of knowledge of the necessary facts, they should have in their possession all the present information which I transmit with my opinion which is based on the belief that the whole of the present attack is set as a trap for the enemy to make us move all our reserves in a hurried strategical disposition which we would later regret.

A summary of this message was seen by Field Marshall Jodl who underlined the words 'in South East and Eastern England' and took it to the Führer. Berlin, in reply to Madrid on 11 June, described GARBO's report in the following terms: 'The report is credible. The reports received in the last week from the ARABAL (GARBO) undertaking have been confirmed almost without exception and are to be described as especially valuable. The main line of investigation in future is to be the enemy group of forces in South Eastern and Eastern England.'[5]

The greatest deception in modern military history was working beyond MI5's wildest dreams. British Intelligence had some inkling of this as early as 28 May when the 'fact that the Germans were in a receptive frame of mind to absorb our cover plan' was indicated in an ISOS intercept in which the Japanese Ambassador in Berlin gave a résumé of a conversation which he had had with Hitler the previous day:

> Speaking of the Second Front, Hitler said that he, himself, thought that sooner or later operations for the invasion of Europe would be undertaken. He thought that about eighty divisions had already been assembled in England (of these divisions about eight had had actual experience of fighting and were very good troops.) I accordingly asked the Fuhrer if he thought that these British and American troops had completed their preparations for landing operations and he replied in the affirmative. I then asked him in what form he thought the Second Front would materialize, and he told me that at the moment what he himself thought was most probable was that after having carried out diversionary operations in Norway, Denmark and the southern part of the west coast of France and the French Mediterranean coast, they would establish a bridgehead in Normandy or Brittany, and after seeing how things went would then embark upon the establishment of a real Second Front in the channel. Germany would like nothing better, he said, than to be given an opportunity of coming to blows with large forces of the enemy as soon as possible. But if the enemy adopted these methods his numerical strength would be dispersed and he (Hitler) intended to watch for this...

That the invasion 'came as a surprise' was evident in another ISOS intercept of 15 June from a despatch from the Japanese Ambassador, Berlin: 'Leaving for the moment the Anglo-American claim that the landing (in France) was a surprise, it is a fact that although the Germans had long been warning their people of the danger of enemy landings, there is a tendency to think that the German military authorities were making preparations with July in their minds and that the present landing occurred rather too early to suit them...'[6]

Harris and MI5 had always argued against the suggestion, from sceptics, that the German High Command 'would certainly pay no attention to GARBO's appreciations and might even consider them pretentious'. 'We argued that this possibility could best be judged by considering the situation in the reverse. Had the German threat to invade England developed into a reality, there could be no doubt that the opinion of CSS [Chief of the Secret Service/SIS] would have considerably influenced decisions taken by the British Chiefs of Staff in their counter-invasion measures, had he at the time been able to produce impressive reports about German intentions reaching him from a large organisation of long standing and reliability operating from Berlin. In such a situation CSS would have been obliged to put forward, with strong recommendations, any conclusions reached by the chief of his trusted Berlin organisation.' In the German case, Harris and MI5 had believed 'there was every reason to suppose that the situation would be similar. After the Normandy landing there would inevitably be certain divergences of opinion in the German High Command as to further Allied intentions. There would be some German leaders who, we anticipated, would draw the conclusions which we were trying to inspire through FORTITUDE. If, therefore, we could, through GARBO and the Abwehr, supply every form of ammunition, for the arguments of those Germans inclined to believe in our cover plan, then we would be assisting those elements to influence their colleagues to the same belief.'

When, after the end of the war, 'we were fortunate enough to discover a great proportion of the OKW files, together with their intelligence reports and summaries, covering the period with which we are now dealing, we discovered ample and abundant evidence to prove that our judgment had not been at fault in the above respect'. Perhaps the 'most unusual document to come to light' was a FHW appreciation of enemy intentions report (the FHW was the Intelligence Department in the German Supreme Command responsible for all intelligence appreciations connected with the Allied armies in the West) in which a conversation between GARBO and his friend in the Ministry of Information was used as an Appendix to the report. The Lagebericht West (situation or intelligence report) to which the GARBO material was appended 'was the highest form of appreciation made in the

German Armed Forces on "enemy" ground forces'. According to a SHAEF appreciation on this document, 'it is a unique case of an agent's report being quoted verbatim in an official report of so high a level'.

Similarly, reported Harris: 'We were to discover that all eye witness reports were incorporated in Daily Situation reports on the Allied Armies published by FHW. Thus, the movement and regrouping of all notional and misplaced formations, the subject of the reports of the GARBO network, became the subject of the daily intelligence reports of the German Supreme Command, to be widely circulated in German official circles, and on which all German appreciations were subsequently based.' An exact copy of the GARBO reports, was, after being retransmitted from Madrid to Berlin, teleprinted on to the German Supreme Command at Zossen where it was distributed to the appropriate intelligence sections. Copies were sent direct to the Commander-in-Chief of the German armies in the West. In addition, he would receive the substance of the same material in the form of the Daily Situation reports of the FHW and fortnightly review of Allied intentions, as published by the OKH (Army High Command.) Changes in the location of formation would sometimes appear in print in FHW reports within twenty-four hours of the information having been transmitted by GARBO. Harris noted that: 'Neither the interception of our wireless deception network nor physical deception, played any substantial part in implementing the work of the agents. The success of wireless deception was dependent on the efficiency of their interception services. It must be realized that prior to D-Day the enormous volume of traffic on the air in a relatively concentrated space was so great, that the task for any interception service to analyse it all would have been an enormous one.' Fortunately, in the case of FORTITUDE (SOUTH), unlike STARKEY and FORTITUDE (NORTH): 'Planning was far less rigid, and it was this flexibility that permitted the deception plan to be developed as reactions were perceived. From the point of view of managing the case it was a far more strenuous and exacting proposition in the first phases, than it would have been had we been implementing a plan worked out to the closest detail. This elasticity in planning, however, made possible the effective prolongation of the threat until after the Pas de Calais had been overrun by Allied troops, when threats to Denmark and later, Western Germany were created, as the German Armies retreated.'[7]

When confronted, during interrogation, with the text of GARBO's crucial message of 9 June, Field Marshall Keitel replied: 'There you have your answer. If I were writing a history I would say, with ninety-nine per cent certainty, that that message provided the reason for the change of plan.' The change of plan was the decision *not* to commit German reserves from Calais to Normandy. Further evidence of the importance of GARBO's 9 June message on German strategy was provided by the OKW War Diary, attached to which were a number of appendices, one of which contained copies of important documents relating to the Normandy invasion which were received from day to day at the OKW. On Jodl's instructions the OKW War Diary was preserved with a view to its probable value to historians in the future, but the appendices were destroyed, so that only the bare headings remained. Of the four 'invasion' documents included for 10 June one was entitled 'News from Madrid' (Nachricht aus Madrid). All GARBO's material was transmitted through Madrid. As Hesekth concluded: 'It is natural to suppose that any message which altered the course of a campaign should have been thought worthy of inclusion in an appendix to the War Diary... Taking the evidence as a whole, the reader will probably agree that GARBO's report decided the issue. But whatever view one may take it must always be remembered that no message would have spurred the Germans to action on the morning of 10 June had they not already been convinced of the presence of FUSAG beyond the Straits of Dover. And the establishment of that force on either side of the Thames Estuary had been the combined achievement of GARBO and BRUTUS.'[8]

It was game, set and match to MI5. If anything ever justified the existence of the Security Service and ensured its reputation in the annals of intelligence warfare this was it. But MI5 had not finished quite yet.

The Germans had been asking the XX agents for reports on damage inflicted by the V1 flying bomb on London. Hugh Astor – who had taken over from Chris Harmer as BRUTUS's case officer – asked for the immediate policy decision regarding the bomb damage reports which were to be transmitted by BRUTUS: 'His reputation is at stake, and by transmitting – or failing to transmit – this information he may make or mar his reputation. We already know that detailed information about the bomb damage is of vital importance to the Germans from an operational point of view, and it seems probable to me that the Abwehr have guaranteed to supply this information, and that their reports will be studied, not only by the operational sections, but by the most prominent persons in Berlin, including Hitler and Göring. If this supposition is correct, then it is true to say that a spotlight is at present focussed upon BRUTUS and that his existence is now known to various big-wigs in Berlin.' Astor believed that, by 'pandering to their present hunger for information about bomb damage, we shall presently reach a stage where high level questions on military matters are addressed personally to BRUTUS'. By supplying this information, it seemed to Astor that 'we would be pandering to the whims of the Germans and improving our position for putting over military deception at a later date'.[9]

On the other hand, however, supplying bomb reports to the Germans could put GARBO's position in jeopardy for he also had a role to play in deceiving the Germans as to what was really happening on the ground in France. The build up of Allied forces in Normandy was proceeding rapidly and it was important to withhold from the Germans information which would disclose that the 1st Canadian Army and the 3rd American Army were in the battle area until approximately D+50 'by when the enemy would probably discover this for themselves'. The problem was that 'it would have been extremely suspicious had the agents in the south and south-east failed to observe the considerable movement of the formations' destined for Normandy. Therefore, it 'was highly desirable that the GARBO transmitter should be forced to be silent for at least ten days' while these forces were moved to France. To make this possible it was decided to have GARBO 'arrested'. The alarming news was transmitted by his imaginary Agent No. 3, then in charge of the wireless station. The Germans immediately instructed the organisation to cease all activities for at least ten days until the repercussions to GARBO's arrest had been observed. 'In this manner we were able to remain silent between D+36 and D+46 which brought this phase of the plan to a satisfactory close.'

FORTITUDE SOUTH II

On 12 July, Madrid received the news from Agent Three: 'Widow just reported surprising news that GARBO was released on the 10th and is back at his hotel... My instructions from him are to give agent 4 (1) ten days' holiday and return immediately to Glasgow and await orders there.' The Germans were informed how, on 4 July, as a result of a conversation which he had heard in a public house about some bombs which had fallen at Bethnal Green during the previous night, GARBO had gone to investigate. He had casually questioned a man in the crowd, who unluckily for him had turned out to be a plain clothes policeman. The latter's suspicions had been further aroused by GARBO swallowing a piece of paper on which he had previously made some notes. In his zeal the police officer who had made the arrest had detained GARBO at the police station for a longer period that he was legally entitled to do without a warrant, a fact that was pointed out to GARBO by one of his fellow prisoners. On the latter's advice he had written a letter to the Home Secretary stating his grievance. He had also invoked the assistance of his employer J (3) at the Ministry of Information. This action had resulted in a marked change in the attitude of the Police.

In an interview with the Chief of the Station GARBO had explained that he had had a conversation several days before with J (3) in which he had questioned the efficacy of the defence measures used against the new weapon. In order to prove his point he had decided to make some personal observations and this had led to his untimely arrest. J (3) was of course able to corroborate the conversation and so GARBO had been able to leave the prison without a stain on his character. In taking leave of the Chief of the Station, the latter admitted that the police had been over-zealous in the fulfilment of their duties and GARBO ended his account of the interview with the remark: 'As I did not understand half of what he was saying, I reacted to his amiability by thanking him for having had me in the prison, which, when I look back now, I see how ridiculous my words must have been.'[10]

The effect of GARBO's arrest was exactly that which MI5 had hoped for. Nearly all the other agents had been asked to report bomb damage. On 12 July, BRUTUS received an incoming message, stating: 'Stop immediately all observation on destruction caused by flying bombs and only communicate to us information on location of troops etc. in accordance with instructions given.' Hugh Astor connected this, straight away, with the arrest of GARBO and the assumption by the Germans that it was a result of him making enquiries about bomb damage: 'It is of interest to note, therefore, that the Germans are now alive to the danger of making enquiries of this type and that they should have been so prompt in warning BRUTUS to discontinue these enquiries. I feel that this is another instance of the high regard in which the Germans hold BRUTUS.'[11] As soon as the Germans had received details of GARBO's arrest and subsequent release, they urged him to 'cease all investigation of the new weapon'. Similarly TATE was informed that messages about troops were of more interest than those about flying bombs.[12]

Masterman, Astor and Marriott had a long talk on 5 July about the proposal, in the deception cover plan, to despatch BRUTUS to France for the purpose of carrying out operational deception in accordance with the wishes of SHAEF, who appeared to want BRUTUS in France roundabout the middle of August or the beginning of September. On the assumption that BRUTUS was primarily regarded as an instrument of deception, and that, other things being equal, the reasonable wishes of SHAEF ought to be complied with, the MI5 men came to the following conclusions:

> 1. That if the greatest possible degree of plausibility is required then we must insist upon the Germans providing BRUTUS with a transmitter in France.
> 2. That it is not possible to get BRUTUS to France anywhere near the date nominated by SHAEF unless we provide his transmitter, whether by allowing him to take his present one or by allowing him to be supposed to have built one for himself in France, and that either of these two methods is stretching German credulity a good deal.
> 3. That it is utterly unplausible [sic] for CHOPIN to be supposed to go to France, and that therefore BRUTUS must go himself.
> 4. That in consequence of paragraph 3, BRUTUS himself must be given some job in France to which he can be posted, and that the job must be such that he has some manifest duties to perform. In other words BRUTUS must be able to give some explanation to the general public of what it is that he is supposed to be doing.

It was the view of Masterman, with which Marriott in the main agreed, that SHAEF would, in fact, find the case much less useful in France than it was at present in England, and that the process of moving BRUTUS 'is bound to de-grade him as an agent'. The Germans were bound to be a very long time in producing the transmitters, and for the next few months therefore BRUTUS would in fact have to be run in exactly the same way as though it had never been suggested that he ought to be sent to France. While it really remained for SHAEF to decide the various outstanding points and for MI5 to advise upon the sort of case which they were likely to have at the end of their machinations, Marriott thought: 'One piece of advice I think we can give them is that if they adopt the less plausible course of allowing BRUTUS to provide his own transmitter, then they ought to reckon with the possibility of having to run the case on innocuous lines for up to a month in order to judge whether the Germans have swallowed the move. It may be that virtually to put the case out of action for a month in this way may persuade SHAEF that BRUTUS had better stay in England.'[13] By 8 August, when Marriott saw Hesketh to discuss BRUTUS's future, he found that SHAEF were not particularly anxious for BRUTUS to proceed overseas, 'and indeed consider that the war is going so well that any traffic which they want put over cannot only be much better done from here, but may also be so urgent that there may not be time for him to play any part unless he stays here'.[14]

The option to send BRUTUS over to France was always on the table – particularly when it was discovered from ISOS that the Germans had arranged for a wireless transmitter which was buried outside Paris to be put at the disposal of BRUTUS. With the wireless set was buried 50,000 French francs. On the Nationale 3 highway between Paris and Meaux there was a milestone which, according to the inscription upon it, was 2.3 km from Claye and 12.4 km from Meaux. The equipment was concealed here 5 metres from a stone in a ditch under a mark in the grass. The equipment was buried 10 cm deep.[15] Chris (now Major) Harmer, was brought back into the frame to, if necessary, retrieve the transmitter but he too was of the opinion that starting up the transmitter in France would 'probably involve the whole case in all those risks of compromise which we are hoping to avoid by closing down BRUTUS himself. Thus, except in case of great necessity, Harmer wishes to abandon his share in the project'.[16]

In the end things had gone so well with the deception plan that events brought about changes in the scheme. As early as the middle of July 'the time had arrived when we could no longer with safety withhold the full story'. Before 9 July, the Germans believed that one division from each of the army corps in the fictitious FUSAG had sailed. Allowing one day for the sea passage MI5 were bound to assume that the Germans would hope to identify all these divisions in France by 16 July. It had by now become very difficult to maintain the press censorship on the whereabouts of General Patton – in reality in France with American forces but, as far as the Germans were concerned, still in Britain as the commander of the imaginary FUSAG. The Ministry of Information thought it would be impossible to keep the lid on the true whereabouts of Patton beyond 20 July. It was decided that FORTITUDE SOUTH II should be put into operation on 18 July. BRUTUS was to deliver a story to the Germans in a series of messages, while GARBO would meet his friend 4 (3) and give his own version in a letter which would reach the Germans at the end of the month and would corroborate what they had already heard from BRUTUS. BRUTUS's report ran as follows:

I learnt at Wentworth that FUSAG has undergone important changes owing to the necessity for sending inadequate reinforcements to Normandy. So far as I know, the Supreme Commander namely Eisenhower decided that it was necessary to send urgently a part of the forces under FUSAG, who would pass under the command of a new army group. These forces will be replaced in FUSAG by new units arriving from America

and by British reserves. No exact details but I can confirm that
FUSAG will include the Ninth American Army, the Fourteenth
American Army and the Fourth British Army. FUSAG, changes in
the command. I suppose that Eisenhower and Patton were not in
agreement over the change in the Order of Battle because Patton
has been replaced by General McNair as command in Chief of
FUSAG. I have discussed, with my colonel, the latest changes
which have caused a good deal of bother at our headquarters. He
tells me that Montgomery demanded immediate reinforcements
in Normandy in such a fashion that it was necessary to send units
from FUSAG which were already in the South of England, notably
the First Canadian Army and a large part of the Third American
Army. The fresh units in FUSAG will take up the duties of the
units which have been despatched. The staff command of FUSAG
remains unchanged. The Fourteenth American Army has already
removed towards East Anglia to the area formerly occupied by
the Third Army. The headquarters are at Little Waltham. The
Fourth British Army is also in the South. My colonel considers
that the fresh units in FUSAG will be ready to take the offensive
towards the beginning of August.

The Germans were being led to believe that the American Third Army
had now transferred to France and, as Jodl stated under interrogation
on 11 December 1945, while he considered the Pas de Calais (FUSAG)
threat to be over by the middle of July when formations of the
American Third Army began to appear in Normandy, he admitted
'reluctantly, as his loyalty to Hitler remained unshaken', that the
continued retention of a large part of the German Fifteenth Army in
the Pas de Calais after that date was 'due to the Führer's own persistent
belief in the imminence of a second landing'. Thus, thanks mainly to
BRUTUS's message, the Germans while recognising that FUSAG had
been depleted with units transferred to Normandy and, therefore,
unlikely to be used in the short term against the Pas de Calais, by now
had bought into the XX deception on such a scale that they found it
difficult to discount FUSAG being reinforced and used against a less
defended part of the Channel.

But even the best plans could go wrong and it depended on the eagle
eyes of those running the XX to make sure this did not happen. On 22
July, Hugh Astor wrote to Marriott to tell him that he was 'somewhat
perturbed by the similarity of the messages sent by GARBO and
BRUTUS relating to the changes in the FUSAG Order of Battle'. In
one instance a letter from GARBO dealing with these changes 'tallies

almost word for word with the information given by BRUTUS'. It seemed to Astor 'preposterous that two agents should have obtained such exactly similar details on so important and secret a matter, and the coincidence is rendered the more grotesque by the fact that both agents forwarded the information on or about the 20th July'. Risking that Marriott might think that 'I am making a mountain out of a molehill, but it seems to me that SHAEF are working under the misapprehension that it is necessary to report the same story through two channels in order to ensure that the Germans can understand it.' The object of installing BRUTUS in FUSAG, Astor pointed out, was to enable him to send reports which could not be adequately covered by the GARBO organisation.[17] Fortunately, if no one had noticed this at SHAEF no one did on the German side either.

By the end of August, British and Canadian forces were approaching the Pas de Calais and, on 8 September, FORTITUDE SOUTH II was formally brought to an end. The deception plan had been an unqualified success. So much so that, on 29 July, GARBO had been informed 'With great happiness and satisfaction,' by Madrid, 'that the Führer has conceded the Iron Cross to you... For this reason we all send you our most sincere and cordial congratulations'. GARBO replied: 'I cannot at this moment ... express in words my gratitude for the decoration conceded by the Führer, to whom humbly and with every respect I express my gratitude for the high distinction which he has bestowed on me, for which I feel myself unworthy'.[18]

While the Great Game was reaching its great climax, ZIGZAG returned to Britain on 27 June 1944 'by his usual route and means'; he landed by parachute in Cambridgeshire.[19] After being flown to Madrid he had been issued with a false Norwegian passport and flown to Paris. There he was told that Graumann had been sent to Russia in disgrace; ZIGZAG refused to divulge his story to anyone but Graumann. He was accordingly sent to Berlin by train, where he stayed one night, and then flown to Oslo where he was greeted by Graumann. ZIGZAG had complete freedom there and bought himself a yacht that he used for sailing around fjords, collecting information on targets for Allied bombing operations. In July, he was flown to Berlin to discuss the possibilities of a sabotage mission. The Germans did not know what they wanted to sabotage – only that they wanted to sabotage something in 'the British factory system'. When ZIGZAG returned to Oslo he found that the Germans there were more interested in discussing a mission to find out about British anti-submarine devices. ZIGZAG took the opportunity to engage in some intelligence gathering as to what the Germans knew about British anti-submarine devices. He was then sent to Berlin again, this time to Luftwaffe HQ, so that he could learn from them about a mission to find out about British night fighter devices.[20] Finally, he was told to report on the damage caused by flying bombs.[21]

ZIGZAG's assessor at Camp 020 – Brown – noted in his report that there was, of course, the 'inevitable girlfriend': Dagmar Lahlum. Chapman led Lahlum to believe he was a German, which led to the girl's embarrassment since any Norwegian associating with Germans were automatically ostracised by their compatriots. ZIGZAG had emphasised that she was not a 'fast' girl but had married a man older than herself who wanted her to stay and home and look after him. She, at twenty-one, was prepared to forgo her amusements. Her husband's unfaithfulness gave the opportunity to divorce him, which was in train when Chapman met her. Some five months after they met, approximately August/September 1943, Chapman told her, when they were alone on his yacht, that he was working for the British. Chapman denied he was under the influence of drink when he told her, or that he was afraid of losing her if he continued to impersonate a German. Dagmar was curious to know more details about his work but Chapman claimed he told her nothing. While Dagmar expressed a certain amount of surprise at this information, she said she had suspected from his accent that he was not German. ZIGZAG had complete confidence in her as she was herself anti-German. When he left Oslo Chapman asked the Germans to look after her and pay her 600 Kroner a month from his money. The relationship with Dagmar was further complicated when it emerged that while Chapman was walking in the street with her, she stopped suddenly and entered into a small tobacconist's shop, returned almost immediately and told him that the Allies had invaded Sicily. The news about Sicily had not at that moment been broadcast in Norway. Alarmingly, it appeared to Brown, therefore, that Dagmar was in contact with the Norwegian underground, at the same time had the confidence of a British Secret Service agent and was being maintained by the German Secret Service.

Brown was of the opinion that the 'courageous and ruthless' ZIGZAG had given satisfaction to his no less ruthless German employers. Chapman did not appear to boast of his exploits, which if true, in Oslo would only serve to enhance the high opinion the Germans had of his ability and courage. He stood out for his financial reward and got it; he was apparently able to match their best drinkers without giving the show away and to lead as hard a life as any of them. He won a shooting match with revolvers during which Chapman shot down sixteen electric light bulbs at 8 metres before his opponent hit the target. He collected 100 Kroner 'and that he got away with this in a German camp says much for his standing and popularity'. There was an incident where he beat up a Norwegian Legionnaire for a fancied slight to his girlfriend; on another occasion Chapman obtained the release of a young friend of Dragma from a crowd of rounded-up students. To do this he had an argument with a German soldier and an officer in the street. Chapman's sailing exploits off Oslo, when he put out against all advice and survived the loss of sails, would only have enhanced his stock and particularly pleased Graumann who was proud of his protégé; indeed, Chapman had 'made' Graumann in the German Secret Service. Be that as it may, noted Brown, Chapman remained a difficult subject with a certain percentage of his loyalties still for Germany: 'One cannot escape the thought that, had Germany been winning the war, he would quite easily have stayed abroad. In England he has no social standing; in Germany, among thugs, he is accepted.' It was not easy to judge the workings of Chapman's mind: 'He is bound to make comparisons between his life of luxury among the Germans where he was almost an law unto himself, and his treatment here, where he has still the law to fear.'²²

This was, effectively, the end of the ZIGZAG case. By now the invasion of Occupied Europe was under way. And Chapman was, more than ever, difficult to control. Ian Wilson reported, in August 1944, that: 'ZIGZAG himself is going to the dogs.' He was claiming to be making large sums of money by backing the winners of dog races that had been fixed. There remained a suspicion that he cancelled an appointment for sending a transmission to the Germans because he saw the opportunity for making a profit on the dog track. ZIGZAG had also been looking at a variety of options for going legit, including opening a West End club which he later modified to Southend. He subsequently dropped this idea once he had been advised that the club was unlikely to survive for more than a month or two. Hopes for a venture into hotels in Southend rested upon overcoming the objections of the local Chief Constable.²³

TAR Robertson was forced to meet with ZIGZAG at the former's club and hear, for himself, the dissatisfaction that the agent now felt regarding the running of his case.²⁴ On 13 August, Robertson, Marriott and Major Ryde discussed the case. The problem confronting them was how to keep ZIGZAG's 'active and adventurous' mind from becoming restive and dissatisfied if he were forced to remain inactive. At the moment it was proving difficult to keep him transmitting false information regarding flying bomb attacks on London: 'ZIGZAG has already shown us that if this state of affairs continues he will go bad on us; he will turn his tortuous mind to working out schemes for making more money, which will almost certainly bring him to the notice of the Police. It would be extremely embarrassing for us if he should be arrested while still on our hands.' Robertson was of the opinion that there was only one possible conclusion: that the ZIGZAG case must be closed down at the earliest possible moment. It was agreed that the position should be made perfectly clear to ZIGZAG that the necessity for closing down the case was no reflection upon him but one forced by the war situation. He was to be paid £5,000 as a final settlement and told that he could not look to MI5 for any future help should he get into trouble with the Police.[25] Robertson agreed with the views of others within MI5 that ZIGZAG was a man without any scruples who would blackmail anyone if he thought it worth his while and would not stop even at 'selling out to the opposition'; nevertheless, he maintained that 'we are bound to give ZIGZAG a fair deal from a financial point of view, at any rate, as he has done a very considerable deal for this country'.[26]

The correctness of the decision to stand down ZIGZAG only seemed to be confirmed when Major Ryde, of MI5, witnessed, on several occasions, ZIGZAG: 'walk up to a Norwegian and address him in Norwegian, I have seen him in the company of highly undesirable characters, speaking to a German Jewess in German, a Frenchman in French. I have heard him discussing, with a man with a known criminal record, conditions in Paris in such a way that it must have been apparent that he has been there within the last few months.' Although Ryde was able to curb these indiscretions when he happened to be present, he had no idea what ZIGZAG said when he was unattended.[27] When Ryde heard of another apparent indiscretion – he was found in the company of the infamous Jimmy Hunt who seemed to be aware of his activities – the Intelligence Officer urged ZIGZAG's dismissal, immediately, on the grounds that he had broken his side of the bargain. But the decision had, in essence, been taken. By now the only work for ZIGZAG was some low-level deception work on the part of the Admiralty – which was the reason the case had been kept going despite Robertson's objections.[28]

The case of ZIGZAG quietly closed in 1944. After the war, Chapman wrote an account of his account of his experiences which was bought by a French newspaper, in 1946; it resulted it him being convicted under the Official Secrets Act. Another attempt to publish resulted, in 1952, in the *News of the World* having an edition pulped after representations from MI5. Not long afterwards, Chapman got in contact with Graumann who held no grudge when he found out about his duplicity. His former Abwehr boss then flew to Britain to attend the wedding of Chapman's daughter.[29] Chapman later became the subject of a film (starring Christopher Plummer and Yul Brynner) and the last that was known of him was that he ran a health hydro in Hertfordshire.[30]

END OF THE ROAD

The disbandment of the 58th and 80th British Infantry Division in April 1945 constituted the last step in the dissolution of FORTITUDE's imaginary armies. The only letter writers who engaged in operational deception during the latter months of the war were GELATINE and BRONX. The former had been 'showing signs of anxiety and depression for some time'. On 7 April she saw that defeat was near and on the 7th complained to the Germans: 'I must know when to stop as I do not want to endanger my position at the last moment. And what happens after that?' Her last letter was posted on 30 April. BRONX 'kept her head' until the end and on 3 May wrote: 'Events succeed each other so quickly that everyone here thinks of the war as being over, but no one knows who is really in command in Germany. It seems to me useless to send you military information, but I think I could, from time to time, send you political observations which would be of use to you in the reconstruction of Germany once this terrible period is over.' Of the three surviving wireless agents TATE, 'whose performances had been so disappointing in the summer, was beginning to receive some slight indication of recognition' before FORTITUDE ended. In November he ceased to operate on MI5's behalf, devoting himself thereafter to naval deception, in which employment he achieved some striking successes.

BRUTUS left FUSAG on 21 August and returned to the Polish Air Headquarters at the Rubens Hotel. He had already expressed some concern about the future of Poland and the treatment of Polish subjects by the Germans. This and the fact that he was no longer at the army group headquarters evidently made the Germans fear that they might soon lose him. They therefore did their best to impress him with the great value which they placed upon his services. 'We thank you profoundly for your excellent work and would like you to thank your friend CHOPIN also, who, despite his age, works so well. Tell him please that once the war is over he will have no further financial difficulties.' These encouraging words did not remove the agent's anxiety regarding developments in his own country. On 11 September he told his masters: 'I am very much depressed. The news of former atrocities committed at the camp at Lublin have recently received much publicity in the press and have the appearance of being

too true. I believe that I have the right to ask for a true statement of
your general policy towards my country.' The Germans were quick
to reassure him: 'Once again I thank you with all my heart for your
excellent work. I implore you not to imagine that I have done nothing
for you. I have passed on all your political propositions, especially
concerning your country, recommending them to accept them.' On
29 September, BRUTUS pointed out how difficult it was for him to
continue: 'My present work at my headquarters takes up a very great
deal of time and I have not the same freedom of movement as before.
The search for information and the lengthy enciphering still further
reduces the time available.' After this date his communications became
very infrequent.[31]

The news reached MI5 that VIOLETTE, the former mistress and
sub-agent of WALENTY, was arrested by the Free French at Luneville
in the autumn of 1944. She was, of course, of the view that BRUTUS
was working for the Germans and was therefore able to compromise
him. VIOLETTE herself did not present a security danger, and she had
therefore been released and allowed to return in liberty to Luneville. In
view of the proximity of Luneville to the German frontier 'and of the
fact that her case must be fairly widely discussed in the neighbourhood,
it is possible that the Germans may learn of her arrest... and may
assume that she has denounced BRUTUS'. The greatest danger to the
case, however, was provided by KIKI. This man was a former member
of the WALENTY organisation and was in fact the first man to be
betrayed to the Germans in November 1941. He was duly arrested by
the Germans, and was compelled under duress to take certain action
which resulted in the arrest of further members of the WALENTY
organisation and the subsequent dissolution of the whole organisation.
KIKI himself proved to be a 'bad hat', being ultimately recruited by the
Germans as an agent and coming to Britain on their behalf.

He returned to France, and had been arrested by the French on
account of his collaboration with the Germans. He was now in the
hands of the police judiciaire, who were likely to put him on trial in
a civil court in the near future. It was known that KIKI had revealed
that BRUTUS's escape from the German prison was facilitated by the
Germans, and that he was sent to England with a political mission
for the Germans. It was not yet known whether KIKI was aware that
BRUTUS also had an espionage mission and that he had been able to
maintain contact with the Germans. Astor warned that this information
'must by now be known to a fairly large number of Frenchmen who
are not intelligence officers'. There were in addition certain other
'unknown dangers'. It was believed that two further members of the

WALENTY organisation were still in prison in France, one at Marseille and the other at Lille. The cause of their imprisonment was not yet known, nor was it known whether they were aware of BRUTUS's mission, though this might quite possibly be the case. There was also a slight risk to the security of the case owing to 'intrigues and allegations' against BRUTUS which had recently taken place in Polish circles in England. Astor warned: 'It will therefore be seen that the security of the BRUTUS case on the Continent is at present in a bad way. It is perhaps easy to exaggerate the dangers, but, though the chances of a leakage back to the Germans may be small, these must nevertheless be faced.' The most immediate danger was undoubtedly provided by KIKI, and steps had already been taken to try to postpone the trial of this man, or at any rate to ensure that the trial was conducted in secret by an intelligence organisation. Astor concluded that: 'There are two courses of action open to us, depending on whether it is decided (a) to close the case, or (b) to continue to run it.'

In the event of (a), Astor suggested, on 9 January 1945, that BRUTUS should inform the Germans of the disclosures made by KIKI and some of the others, explaining that they had resulted in a further investigation into his escape. He would explain that in view of this development it was no longer possible for him to maintain his position and that his best defence would be to make a partial confession of his mission. He would say that he was proposing to tell the British authorities that the allegations against him were true and that he was sent to Britain with a political mission to ferment trouble in Polish circles; and that on arrival he started to carry out this mission, with the result that he was arrested in the summer of 1942. He would tell the British that as a result of this arrest he saw the error of his ways and 'had been a good boy ever since'. He would plead for mercy, referring to his excellent work as WALENTY and pointing out that he had been subjected to great nervous strain while under German arrest.

This scheme 'has the advantage that it will provide cover against any future allegations or publicity which may be made about BRUTUS's arrival in this country and should prevent the Germans from ever realising that he has been working under control. Furthermore, the possibility of resuming wireless traffic, either from this country or from the set in France is not altogether excluded'. In the event of (b), it would be necessary to explore fully into the situation at present existing in France and to make the necessary arrangements for the trial of KIKI to receive the minimum of publicity. It would also probably be found possible to devise a plan to safeguard BRUTUS against future denunciations. Although BRUTUS had not been as active as previously the stakes were still high for MI5 realised that in the event of BRUTUS becoming blown: 'The whole of FORTITUDE would also be compromised and the Germans would become aware of our deception technique. The strategic deception... would therefore be compromised.'[32]

A meeting was held to discuss Astor's concerns. The meeting was attended by, among others, Colonel Bevan, Colonel Wild and Colonel Fleetwood Hesketh from Operational Deception and TAR Robertson, Marriott, Masterman, Tommy Harris and Astor. Marriott explained the dangers which had arisen in France on the basis of Astor's note the previous day. The far-reaching effects of BRUTUS being blown were duly understood and appreciated by all present. Colonel Bevan stated that the Combined Chiefs of Staff regarded strategic deception as Top Secret, but that they were fully alive to the possibility of it becoming blown to the enemy, and said that this was a risk which they were prepared to face. Bevan and Colonel Wild both agreed that the danger of blowing a future deception plan was not comparable to the danger of blowing FORTITUDE in the pre-D-Day period as it would reveal little intelligence of value to the enemy. It was therefore agreed that the case of BRUTUS should be continued, and that all efforts should be made to arrange for the trial of KIKI to receive the minimum publicity, and that if need be representations should be made on the highest level. Wild, who was due to return to Paris that day, agreed to undertake the preliminary moves with the French, and to explore how the affair could best be handled.[33]

On 23 January another meeting was called by Colonel Wild, which was attended by Bevan, Robertson, Masterman, Marriott, Hugh Milmo, Major Wells of SOE and Astor. Wild had originally summoned the meeting so that everybody should be acquainted with the recent dangers which were supposed to be confronting the case of BRUTUS, and so that these dangers could be carefully considered and a decision taken as to whether the case should be continued and, if so, what measures should be adopted to preserve its security.

Colonel Wild began by explaining that four members of the WALENTY organisation were at present under arrest in France for collaborating with the Germans, and that they were all aware of the fact that BRUTUS's escape from German imprisonment had been facilitated and that he was in fact a German spy. Wild appeared to have little idea as to the charges levelled against these four persons or the extent of their allegations against BRUTUS. He merely insisted that they were in a position to compromise BRUTUS, and that a certain Roger Bardet was a particular danger in this respect. He had clearly not examined the cases of any of these agents with a view to discovering whether the dangers could be neutralised, but had been influenced both by the French and by Chris Harmer, whom he met in Paris, into believing that the danger was serious.

Wild continued to explain that following the decision taken at the previous meeting he had approached General Eisenhower and had succeeded in obtaining the concurrence of all parties in France to the four agents being sent to the UK. The object of these manoeuvres was to prevent the four agents from being publicly tried in France, but the further consequences of the manoeuvre were not apparently given any serious consideration. Wild was, however, aware that there was a danger of the arrest of two of the agents becoming known to the Germans through a leakage by means of their respective mistresses, and he prepared a plan to meet this contingency. Wild then admitted that, in making the above arrangements, he had acted hastily, and now appreciated that he had taken the wrong course of action. He felt that the correct course would now be for the four agents to remain in France, and to let the French legal procedure run its course and BRUTUS face the music. If BRUTUS was able to survive the storm, '*tant mieux*'; if not, '*tant pis*'.

At this point all of Wild's observations were 'rendered irrelevant' by the late arrival of Captain Vaudreuil, who brought 'hot intelligence' direct from Paris. To the surprise of one and all, he announced that KIKI and Bardet had been subjected to intense interrogation, as a result of which their innocence of collaborating with the enemy had been established. The other members of the WALENTY organisation who had been arrested on the suspicion of collaboration were either unaccounted for after hitherto been believed to be in prison in Marseille or no longer believed to present any great danger to the case of BRUTUS.

This new information came as a complete surprise and 'caused such stupefaction that the original purpose of the meeting was forgotten'. The meeting then proceeded to discuss what course of action should be taken with regard to KIKI and Bardet. Neither B1B nor Wells of SOE were convinced by Vaudreuil's story of their innocence, and they pointed out that if these two agents were released, as suggested by Vaudreuil, and allowed to come to England as free men, it would be impossible to interrogate them under favourable circumstances. Vaudreuil acquiesced, and it was decided that the two men should not be released until full reports of their interrogation had been brought to over. In the absence of the full reports regarding these four sub-agents in France, it was still impossible to assess the dangers which existed to the security of the BRUTUS case, but there was every reason to hope and believe that the dangers were less than was supposed ten days before. But, in truth, the BRUTUS case had, more or less, run its course not because of an increased security risk for, as Astor recognised, while:

> There is no doubt in my own mind that it is perfectly possible to continue to run the case with the same degree of safety as hitherto, but certain parties show a singular lack of interest in the continuance of the case, not on account of the dangers surrounding it, but because it is thought unlikely to serve any useful purpose.[34]

In fact what turned to be BRUTUS's last message had already been sent – on 2 January 1945.

The GARBO case was also drawing to a close. As the Germans retreated, through 1945, GARBO informed them that he had broken up his organisation. On 3 May GARBO sent a message with a request to the Germans to destroy his papers ended on an optimistic note. 'I have absolute confidence, in spite of the present crisis which is very hard, that our struggle will not terminate with the present phase and that we are entering into what is developing into a world civil war which will result in the disintegration of our enemies.' On the 6th the Germans replied: 'Grateful for your latest messages and, especially, your offers of unconditional collaboration. The heroic death of our Führer clearly points the course which must be followed. All future work and efforts, should they be carried out, must be directed exclusively against the danger which is threatened by a coalition with the East... We, therefore, fully approve your plan to return to Spain where, when once you have arrived, the plan for a new organisation directed against the East, can be dealt with.' On the 8th GARBO was told that if he should succeed in reaching Madrid he was to frequent the Café Bar La Modrena, 141 Calle Alcala every Monday between eight and half-past eight in the evening starting on 4 June. He was to be seated at the end of the café and to be carrying the newspaper, *London News*. A person would meet him there who would say that he had come on behalf of Fernando Gomez. On the same day GARBO sent his last message: 'I understand the present situation and the lack of guidance due to the unexpected end of the military struggle. News of the death of our dear Chief shocks our profound faith in the destiny which awaits our poor Europe, but his deeds and the story of his sacrifice to save the world from the danger of anarchy which threatens us will last for ever in the hearts of all men of goodwill. His memory, as you say, will guide us on our course and today, more than ever, I affirm my confidence in my beliefs and I am certain that the day will arrive in the not too distant future when the noble struggle will be revived, which was started by him to save us from a period of chaotic barbarism which is now approaching.'

Soon after the war ended, GARBO made his way to Spain through Canada, the West Indies and South America. He eventually found Kuehlenthal, his master, in the small town of Avila. 'Kuehlenthal was overcome by emotion when he welcomed GARBO to his sitting room. He told him how he had visualised this reunion and marvelled at GARBO's ability to overcome the apparently impossible obstacles which must have been in his way.'[35] Kuehlenthal said that all the members of the German Secret Service in Spain were either disbanded or out of touch with one another. He said that his old friend Canaris had been executed by the Nazis themselves and that most of his superior officers were either dead or had been arrested. It was therefore difficult for him to plan anything at the moment as there was no organisation left; he would have to wait a while. GARBO told him that he was thinking of settling down in South America 'and he gave me the Barcelona address of some people he thought I might find helpful should I think of importing Spanish goods'. After this GARBO went on to Lisbon and met up with Tommy Harris, who could not believe that he had just been to see his German contacts in Madrid: Harris 'found it utterly incredible and was amazed at my audacity. To me it had been final irrevocable proof that my double identity, ARABEL–GARBO, had been an impeccably kept secret right to the end. I found Lisbon as charming and welcoming as ever, filled with happy memories and of people I will never forget.'[36]

It was only with the end of the war in Europe that the Security Service was able to piece together what had happened to Johnny Jebsen. By August 1945, through various interrogations, MI5 had learned a little more about him, although his ultimate fate was still unknown. From Kuebarth and other Abwehr sources it was clear that he was kidnapped in Lisbon at the end of April 1944 at the instigation of Hansen and Kuebarth and was returned to Berlin. There was an indication, through a message smuggled out from the camp at Oranienburg by a member of SOE who had since been shot, and in whom Jebsen seemed to have partly confided, that Jebsen was still alive in Oranienburg early in 1945. Another indication that Jebsen was still alive long after his arrest was that a Greek business contact of his was questioned at the end of 1944 at the Gestapo prison 8 Albrechtstrasse, Berlin, about his financial dealings.[37] But the interrogation of Schreiber, his kidnapper, proved most enlightening. In a conference Schreiber claimed to have assured those giving him his order – Kuebart and Weiss – that he would try everything in his power to get Jebsen onto German soil in compliance with the order, but would not resort to any extreme measures. The discussions, in Madrid, led to no clear suggestions as to how Schreiber was to execute the order. Kuebart and Weiss returned to Berlin and Schreiber proceeded to Lisbon. In Lisbon, Schreiber learned that a close friend of Jebsen's, Moldenhauer, had arrived and was staying with him. Schreiber claimed Moldenhauer was an agent for Ast Cologne. Aware of Moldenhauer's good connections with Allied circles, Schreiber concluded that Jebsen and Moldenhauer were planning to desert to the Allies together in the very near future. He therefore felt it necessary to act sooner than he had intended and also to include Moldenhauer in the abduction, who otherwise might become suspicious and upset the plans. If innocent, Moldenhauer would have no trouble clearing himself with the military authorities in Berlin. Schreiber decided to call both Jebsen and Moldenhauer to his office for a meeting in the late afternoon of 30 April. At that time the office would be completely deserted. They would be knocked out and while unconscious placed in two large trunks in which they could be shipped by car the same evening over the Portuguese-Spanish and Spanish-French borders to Biarritz. To guard against all possible surprises at the borders Schreiber also decided to drug them by injections. Two assistants would be necessary to carry out the action. Schreiber chose Bleil, a signal officer of KO Portugal, in whose name the car was registered and who, according to Portuguese law, had to accompany the car on a trip across the border and Karl Meier, a civilian motor officer of KO, who was thoroughly familiar with the car and if necessary could repair it. Schreiber sent a wire to Hansen in Berlin to the effect that the sudden appearance of Moldenhauer supported their suspicions and necessitated his inclusion in the affair and that the planned action would be initiated without delay.

At noon 30 April, Schreiber and Meier purchased the two trunks, which Schreiber claimed were large enough for a grown person and were fitted with adequately large openings for ventilation. The sleeping drug for the injections Schreiber obtained in a Lisbon pharmacy. Upon his return from Lisbon, Schreiber had asked Jebsen to call at his office on the afternoon of 30 April, using as a pretext his intention of giving him detailed information about a decoration which Berlin wished to bestow on Jebsen. He had also asked him to bring along his friend Moldenhauer, ostensibly to question him on his missions. At 6 p.m. Jebsen and Moldenhauer arrived together at Schreiber's office. Schreiber carried on a general conversation with both of them for a short while and then called Jebsen into another room. There he claims to have informed him of the true outcome of the discussions in Biarritz and of Hansen's order to have him brought to Berlin by force, since he would not go of his own free will. Jebsen made a move for the door and Schreiber knocked him out. Meanwhile Meier had also overpowered Moldenhauer in the adjoining room. According to Schreiber, he then informed both Jebsen and Moldenhauer, after they had recovered in the presence of Bleil and Meier, how he intended to get them across the border and both of them submitted to the injections. The party started out at about 9 p.m. to Bardajoz with the two drugged men in the trunks and Schreiber, Bleil and Meier as the other occupants of the Studebaker sedan. The Portuguese-Spanish border was crossed without incident between midnight and 2 a.m., since Bleil and Meier knew border conditions and officials personally from previous trips both here and at the Spanish-French border in Irun. The trip through Spain was only interrupted by a few rests in the open and the Spanish-French border at Irun was crossed at about midnight of the following night without incident. In Biarritz, Jebsen and Moldenhauer were immediately turned over to the local Stellen Leiter, Obst/Lt Fuchs. In November 1944 in Lisbon Schreiber heard a rumour that Moldenhauer had recently been seen in the Hotel Ritz in Madrid.[38]

The next interrogation that proved of interest was that of Frau Petra Vermehren on 16 January 1947. Frau Vermehren first came to know Jebsen when he was a student at Freiburg University, through her two sons who were also students there. That was in the year 1938. Later Frau Vermehren was a journalist in Spain. She heard that Jebsen had gone to Berlin and was working for the Abwehr. He travelled a great deal, posing as a businessman, travelling to Belgrade and many other cities. One day she received a telephone call from Jebsen in Madrid. He appeared to be very nervous. He asked if he could come and see her in Lisbon where she was working. When they met he confided in her that no one must know where he was, as the Gestapo were looking for him, as he had divulged information about V weapons to the British Secret Service. Jebsen stayed some considerable time in Lisbon often visiting Frau Vermehren's hotel. She often saw him in the company of a Mr Popov, whom she knew to be a British agent. About this time one of Frau Vermehren's sons who had been working in Turkey for the Abwehr, decided to work for the British instead. Frau Vermehren was recalled to Germany. Jebsen tried to persuade her not to go.

He said that he was on friendly terms with Lord Rothschild, who he said had asked him to come to England. Frau Vermehren left by plane for Germany and was arrested at the Tempelhof aerodrome Berlin. She was taken first to the Kurfurstendamm and then to a hotel in Potsdam, where her husband and son and daughter joined her. Apart from the daughter who was sent to Ravensbruck, they were all sent to Oranienburg concentration camp.

In Oranienburg the men prisoners were not allowed to shave themselves. Frau Vermehren who said she was the only woman in the camp at the time received word from her son who was in solitary confinement through the camp barber, that Jebsen had arrived at the camp. She thereupon found the cell where he was and every day threw a stone against the window until she attracted his attention. She first saw Jebsen in September, though she believed that he came first to the camp in July, but that as one of his ribs had been broken during an interrogation he lay on his bed for the first month or two. He told her that the Gestapo had abducted him and smuggled him out of Spain in a box because he had divulged information to the British. Mauldenhauer who was also a friend of Jebsen's in Spain arrived in the camp. In February 1945 she saw Jebsen for the last time. An escort was sent from Berlin and both he and Moldenhauer were taken away. Though she made discreet enquiries through the camp staff she was unable to obtain any information as to his fate. On 12 April, Moldehauer returned to the camp. He seemed surprised that Jebsen had not returned. He said he thought it possible that he may have been sent to Sachsenhausen. On 15 April owing to the advance of the Russians the inmates of the camp were marched away. Those prisoners who were left behind were shot. Frau Vermehren and her husband who were only held as hostages were not. It was thought that Moldehauer was shot. Frau Vermehren eventually escaped and made her way first to Lubeck and finally to Hamburg. She believed that Jebsen was dead. Laura Jebsen, his wife, had heard nothing from her husband 'but refuses to believe that he is dead'.[39] Nothing was ever heard of Johnny Jebsen again. His ultimate fate remained a mystery but it appeared certain that he did not survive his imprisonment. It seems he never betrayed his friend TRICYCLE nor his new loyalty to the British.

15

The ROCK

While the liberation of Europe was the mainstay of the Rolls Royce of XX activity during the war, the Security Service was also involved in a number of less glamorous, but important sideshows. One of these concerned the Rock of Gibraltar which had a land border with Franco's Spain but had been a British colony since the 1700s – much to the anger of the Spanish. In September 1942, David Scherr – who, as a part of the District Security Office, represented the Security Service in British this overseas territory – was interviewing Antonia Chozas Avila (later known as The WITCH) in a room in the Hotel Cecil, The Campo, Gibraltar, using the pseudonym of 'Captain Woodford'. The WITCH, a German sabotage agent, had demanded an interview with the Governor of the Rock of Gibraltar, in order to reveal certain information to him, and Scherr was supposed to be His Excellency's personal assistant (whose real name *was* Woodford). Just as the interview was drawing to an inconclusive end, Scherr was called into the next room 'to cope with a most extraordinary visitor'. This was a woman in her thirties, 'whose dress, mannerisms, speech and general appearance made her a rather seedy but not unattractive imitation of the seductive female spy of the thrillerette type'. She sat down in front of the office desk, crossed her legs ('adjusting the hem of her skirt to reveal them to the best advantage'), slowly lit a cigarette, inhaled, 'breathed out the smoke in the approved furtive, reticent fashion, looking down her long and aquiline nose' at the same time, then smiled across at 'her interrogator-to-be' and said, in 'cosmopolitan' English: 'I am the QUEEN OF HEARTS. Who are you?' Scherr replied: 'My name is WOODFORD. Pleased to meet you. What can I do for you?' and 'Thus began a curious series of episodes which were not without profit either to the QUEEN or to the Security Intelligence Department of the Defence Security Office' – basically MI5 in Gibraltar.

The QUEEN had a sister in Paris married to a German officer. The QUEEN's husband had been sent to Puente Mayorga, a small fishing village, probably, so Scherr thought, to have something to do with the use of Puente Mayorga as an advanced base for underwater sabotage operations by the Italians. Meanwhile, the QUEEN had got herself recruited by the Germans in Madrid to go to the Argentine as their agent, but – 'suspecting, no doubt, that she would double-cross them – they withdrew their offer, whereupon she double-crossed them'. However, the Section V representative, from SIS, in Madrid did not trust her, 'so she had come down into the Campo almost at her wits' end for money'. Although 'mercenary and highly imaginative, the QUEEN was of some use to us in the Campo', and got a XX agent NAG to do 'a little spare-time spying for her' (in her capacity as a German agent). Thus 'we had NAG and the QUEEN reporting against one another, though the QUEEN played more fairly with NAG than she did with us'. She was trying to get him to supply her with a respirator from Gibraltar but 'she kept this quiet from us'. On the other hand she compromised the British later by warning Scherr of some impending sabotage (actually 'a fake which we were then preparing to do on NAG's behalf in a tunnel at Hay's Level on the Upper Rock. After this warning we had to change our plans and choose another target for NAG') 'to be committed by NAG, whom she eventually named, and at the same time warned NAG never to re-enter Gibraltar as she knew that he would be immediately arrested if he did so!' The QUEEN's 'best coup financially' was her handing to MI5 a radar questionnaire of German origin, for which 'Head Office' in London authorised a payment of £100. 'This must have been a pleasant change from the rewards of a pound or so and a bag of peppermints now and again, which was all that we paid her normally for the results of her complicated intrigues.' By 1944 'she was looking and behaving so much like a spy that the Spaniards relieved her husband of his post', for he worked as an official for the Spanish, 'expelled the QUEEN from the Campo, and the two went off to Seville'.

For Scherr and MI5, by far 'the most enterprising, courageous and trustworthy of our XX sabotage agents' in Gibraltar was NAG. In May 1943, NAG was approached by a secret agent – BRIE – of the German sabotage organisation operating from Spain against Gibraltar, who attempted to recruit him to place a time bomb aboard HMS *Manxman* in HM Dockyard, Gibraltar. Alternatively, he was to place it in the Dockyard Armament Magazines or oil fuel deposits. NAG, who was then employed in HM Dockyard, immediately reported to the Gibraltar authorities, offering his assistance. For many months he operated under British direction in the course of which, at considerable risk to his own safety and to that of his wife, he obtained extremely valuable information, 'penetrating the enemy organisation single-handed with remarkable skill, unflagging energy and unflinching courage'. In the course of this work, he personally obtained and handed over to the Gibraltar authorities no less than six items of German sabotage equipment including high explosive bombs. Other sabotage material, including more high explosive bombs, all of which were intended for use in HM Dockyard, he destroyed on instructions from MI5.

During the course of more than two years of 'devoted voluntary service to the British cause', he obtained the confidence of the leaders of the German sabotage organisation in Spain – Friedrich Baumann and his assistants – even to the extent of receiving a course of instruction in sabotage technique in Madrid. He was able to identify a very large number of enemy sabotage agents, some of whom operated entirely in Spain, while others entered Gibraltar and were obtaining access to HM Dockyard as workmen, and also to other important sabotage targets on the Rock. As a result of NAG's information, the Gibraltar authorities were able to exclude or otherwise neutralise these enemy agents, and to achieve throughout a critical period of the war a very high degree of protection for the many sabotage targets 'with which this important base is studded'.

In one case, before NAG had succeeded in actually identifying the enemy agent, an act of sabotage took place on 30 June 1943, when an explosion occurred at the Naval Oil Stores on Coaling Island, Gibraltar. Considerable damage was done, and the agent responsible was paid 40,000 pesetas (approximately £1,000). NAG 'volunteered to bring the culprit to book, and his efforts were crowned with success'. Within a month he had discovered the agent's name (José Martin Munoz) and full details of how the act had been carried out. He also warned the Gibraltar authorities that Martin had another high explosive bomb hidden in a café in Gibraltar with which he planned to blow up one of HM ships in the Dockyard. NAG's 'splendid work' at this juncture was greatly assisted by an elaborate fake act of sabotage which the District Security Office arranged on his behalf. As a direct result of NAG's 'energetic and courageous action', Martin was soon arrested, his second bomb discovered, and a full confession made, which corroborated in every detail NAG's information. Martin was executed in January 1944 and a series of strong diplomatic protests was initiated by His Majesty's Government to the Spanish Government against the 'criminal and nefarious' activities of Martin's accomplices and against leading personalities in the German sabotage organisation in Spain. These protests were based to a very large extent on the accurate information obtained by NAG. This, in turn, led to the disintegration of the German organisation against Gibraltar, many of its known agents having to flee from the Gibraltar area. Meanwhile, NAG 'skilfully retained the confidence of the Germans', and kept the Gibraltar authorities informed of every attempt by the enemy to set up a new organisation. Typical of them all was the work done by NAG in discovering the plans of one such Falangist who held the position of secretary of the labour exchange in the neighbouring town of La

Linea, in which capacity he was able to send his sabotage agents into Gibraltar. Thanks to NAG, 'not a single one of these agents was successful, and all the targets chosen have been protected'.

Scherr pointed out that, over two years, NAG had to associate with 'thugs, desperadoes, Falangist gunmen and other criminal types, who would not hesitate to slit his throat or shoot him in the back if they had had the slightest idea of his work for our case'. Most of his activities were carried on the Spanish mainland, where 'the whole trend of official policy has been frankly pro-German, and where, to be suspected of having worked for – or even of having undue sympathy for us – has meant imprisonment, beatings up, and the consequent ruin of the individual's family. Moreover, by the irony of circumstances, NAG's association with Falangists on our behalf led to his acquiring a reputation which in itself was a danger to him, since, at any moment, he was liable to be shot by some enthusiastic anti-Falangist, unaware of NAG's real record.' In September 1945, NAG was recommended by His Excellency the Governor and Commander-in-Chief, Gibraltar, for the award of the King's Medal for Courage in the Cause of Freedom.

There were nearly 200 XX agents used by MI5 in Gibraltar. They divided, broadly, into counter-espionage and counter-sabotage agents. A further distinction between 'plain' agents and XX agents was not in fact very clear-cut. 'It sometimes happens that an agent previously quite "plain" is in process of becoming a XX agent; or that an enemy agent, of whose innate loyalty to his cause we had reason to doubt, is in process of being doubled back to work for us.' The very first paid agent on the DSO's records was 'F', who began working for the British before the Spanish Civil War. Under cover of his commercial activities, F built up an organisation which was used for both espionage and counter-espionage purposes. The principal members of this organisation were the two brothers F.1 and F.2 (also known as the FRUITIES), Spaniards of Monarchist sympathies and pro-British outlook, resident in the Campo. These two had been for many years on good terms with important personalities in the Campo, being well-known and connected with prominent Falangists such as the Mayor and Chief of Falange in La Linea (Lutgardo Macias Lopez), the head of the Falange information service there (Francisco Escobar Mata), and with Emilio Plazas Tejera and members of his sabotage gang.

In 1940, following some information from French sources, the then DSO began to suspect that F was double-crossing the British in favour of the Spaniards; and F was detained in Casablanca and badly treated by his French interrogators who made a strong effort to substantiate their original denunciations: 'It is difficult to avoid the conclusion that in fact an injustice was done; that F's loyalty was to the British and not to the Spaniards; and that the denunciations were based on F's having had to chicken-feed the Spaniards to justify the activity of his group' noted Scherr. F returned to Gibraltar in very poor health and was at once evacuated, with other Gibraltarians, to Madeira. In the meantime, his brother, who had already been working with him both commercially and secretly, took over the leadership of the group and was given the same symbol. For five years these men reported, daily, on matters of counter-espionage interest in the Campo area: 'Though sometimes their information has appeared too fantastic to be true we have hardly ever been able to regard it simply as a figment of their imagination; and indeed on very many occasions their information has been confirmed by Top Secret Sources from London, by independent and thoroughly reliable agents quite unknown to them, and in other ways. Perhaps their most daring and most useful escapades were early in 1942, when, in association with the XX agent STUFF, they penetrated the PLAZAS Sabotage gang to good (though temporary) effect.'

On the counter-espionage side, the F Group was used in Operation COPPERHEAD just before D-Day. In this operation, General Montgomery had to pass through Gibraltar and on into the Mediterranean theatre in such a way as to lead the enemy to believe that the Allied landings in Europe were to take place from that theatre. Every care had to be taken that the news of the arrival in Gibraltar got quickly to the enemy. To this end, the F Group reported the incident to Francisco Escobar Mata of the La Linea Falange, and to make doubly sure, the DSO arranged for Commandante Ignacio Molina to see 'Monty', for a second or two, in the Governor's residence. 'The trick worked, and the news was with the enemy within a matter of minutes. What they did not know, and what only a tiny handful of persons in Gibraltar knew, was that 'Monty' who arrived on the Rock on that occasion was not the real one at all, but a very clever impersonation, which even deceived many who knew General Montgomery personally!'

Scherr had risen through the ranks to become, by 1942, Security Intelligence Officer in the District Security Office. But the credit for the effective counter-espionage machine that operated, in Gibraltar, during the war belonged to the foresight of his predecessors who set up the machinery. Before November 1935, the Colonial Government, Fortress Headquarters and HM Dockyard in Gibraltar each dealt with security matters in its own sphere: there was little co-ordination of security matters as a whole, and practically no means of obtaining security intelligence. In November 1935, Captain K.W.D. Strong, who had previously held the appointment of Defence Security Officer at Malta, was sent out for three months, by MI5, to start a similar central security organisation in Gibraltar. He made a survey of conditions in Gibraltar from the security standpoint, and left his suggestions for a rudimentary organisation to Captain E.A. ('Tim') Airy to develop. In February 1936 the DSO's staff consisted only of a quarter-master-sergeant from Fortress Headquarters employed on issuing military permits, and a borrowed military clerk. In June 1936, however, Captain Airy visited Malta to study the security problems affecting the two colonies. The security organisation in Malta was already at that time nine years old. He concluded that, owing to the geographical situation of the Colony, it was essential to employ agents *outside* Gibraltar – in Spanish territory and, technically, SIS's stomping ground too – in order to collect information concerning foreign espionage and undesirable political activity. He found therefore that he needed to work in far closer collaboration with SIS than was necessary to his counterpart in (the more remote) Malta. This inevitable extension of security interest beyond British territory was noticeable as early as September 1936, when the District Security Officer was writing to HM Consul at Tetuan: 'Although my duties are really limited to Gibraltar itself, I find that many persons living in the neighbourhood in Spain and also in Morocco are constantly visiting Gibraltar. Their activities are therefore of great interest to me. Similarly local events in Morocco are also very interesting to me, as a knowledge of these is often useful here.'

By 1937, the District Security Office was paying special attention to personnel employed in HM Dockyard, following up the contact made in 1935/36 between Captain Strong and the then newly-appointed Staff Officer (Intelligence), RN. The latter's work was principally to act as a Collecting Officer for the Western Mediterranean and the Atlantic coasts of Spain and France, and to organise a contraband control scheme in case any need for it were to arise. In the Dockyard, the person responsible for the employment of labour was the Civil Secretary (then Mr A.N. Deane) to the Admiral Superintendent. In order to assist the DSO to cope with possible sabotage or espionage inside the Dockyard, the Civil Secretary was directed, in September 1937, by the Admiral, to begin a card index of all types of employees who might be considered potentially dangerous. The information obtained was passed to the Commissioner of Civil Police and to the District Security Officer who was thus able to add his own records, that were very scanty at that time, and to make recommendations to the

Civil Secretary regarding the dismissal of unsuitable employees, and to the Commissioner of Police regarding the exclusion from the Fortress of undesirable foreigners. One result of the District Security Officer's Malta visit in 1936 was the adoption by the District Security Office Gibraltar of a system of personal history files on suspect individuals, though owing to inadequate staff Captain Airy was unable to develop this scheme for some considerable time.

In April 1937, however, a Staff Sergeant (from the Royal Army Service Corps) was sent out from Britain to act as permanent confidential clerk to the District Security Officer whose appointment had now been confirmed as permanent. By June 1938, the District Security Officer was reorganising his existing records into a number of different card index systems and files. By this time, the work of the office had considerably increased. There was now a paid secret agent to be contacted discreetly and frequently, the card index was being reorganised, the personal files had to be compiled, arrivals and new employees had to be checked daily. All this kept Staff Sergeant Holden busy and 'necessitated the first of those many urgent and agitated requests for extra staff with which successive' District Security Officers 'at Gibraltar have bombarded Head Office'.

As the threat of war drew nearer, the unsuitability of the District Security Officer's office premises in Governor's Parade became more evident, and, in 1938, arrangements were made for a move to premises alongside the Central police station in Irish Town, which were previously used as City Council slipper-baths, though this move did not actually take place until June 1940. In December 1938 eleven men were selected to form the basis of the Gibraltar Security Police, to look after the Upper Rock. This police force later took over the frontier from the Civil Police, and was expanded considerably. By 1939, the Defence Security Office 'was therefore on a sure foundation and the machine was functioning with reasonable efficiency, though lack of staff still prevented the full and proper development of the work'.

The District Security Officer had become the central authority on all security matters affecting Gibraltar as a whole, but executive control continued to be exercised by the various departments. The District Security Officer acted in an advisory capacity, collecting security intelligence and passing on to the departments such items as would interest them. In his relations with the Commissioner of Police, 'which have from the beginning been close and friendly,' the District Security Officer had been to some extent able to use the services of the small CID Section, under Detective Inspector Gilbert. In the early years of the organisation, this was indeed the DSO's only channel of receiving security information, and it was to Gilbert that the DSO had to turn when he wanted any suspect shadowed or interrogated, any confidential enquiries made, or any photographic work done. 'This practice was not entirely satisfactory, for a number of reasons.' Gibraltar was a small place, and Gilbert was well-known. His assistants 'have not always been discreet', and Gilbert himself 'cannot be relied upon absolutely to keep his mouth shut'. However, there was no better alternative until after the outbreak of war and the arrival of the Field Security Personnel on the Rock.

It was in July 1940, after the British attacked French naval units at Oran, Mers-el-Kebir, and Dakar (so that they would fall into Germans hands following the Armistice), that the French made reprisal bombing raids on Gibraltar. The Italians, too, 'at last put in an appearance, dropping their bombs mostly in the sea and in La Linea, where casualties were caused and unsuccessfully attributed by Falangists to English gunfire'. During the summer of 1942, Mr (later Lieutenant Colonel) Philip Kirby-Green joined the staff of the District Security Officer and became his deputy in place of Major Gray who returned to the UK in September 1942. Captain Thomson was also about to leave. David Scherr, who was then Company Sergeant-Major of No.54 Field Security Section, and acting OC of the Section since July, had already applied for a commission, and accepted Lieutenant Colonel Medlam's offer of an immediate appointment as Intelligence Officer to take over security intelligence work from Thomson in Gibraltar. On 1 September 1942 he took up the appointment of Security Intelligence Officer (SIO) in the Defence Security Office. Apart from the office records, Scherr took over from his predecessor 'absolutely nothing in the way of agents or even casual informers'. There were no cases current at the time to hand over. Scherr, therefore, felt 'free to develop his own organisation along his own lines. This sense of "glorious isolation" had its advantages though as the work grew in quantity and complexity the disadvantages of working as a single individual became more and more obvious.' On taking up the appointment Scherr set himself the following aims: (a) Collection of security intelligence relating to the activities of enemy sabotage organisations operating in Spain against Gibraltar and (b) Collection of security intelligence relating to the activities of enemy espionage organisations operating in the Campo area against Gibraltar.

It was obvious from the start that priority would have to be given to aim (a), in view of the following facts: '1. The known existence of at least one active enemy sabotage organisation (the PLAZAS Gang), already responsible for nine acts of sabotage or attempted acts of sabotage in Gibraltar from early 1941 to midsummer 1942; 2. The extent of pro-German sympathy on the part of Spanish officials, especially in Falangist and military circles, at a time when our fortunes were militarily still at rather a low ebb; 3. The possibility of doing grave damage to our war effort by the introduction of a bomb into Gibraltar and its use there, by any one of the thousands of Spanish workmen entering daily.'

By comparison, the dangers of allowing enemy espionage to continue were very much smaller than those which would have been incurred had the threat of sabotage been ignored. 'Obviously one uneducated Spanish labourer can do little harm as a spy but can do a great deal of harm as a saboteur.' Right from the beginning Scherr 'found [it] necessary to ignore the barrier which in theory exists between British and Spanish territory'. In so doing he was not aware that eight years before, the then District Security Officer had made the same decision. Although strictly speaking the interests of the Security Service were limited to the protection of Gibraltar against subversive enemy action, it was necessary for Scherr 'to see clearly from the beginning that such protection could not be achieved or maintained unless he were able to penetrate the actual enemy organisations. This penetration inevitably meant taking a very keen interest in what was going on outside the confines of British territory, particularly in the Campo de Gibraltar. In this district much of the enemy sabotage and espionage was obviously being planned and carried out.' In the case of sabotage: 'One attached such importance to the successful penetration of the organisations that one had to be prepared to allow an Agent to anywhere in Spain, or for that matter say to Spanish Morocco, provided that in so doing information was obtained which would protect Gibraltar.' In order to pursue these aims, the following methods suggested themselves to Scherr and were those actually used as the basis on which his embryo department was built:

1. Organisation of an informer service and recruitment of Double Agents.
2. Liaison with the work of the Field Security Sections in relation to the observation of suspects, in Gibraltar.
3. Supervision of the card-index and filing system.
4. Recommendation for consideration of Defence Security Officer of counter-espionage and counter-sabotage measures in Gibraltar, including Exclusion and Inclusion Orders.
5. Liaison with MI6 (Section V) representative.[1]

After a few months (September to December 1942) it became apparent that for the time being, at any rate, counter-espionage – as distinct from counter-sabotage – information in the Campo de Gibraltar would have to be left strictly to Section V whose job it was, in order to enable Scherr to concentrate on counter-sabotage information. By the end of the war there were approximately 16,000 cards in the Index, and some 800 personal photographs collected by Scherr. In September 1942: 'We were not in contact with a single sabotage agent. By May 1943, the result of our concentration on counter-sabotage was that we were in contact with no less than nine sabotage XX (or potential XX) agents, had amassed much information, and had made an already extensive collection of sabotage material.' The work involved in 'contacting and keeping satisfied all these nine persons was no easy task, and it sometimes proved impossible to meet some of them as often as was desirable'. The sabotage informers then current were BRIE, COCK, GON, NAG, WIG, OGG, PAT, ENO and JOE. The District Security Officer called these people 'The Crazy Gang'.[2]

COCK was, according to Scherr, a 'rogue' and one of La Linea's first Falangists. He was an old associate of Plazas, the organiser of the German sabotage groups operating in the Gibraltar area from 1940 to 1943. COCK, who was working as a labourer in HM Dockyard, was responsible with Fermin Mateos Tapia for the successful sabotage to the trawler *Erin* in January 1942, after which incident neither of the two men returned to work. In March 1942, COCK wanted to make some money, and approached a Gibraltar dockyard policeman in La Linea with an offer of information. COCK was contacted in La Linea by representatives of the District Security Officer – three NCOs of No. 54 FS Section were used at various times for this purpose: Sergeant (later Lieutenant.) J.W. Pethybridge, Corporal (later Captain.) E. Markee and Scherr. They succeeded in identifying him and in obtaining from him information about sabotage material in the dockyard and about the movements of Plazas. COCK denounced Juan Dodero Navarro as a saboteur. The material was found in the dockyard in the place indicated by COCK and Dodero was detained and interrogated. Dodero in turn denounced Fermin Mateos Tapia, but claimed that he himself was innocent. As there was no evidence against him he had to be released, but was excluded from the Rock as a precautionary measure.

Contact with COCK was maintained, until in June 1942, he told Scherr that a bottle labelled *Neurocalcina Vitaminada* (he said) contained an incendiary liquid prepared by the Germans for Plazas to give to Dodero, and had been stolen by him from a store of sabotage material in Algeciras. 'This bottle cost us several hundred pesetas, and was smuggled into Gibraltar gingerly and with trepidation. On analysis, it was found to contain "sanitary water", such as is used for street cleaning in Gibraltar. After this incident we made up our minds not to bother with COCK any more and in future not to pay for sabotage material before it had been properly analysed.' However, COCK 'was not to disappear from the scene for long.'

In September, after a period of apparent inactivity, COCK approached an unemployed Spaniard in La Linea and suggested that he should get a job in Gibraltar and take part in sabotage. COCK then went off to Seville in order to inform the Germans of his plans. In his absence, the Spaniard (later called FROG) got into touch with the Security Service via his mother, who worked in Gibraltar as a charwoman. Accordingly, in October, Scherr recruited FROG and his younger brother BULL as the first XX sabotage agents of what was to become the 'Crazy Gang'. 'In a way,' recalled Scherr:

> this was a misnomer. The gang consisted of, for the most part, genuine ruffians armed with genuine bombs, directed by the full resources of the German sabotage organisation in Spain, egged on by the hope of glittering rewards, and protected and encouraged by powerful officials of their own nationality. Take this gang, and give it the opportunities for sabotage and you have a very real, a very pressing, and a very dangerous threat to the security of the Rock. On the other hand, the cloak-and-dagger tactics, the incompetence, bravado, stupidity, mutual suspicion and internecine rivalry displayed by many members of the gang make it easy to understand why an exasperated... [District Security Officer] reading the... complicated counter-sabotage reports, could hardly have failed to choose that name for the group.

In November, COCK was back in La Linea and, having again come to the conclusion that it would be both safer and more lucrative to double-cross the Germans, ordered FROG to contact the British to this end. FROG, 'a man of small initiative', neither told MI5 of COCK's change of attitude, nor told COCK that he was already in touch with them. 'Luckily he did confide in his younger brother BULL, who independently and secretly kept us informed of the true state of affairs, warning us that neither FROG nor COCK was completely trustworthy. BULL offered to act as a check on them, and we accepted his offer.' FROG brought into Gibraltar for MI5 two of COCK's incendiary bombs, before the end of the year. 'Finally [he] informed us, when we had exerted some pressure upon him to do so, that COCK wanted us to provide him with a fake act of sabotage that would justify to the Germans his loss of the bombs, and would earn him their confidence and esteem, enabling him to provide us with further sabotage material and information regarding the German organisation.'

For some two months there was a difference of opinion in the Defence Security Office as to the policy to be adopted. The District Security Officer, 'bearing in mind COCK's black record and FROG's obvious untrustworthiness', was all for getting as much sabotage material out of the pair as possible without bothering to build COCK up in the German organisation. Scheer, 'perhaps because somewhat younger and more optimistic, and having to meet these agents personally, was anxious to have the plan put into operation if only as a single experiment'. Eventually a compromise was reached whereby when COCK had handed over more sabotage material (of which BULL had already informed the Office), 'we would arrange a fake act of sabotage for him. We paid FROG only £5 in all for all his work and for bringing in the two bombs. In contrast to this niggardly sum, it should be borne in mind that when COCK eventually claimed the German reward for the fake act, he was given a total sum of 10,500 pesetas (approximately £260)'.

In other words ('assuming that our £5 reward was at the rate of £2.10s per bomb'), it was more than ten times more lucrative to be a saboteur, in this instance, than to be a XX agent. 'On the other hand, of course, it is not so risky to be a XX agent! Moreover, the staging of the fake is itself our contribution to the XX agent's reward, and an essential contribution.' It followed, in Scherr's opinion, that without the staging of fake sabotage no long-term penetration of the enemy organisation would have been possible, since would-be XX agents would have fallen into one of two classes: either those who were genuinely pro-British and handed in their bombs until the Germans lost all trust in them and they were eliminated from the organisation; or those who were entirely mercenary and preferred to do real sabotage for high rewards if the British could not or would not provide them with sufficient fakes.

By the end of 1942, the Office had decided that BULL was the only really useful and reliable one of the two brothers, and from then onwards FROG played a more and more insignificant part in the counter-sabotage story, 'emerging from lazy obscurity only at long intervals to make an inadequate verbal report of some outstanding incident, or to ask for a permit to sell fruit from a street-barrow, or to appear in the police-court on a charge of selling his fruit at unauthorised times... !' In December 1942 the Office obtained from FROG and BULL a large and heavy high explosive bomb disguised as a car battery, and on New Year's Eve brought in two more of these bombs, which had been specially prepared by Mateos for blowing up the caissons of the two largest dry docks in Gibraltar Dockyard. These bombs were given to FROG and BULL for the Office, by COCK.

The bringing-in of bombs to Gibraltar kept Scherr 'quite busy for some months to come, but it was usually a simple business of putting the bomb into a raincoat pocket and walking out of Spain with it'. On this first occasion the operation was more complicated, for a number of reasons. In the first place, these bombs were much too heavy and too bulky to be carried in a raincoat packet: some kind of vehicle would be needed. In the second place: 'We did not then know enough about BULL to be sure he was not leading us into a trap; while we did know enough about COCK to make us very suspicious of him.' In the third place, it was essential for the actual vehicle in which the bomb was to be carried over the frontier not to be seen by any of the XX agents, and for the hand-over and the transfer to be done in secrecy. In the fourth place, the whole operation had to be carried out and completed before the closing of the frontier at half past nine at night. It was done in the following way: with one companion, Sergeant Pethybridge, Scherr went to La Linea early one evening. After making: a number of obvious calls at bars and cafés in the town, in order to get 'into character', we took a gharry to a lonely tavern on the sandy outskirts of La Linea, called the Bar Andalucia. The gharry-driver had been chosen with care as the most decrepit and unobservant we could find. It was already dark; there was neither Moon nor street-lighting. A few yards away from the garish lights of the Bar Andalucia was a dark street corner at which, three quarters of an hour later, we were to have our rendezvous with BULL and the bomb.

We entered the Bar, and spent the interval playing the fool and the piano, singing drunken ditties, and generally behaving like two intoxicated dockyard workmen on the spree, until to the relief of the barman and waiters (and to our relief also) the time came to leave. We staggered out, still singing, into the gharry, the driver took the reins, and off we moved into the darkness towards the appointed place. 'Stop!' we cried to the driver as we reached the corner. He stopped. It was pitch-black. 'I've left my wallet in the bar and I must go back and fetch it,' said the writer, about to clamber down on to the sand and run back, while P. kept the driver's attention. The plan was then to take the bomb in the darkness from BULL, put in the gharry, and proceed on our way.

Unfortunately, the gharry-driver, thinking the writer was too drunk to walk the few yards back to the Bar, obligingly turned the gharry round and jogged us back there, leaving BULL, FROG and their bomb stranded on the corner. After returning to the bar, looking for the wallet, finding it in another pocket, apologising, and having another round of drinks we again set off, thinking very hard how to get the bomb aboard now. At the corner the writer dropped his raincoat out of the gharry (these vehicles have no sides to them), and tumbled out after it.

'Whoa !' shouted P. The driver stopped, mumbling to himself, but not unused to antics of this kind on the part of 'esos ingleses del arsenal'[English dockyard workers]. In the darkness, FROGand BULL padded up in their rope-soled sandals, and lifted the 'battery' and the raincoat on to the gharry while P. was keeping the driver busy with some tomfoolery, and off we went to a bar even further out of town called the 'Bola de Oro', on the Avenida de Espana.

Here we had a car parked in the shadows, and a pair of trustworthy accomplices in the shape of two Gibraltarian youths, both very good types. While P. took the driver into the bar to give him a drink we rapidly transferred the bomb from the gharry to a secret cache under the back seat of the car – which incidentally belonged to the Cuban Consul in Gibraltar...! From then onwards the operation was plain sailing, or rather, plain driving.

This plan had worked so well that within two or three days we repeated it, using another gharry, of course, in order to obtain the other two 'batteries'.

The District Security Officer, 'now convinced that COCK was playing straight with us', authorised the preparation of the fake sabotage for which COCK had been clamouring for so many weeks, and after a great deal of staff work, a convincing fire took place in January on an old hulk in the Commercial Anchorage which, for the purposes of XX work, was supposed to have been a fully-loaded petrol and oil lighter. This fire was notionally the work of BULL, and COCK therefore took BULL up to Madrid to be introduced to the Germans running the organisation, with MI5's approval. Before they left, a second fake was arranged for COCK and BULL: the explosion of a 'hush-hush' trawler called the *Honjo*, which was in reality an old and worthless hulk which was towed out to sea and sunk with some SOE explosives that also had to be destroyed. 'This fake nearly came to grief because the hulk almost sank before the explosion took place!'

While all this had been going on, in the winter of 1942/1943, another XX agent had appeared on the scene known as BRIE. The WITCH (BRIE's mother) wished to lodge some information with the British authorities in September 1942. She lost her nerve on that occasion, but before the end of the year had plucked up courage enough to put Scherr in touch with her son BRIE. This 'did need a certain amount of courage on her part, as she knew full well that BRIE was a German sabotage agent and intended to go on being one. For the moment we knew only his past record, not his future intentions. It was too good a chance to miss', so Scherr went over to Spain to interview BRIE on a number of occasions, obtaining from him much technical information about sabotage material used by Abteilung II in Spain and also many details of the past activities of the various members of the Plazas gang, whose secretary and second-in-command had obviously been BRIE himself. Now that the Plazas had vanished from the district, BRIE (like COCK) was anxious to cash in personally, either by continuing to carry out sabotage, or by 'XX-ing the Germans, or even by XXX-ing the British'.

Thus, by January 1943, BRIE was in touch with MI5, and kept them informed of the activities of COCK and other persons known to him to be (or to have been) German sabotage agents. At the same time, unknown to BRIE, COCK was in touch with MI5 and the Germans, and 'though we did not trust him entirely we had some measure of control over him through his assistant BULL, who was rapidly building himself with our help a strong position inside the new sabotage organisation that was to succeed the remnants' of the Plazas group. BRIE offered to get in touch 'again' with the Germans, and suggested that he should travel up to Madrid with COCK and BULL so that he could keep an eye on them and report back to MI5 on their plans. 'We thus had the fantastic situation in which all three agents were XX-ing the Germans and one another, and from their subsequent reports we could judge with what kind of men we were dealing.'

BULL's was by 'far the fullest, truest, most conscientious report; COCK's the most slapdash and vague; BRIE's the most cunning and misleading'. All three came back with fresh plans for sabotage material, which MI5 proceeded to collect from them as soon as possible. BRIE was by far the best educated of the trio, 'and would have made an excellent leader of the new organisation from our point of view, had we been able to trust him. COCK was obviously not capable of running any organisation'. BULL, though energetic and reliable, was due to be called up for his military service within a couple of months. So MI5 decided to build up BRIE, in the hope that he would be able to bring under his control all the independent saboteurs then functioning in the area, such as Fermin Mateos Tapia.

A fake act of sabotage in a supposed ammunition tunnel was carried out by MI5 in March 1943 on BRIE's behalf, and before he went up to Madrid to claim his reward Scherr met him to give him a directive. 'The meeting was a memorable one.' It was no easy matter to find a safe place in Spain to meet a XX agent. After much thought Scherr decided to meet BRIE 'by chance' in Algeciras cemetery. It was pouring with heavy rain when Scherr arrived at the cemetery gates, about a mile and a half outside the town, accompanied by Sergeant Pethybridge. Explaining to two 'grizzled' sextons at work in a chapel just inside the entrance that they wanted to look round for the grave of an imaginary great-aunt of P's named María de la Concepción Gomez, 'we trudged round in the mud under the dripping cypresses, getting wetter and wetter, and wondering where BRIE was. Spanish cemeteries are built on the principle of the walled-in courtyard. The walls are some ten feet high and about as thick, and the coffins are usually not buried underground but put into niches in the walls. Sometimes the niche has a glass window so that you can see inside. In this cemetery there were three such courts, and after spending over half an hour exploring every nook and cranny in them, and finding no trace of BRIE, we said a moist goodbye to the sextons and turned to go.' At that moment, BRIE arrived, 'and we had to think up some excuse to justify to the sextons our renewed interest in their most damp and gloomy graveyard. Luckily most Spaniards are half-convinced that the English are crazy, and our lunatic desire to go and have another look for great-aunt María's elusive grave merely confirmed the impression already made on the old men's minds, and they took no further notice of us.' So BRIE and the two Britons went into the only dry place in the rest of the cemetery – the mortuary; 'and while the water fell from our clothes in puddles on the stone floor, and the rain was pouring down into the clay soil outside', Scherr drew on the cold stone slab (where the coffins rest before being sealed up in their niches) a detailed plan of BRIE's target area, the Green Lane ammunition tunnel, now supposed to have been reduced to ruins by BRIE's sabotage. This 'macabre incident was our last meeting with BRIE'. On his return from Madrid he began planning sabotage in real earnest.

Early in 1943, then, the 'relics' of the old Plazas gang were all trying to strike out on their own behalf as independent saboteurs, and of these individuals MI5 were in touch with BRIE and with the COCK/BULL set-up. From the German point of view, Scherr thought that there must have been a good deal of administrative confusion up in Abteilung II headquarters Madrid. As the individual plans of Abt.II agents developed it became operationally vital for the Germans to co-ordinate them so as to avoid two or three carefully prepared acts of sabotage taking place on the same target. Obviously, concluded Scherr, the Germans needed a new leader in place of the absent Plazas. For 'our part, we could turn the appointment of a new leader to our own advantage if the Germans would accept one of our XX agents. We too found the individual members of the Plazas group difficult to control separately, and preferred to have a good, firm leader at the top provided he were in our pocket. At the same time we would continue to keep the activities of our XX agents secret from one another, and in this way would be able to exercise an independent check on them all.'

MI5's first choice, BRIE, 'was already proving untrustworthy and preparing to XXX us'. BULL, therefore, introduced to the Germans, as a suitable leader for their organisation, the agent GON, who had already been recruited by MI5. The Germans, impressed by GON's apparent qualifications, duly appointed him to take charge of the whole of their sabotage operations against Gibraltar. This appointment came as a shock to the other members of the gang, who had been much more closely associated with Plazas than GON had been; but they had, for the moment, no alternative but to accept his leadership. For many months GON remained in this advantageous position. No act of sabotage was to be planned, still less committed, without his prior knowledge and approval. He reported all this information to MI5 accurately and secretly, enabling them to take adequate counter-measures. He also gave MI5 the sabotage material with which the Germans had entrusted him, consisting of a high explosive bomb and two incendiaries. After a while it became clear, however, that GON was not in complete control. One by one the other members broke away and reformed, leaving GON only nominally in charge. 'This was probably due only to impatience and jealousy, not to suspicion of him as a British agent.' In August 1943, following the arrest in Gibraltar of the sabotage agents Martin Munoz and Cordon Cuenca, action was at last taken by the Spanish authorities against some of the German agents of Spanish nationality who were organising sabotage in the Gibraltar area, and a number of imprisonments were made.[3]

As early as January 1943 it had been necessary for Scherr to request assistance, and in May help 'became imperative'. On 18 May Lance Corporal L.E. Bush was detached from No.54 FS Section on permanent loan to the Security Intelligence Officer – Scherr. 'A capacity for really hard work, an unruffable temperament, a deep and extensive first-hand knowledge of Spanish life, language and customs, and a patient understanding of the Spanish character', all combined to make Louis Bush 'an invaluable member of what was to become our Security Intelligence team'. In June 1943, Corporal W. Bulman, also from No.54 FS Section, joined Scherr's security intelligence team, and in October of the same year was commissioned. In July 1945, Bullman joined the Security Service. The acquisition of 'Billy' Bulman was 'another stroke of exceptional good fortune, in view not only of his first-class technical ability (bi-lingual speech and shorthand, and the accumulated experience of many years' residence and business in Spain) but also his own pleasant and friendly personality, reinforced by an engaging Yorkshire shrewdness and forthrightness'. As Scherr recalled:

Our days and nights were long and very full. The inexorable mechanics of contacting secret agents soon studded the passing hours with urgent interviews with queer people and rendezvous in peculiar places. Before it was light enough to see in the mornings, there was someone to meet on his way to the dockyard, or a long wait at the frontier to receive a message; at all hours of the day and night, in fair weather and in foul, the series of successive and furtive encounters and whispered colloquies with one member of the 'Crazy Gang' after another had to go on: in deserted alleyways, empty stables, ploughed fields, public lavatories, lorries, motor-cars, vacant houses, gardens, coal-stores, allotments, cabarets, inns, pine-woods, cane-breaks, tunnels, cemeteries and sand-dunes; in the Dockyard, on the Upper Rock, in the town, at Waterport, and over in Spain – a tedious journey on foot there and back; until the early hours of the morning came, and one went to bed racking one's brains for discreet places for the morrow's meetings, after reading, translating, recording and commenting on the information received during the day. Often one came away from these interviews loaded with bombs in one pocket and detonators or igniters in another, and slipped away from one XX agent just in time to keep a rendezvous with another. And there was always the nagging fear that one had forgotten something important – some decision to be made, some sabotage material to be collected, some information that <u>had</u> to be prepared for use as 'Chickenfeed', some scheme for a fake sabotage to be engineered without fail by a particular date, some favour for an agent, some vital instructions to prepare and pass over.

By May, six of the nine XX agents mentioned were clamouring for fake sabotage, and there was always the implied threat, with those one did not trust (and which of them could one trust?), that if we would not provide the fake, they would proceed with the reality.

There was no time to sit and think calmly and plan ahead a co-ordinated scheme of action. We had to rely in those days almost entirely on snap judgements, and it was sheer good fortune that we did not make too many mistakes.

By March 1944 it was calculated that the Security Intelligence Department had on its records the names of nearly 200 informers, of whom 100 were active and regular informers, 75 were more or less casual informers, some of them inactive at that time, while the remaining few had been dismissed or had permanently ceased to function as agents. Out of this total of nearly 200 only 20 names were taken over from Section V in February 1944, and of those 20, 10 were quite inactive and remained so. More than two thirds of the total number were agents being run by Scherr's MI5/SID prior to his taking over Section V in Gibraltar, the remainder having been recruited in February and March 1944. As far as payment was concerned, only 19 out of the whole total were retained on permanent fee; 43 were paid according to results; and the remainder (over 125) received no payment at all for their services. In running a XX agent, so-called:

'chicken-feed' information often had to be provided, to justify the agent in the eyes of the enemy. Espionage questionnaires of enemy origin produced by the agent were sent by the S.I.D to M.I.5 in London: as they arrived and in some cases special answers were prepared in England for passing over to the enemy. This naturally took some time, and as information required by the enemy was needed quickly it was arranged to have a pool of suitable low-grade 'chicken-feed' available here, into which we could dip as required. The sources of this pool were twofold (1) Local information was supplied by the F.S. Sections here in general bi-weekly batches, which were 'vetted' in conference by

Intelligence Officers representing the three services and were then put into the pool. Secondly, technical information was extracted from magazines such as 'Flight', 'The Aeroplane', 'Aircraft Recognition' 'The Illustrated London News', and so on sent out from Head Office by air, and adapted for use by agents. Records of items fed to an agent were very carefully kept and cross-indexed to enable the item to be recognised should it recur in an intercepted enemy report. Recognition of such an item of "chicken-feed" is, of course, one of the surest ways of knowing the extent to which one has actually penetrated an enemy organisation.

The three officers of the SID worked in very close liaison together so that, as far as the handling of cases was concerned, each one was *au fait* with what was happening and could take over at short notice. Short-term decisions and long-term policy were both usually thrashed out in conversation, as all three sat in the same office. However, as far as possible 'we have tried to leave each officer to develop his particular cases and contact his agents, the chief difficulty being simply that there were too many agents, most of the time, to be dealt with satisfactorily. Whatever theoretical objection may be raised to this large number of agents, the point is that most of the really important ones were agents not of our own choosing but men or women recruited by the enemy to do sabotage or espionage, who preferred to work at XX agents for us instead. Thus the alternative was either to accept their offer and turn them round; or to refuse it and treat them as enemies. The majority of them were not hostile, and to accept them as XX agents was in fact our principal means of self-protection'.[4]

The Gamma Men

The MI5/DSO/SID organisation worked spectacularly well against the Germans – but it was not all good news for the British. The Italian sabotage organisation against Gibraltar was 'infinitely better, and more successful', than its German counterpart. The Italian success was due to a large extent to the use of trained operational personnel of their own nationality, in contrast to the German reliance on Spaniards. The story of Italian sabotage against Gibraltar was therefore chiefly concerned with the activities of the 10th Flotilla M.A.S. (Motoscafo anti-sommergibile). On the night of 30 October 1940, two human torpedoes – or Gammamen – launched from an Italian submarine made an unsuccessful attempt to penetrate the Gibraltar harbour defences. Two prisoners were taken, one of the human torpedoes was destroyed, and the other went ashore in Spain. The crews who manned these torpedoes belonged to a special underwater sabotage unit of the Italian Navy, called the 10th Flotilla MAS under Commandante Borghese. Courses in practical training were held at Spezia, and a course in theory was held at the Accademia Navale at Leghorn. The training included the manoeuvring of human torpedoes at a maximum depth of ten metres below the surface. The normal method of approach was to travel on the surface until about 80 to 100 yards from the target, and then to submerge. Under the hull of the ship the MAS men would then leave their detachable warheads and any other bombs they carried, and then escape to the Spanish shore, using the torpedo to carry them to safety. They were given Spanish money, and instructed to get as close as possible to the shore at Puente Mayorga when returning from the attacks, and then to abandon their torpedoes. At least one of the men who took part in this first attack, a naval lieutenant named Lino Visentin, escaped in this way to Puente Mayorga, where he made his way to a pre-arranged rendezvous and was picked up by the 'arch-organiser' of these operations, 'an astute and capable' Italian engineer, long resident in the Campo de Gibraltar, named Giulio Pistono. He was taken by car to Pistono's house at Pelayo south of Algeciras and from there returned to Italy to take part in later attacks of a similar nature.

The next year (1941), a similar attack took place. Three human torpedoes were launched from a submarine commanded by Borghese himself, which lay in the Bay off Puente Mayorga. This time the targets were merchant ships in the Commercial Anchorage. Visentin led the attack and was himself responsible for the damage to the tanker *Denbighdale*. The *Fionashell* and *Durham* were also damaged. The method of attack and escape were the same as in October 1940, and after destroying their torpedoes the crews were again picked up by Pistono near Puente Mayorga, taken to Pelayo, and from there transferred to Italy. On this occasion the Defence Security Office obtained, after the attack had taken place, a number of reports to the effect that Italian naval personnel numbering up to eight men had swum out of the sea near the ex-Hotel Principe Alfonso early in the morning of 20 September, wearing special diving suits; that they had been taken into custody by the carabineers and afterwards handed over to an official of the Italian Consulate at Algeciras, who had driven them off in his car. These reports were substantially correct, and the official concerned 'was none other' than Pistono, who had been appointed 'Chancellor' of the Consulate to give him suitable cover and protection for his activities. In December 1943 the DSO obtained confirmation of reports which had reached it in 1940 and 1941 from the F group, to the effect that the Italian ship *Fulgor* in Cadiz harbour was in contact with Italian submarines: 'Naturally enough, prior intelligence of impending operations of this kind was impossible to obtain, as knowledge of the operations was limited to very few persons, most of them Italian.' Counter-measures were therefore chiefly operational, and undertaken by the XDO (Extended Defence Officer), RN, whose patrols covered the Commercial Anchorage at nights, dropping depth-charges, examining Spanish fishing boats, and spotlighting the surface to reveal suspicious objects. Their work was hampered by the large number of ships to be protected, by the extensive area of the Anchorage, and by the necessity of keeping at least a quarter of a mile away from the Spanish coastline to avoid infringing Spanish 'neutrality'.

The Italians, though, 'were not satisfied with the results of their operations, and began to plan something better'. In June 1940, the Italian tankers *Olteera* and *Lavoro* had been scuttled in Gibraltar Bay by their crews, who returned to Italy. In June 1942, Lieutenant Visentin came aboard the tanker to prepare it as a base against British and Allied shipping in Gibraltar harbour and Commercial Anchorage. Meanwhile, shore-based operations would take place which would also involve the use of the *Olteera*. With Visentin arrived three special operatives camouflaged as carpenters and cooks, who were to prepare the *Olteera* for future use as a human-torpedo base, and also a doctor travelling as a 'mess-waiter', who was to live aboard and give medical attention as required to the ship's crew and special operatives. Visentin announced that until structural alterations had been completed aboard the tanker, and torpedoes had arrived, attacks would be carried out from the Spanish beach. He made observations of the movement of shipping in the Bay, particularly at night, co-ordinating his results with the routine work of the Italian espionage and observation 'Mission' in Algeciras and with its outpost in La Linea, reporting back to Rome by radio from the Italian Vice-Consulate in Algeciras. He decided that the best conditions for a shore-based attack were lack of moonlight, and slightly heavy seas with some wind to drown any noise. Pistono made himself entirely responsible for organising the shore arrangements, and frequently visited the *Olteera* to confer with Visentin. Their chief concern was to avoid being caught when starting off, lest the expedition came to the notice of any Spaniards working for the British. If caught on their return journey, crews were to say that they had come from a submarine. Meanwhile, material had been assembled at Pistono's house at Pelayo. It was again decided to make use of Puente Mayorga, and Pistono installed an Italian engineer named Ramagnino in a house there named the Villa Carmela. Ramagnino provided sketches and diagrams to be shown beforehand to the men, to assist their return to the beach at Puente Mayorga; and this time his house was to be used as an advanced operational base from which to carry out the attack.

During the first two weeks of July 1942, the twelve men who were to take part in the next attack began to assemble in the area. Some nine or ten men were put up on board the *Olteera* for about a week. They remained hidden during the day, keeping observation on their targets from the Captain's quarters and the bridge. On Sunday 12 July, after the midday meal, two boatloads went ashore, each with some half a dozen men. Some were taken by Pistono in a car to Puente Mayorga and left at the Villa Carmela. The rest of the party again divided into two groups, one travelling by bus and the other on foot, their destination being the same house at Puente Mayorga. On the evening of 13/14 July the saboteurs dressed themselves in the Villa Carmela. They wore underwater equipment, with overalls on, carried three bombs each, had their faces blackened, and had draped camouflage netting over their heads. They crawled at night down to the Mayorga stream and so out on to the beach, entering the sea in pairs at different times, starting about eleven o' clock, according to the distance they had to travel. The men were all instructed to return to Puente Mayorga after the operation. If they failed to land there and were caught elsewhere, they were to say that they had come from a submarine. As a result of this attack, four ships were seriously damaged: The *Baron Kinnaird*, *Shuna*, *Baron Douglas*, and *Empire Snipe*. Five of the twelve men got back to Puente Mayorga and were taken off in Pistono's transport 'safe and sound.' The remaining seven landed on the beach nearby. The seven Gamma-men remained in Seville about six weeks, until it was decided to use some of them in another attack in the Gibraltar area.

At the end of August 1942, three Gamma-men from Seville arrived aboard the *Olteera*, where they stayed until the afternoon of 15 September, when they were taken as before to Villa Carmela. That night the three shallow-divers again made their way down the stream and entered the water. Only one ship, the *Ravenspoint*, was damaged. One of the Gamma-men had managed to place his bombs under the ship in the centre of the keel; the other two had been unable to use their bombs owing to the presence of Spanish fishing boats and British naval patrol launches. One of the two had his leg injured by the propeller of one of the launches. During the operation, Pistono was waiting at Puente Mayorga with two cars to pick up the returning shallow-divers. On arrival at the beach, the men discarded their rank badges (worn during attacks to show that they were operational personnel of the Royal Italian Navy, and not plain-clothes agents) and shallow-diving suits.

Overall the intelligence gathering operation conducted by the DSO – and other agencies – was a complete failure. British naval opinion at the time held it unlikely that either the July or the September 1942 attack could have originated from a submarine. A sample 'limpet-mine' was seen floating near the *Shuna* and was recovered. It was considered probable that both attacks were carried out by saboteurs setting out from the Spanish coast either swimming or in small craft, and then diving down to the ships' bottoms in order to place their bombs. On the whole, the DSO had to admit that 'our information regarding the July attack was good, so far as it went, but related almost entirely to an account of events subsequent to the attack. The little information purporting to refer to preparations made for the attack either came too late for us to warn the Royal Navy in time, or was quite irrelevant.' The Italians appeared to have spread a cover-story of a submarine in Getares Bay 'which tended to obscure the real facts'. But a large number of accounts from different sources were received reporting the arrival on the Spanish shore of the Bay of Gibraltar of six or seven Italians dressed in shallow-diving gear, early in the morning of 14 July. Other reports told of their being taken away by car to Seville after being held by carabineers, and SIS reports from Seville related some of the experiences of these Italians in that city. 'All this made a clear enough picture of what happened to the Gamma-men after the July attack: more vital was to find out how the attack had been carried out.' Concerning this, there were a number of clues in a mass of confusing and vague reports including one from a 'casual source reported that the house called Villa Carmela was suspected of having lodged the Italians who took part in the attack' and:

> Our sabotage XX agent STUFF reported that Carlos CALVO Chozas, second-in-command to the German sabotage chief in the Campo area (Emilio PLAZAS) had visited the farmhouse on the Villa Carmela ground to investigate the disposal of certain 'rubber-suits' left hidden by the Italians there. CALVO was trying to get hold of them for the use of the PLAZAS gang, who were working quite independently of the 10th Flotilla M.A.S.

Following this information, it was discovered that the owner of the Villa Carmela was in fact a British subject named John Louis Bernard Medina, then evacuated to Madeira. A nephew of his working in HM Dockyard was interrogated, but could throw no light on the then tenant of the Villa nor on any activities therein, as the house was in the hands of a Spanish estate-agent, and the nephew had neither occasion nor desire to visit it. He did however know that it was occupied by an Italian: 'In retrospect, there seems no doubt that this should have been more closely followed up, in July 1942, instead of leaving the Italians to use British property once again within another two months as a sabotage-base against Gibraltar.' No relevant reports were received prior to the second shallow-diving attack in September 1942, but once again a number of substantially accurate reports were received from agents and from casual informers after the attack was over, describing the arrival of the saboteurs out of the sea. 'Most striking of all' was some information, less than a week old, from the QUEEN of HEARTS confirming the use of the Villa Carmela and showing complicity on the part of Spanish officials who had foreknowledge of the attack.

The QUEEN's husband worked as an official for the Spanish at Puente Mayorga, and in that capacity sent a report to the Ministry of Marine on the explosions that took place in the Commercial Anchorage. This report knowingly gave a false account of what occurred, saying that the attack had been made from a submarine, whereas he knew that it had in fact been carried out by shore-based shallow-divers. He did, though, include in this false report a true account of an incident involving a Spanish fisherman known as Coca who had stumbled across the three divers just as they were about to enter the sea at the mouth of the Mayorga stream, between eleven and twelve midnight on the night of 14/15 September: 'that is to say, before the attack had taken place. Italian consular officials had offered him one thousand pesetas to keep quiet about what he had seen, and on his proving obstinate they beat him up on the spot.' This fisherman had a sister who was employed by the QUEEN as housemaid. The QUEEN's report to the DSO was based on Coca's story as well as on what she herself had been able to find out from her husband and on her own account. She stated that part of the Italian shallow-diving gear had been washed ashore on 15 September, and offered to get this gear 'if we would pay her well. She also offered to warn us in advance of the next attack.' Elaborate arrangements were made to this end on our side, including coded telephone messages between the QUEEN and 'Captain Woodford'. The QUEEN, who was expecting a child in the near future, was to ring up a certain number in Gibraltar and ask for the 'doctor', leaving a code message the exact wording of which varied according to the time and place either of the next shallow-diving attack or of the interview in which she would hand over the gear – but unfortunately nothing came of either of her schemes. The QUEEN, though, stated that the attack was organised from the Villa Carmela, and she believed that previous attacks had started from there. From the Villa, divers made their way in darkness to the left bank of the stream hid in the bushes until the time was ripe, and then set out from the mouth of the stream into the Bay. When they returned they were put up temporarily in the Villa, unless they were 'arrested' on the shore. 'This information reached us too late to be of use', as the Italians now changed their tactics and used human torpedoes from the tanker *Olteera* in Algeciras harbour for their future sabotage attacks against shipping in the Commercial Anchorage.

On the night 7/8 December 1942 the first human-torpedo attack from the *Olteera* was to be launched. Three torpedoes would set out, each with a crew of two men. Visentin, leading the attack, would be in charge of the first torpedo. The six men had travelled from Madrid to Pelayo, arriving on board the tanker one night about a week before the attack was due to start. It was through a trap-door in the fore-peak of the *Olteera* that human torpedoes were launched. The tanker now had a specially constructed launching chamber and a trap door 4ft x 4ft below the water line in the bows, through which the two-man torpedoes would leave the ship. A large portion of one of the forward bulkheads had been removed to enable the machines to be assembled and stored until the moment arrived to lower them into the flooded portion of the hull. An Italian human torpedo was operated by a crew of two. The leader sat in front and steered. His assistant sat behind him.

'There was great excitement and enthusiasm', the targets being HMS *Nelson* and HM aircraft-carriers *Furious* and *Formidable*. The expedition had to penetrate the harbour defences and attack their targets right inside the harbour. Torpedoes were timed to leave for the attack at half-hourly intervals from midnight onwards on the night 7/8 December. Each torpedo was pushed out of the flooded chamber through the hatch in the ship's side under the water-level. The crew then swam out of the chamber and boarded the torpedo, surfacing immediately in Algeciras harbour in order to make final adjustments before the attack began. Each torpedo carried a complete warhead and an incendiary bomb with which to ignite surface oil and petrol. Shortly after leaving, No.1 torpedo returned with defective rudder transmission. When this had been repaired, No.2 returned for the same reason and was also put right. Adjustment was made to No.3 before it left. 'The attack was a failure.' Visentin and his assistant were killed and their bodies found by the Royal Navy, who also took prisoner both the crew of No.2 torpedo. The only man who returned to the *Olteera* was the leader of the third torpedo, who said that halfway into the Bay he had had to submerge quickly owing to the presence of patrols and the dropping of depth-charges. He had lost his assistant and had to return to the tanker.

After a short period of inactivity aboard the *Olteera*, preparations began for the next attack. Three torpedoes had been assembled, and the crew tested them in Algeciras harbour on or about 6 May. On the night of the 8th, each torpedo was ready equipped with two half-heads and one bomb. The first torpedo set off between eleven and half past eleven that night, and the other two followed at regular intervals. The crews, had, as usual, been given Spanish money and instructions to make for the Spanish shore at Puente Mayorga should the need arise. This time all three torpedoes plus their crews had returned safely to the *Olteera* by half past four the next morning. A white sheet was hung out on deck as each torpedo returned, as a signal to watchers in the Italian Vice-Consulate ashore. The attack was considered by the Italians only a partial success. But from 'our point of view, we lost three ships': The *Camerata*, *Mahsud*, and *Pat Harrison* were damaged and had to be beached. One bomb (damaged) was discovered clamped to the port bilge-keel of the *Camerata*, and clamps similar to those holding this bomb were found on the bilge-keels of the *Mahsud* (one), *Camerata* (two), and *Pat Harrison* (three). On the morning of the 9th, all the torpedo crews left the *Olteera*.

In July 1943, preparations began for yet another torpedo attack from the tanker. The same procedure was followed as for the 8 May attack. On the night of 4 August, three torpedoes set out, each with one complete warhead, this time not carrying any bombs. All three torpedoes returned to the *Olteera* after the attack. Lights were used to signal the safe return of each torpedo. Damage was done to the Norwegian tanker *Thorshovdi*, the British *Stanridge* and U.S. *Harrison G. Otis* the first explosion occurring at approximately 4.15 a.m. 5 August 1943. One was prisoner taken. The five survivors left for Pelayo at 6 a.m. the same morning. After the attack Pistono had a rubber dinghy placed on the beach at Puente Mayorga. The object was to give the impression to any Spaniards working for the British that a submarine had been used for the attack. On or about the 15th, further instructions came through from the Gobierno Militar via the Italian Consulate that the crew of the *Olteera* was to return to Italy. Pistono 'explained that this was the result of pressure by the British authorities. It was however the Spaniards, not the British, who were applying the pressure.' During September and part of October 'strenuous attempts' were made by the Italians and the Spaniards to destroy all traces of the operations that had taken place aboard the *Olteera*, but their work was still unfinished when on Monday 11 October 1943, the tanker was taken in tow by tugs from Gibraltar and anchored in the Commercial Anchorage. One man, Denegri, stayed aboard her, 'having just previously offered his assistance to us via the British Vice-Consul in Algeciras, and was interrogated by officers of the Security Intelligence Department of the Defence Security Office'. His information provided most of the details above.

As the DSO began its investigation into what was a significant intelligence failure, it noted that, first and foremost, 'we must put Spanish complicity, including in this term all those factors which made the Campo de Gibraltar, from the counter-sabotage viewpoint, practically enemy territory'. Secondly, the Italian organisation was disciplined and co-ordinated, and efficiently manned by trained Italian naval personnel whose morale and courage were of a high order. Thirdly the security of the Italian operations and the plausibility of Pistono's deception plans 'could hardly have been improved'. Fourthly, there was 'the immense physical difficulty of protecting the Commercial Anchorage and its shipping from sabotage attacks'. And: 'One cannot help contrasting the Italian record with the dismal failures of the Abwehr in the Gibraltar area. The German chose really a much simpler task than the Italians – the introduction into Gibraltar, and use there, of bombs carried by secret agents entering as workmen. But they worked with Spaniards, and for the most part with very poor quality Spaniards at that.' While the Italians themselves were not satisfied with the results of their attacks:

> they had immeasurably more cause for satisfaction than had the combined British Intelligence Services over their own counter-measures. The events recounted... make humiliating reading from the British viewpoint. There is no point now in trying to proportion the blame as between one service and another, or to call attention to individual shortcomings. What does need emphasising is the threefold fact that even after more than three years of 'total' war our knowledge of the Italian set-up in the Campo was extremely scanty, vague and inaccurate; that our sources of information in Algeciras were wretchedly inadequate; and that there was not enough co-ordination of effort on the part of the separate organisations which were involved in preventing these attacks in one way or another, or which might have been induced to involve themselves. One is thinking mainly of Naval Intelligence, S.I.S., S.O.E., Section V, R.S.S., and the Security Service.

All of these had, could have had, or should have had (as the case may be) a finger in this particular counter-sabotage pie, as there were far too many plums in it for one single digit ever to cope with satisfactorily.

Thus in July 1942, though we all had strong reason to suspect that the Villa Carmela – British property! – had been used by Italian shallow-divers both before and after their attack on shipping in the Commercial Anchorage on the 14th, we were apparently powerless to prevent a repetition of exactly the same tactics in September, we could – so it seemed – neither frighten off the Italians, nor bring pressure to bear via the owner or the Spanish house-agent, nor find any adequate manner in which to protest to the Spanish authorities, nor have the Villa watched, nor even identify accurately the persons normally resident or visiting there.

Equally startling in retrospect 'is our entire and stubborn blindness in the face of the obvious: our failure up to the last moment' to suspect that the Italian tanker *Olteera*, 'right under our noses in Algeciras harbour, might have some connection with the series of Italian underwater sabotage attacks'. Yet however confused the evidence had been, some important clues were made clear right from the first *Olteera*-launched attack in December 1942. For instance, the Royal Navy were positive that no submarine was involved, and that the attacks had been launched from a local base. 'We knew they were Italian because Italian prisoners were taken.' The use of human-torpedoes was strongly suspected, but technical opinion held that any such torpedoes could not possibly be launched from a river mouth or from the flat, sandy shores of the Bay. 'We knew that at least one of the saboteurs in the December 1942 attack had come from Spain before the attack, as he had dirty peseta notes in addition to his clean batch of new ones, and also carried a Zaragoza newspaper of fairly recent date.' Every one of these clues pointed to the *Olteera*, 'but none of us saw the obvious answer until it was too late to matter very much. By "we" and "us" in these last two paragraphs the writer means the officers of all the relevant services here on the Rock, including of course the writer himself.'[5]

Select Bibliography

The National Archives

CAB – Cabinet Office
DEFE – Ministry of Defence
FO – Foreign Office
KV – Security Service
WO – War Office

Imperial War Museum
Lady Constance Kell Memoir
Sir Vernon Kell Diary

Bloody Sunday Inquiry
Witness Statements

Northern Ireland Political Collection
British Government–IRA exchanges

Secondary Sources
Christopher Andrew, *Her Majesty's Secret Service: The Making of the British Intelligence Community* (Viking 1987).
Christopher Andrew & Oleg Gordievsky, *KGB: The Inside Story* (Harper 1991).
Christopher Andrew Vasili Mitrokhin, *The Mitrokhin Archive: The KGB in Europe and the West* (Penguin 1999).
Christopher Andrew Vasili Mitrokhin, *The Mitrokhin Archive II: The KGB and the World* (Penguin 2005).
Tom Bower, *The Perfect English Spy: Sir Dick White and the Secret War 1935–90*.
John Bulloch, *The Origin and History of the British Counter-espionage Service MI5* (Corgi 1963).
Jason Burke, *Al Qaeda: The True Story of Radical Islam* (Penguin 2007).
Bryan Clough, *State Secrets: the Kent-Wolkoff Affair* (Hideaway Publications Ltd 2005).
Eamon Collins & Mick McGovern, *Killing Rage* (Granta Books 1998).
Andrew Cook, *M: MI5's First Spymaster* (Tempus 2006).
Philip Davies, *MI6 and the Machinery of Spying* (Routledge 2004).
Richard Deacon, *'C'. A Biography of Sir Maurice Oldfield* (London 1985).
Kevin Fulton, *Unsung Hero* (John Blake 2008).
Peter Hennessy, *The Secret State: Whitehall and the Cold War* (Penguin 2003).
Mark Hollingsworth and Nick Fielding, *Defending the Realm: Inside MI5 and the War on Terrorism* (Andre Deutsch 2003).
Oliver Hoare (ed), *Camp 020: MI5 and the Nazi Spies* (The National Archives 2000).
Ed Husain, *The Islamist: Why I joined radical Islam in Britain, what I saw inside and why I left* (Penguin 2007).
Martin Ingram & Greg Harkin, *Stakeknife: Britain's Secret Agents in Ireland* (O'Brien Press 2004).
Alan Judd, *The Quest for 'C': Mansfield Cumming and the Founding of the Secret Service* (Harper Collins 1999.
David Leigh, *The Wilson Plot: How the Spycatchers and Their American Allies Tried to Overthrow the British Government* (Pantheon 1988).
Ben Macintyre, *Agent Zigzag: The True Wartime Story of Eddie Chapman: Lover, Traitor, Hero, Spy* (Bloomsbury 2007).
J.C.Masterman, *On the Chariot Wheel: An Autobiography.*

J.C.Masterman, *The Double-Cross System.*

Anthony Masters, *The Man Who Was 'M': The Life of Maxwell Knight* (Basil Blackwell 1984).

Joan Miller, *One Girl's War: Personal Exploits in MI5's Most Secret Station* (Brandon 1986).

Sean O'Callaghan, *The Informer* (Corgi 1999).

Sean O'Neill & Daniel McGrory, *The Suicide Factory: Abu Hamza and the Finsbury Park Mosque* (Harper 2006).

Melanie Philips, *Londonistan: How How Britain Is Creating a Terror State Within* (Gibson Square 2006).

Juan Pujol & Nigel West, *Garbo: The Personal Story of the Most Successful Double Agent Ever* (Grafton 1986).

James Rennie, *The Operators: On the Streets with Britain's Most Secret Service* (Leo Cooper Ltd 2004).

Stella Rimington, *Open Secret: The Autobiography of the Former Director General of MI5* (Arrow 2002).

Michael Smith, *The Spying Game. The Secret history of British Espionage* (Simon & Schuster 2002).

Peter Taylor, *The Guardian,* March 18 2008

Mark Urban, *Big Boys' Rules: SAS and the Secret Struggle Against the IRA* (Faber and Faber 2001).

Nigel West, *MI5: British Security Service Operations, 1909–45* (Triad 1983).

Nigel West, *A Matter of Trust: MI5, 1945–72* (Coronet 1987).

Nigel West, *MI6: British Secret Intelligence Service Operations, 1909–45* (Grafton 1985).

Nigel West, *The Crown Jewels: The British Secrets at the Heart of the KGB's Archives.*

Nigel West, *Mask: MI5's Penetration of the Communist Party of Great Britain.*

Lawrence Wright, *The Looming Tower: Al Qaeda's Road to 9/11 (Penguin 2007).*

Peter Wright with Paul Greengrass, *Spycatcher: The Candid Autobiography of a Senior Intelligence Officer* (Viking 1987).

Notes

Chapter 1
1. KV 2/446, Special Branch report, 18 August 1939.
2. KV 2/445, SNOW, BISCUIT, CELERY, GW and SUMMER.
3. KV 2/446, Special Branch note, 14 February 1939.
4. KV 2/446, Special Branch note, February 1939.
5. KV 2/446, Letter to Squadron Leader Plant, 30 January 1939.
6. KV 2/446, Letter A from Major Boyle, 2 February 1939.
7. KV 2/446, Note to Hinchley-Cooke, 24 March 1939.
8. KV 2/445, SNOW, BISCUIT, CELERY, GW and SUMMER.
9. KV 2/446, Statement by Special Branch, 6 September 1939.
10. KV 2/445, SNOW, BISCUIT, CELERY, GW and SUMMER.
11. KV 2/446, Note, SNOW, nd.
12. KV 2/446, Note, 14 September 1939.
13. KV 2/446, Re: SNOW Case B.3 19, September 1939.
14. KV 2/446, Report on Interview with SNOW, 21 September 1939.
15. KV 2/446, 23 September 1939.
16. KV 2/445, SNOW, BISCUIT, CELERY, GW and SUMMER.
17. KV 2/446, Note, 23 September 1939.
18. KV 2/446, Note, 27 September 1939.
19. KV 2/446, Note, 29 September 1939.
20. KV 2/446, Note, 11 October 1939.
21. KV 2/446, Note, 17 October 1939.
22. KV 2/446, Note, 18 October 1939.
23. KV 2/446, Note, 30 October 1939.
24. KV 2/446, Note, 26 October 1939.
25. KV 2/446 Note, 30 October 1939.
26. KV 2/446 Note, 26 October 1939.
27. KV 2/445, SNOW, BISCUIT, CELERY, GW and SUMMER.
28. KV 2/446, Notes on first contact with CHARLIE.
29. KV 2/446, Note, 7 November 1939.
30. KV 2/445, SNOW, BISCUIT, CELERY, GW and SUMMER.
31. KV 2/446, Notes re: Snow's £5 notes by Lt. J.R. Stopford, 19.11.39.
32. KV 2/446, Note by Lt. J.R. Stopford on Identification of Mrs KRAFFT on 7.12.39.
33. KV 2/445, SNOW, BISCUIT, CELERY, GW and SUMMER.
34. KV 2/446, Note, nd.
35. KV 2/445, SNOW, BISCUIT, CELERY, GW and SUMMER.
36. KV 2/448, Robertson note, 23 May 1940.
37. KV 2/448, BISCUIT.
38. KV 2/448, Robertson note, 27 May 1940.
39. KV 2/448, Robertson note, 23 May 1940.
40. KV 2/448, Robertson note, 27 May 1940.
41. KV 2/448, Robertson note, 23 May 1940.
42. KV 2/448, Robertson note, 27 May 1940.
44. KV 2/448, Robertson note, 23 May 1940.
44. KV 2/445, SNOW, BISCUIT, CELERY, GW and SUMMER.
45. KV 2/448, Robertson note, 27 May 1940.
46. KV 2/448, Robertson note, 23 May 1940.
47. KV 2/445, SNOW, BISCUIT, CELERY, GW and SUMMER.

Chapter 2
1. KV 4/8, Report in the Operations of Camp 020 & Camp 020-R (B.I.E) in Connection with the Interrogation of Enemy Agents During the War 1939–1945.
2. Oliver Hoare (ed), Camp 020: MI5 and the Nazi Spies [hereafter Stephens], p.107.
3. Ibid. p.109.
4. Ibid. pp.126-127.
5. Hoare (ed), p.6.
6. Ibid. p.8.
7. KV 4/8, Report in the Operations of Camp 020 & Camp 020-R (B.I.E) in Connection with the Interrogation of Enemy Agents During the War 1939–1945.
8. Stephens, op.cit. p.35.
9. KV 4/8, Report in the Operations of Camp 020 & Camp 020-R (B.I.E) in Connection with the Interrogation of Enemy Agents During the War 1939–1945.

10. Stephens, op.cit. p.32.

11. KV 4/8, Report in the Operations of Camp 020 & Camp 020-R (B.I.E) in Connection with the Interrogation of Enemy Agents During the War 1939–1945.

12. Stephens, op.cit. p.46.

13. KV 4/2, The Security Service. Its Problems and Organisational Adjustments 1908–1945, Volume 2.

14. KV 4/8, Report in the Operations of Camp 020 & Camp 020-R (B.I.E) in Connection with the Interrogation of Enemy Agents During the War 1939–1945.

15. Stephens, op.cit. pp.107-109.

16. KV 4/8, Report in the Operations of Camp 020 & Camp 020-R (B.I.E) in Connection with the Interrogation of Enemy Agents During the War 1939–1945.

17. Stephens, op.cit. p.124.

18. KV 3/76, German Espionage from 1939 – Objectives in Great Britain, Volume 1.

19. KV 3/76, German Espionage from 1939 – Objectives in Great Britain, Volume 1.

20. KV 3/76, German Secret Service Report No.2, December 1940.

Chapter 3

1. Bower, op.cit. p.21.

2. Ibid. pp.35-36.

3. KV 4/1, The Security Service. Its Problems and Organisational Adjustments 1908-1945, Volume 1.

4. CAB 63/193, Second Report Dealing with the Security Service (MI5).

5. KV 4/1, The Security Service. Its Problems and Organisational Adjustments 1908-1945, Volume 1.

6. CAB 63/193, Wilson to Bridges, 22 May 1940.

7. IWM, Kell, Diary.

8. KV 4/2, The Security Service. Its Problems and Organisational Adjustments 1908-1945, Volume 2.

9. Liddell, Diary, 11 June 1940.

10. IWM, Kell Papers, Constance Kell memoir, p.229.

11. CAB 21/3498, The Security Executive. An Outline of its Course and Functions.

12. CAB 21/3499, Ministerial Responsibility for the Security Service, 2 December 1943.

13. Liddell, Diary, 22 May 1940.

14. Liddell, Diary, 27 August 1940.

15. Liddell, Diary, 18 November 1940.

16. Liddell, Diary, 20 November 1940.

17. Liddell, Diary, 25 November 1940.

18. Liddell, Diary, 26 November 1940.

19. Liddell, Diary, 27 November 1940.

20. Liddell, Diary, 6 December 1940.

21. KV 4/88, Report on the Security Service, 13 February 1941.

22. CAB 123/135, War Office to Lord President, 20 February 1941.

23. CAB 123/135, Anderson to Prime Minister, 19 February 1941.

24. CAB 123/135, Petrie to Swinton, 19 February 1941.

25. CAB 123/135, Swinton to the Lord President, 18 February 1941.

26. CAB 123/135, Lord President to Prime Minister, 24 February 1941.

27. CAB 123/135, Prime Minister's Personal Minute, 1 March 1941.

28. CAB 123/135, Petrie to Swinton, 4 March 1941.

29. CAB 123/135, Swinton to Petrie, 5 March 1941.

30. CAB 132/135, Petrie to Anderson, 4 April 1941.

31. CAB 123/135, Anderson to Prime Minister, 4 April 1941.

32. KV4/20.

33. Nigel West, MI5 p.168.

34. CAB 63/193, Second Report Dealing with the Security Service (MI5).

35. KV 4/2, The Security Service. Its Problems and Organisational Adjustments 1908-1945, Volume 2.

36. Bower, op.cit. pp.44-45.

37. Oliver Hoare (ed), Camp 020: MI5 and the Nazi Spies [hereafter Stephens], pp.14-15.

38. KV 4/2, The Security Service. Its Problems and Organisational Adjustments 1908-1945, Volume 2.

39. DNB, Michael Kitson rev. Miranda Carter, Sept 2004.

40. KV 4/2, The Security Service. Its Problems and Organisational Adjustments 1908-1945, Volume 2.

41. KV 4/123, Security Service Fortnightly Intelligence Summary No.57.

42. KV 4/2, The Security Service. Its Problems and Organisational Adjustments 1908-1945, Volume 2.

43. KV 4/123, Security Service Fortnightly Intelligence Summary No.57.

44. Liddell, Diary, 9 October 1940.

45. Liddell, Diary, 10 October 1940.
46. Liddell, Diary, 28 October 1940.
47. Liddell, Diary, 7 November 1940.
48. Liddell, Diary, 10 November 1940.
49. Liddell, Diary, 20 November 1940.
50. Liddell, Diary, 2 December 1940.
51. KV 4/123, Security Service Fortnightly Intelligence Summary No.57.
52. KV 4/123, Security Service Fortnightly Intelligence Summary No.57.
53. KV 4/2.
54. KV 4/123, Security Service Fortnightly Intelligence Summary No.57.
55. KV 2/445, SNOW, BISCUIT, CELERY, GW and SUMMER.
56. KV 4/2, The Security Service. Its Problems and Organisational Adjustments 1908-1945, Volume 2.
57. KV 4/123, Security Service Fortnightly Intelligence Summary No.57.
58. J.C. Masterman, *The Double-Cross System*, p.113.
59. KV2/94.
60. KV 4/2, The Security Service. Its Problems and Organisational Adjustments 1908-1945, Volume 2.
61. Liddell, Diary, 12 October 1939.
62. KV 4/2, The Security Service. Its Problems and Organisational Adjustments 1908-1945, Volume 2.

Chapter 4
1. KV 4/2, The Security Service. Its Problems and Organisational Adjustments 1908-1945, Volume 2.
2. Bower, op.cit. p.42.
3. Liddell, Diary, 7 October 1940.
4. Bower, op.cit. pp.42-43.
5. Stephens, op.cit. pp.155-156.
6. Ibid, pp.164-166.
7. KV 4/2, The Security Service. Its Problems and Organisational Adjustments 1908-1945, Volume 2.
8. KV 4/63, Note for the JIC.
9. KV 4/63, Memorandum on the 'Double-Cross' System, 27 December 1940.
10. Liddell, Diary, 17 September 1939.
11. Liddell, Diary, 30 September 1939.
12. J.C. Masterman, *On the Chariot Wheel: An Autobiography*. pp.222-223.
13. Ibid, p.237.
14. Ibid. p.viii.
15. KV 4/2, The Security Service.

Its Problems and Organisational Adjustments 1908-1945, Volume 2.
16. KV 2/845, SKOOT, 4 January 1941.
17. KV 2/845, The Story of SKOOT.
18. KV 2/845, SKOOT, 4 January 1941.
19. KV 2/845, Note, 21 January 1941.
20. KV 2/845, SKOOT, 4 January 1941.
21. KV 2/845, SKOOT's Questionnaire, 31 December 1941.
22. KV 2/845, Note, 2 January 1941.
23. KV 2/845, B.2a Note, 2 January 1941.
24. KV 2/845, Report on Interview with SKOOT, 7 February 1941.
25. KV 2/846, Memorandum to S.I.S. (Major Cowgill) re TRICYCLE, 25 March 1941.
26. KV 2/845, Report on Interview with SKOOT, 7 February 1941.
27. KV 2/845, B.2a Report, 7 February 1941.
28. KV 2/845, Report on Interview with SKOOT, 7 February 1941.
29. KV 2/846, Memorandum to S.I.S. (Major Cowgill) re TRICYCLE, 25 March 1941.
30. KV 2/845, Extract from Weekly Summary, 6 February 1941.
31. KV 2/846, Memorandum to S.I.S. (Major Cowgill) re TRICYCLE, 25 March 1941.
32. KV 2/845, SKOOT, 10 January 1941.
33. KV 2/845, B.2a Report, 12 February 1941.
34. KV 2/845, Robertson note ,9 February 1941.
35. KV 2/845, Luke note, 13 February 1941.
36. KV 2/845, Copy of Letter Written in Secret Ink by SKOOT.
37. KV 2/856, Memorandum to S.I.S. (Major Cowgill) re TRICYCLE, 25 March 1941.
38. KV 2/845, Luke note, 13 February 1941.
39. KV 2/845, SKOOT, 23 February 1941.
40. KV 2/846, Memorandum to S.I.S. (Major Cowgill) re TRICYCLE, 25 March 1941.
41. KV 2/846, Popov to G.F. Luke, 3 March 1941.
42. KV 2/846, Memorandum to S.I.S. (Major Cowgill) re TRICYCLE, 25 March 1941.
43. KV 2/847, TRICYCLE's Report, 1 May 1941.

44. KV 2/849, TRICYCLE's last Visit to England. (Events from April 30th to June 26th 1941).
45. KV 2/852, TRICYCLE, Revised Summary up to Departure from Lisbon to USA on 11.8.1941.
46. KV 2/849, Memorandum for [BALLOON].
47. KV 2/852, TRICYCLE, Revised Summary up to Departure from Lisbon to USA on 11.8.1941.
48. KV 2/849, GELATINE, 16 September 1941.
49. KV 2/849, GELATINE, 26 September 1941.

Chapter 5
1. KV 2/445, SNOW, BISCUIT, CELERY, GW and SUMMER.
2. KV 2/60, The SUMMER Case.
3. KV 2/60, Resume on [blanked out], 10 September 1940.
4. KV 2/60, The SUMMER Case.
5. KV 2/445, SNOW, BISCUIT, CELERY, GW and SUMMER.
6. KV 2/60, Memo to White, 14 January 1941.
7. KV 2/60, Report on SUMMER.
8. KV 2/60, Memo to White, 14 January 1941.
9. KV 2/445, SNOW, BISCUIT, CELERY, GW and SUMMER.
10. KV 2/1066, RAINBOW, 14 April 1940.
11. KV 2/1066, Gunther SCHUTZ note, 28 January 1940.
12. KV 2/1066, RAINBOW, 14 April 1940.
13. KV 2/1066, 28 January 1940.
14. KV 2/1066, RAINBOW, 14 April 1940.
15. KV 2/1066, RAINBOW nd.
16. KV 2/61, TATE.
17. KV 2/60, Personal descriptions of TATE, SUMMER and Richter and TATE's contacts.
18. KV 2/61, TATE.
19. KV 2/60, Personal descriptions of TATE, SUMMER and Richter and TATE's contacts.
20. KV 2/61, TATE.
21. KV 2/60, Personal descriptions of TATE, SUMMER and Richter and TATE's contacts.
22. KV 4/92, B1.A Case Summaries.
23. KV 2/61, TATE.
24. KV 2/61, Interrogation of TATE by Major Stephens at Latchmore House,

21 September 1940.
25. KV 2/61, TATE.
26. KV 2/61, Interrogation of TATE by Major Stephens at Latchmore House, 21 September 1940.
27. KV 2/61, Interview by Major Stephens, 23 September 1940.
28. KV 2/61, TATE.
29. KV 4/92, B1.A Case Summaries.
30. Masterman, *Double-Cross*, op.cit. p.93.
31. KV 2/61, Robertson to Stephens, 28 April 1941.
32. KV 2/61, Message sent 8.30 a.m., 21/5/4.
33. KV 2/61, Message received, 8.50 a.m., 21/5/41.
34. KV 2/61, Message sent, 12.30 p.m., 21/5/41.
35. KV 2/61, Message received, 12.45 p.m., 21/5/41.
36. KV 2/61, Message received by TATE, 22 May 1941.
37. KV 2/61, Message sent by TATE, 23rd May 1941.
38. KV 2/61, Message received by TATE, 23rd May 1941.
39. KV 2/61, Note, 27 May 1941.
40. KV 2/61, Message received by TATE, 28th May 1941.
41. KV 2/61, TATE, 28 May 1941.
42. KV 2/61, W.E. Luke Note, 28 May 1941.
43. KV 2/61, Note, 30 May 1941.
44. KV 2/61, Message sent, 30th May 1941.
45. KV 2/61, Message received, 30th May 1941.
46. KV 2/61, pp.164-166.
47. KV 2/61, TATE, 8 July 1941.
48. KV 2/61, 10 December 1941.
49. KV 4/92, B1.A Case Summaries.
50. KV 2/61, TATE, 3 July 1941.
51. TATE, 7 July 1941.
52. TATE, 22 September 1941.
53. KV 2/1066, TATE, 8 August 1942.
54. KV 2/61, Plan CARTER-PATERSON Objects.
55. KV 2/6, TATE, 21 August 1942.

Chapter 6
1. KV 2/445, SNOW, BISCUIT, CELERY, GW and SUMMER.
2. KV 2/674, 7th April 1940.
3. KV 2/674, B.3 Note, 7 April 1940.
4. KV 2/674, Statement.
5. KV 2/647, B.3 Report, 6 April 1940.
6. KV 2/674, B.3 Report, 9 April 1940.

7. KV 2/647, W.2 Report, 10 December 1940.

8. KV 2/674, B.2A, 20 January 1941.

9. KV 2/674, 2nd B.2a report, 17 January 1941.

10. KV 2/674, B.2a, 17 January 1941.

11. KV 2/674, SNOW and CELERY, 30 March 1941.

12. KV 2/674, Report on SNOW and CELERY.

13. KV 2/674, Report, March 28th, 1941.

14. KV 2 /674, CELERY Statement.

15. Note on the Interrogation of Snow, 3 April 1941.

16. KV 2/445, SNOW, BISCUIT, CELERY, GW and SUMMER.

17. Note on the Interrogation of Snow, 3 April 1941.

18. KV 2/674, R.T. Reed report, 1 April 1941.

19. KV 2/674, Note, 1 April 1941.

20. KV 2/674, Interrogation, 8 April 1941.

21. KV 2/674, CELERY, 10 April 1941.

22. KV 2/647, Part Three.

23. KV 2/450, Masterman to Merriott, nd.

24. KV 2/450, Conference 10 April 1941.

25. KV 2/445, Major Ritter's Final Report (translation), 31 July 1941.

26. KV 2/445, SNOW Interogations, 7.4.42–10.4.42.

27. KV 2/450, Robertson, 18 August 1941.

28. KV 2/450, Masterman note, 14 August 1941.

29. KV 2/445, Note on the Memorandum 'Dr Rantazu's Meeting with SNOW and CELERY in Lisbon, November 1941.

30. KV 2/450, Note, 14 August 1941.

31. KV 2/450, Note on the Case of SNOW JUNIOR, 19 August 1941.

32. KV 2/445, SNOW, BISCUIT, CELERY, GW and SUMMER.

Chapter 7

1. KV 2/1067, The Case of MUTT & JEFF.

2. KV 2/1067, MUTT & JEFF.

3. KV 2/1067, The Case of MUTT & JEFF.

4. KV 2/1067, MUTT & JEFF.

5. KV 2/1067, The Case of MUTT & JEFF.

6. KV 2/1067, MUTT & JEFF.

7. KV 2/1067, The Case of MUTT & JEFF.

8. KV 2/1067, MUTT & JEFF.

9. KV 2/1067, The Case of MUTT & JEFF.

10. KV 2/1067, MUTT & JEFF.

11. KV 2/94.

12. Masterman, *Double-Cross*, op.cit. p.117.

13. KV 2/94.

14. Masterman, *Double-Cross*, op.cit. pp.118.

15. KV 2/326, The MULLET-HAMLET Case by A.H. Robertson, 3 February 1943.

16. KV 2/326, Harmer memo, 15 September 1942.

17. KV 2/326, Robertson to Liddell, 17 September 1942.

18. KV 2/326, Masterman to Liddell, 18 September 1942.

19. KV 2/326, Instructions to MULLET, 14 December 1942.

20. KV 2/326, The MULLET-HAMLET Case by A.H. Robertson, 3 February 1943.

21. KV 2/325, The PUPPET-HAMLET Case by A.H. Robertson, 20 April 1943.

22. Masterman, op.cit. p.119.

23. KV 2/326, Note by Major Foley.

24. KV 2/325, 3 February 1943.

25. KV 2/327, The PUPPET-HAMLET Case, 21 April 1943.

26. Masterman, op.cit. pp.119-120.

Chapter 8

1. Masterman, *Double-Cross*, op.cit. p.120.

2. KV 2/94.

3. Masterman, *Double-Cross*, op.cit. p.120.

4. KV 2/94.

5. Masterman, *Double-Cross*, op.cit. p.120.

6. KV 2/94.

7. Masterman, *Double-Cross*, op.cit. p.121.

8. KV 2/94.

9. Masterman, *Double-Cross*, op.cit. p.121.

10. KV 2/94.

11. Masterman, *Double-Cross*, op.cit. p.121.

12. KV 2/94.

13. KV 4/247, WALENTY Report, 30 November 1942.

14. KV 2/928, Summary of VICTOIRE's Memoirs.

15. KV 4/247, BRUTUS Summary.
16. KV 2/928, Harmer memo.
17. KV 4/247, WALENTY Report, 30 November 1942.
18. KV 4/247, APPENDIX A, WALENTY's Original Story and Annexes.
19. KV 4/247, WALENTY Report, 30 November 1942.
20. KV 4/247, BRUTUS Summary.
21. KV 4/247, WALENTY Report, 30 November 1942.
22. KV 4/247, APPENDIX A, WALENTY's Original Story and Annexes.
23. KV 4/247, BRUTUS Summary.
24. KV 4/247, APPENDIX A, WALENTY's Original Story, and Annexes.
25. KV 4/247, APPENDIX C, WALENTY's reconstructions of the two documents he wrote in prison for the Germans.
26. KV 4/247, APPENDIX A, WALENTY's Original Story and Annexes.
27. KV 4/247, APPENDIX C, WALENTY's reconstructions of the two documents he wrote in prison for the Germans.
28. KV 4/247, APPENDIX A, WALENTY's Original Story and Annexes.
29. KV 4/247, WALENTY Report, 30 November 1942.
30 KV 4/247, Marriott to Robertson, 5 December 1942.
31 KV 2/247, BRUTUS Supplementary Report.

Chapter 9
1. KV 2/41, Summary of the GARBO Case, 1941-1945 by Tomas Harris. See also *GARBO: the Spy Who Saved D-Day* with an introduction by Mark Seaman.
2. Juan Pujol and Nigel West, *Garbo: The Personal Story of the Most Successful Double Agent Ever*. pp.25-26.
3. Ibid. pp.64-65.
4. KV 2/41, Summary of the GARBO Case 1941-1945, Chapter 6.
5. Pujol and West, op.cit. pp.105-108.
6. Ibid, pp.116-118.
7. Ibid. pp.242-243.
8. KV 2/41, Summary of the GARBO Case 1941-1945, Chapter 9.

9. Masterman, *Double-Cross*, op.cit. p.114.
10. KV 2/1444, B1.A note, 14 February 1943.
12. KV 2/1444, The Polish Case Against CARELESS, 15 March 1943.

Chapter 10
1. KV 2/41, Summary of the GARBO Case 1941-1945, APPENDIX XXIX.
2. KV 2/457, Chapman, 7 January 1943.
3. KV 2/459, Second Interim Report on the Case of Edward Arnold Chapman, 10 July 1944.
4. KV 2/455, Statement of Edward Chapman, 16 December 1942.
5. KV 2 456, Note, 29 December 1942.
6. KV 2/455, Operation NIGHTCAP, 1 October 1942.
7. KV 2/455, NIGHTCAP, 2 October 1942.
8. KV 2/455, Sergeant Joseph S. Vail statement.
9. KV 2/457, Chapman, 7 January 1943.
10. KV 2/455, Chapman to the Commandant, 18 December 1942.
11. KV 2/455, Chapman, 17 December 1942.
12. KV 2/457, Chapman, 7 January 1943.
13. KV 2/456, Letter from Major R.M. Spier, 28 December 1942.
14. KV 2/456, Instructions to FSP.
15. KV 2/456, ZIGZAG, 26 December 1942, Marshall memo.
16. KV 2/456, ZIGZAG, 28 December 1942.
17. KV 2/457, L.C. Marshall note, 8 January 1943
18. KV 2/458, SLA (Mr Hale), 14 February 1943.
19. KV 2/457, ZIGZAG, Note R.T. Reed, 7 January 1943.
20. KV 2/459, R.T. Reed, 15 March 1943.
21. KV 2/458, SLA (Mr Hale), 14 February 1943.
22. KV 2/459, R.T. Reed, 15 March 1943.
23. KV 2/458, SLA (Mr Hale), 14 February 1943.
24. KV 2/459, R.T. Reed, 15 March 1943.
25. KV 2/458, SLA (Mr Hale), 14 February 1943.
26. KV 2/459, R.T. Reed, 15 March 1943.

27. KV 2/457, ZIGZAG, 11 January 1943.
28. KV 2/459, R.T. Reed, 15 March 1943.
29. KV 2/458, L.G. Marshall, Memo, 2 February 1943.
30. KV 2/458, ZIGZAG, Report of Activities in Liverpool, 3 March 1943.
31. KV 2/459, R.T. Reed, 15 March 1943.
32. KV 2/458, ZIGZAG, Report of Activities in Liverpool, 3 March 1943.
33. KV 2/459, ZIGZAG, 9 March 1943.
34. KV 2/459, ZIGZAG, 21 March 1943.
35. KV 2/459, ZIGZAG, 16 March 1943.
36. KV 2/459, Second Interim Report on the Case of Edward Arnold Chapman, 10 July 1944.
37. KV 2/459, ZIGZAG, 28 March 1943
38. KV 2/459, Second Interim Report on the Case of Edward Arnold Chapman, 10 July 1944.
39. KV 2/459, D.I Wilson, Memo, 12 July 1944.
40. KV 2/461, Plan DAMP SQUID 1, 8 April 1943.
41. KV 2/461, Wood to Rothschild, 14 April 1943.
42. KV 2/461, Rothschild to Wood, 15 April 1943.
43. KV 2/461, ZIGZAG, 24 April 1943.
44. KV 2/461, ZIGZAG, 26 April 1943.
45. KV 2/459, White to Robertson, 5 May 1943.
46. KV 2/247, BRUTUS, 19 June 1943.
47. KV 4/247, BRUTUS, Supplementary Report, 31 December 1944.
48. KV 4/247, BRUTUS, 20 August 1943.
49. KV 2/24, BRUTUS, Supplementary Report.

Chapter 11
1. Nigel West, *MI6 British Secret Intelligence Service Operations 1909-45*, p.44.
2. Ibid. pp.62-63.
3. Ibid. p.131.
4. Ibid. p.129.
5. KV 4/2.
6. KV 4/120, Petrie to C 7, April 1942.
7. KV 4/120, Petrie to C 17, April 1942.
8. KV 4/120, Case for Uniting Section V and B Division Work.
KV 4/120, C to Petrie, 11 May 1942.

10. KV 4/120, Petrie to C 5, June 1942.
11. KV 4/120, C to Petrie, 28 June 1942.
12. KV 4/120, White to Petrie, 1 July 1942.
13. KV 4/120, Memorandum on MI5/MI6 Joint Section for Counter-espionage.
14. KV 4/120, Note of Meeting held at 3 pm on Wednesday, July 22nd, 1942, to discuss proposals as to co-ordinating Section V of SIS and B Division of MI5.
15. KV 4/120, Milo to DGSS, 27 July 1942.
16. KV 4/120, ADB1 (DG White) to DGSS through DB (Liddell), 10 August 1942.
17. KV 4/120, DB to DGSS, 12 August 1942.
18. KV 4/120, Switzerland B1.B, 7 August 1942.
19. KV 4/120, DB to DGSS, 12 August 1942.
20. KV 4/120, Draft letter to Brigadier Menzies.

Chapter 12
1. KV 2/852, TRICYCLE in America, August 1941–October 1942.
2. KV 2/849, Note to Masterman, 12 April 1942.
3. KV 2/849, Marriott to Foley, 13 May 1942.
4. KV 2/849, TRIBAGE Organisation, 10 May 1942.
5. KV 2/849, TRICYCLE/BALLOON/GELATINE, 12 May 1942.
6. KV 2/849, Robertson to Foley, 16 May 1942.
7. KV 2/849, TRICYCLE, 14 July 1942.
8. KV 2/849, Summary of TRICYCLE's Interrogations on 23 and 24 October 1942.
9. KV 2/852, TRICYCLE in England, 21 October 1942 to date.
10. KV 2/852, METEOR and TRICYCLE, 28 April 1943.
11. KV 2/868, DREADNOUGHT and his Contacts with the German Intelligence Service, 24 August 1944.
12. KV 2/868, DREADNOUGHT and the Mihailovic Movement.
13. KV 2/868, DREADNOUGHT and his Contacts with the German Intelligence Service, 24 August 1944.
14. KV 2/868, The Yugoslav group of B1.A. agents: TRICYCLE, DREADNOUGHT, METEOR,

VELOCIPEDE, THE WORM and FREAK.

15. KV 2/868, DREADNOUGHT and his Contacts with the German Intelligence Service, 24 August 1944.

16. KV 2/868, The Yugoslav group of B1.A agents: TRICYCLE, DREADNOUGHT, METEOR, VELOCIPEDE, THE WORM and FREAK.

17. KV 2/868, The Yugoslav group of B1.A. agents: TRICYCLE, DREADNOUGHT, METEOR, VELOCIPEDE, THE WORM and FREAK.

18. KV 2/859, TRICYCLE, Summary from 1.4.43 to 26.2.44.

19. KV 2/852, METEOR and TRICYCLE, 28 April 1943.

20. KV 2/852, TRICYCLE, 2 May 1943.

21. KV 2/868, The Yugoslav group of B1.A agents: TRICYCLE, DREADNOUGHT, METEOR, VELOCIPEDE, THE WORM and FREAK.

22. KV 2/859, TRICYCLE, Summary from 1.4.43 to 26.2.44.

23. KV 2/859, DREADNOUGHT and his Contacts with the German Intelligence Service, 24 August 1944.

24. KV 2/859, TRICYCLE, Summary from 1.4.43 to 26.2.44.

25. KV 2/859 DREADNOUGHT and his Contacts with the German Intelligence Service, 24 August 1944.

26. KV 2/859, TRICYCLE, Summary from 1.4.43 to 26.2.44.

27. KV 2/852, TRICYCLE, 28 April 1943.

28. KV 2/852, TRICYCLE, 2 May 1943.

29. KV 2/859, TRICYCLE, Summary from 1.4.43 to 26.2.44.

30. KV 2/855, Astor note, 7 October 1943.

31. KV 2/855, Harris note, 8 October 1943.

32. KV 2/855, Wilson memo, 8 October 1943.

33. KV 2/859, TRICYCLE, Summary from 1.4.43 to 26.2.44.

Chapter 13

1. KV 4/4, History of the Operations Section.

2. KV 4/4, The Inter-Services Security Board.

3. KV 4/4, History of the Operations Section.

4. KV 4/4, Security Service: Charter of the Operations Section.

5. KV 4/4, History of the Operations Section.

6. KV 4/79, Summary Exercise HARLEQUIN.

7. KV 4/79, Observations on Exercise HARLEQUIN and Operation STARKEY, 13 September.

8. KV 2/41, Summary of the GARBO Case 1941–1945, CHAPTER XXIII.

9. KV 2/41, Summary of the GARBO Case 1941–1945, CHAPTER XXIV.

10. KV 4/2.

11. KV 2/41, Summary of the GARBO Case 1941–1945, CHAPTER XXIV.

12. KV 4/2.

13. WO 208/4374, FORTITUDE: A History of Strategic Deception in North Western Europe April 1943 to May 1945.

14. KV 4/2.

15. WO 208/4374, FORTITUDE: A History of Strategic Deception in North Western Europe April 1943 to May 1945.

16. KV 2/858, TOP SECRET, nd.

17. KV 2/858, The Gruppe III Investigation and ARTIST's Present Position, 27 April 1944.

18. KV 2/858, TRICYLE/ARTIST, 17 May 1944.

19. KV 2/858, TOP SECRET, nd.

20. KV 2/858, TRICYLE/ARTIST, 17 May 1944.

21. KV 2/858, Effects of the removal of ARTIST on Deception Plans, 9 May 1944.

22. KV 2/858, Harris memo to Robertson and Marriott, 9 May 1944.

23. KV 2/858, Note, nd.

24. KV 2/859, TRICYCLE, April 1943–May 1944.

25. KV 2/858, TRICYLE/ARTIST, 17 May 1944.

26. WO 208/4374, FORTITUDE: A History of Strategic Deception in North Western Europe April 1943 to May 1945.

Chapter 14

1. WO 208/4374, FORTITUDE: A History of Strategic Deception in North Western Europe April 1943 to May 1945.

2. KV 2/272, Plan for BRUTUS, 26 May 1944.

3. WO 208/4374, FORTITUDE: A

History of Strategic Deception in North Western Europe April 1943 to May 1945.
4. KV 2/41, Summary of the GARBO Case 1941-1945, CHAPTER XXIV (B).
5. WO 208/4374, FORTITUDE: A History of Strategic Deception in North Western Europe April 1943 to May 1945.
6. KV 2/41, Summary of the GARBO Case 1941-1945, CHAPTER XXIV (A).
7. KV 2/41, Summary of the GARBO Case 1941–1945, CHAPTER XXIV.
8. WO 208/4374, FORTITUDE: A History of Strategic Deception in North Western Europe April 1943 to May 1945.
9. KV 2/72, Astor to Marriott, 27 June 1944.
10. WO 208/4374, FORTITUDE: A History of Strategic Deception in North Western Europe April 1943 to May 1945.
11. KV 2/72, Astor to Marriott, 15 July 1944.
12. WO 208/4374, FORTITUDE: A History of Strategic Deception in North Western Europe April 1943 to May 1945.
13. KV 2/72, Marriott note, 5 July 1944.
14. KV 2/72, Marriott note, 10 August 1944.
15. KV 2/72, Astor note, 28 September 1944.
16. KV 2/72, Marriott note, 8 November 1944.
17. KV 2/72, Astor to Marriott, 22 July 1944.
18. WO 208/4374, FORTITUDE: A History of Strategic Deception in North Western Europe April 1943 to May 1945.
19. KV 2/459, ZIGZAG, Milmo to Stephens, 28 June 1944.
20. KV 2/459, ZIGZAG, 29 June 1944.
21. KV 2/459, ZIGZAG, Milmo to Stephens, 28 June 1944.
22. KV 2/459, Second Interim Report on the Case of Edward Arnold Chapman, 10 July 1944.
23. KV 2/460, ZIGZAG, 6 August 1944.
24. KV 2/460, ZIGZAG, 15 August 1944.
25. KV 2/60, ZIGZAG, 14 August 1944.
26. KV 2/460, ZIGZAG, 15 August 1944.
27. KV 2/460, ZIGZAG, 13 September 1944.
28. KV 2/460, ZIGZAG, 24 October 1944.
29. West, *MI5*, op.cit. p.236. Ibid. p.242.
30. Ibid. p.242.
31. WO 208/4374, FORTITUDE: A History of Strategic Deception in North Western Europe April 1943 to May 1945.
32. KV 2/72, Astor note, 9 January 1945.
33. KV 2/72, Note, 12 January 1945.
34. KV 2/72, Astor note, 25 January 1945.
35. KV 2/41, Summary of the GARBO Case, 1941–1945.
36. Pujol and West, pp.249-250.
37. KV 2/860, Note, 2 August 1945.
38. KV2/861, Note of Schreiber's interrogation.
39. KV 2/861, Interrogation by J. Flinn.

Chapter 15
1. KV 4/260, The 10th Flotilla M.A.S.
2. KV 4/259, History of the Security Intelligence Dept. of the Defence Security Officer Gibraltar, 1939–1945.
3. KV 4/260, The 10th Flotilla M.A.S.
4. KV 4/259, History of the Security Intelligence Dept. of the Defence Security Officer Gibraltar, 1939–1945.
5. KV 4/260, The 10th Flotilla M.A.S.

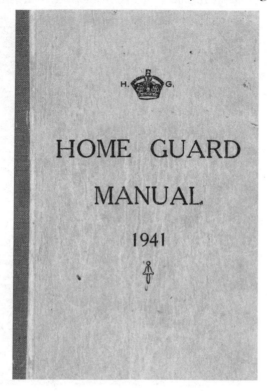

Also available from Amberley Publishing

A fabulous slice of wartime nostalgia, a facsimile edition of the propaganda booklet issued following victory in the Battle of Britain

First published in 1941, *The Battle of Britain* was a propaganda booklet issued by the Ministry of Information to capitalise on the success of the RAF in defeating the Luftwaffe. An amazing period piece, hundreds of thousands of copies were printed and sold for 6d and it became one of the year's best selling books. It is the first book to embed in the public imagination the heroics of 'The Few'.

£4.99 Paperback
25 illustrations
36 pages
978-1-4456-0048-2

Available from all good bookshops or to order direct
Please call **01285–760–030**
www.amberleybooks.com

Also available from Amberley Publishing

'A poignant and evocative account of what it felt like to be a young fighter pilot in the Battle of Britain'
JULIA GREGSON, *bestselling author & daughter of Barry Sutton*

Fighter Boy

Life as a Battle of Britain Pilot

BARRY SUTTON

The Battle of Britain memoir of Hurricane pilot Barry Sutton, DFC

At 23 years of age, Barry Sutton had experienced more than the average person experiences in a lifetime. This book, based on a diary he kept during the war, covers September 1939 to September 1940 when he was shot down and badly burned.

£20 Hardback
20 illustrations
224 pages
978-1-84868-849-0

Available from all good bookshops or to order direct
Please call **01285-760-030**
www.amberleybooks.com

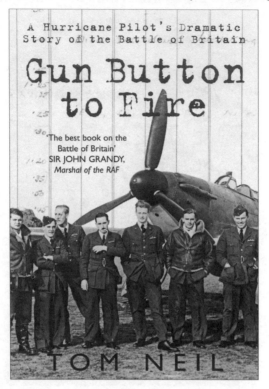

Also available from Amberley Publishing

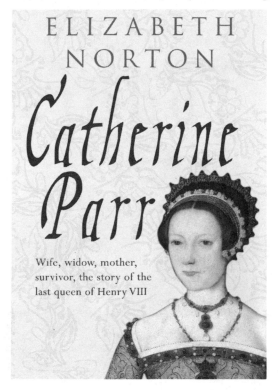

ELIZABETH
NORTON

Catherine Parr

Wife, widow, mother,
survivor, the story of the
last queen of Henry VIII

Wife, widow, mother, survivor, the story of the last queen of Henry VIII

The sixth wife of Henry VIII was also the most married queen of England, outliving three husbands before finally marrying for love. Catherine Parr was enjoying her freedom after her first two arranged marriages when she caught the attention of the elderly Henry VIII. She was the most reluctant of all Henry's wives, offering to become his mistress rather than submit herself to the dangers of becoming Henry's queen. This only served to increase Henry's enthusiasm for the young widow and Catherine was forced to abandon her lover for the decrepit king.

£18.99 Hardback
40 illustrations (20 colour)
240 pages
978-1-84868-582-6

Available from all good bookshops or to order direct
Please call **01285-760-030**
www.amberleybooks.com

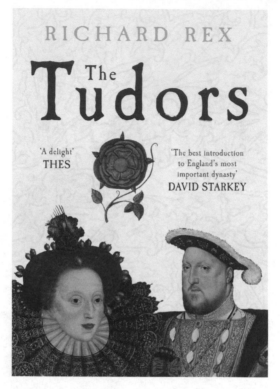

Available from March 2010 from Amberley Publishing

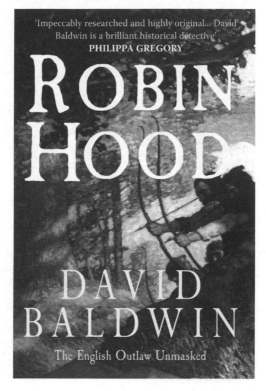

The identity of Robin Hood is one of the great historical mysteries of English history — until now

'Impeccably researched and highly original... David Baldwin is a brilliant historical detective'
PHILIPPA GREGORY

David Baldwin sets out to find the real Robin Hood, looking for clues in the earliest ballads and in official and legal documents of the thirteenth and fourteenth centuries. His search takes him to the troubled reign of King Henry III, his conclusions turn history on it's head and David Baldwin reveals the name of the man who inspired the tales of Robin Hood.

£20 Hardback
40 illustrations (20 colour)
320 pages
978-1-84868-378-5

Available from March 2010 from all good bookshops or to order direct
Please call **01285-760-030**
www.amberleybooks.com

Also available from Amberley Publishing

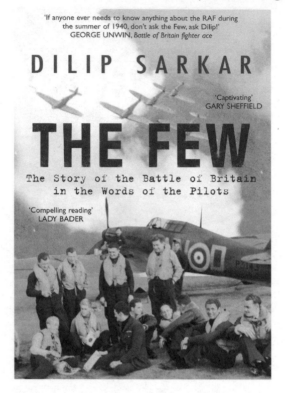

The history of the Battle of Britain in the words of the pilots

Also available from Amberley Publishing

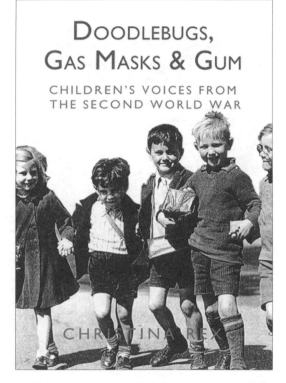

DOODLEBUGS,
GAS MASKS & GUM

CHILDREN'S VOICES FROM
THE SECOND WORLD WAR

CHRISTINA REX

A child's-eye view of life in wartime Britain

'A rich compilation of the recollections of childrens' lives' JULIET GARDINER

Six years of conflict, where military manoeuvres, bombs and exhortations to greater dedication to the War
Effort were a daily staple, became the normality of our childhood after September 3rd 1939. For young
children, this was a time of great excitement.

£14.99 Paperback
80 illustrations
192 pages
978-1-84868-085-2

Available from all good bookshops or to order direct
Please call **01285-760-030**
www.amberleybooks.com

Available from November 2010 from Amberley Publishing

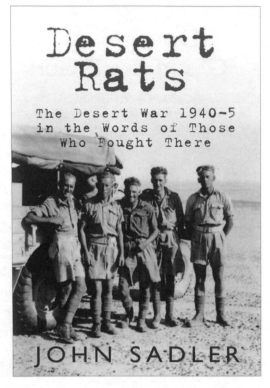

The story of the last surviving 'Desert Rats' in their own words
and their experience of war in North Africa

From 1940-3 Britain was engaged in a life and death struggle with the Axis powers
in North Africa, a titanic, swaying conflict that surged back and forth across the
barren wastes of Egypt, Libya and Tunisia. Those British servicemen who were to form the legendary
'Desert Rats' were, for the most part, not professional soldiers; they were drawn from all walks of civilian life.
They were ordinary men who did extraordinary things in most extraordinary circumstances.

£20 Hardback
80 illustrations
320 pages
978-1-84868-337-2

Available from November 2010 from all good bookshops or to order direct
Please call **01285-760-030**
www.amberleybooks.com

Also available from Amberley Publishing

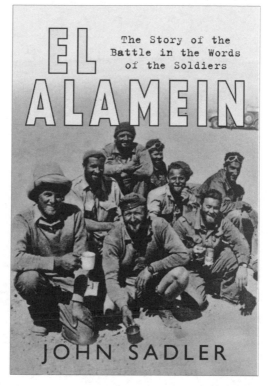

The Story of the
Battle in the Words
of the Soldiers

EL ALAMEIN

JOHN SADLER

*This is the story of El Alamein and the British soldiers who
fought in it*

'There was for me no excitement in the charge. I'd seen it all before, and after a certain time you look
round the faces of your mates and you realize with a shock how few of the original mob are left. Then
you know it's only a matter of time before you get yours. All I wanted to do was to get across that bloody
ground and through the guns.' *BRITISH INFANTRYMAN*

The epic battle in Egypt between the Axis forces led by Rommel 'the Desert Fox' and Britain's 'Desert
Rats' in the words of the soldiers themselves.

£20 Hardback
50 illustrations (15 colour)
336 pages
978-1-84868-101-9

Available from all good bookshops or to order direct
Please call **01285-760-030**
www.amberleybooks.com

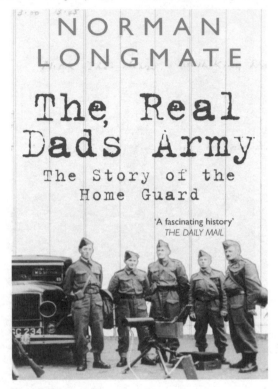

Also available from Amberley Publishing

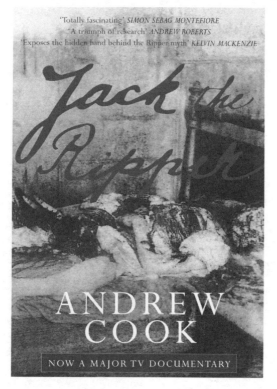

Finally lays to rest the mystery of who Jack the Ripper was

'Totally fascinating' SIMON SEBAG MONTEFIORE
'A triumph of research' ANDREW ROBERTS
'Exposes the hidden hand behind the Jack the Ripper myth' KELVIN MACKENZIE

The most famous serial killer in history. A sadistic stalker of seedy Victorian backstreets. A master criminal. The man who got away with murder – over and over again. But while literally hundreds of books have been published, trying to pin Jack's crimes on an endless list of suspects, no-one has considered the much more likely explanation for Jack's getting away with it... He never existed.

£9.99 Paperback
53 illustrations and 47 figures
256 pages
978-1-84868-522-2

Available from all good bookshops or to order direct
Please call **01285-760-030**
www.amberleybooks.com

Also available from Amberley Publishing

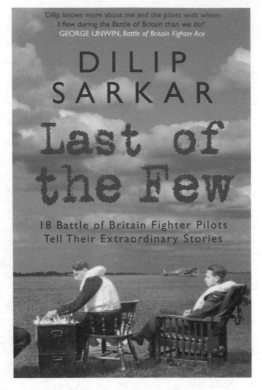

'Dilip knows more about me and the pilots with whom
I flew during the Battle of Britain than we do!'
GEORGE UNWIN, *Battle of Britain Fighter Ace*

DILIP
SARKAR

Last of
the Few

18 Battle of Britain Fighter Pilots
Tell Their Extraordinary Stories

*18 Spitfire and Hurricane fighter pilots recount their experiences
of combat during the Battle of Britain*

'Dilip knows more about me and the pilots with whom I flew during the Battle of Britain than we do! If
anyone ever needs to know anything about the RAF during the summer of 1940, don't ask the Few, ask
him!' GEORGE 'GRUMPY' UNWIN, Battle of Britain fighter ace

£20 Hardback
60 illustrations
240 pages
978-1-84868-435-5

Available from all good bookshops or to order direct
Please call **01285-760-030**
www.amberley-books.com

Available from February 2011 from Amberley Publishing

The history of MI5 during the era of the Cold War, the IRA and international terrorism

Despite an outstanding record against German and Soviet espionage, the book reveals MI5's greatest failure: how and why it failed to prevent Soviet agents like Anthony Blunt, penetrating the heart of the British establishment, including MI5 itself. The authors look in detail at MI5's role in the post-Cold War world; in particular, they consider its changing role as it took on the main responsibility in countering terrorist threats to Britain. Controversy has never been far away during MI5's battle against the IRA, which included sending deep penetration agents into the heart of Northern Ireland's terrorist organisations. And in the twenty-first century, MI5 has had to face the deadliest terrorist threat of all – from Al Qaeda. The book looks at MI5's attempts to prevent mass murder on the streets of Britain, including the failure to stop the 7/7 bombings in London in 2005.

£9.99 Paperback
384 pages
978-1-4456-0267-7

Available from February 2011 from all good bookshops or to order direct
Please call **01285-760-030**
www.amberleybooks.com

About the Authors

Thomas Hennessey is Reader in History at Canterbury Christ Church University. His other books include *A History of Northern Ireland, 1920-96*; *Dividing Ireland: World War One & Partition*; *The Evolution of the Troubles 1970-72*; *The Northern Ireland Peace Process: Ending the Troubles?* and *Northern Ireland: The Origins of the Troubles*. He lives in London and Canterbury.

Claire Thomas is a historian who specialises in the early years of the Cold War. She is currently working on a history of Britain's involvement in the Korean War. She lives in Folkestone.

Also available from Amberley Publishing

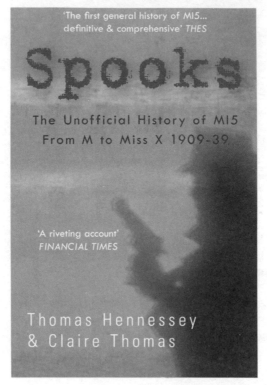

'The first general history of MI5...
definitive & comprehensive' *THES*

Spooks

The Unofficial History of MI5
From M to Miss X 1909-39

'A riveting account'
FINANCIAL TIMES

Thomas Hennessey
& Claire Thomas

The real history of MI5

'PO Box 500, London W2' – the nondescript address from behind which one of the world's most famous secret services hid: MI5. Drawing on previously secret sources, this book lifts the lid on Britain's Security Service in its battle against German and Soviet espionage. It tells the sensational stories of the officers and agents and the enemies they confronted, from MI5's creation in 1909 under the direction of Vernon Kell, Britain's first spymaster.

Building on the service's wartime success, Maxwell Knight ('M'), MI5's charismatic and eccentric agent runner, penetrated Soviet and Fascist spy networks during the 1920s and 1930s. His agent, 'Miss X', was instrumental in breaking the Percy Glading spy ring run by the Soviets, while the beautiful Joan Miller and 'Miss Z' helped bring to justice Tyler Kent, who was passing information to the Axis powers.

£9.99 Paperback
384 pages
978-1-84868-526-0